THE HONGKONG BANK IN THE
PERIOD OF IMPERIALISM
AND WAR, 1895–1918
WAYFOONG, THE FOCUS OF WEALTH

VOLUME II OF
THE HISTORY OF THE HONGKONG
AND SHANGHAI BANKING
CORPORATION

THE HISTORY OF THE HONGKONG AND SHANGHAI BANKING CORPORATION

FRANK H.H. KING

VOLUME I

The Hongkong Bank in Late Imperial China, 1864–1902: On an even keel

VOLUME II

The Hongkong Bank in the Period of Imperialism and War, 1895–1918: Wayfoong, the Focus of Wealth

VOLUME III

The Hongkong Bank between the Wars and the Bank Interned, 1919–1945: return from grandeur

VOLUME IV

The Hongkong Bank in the Period of Development and Nationalism, 1941–1984: from regional bank to multinational group

For a list of contents for each volume, please see pages v–vii

Shanghai, with the signatures of A.G. Stephen and I.S. Law

Peking, with the signatures of R.C. Allen and N.H. Prockter.

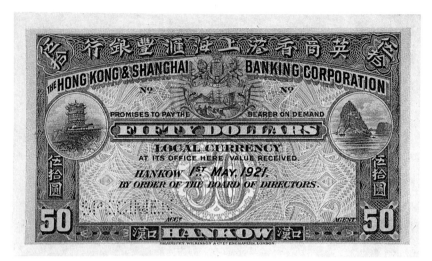

Hankow, specimen.

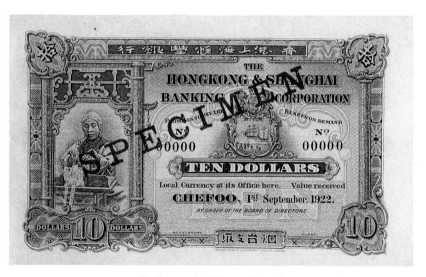

Chefoo, or, in Chinese, Yentai.

THE HONGKONG BANK
IN THE PERIOD OF
IMPERIALISM AND
WAR, 1895–1918

WAYFOONG, THE FOCUS OF WEALTH

VOLUME II OF
THE HISTORY OF THE HONGKONG
AND SHANGHAI BANKING
CORPORATION

FRANK H.H. KING
Professor of Economic History, University of Hong Kong

with

DAVID J.S. KING and CATHERINE E. KING

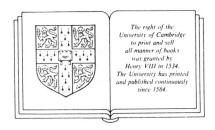

The right of the
University of Cambridge
to print and sell
all manner of books
was granted by
Henry VIII in 1534.
The University has printed
and published continuously
since 1584.

CAMBRIDGE UNIVERSITY PRESS
Cambridge
New York   New Rochelle   Melbourne   Sydney

Published by the Press Syndicate of the University of Cambridge
The Pitt Building, Trumpington Street, Cambridge CB2 1RP
32 East 57th Street, New York, NY 10022, USA
10 Stamford Road, Oakleigh, Melbourne 3166, Australia

First published 1988

Printed in Great Britain at the University Press, Cambridge

Copyright acknowledgements

Extracts from P.G. Wodehouse, *Psmith in the City* and 'My Banking Career', are reprinted by permission of the author and the author's agents, Scott Meredith Literary Agency, Inc., 845 Third Avenue, New York, New York 10022 (American rights) and by permission of the Trustees of the Wodehouse Trust no. 3 and Century Hutchinson (other rights).

Extracts from Bruce Tytler, *Here, There & (Nearly) Everywhere* (London, Weidenfeld and Nicolson, 1979), are reprinted by permission of his estate.

Data from *China's Foreign Trade Statistics, 1864–1949*, by Hsiao Liang-lin (Harvard University, East Asian Research Center, 1974), are published with the permission of the Council on East Asian Studies, Harvard University.

Illustrations from *The Railway Magazine* are republished with the kind permission of John Slater, editor.

The illustration from the collection of Jeffrey Richards is published with his permission. It was recently included in Richards and John M. MacKenzie, *The Railway Station, a Social History* (Oxford, 1986).

British Library cataloguing in publication data
King, Frank H.H.
The History of The Hongkong and Shanghai
Banking Corporation.
Vol. 2: The Hongkong Bank in the Period of Imperialism and War, 1895–1918:
Wayfoong, the Focus of Wealth.
1. Hongkong and Shanghai Banking Corporation
– History
I. Title   II. King, David J.S.   III. King, Catherine E.
332.1'2'095125   HG3354.H6

Library of Congress cataloguing in publication data
King, Frank H.H.
The Hongkong Bank in the Period of Imperialism and War, 1895–1918:
Wayfoong, the Focus of Wealth.
(The History of The Hongkong and Shanghai Banking
Corporation; v. 2)
Bibliography.
Includes index.
1. Hongkong and Shanghai Banking Corporation – History.
2. Banks and banking – China – history – late Ch'ing, early Republic.
3. East Asia – Economic conditions.   I. King, David J.S.
II. King, Catherine E.   III. Title.   IV. King,
Frank H.H. History of The Hongkong and Shanghai
Banking Corporation; v. 2.
HG 1571.K56   VOL. 2   332.1'5' 095125.5   87–6349
[HG3354.H65]   [332.1'5'095125]

ISBN 0 521 32707 5

CONTENTS OF VOLUMES
I, II, III, AND IV

VOLUME IV. THE HONGKONG BANK IN THE PERIOD
OF DEVELOPMENT AND NATIONALISM, 1941–1984:
FROM REGIONAL BANK TO MULTINATIONAL GROUP

TABLE OF CONTENTS
VOLUME II

LIST OF ILLUSTRATIONS

LIST OF TABLES

PREFACE

... the Bank is neither a philanthropic nor a systematic swindling institution.
                    A.D. Brent to the Editor, *Peking and Tientsin Times*, 1901

The Hongkong and Shanghai Banking Corporation in the course of its history has had more than one Chinese name, but one has become standard -- 'Wayfoong' (*hui-feng*). It can be translated as 'focus of wealth'. This second volume of the Bank's history deals with those strangely hectic years from 1895 to 1914 when the Bank became increasingly involved as lead manager or co-manager in the public issue of major loans designed to finance economic development in China, Japan, and Siam. Funds were also sadly needed for less productive purposes, and in this too the Bank cooperated with Imperial and Republican China to tap the capital markets of Europe in successful efforts to obtain the funds required for indemnities and reorganization under conditions compatible with China's integrity and sovereignty.

Europeans sought to bring to China the benefits of free trade and modernization, but they themselves could not remain true to their principles, and the Bank, like Europe itself, turned its attention from Far Eastern development to the realities of the Great War. Thus the story of the Hongkong Bank's leadership and the formation of an international China Consortium operating from the Bank's London Office and inspired by Sir Charles Addis, its London Manager, ends, without doubt, in 1914. The years 1914–1918 are a sad postscript.

Volume I of this history was focused on the Hongkong Bank as a China-coast bank, founded by taipans of British, Parsee, American, Norwegian, and German nationality to serve the regional trading communities and the local economies of the Treaty Ports and colonial settlements of Asia east of India. In the course of its growth from the Hong Kong and Shanghai based operation, which in 1865 was capitalized at $2.5 million (=£0.6 million), to the retirement of Sir Thomas Jackson in 1902, when published shareholders' funds were $25.9 million (=£2.4 million), the Bank, as an Eastern exchange bank, had established offices not only in the Far East and Southeast Asia but also in France, Germany, India, and the United States. Most importantly, it had gained a position and a sound reputation in the City of London itself, where its two able Shanghai Managers, David McLean and Sir Ewen Cameron, had in succession brought to the City the Bank's Eastern expertise and successfully challenged the great houses of issue in the field of China finance.

The fall of silver and the dramatic changes in the China trade had had their impact on all Eastern exchange banks; several failed. The Hongkong Bank, successfully implementing a policy described as maintaining an 'even keel', that is, matching sources and uses of funds in both the gold (sterling) and silver currency areas in which it operated, had minimized exchange risks and emerged as the premier British overseas bank in the East.

This story is continued in the present volume as silver prices rise, then stabilize, and finally move towards peaks as an immediate consequence of post-war restoration of the free silver market. The first part of this volume is then a continuation of Volume I, the account of the Bank as an exchange bank, of its staff, and of its branches. Nevertheless, even here there is a new feature. The Bank's expertise was at last being tapped; its Managers were consulted, appointed to the Legislative Councils and to international commissions. The Bank's success was bringing not only financial rewards to shareholders but public responsibilities.

It was not only the Bank that had changed. From the early 1850s to 1895 Europeans could feel reasonably at ease relative to the East. Relations with the Chinese Empire had been stabilized in the context of British domination of its limited though growing foreign trade. Foreign relations, it is true, remained on an unstable basis, but for the time this could be set aside, at least until the full potential of the recently won 'rights' had been realized. The treaties on which these relations were based still fell short of Chinese recognition of the normal rights of sovereign intercourse; they remained, as the Chinese were later to claim, 'unequal', but the balance was still in China's favour.

Japan also had been 'opened' but was pursuing its own course; Siam appeared comfortable with a relatively benign, though hardly costless foreign tutelage which nevertheless remained under ultimate Siamese control; and other territories were subject to colonial supervision of varying types.

All this was now threatened. In 1895 China had been defeated in the First Sino-Japanese War, Europe was expansionist minded, the ambitions or fears of rival governments being reflected in the maze of interconnecting sometimes cooperating sometimes rival consortiums of varying composition. Funds from South Africa's Rand could find their way into Burmese ruby mines or Chinese railways. Concession hunters obtained options which obstructed the legitimate development of mining, rival political concessions forced tortuous subsequent negotiations before planned railway construction could begin, while the impact on Eastern Governments undermined the world political balance. In the age of 'imperialism' China was caught in a trap of its own making.

Through all this the Hongkong Bank steered a steadying course from its first agreement in 1895 with its German rival in the East, the Deutsch-Asiatische Bank, to the formation of the Six Power Groups (often referred to prematurely but conveniently as 'the China Consortium') in 1912. As early as 1874 the Bank had established itself as an agent of Imperial China, the London Managers through their Consultative Committee maintained contact with the City, but in the early years the sums involved had been small, China had not been threatened politically, and the Bank operated, as it would always wish to operate, on a private-sector commercial basis. The dramatic adaptation of the Bank to the methods necessary in a new world of concessions, political involvement, and international cooperation is the main theme of this volume.

In the 1870s the Hongkong Bank had been successful in bidding for British Government 'Treasury Chest' business and for the principal account of the Hong Kong Government; by 1895 the Bank had become the virtually permanent banker to the British Government in China and shared the task with the Chartered Bank in the Straits Settlements. Despite long-running disputes with the British Treasury, Managers were asked for advice on British financial interests in the East. With the post-1895 changes this relationship took on greater significance; the range of an exchange bank's interests and responsibilities developed in the context of Government's greater involvement in direct political and economic negotiations with the Imperial Government of China. At the same time the Hongkong Bank sponsored (with Jardine, Matheson and Co.) the founding of the British and Chinese Corporation, a company designed to bring together British China interests.

To recount these events in context, this volume has to reach back to 1895, overlapping in part the years covered by Volume I. The second part of Volume II covers these significant financial/political developments; the climax is the China Consortium, with its central office in the Bank's London Office at 9, Gracechurch Street, and its 'head', the London Manager, Sir Charles Addis.

The Hongkong Bank was a British overseas bank; even when a German, the Bank's Chairman for the year, presided at the proprietors' semi-annual meetings, he would stress and praise its role in the fostering of British trade. Nevertheless, in the increasing European rivalry which accompanied the apparent European cooperation in Eastern finance, the Bank was open to popular British criticism for its open German connections. With the outbreak of war in August 1914 this criticism took a bitter turn. The Bank, however, steered as reasonable a course as possible and continued to serve Allied interests throughout. There was a cost. The Bank for a time lost that spirit of internationalism which, while free trade had prevailed, had been the basis of Hong Kong's prosperous role as entrepôt for South China and as the operational base for British interests in East Asia.

The extended almost political role of the Hongkong Bank is at first glance fully described in public archives, particularly in the Public Record Office, London. And yet despite the mass of correspondence, memorandums by Bank Managers, minutes of meetings between consortium banks, details of the founding and progress of the British and Chinese Corporation and its associated Chinese Central Railways, an appreciation of the Bank's role has been singularly lacking. The reason is now clear. The public archives present the Bank's public face, the correspondence is by officers otherwise unknown and often misidentified, and the public officials themselves are not always accurate in their comments. The emotional attacks of 'scaremonger' journalists and later of Chinese nationalists, their apologists, and their successors have distorted the record. The failure of serious scholars to attempt a correction is due in part, it is fair to add, to the absence of a Hongkong Bank archive, without which a balanced interpretation of the Bank's role has proved impossible.

The principal contribution of this volume is the reinterpretation of events in a period of 'imperialism' and war on the basis of information from the Board of Directors' minutes, the Charles Addis papers, the J.O.P. Bland papers, the surviving but incomplete correspondence which has been rediscovered and catalogued for the use of scholars in the 'Group Archives', and from related sources which had previously been left aside. The history of an Eastern exchange bank merges with the total story of European involvement in the affairs of China. So important was the role of the Hongkong Bank, so intimate were the relations of its London Manager, Sir Charles Addis, with the Foreign Secretary and the Foreign Office, and of its Peking Manager, E. Guy Hillier, with Ch'ing dynasty officialdom, that the broader history cannot be properly understood without the input from the archives of The Hongkong and Shanghai Banking Corporation. The events described, however, have already inspired legends; one interpretation has, for example, encouraged the protests of Chinese nationalists. China's unpaid public debts remain as testimony of the efforts made to assist in China's modernization; they remain an equally convincing testimony of China's misconceived rejection of these efforts.

The Hongkong Bank's role in Eastern finance was not confined to China. Less controversial was the assistance rendered to Japan and Siam, while on a smaller scale the Bank continued the finance of local joint-stock enterprises.

Nevertheless, it is the China role which has attracted the greatest general interest. In Volume II the Hongkong Bank reached a pinnacle; its public role was constructive, its advice highly regarded, and its contribution undoubted. Yet its role was even then controversial; later the Bank would be criticized. In the inter-war period, described in Volume III, the focus would for a time be once again on exchange banking; there would be a return from grandeur.

Despite the broadly based interest of the present volume, this remains a commissioned business history of a commercial bank. Events of historical significance have been chosen for and explained on the basis of their relevance to the Hongkong Bank. The study remains, nevertheless, 'at arm's length' and includes, on the instructions of the Chairman, Sir Michael Sandberg, 'warts and all'. This is consistent with the co-sponsorship of the project by the University of Hong Kong, where it was administered subject to normal academic principles by the Centre of Asian Studies.

In fulfilling this commission I was granted full access to the Bank's reconstituted archives, subject only to respect for the legally protected rights of the Bank's customers. The history is nevertheless written on the basis of the published accounts. Inner reserves and true profits were known only to the Chief Manager and the officer responsible for keeping 'Head Office books'; they were not recorded on a regular basis and the task of recasting the accounts was not practical. Where true figures are by chance available they have been cited by way of illustration. The published figures are, however, those on which the Bank operated and on which it was judged by contemporaries; their use in this history does not distort the record of the Bank.

A NOTE ON ROMANIZATION

The present official romanization system of the Chinese language as prescribed by the authorities of the People's Republic of China is '*pinyin*'.

In this history as a general principle all Chinese characters are either 'decoded' according to a system known as 'modified Wade-Giles' or are cited in the form customary at the time and familiar to the persons who made this history. This approach, with its usual exceptions, has been explained in Volume I. A Glossary has been appended which relates the form in the text to *pinyin* and to Chinese characters.

Centre of Asian Studies,   FRANK H.H. KING
University of Hong Kong.

July 15, 1986

ACKNOWLEDGEMENTS

My acknowledgements for assistance covering the entire history project are listed in Volume I, and what follows is generally confined to work on Volume II. I restate, however, my appreciation to those most closely involved.

This history was commissioned by The Hongkong and Shanghai Banking Corporation. I am grateful to the Bank's Chairman, Sir Michael Sandberg, for his willingness not only to commission a history early in his tenure as chief executive officer, but also for his continued support as the project was extended from time to time.

Rayson L. Huang, Vice-Chancellor, University of Hong Kong, authorized this cooperative research project within the Centre of Asian Studies; the Committee of Management, the Director, and staff of the Centre provided administrative support, and the staff of the Secretary's Office and Finance Office in the University gave prompt assistance and advice.

Leslie Pressnell accepted the appointment of consultant to the project, read every chapter, and advised in detail. S.W. Muirhead, for some time Controller Group Archives, commented thoroughly on all aspects of the drafts; A.I. Donaldson and the staff of Group Archives saw this volume through the final stages. Geoffrey Jones advised me on specific difficulties encountered.

Parts II and III of this volume were written on the basis of reports prepared by David J.S. King. His research covered important material not all of which could be incorporated in the main history; his reports are therefore listed in the Bibliography. He also translated material kindly supplied by Sr. Edóardo Verdiani, from Florence, relevant to the Pekin Syndicate. David King's work was primarily in Hamburg and Bonn but he also undertook research in Paris, Lyons, and London. All matters relating to the Bank's staff were written on the basis of the research and analysis undertaken by Catherine E. King (esp. in this volume, Chapter 3); she also acted as editorial associate.

Not all the senior assistants prepared full research papers. Elizabeth Ng Wai Yee covered the records in London, where she spent several months, primarily in the PRO. Others involved in Volume II include Gary Watson

(Toronto, J.O.P. Bland papers), Eveleyne André (Belgium), Wang Ke-wen (Hoover Institution, Stanford), and R.J.H. King (Harvard and Boston area libraries).

Hong Kong University undergraduate assistants for Volume II include: Lee Chun Wah and Cheng Yim-mei (statistics and economics), Kitty Yu Wai Hing (translation), Pauline Chow Lo Sai (history), and Lau Wai Keung (statistics).

In the early stages of the project the Centre of Asian Studies held a conference, bringing together research related to the history of the Hongkong Bank. As far as Volume II is concerned most of this work deals with the branches, especially as described in Chapter 2. The published contributions are listed in the Bibliography and referred to both in footnotes and end-notes. Additionally, there were some who submitted research reports, and I should mention those of Chee Peng Lim and his colleagues, W. Evan Nelson and his Singapore assistants, J.T.M. Van Laanen, H.L.D. Selvaratnam (through the Marga Institute, V. Kanesalingam, Associate Director), Thiravet Pramu-anratkarn, Roy C. Ybañez (through the U.P. Business Research Foundation and Fanny Cortes-Garcia), and Claude Fivel-Démoret.

Information on the Bank's Hong Kong compradores comes almost entirely from the research of Carl T. Smith. Takeshi Hamashita has provided me with considerable material in Japanese and advice on using it; C. Fivel-Démoret undertook research in Lyons and Paris. G. Kurgan-van Hentenryk was as helpful personally as was her monumental study of Belgian interests in China. From Liverpool Patrick Tuck sent me extracts from his notes on the Hongkong Bank and the Missions étrangères de Paris in the East. Kanji Ishii checked Japanese sources relative to the rival British companies of 1905/06. In Manila Lewis E. Gleeck of the American Association of the Philippines introduced me to several useful sources. The Siam Commercial Bank searched its files for relevant material.

In the course of the project several important private sources appeared for Volume II. Most important were the papers of Sir Charles S. Addis which, through the generosity of Robina Addis and the late Sir John Addis, have been deposited in the Library, the School of Oriental and African Studies, University of London. I am grateful to Roberta A. Dayer for introducing me to this important source. Sir Michael Sandberg commissioned a catalogue of the Addis Papers, to be undertaken by Margaret Harcourt Williams (published in 1986); Mrs Harcourt Williams also checked my references to and quotations from the Addis Papers against the completed catalogue and undertook several separate research tasks for this volume. Charles P. Addis supplemented the Addis collection with important items.

Rosemary Seton, the Archivist at SOAS, was helpful with this and with other materials, including the Swire Papers and the Archive of the China Association.

Sir Carl Meyer was a member of the Bank's Consultative Committee; Sir Anthony Meyer kindly permitted his grandfather's letter books to be shipped to Hong Kong for examination. I record my appreciation to P.H. Blagbrough and Ms J.M. Lowe of Matheson and Co. for locating and granting access to the files of the British and Chinese Corporation and the Chinese Central Railways. My earlier research on the banking aspects of this period had been facilitated by a grant in 1966 from the Social Science Research Council, New York.

Acknowledgement must be made to those who sent various papers, photographs, and smaller collections, some of which have been deposited in Group Archives. The autobiography of H.E. Muriel was already in the Bank's archives; permission to quote from it has been granted by his daughter, Margaret Forgan. The Peking reports of A.D. Brent and related material were made available through the thoughtfulness of his nephew, Brent Hutton-Williams. In Germany, Manfred Pohl of the Deutsche Bank brought our attention to several sources. We are also grateful for access to the minute books of the Ost-Asiatischer Verein in Hamburg. C. Schultz granted D.J.S. King access to the archives of one of the Bank's founding companies, Siemssen and Co. Also in Hamburg David was assisted by Senator Jan Albers (Kunst and Albers material) and Herr Gabrielsson of the Hamburg Staatsarchiv; in Bonn Maria Keipert granted him access to the important archives of the Auswärtiges Amt.

The list of archives consulted as shown in the Bibliography is also a list indicating that the Archivists concerned materially assisted in the success of this project.

FRANK H.H. KING

STATEMENT ON DOLLARS AND EXCHANGE

All dollars in this history
unless specifically stated otherwise
are
HONG KONG DOLLARS.
One billion=1,000 million
One lac=1,00,000

The Hong Kong/London exchange rate is quoted as so many shillings and pence per dollar, e.g. $1.00=4s 6d. From this it follows that:

A **fall** in exchange will result in a dollar exchanging for fewer shillings and pence and is evidence of a depreciation of the Hong Kong dollar *vis à vis* sterling.

A **rise** [improvement, increase] in exchange will result in a dollar exchanging for more shillings and pence and is evidence of an appreciation of the Hong Kong dollar *vis-à-vis* sterling.

The Shanghai exchanges are similarly quoted in terms of a Shanghai tael.

'Silver' may refer in the popular business jargon of the day to units of account payable in silver bullion or coin. Thus a 'silver' loan is a loan denominated in e.g. Hong Kong dollars or Shanghai taels.

'Gold' may refer to sterling and/or to other currencies on a gold standard.

'The exchanges' or other similar term refers, unless modified, to the foreign exchange rates and the markets which determine the rate at which one currency can be bought in terms of another.

All dollars in this history
unless specifically stated otherwise
are
HONG KONG DOLLARS.

ABBREVIATIONS

AA	Auswärtiges Amt
ACDC	American China Development Corporation
Bank	Hongkong and Shanghai Banking Corporation
BE	Buddhist Era
B&CC	British and Chinese Corporation, Ltd
CCB	Capital and Counties Bank
CCR	Chinese Central Railways, Ltd
C–K terms	terms found in the agreements relative to the Canton–Kowloon Railway
CIO	Companie Internationale d'Orient
CMSNCo	China Merchants' Steam Navigation Company
Chartered Bank	Chartered Bank of India, Australia and China
d	pence
D/A	documents against acceptance
DAB	Deutsch-Asiatische Bank
DB	Deutsche Bank
D/P	documents against payment
FMS	Federated Malay States
Fr	French francs
HkTs	Haikwan taels
HMG	His Majesty's Government
Hongkong Bank	Hongkong and Shanghai Banking Corporation
HSBC	Hongkong and Shanghai Banking Corporation 'Heart and Soul Breaking Corporation'
IBC	International Banking Corporation
IMC	Imperial [*then* Chinese] Maritime Customs
KfAG	Konsortium für Asiatische Geschäfte
Mercantile Bank	Mercantile Bank of India, Limited (after 1892)
NYK	Nippon Yusen Kaisha [Japan Mail Steamship Company]

OAV	Ost-Asiatischer Verein
OBC	New Oriental Bank Corporation, Ltd
OGSF	Officers Good Service Fund
P/A	Power of Attorney
P&O	Peninsular and Oriental Steam Navigation Company
PB	Parr's Bank
PNB	Philippine National Bank
s	shillings
ShTs	Shanghai taels
Tcs	Ticals
TJ	Sir Thomas Jackson
T–P terms	terms as found in the agreements relative to the Tientsin–Pukow Railway
Ts	taels
TT	telegraphic transfer
¥	yen
YSB	Yokohama Specie Bank
$Gold	US unit of account contrasted with the silver-based Hong Kong dollar unit of account
£	pound sterling unit of account

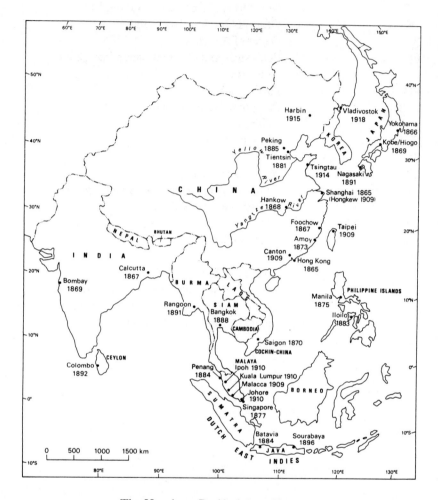

1. The Hongkong Bank's Asian offices, 1918

Part I

THE HONGKONG BANK
AS EASTERN EXCHANGE BANK,
1902–1914

The capture of the trade arising out of [British] investment was the main objective of [Sir Ewen] Cameron's policy. Loans were never to be considered as an end in themselves, but only as a means of promoting China's foreign trade. [Sir Thomas] Jackson held strongly to this view.

Sir Charles Addis to V.M. Grayburn, 1933

In this key period of 'imperialism' in the nearly twenty years prior to the Great War of 1914–1918, the Hongkong and Shanghai Banking Corporation played a vital and constructive role in Far Eastern development finance, as the joint promoter of the British and Chinese Corporation and the Chinese Central Railways, and as the lead bank in the expanding international China Consortium which was responsible, *inter alia*, for the politically controversial Reorganization Loan of 1913. The 'local bank', founded by Hong Kong taipans in 1864, had become a leading actor among the international consortiums which were formed between the First Sino-Japanese War and the end of the Great War, years which witnessed the foredoomed reforms of 1898, the traumatic Boxer Uprising of 1900, the death of the Empress Dowager, Tz'u Hsi (1908), the abdication of the last Ch'ing Emperor in 1912, the rule of Yuan Shih-k'ai (1912–1916), and the beginning of the Warlord period.

Volume I set the stage and told the Bank's own story to the retirement of its famous Chief Manager, Sir Thomas Jackson, in 1902. Volume II is presented in three distinct parts, each requiring a separate approach, yet all contributing to an understanding of the Bank and its role. The first deals with the Bank as exchange bank, taking it from the beginning of 1902 to August 1914; J.R.M. Smith and (Sir) Newton J. Stabb proved able successors to Jackson, and the Bank flourished. The successful rights issue of 1907 increased the Bank's paid-up capital to $15 million and there was a virtual doubling of shareholders' funds from $25 million (=£2.4 million at 1s:10¼d) to $50.3 million (=£4.7 million at 1s:10⅝d) from the end of 1901 to December 1914. Total assets increased by 70% and dividends were more than maintained, while the total distribution increased in both sterling and dollar terms (see Chapter 1, esp. Tables 1.4A and B).

The stated basis of exchange banking was the profit from the turnover of funds in the finance of trade. The growth of trade was therefore a factor in such a bank's prosperity; the growth potential in China, even allowing for the gross exaggeration of expectation, which characterized, then as now, any discussion of the China trade, was enormous. The directors and management of the Hongkong Bank not only accepted this, they were in a unique position with their Hong Kong Head Office and their London connections to be effective in encouraging China's 'modernizers' in their ambitions. From carefully scrutinized overdraft facilities to the raising of foreign loans, the Hongkong Bank became increasingly involved. The prize would be not only the short-term benefits of commissions and underwriting fees but also the finance of the materials of development and of the resulting growth of trade.

Part II reflects the first part of the title of the volume. In the Period of 'Imperialism' the Bank proved capable of adjustment and leadership; there were those who had noted its past ability to issue 'small' loans but doubted its

3

capacity to lead manage the new demands of the East, but, as far as China and Siam were concerned, the Bank under its formidable London Managers, Sir Ewen Cameron and later Sir Charles S. Addis, succeeded in the task. The Bank participated in the issue of Japanese loans, but in consortiums of varying composition, usually managed by Parr's Bank.

The positive story ends in 1914, and Part III refers to the second half of the volume's title. This is an account of the Hongkong Bank in the Great War. As if to stress the tragedy, Part III begins, in Chapter 9, with a review of the Bank in the tradition of internationalism – in the tradition of Hong Kong itself. The cooperative, multinational approach so carefully fostered by the Bank was shattered. The jingoists had for a time succeeded. The Bank's accounts, however, described reasonable growth in dollar terms, although the sudden war-end appreciation of silver distorted the sterling figures. The dollar value increase in shareholders' funds during the Great War was 8%; this translated to 93% in sterling equivalents (see Table 10.5).

Each Part of Volume II is furnished with its own introduction. This, however, being the introduction to the first part, serves also for the volume itself, briefly reviewing the history of the Bank to 1902 and restating those general issues which remain relevant in the period now under consideration.

The Hongkong Bank, 1864–1901

The Hongkong Bank was promoted by Hong Kong based merchants and incorporated with an initial paid-up capital of $2.5 million under a Hong Kong general companies ordinance, subsequently disallowed, with the stated purpose of acting as a local bank (in the sense that the Indian Presidency banks were 'local' banks) for Hong Kong and the Treaty Ports of China and Japan. It was granted the right to issue banknotes. By 1866 the Bank had been reincorporated by special Hong Kong ordinance consistent with the provisions of the Colonial Banking Regulations, its subscribed capital was $5 million, and its purposes were more broadly conceived to include exchange banking. It may therefore be characterized as a British overseas bank in the tradition of the Royally chartered banks, an Eastern exchange bank, and a local (Presidency type) bank with Head Office and Board of Directors in Hong Kong.

The Bank's initial success reflected the fact that the promoters had identified a real economic need. The senior taipans of the Eastern hongs were resident in the East; the decision makers needed a bank which was itself capable of immediate and therefore local decision making. Nevertheless, the directors recognized the importance of London and established an office there, an office which under David McLean, Thomas Jackson, and Ewen

Cameron had become capable of providing the basis for the major operations required in the period from 1895.

Poor investment decisions and uninspired exchange operations endangered the Bank in 1874/75, the low point in its history. A conservative write-off policy and the ability of Jackson as the new Chief Manager enabled the rapid recovery, and in 1883 the first rights issue led to a paid-up capital of $7.5 million and shareholders' funds of $12.6 million (=£2.2 million). As silver declined and disruption overtook the Eastern trade, the Bank had weathered another crisis by the end of the decade, but in 1890 the directors were able to announce a second rights issue, raising the capital to $10 million, although consequent 1892 shareholders' funds of $16.6 million were equivalent to only £2.6 million. The exchange had fallen from 3s:2½d to 2s:10⅝d between June 1891 and June 1892.

The Bank, under its only French Chief Manager, Tahiti-born François de Bovis, suffered heavily from trade failures – including that of an important constituent, the American hong of Russell and Co. – from the defalcation of the Hong Kong compradore, and from the fall in the exchange, despite the general success of its 'even keel' policy. 'TJ' was recalled from London. Under his leadership the Bank once again recovered; by 1895, however, although shareholders' funds were back to $14.9 million, the sterling equivalent was only £1.5 million; exchange had fallen from 4s:1½d to 2s:od. Jackson focused on building up the reserves and probably for the first time 'true' profits were understated. The Bank's consequent inner reserves were revealed in the December 1898 accounts, enabling year-end payments into published reserves sufficient to create a fund equivalent in value to paid-up capital. On December 31, 1901, shareholders' funds were $25.9 million (=£2.4 million at an exchange of 1s:10¼d).

J.R.M. Smith inherited a prosperous bank in 1902. But Jackson had left more than this. The Bank had firmly established itself throughout the region. In 1874 the directors had authorized the first publicly issued loan guaranteed by the Imperial Government of China. Moving north from Shanghai in the 1880s the Bank had established offices in Tientsin, the base of Viceroy Li Hung-chang, and in Peking, the imperial capital. Through its Tientsin compradore, Wu Mao-ting, the Bank established contacts directly with the imperial authorities. Its Peking Manager, E.G. Hillier, learned much before blindness overtook him, and he remained the Bank's agent in the capital until his death in 1924. Here too in 1886–1888 young Charles Addis had his apprenticeship; he would continue his official contacts in Shanghai and in London, where, from 1905, he was a joint Manager. The Tientsin and Peking Managers encouraged ideas of modernization, Wu Mao-ting himself became an industrialist and railway director, but China's immediate needs were elsewhere and her Government was incapable of the necessary leadership.

Sir Robert Hart, the Inspector-General of China's Imperial Maritime Customs, wrote to his London manager that the Hongkong Bank 'understood China'.

One key to the Bank's position was obviously its Eastern head office. Equally important was its base in a silver-using area. Its accounts were in silver; the main sources of its funds were silver; it could afford to 'understand' and provide China with the financial services she required on an emergency basis. The Managers did not do business directly with the Chinese, however; they operated through their compradores. Nevertheless they became aware of Chinese practices and they were prepared to adjust to meet Chinese requirements, although adjustments were not always easy or without occasional litigation. When the Chinese Government approached with requirements alien to the normal practices of the London capital market, the Bank could act as interface, accepting Chinese conditions but offering London terms to potential bondholders.

The Bank's position in the East, however, was also a source of potential weakness when dealing with London. This was overcome on several levels. McLean obtained sterling funds for financing the Bank's London trade requirements; he worked through an Advisory or Consultative Committee which brought him into contact with the City. The Board of Directors in Hong Kong together with the Chief Manager remained aware that, with London shareholders and the need to raise part of any new capital issue in London, the Bank's sterling image had become of great importance, despite the fact of its silver accounts. When McLean retired in 1889 Jackson went Home from the East, but he was recalled on three occasions and the third time he remained in Hong Kong until 1902. Meanwhile the Bank had become, as a result of open tender, the British Government's banker in China, Japan, and Hong Kong. After Jackson's return to Hong Kong in 1893, London was managed by Cameron and the vital links of confidence, based on the Bank's formal relationship with the 'Treasury Chest', were forged with the Foreign Office.

This brief survey provides some background for what will follow. The key elements for success were the British overseas banking tradition, the Bank's competence as an Eastern exchange bank, its intimate Chinese contacts, its local management and Board of Directors, its strong London representation, and its well-earned reputation.

The issues

In Volume I two themes were developed as vital to the Hongkong Bank's history: (i) the colonial banking tradition and (ii) the regional focus.

As for the first, by 1900 the main controversies had been resolved. The Treasury still took its 'gatekeeper' function seriously. It examined the Bank's performance before authorizing an increase in capital, it continued unsuccessfully to urge the Hong Kong Government to take over the banks' note issue, but the problem of an excess issue, 100% backed by coin or specie, had been resolved. The position relative to one-dollar notes remained unchanged until 1912 when Hong Kong arguments finally prevailed and the Hongkong Bank was permitted to increase the issue. The Treasury remained throughout the Bank's ultimate regulator.

The stability of this position throughout the period makes it possible to omit further discussion on 'The Bank and the Regulators', a subject considered at length in Volume I. The problems of the Hamburg Branch in the Great War is admittedly a special case (see Chapter 11).

Although the directors had long been aware of possible pressure for transferring Head Office to London, the question did not become one for serious public discussion until the late 1890s when the Bank became increasingly involved in the issue of Eastern loans in London. The Board itself never formally considered the proposition; the discussion was speculative and often encouraged by those who felt aggrieved at the Bank, its directors, or both. Instead the Bank strengthened its position in London through a strong management and a reinforced Consultative Committee. The regional focus of the Bank remained unimpaired.

Corporate history

As the corporation developed from a Hong Kong and Shanghai operation and grew from a bank capitalized at $2.5 million to a regional and London financial institution with paid-up capital of $15 million, the nature of the organization changed and personnel policy was no longer a question of picking up the right people on the China coast.

The Bank was operated by a London-recruited foreign, or 'Eastern', staff working with two 'native' staffs: (i) an intermediate clerical group, the 'Portuguese', 'burghers', 'Home' staff, or equivalent and supplemented by local 'British' staff and (ii) a Chinese, Sinhalese, etc. staff responsible to locally guaranteed compradores (or their equivalent) for the handling of funds or for more menial tasks. This three-tiered system, formalized by the 1880s, survived into the 1950s; it appeared to solve several key problems. By depending on a certain 'class' of young man personally recommended, by indoctrinating or socializing them through a period of clerkship first in London and then in the East, the Bank developed a team, or, as the Eastern staff Bankers themselves called it, a 'family'. Even though the Eastern staff grew in the period 1902–1914 from 156 to 214, even though the size of major branches prevented the early intimacy of Manager and 'banker's assistant', control of junior staff and, indeed, control of distant offices, continued to depend on this 'family' concept (see Chapter 3).

The system had its limitations, however. There was a consequent 'non-professionalism' which came to be questioned in the context of German competition. There was also, it seemed to critics, an absence of opportunity for specialization, evidenced in the inability to replace men with the self-taught qualifications of Charles Addis and E.G. Hillier from within the service. There were suggestions for 'up-grading' the staff, which, in the context of Treaty Port life, were doomed to fail.

The Bank's exchange position was a key to its success; it was also the key to predicting the course of exchange rates, knowledge of which would be of significant value to Hong Kong merchants including the merchant directors. The directors recognized that, if the Board were to remain in Hong Kong, they would have to withdraw from active management. The Board had instituted profit sharing with Jackson shortly after his return in 1893; the practice continued. The Chief Manager was no longer primarily an executive secretary to the Board and an office manager; he was responsible for the banking activities of the Bank, although no formal delegation would be minuted until 1962. There was still but little broadening of middle management except in Hong Kong, Shanghai, and London; a Head Office hierarchy was not yet throwing up its own Chief Manager, but the necessary beginnings were made.

Branches can be compared to separate banks operating with a common capital and responsible to the same directors through a chief executive. There had been many Eastern failures caused by directors incapable of controlling their branch Managers, and in its early years the Hongkong Bank had not been immune to this problem. The difficulties had arisen, however, mainly with Managers selected before the London-based recruiting system had been fully developed or from outside the system, as in Batavia or Lyons. Comprehensive consideration of this problem would require a full-scale history for each branch. This has proved impractical; instead the fortunes of selected branches are considered in Chapter 2, the stories reaching back as necessary to the pre-1902 years.

The Bank and Hong Kong

Although the Board of Directors had virtually abdicated their banking role, they quite definitely represented the Bank. The Chief Manager was neither a member of the Legislative nor the Executive Council; his advice was sought on matters related to the currency, on the content of ordinances related to banking, and on such esoteric questions as to why the Hong Kong dollar was so often quoted at a premium over its relative silver value, but he did not present himself as a general community leader – nor, with certain exceptions, for example, T.S. Baker in Singapore, did the Managers elsewhere.

The Hongkong Bank remained the Government's banker and was responsible for over 80% of the local note issue. It remained concerned with the local economy, sufficiently so that the Board required a list of advances to public companies to be submitted by the Chief Manager. There was never, however, a question of a crisis comparable to those of 1874 or 1892; the Bank was sufficiently strong to render assistance without endangering its own position.

The Bank as adviser

With the continued fall of silver in the 1890s Eastern Governments were forced to consider the implications on their external trade, in the course of which the alternative of a gold standard or gold exchange standard would receive consideration – and, in several cases, implementation. China, and therefore Hong Kong, stayed nominally at least on silver. Independently there were developments which threatened the position of Eastern exchange banks as Government banks. In India, the Philippines, and Siam, for example, national or Government-sponsored banks were founded to take back the revenues from the private-sector, foreign-based, exchange banks. These new institutions were, however, also involved in the private sector, they were competitors of the exchange banks. In a later period the Imperial Bank of India, the Siam Commercial Bank, and the Philippine National Bank would find their roles curtailed in turn; they would not, unlike the Bank of England, become their country's central bank.

These simultaneous developments created problems of policy and implementation, and the various legislative bodies, the British Treasury, and responsible colonial authorities sought the advice of exchange bankers. The advice received was not always disinterested. The exchange bankers sought to exclude the new national banks from exchange operations; their comments on the monetary standard were often biased by an inability to work out the potentials of major change and a consequent and understandable tendency to prefer the *status quo*. Hongkong Bankers were, however, involved, and their contributions are part of the history of the Bank.

Following the Boxer Uprising the tendency of the Powers to meddle in Chinese affairs extended to the currency, and various commissions were established and reform proposals considered. In this Hongkong Bankers participated at both the practical local level and the comprehensive policy level. Here common sense proved useful, a gold standard was not attempted, and the currency system remained, with a few exceptions, in its diverse but workable confusion until 1935. These and related topics are considered in Chapter 4.

The Bank and China

Sir Newton Stabb might state his aversion to political involvement, but the Hongkong Bank could no longer operate in China on a solely commercial basis; it had to consider overall British policy, at least to the extent that it was affected by spheres of interest and Chinese-granted concessions. British policy was not, however, single-purposed; the Hong Kong Government, for example, had concerns which were not of the highest priority in the Foreign Office. Furthermore, policy could be influenced, and, to the extent that commercial negotiations affected *de facto* the course of policy, financiers might not be without influence even on Foreign Service officers, who, like their fellow-classicists in the Chinese Mandarinate, were not particularly commercially oriented.

The Bank's China-related activities were changed in 1895 by several factors, including the increased financial demands of the Imperial Government, the growth of international rivalry based on political rather than commercial factors, and the tradition by which the Chinese authorities granted commercial privileges or concessions through Governments. The position was further changed by events subsequent to the Boxer Uprising, with the increase in international loan obligations, and by the breakdown in the collection of customs revenues following the 1911 Revolution. The Hongkong Bank, as banker to the British Government, was a custodian bank for Boxer Indemnity funds; as the leading foreign bank, it found itself, as a consequence of Chinese Government decisions, the principal custodian of a large volume of official funds; as participants in the British and Chinese Corporation and the Chinese Central Railways, who were trustees to bond-holders, the Bank was responsible for advice on the safeguarding of the bondholders' security; as the largest bank in China's principal money market of Shanghai, it could not avoid responsibility in times of financial chaos.

In brief, the Bank's involvement in China had changed from that of trade finance with an ability to handle occasional government loans to a comprehensive presence, certain aspects of which would be subject to disapproval by contemporaries, others would become controversial in a period of nationalism. And yet, when examined carefully, the Bank's involvement remained compatible with a primarily private-sector orientation. The political causes of the Bank's increased role in China lay beyond the scope of the Bank's authority; the implementation of policies originating elsewhere was later mistaken for the policies themselves. When the Chinese authorities requested the Bank, as bankers, to receive the post-1911 customs revenues, the proposal seemed one of simple convenience. With the outbreak of civil war and with disputes relative to recognition, Chinese funds in a foreign bank were subject to Legation decisions as to who constituted the authority on which the Bank was legally authorized to act.

But the Bank's most important role relative to China resulted from its development of and leadership in the international Groups which dominated China's foreign borrowing between 1895 and 1914. The initial concepts and consequent adjustments as China itself developed new political priorities are, together with the technical banking consequences, the subject of Part II of this volume.

The contents of Parts II and III are considered in introductions preceding Chapters 5 and 9 respectively.

1

THE CORPORATION, 1902–1914

> It appears to me, gentlemen, that the mantle of the late Sir Thomas Jackson of
> happy memory has fallen very gracefully upon the shoulders of Mr Smith . . .
>
> Murray Bain, 1903

The photographer had problems enough arranging the team for the 1906 annual group photograph down at the Hongkong Bank's New Beckenham playing fields when the Captain of Sports inexplicably insisted on the inclusion of a short, roundish man clad in bowler hat and reach-me-down sort of suit, presumably the groundsman in his Sunday best. This required some negotiation and, when objections to the presence of the supposed 'groundsman' proved ineffective, the photographer began lecturing the intruder on deportment.[1]

The reason for the resulting mirth would have been obvious to anyone able to recognize James Ross Middleton Smith, the Chief Manager of the Hongkong Bank, then on Home leave.

As the Board were to minute on Smith's death in 1918, 'He shunned publicity and public thanks, but those who knew him best will remember many instances of unostentatious kindness and generosity.' The Board further noted, 'He conducted the affairs of the Bank with marked ability and success until his retirement at the end of 1910.' Smith's successor, Newton Stabb, had commented, 'It is no easy matter to follow a man like Smith. There are very few like him. He has done magnificent work for the Bank and the Staff have a great deal to thank him for.'[2] But this merely heightens the mystery of the man who succeeded Jackson; who was Smith and why was he Chief Manager?

THE SUCCESSION – SMITH AND STABB

Smith succeeds Jackson

On March 15, 1882, J.R.M. Smith and V.A.C. Hawkins left England for the East together, in 1884 Smith in Shanghai and Hawkins in Hong Kong received additional pay for their handling of tasks usually assigned a more senior officer, and in 1902 they were both in Hong Kong, both eligible to be appointed Chief Manager as Jackson's successor. But before the Board chose between them, there must have been some elimination of others; in early 1902 Smith was sixteenth and Hawkins seventeenth on the seniority list.

The following analysis is based on the assumption that 'health' or physical capability to withstand the pressures, a criterion specifically mentioned in the Board's announcement of Jackson's successor, was consistent with the unspoken decision to pass the chief managership on to the next generation and that 30 years in the East was considered normal, although certainly not binding.

The senior member of the Eastern staff in 1902 was W.H. Harries who had left London 32 years before and had spent all but seven years of his 'Eastern' career in San Francisco. From a practical point of view, neither he nor his Accountant M.M. Tompkins were eligible. Tompkins had been recruited into the Bank in 1875 in San Francisco; he had never served elsewhere and was in reality 'local staff'.

R.H. Cook (East in 1872), C.B. Rickett (joined in the East in 1874), and E.H. Oxley (East in 1874) had been appointed Agents in smaller though not necessarily unimportant agencies, but they had little Head Office experience and had in any case been more than 28 years in the East. J.P. Wade Gard'ner (East in 1873) had been Acting Chief Manager for a few months in 1890 and, since then, had been reasonably successful as Manager Shanghai. But he too had been long in the East; the New York Office, in succession to A.M. Townsend (East in 1870), was a more appropriate appointment for him. R. Wilson (East in 1877) was in Colombo, P.E. Cameron (East in 1880) had only recently been appointed to Calcutta, and David Jackson (East in 1878), TJ's younger brother, however successful in Yokohama, did not have a uniformly brilliant record. G.W. Butt (East in 1878) had for the first time brought sound management to Singapore, but there is no evidence that he was considered, and indeed he left the East for a London Office appointment, possibly on health grounds, in 1903.

H.M. Bevis (East in 1875), the Manager Shanghai, and but recently the Acting Chief Manager during Jackson's leave in 1900, had all the qualifications except, perhaps, his already lengthy service in the East. His health would soon deteriorate, but although this became apparent to his colleagues in Shanghai perhaps as early as 1902 there is no evidence that this was already noticed in Hong Kong and Bevis himself was upset by the Board's decisions on both the succession and the related assignments.

The four others senior to Smith, including F.W. Barff (joined in the East in 1880), had nothing approximating the necessary experience. With hindsight the focus on Smith and Hawkins must have been obvious.

Since both these officers were prima facie potential chief managers, and since they were of a seniority which would seem to suggest ten further years of service in the East, there is no need to consider those junior to them in any detail. Even Charles Addis (East in 1883), who confided such matters to his diary, did not suppose he, as Sub-Manager Shanghai, was neglected.

An examination of the careers of Smith and Hawkins, while it reveals similarities, also points to differences, very much in Smith's favour. Both served as Sub-Manager Hong Kong and Hawkins had been Chief Accountant, but Smith had been Sub-Manager Shanghai; Hawkins was briefly Manager Batavia, but otherwise he never left Head Office, whereas Smith had opened and managed the Bangkok and Rangoon agencies and was for three years Inspector of Branches as successor to John Walter.

There had been a certain element of chance in Smith's career; Jackson's original plan in 1888 had been for R. Wilson, then Accountant in Shanghai, to open Bangkok, but with A. Leith's sudden illness, Wilson was diverted to Tientsin; W.N. Dow (East in 1880) was the second choice, but Rickett in Penang went on leave, and Dow with his Straits experience was sent there as acting Agent; Jackson then turned to Smith who thus became the first of his 'year', of his seniority, to receive an appointment.

On January 22, 1902, the directors had an extraordinary meeting in the office of the Chairman, Robert Shewan, of Messrs Shewan, Tomes and Co.; if Jackson were present, no mention is made of it, and he did not write the minutes. It was then that the decision, after taking into account all factors, including age, health, and ability, was made in favour of Smith. The reference to 'age' suggests that Wade Gard'ner and Bevis were considered. The former was, in fact, noted in the minutes and there recommended, as already stated, for New York. That the directors were aware of Hawkins' claim is evidenced by their award to him of a *solatium* in the form of a salary increase; he was appointed Inspector of Branches until either Shanghai or San Francisco should be available.

The directors formally recorded the agreement that Smith might choose his own Sub-Manager.

These decisions were confirmed at the next official meeting of the Board. The status of, or the need for, the 'private' meeting is not clear. Its minutes are written in normal sequence in the official minute book, but the subsequent 'confirmation' and the absence of Jackson as 'secretary' are significant.

The best explanation is that Hawkins, who was socially prominent and long visible in Hong Kong, had been a satisfactory Sub-Manager but that he either lacked the talents for a Chief Manager or else had earned the disapproval of some of the Board members. Certainly Addis had scant regard for Hawkins' capabilities; he thought highly of Smith. The choice was Smith, but the need to handle Hawkins' claims properly forced the directors to hold a confidential meeting without the presence of the Chief Manager.

Support for this interpretation may be found in the explanation the Bank's Chairman presented to the proprietors at the February 1902 meeting:

In making this selection [of Mr Smith] your directors were solely guided by considerations as to the qualifications of the various candidates, not only mentally but physically also, for it requires a strong man in every respect to undertake the responsibilities of such a post under the conditions of the climate and of life generally that prevail in this place. All such claims as those of seniority, age, etc., were made subordinate entirely to the one object we had in view of obtaining the best and most suitable man for the position.

There is no record of Jackson's own position. The list of Smith's appointments suggests that Jackson may have been consciously preparing him for the succession; this is the most likely interpretation of the events. But it is unquestionably possible that Jackson was grooming his Sub-Manager Hawkins for the succession; if so, there were two problems: first, Hawkins' abilities were not universally acknowledged in the Bank and, secondly, Hawkins would appear to have been a cousin of Jackson's. The private meeting would save Jackson from any embarrassment or, perhaps, responsibility for a choice that must be that of the directors.

When Jackson visited Shanghai en route Home, a puzzled Addis recorded that he seemed despondent and would not talk either of the Bank or of Addis's career; as if, somehow, these were no longer matters of which he had knowledge. One obvious interpretation is that Jackson was suffering the pain of leaving Hong Kong and all it had meant to him, but there are other interpretations which these thoughts and the subsequent association of Jackson and Hawkins on the board of the Imperial Bank of Persia make possible.[3]

The appointment of Newton Stabb

When Smith retired in 1910 on grounds of health, the appointment of Newton Stabb (East in 1891), then 42nd on the seniority list, was unusual in that he was junior to his two successors as Chief Manager, A.G. Stephen (East in 1885) and A.H. Barlow (East in 1891). It can be argued, however, that it was the latter appointments which were open to question; Stabb, after all, was just ten years junior to Smith and on the same grounds of age, health, and qualification was eligible; he was also well-positioned. Unfortunately of the two Hongkong Bank Board Minute Books lost during the Pacific War, one covers the crucial period of Stabb's appointment, but the situation can be partially reconstructed.

If the Board's policy in both 1902 and 1910 were to pass the chief managership on to the next 'generation', this simplifies analysis by eliminating say 22 of those senior to Stabb, including Stephen and, indeed, Charles Addis and H.E.R. Hunter (East in 1882). Nevertheless, these last two were marginal, and their position must be considered.

In March 1902 Addis learned of the Board's decisions – Smith, Hawkins and Wade Gard'ner were mentioned, but there was no reference to Addis or to the sub-managership in Hong Kong. Would Addis be called down to assist Smith? Writing in their joint diary, Mrs Addis recorded on May 8, 'Mr H. Hunter is to be sub-manager at HO. "The blow has fallen." Nevertheless I believe it is only that better things are in store for us.'[a]

In selecting Hunter as his Sub-Manager Smith had exercised the option promised by the Board; it was a sound choice. Hunter was an extrovert and socially oriented bachelor, the right counter to Smith; he had first shown his ability in his Borneo survey (see Vol. I, p. 424) and had held responsible posts as Agent Bangkok and Sub-Manager Shanghai. Addis himself does not express disappointment; his role in Shanghai was a demanding one which no other Bank officer was prepared for, involving as it did intimate concern with loan and railway negotiations, relations with Chinese officials over reparations payments and other matters with which Addis was to remain involved throughout his career. He turned down an offer from the American International Banking Corporation to be manager for £4,000; his Manager, Bevis, advised him that he would be Chief Manager some day.

Whatever long-run plans Smith may have had for the succession were upset by death and health factors which could not have been foreseen. In July news came that David Jackson had died in Yokohama of aneurism of the heart – 'He was an able chap and very kind hearted,' Addis wrote.[4] Smith replaced him with V.A. Caesar Hawkins, eventually made Harry Hunter the Inspector of Branches, and positioned J.C. Peter (East in 1884) as Sub-Manager in Head Office.

In March 1904 Addis was on Home leave and, Bevis, his health deteriorating, was soon to follow. Thus Smith was no doubt already planning to replace Bevis with Addis in 1905. The serious illness and consequent resignation early that year of Sir Ewen Cameron, the senior London Manager, upset the plans; Addis was instructed to cancel his bookings on the P&O and act as the junior of the two London Managers under A.M. Townsend. At first a temporary assignment, it was soon confirmed, thus technically eliminating Addis from the Eastern staff.

Into the Shanghai vacancy Smith then sent Harry Hunter who was replaced as Inspector by W. Adams Oram (East in 1882), another of Addis's contemporaries. When Smith took leave in 1906 he confirmed his high opinion of

---

[a] Presumably she was not thinking specifically of the ultimate consequences of their confirmation by the Bishop of Shanghai that afternoon – although she recognized that '... now we "belong to the Church" '.

Hunter by recommending him to the Board as Acting Chief Manager; Hawkins was passed over once more.

Addis met Smith several times in London. 'The little man looks well and even robust but sad a wee. I fancy he is concerned about his health in some way . . .'[5] Then just before his departure in December 1906 Smith had another long talk with Addis 'about his successor as Chief Manager. I was virtually offered and declined the succession. I believe I can be of more use to the Bank in London. But who could have believed I would ever refuse the Chief Managership of the HSBC!'[6] Addis was the fourth in the Bank's history known to have refused – following McLean, Cameron, and Walter (see Volume I).

For a time nothing relevant changed. Then in May 1909 J.C. Peter, the Sub-Manager in Hong Kong, took a Home leave which extended through April 1911, by which time many developments had occurred. The young Newton Stabb, who had been Sub-Accountant in Hong Kong and then as late as 1907 was Agent Saigon, returned from leave and replaced Peter as Sub-Manager.

Smith again took Home leave in 1910; V.A.C. Hawkins had resigned in 1907, A.H. Barlow was Agent Bangkok, Hunter was doing important work as Manager Shanghai, Peter was on extended leave. Thus Stabb was appointed Acting Chief Manager. When Smith resigned in London, Stabb was confirmed in the post.

Whether Hunter was approached is not known, but he might well have refused and, in any case, his health broke down in 1911 and he retired to London, where he became a director of Hambro's Bank and of the Imperial Bank of Persia. He was succeeded in Shanghai by A.G. Stephen, who had previously been Manager Manila.

If Smith had been the obvious choice, barring the possibility of Hawkins, Stabb owed his early succession in no small part to the particular circumstances, but there were already signs that he was under consideration. In 1899, Addis and Wade Gard'ner had written of Stabb officially: 'Excellent man in every respect. He proved himself a man of first rate ability. We have the highest opinion for his capacity and judgement.' In 1909 Addis noted Stabb as one of the up and coming men in the Bank.

Nevertheless, a close examination of the seniority list suggests not only names like Stephen, Manager Manila, or J.C. Peter, but also less certain but quite possible choices with equal experience. What specifically was Stabb's background?

Five years younger than his successor, A.G. Stephen, John Newton Stabb was born in 1868 in St John's, Newfoundland, and moved with his family to New York in 1873 where he eventually attended Brooklyn Polytechnic

Institute following earlier schooling in Devon, his ancestral home. The family had emigrated from the Torquay area in the eighteenth century but had maintained contact – a cousin, G. W. Stabb, from Torquay was to serve with the Bank from 1930 to 1960. Newton Stabb himself joined the Hongkong Bank in New York and was sent to London Office for training by A.M. Townsend. In 1909 Stabb married Ethel Mary, the daughter of A.M. Townsend, her mother being the sister-in-law of Ewen Cameron; thus Stabb had certainly married into the Bank.

If the only surviving formal reference to Stabb is the personnel report cited above, the unofficial references to him are all favourable, and there is one which must stand as evidence for the reasons behind his early promotion. Writing in 1952 A.S. Henchman, former Shanghai Manager, confirmed that in contemporary opinion H.M. Bevis, while popular, was 'not renowned for anything beyond the humdrum', although in fairness one should recall that his health had already seriously deteriorated. However, as Henchman noted, this provided the Bank the opportunity to take note of Newton Stabb:

Shanghai taipans have told me that if they required anything of real importance in those days they ignored the Manager's Room and went to this junior [Stabb] in the Telegram Department. It was not long before 'Beano' as we called him was installed at a desk behind Bevis and, according to the brokers, any offer entailing a real knowledge of exchange was telegraphed to him by a kind of code-signal for acceptance or refusal by Bevis who in the meantime had assumed an air of profound consideration until the signal came through.

. . . In [1903] Stabb appeared suddenly at Hong Kong during the reign of J.R.M. Smith. He was put in charge of the Book Office and when the Compradore [Lau Wai Chun] 'went wrong' took over the Cash Department where I was working as a junior. He was brilliant and capable in everything he touched.[7]

These comments receive some corroboration in a diary entry by Charles Addis dated Shanghai, June 30, 1902: 'With Bevis away and no Stabb at my right hand I had a heavy day of it.'[8]

Thus it is only possible to conclude that the Board, like his Shanghai superiors in 1899 and all others after them, found him convincing. His subsequent performance proved their judgement to have been sound.

THE SHAREHOLDERS, THE BOARD, AND THE LONDON COMMITTEE

With two new Chief Managers the Board might be expected to have played a more important role in the management of the Bank, but this did not occur. In 1910 the Board did revert to a sub-committee system and there is the feeling that the regular weekly meetings had become formalities, justifying Stabb's promise to Swire's that permitting their manager in Hong Kong to join the Board would involve little more than fifteen minutes of his time each week. The Board were kept informed of developments, their approval sought in certain formal situations, but in general their role remained non-executive, keeping the 'management' – a term coming more into use in the minutes – in touch with the requirements of constituents. As the Bank's role in China and Japan loans increased, so the role of the London Office became more significant. The role of the London Consultative Committee was consequently enhanced, but only in its own sphere; it would never challenge the Board in Hong Kong.

The shareholders

Under the terms of its charter and articles of association the Hongkong Bank was not obliged, as provided by the Companies Act, to furnish information about the shareholders. Nevertheless, the Bank apparently circulated a printed list of shareholders (but not the number of shares each held) with their addresses as stated on the register. Of these lists only two had been located, as of the time of writing this history – December 1905 and 1916. On the basis of these samples, the following rather surprising information is revealed.

There were 3,306 names on the 1905 list, although a few of these may be variations. The important fact is, however, that 2,533 or 77% gave an address in the British Isles. If the London Register had been open for unlimited transfers, it would have held at least three-quarters of the names and certainly well over 50% of the total shares. With a determined policy of maintaining the Head Office in the East, this was a significant statistic for the Board to keep in mind.

Of the 505 names listed with a Far East (including the Philippines) address, 109 were native to the country of residence. Some 59 were Chinese, 28 Portuguese, and 11 Filipino. And 13 were Indians resident in Hong Kong. There were nationalistic articles written which claimed the Bank would not permit Chinese to own shares; given the open market this claim is prima facie incorrect, but the evidence of Chinese names is reassuring.

Shareholders with addresses elsewhere may be found in the Straits Settlements, Siam, and the Dutch East Indies (31 names), India, Ceylon, and Burma (31), elsewhere in the British Empire (9), the United States (23), and Europe (163).

There were 91 shareholders with German-sounding names, and one must assume that a high percentage of these were in fact German. When Sir Charles Addis was asked by the Foreign Office for a list of German holdings during the Great War, he too had trouble distinguishing nationality on the basis of name, but a safe conclusion would be that in 1905 the Germans held only a small equity interest in the Bank.

The correspondence of staff members, at least in the early years of the Bank, suggests that some at least bought Bank shares on the basis of 'insider' information. In December 1905 there were 49 members or former members of the Hongkong Bank staff who owned Bank shares. The list is composed primarily of senior Managers.

Of the names on the share list 35% were the names of ladies; 705 married women and 451 single, plus 23 names which were listed '. . . and wife'. But in view of the fact that the holdings of each shareholder are unknown, little further may be said.

The shares were expensive, say £94, although this is admittedly a high (see Table 1.5). But even when shares had been in the £60s earlier in the decade, they were not items for general savings; the high price per share, and thus the significance in absolute terms of any percentage fluctuation, would discourage many. The absence of a large number of 'native' shareholders would also reflect the foreign nature of shareholding itself. As for the high percentage of women's names, this would not as yet reflect the concern with Estate Duty; it might be a consequence of late marriages in the East, young wives and consequently many widows, but this is simply conjecture – the statistic is in any case not an unusual one. The main facts are (i) the importance of the shareholders resident in the British Isles, (ii) the relatively few German names, and (iii) the presence of Chinese shareholders.

Composition of the Board of Directors (Table 1.1)

The only new company represented on the Hongkong Bank's Board during this period was Butterfield and Swire, from April 1914. Bradley and Co. were not represented continuously on the Board; otherwise there was no change in representation until the Great War.

There were other changes.

First of all, the addition of the Swire interests, Butterfield and Swire, including Taikoo sugar and important shipping connections, was a major breakthrough. John Samuel Swire (1825–1898), known as 'the Senior', had been suspicious of too close a connection with a bank on whose directorate Jardine Matheson was represented. Stabb had written personally to John Swire (eldest son of and successor to 'the senior') in London noting not only that there was 'scarcely any work attached to the position' of director but also appealing on the grounds that 'I do not want [the vacancy] filled except by a Britisher.'[9] Once elected, G.T.M. Edkins, Swire's senior manager in China, who had that same year been refused permission by his London principals to accept the Governor's invitation for an appointment to the Legislative Council, played a full role, becoming Chairman of the Bank in 1921.[b]

With the virtual fixing of company representation, that is, the replacing of a resigning director with another representative of the same company, the practice of substitution during Home leave developed. Thus the period is characterized by a significant increase in turnover, which cannot but have affected the grasp the directors possessed of the Bank's affairs. Turnover had a secondary impact on the rotation of the chairmanship and deputy chairmanship, with mid-year changes and seniority affected by absences on leave, making the determinants of the succession difficult to ascertain. Possibly for these reasons Jardine, Matheson and Co.'s representatives on the Board were elected chairmen for four of the twelve years; Reiss and Co. were also over-represented; and on three occasions there were two-year chairmanships.

The last German to be Chairman of the Hongkong and Shanghai Bank was A. Haupt of Melchers and Co. in 1907; in 1908 E. Goetz of Arnhold, Karberg and Co. was elected Deputy Chairman, but he resigned on leaving Hong Kong in July.

An analysis of Table 1.1 will confirm that Germans were not being elected Chairman in turn, but the real confrontation did not develop until 1913, when both the Chairman and the Deputy Chairman resigned in mid-year on leaving the Colony. As noted already Stabb was unwilling to see a vacancy on the Board filled by a German; he was equally unwilling to have a German Chairman.

Apparently the obvious choice was C.R. Lenzmann of Carlowitz, a company which by then was highly (and unreasonably) controversial in British trading circles, including the China Association. 'It will be difficult', Stabb had written to Addis, 'to know whom to make Chairman as we cannot put up a German.'[11] The problem presumably arose at this time through the fore-knowledge that F.H. Armstrong of Reiss and Co. and C.H. Ross of Jardine Matheson would not in fact serve out their terms. The selection of S.H. Dodwell to succeed them reflected the gravity of the situation, since Dodwell had not even been a member of the Board until late Spring of the year.

Throughout this period the Hongkong Bank remained otherwise in close

---

[b] The Governor had first invited Newton Stabb to membership on the Legislative Council, but 'after giving careful consideration to the matter [Stabb] informed me that he was unable to spare time to undertake the duties'. (Stabb's refusal was part of an overall policy and consistent with the Bank's refusal to permit their Shanghai Manager to stand for election to the Municipal Council.) Stabb nevertheless served briefly as a substitute on the Legislative Council in 1919. The Governor then invited Edkins and, when he declined, turned to Edward Shellim of D. Sassoon, Sons and Co., noting that Shellim had 'strong claims to the seat by reason of long residence in the Colony, of the large mercantile interests which he represents and of his business ability. He has for three terms been Chairman of the Hongkong and Shanghai Banking Corporation.'[10]

Table 1.1 *The Hongkong and Shanghai Banking Corporation Boards of Directors, 1902–1914*

February 1902

R. G. Shewan	Shewan, Tomes and Co.	*Chairman* 1902/03
J. J. Bell-Irving	Jardine, Matheson and Co.	*Deputy Chairman* (i) 1902
A. Haupt	Melchers and Co.	(ii) 1902
A. J. Raymond	E. D. Sassoon and Co.	(iii) 1902/03
D. M. Moses	D. Sassoon, Sons and Co.	
R. L. Richardson	Bradley and Co.	
G. W. Slade	Gilman and Co.	
N. A. Siebs	Siemssen and Co.	
H. E. Tomkins	Reiss and Co.	
H. Schubart	Carlowitz and Co.	
E. Goetz	Arnhold, Karberg and Co.	

11 members

Resigned: R. L. Richardson (March)   Elected: G. H. Medhurst (Dodwell)
J. J. Bell-Irving (May)   C. W. Dickson
G. W. Slade (September)   G. Balloch
A. Haupt (November)   C. Michelau

February 1903

A. J. Raymond	E. D. Sassoon and Co.	*Chairman* 1903/04
H. E. Tomkins	Reiss and Co.	*Deputy Chairman* 1903/04
D. M. Moses	D. Sassoon, Sons and Co.	
N. A. Siebs	Siemssen and Co.	
H. Schubart	Carlowitz and Co.	
E. Goetz	Arnhold, Karberg and Co.	
G. H. Medhurst	Dodwell and Co.	
C. W. Dickson	Jardine, Matheson and Co.	
G. Balloch	Gilman and Co.	
C. Michelau	Melchers and Co.	
R. G. Shewan	Shewan, Tomes and Co.	

11 members

Resigned: D. M. Moses (March)   Elected: E. Shellim
G. Balloch (May)   H. A. W. Slade
G. H. Medhurst (July)   E. S. Whealler
R. Shewan (August)   C. A. Tomes
C. Michelau (January 1904)   A. Haupt

February 1904

A. J. Raymond	E. D. Sassoon and Co.	*Chairman* 1904/05
H. E. Tomkins	Reiss and Co.	*Deputy Chairman* 1904/05
N. A. Siebs	Siemssen and Co.	
H. Schubart	Carlowitz and Co.	
E. Goetz	Arnhold, Karberg and Co.	
C. W. Dickson	Jardine, Matheson and Co.	
E. Shellim	D. Sassoon, Sons and Co.	
H. A. W. Slade	Gilman and Co.	
E. S. Whealler	Dodwell and Co.	

Table 1.1 – *cont.*

C. A. Tomes	Shewan, Tomes and Co.	
A. Haupt	Melchers and Co.	

11 members

Resigned: C. W. Dickson (May)   Elected: W. J. Gresson
           C. A. Tomes (July)   R. Shewan

February 1905
H. E. Tomkins	Reiss and Co.	*Chairman* 1905/06
H. A. W. Slade	Gilman and Co.	*Deputy then Chairman* 1905
A. Haupt	Melchers and Co.	(ii) *Deputy Chairman* 1905/06
N. A. Siebs	Siemssen and Co.	
H. Schubart	Carlowitz and Co.	
E. Goetz	Arnhold, Karberg and Co.	
W. J. Gresson	Jardine, Matheson and Co.	
E. Shellim	D. Sassoon, Sons and Co.	
E. S. Whealler	Dodwell and Co.	
C. A. Tomes	Shewan, Tomes and Co.	
A. J. Raymond	E. D. Sassoon and Co.	

11 members

Resigned: E. S. Whealler (March)   Elected: G. H. Medhurst
         H. E. Tomkins (May)   F. Salinger
         W. J. Gresson   C. W. Dickson
         H. Schubart (November)   C. R. Lenzmann

February 1906
A. Haupt	Melchers and Co.	*Chairman* 1906/07
C. W. Dickson	Jardine, Matheson and Co.	(i) *Deputy Chairman* 1906
G. H. Medhurst	Dodwell and Co.	(ii) *Deputy Chairman* 1906/07
N. A. Siebs	Siemssen and Co.	
E. Goetz	Arnhold, Karberg and Co.	
E. Shellim	D. Sassoon, Sons and Co.	
C. A. Tomes	Shewan, Tomes and Co.	
A. J. Raymond	E. D. Sassoon and Co.	
F. Salinger	Reiss and Co.	
C. R. Lenzmann	Carlowitz and Co.	
H. A. W. Slade	Gilman and Co.	

11 members

Resigned: E. Shellim (March)   Elected: D. M. Nissim
         F. Salinger   H. E. Tomkins
         C. W. Dickson (May)   W. J. Gresson (June)
         H. A. W. Slade (September)   G. Balloch

February 1907
G. H. Medhurst	Dodwell and Co.	*Chairman* 1907/08
W. J. Gresson	Jardine, Matheson and Co.	*Deputy Chairman* 1907
N. A. Siebs	Siemssen and Co.	
E. Goetz	Arnhold, Karberg and Co.	
C. A. Tomes	Shewan, Tomes and Co.	
A. J. Raymond	E. D. Sassoon and Co.	

Table 1.1 – *cont.*

C. R. Lenzmann	Carlowitz and Co.
D. M. Nissim	D. Sassoon, Sons and Co.
H. E. Tomkins	Reiss and Co.
G. Balloch	Gilman and Co.
A. Haupt	Melchers and Co.

11 members

Resigned: N. A. Siebs (March)   Elected: F. H. A. Fuchs (April)
          D. M. Nissim (April)   E. Shellim
          W. J. Gresson (May)   H. Keswick (*Deputy Chairman*)
          G. Balloch (June)   H. A. W. Slade
          A. Haupt (December)   G. Friesland (January 1908)

February 1908

H. Keswick	Jardine, Matheson and Co.	*Chairman* 1908
E. Shellim	D. Sassoon, Sons and Co.	*Chairman* 1908/09
E. Goetz	Arnhold, Karberg and Co.	*Deputy Chairman* 1908
C. A. Tomes	Shewan, Tomes and Co.	
A. J. Raymond	E. D. Sassoon and Co.	
C. R. Lenzmann	Carlowitz and Co.	
H. E. Tomkins	Reiss and Co.	
F. H. A. Fuchs	Siemssen and Co.	
H. A. W. Slade	Gilman and Co.	
G. Friesland	Melchers and Co.	
G. H. Medhurst	Dodwell and Co.	

11 members

Resigned: A. J. Raymond (February)   Elected: C. S. Gubbay
          G. H. Medhurst (March)   E. G. Barrett
          F. H. A. Fuchs (May)   C. G. R. Brodersen
          H. Keswick (July)   W. J. Gresson (*Deputy Chairman*)
          E. Goetz   W. Helms
   Died: C. G. R. Brodersen (October)   H. A. Siebs

February 1909

W. J. Gresson	Jardine, Matheson and Co.	*Chairman* 1909/10
H. E. Tomkins	Reiss and Co.	*Deputy Chairman* 1909/10
E. Shellim	D. Sassoon, Sons and Co.	
C. A. Tomes	Shewan, Tomes and Co.	
C. R. Lenzmann	Carlowitz and Co.	
H. A. W. Slade	Gilman and Co.	
G. Friesland	Melchers and Co.	
C. S. Gubbay	E. D. Sassoon and Co.	
E. G. Barrett	Dodwell and Co.	
H. A. Siebs	Siemssen and Co.	
W. Helms	Arnhold, Karberg and Co.	

11 members

Resigned: G. Friesland   Elected: J. W. Bandow
          H. A. W. Slade (February 1910)   G. Balloch

Table 1.1 – *cont.*

February 1910

H. E. Tomkins	Reiss and Co.	*Chairman* 1910
G. Balloch	Gilman and Co.	*Deputy then Chairman* 1910/11
C. A. Tomes	Shewan, Tomes and Co.	
then R. Shewan		*Deputy Chairman* 1910/11
C. R. Lenzmann	Carlowitz and Co.	
E. Shellim	D. Sassoon, Sons and Co.	
C. S. Gubbay	E. D. Sassoon and Co.	
E. G. Barrett	Dodwell and Co.	
H. A. Siebs	Siemssen and Co.	
W. Helms	Arnhold, Karberg and Co.	
J. W. Bandow	Melchers and Co.	
W. J. Gresson	Jardine, Matheson and Co.	

11 members

Resigned: W. Helms   Elected: F. Lieb
   E. G. Barrett   G. H. Medhurst
   H. E. Tomkins   F. H. Armstrong
   C. S. Gubbay   S. A. Levy
   W. J. Gresson   H. Keswick
             A. Forbes (Bradley & Co.)

February 1911

H. Keswick	Jardine, Matheson and Co.	*Chairman* 1911
G. H. Medhurst	Dodwell and Co.	*Deputy then Chairman* 1911/12
E. Shellim	D. Sassoon, Sons and Co.	*Deputy Chairman* 1911/12
R. Shewan	Shewan, Tomes and Co.	
C. R. Lenzmann	Carlowitz and Co.	
H. A. Siebs	Siemssen and Co.	
J. W. Bandow	Melchers and Co.	
F. Lieb	Arnhold, Karberg and Co.	
F. H. Armstrong	Reiss and Co.	
S. A. Levy	E. D. Sassoon and Co.	
A. Forbes	Bradley and Co.	
G. Balloch	Gilman and Co.	

12 members

Resigned: J. W. Bandow   Elected: G. Friesland
   E. Shellim   W. Logan
   H. Keswick   C. H. Ross
   W. Logan   E. Shellim
   S. A. Levy   C. S. Gubbay

February 1912

E. Shellim	D. Sassoon Sons and Co.	*Chairman* 1912/13
F. H. Armstrong	Reiss and Co.	*Deputy Chairman* 1912/13
R. Shewan	Shewan, Tomes and Co.	
C. R. Lenzmann	Carlowitz and Co.	
H. A. Siebs	Siemssen and Co.	
F. Lieb	Arnhold, Karberg and Co.	

Table 1.1 – *cont.*

C. S. Gubbay	E. D. Sassoon and Co.
A. Forbes	Bradley and Co.
G. Balloch	Gilman and Co.
G. Friesland	Melchers and Co.
C. H. Ross	Jardine, Matheson and Co.
G. H. Medhurst	Dodwell and Co.

12 members

Resigned: C. R. Lenzmann   Elected: C. G. Laurenz
    G. Balloch   W. L. Pattenden
    G. H. Medhurst (August)   S. H. Dodwell
    A. Forbes (November)   J. A. Plummer

February 1913

F. H. Armstrong	Reiss and Co.	*Chairman* 1913
C. H. Ross	Jardine, Matheson and Co.	*Deputy then Chairman* 1913
G. H. Medhurst	Dodwell and Co.	
then S. H. Dodwell		*Deputy then Chairman* 1913/14
R. Shewan	Shewan, Tomes and Co.	
C. R. Lenzmann	Carlowitz and Co.	
H. A. Siebs	Siemssen and Co.	
F. Lieb	Arnhold, Karberg and Co.	
C. S. Gubbay	E. D. Sassoon and Co.	
J. A. Plummer	Bradley and Co.	
W. L. Pattenden	Gilman and Co.	
G. Friesland	Melchers and Co.	
E. Shellim	D. Sassoon, Sons and Co.	

12 members

Resigned: F. H. Armstrong (April) Elected: P. H. Holyoak
    C. H. Ross (May)   D. Landale (*Deputy Chairman*)
    F. Lieb (October)   E. Goetz
    G. R. Laurenz (December)   C. Landgraf (January 1914)

February 1914

D. Landale	Jardine, Matheson and Co.	*Chairman* 1914/16
W. L. Pattenden	Gilman and Co.	*Deputy Chairman* 1914/16
S. H. Dodwell	Dodwell and Co.	
R. Shewan	Shewan, Tomes and Co.	
C. Landgraf	Carlowitz and Co.	
H. A. Siebs	Siemssen and Co.	
E. Goetz	Arnhold, Karberg and Co.	
C. S. Gubbay	E. D. Sassoon and Co.	
J. A. Plummer	Bradley and Co.	
G. Friesland	Melchers and Co.	
E. Shellim	D. Sassoon, Sons and Co.	
P. H. Holyoak	Reiss and Co.	

12 members

Table 1.1 – *cont.*

Died: G. Friesland (Melchers)	Elected: F. Lieb (April)
Resigned: E. Goetz (April)	G. T. Edkins (Butterfield and Swire)
	J. E. A. Widmann (Melchers)
J. E. A. Widmann (Melchers, August)	
F. Lieb (Arnhold, Karberg and Co.)	
H. A. Siebs (Siemssen and Co.)	
C. Landgraf (Carlowitz and Co.)	

association both as a commercial bank and as a merchant bank with its German constituents and associates; at times the Bank was on the defensive, called on to prove itself British. The gossipy and irresponsible Peking correspondent of *The Times*, G.E. Morrison, wrote frequently of the Bank's policy being 'dominated' by its German directors, and there is no doubt some took his jingoism seriously. The Bank, on the other hand, failed to appreciate the full implications of the deterioration in 'popular' Anglo-German relations, assuming that its position was still understood in terms of Hong Kong as an entrepôt, free and open to all.

Nor in those years did the Bank consider its 'corporate image', except perhaps in the concern shown over the composition of the Board of Directors.[12] Certainly the events of August 1914 were not foreseen by either directors or senior management.

The changed role of the London Committee

The formal invitation to the Hongkong Bank's Annual London Dinner in 1909 began, 'The London Committee and Managers . . .' There was no parallel in Hong Kong either to the annual dinner or to this significant mode of address.

The Board of Directors had often minuted that a certain matter was left to the discretion of Ewen Cameron as senior London Manager. Or, they might decide that such discretion was to be used after consulting the London Committee. But in the period after 1902 the Board, especially in matters concerning details of major loans, might rule that the decision was to be 'left in the hands of the London Managers and London Committee'.

The London Committee had come a long way from its limited role as defined by McLean in 1875 – 'examine the bill Schedules sent home and those sent out and to give me the best information about the names etc. and also the general working of the London office . . .'[13] But the Committee itself had changed, as Table 1.2 clearly reflects.

Table 1.2 *The Hongkong and Shanghai Banking Corporation London Consultative Committee, membership, 1903–1914[a]*

1903		
Sir Thomas Jackson, Bart	Chairman	
	retired HSBC Chief Manager	
	Director, London & County Bank	1903–1915
William A. Jones	Director, London & County Bank	1891–1905
Carl Meyer	formerly N. M. Rothschild and Sons	
	Chairman, Pekin Syndicate	1899–1916
William G. Rathbone	Director, P&O SN Co.	1900–1919
John Walter	retired, HSBC staff	1902–1906

	RESIGNED ETC.:	APPOINTED:
1905	William A. Jones	
1906	John Walter	Sir Ewen Cameron
1908	Sir Ewen Cameron	
1912		J. R. M. Smith
1912		Henry Keswick

1912		
Sir Thomas Jackson, Bart	Chairman	–1915
Sir Carl Meyer, Bart		–1916
William G. Rathbone		–1919
J. R. M. Smith	retired HSBC Chief Manager	–1918
Henry Keswick	Director, Matheson and Co.	–1919

[a] cf Volume I, Table 13.6.

However mischievously put, Alexander Michie, playing all three witches to Addis's Macbeth, had whispered to the young Addis in 1888 that (i) the Bank was growing too big for Hong Kong and that a sudden crisis would force a move to London, (ii) the directors, while the best Hong Kong could supply, were too narrow, too dependent on the Bank to be proper guides, and he concluded (iii) –

the man required for London will be a man of affairs, able to hold his own in society and not merely an exchange hack, and looking round I think there is probably no one so well fitted as yourself by general culture to hold that post. Make that then your objective and when the cry comes for a change of management to London, do not resist it for it is bound to come . . .[14]

Addis was quick to note in his journal, 'Cameron thinks a change of management to London would be a mistake, even with a Hong Kong local committee.' But was the seed of an idea sown? Addis out of all expectation had become junior Manager London in 1905; in 1912 he succeeded Townsend as senior Manager. Glamis then Cawdor he had, would he be Chief Manager – in London – thereafter?

Michie had diagnosed the problem, but there were other remedies. In the crisis of 1874/75 the London shareholders were successful in having McLean sent out from London to report; in 1890–1892 the lesson was learned that for an Eastern bank Hong Kong was safer than London; yet, Michie could not be gainsaid, in the 'Age of Imperialism', the years of the great loans to China, Japan, and Siam, there had to be a credible management in the financial market of the world, the directors in Hong Kong were not only insufficiently qualified to supervise such activities but they were, as Michie foresaw, incorrectly sited. And yet the Head Office remained in Hong Kong.

It remained because only half the problem had been stated. The Hongkong Bank remained a regional exchange bank; its source of funds was regional, it financed intra-regional trade, and its inter-regional trade was only partly to London; from Hong Kong the Bank looked to Lyons and Hamburg, to San Francisco and New York; its Eastern-based constituents required its facilities; its shareholders, and just under 50% of the shares were on the Eastern registers, supported them. Operating in silver, the Bank needed a silver base.

At the same time, as the British representative on the successive international China consortiums, it was also true that, dealing in the world's capital market, the Bank required a London base.

The solution had in part already been found with the departure from the East of Ewen Cameron, the Manager most skilled in merchant banking; the Board now took the next essential and logical step; they transformed the Consultative Committee *de facto* into a virtual second but always subsidiary 'board' and they instructed their London Managers to work with this 'board' in City of London affairs even as the Chief Manager worked with the Hong Kong Board on commercial and exchange bank matters. For the loans floated in London, Hong Kong took London advice; for exchange banking, and, indeed, for sovereign-risk silver loans issued in the East, the Hongkong Bank remained very much under the direction of its Board in Hong Kong operated by the Chief Manager, by the Manager Shanghai, and by able Managers and Agents throughout the region the Bank knew best.

And afterwards in the inter-war years, when the loans had been made and the nations turned within themselves to their own declining empires, what then would be the London Committee's role? By then Sir Charles Addis was successor to Jackson as Chairman of a Consultative Committee which had lost its lustre, of a committee which served a Bank which had returned to Hong Kong, worrying over the remains of its imperial role, but destined for a period to do what it had in any case always done best, exchange banking, and to play a less dramatic part in world affairs – except, always, in China.

And yet for Addis the prophecy of Michie still proved relevant, not in the tendency of journalists and officials to confuse his chairmanship of a London Committee with that of the Hongkong Bank itself, a usurpation by default which Hong Kong resented, but by his contribution to inter-war finance as director of the Bank of England, director of the Bank of International Settlements, British director of the Reichsbank, confidant of Montagu Norman, of J.M. Keynes, and of R.G. Hawtrey, and the consultant to the British Government on financial and Chinese affairs to the end.

The Board of Directors had for some time been concerned that the London Committee should be able to play a leading role in the Hongkong Bank as a merchant bank. While retaining the link with the London and County Bank and its successors – the London, County and Westminster etc. – first through W.A. Jones and then through Thomas Jackson himself, the Board also approved the appointment to the London Committee of Carl Meyer (later Sir Carl Meyer, Bart) and William Rathbone, both able financiers.[c] By agreeing to John Walter's succession to the place of G.E. Noble in 1902, the Board confirmed its policy of bringing the Committee into closer contact with the London Office, with the varied needs of the Bank in London, staffing, buildings, and financial. Walter had agreed to resign his seat on the retirement of Cameron, should Cameron wish to replace him; the Board took advantage of this in 1906.

With the retirement of Sir Thomas Jackson in 1902 the Board were able to take the final step in the transformation of the London Committee. By appointing him Chairman at a realistic salary of £1,500, that is, six times the basic remuneration of the Chairman of the Hongkong Bank itself, and by confirming that he was no longer a member of the Bank staff, the Board had set up an independent authority operating a committee of experts, linked to the working of the Bank and available for authoritative consultation on the problems confronting the Bank in London.

Nor was there much opportunity for a conflict of authority. The Board and the Committee worked in two different fields in two different places, each dominant in its own specialization. The ultimate authority rested with the Board in Hong Kong; this was never challenged as there was, in fact, no need to do so.

Working in association with the Committee in London were the two London Managers. In McLean's day, McLean had been Manager and William Kaye had been Sub-Manager. But with Jackson and Cameron both in London, the Board had agreed that Cameron could sign as 'Manager',

[c] The knighting of Carl Meyer in 1910 gave rise to an anti-Semitic outburst from G. E. Morrison, the *Times* correspondent in Peking, who apparently had hoped for such an honour: 'There is no chance of my being knighted – none whatever. At one time there was some such talk, but those honours are reserved for Jews, Railway Conductors and loyal Britishers who sing "God Save the King" in broken English like Carl Meyer and the Abrahams, Isaacs, and Jacobs.' What Morrison saw as the close connection of the Hongkong Bank with both Jews and Germans seemed to particularly upset him.[15]

although Jackson was in charge; hence the tradition of two 'Managers' and, indeed, as the office grew, there was need for Sub-Managers as well.

As it happened, one of the two Managers was more experienced in merchant banking; first it had been Cameron. His 'junior' had been John Walter and then A.M. Townsend. The appointment of Charles Addis as junior Manager in 1905 carried with it membership, replacing Cameron, on the boards of the British and Chinese Corporation, Ltd, the Bank's jointly promoted venture with Jardine, Matheson and Co., and the Chinese Central Railways, Ltd (see Part II). Although Townsend was involved in loan negotiations, especially those dealing with Japan, Addis was the principal Manager concerned. When in turn he became senior, Addis's position was *de facto* confirmed by the appointment of H.D.C. Jones as junior Manager. Jones was strictly an exchange banker. Addis would be assisted by Murray Stewart, brought back to the Bank for this purpose; Addis's operations were virtually outside the normal work of the Bank with which he nevertheless remained very much in touch and involved.

The changes resulting from Sir Newton Stabb's appointment as Manager London in 1921 require a separate discussion. This is undertaken in Volume III.

The policies of the Board of Directors

To say that there were two banks would be an exaggeration; there were two functions, separated efficiently to meet apparently conflicting requirements. They might today be managed by establishing a separate company, a Wardley for example, but in the 1900s the solution was found in a redesigned London Committee and a specially qualified London management.

But policy for the Bank was set in Hong Kong, and the Board, no doubt guided by an increasingly experienced management, made the decisions which affected the corporation as a whole.

Establishment of new agencies

The Board displayed its traditional caution with reference to the establishment of new offices, using the alternative method of appointing merchant agents where possible, for example, Jardine Matheson in China's developing northeast provinces which constitute Manchuria. There were two areas of expansion, however, China and the Malay States, and a total of nine agencies were opened in the pre-war decade (see Table 2.1).

After an exhaustive study, management did not recommend opening in Chungking, but the Board did agree to establish agencies in Hongkew, Canton, and Tsingtau, each of which has its own history.

Kobe/Hiogo. Before taking action, however, the Board were determined that management should act in strict accordance with the terms of the ordinance. They did not want the vilifications of 1890 repeated (see Volume I, Chapter 11). In 1904 A.M. Townsend as London Manager had entered into a detailed correspondence with the Treasury to explain to them that Hiogo had been incorporated into Kobe and that the Bank accordingly wished permission to change the official location name of its agency from Hiogo to Kobe. He forwarded a letter from the Agent, J. McLean:

Letters of Credit issued by other Banks would indicate that we have no Branch at Kobe.

Many people have an idea that Kobe and Hiogo are different places some distance apart and strangers carrying Letters of Credit find under the heading Kobe – either the Chartered or Specie Bank, naturally they go to one of these banks though in many cases they would prefer to come to us.[16]

The Treasury were somewhat bemused by all this, but the approval was given for the change.

More important was Addis's representation to the Treasury in 1906 requesting permission to open in Canton, Dalny (Dairen), Newchwang, Tsingtau (Kiaochow), and the Malay States. The Treasury minutes indicate acceptance that all these were 'within the natural sphere of the Hongkong and Shanghai Banking Corporation', except that ' "The Malay States" seems rather a wide geographical "place" ' and that some caution should be used since the Bank might be building up an argument in preparation for the renewal of their charter in 1908. A month after this last minute, on October 27, 1906, the necessary formal permission was signed, although this did not actually require that the Bank take any immediate action.[17]

Hongkew. Before this the Board had acted on the question of Hongkew, that part of Shanghai across Soochow Creek and along the Whangpoo; as such it (i) needed no special authorization being in Shanghai but (ii) is no further from the Bund than say West Point (for Jardine interests) is from central Hong Kong. Until the Kowloon sub-agency was opened in 1929 the Hongkong Bank had no other two-office city, and the Board's 1906 agreement to the opening of a sub-agency in Hongkew must be ascribed to the eloquence of H.E.R. 'Harry' Hunter.

With the Chief Manager safely on the boat sailing for London, Harry Hunter just down from Shanghai made his appeal at the May 29 Board meeting, the first he attended as Acting Chief Manager. Arguing that a 'branch' at Hongkew would further the development of the Settlement and be a convenience to a large private connection the Bank had in Hongkew, Hunter was successful and the office was established, providing, among other things, an opportunity for a young Bank officer to obtain further experience in semi-independence. The first Sub-Agent to be named on the Staff Lists, A.F. Warrack in 1909, had been eleven years on the Eastern staff.

Canton. The Hongkong Bank had a long relationship with Deacon and Co., their Canton agents. Three Deacon brothers served as tea tasters for Augustine Heard and Co. between 1847 and 1857; Albert Deacon, who had come to China in 1852, then founded his own firm and on return to London went into partnership with his brother as Messrs E. and A. Deacon; Albert was appointed a member of the Bank's first London Committee. In Canton the Hong Kong firm had acted as agents for both the Hongkong and the Mercantile Banks.

In October 1906 J.O.P. Bland, representing the British and Chinese Corporation, agreed in Peking that monies payable by the planned Canton–Kowloon Railway to the Hongkong Bank should be receivable in Canton or Hong Kong at the discretion of the Viceroy, and this provision was subsequently incorporated into Article 14 of the 1907 Loan Agreement.[18] The possibility of large sums being paid into a merchant agent would alone have been sufficient for the Bank to consider a Canton office, but in January 1908 Deacon's compradore absconded and, as a result, the Hongkong Bank suffered some considerable loss since the compradore had access to the Bank's Canton funds. This loss coincided with progress on the Canton–Kowloon Railway project and, although the latter is not specifically referred to by the Board, it was obviously the underlying factor in, as the defalcation was the proximate cause of, the Board's ultimate decision to open in Canton.

The foreigners in Canton had been relegated by the anti-foreign Cantonese to a riverine sandbank, which they duly built into a prosperous trading and residential base known as Shameen, and there in 1904 the Board, recognizing the limited area involved, had had the foresight to purchase land in anticipation of need. Thus in July 1908 they were able to authorize the opening of the Bank's own office with R.R. Hynd (East in 1891) as the first Agent.

Tsingtau. Consideration of a branch in Tsingtau began at least as early as 1903 when Charles Addis was Sub-Manager in Shanghai. The question arose again the following year and Cameron as London Manager asked Addis, who was then Home on leave, to go to Hamburg to discuss the whole question of Julius Brüssel's health (Brüssel, a German citizen, was then Manager Hamburg) as well as Tsingtau. Addis's report is addressed to Smith as Chief Manager and involves a basic policy recommendation: the Hongkong Bank should be ruled in its decisions by commercial not political arguments.

'To open a branch in Tsingtau has long been a hobby of Brüssel's', Addis wrote, but the Hamburg Manager's arguments were based on the premiss that as the Hongkong Bank was the premier bank in the East it had a duty to open; Brüssel also stressed the satisfaction that such a move would give 'our German friends, commercial and official'. Addis accepted that the German merchants, Frickssen (A.K.) and Arnhold, Karberg and Co., were dissatisfied with their arrangements with the Deutsch-Asiatische Bank (DAB) and could be depended upon to give their business, even Government business, to the Hongkong Bank at equal rates, but Addis realistically warned that such an understanding might not last and that inevitably once the Hongkong Bank was there and unable to withdraw easily there would be a natural tendency for the German officials to favour 'their own' bank.

The attraction of the Hongkong Bank to Tsingtau merchants was then, first, as a foil to the DAB and, secondly, as a sign of recognition and stability for the German colony in North China, assisting them perhaps to consolidate their position in Shantung. But to all of this Addis concluded:

If I am right in thinking that the proper principle for us to go on is a commercial one and that we ought, therefore, only to open in places where an Agency is likely to pay its way either immediately or in the near future, then Tsingtau should wait.

It is quite possible that important commercial developments may follow the railway extension in Shantung. The exports of straw braid and pongees from Tsingtau are increasing and there may be mineral exports to come. All this is worth watching with a view to opening as soon as such a step is justified by the trade of the place. But in my opinion the time is not ripe for that yet; nor, with a [Russo-Japanese] war in progress can we consider it propitious. It would be more prudent to wait and see the outcome of events.[19]

The total foreign trade of the port as recorded by the Maritime Customs in 1904 was HkTs4.3 million; in 1913 it was HkTs28.4 million, and the Bank had the basis for a reconsideration. By 1912, as a first step, the Board had sent A.D. Brent as Agent; in January 1914 they authorized the establishment of an agency under G.G.S. Forsyth (East in 1896) with D.C. Edmondston (East in 1912), a junior with a 'good knowledge of German' and who subsequently became Manager Hamburg in 1921 with only nine years seniority.[d] By establishing an office in Tsingtau on the eve of the Great War the Hongkong Bank was positioned before the conflicting claims of the Japanese and later the Chinese authorities could seriously affect their right of presence.

Taipei.　In any consideration of new China branches, note should be made of the Hongkong Bank's own sub-agency in Taipei apparently established in

---

[d]　With the reluctant approval of the Board and at the request of H.M.'s Minister in Peking, Brent served for three months, 1911/12, as acting Vice-Consul in Tsingtau on the understanding that it involved only one hour's work a day.

1909, replacing its former merchant-agency relationship in Tamsui. At the time Formosa was under the occupation of the Japanese and the Bank's sole Eastern staff member assigned to the sub-agency was listed as a member of the Yokohama office staff, to which branch he reported. The growing trade of the respective ports was sufficient commercial justification for the Bank's decision.

Manchuria. The Bank also reacted in stages to the growing trade of the Northeast Provinces. In 1911 the Bank sent its own staff officer to Dairen (Dalny) and in 1913 two officers to Harbin to work with the merchant agents. These officers were at first listed as if members of the Bank's Shanghai staff, but they were listed separately when full agencies were established in 1922 and 1915 respectively.

Malaya. Developments in Malaya, both in the Straits Settlements and in the Malay States, were the consequence of the rubber boom which peaked in 1910 driving prices from the four shillings prevailing at the beginning of the decade to a record twelve or even thirteen shillings a pound. Both rubber and tin production were expanding and the latter especially brought Chinese workers and with them China connections. With the energetic and ambitious T.S. Baker (East in 1883) then the Singapore Manager, expansion north was inevitable; the Bank had to move into Ipoh and Kuala Lumpur if only to secure the business its Penang agency had developed; the move to Malacca was prompted at least in part by the demands of planters then served by Singapore, that to Johore Bahru was also partly in response to the requirements of the Sultan and his Government with whom the Bank had long had associations. In fact the three new Malay States sub-agencies – in Ipoh, Kuala Lumpur, and Johore Bahru – were to open within weeks of each other in early 1910.

   The Chartered Bank had early been encouraged to establish in the Malay States through promises of Government business and accommodation, and the Hongkong Bank's entry into Malacca, encouraged by the Straits Settlements Governor, Sir John Anderson, was facilitated by the offer of temporary accommodation and the deposit of Government funds, including those of the Municipal and Rural Boards, with the Bank.[20] The Government of the Federated Malay States (FMS) was also anxious for the Bank to establish in the administrative capital of Kuala Lumpur and promised to share Government business with the long-established Chartered Bank and to assist the Bank in finding accommodation. In 1912 the Bank decided to build in the Old Market Square, and this remained its Malayan headquarters until construction of a new building on the same site in 1973. Similarly there was assistance in Ipoh, but business alone was sufficient to justify the new agencies. The first

Sub-Agent in Ipoh was A.C. Hynes (East in 1897), the Bank's Chief Manager, 1926–1929.

By these initiatives the Hongkong Bank had moved up country from the ports and established itself as a 'local bank'. In 1912 the Mercantile Bank was induced to establish a branch at Kota Bharu on the peninsula's East Coast, setting a base for further expansion, supplementing the Hongkong Bank's moves which, with the merger of the two banks after 1959, provided the nation-wide coverage which enabled the Hongkong Bank Group to participate in the development of the Federation of Malaysia.

Thus the geographical expansion of the Bank in China may be described as 'cautious', that in Malaya as historically significant.

Other policies

During the period 1902 to 1914 the Hongkong Bank renewed its charter of incorporation and in 1907 obtained a 50% increase in its paid-up capital, from $10 to $15 million, by a rights issue. Further amendments to the basic charter were authorized in 1914. The problem of the excess issue of banknotes and of the one-dollar note issue arose from time to time, but the Board had Addis negotiating in London as well as the Chief Manager in Hong Kong. These and related matters were not, as far as the Board was concerned, controversial, and are better considered in the chronology below.

In connection with the issue of new shares the Board discovered, somewhat belatedly, that, if they excluded the clause on the scrip stating the exchange rate, they would be free to pay dividends at the rate of the day; in effect they had been doing this all along, but they had had to state their decision on two separate lines of the accounts, one showing the dollar equivalent of dividend calculated at $1 = 4s:6d, the other showing the additional amount necessary to actually pay the dividend at the rate of the day. From 1908 this complication was eliminated.

The Bank had been paying dividends income tax free for those shares on the London Register. In 1903 the Board, on the recommendation of the London Committee, agreed to pay the tax for those resident in the United Kingdom even if their shares were on the Hong Kong Register, thus placing all shareholders on an equal footing. However, the increase in tax forced reconsideration of the best way to achieve equality; it was agreed that dividends would be paid subject to tax, and the adjustment will be described below in connection with the mid-1914 accounts.

The dividends continued to be quoted in sterling, however, until 1972. This apparent anomaly could no longer be explained in terms of the complications arising from the original par exchange rate; the fact is the Bank's performance was judged in London.

The published reserves remained cushioned by unappropriated funds in

Head Office and branch contingency accounts and by the writing down of securities to market price or below out of current profits. The surplus on contingencies accounts, which eventually totalled more than $3 million, was maintained by the traditional custom of writing off all possible losses from current earnings, despite the existence of the unappropriated amounts.

Jackson's 'third reserve' of $8.9 million remained unmentioned and, given other policies, would seem not to have been touched. Since it cannot be identified, it has to be omitted from the analysis (see Chapter 13, Volume I).

Bank premises account was periodically written down on the grounds that it was Board policy to keep any non-income bearing account at a nominal level.

On the remuneration of its Chief Manager the Board proceeded cautiously, offering Smith, as previously noted, a flat £5,000 per annum. His performance was such as to warrant a bonus of £1,000 at the end of 1903, £2,000 at the end of 1904, and this was followed in 1905 by new terms which were, in fact, a modification of the Board's previous arrangement with Jackson: Smith was to receive the £5,000 plus 1% of the amount paid away to reserves and paid out in dividends. This was eventually amended in 1908 to be a minimum of 1% depending on performance. With Stabb the Board began anew, but eventually granted him the 1% in addition to the basic £5,000.

Other personnel policies will be considered in Chapter 3 below.

THE CHRONOLOGY, 1902–1914

The setting

Silver

In the last eight years of Jackson's administration of the Hongkong Bank, from 1893 through 1901, the sterling value of the dollar fell 26% from 2s:6d to 1s:10¼d. In February 1903 the general committee of the China Association held a discussion on silver's future. The experts, noting that Japan and the Philippines were already on 'gold', predicted correctly that the Straits Settlements and Siam would soon follow. From this T.H. Whitehead, the Chartered Bank's former Hong Kong manager, basing his argument on the fact that silver had been abandoned by several countries as a standard of value and assuming that silver would in consequence not be used for coinage, predicted that the price of silver must continue to fall.[21]

Thomas Jackson was present. He foresaw that to go off silver did not necessarily mean that the country would abandon the use of a silver coinage or that China would cease to create a demand for the metal; he, surprisingly, concluded that a rise in the price of silver and in the China exchange within the following twelve months was probable.[22]

The following month the price of silver rose slightly; by mid-year it had reached 2s:6d per ounce and the exchange had risen a net 5.3% in six months. Jackson's prediction had been made at virtually the record low point; indeed the Bank's end-1906 accounts used a rate, 2s:3⅛d, which was 43% in excess of the 1s:7d prevailing at the end of 1902. At this point there was again a decline in the exchange paralleling a fall in the price of silver as India ceased buying and an American financial crisis forced up the Bank rate to 7%. There were rallies in 1909 and 1912 for which Indian factors were mainly to explain, and in which in the latter year the Hongkong Bank played a dramatic role. The rate in June 1914 was still approximately 20% above the record lows which marked the beginning of J.R.M. Smith's tenure as Chief Manager (see Table 1.3).

Within each half-year there were often severe fluctuations which were considerably greater than the figures in Table 1.3 suggest; similarly, the appearance of a 'plateau' from 1894–1917 as seen from a superficial glance at Figure 1 was operationally a delusion. The movements, however, required considerable shipments of bullion and other profitable operations to counter speculators, and these exchange rate variations became part of the normal hazards of the Bank's operations. They placed a heavy burden on the key Managers; mastery of exchange operations became the one essential qualification for the Chief Manager, a London Manager, and the Shanghai Manager. Smith, Townsend/Addis, and Hunter were a team, as were Stabb, Addis, and Stephen later.

The Bank was still said to be operating on an 'even keel', but the term was subjected to a subtle change of meaning. Originally, in the early 1880s, it had been used to assure constituents and shareholders that the Bank's sources and uses of funds were matched in the two major currency areas – gold/sterling and silver/dollar. Statistical tests (see Volume I, introduction to Part II) are compatible with this explanation through the period 1902. Subsequently the Bank took positions in sterling or silver, the former particularly marked as silver declined from its post-Great War peak (see Volume III), and no statistical test will support a simple sources/uses of funds explanation of the term 'even keel'. The brief decline in the value of shareholders' funds in 1919 during the height of the silver boom reflects the impact of the Bank's sterling reserve holdings (see Figure 2). The term was becoming a slogan, a statement that the Bank was aware of the risks and was taking (unspecified) precautions. The term, in other words, no longer carried a specific operational significance.

The accepted explanation of the improved fortunes of silver is precisely in its use for coinage in countries 'off silver'. The fall which began in 1913 continued through mid-1915; it might have been more serious but for the action taken by the Hongkong Bank as leader of a syndicate formed on the

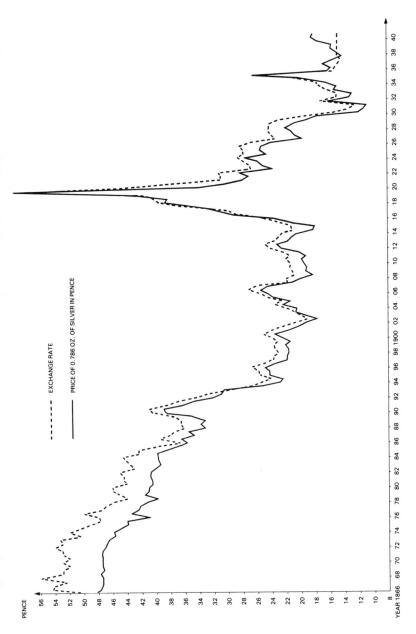

PENCE

EXCHANGE RATE

PRICE OF 0.786 OZ. OF SILVER IN PENCE

Figure 1 Exchange rate (Hong Kong on London) and the price of silver (London), 1866–1940

39

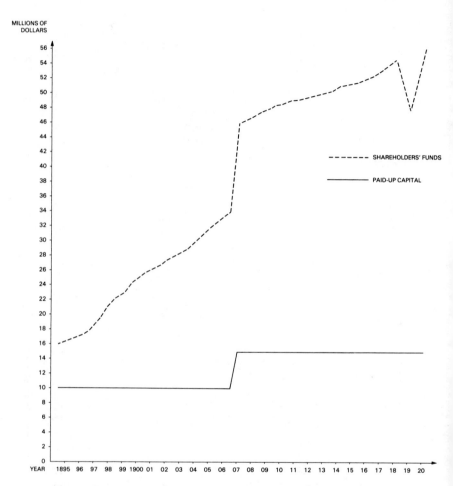

Figure 2 Shareholders' funds and paid-up capital in dollars, 1895–1920

failure of the Indian Specie Bank, but that story requires separate handling at the appropriate time, as does a consideration of the impact of these events on the accounts of the Bank.

Banking

That there were new banks operating in China during the years before the 1914–1918 war is well-known, but unfortunately it is difficult to assess their impact on the operations of the Hongkong Bank. That the new banks were for the most part 'national' in the sense that they were founded to finance a particular country's intended investments in China or to float or service their loans is equally true, but this did not mean they were necessarily also successful in cornering the trade finance of their nationals, who might still prefer the well-established exchange banks. Certainly the newcomers were involved in the international loans and the railway concessions, but it was the Hongkong Bank's boast that, where hands were not tied, business of all nationalities came to the Hongkong Bank.

The earlier arrival of the Deutsch-Asiatische Bank and the Banque de l'Indo-Chine has been noted in Volume I. There had been minor Russian banking ventures in the North, but the first serious development was the founding of the Russo-Chinese Bank in December 1895; this was merged with the Banque du Nord in 1910 to form the Russo-Asiatic Bank, and behind the Russians were the expertise and finance of European capitalists, especially the French Crédit Lyonnais and Banque de Paris et des Pays Bas (with Belgian associations); the Disconto-Gesellschaft was also involved through the St Petersburg International Bank.[23]

American national, that is, Federally chartered, banks were not permitted overseas branches before 1914, but special banks for overseas operations could be incorporated. The Guaranty Trust of New York was behind the Cathay Trust Company; in 1902 the Connecticut-chartered International Banking Corporation (IBC) began the development of a branch network in the East and established an excellent reputation on its own before the National City Bank of New York acquired a majority interest in 1915. IBC's chairman and president General Thomas H. Hubbard 'copied the structure and raided the personnel of the British overseas banks', and by 1914 IBC had, in addition to offices in New York, London, Panama, and San Francisco, a network of sixteen branches in China, Japan, the Philippines, Singapore, and Hong Kong.[24] In 1903 the Nederlandsche Handels Maatschappij opened a branch in Shanghai and the Crédit Foncier de l'Extrème Orient opened in 1907. Lloyds Bank was present through the so-called 'Peking Group', but it did not operate a separate banking facility in the Far East. These banks, with the Yokohama Specie Bank, feature in the complex combinations which

Table 1.3 *The price of silver and the Hong Kong exchange, 1902–1914*

Year	d/ounce of silver	\$=x s/d[a]	% change in 6 months
1872 June	60.0	4/6	–
1877 October	54.6	3/11$\frac{1}{8}$	–
1901 December	25.8	1/10$\frac{1}{4}$	–
1902 June	24.4	1/8$\frac{1}{2}$	−7.9
1902 December	22.6	1/7	−7.3
1903 June	24.6	1/8	5.3
1903 December	26.4	1/8$\frac{7}{8}$	4.4
1904 June	26.1	1/9$\frac{15}{16}$	5.1
1904 December	28.6	1/11$\frac{9}{16}$	7.4
1905 June	27.1	1/10$\frac{1}{2}$	−4.5
1905 December	30.3	2/0$\frac{9}{16}$	9.2
1906 June	31.1	2/1$\frac{1}{2}$	3.8
1906 December	32.4	2/3$\frac{1}{8}$	6.4
1907 June	31.1	2/2$\frac{3}{16}$	−3.5
1907 December	26.8	1/9$\frac{1}{3}$	16.9
1908 June	25.4	1/9$\frac{7}{8}$	0.6
1908 December	23.2	1/8$\frac{3}{4}$	−5.1
1909 June	24.4	1/9$\frac{1}{8}$	1.8
1909 December	24.3	1/9$\frac{1}{2}$	1.8
1910 June	24.8	1/9$\frac{3}{8}$	−0.6
1910 December	25.4	1/10	2.9
1911 June	24.6	1/9$\frac{1}{2}$	−2.3
1911 December	25.7	1/10$\frac{1}{4}$	2.9
1912 June	28.6	2/0$\frac{1}{16}$	8.8
1912 December	29.7	2/0$\frac{7}{8}$	3.4
1913 June	27.7	1/11$\frac{5}{8}$	−5.0
1913 December	27.3	1/11$\frac{3}{16}$	−1.8
1914 June	26.3	1/10$\frac{5}{8}$	−2.4
1914 December	23.3	1/9$\frac{1}{8}$	−6.6
1915 December	27.1	1/11	8.9[b]
1901 (Dec) – 1914 (June)			1.7
1872 (June) – 1914 (June)			−58.1

[a] Rate quoted in HSBC semi-annual reports.
[b] Percentage change in 12 months.

attempted to finance China's modernization. In contrast two companies established in 1905 and intended to finance Japanese trade and development, the Anglo-Japanese Bank and the British and Japanese Finance Corporation, had brief and insignificant histories.

The Chinese Revolution of 1911 did not in itself affect the status of foreign banks, which were then protected by extraterritorial status as defined by treaties. Indeed, the last years of the Manchu dynasty saw the decline of the so-called 'native banking system', as provincial and customs authorities founded semi-official banks and used post office facilities for revenue deposit and transmission. The Revolution caused the final collapse of the Chinese remittance, or Shansi, banks.

China's modern banking sector was in embryo and hardly prepared to fill the vacuum. The Bank of Communications (Chiao-t'ung Bank) and the Bank of China – the latter evolved from the Ta Ts'ing Bank – were contending for central bank status which, in the end, neither achieved. The Imperial Bank of China was temporarily in eclipse, and the crisis in the Shanghai money market in 1910/11 weakened the system; nevertheless the potential was obviously there.

The foreign exchange banks were not equipped and never intended to penetrate China as commercial banks; their resources were barely adequate for the limited role they actually played in the interior through the native banking system. However, the increased preference for banknotes and the random issue of inadequately secured notes by various Chinese banks from the early 1900s encouraged the use of Hongkong Bank banknotes at a time when the Bank was withdrawing its note issue in the Straits and, indeed, in China itself. Thus it was the Hong Kong issued notes of the Bank which moved up the railways and through the trading network of the South as one form of stable currency available to the producers of the region.

In Japan the Japanese had long established a banking system which served their requirements as foreign trade increased in tonnage and value. In 1903, for example, there were 2,491 banking offices in the country with a total paid-up capital of Yen 380 million, but even in Japan (and despite the lapse of extraterritoriality in 1899) there was room for foreign exchange banks.[25] In addition to the Chartered Bank and the Hongkong Bank there were German, Russian, Dutch, and French newcomers. The increased activity of the Yokohama Specie Bank notwithstanding, the Japanese still had need of foreign banking facilities. Indeed, in the special field of public loans, the Hongkong Bank was involved with Japanese loans to a greater total nominal value than that of the Chinese issues.[26] There was, however, an essential difference. In Japan the foreign banks served a supplementary role; in the London market the Yokohama Specie Bank was always a member of the issuing Group. With China loans the Hongkong Bank acted as the sole member of the British Group until 1913; there were no Chinese banking participants until the 1930s. To write of the Hongkong Bank as a China bank is to make a qualitative statement about the Bank's role rather than a quantitative statement of its loan business.

While the Hongkong Bank was a leader in both China and Japan, the

French and Dutch financial institutions controlled the bulk of the trade between Europe and their colonies in the East. Exceptions were the finance of trade with British interests and intra-regional trade and the related movement of funds, for example, remittances by Overseas Chinese. In the Philippines the long-established Hongkong and Chartered Banks found themselves competing with newly arrived American institutions; the Hongkong Bank's New York agency proved invaluable.

In Siam the Bank faced German intrigue, but it worked in cooperation with a strongly independent but friendly Government which feared in particular French financial involvement. The Bank was in India primarily to finance the India–Far East trade and consequently gave first priority to foreign exchange operations. It was not therefore affected by Indian banking competition *per se*, but one should note that the Mercantile Bank of India took over David Yule's Bank of Calcutta in 1906 – Yule was the sole holder of its common stock. Further south in Ceylon, where the Hongkong Bank was a late-comer, there is no question but that it continued to play a secondary role in extremely competitive situations.

The banking scene was, then, a changing one, but the national orientation of the new banks and the primary concern many of them had for major loan and investment activities as well as the undeveloped state of the local banking systems – Japan excepted – left the British exchange banks, and the Hongkong Bank in particular, considerable room for growth. Indeed, in 1907 the Hongkong Bank felt it necessary to increase its capital from $10 million to $15 million; the Board wished to avoid accusations of overtrading.

The growth of trade and foreign investment

The average annual compound rate of growth of China's foreign trade between 1902 and 1914 inclusive was just over 6%; this compares with the growth of the Hongkong Bank's assets at say 4.4% per annum or of shareholders' funds at 5.3% during the period from Jackson's departure to the outbreak of war in 1914. This in turn compares with the previous period considered, 1893–1901, as follows: the growth of China's overall foreign trade was 6.5% per annum, that of the Bank's shareholders' funds and assets varying between 3.5% and 7.5% depending on how the exchange factor is weighted. In view of the random factors involved, it would only be safe to conclude that the Hongkong Bank appears to have kept its share of the China market.

In the years before the Great War there was a decline in Britain's share of the China trade and in the percentage of British shipping visiting China ports. In view of the Bank's international constituency on the China coast, however, this factor should not, *a priori*, have affected the Bank's business.

The development of the export economies of Siam, the Malay States, and the Netherlands East Indies had already caused significant percentage increases in trade, but then the beginnings had been small, and the details can be considered in the following chapter which provides glimpses of the various branches.

The semi-annual speeches of the Hongkong Bank Chairman frequently refer to the depressed state of trade, especially in China. Certainly the high hopes of most traders to the East were still not realized, despite the renegotiation of trading regulations and the supposed curtailing of the *likin* transit tax incorporated in the MacKay Treaty of 1902; the disinterest of the Confucian official had given way first to the chaos of reaction. There was then a pause while China appeared to be reorganizing preparatory to reform of the currency, creation of a nation state political structure, and the ordering of railways. On the eve of what foreigners saw as the success of these policies came the Revolution and the disorganization of the national economy which continued, with the interlude of President/Emperor Yuan Shih-k'ai's brief effectiveness, until the late 1920s, when again there was hope tempered by the concern with nationalism.

Those who had hopes for a spectacular growth in the China trade were once again frustrated. If they were British they might turn, not on the Chinese, but on the Germans to explain why prosperity and stable growth in the China trade had not been accomplished after the concessions China made following the Boxer Uprising.

Growth rates and accounts – 1902–1914 (Tables 1.4–1.6)

An overall survey of the Bank's dividends may be seen in Figures 3 and 4. They suggest a focus on the sterling value and the consequently greater fluctuations in the total dollar payout during the decline of silver; they also reflect the confusion of a silver-based bank declaring its dividends in terms of sterling. Originally, this was done for a simple legalistic reason: the fixed exchange rate between dollars and sterling marked on the Bank's scrip. The Bank nevertheless had only to decide what dividend to pay in silver, translate that into sterling at the rate of the day, and then make the declaration in sterling. But by the 1900s with a high proportion of the market judging the Bank by its sterling performance, the Bank had to attempt at least to reverse its thinking; it had to consider first the sterling dividend it ought to pay, and let the dollar payout fluctuate accordingly. The limits to this will be seen in Chapter 10 dealing with the appreciation of silver late in the Great War.

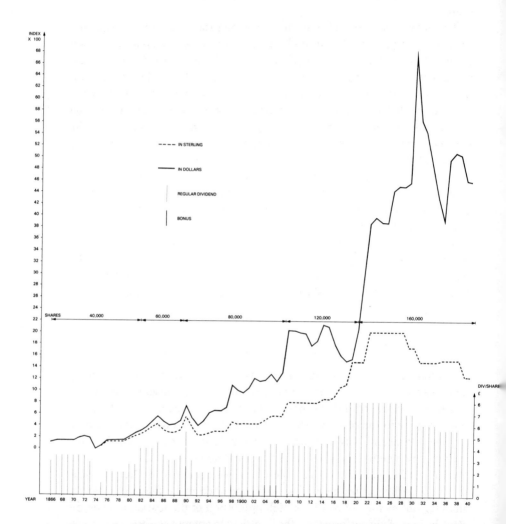

Figure 3 Sterling dividends and annual payout in dollars and sterling (1866=100),
1866–1940

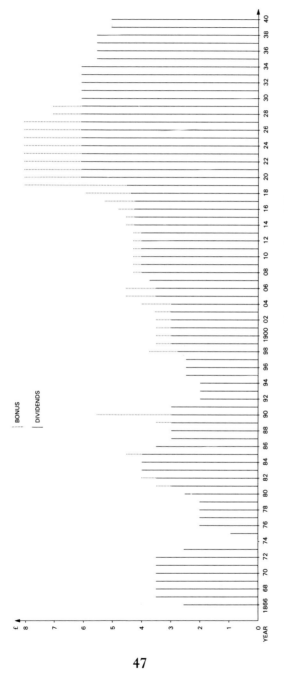

Figure 4 Annual dividends/share and bonuses in sterling, 1866–1940

47

Table 1.4A *The Hongkong and Shanghai Banking Corporation*
Key indicators, 1902–1914

(in millions of dollars unless otherwise indicated)

Year	Assets $	= £	Reserves[a] (i)	+ (ii)	Net Earnings	To Reserve	To Dividend @£2[b]	Rate $1 =xs/d
1901 Dec.	248.8	23.1	10.0	4.25	2.39	0.50	1.73	1/10$\frac{1}{4}$
1902 June	271.4	23.2	10.0	4.75	2.12	0.50	£1$\frac{1}{4}$ 1.41	1/8$\frac{1}{2}$
1902 Dec.	280.9	22.2	10.0	5.50	2.78	0.75	£2[b] 2.02	1/7
1903 June	252.8	21.1	10.0	6.00	2.16	0.50	£1$\frac{1}{2}$ 1.44	1/8
1903 Dec.	267.8	23.3	10.0	6.50	2.34	0.50	£2[b] 1.84	1/8$\frac{7}{8}$
1904 June	260.0	23.8	10.0	7.00	2.10	0.50	£1$\frac{1}{2}$ 1.31	1/9$\frac{5}{16}$
1904 Dec.	274.8	27.0	10.0	8.00	3.25	1.00	£2$\frac{1}{2}$[b] 2.04	1/11$\frac{9}{16}$
1905 June	314.0	29.4	10.0	8.50	2.22	0.50	£1$\frac{3}{4}$[c] 1.49	1/10$\frac{1}{2}$
1905 Dec.	290.8	29.8	10.0	9.50	3.16	1.00	£2$\frac{1}{4}$ 2.15	2/0$\frac{9}{16}$
1906 June	266.3	28.3	10.0	10.25	2.10	0.75	£1$\frac{3}{4}$ 1.32	2/1$\frac{1}{2}$
1906 Dec.	264.1	29.8	10.0	11.00	2.72	0.75	£2$\frac{1}{4}$ 1.95	2/3$\frac{1}{8}$
1907 June	289.3	31.6	10.0	11.75	2.12	0.75	£1$\frac{3}{4}$ 1.28	2/2$\frac{3}{16}$
1907 Dec.	299.5	27.1	15.0	13.50	3.15	0.50[d]	£2[e] 2.43[f]	1/9$\frac{3}{4}$
1908 June	333.8	30.4	15.0	14.00	3.40	0.50	£2 2.63	1/9$\frac{7}{8}$
1908 Dec.	384.0	33.2	15.0	14.50	3.64	0.50	£2$\frac{1}{4}$ 3.12	1/8$\frac{3}{4}$
1909 June	345.6	30.4	15.0	15.25	3.49	0.75	£2 2.73	1/9$\frac{7}{8}$

1909 Dec.	359.7	32.2	15.0	15.50	3.31	0.25	£2¼ 3.01	1/9½
1910 June	377.3	32.8	15.0	16.00	3.36	0.50	£2 2.69	1/9⅜
1910 Dec.	346.3	31.7	15.0	16.25	3.22	0.25	£2¼ 2.95	1/10
1911 June	359.1	32.2	15.0	16.75	3.19	0.50	£2 2.68	1/9½
1911 Dec.	394.5	36.6	15.0	16.75	2.84	0.00	£2¼ 2.91	1/10¼
1912 June	380.8	38.2	15.0	17.00	2.92	0.25	£2 2.39	2/0 1/16
1912 Dec.	382.2	39.6	15.0	17.20	3.07	0.20	£2¼ 2.61	2/0⅞
1913 June	387.6	38.2	15.0	17.45	2.99	0.25	£2 2.44	1/11⅝
1913 Dec.	408.6	39.5	15.0	17.65	3.32	0.20	£2¼ 2.79	1/11 3/16
1914 June	419.8	39.6	15.0	18.00	3.52	0.35	£2:3^g 2.74	1/10⅝
1914 Dec.	435.2	38.3	15.0	18.00	3.81	0.00	£2:8 3.27	1/9⅛

Shareholders' funds (1901 Dec.) = \$25,938,000 (@ 1/10¼ = £2,432,000)
Shareholders' funds (1914 June) = \$50,340,000 (@ 1/10⅝ = £4,746,000)

[a] Reserve Fund: in millions of dollars: (i) silver reserves (ii) gold reserves.
The figure for the Reserve Fund *includes* the amount transferred at the end of the period as approved by the shareholders at the subsequent meeting.
[b] Dividend rate is £1:10 plus bonus.
[c] New dividend rate of £1:15 plus bonus where applicable.
[d] Plus premium on new shares of which £5 million was added to the sterling reserve and \$1.25 million to the silver reserve.
[e] New dividend rate of £2 plus bonus where applicable.
[f] Quoted on the abstract of accounts in a single figure for the first time, i.e. without reference to the 4/6 rate.
[g] New rate of £2:3 but **not** tax paid, and the additional three shillings is designed as compensation. Add bonus where applicable.

49

Table 1.4B *The Hongkong and Shanghai Banking Corporation Dividends, 1902–1914*

Year	Interim			+ Final			+ Bonus[a]		= Total		Payout		Ratio	% of book value	
	£	@	= $	£	@	= $	£	= $	£	= $	£	= $ (millions)	%	£ (percent)	$
1902	1:10	1/8½	**17.56**	1:10	1/7	**18.95**	0.10	**6.32**	3:10	**42.83**	0.28	**3.43**	70	13.0	**12.6**
1903	1:10	1/8	**18.00**	1:10	1/8⅞	**17.25**	0:10	**5.75**	3:10	**41.00**	0.28	**3.28**	73	11.4	**11.6**
1904	1:10	1/9 15/16	**16.41**	1:10	1/11 9/16	**15.28**	1:00	**10.19**	4:00	**41.88**	0.32	**3.35**	63	11.0	**11.3**
1905	1:15	1/10½	**18.67**	1:15	2/0 9/16	**17.10**	1:00	**9.77**	4:10	**45.54**	0.36	**3.64**	68	11.2	**11.6**
1906	1:15	2/1½	**16.47**	1:15	2/3⅛	**15.48**	1:00	**8.85**	4:10	**40.80**	0.36	**3.54**	68	9.7	**9.9**
1907	1:15	1/2 3/16	**16.04**	2:00	1/9¾	**22.07**	–	–	3:15[b]	**38.11**[b]	0.36	**3.71**	70	10.9	**10.0**
1908[c]	2:00	1/9⅞	**21.94**	2:00	1/8¾	**23.13**	0:05	**2.89**	4:05	**47.96**	0.51	**5.76**	82	12.6	**12.3**
1909	2:00	1/9⅛	**22.72**	1:00	1/9½	**22.33**	0:05	**2.79**	4:05	**47.84**	0.51	**5.74**	84	11.9	**12.0**
1910	2:00	1/9⅜	**22.46**	2:00	1/10	**21.82**	0:05	**2.73**	4:05	**47.01**	0.51	**5.64**	86	11.5	**11.6**
1911	2:00	1/9½	**22.33**	2:00	1/10¼	**21.69**	0:05	**2.71**	4:05	**46.73**	0.51	**5.59**	93	11.3	**11.5**
1912	2:00	2/0 1/16	**19.95**	2:00	2/0⅞	**19.30**	0:05	**2.41**	4:05	**41.66**	0.51	**5.00**	83	9.9	**10.1**
1913	2:00	1/11⅝	**20.32**	2:00	1/11 3/16	**20.70**	0:05	**2.59**	4:05	**43.61**	0.51	**5.23**	83	10.6	**10.5**
1914[d]	2:03	1/10⅝	**22.81**	2:03	1/9⅛	**24.43**	0:05	**2.84**	4:11	**50.08**	0.55	**6.01**	82	12.2	**11.8**

Bold face = $ equivalent.
[a] Bonus is at same rate of exchange as final dividend.
[b] Includes proportionate dividend on 40,000 new shares.
[c] Figures reflect full effect of the increase in the number of shares.
[d] Dividends include offset for UK income tax.
Source: Tables 1.3 and 1.4A.

Dividends and growth

In 1907 there was a rights issue which at £30 a share and an exchange rate of 2s:2³⁄₁₆d would add some $11 million to shareholders' funds. The Bank had once again selected the most appropriate time; exchange was at a twenty-four year peak (1893–1916). Therefore the average annual growth rate of shareholders' funds over the period from approximately the retirement of Jackson, January 1, 1902, to the beginning of the Great War, June 30, 1914, was 5.3%, but as this passes over the date of the capital issue, the growth rate states nothing about the operating success of the Bank. In the period from Jackson to the last accounts before the addition of the new capital in June 1907, when shareholders' funds were $33.8 million, the average annual rate of growth of shareholders' funds was 4.9%; this compares with a growth rate of 1.5% for the rest of the period, January 1, 1908 (shareholders' funds=$45.8 million) to June 30, 1914.

The reason for this is not difficult to appreciate, nor did it surprise contemporaries. The dividend rate had been £1:10s per half-year plus a usual bonus of ten shillings, that is £3:10s per annum. In June 1905 the Board raised the 'normal' semi-annual dividend to £1:15s with a 'normal' year-end bonus of £1 or an annual payout of £4:10s per share. This increase was possible partly because of the rising exchange rate, and it is notable that the annual dividend payout as a percentage of net published earnings was within the range of 63% to 70% throughout. Despite the increase in capital the dividend was actually raised to £2 per half-year at the end of 1907 in lieu, the Chairman stated, of the usual year-end bonus; but by the end of 1908 a bonus of five shillings was added for a total annual payout of £4:5s per share on an increased number of shares and at a lower exchange. As the exchanges fluctuated in this period, the total payout on the increased capital required ranged from 82% to 93% of net earnings as defined in the accounts (see Table 1.4B).

This is also reflecte din the additions to reserves, which, as Table 1.4A shows clearly, dropped after the increase in capital. Either calculation is a consequence of the Board's decision to maintain a high level of dividends relative to published earnings. With published reserves valued at twice the amount of paid-up capital, half in sterling and half in silver, the arguments for further shareholder 'sacrifices' could no longer expect a friendly audience. The shareholders had participated in the growth of the Bank; they now wished to participate in the consequences, while still permitting some further augmentation of the reserves at a time when the exchanges were, admittedly, unstable.

The use of shareholders' funds calculated in dollars as the basis for describing growth minimizes the impact of extraordinary factors which make many of the other series, those in Tables 1.5 and 1.6, difficult to interpret. Apparently random changes in assets, bullion, and deposits often reflect the impact of major loans; changes in the note issue may reflect the proximity of Chinese New Year (which is a lunar festival at which time debts were settled in cash) or at the end of 1911 the increase in the note issue is consequent to a pile-up of remittances from Overseas Chinese which remained unutilized by the recipients, a consequence of the unsettled times. The bills and loans reflect changes in the method of financing trade or the number of bills held to maturity given the rate of interest in the London market. The share price differentials as between London and Shanghai are partly due to changes in expectation relative to the exchanges and partly to the non-transferability of shares between the London and Eastern registers.

Earnings and dividends

The 'net earnings' are the published profits of the Hongkong Bank. The actual net profits were brought before the Board of Directors who allocated them partly before and partly after determination of the published figure; those before included a transfer to Contingencies Account of which over $3 million was unappropriated and therefore constituted an 'inner reserve'. Other pre-publication allocations were actually costs of operations reserved for the discretion of the Board and thus not really 'profits', for example, bonuses to the Eastern staff, bonuses to Managers, allocation to the Officers Good Service Fund; items allocated on the published abstract of accounts included allowances for the writing down of the Premises Account and directors' remuneration.

The Board had resolved to keep the sterling reserve equal to the paid-up capital; when consols began to decline the Board developed the practice of writing them down out of current profits. This does not appear in the accounts, but shareholders were informed and could in any case calculate the amounts involved from the information provided. Thus in announcing the recommendation of a dividend plus bonus for the six months ending December 1911 resulting, exceptionally, in a payout in excess of current earnings, the Chairman of the Bank made the point that the adjustment of the reserves had been costly and that one could argue as to whether current earnings were not in fact higher than stated (see Table 1.4A).

This discussion reflects the reluctance to vote dividends out of reserves of any kind. One purpose of reserves as stated in the Bank ordinance was the equalization of dividends; when this use was seen to be unacceptable in the market a special reserve marked 'for equalization of dividends' was established at a not particularly happy moment in the Bank's history. It was soon exhausted and not reestablished. In consequence, the Board permitted the amount in Profit and Loss Account held over to rise to an amount in excess of $2 million for equalization of dividends. But when this was touched, as it was at the February 1912 meeting, the Board considered the situation required delicate handling. One staff member, misunderstanding the situation, resigned in indignation and, on receiving no explanation from the Board, in January 1913 called a public meeting in London – but that story will be told below.

The note issue

From Table 1.6 it is possible to calculate the total note issue of the Hongkong Bank by adding the authorized issue (= the paid-up capital) to the amount under 'Excess Notes'. Thus the total issue for June 1907 was $18.1 million; for December 1907, $15.7 million; it was between these dates that the paid-up capital rose from $10 to $15 million. In June 1910 the total issue was $14 million; there was no excess issue and the authorized issue was $1 million less than the maximum permitted under this category.

The progress of the Hongkong Bank, 1902–1907

An overall view of the growth of shareholders' funds in the period from 1895 to 1918 is provided by Figures 5–6 (see also Figure 2 above). These Figures illustrate the developments described in Volume I, Chapter 13, in the present section, in a further section dealing with 1908–1914 below, and in Chapter 10 below.

At the end of 1902 Head Office remained the most 'profitable' 'branch', followed by Shanghai. As a consequence of the profits of a Japanese loan, Yokohama came next, followed by Manila. But the figures are subject to considerable interpretation and it is perhaps wiser to conclude that the main sources of net income to the Bank were (i) Hong Kong and Shanghai and their dependent agencies, (ii) Yokohama, (iii) Manila and Singapore, depending very much on special developments from time to time, and (iv) special events, such as loans, which by being credited, according to the particular circumstances, on Head Office books, on Yokohama accounts, etc., make analysis difficult. An unadjusted list of branch profits as taken over by Head Office would read well, but without knowledge of the amounts retained for contingencies, the exchange rates used and the special events occurring – for much of which the evidence no longer remains – the conclusions drawn from such a list must be tentative (see Table 1.7).

Perhaps one important point to note is the relative absence of losses, which, as one shareholder noted at the semi-annual meeting, had so vexed and frustrated the Bank in the past. The sudden increase in bills receivable in mid-

Table 1.5 *The Hongkong and Shanghai Banking Corporation*
Earnings and share prices, 1902–1914

Year	(i) Net earnings $ 000	(ii) £ Dividends/share	(iii) Book value $	(iv) Book value £	(v) Share price Shanghai (Ts)	(vi) Share price London (£)	(vii) M/B ratio $	(viii) M/B ratio £	(ix) Rate $1 = xs/d
1901 Dec.	2.39		324	30.1	620	64	1.91	2.13	1/10 1/4
1902 June	2.12	£1½	330	28.2	600	63	1.82	2.23	1/8 1/2
1902 Dec.	2.78	£2	340	26.9	644	64	1.89	2.38	1/7
1903 June	2.16	£1½	346	28.8	680	64	1.96	2.22	1/8
1903 Dec.	2.34	£2	352	30.6	665	62	1.89	2.02	1/8 7/8
1904 June	2.10	£1½	359	32.8	660	68	1.84	2.07	1/9 5/16
1904 Dec.	3.25	£2¼	372	36.5	713	71	1.92	1.95	1/11 9/16
1905 June	2.22	£1¾	381	35.7	808	86	2.12	2.41	1/10 1/2
1905 Dec.	3.16	£2¼	393	40.2	865	94	2.20	2.33	2/0 9/16
1906 June	2.10	£1¾	403	42.8	815	92	2.02	2.15	2/1 1/2
1906 Dec.	2.72	£2¼	412	46.6	825	95	2.00	2.04	2/3 1/8
1907 June	2.12	£1¾	422	46.1	873	79	2.12	1.76	2/2 3/16
1907 Dec.	3.15	£2	381	34.5	740	80	1.88	2.24	1/9 3/4
1908 June	3.40	£2	385	35.1	770	79	1.93	2.16	1/9 7/8

1908 Dec.	3.64	£2¼	390	33.7	865	83	2.11	2.35	1/8¾
1909 June	3.49	£2	396	34.8	1015	97	2.46	2.67	1/9⅛
1909 Dec.	3.31	£2¼	398	35.7	1020	92	2.47	2.49	1/9½
1910 June	3.36	£2	402	35.8	950	90	2.27	2.42	1/9⅜
1910 Dec.	3.22	£2¼	404	37.1	915	88	2.20	2.31	1/10
1911 June	3.19	£2	409	36.6	918	88	2.17	2.32	1/9½
1911 Dec.	2.84	£2¼	408	37.6	900	83	2.15	2.14	1/10¼
1912 June	2.92	£2	410	41.1	830	84	2.03	2.04	2/0 1/16
1912 Dec.	3.07	£2¼	412	42.7	810	84	1.99	1.99	2/0⅞
1913 June	2.99	£2	415	40.8	815	81	1.96	1.98	1/11⅝
1913 Dec.	3.32	£2¼	416	40.2	795	80	1.89	1.97	1/11 3/16
1914 June	3.52	£2:3	419	39.5	830	84	1.94	2.08	1/10⅝

(i) Net earnings in millions of Hong Kong dollars from Table 1.4A.
(ii) Dividends declared in pounds sterling, see Table 1.4A.
(iii) Book value = shareholders' funds, i.e. paid-up capital + reserves (including amounts paid in from net earnings) + retained profits, divided by the number of shares outstanding.
(iv) Column (iii) converted into pounds sterling at rate of semi-annual report.
(v) Shanghai shares were quoted at so much percent premium, which is added to the par value of shares, i.e. $125; the dates are mid-July and mid-January.
(vi) London prices for shares on the London register.
(vii) Equivalent to (v) divided by (iii).
(viii) Equivalent to (vi) divided by (iv).
(ix) The rate used in the semi-annual Hongkong Bank accounts.

(in millions)

Table 1.6 *The Hongkong and Shanghai Banking Corporation*
Cash, selected balance sheet items, and ratios, 1902–1914

Year	Assets $	Assets Index	Cash and bullion $[a]	C/A ratio	Net earnings $	E as % of A	Excess notes[b]	Deposit Liabilities in silver $	gold £	Total $[d]	Loan etc. $	Loan/D ratio	Bills rec. $	Bills pay. $
1901 Dec.	248.8	100	57.2	0.23	2.39	0.96	3.0	125.5	6.0	189.8	74.7	39	95.8	18.2
1902 June	271.4	109	60.2	0.22	2.12	0.78	4.6	131.2	5.9	200.5	88.5	44	99.3	28.2
1902 Dec.	280.9	113	52.0	0.19	2.78	0.99	6.6	132.8	7.0	220.7	98.8	45	107.6	14.4
1903 June	252.8	102	42.6	0.17	2.16	0.85	3.1	119.4	6.6	198.0	96.6	49	90.1	12.3
1903 Dec.	267.8	108	54.7	0.20	2.34	0.87	6.3	120.9	6.9	200.6	89.9	45	101.1	20.9
1904 June	260.0	104	52.8	0.20	2.10	0.81	4.9	122.6	6.8	199.5	87.1	44	99.8	15.3
1904 Dec.	274.8	110	51.7	0.19	3.25	1.18	6.4	119.5	8.8	213.9	85.6	40	115.0	12.4
1905 June	314.0	126	57.8	0.18	2.22	0.71	6.0	127.3	11.3	248.6	104.2	42	126.9	17.4
1905 Dec.	290.8	117	63.5	0.22	3.16	1.09	9.1	123.8	9.7	222.0	91.1	41	113.7	16.2
1906 June	266.3	107	50.5	0.19	2.10	0.79	4.3	118.4	9.5	208.2	94.0	45	100.8	10.2
1906 Dec.	264.1	106	51.9	0.20	2.72	1.03	6.1	118.3	9.3	199.2	93.0	47	99.0	13.9
1907 June	289.3	116	55.8	0.19	2.12	0.73	8.1	121.5	10.8	222.5	89.8	40	123.6	13.5

Date													
1907 Dec.	299.5	120	54.6	0.18	3.15	1.05	0.7	130.1	9.7	224.1	101.6	45	118.0	11.5
1908 June	333.8	134	62.4	0.19	3.40	1.02	1.5	140.7	10.2	255.7	109.9	43	135.5	12.5
1908 Dec.	384.0	154	70.2	0.18	3.64	0.95	5.0	152.9	12.6	298.6	120.1	40	162.8	15.5
1909 June	345.6	139	72.6	0.21	3.49	1.01	-0.8^c	157.4	9.7	267.1	113.0	42	130.8	14.1
1909 June	359.7	145	69.1	0.19	3.31	0.92	0.0	160.7	10.0	272.4	108.5	40	147.9	21.5
1910 June	377.3	152	72.9	0.19	3.36	0.89	-1.0^c	183.0	9.6	290.7	144.6	50	125.6	21.5
1910 Dec.	346.3	139	69.3	0.20	3.22	0.93	0.1	167.3	8.9	264.1	125.3	47	121.9	14.8
1911 June	359.1	144	74.1	0.21	3.19	0.89	2.7	173.7	8.8	271.4	125.3	46	130.0	18.3
1911 Dec.	394.5	159	73.9	0.19	2.84	0.72	10.3	191.0	9.9	298.3	122.1	41	160.0	10.6
1912 June	380.8	153	69.3	0.18	2.92	0.77	7.7	183.4	9.8	281.5	140.3	50	123.4	9.4
1912 Dec.	382.2	154	63.1	0.17	3.07	0.80	9.8	191.5	10.0	288.4	140.0	49	135.7	6.0
1913 June	387.6	156	78.6	0.20	2.99	0.77	8.4	188.7	9.3	281.7	139.1	49	124.6	19.9
1913 Dec.	408.6	164	70.0	0.17	3.32	0.81	9.8	195.4	10.1	298.2	141.7	48	148.0	19.9
1914 June	419.8	169	80.5	0.19	3.52	0.84	7.5	202.8	10.6	313.2	146.9	47	142.2	16.6
1914 Dec.	435.2	175	97.4	0.22	3.81	0.88	12.2	210.5	10.5	329.3	141.5	43	150.9	17.4

^{a} Includes arbitrary amounts against note issue.
^{b} Add $10m for total note issue through June 1907.
Add $15m for total note issue from December 1907.
^{c} I.e. less than $15m, the 'authorized issue'.
^{d} Includes gold deposits at rates shown in Table 1.4A.

E = earnings D = deposits.
A = assets Bills rec. = BR = bills receivable.
Loans etc. = Bills discounted, loans and credits.
Bills pay. = BP = bills payable, including 'drafts on London Bankers and short sight
drawings on our London Office against bills receivable and bullion shipments'.

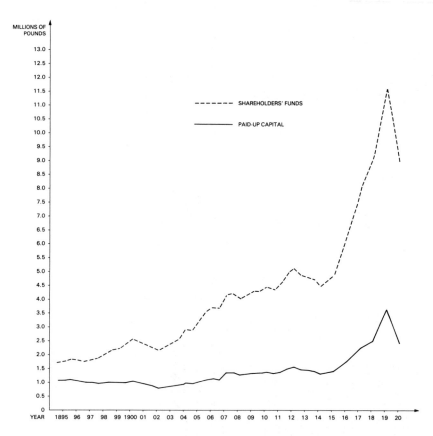

Figure 5 Shareholders' funds and paid-up capital in sterling, 1895–1920

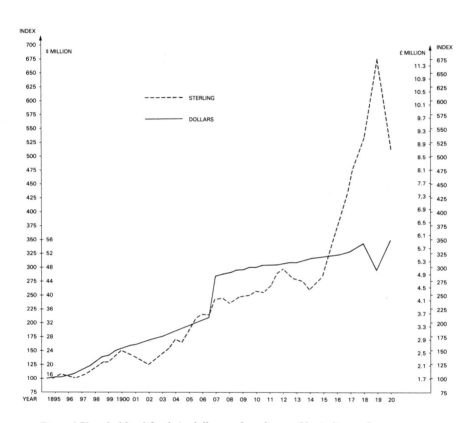

Figure 6 Shareholders' funds in dollars and sterling and by indices, 1895–1920

Table 1.7 *The Hongkong and Shanghai Banking Corporation Profit and Loss Account, 1902*

Net branch/agency profits (thousands) (as reported to Head Office)		Reconciliation (millions)	
Head Office, Hong Kong	922,378	Total funds available	4.396
Shanghai	800,000	Less allocations	
Yokohama	750,000	before publication	0.175
Manila	400,000	Less amount carried	
Singapore	150,000	forward	1.432
Bangkok	120,000		
Batavia	100,000	= Published earnings	2.789
Colombo	20,000		
New York	−21,340	Less allocations	
Rangoon	−12,500	after publication	2.786
Other accounts	−269,754		
		= Increased amount	
Total ½-year profit	2,958,784	carried forward on	
From previous ½-year	1,437,740	published accounts	0.003
Total funds available	4,396,525	*Inner Reserves:*	
(i) allocations before publication		Surplus on	
To Managers	25,000	Contingencies	
10% bonus to staff	150,000	Account	1.780
(ii) allocations after publication		Value of securities	
To dividends	2,021,052	held as reserves	
To reserves	750,000	understated by	7.000
To directors	15,000		
To amount			
carried forward	1,432,472		

Slight discrepancies remain due to the fact that the unpublished figures may have been adjusted before the final accounts were signed. The source is the minutes for 13 January 1903 when the figures were first presented to the Board for discussion.
Note: Each half-year had special problems – this account is merely illustrative and is not to be considered typical.

1902 is not specifically explained, but for the year 1902 the total trade of China alone increased by HkTs112 million and Chinese importers fixed their exchange ahead in anticipation of a further decline in exchange. China's black tea exports had been declining since 1895 and were particularly low in 1901 and again in 1902, but the trend was upwards, and the Bank's Chairman was unduly pessimistic at the meeting; he was correct, however, in supposing that other exports were growing in importance.

In the first half of 1903 with silver tending upwards, Smith was tested and passed. As Murray Bain, the veteran proprietor of the *China Mail*, put it, 'It appears to me, gentlemen, that the mantle of the late Sir Thomas Jackson of happy memory has fallen very gracefully upon the shoulders of Mr Smith . . .' Hong Kong was accepting Smith; he would be able to look out without qualms on the statue of Sir Thomas once it was installed in full view of his office. The fall in deposits and the offsetting entries, including a net fall in the total assets of the Bank, which marked this half-year were the result of the withdrawal of loan funds and temporary Government accounts independent of normal commercial operations.

Although marred by the outbreak of the Russo-Japanese War and the consequent unfavourable impact on the Bank's operations in northeast China, 1904 was another generally successful year. It was the year of Japanese and Siamese loan issues, and of the consequent temporary increase in gold deposits. The year-end bonus was doubled from ten shillings to one pound, and the bonus to staff, which had been running at 10%, was increased to 15% of salaries.

At the mid-1905 meeting a shareholder specifically referred to the increased value of the Bank's shares, which undoubtedly reflected the improved year-end bonus and the anticipation, correct as it turned out, of a higher regular dividend. Reference was made to a depression in trade in South China and in fact the Bank had suffered through the difficulties of its Hong Kong compradore, as will be discussed in the following section. The rise in gold deposits was temporary and due to loan proceeds on current account.

The decline in silver deposits noted in the December 1905 accounts was offset by an increase in the note issue, reflecting what the Chairman referred to as the 'year-end demand for money', for cash as opposed to current accounts. This was one of the major management problems – coping with the routine of banking operations, providing not only for the requirements of regular constituents but also for the seasonal preferences of the population of Hong Kong and the Canton Delta region. The notes were not, it should be remembered, legal tender either in Hong Kong or elsewhere, making any estimate of demand for them particularly difficult. An underestimate of demand would result in their being quoted at a premium.

The rising exchange rate reduced the silver value of the Bank's sterling reserves; consequently in the first half of 1906 the Board authorized the purchase of £28,000 2½% consols out of current profits. The Chairman reminded the shareholders that changes in various account items might reflect changes in the exchange rate and that the true measure of the Bank was in its turnover and profits. The former he reported to be increasing; the latter, sufficient to maintain the recently increased dividend – but only, one should note, in terms of sterling at the higher exchange rate.

Not that Jackson was forgotten, especially with the unveiling of his statue. One old Parsee friend wrote:

You must be knowing that poor Hong Kong is now passing through a series of misfortunes never known before. Typhoons, fires, failures, one after the other seem to rival one another. The typhoon of 18th September has disorganized all trade. Add to this the troubles of the yarn and opium merchants . . . Everybody says that at such a time you ought to have been in Hong Kong. There is a general opinion all round that a mere telegram of your departure from London for Hong Kong will make the whole place ablaze with enthusiasm and joy for coming prosperity. Chinese and foreigners all alike will have TJ to relieve Hong Kong . . . I cannot forget that on the day Sir Matthew Nathan [the Governor] opened your statue, we drank champagne to our hearts' content.[27]

Indeed Hong Kong had more to celebrate than the 'opening' of Jackson's statue. Situated as it was on the open space between the Bank and the harbour, the occasion was a reminder that on Jackson's advice the Board had agreed to cooperate with the Government in providing a central city park area, adorned by statues, which today (1987) has been developed into a great public facility, with only the statue of Jackson remaining to remind the citizens of its origin and to give meaning to the name of Statue Square.

The last sentence in the letter sets the tone; this is in reality a kind letter to an old man, retired but not forgotten. In the same letter there is praise of Smith and no one thought to blame the typhoon on the Acting Chief Manager, Harry Hunter. On the contrary, in July 1906 the Board had voted him $10,000 for a brilliant job in Shanghai, they later voted him an honorarium of $12,500 for his seven-month performance as Acting Chief Manager. Even though some 12% of the net published earnings of $2.7 million could be ascribed to profits on the Siamese Loan, the Chinese 5% Loan, and the City of Tokyo Loan, the figure was evidence of successful management despite unprecedented fluctuations in the price of silver.

Nevertheless, one cannot blame the more traditionally minded for burning joss sticks before the statue of one so successful, even if neither Hunter nor Smith had need to do so.

Smith had returned from his New Beckenham photography session by mid-January 1907 in time to handle the problems related to the proposed rights issue and face the consequences later in the year of a 7% Bank rate in London.

The year 1907 was a uniformly bad one. The American financial crisis was felt particularly in the silk trade and affected the Lyons agency of the Bank. The high cost of finance caused a depression in the China trade resulting in a high level of stocks on the China coast, and famine in India led to that country ceasing to import silver which in turn caused the severe fluctuations of 25% in its price and a net fall of 17% in the exchange over the year. The Bank's net earnings of $3.15 million in the second half of the year must be considered therefore as a tribute to the management of J.R.M. Smith and his colleagues, reflecting the Bank's status as an exchange bank, as well as the profitability of its loan issues.

The failure of the third compradore, 1906[e]

By a rather complex sequence of events, foreign zeal for the reform of China led the Hongkong Bank's compradore, Lau Wai Chun, into bankruptcy. The officials of the Chinese Empire were all the products of classical studies – as indeed were those of the British Empire. But following the Boxer Uprising the classical students of the British Empire prevailed upon the classical students in the Chinese Empire to amend their examination system to conform more with the needs of modernization. The introduction of a new examination in China was followed at a leisurely (but ultimately more effective) pace in Britain. Charles Addis's frustrations relative to a new business degree in universities will be considered in Chapter 3 and in Volume III.

The impact of reform in China is a subject for other histories. Here it should be noted that there was a large syndicate in Kwangtung and Hong Kong, the Wei Sing lottery, which was based on betting on the results of the Provincial examinations. As the nature of the examinations was changed, the public lost confidence in the lottery and the syndicate found itself short of funds, which it remedied by means of dubious financial operations.

One weakness of the compradoric system already considered in Volume I, Chapter 14, was the dependence of the compradore on his guarantors and of the inadequacy of the security in cases of general failure or of illegal transactions. By March 1905 the Bank compradore's position had reached a point where J.R.M. Smith felt himself not justified in offering further assistance. But unlike the former Chief Manager, François de Bovis, when faced with a similar crisis, Smith recognized the problem and brought it to the Board; they appointed a sub-committee and subsequently approved further support of the compradore.

The Bank offered to guarantee $40,000 due the Bank of Taiwan, and, if the compradore could not raise the $90,000 for a compromise arrangement with his other debtors, the Bank would extend this credit to him – on the condition, however, that no further claims against him appeared.

To worsen the situation, a month after the Bank agreed to help the compradore, a shroff absconded with $52,747.71. The compradore was also

---

[e] This account and the one below on the fourth compradore are based on the version presented by Carl T. Smith at the Hongkong Bank History Conference in 1981 and published as, 'Compradores of The Hongkong Bank', in King, ed. *Eastern Banking* (London, 1983), pp. 104–06 and 108–10, for which grateful acknowledgement is made.

responsible for this amount and already all his security was needed to cover his other liabilities to the Bank. A few days later irregularities in the cash balance were found. Without the Bank's approval he had paid sums to his creditors. On June 13, 1905, the Board decided to replace the compradore as soon as a suitable person could be found for the position.

No acceptable candidates came forward, so the Bank was forced to continue for the time being with Lau Wai Chun. But in March 1906 the legal advisers to the Bank said Lau should file for bankruptcy and, at the same time, resign. The Bank then had the task of finding a new compradore. They in fact took on Lau Pun Chiu, formerly with E.D. Sassoon and Co. and probably a distant relative of Lau Wai Chun. Since compradores were often related and since many of the former compradore's family were employed in the Bank, the choice was a natural one. But by 1912 Lau Pun Chiu had himself got into difficulties.

The charter, the capital, and the note issue

The Board faced three problems which were, in fact, 'solved' simultaneously – extension of the charter, which was due to expire in 1908, permission to increase the capital of the Bank, and the right to increase the authorized and continue an 'excess' note issue. Only the conditions under which the last would be granted proved an issue of contention. The Treasury acted, as indeed it had done in 1865–1866, on the basis that the Bank was a going concern and that there was no need to exercise its 'gatekeeper' function, especially so since the revised principles of the note issue had been decided under separate legislation, which it was now only necessary to adjust and inject into the Bank's own charter.

The extension of the Bank's incorporation was not considered as a separate issue; thus only two topics remain for full consideration.

An increase in capital

The Chairman, A. Haupt of Melchers and Co., recommended an increase in the Bank's capital in a January 1906 memorandum which stressed the significance of the ratio between shareholders' funds, that is, capital plus reserves, and deposit and note liabilities. In 1890, when the Board had last recommended a capital increase to the shareholders, capital and reserves had been 12.5% of deposits plus notes; end-1906 figures were not yet available but end-1905 figures showed the relationship was then 12.2%, which Haupt considered sufficient proof of the need for a capital increase.

A picture of the capital/shareholders' funds position in the period 1895–1920 can be seen in Figure 7.

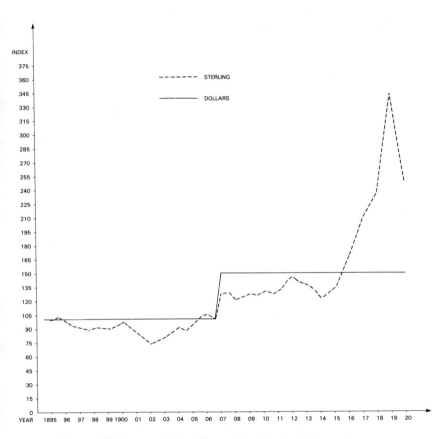

Figure 7 Paid-up capital in dollars and sterling by indices, 1895–1920

The history of the years immediately following the capital increase supports the wisdom of the decision; the note issue increased erratically but dramatically, deposit liabilities were a third higher, loans increased accordingly so that the loan/deposit ratio remained in the same range of 40–50%, and the earnings as a percentage of assets dropped only slightly. The Chairman's declared reasoning could nevertheless be faulted on a short-run basis. During 1906 both the note issue and the unusually high deposit figures had fallen and the comparable ratio at the end of December was 14.4%.

The note issue was really the problem.

In Hong Kong banknotes were already passing at a premium of up to 3% against silver legal tender and, while the Bank could, given extension of the relevant legislation, issue 'excess' notes on deposit of 100% backing in silver, this could prove a costly process. With the increase in capital the permitted 'authorized' note issue would, the Board hoped, be automatically increased by an equal amount. The Bank's own ordinance provided for an authorized issue equal to paid-up capital.

The basis on which the proposal was put to shareholders, however, was purely in terms of sound banking practice: the capital and reserves of the Bank were inadequate to cover any expansion of the Bank's role at a time when trade was bound to increase and competition must be met.

In January 1906 the Board agreed on the basis of Haupt's memorandum that the Chief Manager should (i) negotiate with Government for a revision to the Bank's 1866 ordinance to permit an increase in authorized capital to $20 million, but (ii) explain that the Governor's approval was sought under a revised charter for an immediate increase, within this new limit, of only $5 million. The procedure was (i) for the Governor to determine the Colonial Office's and Treasury's preliminary views, which if favourable would (ii) permit the Bank to call an extraordinary meeting of shareholders, leading, when all parties were in agreement, to (iii) the passage of an ordinance in the Hong Kong Legislative Council.

The Board proposed that the new capital be obtained through a rights issue of 40,000 new shares allotted on the basis of one new share for every two of the 80,000 old shares, that the price should be £30 and that the rate of exchange for those on the Eastern registers should be the Bank's rate for demand bills on London on the date payment was due. The Chairman reported to the Board that he had the support of the London Committee for the proposals.

Given the par value of the shares as $125, at the rate of exchange mid-year, the equivalent in sterling was £13:12s:7d, and the price of £30 included a premium of 120%. On the other hand book value at mid-year was £42:16s and the share price was over £90. The effect of the transaction would be to grant present shareholders an opportunity to gain from the growth of the

Bank's capital and the high price of its shares either by selling their rights to the new shares and thus diluting their equity in the Corporation for a more than proportionate capital gain, or by exercising their rights, retain their proportionate share of an equity the value of which would have increased in excess of the £30 price they would have paid for the new shares.

The difference between say £92 and the par value of a Hongkong Bank share of £13:12s:7d would be split between the shareholder selling (or exercising) his rights and the Bank receiving the £30.

> In fixing the price of this proposed new issue [Haupt wrote] we have not only to think of the interests of our Shareholders but we must also consider what is best for the future welfare of the Bank. . . . I am sure you will agree with me that this price [£30] confers on shareholders a liberal bonus, but one to which I think they are fairly entitled as a reward for the way in which they have supported us in adding so largely to our reserves in the past. At the same time though the premium per share appears small, it will, in the aggregate, form a substantial addition to reserve funds.

This was in effect a partial capitalization of the reserves; the net result, however, was a dilution of the stock, since the book value consequently declined, although the sudden fall in exchange affected the sterling book value considerably more than the silver value (see Table 1.5).

The agenda for the Extraordinary Meeting, which was scheduled for May 31, 1907, that is, after the Bank had obtained the Government's preliminary agreement, was designed to obtain shareholder approval for an ordinance which would both authorize the permissible limit of the Bank's capital to $20 million and for a proclamation which would specifically authorize the immediate issue of 40,000 new shares for an additional $5 million capital. The shareholders approved, and payments for the new shares were subsequently ordered to be made by instalment on July 1 and October 1.

Thus by the end of 1907 the accounts show the additional capital and the allocation of the bonus, the difference between par and £30, to the reserves: £500,000 to the sterling reserves (@2s=$5 million) and $1,250,000 to the silver reserves. The Bank remained on an 'even keel'.

The note issue
When the capital of the Bank had been last increased, to $10 million in 1890, the action was taken within the terms of the original ordinance without need of amendment. Under its terms the Bank was required to hold a reserve in specie equivalent to one-third its note issue. As a requirement for the 21-year extension of its charter, the Bank had been obligated to deposit securities valued at $2.5 million with the Government, that is to the extent of one-third of its note issue, which was assumed to stand at the limit of paid-up capital, then $7.5 million. With the increase in capital to $10 million in 1890, the

Government had insisted that the Bank deposit one-third of the additional $2.5 million capital, again on the assumption, correct in the event, that the note issue would soon reach the authorized limit.

The paid-up capital was now about to be increased by a further $5 million. The Bank hoped that the provisions in its ordinance, which would automatically increase the authorized note issue to $15 million, but with the additional requirements negotiated in 1886 and 1890, that is, the deposit of securities worth one-third of the additional capital, would prevail.[28]

The Colonial Office minuted, 'I thought they would want this. We cannot allow an extension of the ordinary ['authorized'] note issue on the present terms (that they deposit securities to the extent of one third with the Crown Agents).'[29] The counter-suggestion from Government was for the Bank to deposit specie equivalent to the entire additional capital with the Crown Agents or the Colonial Treasury. Charles Addis, the Bank's junior London Manager, negotiated successfully for this provision to be modified, permitting, at the discretion of the Bank, the right to deposit up to one-third in securities.[30] Addis warned Smith that this was as far as the Colonial Office and Treasury would go, and the Bank accepted the terms.[31]

In consequence the Bank would have an authorized note issue limit of $15 million against which they were obliged to hold one-third in specie at the office of issue and to have on deposit with the Crown Agents or the Hong Kong Government securities and cash valued at $8.3 million of which $5 million could be in approved securities.[f] The Bank was thus deprived of some further flexibility and its cash, which had in any case been held at a high level against the possibility of sudden encashment of its notes, would now be partly under the control of the Government.

As for the 'excess' issue, the provisions for this were due to expire in 1907. Since the relevant special ordinances permitting the excess issue dealt in fact only with the Hongkong Bank, the provisions were incorporated, unchanged, into the revised 1907 ordinance.

The ordinance

On June 6 the Hon. Henry Keswick, senior partner of Jardine, Matheson and Co. and, as it happened, Deputy Chairman of the Hongkong Bank, moved the first reading of a bill in the Legislative Council entitled:

An Ordinance to authorize the Hongkong and Shanghai Banking Corporation from

---

[f] This is calculated as follows: by the former agreements – first $2.5 million in securities had to be deposited, then when the capital was increased by $2.5 million to $10 million a further one-third of the addition (=$0.83) was required; then finally an amount equivalent to the entire 1907 capital increase, that is $5 million was required in securities or coin. This gave a total security in the hands of the Government for the $15 million note issue of $8.3 million, but only one-third of the issue or $5 million could be secured by interest-bearing securities.

time to time to increase the Capital of the said Corporation from the sum of Ten Millions of Dollars to a sum not exceeding the sum of Twenty Millions of Dollars, and to continue incorporated for a further term of 21 years; and to continue in force for a further period of 21 years the provisions of Section 3 of the Hongkong and Shanghai Banking Corporation Ordinance, 1899, with regard to the Excess Issue of Bills and Notes payable to bearer on demand.[32]

Arguing that 'it is most desirable to have this leading Bank closely identified with the Colony', Keswick moved the second and third readings and the Bill was agreed to on June 13, 1907.

As the ordinance (No. 6 of 1907) was passed as previously approved by the Home authorities in London, there was no need for the 'suspension' clause which was usually attached to bills dealing with 'reserved' subjects and which provided time for consideration and advice to Her Majesty as to disallowance; thus the Officer Administering the Government, F.H. May, was free to give immediate consent for the requested increase in the Bank's capital from \$10 to \$15 million, which he did by Proclamation on June 15 and confirmed as in effect by Proclamation of June 20.[33] A further \$5 million increase in the Bank's capital would be authorized under the provisions of this ordinance in 1921.

There was apparently no question but that the Bank's ordinance would be renewed, that the capital would be increased, and that the note issue would be increased *pari passu*; the only problem was the security for the note issue on which opinions had changed since 1865, but the Treasury's demands were a consistent development from the arguments raised in 1886 and 1890.

The question of the shareholders' reserve liability was at no point raised in these deliberations by any of the parties involved. With published reserves equal to an amount already close to 200% of paid-up capital, the matter apparently did not seem one of immediate concern.

From 1908 to the outbreak of war

During the period from 1908 the Bank was operating on an enhanced capital; this meant that, for any given dividend, the sum paid out to shareholders overall would be greater. There was in addition an average – considering the period 1902–1907 against 1908–1914 – 7% increase in dividends per share, but earnings were up only 42% against a capital increase of 50% and the exchanges were on the average less favourable in the second period (see Table 4.1). The fall in the market value of consols and other sterling gilt-edged securities and the policy of the Bank to write down the book value accordingly out of current profits were further drains on net earnings. These factors forced a fall in the rate of growth of the published reserve funds; nevertheless the Bank maintained a sound position and was not prevented from any particular course as a consequence of these policies.

By the end of 1908 the unappropriated surplus on Contingencies Account was $3.7 million and the directors were transferring a high proportion of the profits from such loans as the Shanghai–Nanking Railway and the Canton–Kowloon Railway to this account, which, while following traditional accounting practices in the handling of profits from extraordinary sources, confirms the view expressed above that the size of the published reserves and the pressure for maintaining the dividends, required the development of hidden reserves. Market psychology did not permit reserves to be used; hence hidden reserves became a necessity, not only for the Hongkong Bank, but for the banking industry in general.

The Bank had also to contend with the growth of a 'Special Charges Account', which, for example, totalled $170,000 for the second half of the year. These were special overheads which had neither been apportioned to the branches nor taken over by Head Office. They included salary of staff on leave, passages, and the first trip out (with allowances) of London Office juniors. But they also included $8,000 for the various *ad hoc* 'pensions' which the Board had from time to time granted and which, unlike the one-time retirement gratuity, could not be taken from the Officers Good Service Fund (OGSF). Offsetting these items but slightly were such detailed items as refunds from unused sleeper berths or from the P&O for a portion of the fare of some junior who, bound originally for Hong Kong, was ordered assigned on an emergency basis to an office en route. All this provides an insight into the detailed problems still brought before the Board of Directors.

In 1908 dear money had given way to cheap and with funds seeking employment, the Bank decided to hold bills until maturity, explaining the sudden growth in 'bills receivable'. There were signs of trade recovery, but excess funds had to be employed in the purchase of relatively low-earning Government securities. In the Chairman's speech the deaths of the Empress Dowager and of the Kuang-Hsu Emperor were alluded to.

At the mid-1909 meeting of Proprietors, the Chairman W.J. Gresson announced and defended the subscription of $50,000 to the University of Hong Kong conditionally upon the full amount required for the Endowment Fund being forthcoming.

Without desiring to enter into the controversy as to the desirability of a University at all, I would point out that the proposition has been most favourably received by the Chinese, including the highest officials, not only in Canton but also in Peking, as is demonstrated by the way they have come forward with subscriptions. If you will reflect on the position held by the Bank in China and its intimate financial relations with the Chinese Imperial Government for so many years, I am sure you will recognize that we have acted in the best interests of the Bank and will approve of our action accordingly. (Applause).

1909 was a year of steady exchanges, expanding trade, and a rise in rubber prices in the Straits Settlements, where the Malacca sub-agency was opened. Harry Hunter's Hongkew sub-agency which had been authorized some three years previously was finally opened; but much of the Chairman's speech was still in terms of 'prospects'. These were realized in 1910.

Long negotiations for railway construction and currency reform loans were coming to fruition in 1910 and early 1911, but in October a nationalist revolution overthrew the dynasty and brought in the Chinese Republic. Addis reacted by ordering the Bank's athletic teams in London to abandon their team colours – imperial yellow with a black Chinese dragon. In China management looked on with apprehension but at the February 1912 meeting the Chairman was able to make one important reassurance, the contending parties in China had been in agreement that customs revenues were to be paid to the order of the Commission of Foreign Bankers in Shanghai, with the Hongkong Bank as the initial repository. Maintaining China's credit, although not necessarily what China should borrow for, was not a political issue; the move was welcomed by investors and their bankers.

There was, however, some delay in repayment of the Chinese 6% Gold Loan of 1895, but the Hongkong Bank agreed to buy the coupons from bondholders against later repayment from the Chinese Government.

As noted in the preliminary comments, the increase in the note issue was due to Chinese holding notes obtained in payment of overseas remittances and failing to put them back in circulation, reflecting the troubled times. The increase in bills receivable was again the consequence of holding them in London until maturity rather than discounting.

As the Chairman's speech touched on the course of silver, he referred briefly to Indian speculation in silver and that story, in which the Hongkong Bank played a role, will be told below.

During 1912 the Hongkong Bank wrote $550,000 off the Premises Account, which nevertheless continued to increase – the account had stood at less than a million at the end of 1901; in mid-1912 it was $2.2 million; at the end of the year it had reached $5.4 million but by mid-1914 it had reached $7.4 million despite continuous write-offs. The Hongkong Bank had purchased the land and was building its new London Office on Gracechurch Street, but it was also meeting the costs of new offices in the Malay States, in Bombay, and in Hankow – having just completed building in Sourabaya. All this deserves separate consideration.

In 1913 Newton Stabb, who had been appointed Chief Manager for three years from January 1911, was offered a further three years; in May 1914 he went on leave and, although during his short leaves A.H. Barlow had taken charge of Head Office, for this longer period A.G. Stephen was called down from Shanghai to become Acting Chief Manager. Thus Stabb was in London at the outbreak of war, and Stephen, wistfully perhaps, cabled on August 3, 'I think in view of gravity of situation you should resume charge here and I proceed Shanghai unless in your opinion your presence more necessary in London in general interests HSBC.'[34] Stabb returned to Hong Kong.

The directors did consider the need to purchase land for an office in Kowloon, but in the event no action was taken because it was agreed sites would always be available. A Kowloon sub-agency was not actually established until 1929.

In the year before the Great War profits had risen, but this was apparently due to net earnings from loans, particularly the Reorganization Loan of 1913, which netted the Bank £103,000, and from such special operations as the silver syndicate, mentioned below. The continued need to write down consols acted as a drag on profits, but the Bank continued to pay an annual bonus to staff (except at the end of 1911) and an additional gratuity to managers at a total annual cost of approximately $240,000.

Finally in 1914 the Bank tackled the growing problem of paying dividends tax free. A.G. Stephen as Acting Chief Manager cabled Stabb that he thought, contrary to Addis, that although there was no necessary connection between the size of the dividend and the change of the tax basis, one should 'start fair'.[35] The Board therefore accepted Stabb's final recommendation to raise the dividend to offset the tax payment, leaving the British-resident shareholder as well off as before – at least for the present half-year. The normal dividend of £2 was accordingly increased by three shillings (see Table 1.4B).

SPECIAL TOPICS, 1912–1914

This survey of the Bank's overall operations from 1902 to 1914 does little justice to its varied and often virtually independent activities in the region and in London. The Bank as seen in the published 'abstract' of accounts and the Chairman's speech is relatively colourless. The purpose of this section is to introduce several topics and problems which characterized the Bank's activities in the last three years of the period under consideration.

The first, advances to public companies, is a commentary on a typical (and uninformed) criticism of the role of exchange banks; the story of the compradore is a continuation of that complex topic; the account of the silver operations on behalf of (a) the India Office and (b) the Hongkong Bank initiated syndicate is by contrast an example of the Bank's ever-increasing involvement in the complexities of international finance and its enhanced role in London; the Bank's finance of the opium trade, although of long standing, again became controversial in a period of nationalism.

The account of W.F. Skene's charges against the management of the Bank, although perhaps out of proportion to its importance, provides an opportunity to review the Hongkong Bank's practices with regard to accounting disclosures and hidden reserves, which, after all, affect any analysis this history presents. Data on the inner reserves have not been preserved and labelled as such, and the resulting limitations to this history should be understood.

Advances to public companies

The Hongkong Bank had been founded in part to assist development on the China coast, but the failure of the firms selected for financial assistance had endangered the future of the Bank. In Volume I, Chapter 6, a shareholder was quoted as referring to the Bank 'having sacrificed a million for the furtherance of local enterprise (laughter)', and the directors reminded themselves that turnover of funds was the source of profit, the 'lock-up' of funds a matter for concern.

Criticism by nationalists has been directed at the 'foreign' banks for their failure to finance fixed investment in the historical development of the economy. The exchange banks were not designed for this task, their capital was inadequate, and their role was to facilitate the operations of enterprises in which entrepreneurs had been willing to provide risk capital.

Nevertheless the Hongkong Bank did in fact contribute to the finance of fixed investment in several ways. By advancing against the shares of public companies the Bank provided liquidity, making possible the investment of others, protecting itself partially at least from the direct consequences of business failure. Even this was financially dangerous.

The Bank also bought locally quoted shares for its own portfolio.

The Bank's sterling reserves were partially in Indian and colonial securities, some of which were designed for the finance of development projects. A 1902 list of securities includes India, Cape of Good Hope, Natal, Canada, Western Australia, and Victoria Government stock and various Indian railway debentures. From time to time the Bank held bonds of China issues it had underwritten, and the OGSF had at one time been partly invested in China Merchants' Steam Navigation Company securities which the Bank had held rather than force on a reluctant market.

The Hongkong Bank was also 'notorious' for standing by its constituents, for seeing them through a crisis. For this it was criticized by some contemporaries since the Bank seemed at times 'quixotic'. In extreme cases the Bank did take possession and then either managed the enterprise for a time, for example the Tschurin Department Stores in Manchuria, or sold off the property, again receiving contrary criticism.

If the theoretical ideal bank credit is self-liquidating, the high marketability of a loan is a reasonably safe substitute in ordinary times. The danger comes from advances to companies which, whether secured or not, cannot easily be withdrawn and are a threat to the Bank's liquidity. A bank might advance to a constituent for several purposes from several branches and might be unaware of its total exposure. With Chinese customers the Bank recognized its vulnerability and operated through the compradore's security, which brought problems of its own as the following section will detail. The Board of Directors were naturally aware of these problems and, at a time when they were withdrawing from active management of the Bank, they nevertheless called for a series of occasional reports on 'Advances to Public Companies' by the two main offices, Hong Kong and Shanghai.

At the end of 1913, for example, advances to such companies totalled approximately $9.4 million or 6.8% of total loans etc. outstanding. Advances to Hong Kong companies totalled $5.3 million, principally to the China Sugar Refining Company and the Hongkong and Whampoa Dock Company, the latter against no specific security. Advances in Shanghai were slightly less than Ts3 million and were more evenly spread. Typical of the companies financed in this way were such factories as the China Flour Mill Company, the Central Garage Company, International Cotton Manufacturing Company, Kiangnan Dock and Engineering Works, Lau Kung Mow Cotton Spinning and Weaving Company, Major Bros, New Engineering and Shipbuilding Works, Shanghai Electric and Asbestos Company, Shanghai Gas Company, Shanghai Tannery Company, and the Shanghai Tug and Lighter Company. The Bank had also advanced to land investment companies and rubber estate companies with head offices in Shanghai.

It was not a dangerously large list, but the Board nevertheless felt they should be provided the information, and the list was, exceptionally, regularly attached to the minutes and so preserved.

The Hong Kong compradores, from Lau Pun Chiu to Ho Sai Wing[36]

The fourth compradore had come to the Bank in 1906 with a minimum of security, and by 1912 there were problems once again.

Lau Pun Chiu granted unauthorized overnight loans from the Bank's funds – as, indeed, had other compradores. A cash shortage of $40,000 first appeared in September 1912. When queried, the compradore replied that it was to have been replaced the day the shortage was discovered, but the person from whom he was to receive the money had not appeared.

This shortage placed the relationship of the compradore to the Bank in question and a meeting was called of the compradore's sureties. They decided to continue their surety and the compradore was retained. Some days later another shortage, of $32,000, was discovered and Lau Pun Chiu did not appear at his office that morning – he had left for Shanghai. His total shortfall amounted to about $152,000, covered by security amounting to $360,000.

In the month between the departure of Lau Pun Chiu and the engagement of a new compradore, the cash department was run with the old staff under the supervision of Mok Kon Sang, son of the compradore of Butterfield and Swire, who was one of the sureties. He was there not only because he was qualified as a compradore but also to look after the interests of the sureties.

The next compradore, Ho Sai Wing (or usually Ho Wing) was a member of what was probably Hong Kong's wealthiest family, and he remained with the Bank until 1946. The Ho family fortunes began when Ho Tung, the eldest of four brothers, joined Jardine, Matheson and Co. at the age of eighteen as an assistant in the compradore department, he rose to the top and was eventually succeeded as the firm's compradore by his brother Ho Fuk. The Ho family developed varied interests in Hong Kong, including a native bank and trade in leather, sugar, and other commodities.

Ho Wing, the new compradore of the Bank, was the son of Ho Fuk but was adopted by Ho Tung. After leaving Queen's College, Ho Wing had toured Europe and, on his return in 1902, became compradore of E.D. Sassoon and Co. From there he became compradore of the Bank. Ho Wing was secured by his father, Ho Tung, for $300,000. His monthly salary was $1,000. Ho Wing did not have the large Chinese clan connections of the previous compradores, but as part of the Ho family he had particularly sound connections, *inter alia*, with various Eurasian families in Hong Kong. The first generation of the Ho family were, as noted above, compradores for Jardine's; the second generation spread itself into other firms. Ho Wing was at the Bank, his brother Ho Sai Iu was compradore of the Mercantile Bank, another brother Ho Sai Kwong succeeded Ho Wing as compradore at E.D. Sassoon and Co., and yet another brother Ho Leung was a compradore at Jardine's. These were all sons of Ho Fuk. Ho Sai Ki, another son of Ho Fuk, became compradore for Arnhold and Co. Ho Sai Wa, a cousin, was an assistant compradore in the Mercantile Bank.

For a time T.P. Tong was joint compradore with Ho Wing. It may have been that Ho Wing did not wish to devote his time exclusively to his compradore post, and hence there was a sharing of responsibility, but this arrangement ceased in 1933.

But as far as Hong Kong was concerned, the Bank's compradore problem had been resolved. This was not true, however, elsewhere; the Bank had problems, for example, in Bangkok in late 1913.

The Hongkong Bank and silver operations

The India Office silver purchases of 1912

At the beginning of 1912 the Indian Government estimated their needs for silver for coinage as 51 million ounces worth £6 million at current prices and equivalent to nearly one-quarter of the world's annual supply.[37] Noting that silver prices had fluctuated some 50% in the previous decade, the India Office were concerned that should information leak regarding Government's purchasing plans, the price would move against them and speculators would take positions adverse to the Government's operations, as indeed the Indian Specie Bank was later to do – to its cost.

The obvious solution was for operations to be undertaken with the utmost secrecy until the silver had actually been purchased; the India Office entrusted the task to Samuel Montagu and Co., and they in turn relied on the Hongkong and Shanghai Banking Corporation to make the purchase in the East. Shipments were invoiced to the Hongkong Bank, London; at the last minute and as the ship approached Bombay or Colombo (for Calcutta), the parties concerned were sent cabled instructions to change the destination and off-load on account of the Hongkong Bank in Bombay or Calcutta. Only at that point would the Indian authorities claim involvement and take delivery.

At the end of October 1912, for example, the Bombay mint master cabled that he had received in one shipment from China through the Hongkong Bank 245 boxes of British silver dollars and 661 boxes of sycee silver with a total value of £400,000. The purchases were accomplished on a rising market between 2s:6$\frac{15}{16}$d and 2s:8$\frac{7}{8}$d, a much more favourable range than had been anticipated. The Hongkong Bank however apparently had difficulties finding the silver on schedule but overall met the extraordinary demands placed upon it.

Speculation did follow news that large shipments of silver had arrived in India, but by this time the balance had been purchased by the Bank in China and the impact of speculation on the market for these specific transactions was minimal. The impact on the Indian Specie Bank, however, was another matter, and the consequence of their failure is related below.[38]

One writer has referred to these transactions as being at 'the centre of one of the gravest political and financial scandals in English social history'.[39] This is surely an exaggeration; there was a family connection between the Under-Secretary of State for India and Samuel Montagu and Co. and, given political tempers at the time, there was consequently a Royal Commission. The Hongkong Bank was not involved in this controversy, but publication of its role should have enhanced its reputation for efficiency and public service.

The 1913 silver syndicate

Sir Charles Addis, the Bank's London Manager, was involved in two London-initiated silver transactions which contributed to the higher 1913/14 net earnings earlier referred to.

In 1913 he recorded in his diary:

> September 22. Over a cup of coffee in Bank of England parlour I sold £1 million silver to the Governor, Walter Cunliffe.
> A bold coup and, I think, a good one.

Unfortunately there are no details in the surviving records.

On November 29, 1913, the Indian Specie Bank, which had speculated in silver, failed with a total eventual loss of Rs3,404,379. The bank defaulted on some £3 million in silver contracts with Sharps and Wilkins. Had the firm attempted to sell this amount of silver on the market, there would have been a serious crisis, and Addis moved quickly to avert it by initiating the formation of a syndicate to take over the contracts and sell over a period of time without disruption to the market.

Neither Lord Rothschild nor the clearing banks would assist on acceptable terms, but the Bank of England was sympathetic and Addis was able to enlist the cooperation of the Chartered Bank and three silver brokers, Mocatta and Goldsmid, Samuel Montagu and Co., and Pixley and Abell, with the two banks acting as co-managers, but with Addis signing for the syndicate. By December 4 the contract was signed and four days later the Bank of England agreed to advance the syndicate £1.5 million on a 5% margin on daily silver prices with bar silver as security. Sharps and Wilkins assigned their rights in claims against the Indian Specie Bank in liquidation to the syndicate, and the latter became responsible on behalf of the Indian bank for contracts totalling £3,053,361 for 26,372,714 standard ounces at a price of 27.787 pence, which the syndicate agreed to buy at 2s:2½d, or 26.5d (=£2,912,000).

On December 9 the Hongkong Bank first put up a total £40,000 with the Bank of England as a 5% margin and, the Bank's own share being £10,987:2s:6d, then claimed the balance from its partners in the syndicate.

By this time Addis had received the congratulations of Sir Felix Schuster as chairman of the India Council Finance Committee and Newman as deputy governor of the Bank of England, but the syndicate's task had just begun. The end came in early April when Addis recorded in his diary on April 2, 'Silver syndicate closed. For four months has disposed of £3 million silver taken over at time of Indian Specie Bank failure. It is a great relief. It added plenty to my work and worry.' The net profit was £16,146:16s:6d of which the Hongkong Bank earned £4,435:18s:9d.[40]

Opium

The Chairman of the Hongkong Bank during 1912 was E. Shellim of D. Sassoon, Sons and Co., and it was his duty to speak to the opium trade. 'So far as this Bank is concerned it, in common with other Eastern Exchange Banks, is interested in the financing of this business [the opium trade], as it has been since its foundation . . .' The specific problem was the impediments placed by Republican Chinese regional officials on the movement of opium from the ports to the consumers. An agreement had been made, of which the Indian Government had taken cognizance, which would over a period of time eliminate the legal trade in opium; the officials in question had anticipated the deadline and some nine months' supply was awaiting shipment inland. The merchants took the position that they had entered into a legal operation and were cutting back within the time allowed. As the Chairman put it:

While fully sympathizing with China in her efforts to suppress opium smoking, the fact should not be lost sight of that a certain period was arranged by China in which to attain that object, therefore those who entered into commitments on the good faith of the agreement being effective have reasonable cause for complaint at the present situation.

And the Hongkong Bank, having financed shipments, could not expect repayment until such shipments were in fact sold.

The Bank had participated in protests against the taxation and other impediments to the trade in opium as recently as 1910; the grounds were always interference with trade contrary to the provisions of the treaties, that the commodity in question was opium was not, as far as the Bank was concerned, a relevant point.[41]

The Bank financed trade; it was for the political authorities to agree on what constituted legitimate trade and for commercial organizations to operate within these agreements – and for them to protest if the agreements were not fulfilled. Thus the Corporation faced the classic issue of responsibility for the consequences of its actions, as the landlord whose property is rented for purposes which, while legal, are considered by some immoral. The Bank's attitude to the problem was amoral; just as a business corporation was not instituted to give its shareholders' funds away for charity – it was for shareholders to give to charity from the dividends paid them – so it was not a corporation's role to take moral positions but rather for its directors and shareholders in their private capacity to take whatever political action they, as citizens, thought desirable. Not only money but bankers are neutral – both these views in their strictest interpretation are being challenged today, but they remain subjects of considerable debate.

The Hongkong Bank was not, then, alone in its attitude; on the disruption of trade, albeit the opium trade in this case, the Bank acted in association with the Chartered Bank, the Mercantile Bank, and the Hong Kong General Chamber of Commerce. The Bank managers urged the British Government either to insist on China enforcing the relevant treaties or to require the Indian Government to suspend the auction of certified opium until the treaties were enforced. Their position, as expressed in 1912 in relation to the developments referred to in the Hongkong Bank Chairman's speech, was simple:

Banks in both India and China felt justified in financing the Merchants as they considered the business was protected by Treaty. . . . Merchants would never have entered into the commitments had they not felt perfectly satisfied they were protected by Treaty rights. [Signed] Wm Dickson, Manager, Chartered Bank of India, Australia and China; N.J. Stabb, Chief Manager, the Hongkong and Shanghai Banking Corporation; and F.C. Macdonald, Manager, Mercantile Bank of India, Ltd.[42]

On this basis the Hongkong Bank had advanced £900,000 to the opium merchants who, with their stocks held up in Shanghai, were on the verge of bankruptcy. The Indian Government meanwhile refused to suspend sales, and, as the British Minister, J.N. Jordan, observed in Peking, 'In all the circumstances I cannot see how serious disaster to the trade is to be averted.'[43]

At this point eleven banks in Shanghai jointly protested the impediments local authorities were placing on the trade; in addition to the three British exchange banks there were the Yokohama Specie Bank, Banque de l'Indo-Chine, Banque Sino-Belge, Netherlands Trading Society, Bank of Taiwan, Deutsch-Asiatische Bank, and the Russo-Asiatic Bank.[44]

The opium problem was one which had aroused emotions since the early days of the private merchants' Canton trade, but it had become complicated by the development of native-grown opium which by 1912 constituted some 90% of the total consumption in China.[45] The priority the Chinese Government was giving, with relative if temporary success, to the suppression of native-grown opium, however, led to international cooperation in China's efforts to prohibit opium imports. The several British and Imperial authorities, for example, had accepted a plan whereby Indian Government-regulated sales of 'certified opium', the basis for the legal export trade, would be decreased periodically until totally eliminated.

But the revolutionary authorities wished naturally to speed the process, and the banks were caught in the middle. The problem was not fully resolved until 1917 when the remaining stocks of 'certified opium' were purchased and destroyed by the Chinese Government.

In the meantime continuation of the trade served as an anti-foreign weapon. In Peking the *Times* correspondent, G.E. Morrison, whose opportunistic attacks on the Hongkong Bank usually focused on its alleged German domination, this time recognized the long-standing Jewish connections of the Bank by using anti-Semitism as his weapon.[46] But the position the foreign traders and their governments were attempting to defend was an impossible one.

The Hongkong Bank's policy as set by the Board was non-involvement in public affairs – except as they affected trade, banking, or monetary policy. Thus its public protests were consistent with its overall trade policy but the application of that policy to this particular commodity, while consistent with the commercial morality of the time, would be subject to justified criticism.

The charges of W.F. Skene

Early in W.F. Skene's brief career with the Bank, the Calcutta Manager, W.K. Dods, had written in his formal report, 'I am sorry to say I cannot recommend this man for promotion . . . he is lacking in steadiness and common sense. His private finances are in an appalling condition and he is continuously at loggerheads with the members of the staff.'[47] Skene had come East in 1898 and had received for many years reasonable reports, serving as Shanghai secretary to the Indemnity Committee in 1904. In 1911 he went on leave in the usual way and then in a letter dated January 9, 1912, resigned from the Bank's service, charging that the Bank was publishing false accounts and that there were funds concealed from shareholders and directors alike. The payment of dividends from these concealed funds was, he claimed, a criminal act with which he could not be associated and he concluded by requesting the Bank to 'indemnify' him for loss of career.

Charles Addis, who had known Skene in Shanghai, had discussed the problem with him in London and recommended that he receive the gratuity usual on retirement. Newton Stabb, the Chief Manager, on the other hand felt sufficiently strongly to bring an adverse recommendation to the Board; they refused the usual gratuity and instructed that Skene be informed the charges were false.

A year later Skene called a public meeting of the Bank's London share-holders in the Criterion Restaurant. Some 30 or 40 persons attended, including the Bank's legal representative who, being invited by Skene to address the meeting first, successfully undermined Skene's credibility by stressing, *inter alia*, Skene's junior status. It was true that Skene had not yet risen high in the service, but with the exception of A.F. Warrack, the senior at the Hongkew sub-agency, neither had any other banker's assistant of 1898 seniority – as Skene, to no effect, was careful to point out.

Skene charged that the Bank issued false balance sheets. Under Jackson the management had concealed profits, placing them in various accounts, such as exchange accounts, contingency accounts, China loan accounts, and certain current accounts.

Smith, Skene claimed, lacked Jackson's finesse in speculation and consequently, he concluded, there had been losses covered by withdrawing funds from the hidden reserves. 'In fact I believe I am correct in saying that ever since the increase in your capital some five years ago your dividends have not been paid out of current profits as you have been led to believe, but with the assistance of these heavy reserves.'[48] Skene's charges can be divided into four major categories: (i) that the directors were kept uninformed, (ii) that there existed hidden reserves, (iii) that there had been losses under Smith, and (iv) the hidden reserves had been used to cover these losses resulting in an overstatement of net earnings which would permit the usual dividend and bonus.

Skene's contention that payment of dividends from 'reserves' – which he perhaps confused with 'capital' – was a criminal act may be dismissed immediately as false. Although there had been some definition of accounting requirements in British company law, they were still admittedly inadequate and the Hongkong Bank was not, in any case, subject to their provisions. The Bank's 1866 Deed of Settlement states:

Art. 151: It shall be lawful for the [Board] to set aside such proportion, as they shall think fit, of the net profits for the purpose of creating, adding to, and maintaining a Reserve Fund for the purpose, as far as desirable, of equalizing the dividends . . . Art. 153: When and so often as the sum at credit of the Reserve Fund shall amount to a sum larger than, in the judgement of the [Board], shall be necessary, it shall be lawful to apply such part of it as may be thought proper as part of the divisible profits of the Company.[49]

Skene was, however, correct in stating that the directors were not fully informed on the immediate state of the Bank. His comparison with joint-stock banks in England was telling but irrelevant; it was acknowledged that the situation in Hong Kong did not permit directors, all of whom had recognized and fully admitted conflicts of interest, to be current either with the Bank's exchange position or with the status of customers' accounts. The comparison was irrelevant because the Board of the Hongkong Bank was non-executive; it did not make the decisions which would have required the withheld information.

The corrective to this situation was to bring the Head Office of the Bank and the Board of Directors to London. Skene recommended this to the meeting.

Skene was also correct in supposing that there were hidden reserves, although whether these were hidden from the directors is impossible to confirm. The directors were aware of (i) the surplus on Head Office Contingency Account plus the amounts held back by branches in unappropriated accounts, (ii) the status of the China, Japan, and Siam loan accounts, (iii) the status of the exchange accounts, and (iv) the difference between market and book value of the Bank's securities. But Skene contended, no doubt accurately, that management had set up a current account in excess of £200,000 equivalent, which was properly a reserve fund; this the directors may or may not have been aware of.

In his study of the Hongkong Bank's financial statements, Professor T.A. Lee has written:

Banks are no strangers to subjective accounting practices and limited disclosure, and it should be no surprise to associate HSBC with such a situation. In fact, it has usually been the case in most developed free-enterprise societies that banks have been allowed legally to 'smooth' their financial results by use of techniques such as 'inner' or 'hidden' reserves and to disclose far less information than is expected or required for other trading concerns. The reason for this approach to reporting requirements is the need to reflect financial stability in banks for the benefit of depositors.[50]

That the Bank had suffered losses was true, but provision had been made from current earnings despite the existence of over $3 million unappropriated in the Contingency Account. Skene referred to Shanghai losses; in this he was also correct, although the Minute Book for that period is missing. In any case, there can be no question of Smith's ability in exchange; indeed, to suppose otherwise would be to suggest that all the directors and such inveterate diary writers as Charles Addis were totally misled. The bonuses voted to the staff and the liberal payments to Smith suggest the directors' complete confidence in management. This is not the same as supposing the directors were fully abreast of every detail.

The only interesting point in Skene's presentation is his charge that dividends since the 1907 capital increase had been paid, in part at least, from hidden reserves. During this period the Bank had transferred $3.7 million to the published reserves, allegedly from current net earnings. They had also written down consols as required from current net earnings. There is thus a considerable margin before dividends can be said to come from inner reserves.

From time to time the Board recommended transfers to Premises Account; such a transfer at the end of 1911 – the six-month period after which no addition to reserves occurred and dividends were paid out of the previous six months' carry-over on Profit and Loss Account – was designed, Skene charged, to mislead shareholders into supposing the half-year had been prosperous, contrary to fact. Had the Board or management desired to disguise the position, it is difficult to understand why they openly paid out dividends in excess of net earnings. The transfer to Premises Account was consistent with a long-established practice and particularly necessary in view of the heavy commitments the Board was making in property development (see discussion below).

Skene made much of the fact that he had discussed this with Charles Addis who had admitted the existence of hidden reserves. But the terms of the Addis 'admission' are limited; there is no suggestion that Addis felt the Bank was involved in any improper deception, and officially the Bank made no response to Skene's charges.

Nevertheless, this was all at a public meeting. The shareholders were partly confused by the personal element, but in the end they voted quite simply (and with one in dissent) that they did not believe Skene. They then passed a mock 'vote of thanks' on the grounds that he had told them their Bank, with its hidden reserves, was better off than they thought it was.[51] As Addis cabled Stabb in Hong Kong, the meeting was a fiasco.[52]

Nothing more was heard of the issues discussed at the meeting or of Skene himself, but from the point of view of the Bank's history certain conclusions may be drawn from so public an airing of the Bank's practices. First, the normal accounting practices, which included hidden reserves, were not questioned by shareholders; second, the suggestion of a move to London was not taken up; and third, the existence of hidden reserves was established.

The one-dollar note issue

The various advisory bodies in Hong Kong, the Finance Committee, the General Chamber of Commerce, and, finally, the Executive Council were advising once again that the permitted limit on the issue of one-dollar notes be raised from $226,000 to $350,000. This view was supported by Newton Stabb, Chief Manager of the Hongkong Bank, who claimed that applications at the counter for one-dollar notes had repeatedly to be refused due to lack of supply.[53]

Previously the argument against the small denomination notes had been based on the absence of unchopped dollar coins passing by tale; now the argument was one of weight, the British dollar had the weight of a crown coin in England but was worth but one-fifth, and the cost of undertaking transactions in coin was one reason why notes in general were at a premium.

But the premium hardly met the cost of a one-dollar issue, and both the Chartered Bank and the Mercantile Bank – the latter having recently been granted through the provisions of Ordinance No. 65 of 1911 the right to issue notes in Hong Kong to help alleviate the general shortage – although acknowledging the need, declined to participate in any such issue on the grounds of cost. The Government had only recently considered and rejected a Government note issue, and, therefore, the whole project now rested (i) on the willingness of the Hongkong Bank to undertake it as a public service and (ii) on the Treasury to permit the increase.

The points advanced by the Officer Administering the Government of Hong Kong, Claude Severn, in his despatch of June 28, 1912, were designed to counter long-standing arguments based on the supposition that 'such notes must be held by the classes least educated'.

The Hongkong Bank had informed the Governor that the demand for one-dollar notes came from the Europeans and the Chinese shopkeepers who served them; it was a matter of convenience since the dollar coins were heavy for value. A transaction involving payment of say $4.00, one less than the five-dollar note, required carrying coins weighing four ounces avoirdupois. 'It is not surprising therefore', Severn added, 'that the standard coin is used rather as a reserve against note issue than as a medium of exchange.'[54]

The Bank and the Chamber of Commerce advised that few if any of the notes circulated outside Hong Kong.

The long-standing argument that the one-dollar note was of small denomination came under attack. Granted it was small to My Lords of the Treasury, but was it small to a Hong Kong 'coolie'? Severn thought not; the poor man's needs were denominated in fractions of a dollar. In any case if all these notes were in a panic surrendered at once, they amounted to but 1.16% of the Bank's total note issue. And, finally, since there were 444,664 Chinese in Hong Kong and only 226,000 one-dollar notes . . .

The Treasury had unfortunately misplaced the files and were under the impression that the Hongkong Bank no longer issued any one-dollar notes. They were also concerned by the argument that foreign notes, mainly notes of the Banco Nacional Ultramarino in Macau, were still circulating in Hong Kong contrary to recent legislative prohibition.[55] However the resulting delay was minimal and on September 2, 1912, the Treasury approved the increased issue, subject as usual to the Bank's agreeing to withdraw in the event of a Government note issue.[56]

In banking as in philosophy the questions which exercise the intellectual ingenuity of one generation may cease to fascinate the next. This particular issue has undoubtedly ceased to fascinate the present generation except, perhaps, as a matter of interest as to how it could ever have fascinated the past. But money was the product with which the Bank dealt, and regulations which affected the former concerned the latter; in the Bank's history the debate must be recounted.

The Hongkong Bank and the Government

The Bank's ordinance and the purchase of land
The purpose of sections 17 and 19 of the Hongkong Bank Ordinance of 1866 was to prevent the Bank speculating or dealing in land; in addition it provided

Table 1.8 *The Hongkong and Shanghai Banking Corporation*
Lands and buildings owned by the Corporation in 1912
(in thousands of dollars)

	cost of land	cost of building	total cost	
Hong Kong				
Bank	140.0	367.9	507.9	
St John's Place			45.0	
Cloudlands	35.5	90.7	126.2	
Reclamation	63.4		63.4	
Cliffs	40.0	116.2	156.2	
Mayfield	40.0	20.0	60.0	
				1,201.6
Shanghai				
Bank			217.0	
Brand Bros property			319.2	
Mackenzie property			384.6	
Cadastral No. 1018				
Hongkew			209.6	
				1,130.5
Yokohama				
Bank			62.5	
No. 160 The Bluff (Manager)			25.0	
No. 70 The Bluff (Sub-Manager)			16.0	
No. 2B			126.0	
				229.5
Singapore				
Mount Echo			13.3	
Bank	134.6	136.4	271.0	
Sub-Manager's house			29.1	
				313.4
Manila				
Bank house			27.9	
Office			82.5	
				110.4
Bombay				
Office			108.8	
				108.8
Rangoon				
Bank			80.5	
Additional site	20.1		20.1	
New building		125.0	125.0	
				225.7
Batavia				
Agent's house			32.7	
New premises			188.4	
				221.0

Table 1.8 – *cont.*
(in thousands of dollars)

	cost of land	cost of building	total cost	
Kobe				
Office and house			18.0	
New buildings			301.4	
Junior mess house			34.1	
				353.5
Hankow				
Office and house			28.4	
				28.4
Nagasaki				
Office and house			19.6	
New building			67.0	
				86.6
Amoy				
Office			37.4	
House			10.0	
Cottage			5.0	
				52.4
Foochow				
Bank	3.5	15.0	18.5	
				18.5
Saigon				
House			13.0	
Premises			68.0	
				81.0
Tientsin				
Office and house			54.6	
New building			58.5	
Startstoff property			118.2	
				231.3
Peking				
Office and house			11.8	
New buildings			217.9	
				229.6
Penang				
House			24.5	
New premises	104.0	234.9	339.0	
Penang Government Hill	1.2		1.2	
				364.6
Iloilo				
House and office			18.9	
				18.9

Table 1.8 – *cont.*
(in thousands of dollars)

	cost of land	cost of building	total cost	
Calcutta				
Bank house			67.0	
				67.0
Canton				
Land and Bank buildings			48.0	
Godown and junior mess			30.0	
				78.0
Sourabaya				
Bank	35.3	67.9	103.2	
Agent's house			40.5	
				143.7
Bangkok				
	26.1	50.4	76.6	
				76.6
Colombo				137.3
Kuala Lumpur				22.3
Malacca				60.0
		Total cost $28,560,700		
		On books at $2,171,000		

Source: CO 129/391, ff. 256–59.

that the Bank could purchase land for its own use but that any such proposed purchase with an annual value over $30,000 had *inter alia* to be sanctioned by the Governor. This sanction the Bank had never sought.

In 1910 the Bank, which was paying an annual rental of £5,500 for its London office on Lombard Street, decided to acquire a freehold site on Gracechurch Street for £250,000. This was a considerable investment and at some stage someone decided to read the ordinance of incorporation. The Bank then requested the required sanction; the Government discovered that the Bank had not previously reported its major property transactions and was in violation of its ordinance; consequently the Bank was instructed to report all its purchases for a *post factum* sanction.[57]

There is nothing in the records to suggest the connection was made, but the affair could have been compared to the retroactive sanction given by the Treasury for the agencies opened by the Bank in what was thought to be a contravention of its charter. The Officer Administering the Government was in fact prevailed upon to sanction the Gracechurch purchase first with the understanding that the Bank would provide a list of all property acquisitions later – two years later as it turned out.

Due, however, to a controversy over the interpretation of the requirement, the Bank decided to simply submit a list of *all* its property acquisitions. And thus, in consequence of these exchanges, the Bank's position relative to its property was regularized and a list of such property has been preserved (see Table 1.8).

The 1914 revision of the Bank's ordinance

In April 1914 the Board began procedures to obtain amendments to the ordinance; these were not in fact completed until after the commencement of the War in August, but they were in no way related to the conflict and therefore their history properly belongs to this chapter.

The Bank had been challenged from time to time on its right to hold mortgages as security, and despite counsel's opinion, the Bank was concerned by the outcome of recent court precedents involving compradores. It sought, therefore, to have section 20 of its ordinance amended to make clear the Bank's right to take any kind of security, including mortgages.

As described by the Attorney General under 'Objectives and Reasons':

The object of this Bill is to amend Section 20 of the Hongkong and Shanghai Bank Ordinance, 1866, so as to enable the [Corporation] generally to take security from its customers for any moneys owing or to become owing to the Corporation, and for any liabilities incurred or to be incurred towards the Corporation and to deal with any securities so taken.

This amendment is considered desirable in order to bring the powers of the Corporation clearly into line with modern banking practice as the wording of the existing section is not entirely free from ambiguity.[58]

The second revision related to the ordinance's requirement that semi-annual meetings of the proprietors be held. The Bank felt that ordinary meetings need be held only once a year and that an interim dividend could be authorized.

In July the Government after correspondence with and approval from London agreed in principle to these non-controversial amendments and an Extraordinary Meeting of proprietors was held on August 22.[59]

The Bill was first advertised in the Press – one English-language and one Chinese-language newspaper – and subsequently introduced into the Legislative Council by the Hon. D. Landale, senior partner of Jardine, Matheson and Co. and Chairman of the Hongkong Bank. With standing orders suspended the Bill passed through its three readings on September 18 and became Ordinance No. 24 of 1914.[60]

Epilogue – Stabb, Addis, and the Chairman's speech

In July 1914 when Stabb was on leave in England Addis wrote, 'He is a fine, manly, modest fellow. I wish he could write as he talks. Able in a way but limited.'[61]

The practical outcome of this problem had been for Stabb, once he had been appointed the Bank's Chief Manager, to ask Addis to write parts of the Chairman's semi-annual 'speech' for presentation at the Ordinary General Meetings.[62] The speech accordingly becomes longer, moving from country to country, surveying the state of relevant affairs; there had already been a tendency in this direction, but now the London end was to be more fully developed and, in addition to comments for example on the native banking crisis in Shanghai, there would be comments on the Bank's involvement in the various consortiums, noting participation, for example, in the 4% £11 million Japanese Conversion Loan and a loan of £6 million at 4½% for the South Manchurian Railway Company, guaranteed by the Japanese Imperial Government.

The eventual development of this 'Chairman's Speech' would turn it into a document pronouncing economic and financial judgement on London and the East. To the extent that it was a record of events it was interesting; on the details of the Bank's participation in these events it was authoritative. But when the speech went beyond this, it also went beyond the competence of the Board, perhaps of the Chief Manager – Stabb was not interested in the politics of banking – and reflected rather the views of Sir Charles Addis in London.

This is not to suggest that either Board or management disagreed with Addis; they had ample opportunity to amend or delete sections of the draft. The problem is to interpret these speeches as acts of the Bank. Was the Chairman just presenting informed views as a public service, as if, perhaps, he were an early news commentator, or are these somehow the adopted views of the Bank presaging policy decisions and consequent action?

Today, many of the topics then carried in the Chairman's speech would be found in reports from specialist departments, carrying the Corporation's disclaimer.

Accepting the contents of the Chairman's speeches from 1910 at least to the early 1930s as official Bank policy statements would be to exaggerate their importance. Except where they touched the working of the Bank narrowly defined, they were rather informed expressions of opinion or summary of facts, as interesting to the members of the Board as they were to the public at large.

2

BRANCHES AND AGENCIES – AN ILLUSTRATIVE SURVEY

> In connection with new agencies I may mention we have received invitations from various influential quarters, where a want of banking facilities is felt, to open branches of this Bank . . . the Board determined that it was not advisable to extend the interests of the Bank, however brilliant the prospects, to places which could not be considered as being directly in contact with or of immediate importance to the trade of China.
>
> Chairman, the Hongkong Bank, 1884

The Hongkong and Shanghai Banking Corporation established its first offices in Hong Kong and Shanghai; that was the purpose of the Bank's founding, to provide banking services for the region from bases in these two great ports, the one British, the other international and strategically located at the gateway to the Yangtze and central China.

To better accomplish the original objectives of the founders, the Bank commissioned merchant hongs to act as agents for the Bank in the outports, networks based on the twin hubs of Hong Kong and Shanghai were developed, and, as the volume of business improved or a merchant hong failed, the Bank's directors authorized the opening of agencies staffed by the Bank's own servants.

The outports also grew; in some cases they were 'outports' only in the context of interport trade terminology. Thus the Bank's agencies in Yokohama (1866), Manila (1875), and Singapore (1877) became branches with their own capital and with responsibilities for their own 'outport' agencies, for example, Hiogo (1869), Iloilo (1883), and Penang (1884). Whatever the original justification had been in establishing the office, whatever the rationale for maintaining it in the context of intra-regional trade finance, a branch – even a sub-agency – of the Hongkong Bank came inevitably to play a banking role locally, to become involved in and have an impact on the local economy apart from immediate trade finance.

This is apparent even in the Indian agencies of Bombay and Calcutta where the expertise of the Bank and its global interests both suggested playing a minimal role, at least in the years before World War II. However, with the establishment of agencies in Rangoon (1891) and Colombo (1892), the Hongkong Bank had organized for itself a second region of interest with its triangular trade relations. In part these Indian, Burmese, and Ceylonese agencies played a role in the Bank's global exchange operations, but they also became oriented to the needs of South Asia increasingly independent of the Bank's basic East Asian operations.

Certainly in Lyons (1881), Hamburg (1889), San Francisco (1875), and New York (1880) the Hongkong Bank's 'impact' was almost entirely linked to the initial concept of the branch or agency, that of serving the Bank's Eastern trade and exchange requirements. But these were 'special agencies', established in countries with developed banking systems and restricted by regulation or custom from full participation – restricted also by the size of the Bank's resources and the greater earnings likely from the employment of funds in the East.

Saigon (1870) was in French colonial territory, but here the Bank was called on to assist in the finance of a Catholic cathedral; the Hongkong Bank's connections with the Catholic Church were close. The accounts of the Procure Générale were international in scope and, as far as East Asia was concerned, were managed in Hong Kong; they were held by the Hongkong Bank. The Banque de l'Indo-Chine came later, but the Catholic authorities saw no reason to change, particularly in a period of growing anti-clericalism among French colonial authorities.[1]

When in 1882 the Conseil Colonial of Cochinchina withdrew a subsidy from the Vicariat Apostolique of Western Cochinchina, the Saigon bishopric, equivalent to two-thirds of its annual income, the mission mortgaged local property most probably to the Hongkong Bank.[2] As the anti-clerical legislation continued, the Société des Missions Etrangères asked the Bank in 1885 not to allow the senior local employee, A. Perrin, to handle their account; he was identified as a Freemason and a member of the Ligue de l'ensignement.[a]

In Netherlands East India the Dutch were paramount, but the Bank's Batavia branch (1884) supplemented by the Sourabaya sub-agency (1896) facilitated the finance of sugar, an export vital to the prosperity of the territory.[b]

If the Bank played a role in these territories, then its impact in say Bangkok and Manila where British investment was significant, or in Japan where its own modernization required exchange banking facilities, or China itself

---

[a] Perrin had joined the Bank in 1872 as a member of the local staff, what later in Shanghai would be referred to as the 'local British', that is, neither Portuguese nor local native. As such he held a key position in the agency until his death on leave in 1914 (see Chapter 3).[3]
[b] For a brief survey of the Bank in the Netherlands East Indies, see the paper by J.T.M. van Laanen in King, ed. *Eastern Banking* (London, 1983), pp. 392–408.

Table 2.1 *The Hongkong and Shanghai Banking Corporation*
Branches and agencies, 1918

	Year of opening		Year of opening
HONG KONG	1865	YOKOHAMA	1866
Foochow	1867	Kobe/Hiogo	1869
Saigon	1870	Nagasaki	1891
Amoy	1873	**Taipei**	**1909**
Bangkok	1888		
Canton	**1909**	CALCUTTA	1867
		Rangoon	1891
SHANGHAI	1865	BOMBAY	1869
Hankow	1868	COLOMBO	1892
Tientsin	1881		
Peking	1885	MANILA	1875
Hongkew	**1909**	Iloilo	1883
Tsingtau	**1914**		
Harbin	**1915**	BATAVIA	1884
Vladivostok	**1918**	**Sourabaya**	**1896**
London	1865	SINGAPORE	1877
San Francisco	1875	Penang	1884
New York	1880	**Malacca**	**1909**
Lyons	1881	**Kuala Lumpur**	**1910**
Hamburg	1889	**Ipoh**	**1910**
		Johore	**1910**

Boldface: offices established in the period 1895–1918.

where even a modest presence taxed the available foreign resources would be of interest not only to students of banking history but also to those concerned with the economic development of the territories involved.

A list of the Bank's offices in the period 1865–1918 is provided in Table 2.1.

From the personnel point of view, these branches and agencies were staffed by officers of a primarily China bank. But once in the distant port, the Manager became a part of that community, responsive to its needs, within the scope permitted by the sources of his funds and Head Office directives.

Head Office was, after all, far away, but fellow-expatriates were no further than the nearby Club. Or a Manager in Iloilo, however distant from China itself, would find the Chinese were there – as were the local sugar planters and their increasing requirements. In Colombo the guarantee shroff substituted for the compradore, the chettiars for the 'native bankers' of Shanghai.

The Bank's peripatetic but lone Inspector would pass through, deplore the state of this or that advance, urge the repayment of the overdrafts, and secure from the Manager the necessary assurances.

The man from Head Office once on the ship, however, the Manager no longer found the arguments for a limited role so compelling; who but the local Manager, he could argue, knew local conditions? The half-yearly profits were wired to Head Office; if these reflected the Manager's banking competence, he might do much, the Inspector's reports notwithstanding.

Whatever the theory, whatever the control system, the Managers of the Hongkong Bank's branches and agencies acted with a relative independence which varied with locality or opportunity. They were part of a banking network which used them, but equally the network was one which they saw as a means to enhance their own agency's funds and their own agency's capabilities to further local enterprise, be it a small brick factory or a medical dispensary.

The branches and agencies of the Hongkong Bank have been considered in their role as contributors to the corporation or as outports in the trade network. In this chapter selected offices of the Bank, excluding those in China, will be considered in their own right with a glimpse at their local impact. In fact each branch is entitled to a full history of its own; as this is impractical, a sampling is the only alternative. Each agency took on local characteristics as the Manager, his 'Eastern staff', his compradore, shroff, *banto*, Portuguese clerks, and 'native' assistants developed a banking business in a community with interests, developments, and pressures of its own. In the Philippines there was the revolution and the coming of the American occupation; in Singapore a push north into the Malay States and the constant supervision of the Colonial Office and the British Treasury; in Ceylon the Bank took a secondary place and witnessed the first signs of change in colonial banking traditions; in Japan the Bank was provided a foretaste of an independent East with the lesson that a role for the foreign exchange bank even then remained.

In the Philippines, Ceylon, the Straits, and China the Bank played a role in monetary and banking policy; this subject is reserved for separate consideration.

THE HONGKONG BANK IN JAPAN[c]

Two propositions have been stated: (i) the Hongkong Bank was a China bank and (ii) branches and agencies, while opened in connection with the China trade, might take on a life of their own. A nice refinement should be made. If that 'life' reached a certain dimension, the branch might well be justified in its

[c] This section could be profitably read with Professor Takeshi Hamashita's study 'A History of the Japanese Silver Yen and The Hongkong and Shanghai Banking Corporation, 1871–1913', in King, ed. *Eastern Banking* (London, 1983), pp. 321–49. Material covered there is not duplicated here, but this section also has benefited from Professor Hamashita's contributions and research.

own terms. If Manila can be justified without reference to China, if Colombo is understandable only in terms of South Asia, then certainly the Bank's history in Malaya – Singapore, the other Straits Settlements and the Malay States – and in Japan can be told without any need to justify it in terms of China, although there was in these places a considerable China connection.

The question is one of optimal allocation of a scarce resource, the capital funds of the Hongkong Bank. This is the question Ewen Cameron, then Manager Shanghai, put to the Board when a Singapore agency was first proposed; this was the basis of the discussion when penetration of Europe was considered after the Great War. Initially the Bank's capital could all be usefully employed in China; but with the rights issues and expansion in the late nineteenth century, and with the garnering of deposits as needed in London, the Bank soon had resources sufficient to develop in Malaya and the East in general.

As the history of the Bangkok branch will illustrate, the local Manager had some discretion if only he could develop local sources of funds. Characteristically these funds were relatively short-term; the demand for funds, in whatever form the application was originally submitted to the Manager, might in reality be for 'permanent' investment and unsuitable for banking as understood in the British tradition or as undertaken by the exchange banks.

There was a way out of this impasse; the Bank could obtain funds as agent in the long-term capital market. This it did not only for the great Empire of China but also for the Philippines' Manila Railway, for the Kingdom of Siam – and for Japan.

A brief survey

The Bank in Japan had its own history. Yokohama was part of that original Treaty Port community which the Bank at its founding was designed to serve; it became part of that foreign establishment which the Japanese called on to assist in their own program of development. Thus the Bank was instrumental in disseminating the use of the silver yen, it served as a model for the constitution of the Yokohama Specie Bank, and also financed Japan's growing trade requirements.

There were always limitations. In 1888 the Bank had made a $250,000 loan to Yanosuke Iwasaki, but when in 1890 this 'valued customer', as he was referred to in the Board of Directors' minutes, sought to borrow one million yen at 7.5% against Japanese securities, the Bank had to reluctantly decline on the grounds that the ownership of these particular securities could not be transferred to a foreigner.[d] As Japan's dependence on foreign institutions

---

[d] Yanosuke Iwasaki was one of the co-founders of the Mitsubishi Bank and with his elder

lessened and with the end of extraterritoriality in 1899, the Bank in common with other foreign firms, continued to play a marginal role, providing as it were a foretaste of the limitations – and the considerable remaining range of available activity – which would be imposed by other countries even before World War II.

The Japanese attitude is reflected in the instructions sent to his overseas managers by Takashi Masuda, director of Mitsui Bussan – a bank to which the Hongkong Bank had lent $700,000 in 1878 – 'You should not lower your head toward the Hongkong and Shanghai Bank but raise your head and associate on equal terms.'[4] This advice, while stating a sound general principle, reflects a characteristic attitude of one of the Bank's best Japanese customers.

The early Hongkong Bank banknotes issued in Japan were typically never accepted by the Japanese authorities; the notes circulated in the foreign enclaves and among foreigners. By the time extraterritoriality was ended, they had been run down; the remaining balance had to be withdrawn. Similarly, the Bank opened a Savings Bank in 1885, operating on rules based on those in Hong Kong and primarily if not exclusively for foreigners.

The Yokohama branch with an assigned initial capital of $1 million and its dependent agencies of Hiogo (Kobe) and Nagasaki returned a profit in normal years equal approximately to two-thirds that of Shanghai or Head Office in Hong Kong. The Bank assigned to its main Japan office a series of its ablest Bankers, Thomas Jackson (1872–1875), W.H. Harries (1875), John Walter (1876–1878, 1881–1884), A.M. Townsend (1879–1880), Edward Morriss (1884–1890), H.M. Bevis (1890–1892, 1897–1899), David Jackson (1893–1896, 1899–1903), V.A. Caesar Hawkins (1903–1907), H.D.C. Jones (1907–1910), and the longest-serving – R.T. Wright (1910–1923), who would be caught in the Yokohama or Kanto earthquake of 1923 and who transferred the main Japanese office to Kobe.

With the foreign trade virtually doubling each decade, from 26 million yen in 1868 to 842 million yen in 1906, the Hongkong Bank prospered despite dramatic failures of constituents and consequent losses, which were on occasion partially offset by taking over the failing firm's office or residence for a Bank Manager or for a junior mess.[e] By 1890 the Board had increased the capital assigned to its Japanese operations to $2.5 million. But this importance is relative – in 1914 for example although there were 20 Eastern staff serving

---

brother, Yatarō Iwasaki, founder of the Mitsubishi Zaibatsu. The 1890 date suggests that the loan was requested in response to the provisions of the new Japanese Bank Act. The Board's wording of their rejection is evidence that the Hongkong Bank was doing a significant business with Iwasaki and was reluctant to endanger the relationship.
[e] In 1881 the Bank took over the premises of Walsh Hall and Co. in Yokohama and Kobe.[5] The Bank took over buildings of W.H. Gill and Co. in 1905. Other firms were Kirby and Co., Ludwig and Co., and Vogel (Ludwig and Traub) 1884, and Adamson, Bell and Co. 1891.

in Japan, this compares with 63 in China, and 25 in the Straits Settlements and Malay States, and 30 in Hong Kong.

In 1891 the Bank's business in Nagasaki entered an 'intermediate' stage; that is, the Bank appointed one of its own staff, A.B. Anderson, as 'agent', but he worked in the offices of the former merchant agents, Messrs Brown and Co., who continued to receive a commission for the use of their facilities, including the treasury. This arrangement was terminated in 1896 with the upgrading of Nagasaki to agency status; indeed it was through this agency that the Bank's business with Chemulpo in Korea was maintained. The Board further authorized the construction of a building for the agency, which, when completed around 1908, became the first building designed in Western classical tradition by a Japanese architect, Kikutarō Shimoda.[6] Located near the former Nagasaki Maritime Customs building, the imposing structure is today a Museum of Folk Art and Culture, the Bank's agency in the city having been closed in 1932.

The Hongkong Bank was represented at Shimonoseki from 1906 by Jardine, Matheson and Co., and the Mitsubishi Bank became its first Tokyo agents in 1912; the Bank did not open an office there until 1924, after the Kanto earthquake.

For some twenty years after 1880, the year the Chartered Bank opened an office in Yokohama, and despite the dramatic increase in Japan's foreign trade, the two British banks had had little foreign competition. It was discouraged, perhaps, by the increasingly dominant role of the Yokohama Specie Bank, by the difficulties Eastern banks were in any case facing, and by the lack of sound information in a period of changing monetary standards and economic fortunes. The New Oriental had failed in 1892 and the Mercantile Bank of India had not yet returned, but in the decade before World War I, the Hongkong Bank faced new competition: the Russo-Chinese Bank in 1898 (closed in 1904), the International Banking Corporation, and the Deutsch-Asiatische Bank in 1905 – the last despite considerable discussion in Germany relative to the formation of a separate German-Japanese bank.

The main attraction for continental banks was the prospect of sharing the development finance, and when this seemed uncertain, business proposals were postponed or abandoned. The Russo-Japanese War also inhibited both German and French participation, since the industrial consortiums supporting the international banks were closely involved with the financing of Russian industrial contracts.

The Hongkong Bank and the Japanese loans

After the loan issued on behalf of the Japanese Government in 1873 by the Oriental Bank, the Japanese did not enter the overseas capital markets again until 1897. From then until 1930 the Hongkong Bank would be involved in the issue of Imperial and municipal loans with a total face value of £250 million, the larger portion of which were for productive purposes.

Although the Hongkong Bank was not the only foreign bank in Japan, it was the 'senior' bank and its China experience had provided it with the expertise to issue major loans in London. Accordingly the Japanese Government first turned to the Hongkong Bank and then, despite German blandishments, remained with them, although there was no question of the Bank becoming, as it were, merchant bankers to the Japanese Government; indeed, the Bank did not attempt to issue the loans even in the London market on its own. For the Japanese loans the Bank participated as a member of a syndicate, usually including Parr's Bank and the Yokohama Specie Bank.

The Hongkong Bank's role in the Foochow Loan of 1874 and in the financing of China's defence efforts during the first Sino-Japanese War precluded it from taking an active role in financing Japanese war requirements.

From 1897 when Japan reentered the foreign capital market the Bank would not have been able to act alone and while often carrying the major burden of the negotiations was, in fact, one of several participants in syndicates which included the Yokohama Specie Bank and, at first, the Capital and Counties Bank (merged with Lloyds Bank in 1918) and the Chartered Bank. Parr's Bank became involved as early as 1899; a manager, A.A. Shand, had earlier served in Japan as a banking adviser and the Japanese do not forget such assistance (see note on p. 146). When Parr's merged with the London County and Westminster Bank in 1918, the Westminster Bank (as it was known from 1923) inherited the relationship. Baring Brothers and N.M. Rothschild and Sons were involved from time to time. Where the loan was also issued in Germany and the United States, the London syndicate received an agreed tranche and the Hongkong Bank was in turn assigned a proportionate share of the London offering. Sir Charles Addis, the Hongkong Bank's London Manager, complained, however, that by this time each bank's share had become miniscule – the Bank was working for the benefit of partners who contributed little towards the negotiations.

References to these loan activities in the minutes of the Board of Directors are inconsistent; one loan will be referred to in detail, even to the fact that negotiations in Tokyo were in large part handled by the Yokohama branch Accountant, T.S. Baker. Other loans were listed only in the semi-annual statement of profits. It is clear that London Office management referred to the London Committee for expert advice, presumably acting only with their approval.

The 1897 Imperial Japanese Government 5% Loan (No. 1 in the Appendix on p. 143) was denominated in yen but as the bondholders were entitled to redemption at the fixed rate of 2s:0½d=Yen 1, the loan was effectively a gold loan. As part of the war loans its purpose was non-productive; the Hongkong Bank could participate despite the Bank's China priority because it was negotiated considerably after the end of hostilities.

As the summary list below will indicate, the remaining issues, other than those for general or re-financing, were for such diverse economic projects as railway construction, steel works, telephone communications, waterworks, harbour construction, the Fusan (Busan)–Seoul Railway, the South Manchurian Railway, the Industrial Bank of Japan, and various projects in the cities of Tokyo, Yokohama, and Osaka (see pp. 143–46).

The German involvement

The Hongkong Bank had made no special agreement relative to Japanese loans with the Deutsch-Asiatische Bank (DAB). The working relationship developed between the two banks would suggest, however, that there might be cooperation in other areas, and indeed the Hongkong Bank did on occasion involve Germany in its Japanese operations. These were always limited and, when combined with German political reluctance to become involved, made full-scale German participation unlikely – as indeed proved to be the case.

The 1899 £10 million loan (No. 2, see below) was issued at an unfortunate time given the position of the London market at the outbreak of the Boer War, and the public only subscribed 12%, the balance being taken up by the four issuing banks. It is not surprising therefore that a second effort, this time by a French-German group, including the Banque de Paris et des Pay Bas and the Dresdner Bank should fail to arrange a loan for £2 million. These two events would encourage the Japanese to stay with a group which had proved willing to meet their commitments even in unfavourable circumstances.

When the Japanese approached the Hongkong Bank and Baring Brothers in 1902 for a £5 million loan (No. 3), the British Group offered participation to the Deutsche Bank and subsequently to the Disconto-Gesellschaft, but these received no encouragement from the German Foreign Office, and despite complaints from German consular officials in Japan, warning of the difficulties the country would face in competition for Japanese industrial contracts, the new loan was again made exclusively by a British syndicate with the Yokohama Specie Bank.

In the spring of 1905, the Hongkong Bank offered the DAB a one-third share in a proposed £30 million 4½% loan (No. 8).[7] As some of the members of the German industrial consortium which was associated with the DAB, the Konsortium für Asiatische Geschäfte (KfAG), were too close to the Russians in their other business activities to risk offending them by lending money to the Japanese during the war, a 'new' consortium was formed, with the approval of the KfAG, omitting several of the regular members, and with one addition, Delbrück, Leo and Co. of Berlin. Michalowsky of the DAB was to negotiate for the German Group, but when he went to London for the negotiations, he found the Japanese had not been informed of a German participation.[8] A.M. Townsend, London Manager of the Hongkong Bank, withdrew the British offer of a share in the loan, offering instead to allow the German Group to underwrite a portion of it against a 2% commission, which the German Group under the circumstances could not accept.[9]

The loan issued on March 29, 1905, was a great success in London; so popular was it that the crowds making application pushed past the police, and the Bank's rugger team had to be called into action to maintain order. Addis noted that Townsend made many enemies by his ignorance of 'old friends' of the Bank whose applications he had refused. A bonus was distributed to the staff involved; Addis recorded his share as £400, virtually a year's salary for a London Office department head, although at this time he had only been four weeks confirmed as junior Manager.[10]

The third Japanese loan in 1905, the £50 million 4% sterling loan (No. 10), had only £6.5 million allocated to London and this was subscribed 30 times over in November.

Roland-Lücke of the Deutsche Bank proposed that the German Group break with the Hongkong Bank and deal directly with the Japanese in conjunction with the British Speyer group which had shown interest.[11] Representatives of this new combination met with the Japanese negotiator Korekiyo Takahashi in London, but were told that talks with the Hongkong Bank and the Americans were already at an advanced stage. The Japanese expressed their thanks for German interest, but could not abandon their 'old friends, who had stood by them in bad times'. Takahashi, according to Müller-Jabusch, was also opposed to the Speyer group because of their attempt to negotiate directly in Tokyo. In March 1905 the loan was closed without the Germans, but the *ad hoc* German 'Japanese' consortium decided to stay together until the end of World War I.[12]

In June, Baring Brothers – German Foreign Ministry (AA) marginal note: 'then not the HK Bank again this time' – offered the Disconto-Gesellschaft through the mediation of Warburg and Co., Hamburg, a participation in a new loan for £30 million (No. 9). The AA gave its approval to the idea.[13] The loan was divided three ways to include an American group; the British Group, which included the Hongkong Bank, would lead in the negotiations. For the Germans the Norddeutsche Bank, not the Deutsche Bank, would negotiate; this, according to the AA note, was to be kept secret from the latter.[14] The German consortium also had to be rearranged to allow for a special participation by Warburg and Co.[15] On July 9 the new loan was issued at 90, and the German portion was nine times over-subscribed.

Then, in November, negotiations began on a loan to convert internal Japanese loans, which would appear to be the £50 million loan (No. 10). But German archival records refer to a loan of £25 million, of which the French were to place £12.5 million, and the remainder was to be divided among the British, American, and German markets, and this would be consistent with the low – £6.5 million – participation of the Hongkong Bank. The negotiations were to be led by the London and Paris Rothschilds, with the German Group represented by Warburg and Co. As usual the German and American Groups would pay a ½ of 1% commission to the British, but the terms would otherwise be equal. The larger French share was due solely to market conditions.[16]

For several years conditions were not particularly favourable for new Japanese loans, and the Hongkong Bank and its traditional partners had no would-be rivals. The Germans were offered participation in the 1912 City of Tokyo Loan (No. 22), which appeared to be designed to further specific city development projects, however the KfAG turned down the opportunity and the German Ambassador later reported that the loan was openly being admitted to be a 'camouflaged' general Government loan to offset an unfavourable balance of trade, a comment reflecting the difficulty of ascertaining the 'purpose' of a loan unless the total financial plans of the various levels of government are considered in their entirety.

The Hongkong Bank also purchased Japanese Treasury Bills issued in sterling and underwrote certain of the loans listed below.

The ineffective rivals, 1905/06

The peaking of Japanese loan demands in 1905 may provide an explanation for the formation of Japanese-oriented financial companies in both England and France. The two incorporated in London – a bank and a finance company – had links with established China interests.

The Anglo-Japanese Bank, Ltd (Nichi-Ei Gingkō), was established in May 1906 with an initial paid-up capital of £1 million; its Japanese promoters included Sōichurō Asano and Kihachirō Ōkura, senior partner of Ōkura and Co. The firm's London manager was a member of the board – as was Baron George de Reuter, a director of the Imperial Bank of Persia. Registered in Japan as a bank, the Anglo-Japanese Bank opened branches in Yokohama and Tokyo, but the Japanese authorities preferred the established relations with

Parr's through the Yokohama Specie Bank, and its activities were not encouraged despite the presence of Dai Ichi Bank's prestigious Eiichi Shibusawa as adviser. Unable to pay a dividend, the bank's shareholders withdrew in favour of the Commercial Bank of London; in 1913 all Eastern interest ceased.

The British and Japanese Finance Corporation, Ltd (Nichi-Ei Kinyū Gaisha), was registered in September 1905 in terms paralleling those of the British and Chinese Corporation (see Chapter 5) and with a subscribed capital of £601,000. There were board-level ties with the Yangtze Valley Company and the Chinese Central Railways, the latter being an associated company of the Hongkong Bank through the B&CC. Rempei Kondō, the president of Mitsubishi's NYK Line, was a director, as were Edmund Davis, Émile Francqui of the Compagnie Internationale d'Orient, and Albert Thys of the Banque d'Outremer, names familiar in China finance.[17]

The decline in Japanese requirements, the attitude of the Japanese Government to 'old friends' cited above, and the subsequent role of the Yokohama Specie Bank in the Sextuple Groups from 1912 explain why these companies did not become real competitors of Parr's Bank, the Hongkong Bank, and the others associated in their syndicates. It is also significant that experience in Eastern finance elsewhere was not the key to success in Japan.

SELECTED AGENCIES

THE PHILIPPINES – TOTAL INVOLVEMENT[f]

The newly arrived junior, J.H. Lind, came respectfully to the counter of the Hongkong Bank's Manila office one day in 1901. The customer, an American 'volunteer', drew out a revolver and asked if the young man's name were Andrew Ross (East in 1899). Fortunately, as a quick rereading of the preceding sentence will confirm, it was not. Ross had been got out of town.

While not alone in faulting American policies following their acceptance of Kipling's plea to take up the white man's burden, Ross was unique in having a journalist friend publish a highly critical personal letter, the text of which was republished in the *Manila Times* under the headline, 'British Resident dares criticize our Administration', and the American then confronting Lind had come up from the provinces specially to settle the matter.

As it happened Ross lived to be Iloilo Agent in the early 1930s.

---

[f] This section is based on the research report of Roy C. Ybañez, 'The Hongkong Bank in the Philippines', copy in Group Archives, which was published in part in *Eastern Banking*, pp. 435–66, and on additional material in Group Archives.

The Hongkong Bank might be a 'China bank' but in the Philippines it was very much involved locally, and in the early 1900s both the Bank and the Philippine Islands were introduced to the American system.

By 1901 the Hongkong Bank had been in the Islands for over 25 years. Although Manila had been seen as within the orbit of the British and American trading hongs based in Hong Kong from the founding of the Bank, the economic impetus for closer banking relations had been caused by the trade in sugar. But sugar, wrote the Hongkong Bank's Chief Manager A.G. Stephen, 'is a very tricky article – it has brought more Eastern firms to grief than any other kind of tropical produce'. As sugar was the Bank's main business in the Philippines, this statement sets the theme. Over the years, however, sugar would prove to be but one of the problems besetting the Bank's Manila office. The drastic political changes in the Philippines, despite specific problems and disagreements, were not in themselves the cause of the Bank's pervasive long-run problems, but rather (i) the hazards of financing firms dealing with and too often speculating in sugar, and also hemp, vegetable oil, and coconut products, (ii) too close involvement with a few major customers, (iii) the effects of a series of major uncertainties, especially the Jurado Case (1887–1904), and (iv) the economic impact of United States-Philippine relations keeping the Bank as it were 'off-balance' throughout.

These were the problems, but a fair balance would require note of the Bank's financing of the Manila Railway, the extraordinary facilities which ensured the continued existence of the long-established British firms in the Islands, and the exchange facilities made available to the Chinese community in their intra-regional trade and their home remittances – the development of wholesale banking, the assistance to industry, and participation in syndicated loans.

Certain of the earlier relations of the Bank with the Philippines including the long-lasting Jurado Case have been considered in Volume I (see especially, Chapter 11). The currency problems will be considered separately in Chapter 4. With these exceptions there follows an outline of the Bank's history in the Philippines.

The Hongkong Bank in Manila, 1865–1898

The agency of Russell, Sturgis and Co.[g]

The inclusion of a Spanish colonial territory in the initial conceptual 'region'

---

[g] Russell, Sturgis and Co. was founded in 1828 as Russell and Sturgis by George Robert Russell and Henry Parkman Sturgis; they were joined in 1835 by Warren Delano. In 1837 Russell Sturgis, elder brother of H.P. Sturgis, joined the firm, creating a confusion as to whether a comma after 'Russell' is appropriate (it is), and it is natural that this quite separate and distinct Manila partnership should be confused with the Canton firm of Russell and Co., especially since they were each other's mutual agents in the two ports.

of the Hongkong Bank's operations is both surprising and explicable. Unlike the Treaty Ports and Japan, there were in Manila no direct subordinate offices of the major Hong Kong based trading firms and there was little significant Manila-Hong Kong foreign-carried trade, but the Philippines' overall foreign trade was dominated on the one hand by the Chinese and on the other by long-established American and British interests, all of whom had associations with Hong Kong and in the case of Russell, Sturgis and Co. had historic ties with the old Canton trade. Although Philippine trade was usually conducted directly with the Continent or the United States, financing was often through Hong Kong; Manila had but one commercial bank, the Banco Español-Filipino, while the Oriental Bank Corporation and the Chartered Bank of India, Australia and China were represented in Manila by agents. There was obvious opportunity for the new 'local' bank.

The designation in March 1865 of Russell, Sturgis and Co., an American house having close connections with Augustine Heard and Co., was the only major patronage success the Heards obtained in the allocation of agencies by the Provisional Committee, but it does reflect the early American influence in the Bank's directorate. The Manila agents, however, failed in 1875, brought down by the same crisis which wrecked the Heards, and the Hongkong Bank decided, as it had done elsewhere, to establish its own agency.

The Board of Directors assigned Manila a capital of $300,000 and were almost immediately faced with a request from the colonial Government in Manila for a loan of some $3–500,000, but the Manila request was not confirmed by Madrid nor was a charge on the revenue granted, and the Bank passed it by.

Little else is recorded of the years 1866 to 1875, although it is known that these were important in the growth of the Philippine sugar trade, and that the Hongkong Bank had become heavily involved in the finance of sugar and sugar processing both in Indo-China and Thailand. When the failure of Russell, Sturgis and Co. forced the Bank to consider opening its own agency, it was the sugar trade which was particularly attractive and determined the Bank's choice of its first 'special agent', the *de facto* Manager, Charles Ilderton Barnes, a former London Office junior who had joined the Bank in 1872 and come East only in 1873.

The Bank's agency in the Spanish period

Barnes had first been sent to Shanghai but he was transferred to Saigon. There and in Siam he gained some knowledge of the sugar business, reporting on the Bank's continually complex problems with both sugar growing and refining. He seemed, therefore, a sound choice for Manila, although, as David McLean was later to warn, 'I am greatly afraid Barnes will let us in . . . not enough experience in business.'[18] McLean as usual proved correct.

Barnes had been born in Faversham (Kent), thus accounting for its otherwise inexplicable use as the telegraphic address of the Bank in Manila.

Although balance sheets are not available for the Spanish period, scattered comments in the minutes and other general sources indicate that the Manila branch did not trade on its 'capital', which was, in fact, only a right to draw on Hong Kong to a total of one million pesos, nor were its deposits sufficient to finance the growing foreign trade of the Islands and that, from these early years, the branch depended on overdrafts in London. This rendered the Bank open to exchange risk unless it could keep its position covered.

However, other risks, not always recognized by bankers on the scene, were involved, stemming originally perhaps from the credit laws enacted by Spain by which Filipinos could not be held to a debt in excess of $25. Merchants in effect bought the growing crop on the basis of estimates, adjusted at the harvest, of its size, with the security being a mortgage on the land. The banks advanced to merchants against produce stored in godowns, usually owned by the merchant, and thus the whole process was subject to (i) contests over the basic validity of the mortgage as security, (ii) speculation on the size and quality of the crop, (iii) fraudulent grading of a particular shipment, (iv) fraudulent removal of goods stored, (v) fluctuating prices with the consequent possibility of the overseas importer failing to honour bills drawn on him, and (vi) major exchange fluctuations during periods when cover was difficult to obtain.

The first recorded Bank crisis, however, was unrelated to banking. On July 21, 1880, there was an earthquake which Barnes reported had turned Manila into ruins, closing the office – presumably the expanded facilities, approved in 1876, on the corner of Anloague (now Juan Luna) and the Callejon de San Gabriel – and for a week the staff lived on sampans.

Business in the 1880s consisted primarily of granting credits secured by commodities and the discounting of promissory notes. Although competition was modified by an agreement among the exchange banks fixing the China exchange rates, the Chartered Bank's history records that the Hongkong Bank had secured the greater part of the exchange turnover, by implication through its closer contacts with the Chinese community.[19]

Although in 1883 the sugar trade was flourishing sufficiently to lead Barnes to successfully recommend the establishment of a Bank agency in Iloilo, the fall in sugar and other commodity prices brought down the Oriental Bank in 1884 and, in the Philippines, caused the Hongkong Bank severe losses. In that year Martin Dyce and Co., the Hongkong Bank's agents in Batavia and sometime correspondents of the Chartered Bank in Manila, failed at a time when the Hongkong Bank's apparent total exposure to the firm in the Philippines was $85,000, of which $14,000 was in the form of unsecured advances. The Bank's exposure rose by $18,000 when it was discovered that the company's sugar exports had been improperly invoiced, showing a higher quality than was actually shipped.

In the same year Reynolds and Co. were involved in a swindle of $65,000 arising from various bank advances of $500,000 on hemp. With the approval of the Board, Barnes decided to bear a portion of the loss, probably $15,000, rather than have the case go to Court, a significant and not particularly auspicious decision. The Board also noted that Barnes had reported 'the failure of Messrs Birchal Robinson and Co. under disgraceful circumstances', not the least of which would be the loss to the Bank of up to $20,000. In 1886 the Chartered Bank and the Hongkong Bank joined to prosecute George Mackenzie and Co., whose fraudulent activities had cost the latter $15,000.

The Hongkong Bank's policy was to make provisions for potential losses by transfers from a branch's Profit and Loss Account to contingencies, finally writing-off the debt only when its full extent was known. In 1886 Barnes found himself with 11,900 bales of hemp in New York and London and the price falling – so one may assume that importers had refused to honour bills drawn on them by the exporting firm, thus leaving the Bank in unpromising possession. Barnes, however, failed to inform Head Office of the situation, intending to debit his Profit and Loss Account when the sale was actually made, reflecting his belief that hemp prices would rise and the loss would be minimal. This was certainly a form of speculation, and Barnes was informed he was acting contrary to the Bank's policy of facing potential losses squarely and providing for them promptly.

These losses must be set against reported gross profits of say $200,000–250,000 a year, but it is clear that the Board were concerned. In London David McLean was becoming restless, urging that Jackson consider dismissing the Manager, and in 1886 the Board dispatched H.M. Bevis to Manila to be temporarily in charge; Barnes was summoned to Hong Kong to explain the situation. The Directors set a limit of $500,000 as the maximum amount of local advances permitted to first class firms. G.E. Noble was then sent from Head Office on an inspection of branches, including Manila, to report on whether any bad advances or doubtful debts remained; he returned on the eve of the collapse of Peele, Hubbell and Co., the last of the great American houses remaining in the Islands.

Meanwhile Barnes returned to the Philippines and followed up on the case of Macleod and Co., in which the Hongkong Bank illustrated its willingness, frequently necessary in the Philippines, to stand by a client and, if possible, see them through. Although this often involved the Bank in costly intervention in the firm's management, taking risks which were really appropriate only for an equity-holder, the alternative was often prolonged legal action, which the Bank, in common with other creditors, sought to avoid. In any case, in 1879 the Hongkong Bank had extended 'amply secured' credit to Macleod and Co.

for the purchase of steamers in Hong Kong, but subsequent difficulties forced the Bank to attempt to recover the steamers, and when Barnes was sent to Cebu in 1886 to ascertain the status of the firm and a particular shipment of sugar, he was also instructed to make contact with a possible purchaser of the steamers. It took negotiations lasting from 1886 to 1896 during which period Macleod and Co. sold off their steamers for various amounts while the Bank continued to carry them as clients before the account was in a satisfactory position. But afterwards the firm remained one of the Bank's permanent constituents, even after its acquisition by International Harvester in 1904. Macleod interests were also connected with Smith, Bell and Co., another long-time constituent of the Hongkong Bank.

The fortunes of the Manila branch had experienced a downturn from 1884, but despite an increase in capital from the original $300,000 to $1 million in 1886, the branch could not recover while prices were depressed and its clients were endangered. The nadir was perhaps 1887:

Your directors only regret having to make such heavy provision as $500,000 for losses, and I would mention that this has become necessary owing to the depressed state of trade in one field of the Bank's operations, the Philippine Islands. It is principally due to the shrinkage in the value of securities pledged to the Bank [Half-yearly meeting, February 26, 1887]

After this the Bank's financial position improved although its legal existence was challenged and it continued to be harassed by the Jurado case until 1903. By 1896 the situation had, however, sufficiently improved that the then Manager received a bonus from the Board for his contribution (second half-year, 1895) to the Bank's overall profits. The net profit on the eve of the Philippine Revolution in 1898 was $500,000.

Although the Board of Directors was concerned with the managership of C.I. Barnes, his resignation a week after the failure of Peele, Hubbell and Co. was undoubtedly due to the death of Blodgett of Warner, Blodgett and Co. and the consequent strong personal appeal by his friend Edwin Warner, the surviving partner, to join the firm, which then became, as it is now, Warner, Barnes and Co. McLean wanted Barnes 'roasted alive', but as a merchant partner Barnes steered his new firm into close cooperation with the Hongkong Bank to mutual benefit.

Barnes was replaced in Manila by A. Edward Cope, formerly Agent in Saigon, who made arrangements with the Bank's co-creditors to compromise and, as noted above, to keep the Bank to the extent possible out of Court. But there was another source of loss – the exchanges. In the end the Directors were forced to withdraw $600,000 from the Reserve Fund to 'meet the losses at the Manila Agency', of which $450,000 was placed to the credit of a Special Contingent Account and $150,000 to the Manila Contingency Account as an additional provision against losses expected from the failures of Peele,

Hubbell and Co., Baer and Suhm, and possibly others. 'Frequent inspections, the last one made by Mr Jackson, have thoroughly sifted the Bank's affairs in the Philippines,' the Chairman assured the meeting. Brave words . . . which were immediately challenged by the inquisitive editor of the *Hongkong Telegraph*, Fraser-Smith, who asked whether the Chairman was confident there would be no further losses in Manila. The Chairman said, 'Yes.'

In September 1887 the Banco Español-Filipino, which had stood by the Bank throughout its difficulties with trade losses, the Jurado case, and the losses sustained through the depreciation of the currency, made a 5% fixed deposit with the Hongkong Bank. The following year the Hongkong Bank began the restoration of its fortunes in the Philippines by its activities in connection with the financing of the Manila Railway, a matter to be considered below.

Despite the setbacks and the harassments, the Manila branch not only returned to profitability but also entered into new types of business, granting loans to leading local firms against sugar, hemp, copra, tobacco, and coffee; the Bank discounted acceptances drawn by such firms on well-established Filipino planters and advanced funds to producers under the guise of 'purchasing' the growing and unharvested crop. Sugar was shipped to China, Canada, and London; copra to Marseilles and hemp to New York. The banks were entering the business of crop loans through the merchant intermediary.

The late Spanish period was characterized economically by the development of tropical export crops and the consequent growth of foreign trade, Britain being by far the largest partner with some 27% of the exports and providing 33% of the imports. An almost equal percentage of exports went to the United States, although imports from that country were minimal. There was also significant trade with China and Spain. In 1891 the Spanish Government imposed tariff protection in the Philippines on behalf of Spanish goods, a principal sufferer being the British textile industry, and British firms in the Islands sponsored a local textile factory which apparently failed during the disturbances following the outbreak of the Spanish-American War. There is no reference to the Bank in relation to the factory.

By the late 1890s the Manila branch had fully recovered from the crises of the 1880s and, as already noted, profits had risen to $500,000 in 1898. The Bank's cash position then was $650,000 in Manila, $300,000 in Iloilo; the Gold Account (the sterling account) was in credit £15,000 offset by the Hong Kong silver account which was $100,000 in debit. Indeed, on the eve of the American entry into Manila, the Bank was able to lend the Banco Español-Filipino $500,000 against funds of theirs deposited in the Hongkong Bank's London Office.

At the half-yearly meeting in August 1898 the Chairman called attention to the state of affairs in the Philippines, 'where the Bank has considerable interests' and did not anticipate any loss; 'I hope that peace will soon be restored and that business may speedily flourish in those most fertile islands.' Six months later he was to regret that a peaceful solution of the question at issue between the 'American and the native' had not been arrived at, but he foresaw a new era of prosperity and noted that the thanks of the shareholders were due to 'the staff there for the manner in which they behaved during most difficult and trying times'.

The whole development of the Philippine economy would soon be redirected during the American period, a story to be considered below.

The Hongkong Bank and the Philippine Revolution

The role of the Bank in the Revolution was, fortunately, one appropriate for a foreign bank – minimal. And yet the Hongkong Bank's name is well-known in Philippine historical literature. The reason is briefly related below, together with a second minor incident.

The revolutionary funds of Emilio Aguinaldo

As every Filipino schoolboy must be aware, General Emilio Aguinaldo deposited his funds in the Hong Kong office of the Hongkong and Shanghai Banking Corporation. It may not be clear, however, why they should know this, given that the information, while true, has absolutely no significance in the history of the Philippine Republic.

Under the provisions of the Peace Convention of December 1897 between the Spanish Administration in the Philippines and the Insurgents under General Aguinaldo, the latter agreed on behalf of those he commanded to lay down arms, supposedly terminating the Revolution. The Government agreed to (i) grant a general amnesty, (ii) introduce reforms, and (iii) pay an indemnity of $800,000. This payment was to be made in three instalments, the first being by a $400,000 draft of the Banco Español-Filipino on the Hongkong and Shanghai Banking Corporation in Hong Kong to be delivered to Aguinaldo on the day he left his headquarters at Biac-na-bato. The balance was payable in two equal instalments timed to coincide with stages in the return to peace.

The draft was delivered as scheduled and Aguinaldo with 26 other Filipinos reached Hong Kong on December 29, 1897; on January 2, 1898, he deposited the proceeds of the draft in the Hongkong Bank and two days later withdrew $200,000 which he deposited in the Chartered Bank at 2% with the understanding he could withdraw $50,000 each quarter. In the following six weeks additional funds were remitted from the Philippines and deposited, but the second and third instalments promised by the Spanish Government were never received; and in the controversies which followed, the Philippine revolutionaries in Hong Kong convened themselves into a new Supreme Council of the Nation, repudiated the Biac-na-bato agreement, and decided that the funds on deposit in Hong Kong should be under the control of Aguinaldo.[20]

In early April a former colleague, Isabelo Artacho, arrived in Hong Kong and demanded half the funds deposited in the Hongkong Bank and the Chartered Bank, although he had previously received a share of the payout from the second instalment in the Philippines. He also demanded an accounting of any funds already expended. Aguinaldo was unwilling to comply because he wished to keep the capital intact and because he had presumably been using some of the monies for purposes incompatible with the intentions of the Peace Convention.

Artacho then sued Aguinaldo and the two depository banks and, in the process, had an injunction restraining Aguinaldo, the Hongkong and Shanghai Bank, and the Chartered Bank from 'dealing with or parting with the possession of the said sum of $400,000 or any part thereof'. The relevant document is probably unique in that it refers to the hero of the Revolution as 'Emilio Aguinaldo of Morrison Hill Road, Victoria', and it was presumably withdrawn when Artacho finally settled with Aguinaldo for $5,000.[21]

Throughout the Hongkong Bank and, presumably, the Chartered Bank were acting simply as banks. Why then do all accounts make mention of the Hongkong Bank? One basic documentary reference for the study of the Revolution is Taylor's *The Philippine Insurrection against the United States*, and one of the documents is the relevant Hong Kong Supreme Court order, which declares that Artacho:

claims on behalf of himself and all others, the leaders of the late insurrection in the Philippine Islands, now living in exile in Hong Kong on account of an agreement with the Spanish government.

A declaration that the defendant holds in trust for plaintiff and for the said leaders of the late insurrection as are now in Hong Kong, a sum of $400,000 deposited by the Spanish government in Hong Kong in the Hongkong and Shanghai Banking Corporation and in the Chartered Bank of India, Australia and China in the name of the defendant, the said Emilio Aguinaldo, for the use of the plaintiff, the defendant, the said Emilio, and others as aforesaid.[22]

Other documents in the collection also refer to the banks, although, as can be seen from the above, not always accurately. There is no evidence that the Spanish Government chose the Hongkong Bank; rather the whole handling of the transaction would seem to have been determined by ordinary commercial considerations, and the documents suggest that Aguinaldo was fully aware of the technicalities of such matters. Thus the Hongkong Bank may not only be acquitted of any political meddling but also of playing any role of interest; it was merely acting as a bank chosen, presumably, for its correspondent relations with the Banco Español-Filipino.

But on account of this non-event the Bank has enjoyed over 80 years of publicity.

The cruise of the keys

Stories of safes and keys are a part of the bankers' tradition or, perhaps, folklore. Some have been verified. The following, which is the only other adventure the Bank's Manila branch reported during the Revolution, dates from about 1898.

When the Accountant, J.J.H. Orman, reported for work in the morning the Manager quickly handed him the keys to the safe, told him to hire a launch, cruise around Manila Bay and not return for a day or so. The Accountant gone, the Manager, H.D.C. Jones, who had had advance warning, was confronted by a group of insurgents demanding the contents of the safe in the interests of the Revolution.

The Manager regretted that he could not open the safe without the keys and that the keys were with the Accountant, who was unaccountably late. The insurgents waited, but the Accountant continued to cruise and the two parties never had a meeting.[23]

The Bank as a foreign guest in the Philippines did not participate in its Revolution but was yet able to manage an adventure story of a kind suitable to banking.

The Bank and the U.S. Administration – first contacts

The relationship between the British exchange bank and the U.S. Administration began early at several levels and with mixed results. Positive reactions came from senior naval and military officials, including Admiral George Dewey and General Elwell S. Otis, who supported the Bank's application to be designated an official depository for War Department and Insular Funds. The Bank was also asked for advice on reform of the Philippine currency, and it is clear from the evidence that the Manager, W. Adams Oram, was properly cooperative and that he was supported in this by Chief Manager Sir Thomas Jackson in Hong Kong and by the Bank's New York Agent, A.M. Townsend. But in its operations the Bank was subject to adverse comment on four major counts: (i) its role in the export of currency to meet the needs of the Boxer Relief expedition in 1900 – this and the following item will be considered in the following chapter, (ii) the charges made in handling the individual remittance and related problems of American military personnel,

(iii) the question of the Bank's being designated a depository for official funds, and (iv) its heavy involvement in the affairs of Mendezona and Co., which appeared to the American examiners as an example of bad banking.

A depository for official funds
The financial problems of the American military and civilian authorities in the Philippines from 1898 were complex and eventually resulted in a full-scale currency reform, but the first step was relatively simple – where to deposit funds, other than in the official Treasury. This was in fact a two-part question since there were (i) U.S. Funds under the control of the Secretary of the Treasury and (ii) Insular Funds, at first under the War Department and then subject to the control of the administration in the Philippines.

As for the first they became covered by an Act of Congress approved on June 6, 1900, which enabled the Secretary of the Treasury to designate one or more banks in the Philippine Islands in which public monies might be deposited, but the Act provided that such an approved depository must provide U.S. Treasury bonds as security to an equal amount, thus a deposit of U.S. funds then in Manila of say $Gold 5 million would require the banks to set aside $Mex 10 million of their resources in the form of Treasury bonds. After initial enquiries, the banks did not pursue the matter. The balance of this section deals therefore with War Department and Insular Funds.

The American Occupation began on July 31, 1899, and within one year receipts of Insular Funds amounted to over $5 million from customs duties, taxes, etc., with disbursements of some $2.5 million. The handling of these funds would, therefore, afford a considerable source of funds to any designated bank.

As early as April 6, 1899, A.M. Townsend, the Hongkong Bank's Agent in New York, requested that the War Department designate the Bank as its fiscal agent in the Philippines. For the next four to five months a series of letters and cables moved back and forth between Townsend, the U.S. Government in Washington, and the U.S. Philippine authorities. The Chartered Bank was apparently being designated sole fiscal agent against the expressed wishes of the military authorities in Manila, who were advocating the appointment of both banks. On April 24 Admiral George Dewey who had previously stated that the Hongkong Bank was 'best known' – he had after all waited outside Hong Kong harbour in Mirs Bay before proceeding to the Battle of Manila Bay, and as Commander in Chief, Asiatic Station, cabled:

NAVY DOES NEARLY ALL EXCHANGE THROUGH HONGKONG BANK

and recommended the Bank both as fiscal agent and as depository for War Department funds. Indeed, Dewey financed his purchase of coal for the fleet prior to sailing to his victory in Manila Bay, May 1, 1898, by cashing a draft with the Hongkong Bank's Head Office.[h] Dewey's position was supported in August 1899 by the Military Governor, Major General Elwell S. Otis, partly on the grounds that the Hongkong Bank alone had a branch in Iloilo.

Despite the Chartered Bank's designation as a fiscal agent, the Secretary of the Treasury advised the Hongkong Bank that the Secretary of War was free to appoint other agents. Townsend then pressed his suit, claiming that the Hongkong Bank had larger and better facilities than the Chartered including the following:

That this bank has for the past thirty years done most of the financial business for the U.S. Government Officials in the Diplomatic, Naval, and Consular Services in the East, and has, I believe, the goodwill of all your officials who have thus been brought into contact with our staff; that I believe this Bank is the only foreign Bank established in the Philippines, elsewhere than at Manila; that this Bank has also Agents at the principal ports in China and Japan; that this Bank is the only Eastern Bank having its own Branches in America (at New York and San Francisco), and that this Bank's Head Office is in Hong Kong with American Firms represented . . . [The Bank has had an agency] in New York for 19 years, encouraging American Trade with the Orient.[25]

This was followed up in May by another letter to the Secretary of War, Russell A. Alger, expressing concern over the commitment to the Chartered Bank and cautioning against granting a monopoly to any one bank, but when the Chartered Bank was officially appointed in June, Townsend was given to understand that his application would only be considered should a second depository prove necessary.

As this would mean the removal of Insular Funds from the Hongkong Bank, the situation had become critical, and the August intervention of the Manila authorities with the War Department secured the Hongkong Bank's appointment, virtually at the last minute, on August 10, with instructions to deposit a bond for $1 million. All formalities were concluded by August 24, nineteen days after the Chartered Bank had been designated the first depository.

The British banks continued as depositories until the founding of the Philippine National Bank in 1916. The history of the Hongkong Bank's role is short and can be recounted here.

On March 31, 1901, the Hongkong Bank held Pesos 8.6 million and the Chartered Bank Pesos 6.3 million in Insular Funds, which given the total resources of the banks was considerable, and the U.S. Comptroller of the Currency expressed his concern.[26] At this point the Hongkong Bank came under special scrutiny because in its inspection returns it listed its capital as

---

[h] The encashed draft was presented to A.G. Kellogg when he 'retired' from the New York staff of the Bank prior to rejoining as a London junior.[24]

that portion formally assigned to the Manila branch, say Pesos 1 million, whereas the Chartered stated its entire corporate capital. This suggested that the status of the Hongkong Bank's Manila branch might be considered as a separate 'bank', and the U.S. authorities asked whether the Head Office would in fact be responsible for it. This special concern ended on receipt of a full legal confirmation of the corporation's total responsibility, and the general problem was handled by Governor William H. Taft, the new U.S. Administrator, who, while noting he had in fact little choice in his handling of funds, wrote in convincing terms of the soundness of both institutions.[i]

With the coming in 1902 of two American banks, the International Banking Corporation and the Guaranty Trust Co., the Philippine Government's business was shared among them; funds with the Hongkong Bank dropped to Pesos 5.45 million by year-end and Pesos 379,000 in subsequent years.

The Mendezona loans

The third point of early contact with American officials was unfortunate and may have set the basis for the increasingly complex banking regulations in the Philippines, but the adverse commentaries on the Manila banks were wholly justified. Credit would be obtained by hypothecating goods to a bank, and, in the absence of communication between banks, further credit would be obtained by hypothecating the same goods to each of the banks, a process apparently limited only by their small number. This at least is what Captain C.F. Parker, 4th U.S. Artillery and Treasurer, Philippine Archipelago, may be excused for supposing.

In the first nine months of 1900 the firm of Mendezona contracted loans and advances totalling over five million pesos through the device of hypothecating 'the same property over and over again; that he had actually taken hemp from the keeping of one of the creditors and put it up as security with another'.[27] Of the total the Hongkong Bank had advanced Pesos 505,000, the major creditors being the Chartered Bank with 1.5 million and the Banco Español-Filipino just over one million, and it was expected that losses of 50% were involved, although the arrangements made by the five major creditors shut out claims of up to one million pesos by smaller creditors.

In November 1900 the Philippine Commission passed an act providing for the examination of banking institutions and in the first report, dated April 22, 1901, which was forwarded to the U.S. Comptroller of the Currency for comment, the Mendezona loans featured prominently.

---

[i] The Banco Español-Filipino (later Bank of the Philippine Islands) was not at that time a viable alternative since the departing Spanish Government had borrowed $2 million from them and their note issue outstanding was a further $2 million, leaving the bank for a time potentially insolvent.

The methods of doing business are stated as being very lax, unbusiness-like and insecure. The loans are classed as secured or guaranteed, and unsecured, but from the report it would seem that there can properly be but one classification for all loans and that the latter. Frequently no note is given to cover loans; mortgages are long, cumbersome documents showing in disjointed manner the amount, time and interest; and when loans are renewed the same is done by a letter to the bank by the party obtaining the loan and the letter is approved if granted by the Director of the bank, and there is made no entry on the mortgage nor on the books of the bank to show the renewal or extension of the loan.

The inspector was also critical of the overdraft system, claiming they left 'the accounts in a confused and unsettled state and will most certainly lead to mischief if continued'. They were and did. He also questioned whether the banks were holding the legally required cash in vault, 25% of the value of demand liabilities.

The response of the Comptroller focused mainly on the condition of the note-issuing Banco Español-Filipino and took a more long-run view of the examiner's report on the Mendezona loans. 'The Comptroller, under the statement rendered by the Hongkong and Shanghai Banking Corporation, and in the absence of further information regarding the condition of the assets of this bank, can take no exception as to its entire responsibility.'[28] It was this report however which noted that the Hongkong Bank held over Pesos 8 million in public monies 'or an amount exceeding the entire outstanding liabilities of the bank of all other nature'. The Comptroller was presumably referring to the Bank in the Philippines because he is concerned with the fact that capital plus reserves is stated as Pesos 1.6 million and recommends investigating the question of the 'liability of the so-called parent bank of the obligations of the Manila branch . . . [which] would seem to be on its face a separate corporation in law'.

The final comment came from Governor Taft who cabled Washington,

no possible question liability Hongkong and Chartered banks for Manila deposits, General Managers both have admitted this by cable and letter . . . both institutions powerful and considered absolutely safe, may refuse to furnish further securities . . . if deposits in those institutions forbidden Treasurer of the Philippine Islands has no place to keep funds . . . (13 August 1901)

The Hongkong Bank in Iloilo

The Board of Directors of the Hongkong Bank did not open up-country or outport branches without due consideration. The finance of trade was negotiated at the main trading centres and often local agents or plantation managers had no authority to deal on their own. In Burma, India, and Ceylon the Bank remained conservative; China and Japan were in a category of their own, and only with the rubber boom of 1909–1910 did the Bank move up-country from Singapore and Penang. But in 1883, reacting to threatened competition from the Chartered Bank, the Hongkong Bank raced to Iloilo and won by a three-day margin.

As the Chartered Bank left two years later (to return only in 1911) the question may arise as to what the Hongkong Bank had won and what led to the establishment of the Iloilo sub-agency. Undoubtedly the presentation of C.I. Barnes, the Bank's Manila Manager, influenced the Hongkong Bank's Board, and, in fact, both banks had shown considerable foresight.

When first opened for foreign commerce by the Spanish authorities in 1855 Iloilo, a town of 6,000, was the centre of local handicrafts and a small port with a token export of sugar. (Nearby Jaro had a population of 30,000.) The following year Nicholas Loney arrived and, in the few years before his premature death at the age of 41 in 1869, had single handedly modernized the production of sugar, built lorchas to transport sugar from the Negros to Iloilo for export, and helped lay the foundations for the wealth which was to be focused on the Iloilo/Jaro area at least through the 1930s. Formerly with Ker and Co., Loney, who was also British Vice-Consul, founded his own company which, in addition to owning a sugar estate, was the agent for Russell, Sturgis and Co., who in turn were agents in Manila for the Hongkong Bank.

The waterfront which he developed is still named Muelle Loney. With its growing wealth and expanding international trade Iloilo became a social and intellectual centre for the Western Visayas, with strong connections with Britain. It was a logical place to establish the agency of a British exchange bank.

The developments which Loney began were to continue, and in March 1883 John MacNab (East in 1872) was appointed the first Agent, a post he held for fourteen years until his retirement as the sixth senior officer in the Bank in 1897. With the shortage of accommodation in the town MacNab found himself rooming with the Chartered Bank's Walter Young and a young British sugar buyer who acted as referee. Both accepted the need to adapt to the needs of the community and both understood the principles of a sound deposit base. Young, who refers to MacNab as Jock McParritch, described a level of competition not frequently admitted in the staid world of nineteenth-century banking:

You see we were both young, full of zeal and frightfully keen on getting deposits from the natives. Our directors had not given us much capital to play with, so Mac and I went out into the highways and by-ways to capture cash from the shy depositor-bird. In this connection Jock did not like my enterprising methods – hence our quarrels.

My little office was situated at the top of the street leading from Jaro into the town. Both in Jaro and in another important place, Molo, there were many merchants but no banks. [MacNab's] office, being lower down the street, was not so favourably placed for nailing hesitating depositors unaccustomed to banks and banking business (it was our job to teach them), so my method was to watch, through the bank blinds, the passing natives and Chinese, and if they looked like taking money to [the Hongkong Bank] I would dart out and capture them and the cash.

If I spotted a likely customer jingling merrily past my hospitable and eager door . . . his cock under his arm . . . and a few bags of silver dollars rattling in his *caramata*, I would pounce out upon him, and before he could cry 'Putanginama' (a reprehensible swear-word much used, alas! by those poor heathen), he would find a neat little pass-book in one hand, a neat little cheque-book in the other, and in his ear a solemn word of warning to keep away from the red-nosed Scotch lobster down the street.

Mac thought this was neither cricket nor conducting banking operations with decorum, so in his wrath he cursed me in his beautiful native language, something like this:

'By Gad! I'd like to skelp that chap! He's nothing but a bally highwayman! My best customer, Cirilo, was passing his dashed pawnshop this morning with five thousand dollars for me, when the blighter bounded into the *caramata*, and before Cirilo knew what had happened, he found the money gone and one of that damned Cockney's pass-books in his hand. That bounder's the limit.'[29]

Despite a fire in 1885 which practically destroyed Iloilo – the Bank's own Treasury and valuables were fortunately untouched – defalcations in 1888, 1904, and 1906, and the death of a junior, H.W. Stedman, in 1904 (then on his first tour East, now buried in the Jaro American cemetery), there is nothing to suggest the Hongkong Bank ever considered closing down its agency. The existence of the Iloilo agency had been used as an argument by the U.S. Philippine Administration in their successful attempt to have the Hongkong Bank designated a depository for Insular Funds.[30] By 1901 at least, the agency was responsible for balance sheet footings typically about 8% of those of the parent Manila branch. This ratio held through the 1920s, declining to less than 5% in the 1930s.

Within the Bank Iloilo has been both an opportunity for a young man with hopes for the future or, at other times, an office for a more senior man to complete his career. Because it is a live community of a size which the newcomer, even the foreign newcomer, could in part comprehend and expect to contribute to, Iloilo has become an integral part of the Bank's folklore, as well known by reputation as the larger branches. Perhaps R.P. Thursfield, the Bank's in-house poet, was exaggerating somewhat about his 1908 assignment, but some look back with sentiments not unlike the following:

> I have been in many cities,
> I have travelled far and wide;
> The Capitals of Europe
> and America I've tried:
> New York, Constantinople,
> Berlin, and Bucharest.
> And I've come to the conclusion I
> Like Yloilo best.[31]

Table 2.2 *The Hongkong and Shanghai Banking Corporation*
Iloilo sub-agency
(in thousands of pesos)

(i) March 31, 1901
(ii) December 31, 1905

Assets	(i)	(ii)	Liabilities	(i)	(ii)
Loans and overdrafts	359.2	582.2	Capital and reserves	n.a.	n.a.
Bills of exchange	100.2	40.4	Due to Head Office		
Cash	1066.1	429.0	and branches	528.3	672.6
Other assets	0.2		Due to Iloilo banks	50.0	–
			Individual deposits:		
			time	275.7	–
			current	402.4	283.8
			Insular Treasurer:		
			current	264.9	79.6
			Bills payable	2.4	1.0
			Other liabilities	1.9	14.6
Totals:	1525.7	1051.6		1525.7	1051.6

Source: U.S. National Archives, Bureau of Insular Affairs, RG 350, file 2879, Banks: Reports, General.

The agency was closed in 1982.

The March 1901 statement of the Iloilo agency reveals a highly liquid position (even excluding Insular Government funds and the 100% reserve against them) financed by overdrafts presumably in Manila and by local deposits. As Table 2.2 indicates, the second column, end-1905, is more typical although Government deposits ceased with the founding of the Philippine National Bank in 1916. Throughout the period to 1940 Iloilo deposits were insufficient to finance loans and overdrafts and maintain an adequate level of liquidity. The agency was, therefore, forced to borrow from Manila and/or Head Office to assist in its financing of trade, particularly sugar exports.

Loans and overdrafts reached a peak in the early war years with November 1914 figures of approximately 2 million pesos compared to 1.2 million in 1934. Sugar exports grew and a large portion of the financing was arranged through the Iloilo agency, which was also involved in the finance of other items, especially the import of rice and consumer goods. A centralization of Philippine commercial, political, and social life in Manila to the detriment of the provinces, however, was already underway; but further, while in Cebu the port was developed, in Iloilo facilities silted up and labour problems plagued the harbour; and the town, while retaining its regional role as the nominal location of considerable wealth, slowly declined – export finance came to be negotiated in Manila, the Chinese importers felt Japanese competition, local banks were able to quote finer rates – and the Iloilo agency became, perforce, something of a 'backwater'; it garnered funds to lend to Manila branch.

Throughout its history the agency was subject to the Manila branch. This meant that all but routine questions were referred, with a recommendation, to the Manager in Manila and often through him to Hong Kong – requests for increases in local staff pay (even one peso a month for a messenger) went to Head Office through Manila, as did requests for leave and related Eastern staff matters. Through regular correspondence Manila and Iloilo kept each other abreast of mutual cash movements and requirements, warnings of any expected heavy drawings, advice on handling common customers, and comments on reports by Government bank examiners. As a 'sub-agency' Iloilo maintained no foreign exchange position, obtaining rates and other necessary information through Manila.

Banking competition and banking business to 1918

Growth of the banking sector

The competition from 'our American cousins' which the Hongkong Bank's Chairman, Robert Shewan, had promised shareholders, had an immediate impact on the Bank's business in the Philippines, which had in any case to adjust to a new banking environment, albeit in a period of trade growth.

On July 14, 1902, the International Banking Corporation (IBC) established offices in Manila. This was followed in 1903 by the Guaranty Trust Company. The IBC was taken over by the National City Bank of New York (now Citibank, N.A.), in 1984 the largest non-Government bank in the Philippines.[32]

The Hongkong Bank maintained its role as a leading bank in the country throughout the American period. It was in fact the top bank at the start of the American regime, with assets totalling $211.46 million at year-end 1900, a position of leadership that, in terms of resources, would shift from time to time to the Banco Español-Filipino. Both banks eventually relinquished this position to the Government-owned Philippine National Bank.

The entry of new banks would also dilute the Hongkong Bank's share of the banking business in the country. In the period 1906 to 1908, the Bank accounted for as much as 40% of total resources in the banking sector. Ten years later (1916–1918) this had dropped to about 10%.[33] The Bank maintained this share until the outbreak of World War II.

More banks were opened in the latter half of the second decade of American rule (1916–1920). Most significant was the opening of the Philip-

pine National Bank in July 1916. This was to parallel developments in other
territories in which the Hongkong Bank operated; the formation of a locally
sponsored bank, which would take over functions as the Government's bank
even if, in some cases, it did not enter immediately into foreign exchange
operations. With the total capitalization of Pesos 20 million subscribed by the
Government, the Philippine National Bank (PNB) was entrusted with the
responsibility of financing development efforts, was made sole depository of
Government funds, and, particularly important as far as the exchange banks
were concerned, immediately established a branch in the United States, in
New York.

The growth and reorientation of trade

United States-Philippine trade policy affected both the direction and rate of
growth of the country's trade and the Hongkong Bank with special agencies in
San Francisco and New York was particularly well situated to play a significant
role while, at the same time, continuing to be a major factor in the sterling
trade of the Islands.

The free trade relations with the United States beginning with the Payne-
Aldrich Tariff Act in 1909 followed earlier American tariff discounts; in 1913,
the Underwood-Simmons Act was passed, abolishing the quotas on Philippine hemp, tobacco, and sugar, and placing rice on the free list; the same laws
provided for unrestricted entry of U.S. goods into the Philippines. Such
policies firmly established the pattern of economic activity in the Philippines
and her dependence on the primary exports of sugar, copra, coconut oil,
abaca, and, to a lesser extent, tobacco. Only rice, the primary staple diet of the
people, would attain the magnitude of production comparable to these
commodities.

The pattern of growth varied among these export products, see Table 2.3.

Sugar experienced a practically unbroken record of growth, such that in the
last year of free trade (1934) sugar accounted for 65% of total export value.

Copra exports suffered a slump during World War I as military operations
disrupted shipping, making it practically impossible to export copra to Europe,
then its primary market. Recovery was made by a shift to the U.S. market, but
subsequently the Depression brought the copra market to another slump.[34]
Likewise, abaca had an uneven pattern of growth.

Bank business – 1899–1920

These first two decades of American rule were the height of development in
the abaca industry, and the Bank did a significant business financing exports
of hemp. Among the Bank's major clients in 1904 were firms in the shipping
industry, also experiencing a period of growth. This included Aldecoa and

Table 2.3 *The Philippine Islands*
Value of primary export products

(in millions of pesos)

Year	Sugar	Copra	Coconut oil	Abaca products	Tobacco products
1899	6.92	1.45		15.99	1.89
1900–1903	5.81	6.65		35.27	2.47
1904–1908	9.41	9.37		38.44	2.26
1909–1913	17.56	23.69		37.07	5.37
1914–1920	40.75	13.67	30.85	67.93	11.69
1935–1937	107.06	29.53	32.95	35.38	6.54

Co., who took over the steamers of Macleod and Co., and Compania Maritima, which does business today. Traditional clients, such as Warner, Barnes and Co., Smith, Bell and Co., and Macleod and Co., received substantial credit accommodation. The above five clients alone accounted for 83% of outstanding loans and overdrafts of the Bank in 1904. The Bank's loan portfolio accounted for 42% of its assets in 1904.

In 1905 Smith, Bell and Co. came close to liquidation as they were pressed by creditors after selling commodities, principally sugar in the United States, on a falling market. Among the major Eastern creditors were the Hongkong Bank, the Chartered Bank, and the Mercantile Bank; the Home creditors included Baring's and the National Bank of Scotland. The Eastern banks agreed to give up any priority to their claim, but insisted on the reorganization of the Manila and London operations through amalgamation into a limited company. This requirement met, the banks accepted 4% bonds in payment of the company's obligations and these were fully repaid by 1917. This very successful example of cooperation between a major customer and its bankers did credit to both sides, which is presumably why the episode features prominently in the company's published history, proudly entitled *Under Four Flags*.[35]

This concentration of business with a few leading firms and therefore concern for the continued soundness of that business was a characteristic pattern for the Bank throughout the American period and afterwards. On several occasions the Bank received mild rebukes from the Bank Commissioner.

The Bank's other activities, such as deposit taking and transactions in bills of exchange, were fairly spread out. Also among the Bank's early clients were Atlantic Gulf and Pacific Company, Siuliong and Co., Ynchausti and Co., and a tobacco firm, Compana Gral. de Tabacos de Filipinas.

Business continued to grow and new clients were acquired as developments occurred in other commodities. Accounts for the second decade included Luzon Rice Mills, Viuda y Hijos p. P Roxas, Strong Machinery Company, Findlay, Richardson and Co., Limpangco and Sons, and the Philippine Vegetable Oil Company. The latter two firms would cause much concern to the Bank as they encountered financial difficulties.

As in Manila, the major clients of the Iloilo branch were Warner, Barnes and Co., Smith, Bell and Co., and Ynchausti and Co. Among the Iloilo clients were Levy Hermanos, Lizarraga Hermanos, Gregorio Montinola, Josè Araneta, and the Compana Gral. de Tabacos de Filipinas. As already noted, the Iloilo operation was limited, accounting for about 10% of Manila resources, but it provided a crucial link to the sugar centrals and the mechanism for verifying stocks offered as security on advances from the Manila office.

Financing the Manila Railway

The Manila Railway has throughout its history had financial difficulties, not always of its own making. Construction was begun by British engineers in 1883 and by 1888 the company attempted to raise a loan of £1 million by public subscription; the Hongkong Bank issued the prospectus and received a commission of £7,500, which McLean noted would pay for half the loss caused by the fall in the Philippine exchanges. The loan was not well received, and the underwriters had to take up £800,000, subsequently selling prematurely on a falling market. Adolf von André, the Hongkong Bank's one-time Chairman, had been involved and some £300,000 of the unsubscribed portion of the loan was placed in Germany.[36]

The Bank was not itself interested in the loan, but Jackson and McLean invested privately, the latter £2,000 @ 3% discount, and he advised Jackson to hold as the bonds would, in his view, rise to par when the syndicate had unloaded.

In November 1906 Harry E.R. Hunter, as Acting Chief Manager, had the Bank take a one-third share in the issue of a £5.3 million loan in New York and London – in partnership with Speyer Bros – to refinance the railway and provide additional cash. The Manila Railway Company, incorporated in New Jersey, had taken over from the old English company, and the Hongkong Bank and Speyer Bros became further involved with a loan of £411,516:6s:8d (=$Gold 2 million) at 4% and 86, secured by the whole of the Southern Lines, Manila-Dagupan, and their equipment. The accounts of the company were kept in Manila and London and the Bank became further involved by granting clean credits to draw on London from Manila at 30 days' sight.

A third loan, for £1,250,000, was undertaken jointly with Speyer Bros in 1908 to finance construction of 444 miles of railway through a highly productive agricultural area of Luzon.

The experience of the Hongkong Bank in the Philippines might be described as 'total involvement'. At a time when British investment predominated, the Bank had made itself essential to the finance of an export-dominated economy; it had also assisted as a merchant banker in the finance of Luzon's main railway. In the process the Bank recorded profits, but this was the result of years of risky development, legal involvements, and adaptation to a new administration.

Then as the Bank settled down in Manila and Iloilo, conditions changed; export continued to be risky but the Bank from the early 1920s had to face the possibility of exclusion and control. The role of a foreign exchange bank in a developing economy had become a matter of serious debate and political concern.

CEYLON – 'NOT NEEDED FOR CHINA'[j]

In 1858 David McLean en route to make his fortune in Australian banking found himself checked in Ceylon; his connecting ship failed to arrive and he learned later it had been wrecked. But in Colombo he heard tales of banking in the East; he changed his plans and sailed for Hong Kong, to become, after serving with the Oriental Bank Corporation, the Hongkong Bank's first Shanghai Manager in 1865.

This is the first, but admittedly marginal, reference to Ceylon in the prehistory of the Hongkong Bank, and it was not until 1882, seventeen years after the founding of the Bank, that the Board appointed agents in the Crown Colony – Delmege, Reid and Co. (now Delmege, Forsyth and Co., Ltd). This firm, with origins in 1865, had American connections; the two Reid brothers had been in Mississippi River commerce and E.T. Delmege was the U.S. consular agent in Colombo at least in 1872. Their business as agents of the Hongkong Bank, one of the partners was to recall, was 'mostly in the way of buying our own Bills of Exchange'. The Bank itself resisted several pleas to open its own staffed agency in Colombo for reasons which may be summarized in the advice the Board received from McLean in London, 'Colombo not required for China business.'

[j] In addition to his contribution in *Eastern Banking*, on 'The Guarantee Shroffs, the Chettiars, and The Hongkong Bank in Ceylon' (pp. 409–20), H.L.D. Selvaratnam prepared two extensive reports (i) on the Hongkong Bank and (ii) on the Mercantile Bank in Sri Lanka. The following account depends heavily on these contributions. The reports are available in the Hongkong Bank Group Archives.

The establishment of the Bank in 1892

The Bank's legal status outside Hong Kong had been regularized, the Board had sanctioned additional agencies cautiously, but the reorganization of their agents (E.T. Delmege joining with A. Forsyth to form a separate merchant house), combined with renewed requests to establish their own agency may have been factors in the final decision to open in Colombo in 1892. Potential Chartered Bank competition may have been a factor and the weakness of the New Oriental Bank may have been noted. Despite the existence of the Chartered Mercantile and the National Bank of India and despite the Bank's lack of expertise in local South Asian banking and the continued absence of a meaningful China connection, the Hongkong Bank commenced business on July 1, 1892, the day the run started on the New Oriental.

Business was underway with the announcement by the Bank's first Manager, L.C. Balfour (East in 1878), to the Colonial Secretary that the branch had opened on July 1. There was also this invitation from the Bank's new Guarantee Shroff, the equivalent of the China-coast compradore, who obviously was playing a community role with very different social status: 'Mr S. Cathiravelu, Shroff (late of the O.B.C.) requests the pleasure of your company on Friday 1st July 1892 at 10 o'clock A.M. at Delmege Reid and Co. Office, Queen Street on the occasion of the opening of the above bank. Current accounts will then be opened.'

The branch was established in the premises of the Bank's erstwhile agents, Delmege, Reid and Co., but shortly afterwards occupied the former premises of the defunct New Oriental Bank in Baillie Street, and there the Bank remained until after World War I. In the 1893 Inspector's report the building is described as 'splendid', with the implication that, at a rental of Rs15,000 a year, it was too splendid, but 'we could not get what we wanted without taking the whole . . . we are in hopes of gradually letting off such portions of the Premises as we do not require'.

In 1919 the Hongkong Bank, in fact, bought property on Princes Street and in 1925 moved into the building they now occupy.

Evidence that the branch was being set up in accordance with the usual careful economy is found first in the fact that the Hongkong Bank participated successfully in the auction to buy the New Oriental Bank's office furniture, secondly, in the permission granted, at Board level, for the Agent, Robert Wilson, to furnish the Bank house at Rs7,500, and finally, in the approval, again at Board level, for Wilson to hire a horse and carriage 'as is the custom at all other tropical agencies'.

As with the main China-coast offices, but with more flexibility, the staff was from the first three-tiered: (i) the Eastern, or British, staff, (ii) the clerical staff, and (iii) the 'compradore' and staff. But whereas on the China coast (ii) would have been Portuguese, in Colombo they were mainly but not exclusively Dutch burghers – in 1924 of the 31 clerks, 23 were burghers, 5 Singhalese, and 3 Tamil, and there were also Tamil, Malay, and Singhalese peons and messengers, and for (iii) the compradore and his Chinese assistants were replaced by the Head Shroff with his Tamil staff. Of the shroff and the 'guarantee' system more will be discussed in relation to the events of 1919, but something should be said here of the burghers.

Ceylon, first occupied in part by the Portuguese, came under Dutch rule until 1795, and the burghers 'retained their national character, their sturdy self-esteem their traditions and high ideas of probity conducted in a very remarkable degree over a long period. They had a practical monopoly of the clerical work in most public departments and commercial houses.'[37]

The longest serving was Terrence R. Frugtniet, who came from the New Oriental Bank and claimed to have opened the doors for business in 1892 – he retired in 1938. Other names confirm the generalization: Vanderwert, Kriekenbeck, Von Hagt, Milhuisen, while de Zilva and Fernando suggest an earlier Portuguese origin. In keeping with the Bank's policy, there were no local officers until the 1950s, but by this time the Dutch burghers were departing Ceylon and reestablishing in Australia, even as so many of the Portuguese left Hong Kong and the China coast for the United States at about the same time. Thus the leadership of the Bank in Sri Lanka passed quickly to the Singhalese and Tamils.

Few records remain of the years before World War I and the correspondence files are available only from 1913, but the basic problems of the branch were apparent from the first. The problems were the overbanking in Colombo and 'keen' competition, dependence on loans to chettiars and the local market, an imbalance in export/import finance and the consequent problem of obtaining cover for sterling bills purchased, lack of back-up facilities in India, a large number of small and expensive current accounts, and general unfamiliarity with the Indian scene are apparent from the first. Loans to chettiars were on occasion secured by mortgages, something which, according to the testimony of the exchange banks, exchange banks never do; with Dutch law applying, the problem of mortgages as security was compounded.

L.C. Balfour, who opened the office, left almost immediately to take charge in Calcutta, after which he left the Bank; his successor Robert Wilson, previously acting Agent in Tientsin, and then briefly Agent in Amoy and Penang, remained ten years. A long stay was particularly important in establishing the Bank as part of the community; the expatriate members of the trading firms and the estates usually remained throughout their careers while

Table 2.4 *The Hongkong and Shanghai Banking Corporation Colombo agency, January 4, 1893*

Assets	Rupees	Liabilities	Rupees
Cash on hand	7,996.40	Current accounts	2,20,470.43
Balance with Bank of Madras	3,30,549.61	Fixed deposits	62,003.52
Bullion (gold sovereigns)	1,422.67		
Overdrafts	77,925.14		
Loans	4,273.35		
Bills receivable	8,123.34		
Bills discounted	1,61,812.20		

bankers had a reputation of being 'birds of passage'. Personal relations were, however, often the basis for obtaining that limited portion of exchange business which was 'discretionary' with or in the gift of local Managers.

The branch in 1893

The agency had been open but six months when it was inspected by Andrew Veitch (East in 1871) en route to Rangoon and a final destination of Yokohama; his report is remarkable for its insights. A covering 'private' letter to John Walter, the Inspector of Branches, states:

The place simply stinks of the old iniquitous style of doing Eastern business, and the struggle of so many banks only tends to a further laxity and departure from sound banking principles.

Perish Colombo say I rather than that we should lend ourselves to a style of business which is unsound and will sooner or later land us in trouble.

On the first day of business after the New Year holidays, January 4, 1893, Veitch found cover in rupees as shown in Table 2.4. The information is insufficient to provide a complete listing of assets and liabilities but, as the branch had no capital assigned, other sources of funds should be assumed to be overdrafts with other branches, probably London. Bills for collection totalled Rs6,738.14.

The Hongkong Bank was in Colombo as an exchange bank. Exports at £4 million were practically equivalent to imports, but the finance of the former was highly competitive and of the latter, being largely self-financed, very little was offered to the exchange banks. Of the total sterling financing of exports, some £2.6 million was offered to the banks on either a clean or D/A basis by brokers who mixed bills of varying quality which the banks, being (as has been said) highly competitive, were for the most part forced to take as a package. Thus to do business the Hongkong Bank would have to accept paper which London 'Opinions' would not sanction.

Even then income from the Hongkong Bank's share of the exchange transactions would be insufficient to cover the branch's overheads and this from the first pushed the Bank into the local market.

The main overdraft (on current account) was for Rs43,700 at 8% on the basis of a deposit of mortgage of property worth Rs3 lacs accepted by the Bank without knowledge of whether the land was free of other encumbrances. That this locked up funds was noted, yet this unusual type of business was sanctioned by Head Office and grew over the years.

The bills discounted included some 250 clean pro notes of the chettiars guaranteed by the Head Shroff, who was himself secured by an amount equal to only 12% of the liability. The Hongkong Bank in Ceylon was dependent on the expert guidance of one man, the Head or Guarantee Shroff, but with his familiarity with the South Indian scene, the Bank was probably better protected than its other branches, Singapore for example, where chetty business was done. Since the business included exchange with southern India where the Bank had no agencies, however, there could be no easy check on the Shroff's opinions.

Nor was the Inspector any more pleased with the relatively large current account balance, noting that it was made up of 'innumerable small accounts of Natives and Chetties'. The signature of the chettiars was verified by the Shroff but that of Singhalese by a peon earning a salary of Rs18 a month. Since cheques drawn on many of these accounts were never in excess of Rs5, we may conclude that accusations made by later politicians about the unavailability of banking facilities to the ordinary citizen were exaggerated as far as the city of Colombo was concerned. Nevertheless, as the report observes, 'a large amount of labour and a maximum of risk is run in tolerating these small accounts', and they were from time to time discouraged.

While worded more formally than the private letter to Walter, Veitch's official report ended with the warning that 'our share of the Sterling Business together with any other *legitimate* & *sound* local Banking to be done will I fear not cover our expenses, even when we have a better hold of this place than as new comers we have at present'. Veitch suggested that Walter drop by the next time he went on leave, and indeed he did inspect in 1897. While reaching similar conclusions as to the overall lack of business prospects, especially given the fact that the Mercantile and National Bank of India had up-country agencies whereas the Hongkong Bank, disregarding the experience of its Iloilo sub-agency in the Philippines, did not, Walter did not comment on the matters which had so concerned Veitch, and the Colombo branch continued in operation.

1 The Chief Managers.
Sir Thomas Jackson (Chief Manager 1876–1888; 1890–1891; 1893–1902;
Chairman, London Consultative Committee, 1902–1915); J. R. M. Smith (1902–
1911); Sir Newton Stabb (Chief Manager, 1911–1921, Senior London Manager,
1921–1931).

ABSTRACT OF ASSETS AND LIABILITIES, HONGKONG & SHANGHAI BANKING CORPORATION,

31st December, 1914.

LIABILITIES.

PAID-UP CAPITAL,		$15,000,000.00
STERLING RESERVE FUND, £1,500,000 @ ex. 2/-.		15,000,000.00
SILVER RESERVE FUND,		18,000,000.00
MARINE INSURANCE ACCOUNT,		250,000.00

NOTES IN CIRCULATION:—

(Authorised Issue against Securities and Coin deposited with the Crown Agents for the Colonies and their Trustees,)	$15,000,000.00	
Additional Issue authorised by Hongkong Ordinances against Coin lodged with the Hongkong Government,	12,247,823.00	
		27,247,823.00
CURRENT { Silver,	$139,190,287.11	
ACCOUNTS, { Gold, £5,846,366. 1s. 11d.=66,076,790.25		205,267,077.36
FIXED { Silver,	$71,358,782.87	
DEPOSITS, { Gold, £4,663,261. 18s. 1d.=52,686,415.83		124,045,198.70

BILLS PAYABLE:—

(Including Call Loans and Short Sight Drawings on London Office against Bills Receivable and Bullion Shipments,)	$ 8,420,301.74	
Drafts on London Bankers,	8,930,113.32	
		17,350,415.06
ACCEPTANCES ON ACCOUNT OF CONSTITUENTS,		7,120,699.67
PROFIT AND LOSS ACCOUNT,		5,894,227.17

Liability on Bills of Exchange re-discounted, £11,584,790. 13s. 6d. of which £9,210,215. 1s. 9d. have since run off.

	$435,175,440.96

ASSETS.

CASH,		$74,281,545.89
COIN lodged with the Hongkong Government against authorised and/or excess note circulation,		15,500,000.00
BULLION IN HAND AND IN TRANSIT,		7,630,216.66
INDIAN GOVERNMENT RUPEE PAPER,		1,367,919.12
COLONIAL AND OTHER SECURITIES,		14,807,913.50

STERLING RESERVE FUND INVESTMENTS, *viz.*:—

£1,200,000 2½ % Consols at 68½,.. £822,000 (of which £250,000 lodged with the Bank of England as a Special London Reserve).		
£330,000 3 % Exchequer Bonds due 1920 at 93	306,900	
£466,500 Other Sterling Securities, written down to	371,100	
	£1,500,000 @ ex. 2/-.	15,000,000.00
BILLS DISCOUNTED, LOANS AND CREDITS,		141,540,884.57
BILLS RECEIVABLE,		150,946,139.08
LIABILITIES OF CONSTITUENTS for acceptances, per contra,		7,120,699.67
BANK PREMISES,		6,980,122.47
		$435,175,440.96

GENERAL PROFIT AND LOSS ACCOUNT, HONGKONG & SHANGHAI BANKING CORPORATION,

Dr.   *31st December, 1914.*   *Cr.*

To AMOUNTS WRITTEN OFF:—			By Balance of Undivided Profits, 30th	
Remuneration to Directors,	$ 15,000.00		June, 1914,	$ 2,089,008.44
„ DIVIDEND ACCOUNT:—			„ Amount of Net Profits for the Six Months ending 31st December, 1914, after making provision for bad and doubtful debts and contingencies, deducting all Expenses and Interest paid and due,	3,805,218.73
Dividend £2. 3/- per Share on 120,000 Shares=£258,000 at 1/9½ = ... 2,931,124.26				
Bonus 5/- per Share on 120,000 Shares = £30,000 at 1/9½ = ... 340,828.40				
	3,271,952.66			
„ BALANCE forward to next half-year,	2,607,274.51			$5,894,227.17
	$5,894,227.17			$5,894,227.17

STERLING RESERVE FUND.

To Balance, ... £1,500,000 @ ex. 2/-. (invested in Sterling Securities).	$15,000,000.00	By Balance 30th June, 1914, £1,500,000 @ ex. 2/- .	$15,000,000.00
	$15,000,000.00		$15,000,000.00

SILVER RESERVE FUND.

To Balance,	$18,000,000.00	By Balance 30th June, 1914,	$18,000,000.00
	$18,000,000.00		$18,000,000.00

N. J. STABB, *Chief Manager.*

A. C. HYNES, *Acting Chief Accountant.*

DAVID LANDALE,
W. L. PATTENDEN, } *Directors.*
P. H. HOLYOAK.

We have compared the above Statement with the Books, Vouchers and Securities at the Head Office, and with the Returns from the various Branches and Agencies, and have found the same to be correct.

J. W. C. BONNAR, } *Auditors.*
F. MAITLAND,

HONGKONG, *9th February, 1915.*

---

2 The abstract of assets and liabilities and other accounts, December 31, 1914. The Bank's reserves, carefully defined in terms of silver or gold, are valued in excess of twice the paid-up capital. The dividends are quoted in sterling.

旧香港上海銀行長崎支店
香港上海銀行長崎支店は明治29年(1896)開設
され昭和6年4月閉鎖までの35年間、外国貿
易港としての長崎の繁栄に大きな役割を果たし
た。この建物は明治40年頃の建築で、設計者
下田菊太郎は明治の建築界に異色の存在として
その才をうたわれたが、これは現在唯一の遺構
である。 昭和51年3月／長崎市

3 The former Hongkong Bank agency in Nagasaki from a recent photograph by Takeshi Hamashita. The building, designed by Shimoda Kikutarō and completed *circa* 1908, was the first in classical style by a Japanese architect.

4 The Hongkong Bank's Manila Office near the Pasig River, 35 Calle Juan Luna, Binondo, *circa* 1885.

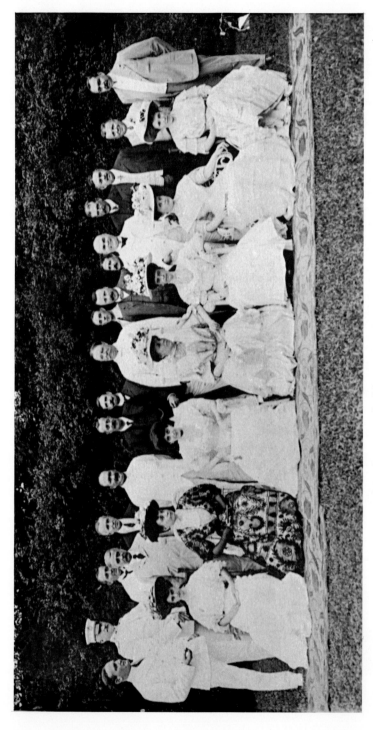

5 A garden party, the Manager's residence, Manila, 1907. The Governor-General, William Howard Taft, is standing in the centre; A. G. Stephen, the Manager, is on his left.

6 Hongkong Bank, Singapore, on Collyer Quay with Johnston's Pier in the left foreground.

7 A. G. Stephen and Mrs Stephen, their sons and staff, Sourabaya, *circa* 1900

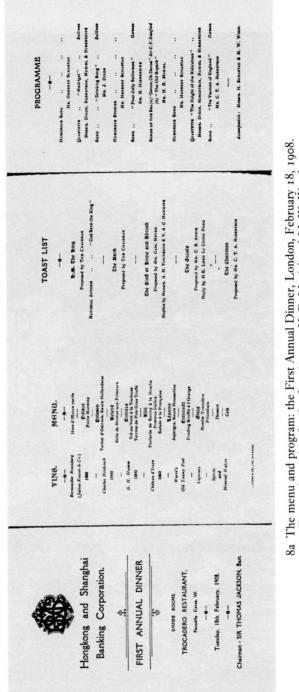

8a The menu and program: the First Annual Dinner, London, February 18, 1908.
Featured together for the first time are H. E. Muriel and M. W. Wood.

9 The London Office Rugby Football Team, 1900/01.
Left to Right (*back row*): Sir Ewen Cameron (Manager, London Office), W. Rodolph, P. Russell, J. Ellerton, F. L. Kendall, W. A. Smith*, H. T. S. Green (Sub-Manager, London Office); (*second row*) T. F. Longmuir, W. Inglis, R. C. Allen, O. J. Barnes (captain), E. R. Hooper, P. G. Wodehouse*, H. N. Steven*; (*front row*) B. C. Lambert, A. Fergusson. (* did not go East).

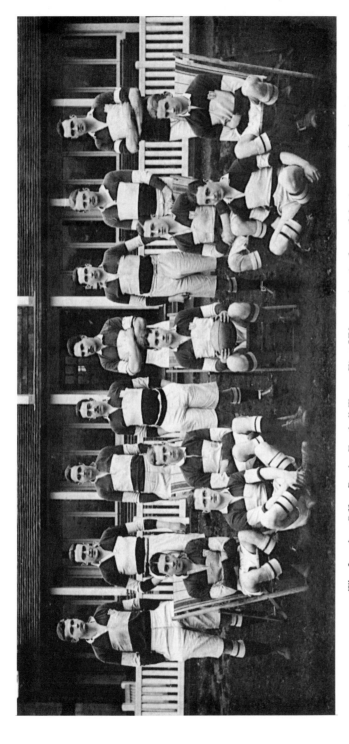

10 The London Office Rugby Football Team, First XV, 1913/14, in front of the just completed New Beckenham club house.

Left to right (*back row*) J. B. Lester[+], E. T. Barnes, P. A. A. Hillier, W. F. MacHutchison[+], B. Good*, J. A. Clark, D. C. T. Twentyman[+], R. L. Moncrieff; (*middle row*) A. M. Duncan Wallace, P. G. Knappett*, H. B. Stone[+], R. B. Kyle[+], J. J. French; (*front row*) R. A. Green, W. R. G. Ebbs[+]. ([+] killed in action * did not go East).

11 'Cliffs', the Peak, Hong Kong, 1910. The residence of the Chief Manager.

The pattern develops, 1893–1914

When the branch opened, Balfour was assigned one Eastern staff assistant. In 1899 another Eastern staff officer was added, but the title 'Accountant' was not used to designate the Number Two until 1904 and a fourth expatriate was added only in 1913. L.N. Murphy (East in 1902), who was to be Manager in the mid-1920s and have supervisory responsibility from Head Office in the early 1930s, was a junior in Colombo from 1908 to 1912. Profit figures (whether meaningful or not) are available irregularly; the figure Rs30,000 appears to refer to a six months' period in 1902, and this may be compared with 1919 annual profits of almost two lacs (Rs1,96,000).

There is reference to the Bank being involved in the finance related to Boer prisoners of war who had been sent to Ceylon. Wilson gave testimony before the 1902 Currency Commission, one of a series of enquiries which was to affect the fortunes of the Bank in the Colony. Also in that year there was the dramatic discovery of Hongkong Bank banknotes worth $258,000, which had been stolen from Singapore and shipped in the false bottom of a crate in transit through the Port of Colombo.

Pre-1914 the Hongkong Bank faced competition principally from the Chartered Bank and the National Bank of India, both London based. The Mercantile Bank of India's main focus was on India, but its Ceylon operations were significant, and it had agencies in Galle, Colombo, and Kandy. The Bank of Madras, a Presidency Bank barred from dealings in foreign exchange, held the bulk of the deposits and was the Government's bank; it was also the clearer – note the Hongkong Bank's clearing account in the 1893 figures in Table 2.4 above – and assisted the Government in its Currency Fund operations.

The monetary system of the British Crown Colony of Ceylon was based on that of India, a policy confirmed by the findings of the 1893 Swettenham Currency Commission, and the Indian silver rupee was the legal tender in which Ceylon Government notes were payable. This required the Government to maintain a portion of the currency reserve, or backing for the note issue, in the form of silver rupees deposited in the Treasury in Colombo. The stock of coin might be depleted when local traders exported rupee coin in making remittances or Tamil workers carried their savings in coin when returning to South India.

This had two consequences. First, on the practical level, the Bank of Madras assisted the Government in managing the reserve and indeed all exchange relationships with India in general. To facilitate the Bank of Madras in carrying out this aspect of central banking the exchange banks limited their own operations to transactions between Colombo and their own branches.

The Hongkong Bank, although it had considered opening a Madras agency in 1892, remained the only Colombo-operating exchange bank without an agency in southern India. The Bank was consequently on occasion at a considerable disadvantage. Secondly, the alternative, minting a Ceylon rupee either as additional or as sole legal tender (or, more broadly, attempting to maintain a separate Ceylon currency), was always a matter for discussion and possible legislation. The exchange banks, the Hongkong Bank included, took a conservative position throughout and supported the Indian link as essential to the island's trade – as those in Hong Kong supported their currency link with China.

In this monetary setting the exchange banks competed for the finance of the growing export trade. Between 1903 and 1912 the export of black tea increased from 142 million to 183 million pounds, rubber from 42 thousand to 15 million pounds (mainly between 1910 and 1912), while desiccated coconut went from 17 million to 31· million pounds. Also important were plumbago, cinnamon, copra, and coconuts. The banks bought the producer's sterling bills, sold sterling in London for India Council Bills – rupee bills of exchange drawn by the Secretary of State for India, purchasable in sterling and payable by the Treasury in India – thus putting themselves in credit in India, and then financing with these funds the import of rice and other basic commodities into Ceylon.

This triangular system as described here is idealized, but information on the Hongkong Bank's specific problems dates only from 1913. Suffice it to add that part of the exchange cover for the sale of sterling export bills was obtained by financing imports from Europe directly to Ceylon, a method which became especially important when the volume of Council Bills was inadequate – and in this financing the Hongkong Bank seemed always to have had difficulties. At other times the Hongkong Bank in Colombo found the break in the triangular finance occurring through lack of sterling to take up Councils allotted and was consequently unable to lay down funds in India sufficient for the needs of the Colombo branch; London had then to be asked to buy in funds on the London market, an operation which could be expensive and in times of tight money, as in 1913, was difficult. The lack of assigned capital put the Colombo branch at a disadvantage, even though London Office gave Colombo a priority in the use of money market funds.

Or in more formal terms:

The rupee surplus of the Bank of Madras and the sterling surplus of the Exchange Banks were set off one against the other by the Exchange Banks supplying the Bank of Madras with rupee credits in India. They were able to do this by buying India Council bills or bar silver in London or by turning over sterling to the Indian branches in exchange for rupee credits in India. India Council bills were those released by the Government of India against payment of sterling in London.[38]

Despite specific problems and constraints, under this system the pre-World War I Colombo branch returned an annual profit.

The Colombo branch was integrated into the South Asian financial system and as its business developed faced towards London rather than Hong Kong. Unlike Calcutta this tendency was not offset by exchange operations with the East. That the branch nevertheless was profitable and contributed to the financial facilities of a developing island economy is a reflection on the low costs of operation, the absence of any formal need for a branch capital, and possibly the fact that many overheads were actually on Head Office books.

In some sense, therefore, those that warned of the 'no China connection' were correct; the office was something of a reasonably profitable anomaly in the Hongkong Bank's system.

SIAM – AWASH WITH FUNDS[k]

The Hongkong Bank pioneered in Siam, establishing the first foreign exchange bank in Bangkok in 1888 (BE 2431) under J.R.M. Smith; the Chartered Bank came in 1893 and the French Banque de l'Indo-Chine in 1897. The Siam Commercial Bank, the first Siamese modern-style bank, was not founded until 1906. The Hongkong Bank served the south of the Kingdom and its tin and rubber exports partly through its office in the Straits Settlement of Penang – the Chartered Bank opened in Phuket itself – but a second Hongkong Bank office was not established in Thailand until the Suapah Road, Bangkok, sub-agency in 1956.

The Bank became the depository of Royal and Government funds, and, with notes in circulation of over Ticals 2.5 million (out of a total 3.3 million of the three exchange banks in 1902), the Manager's main problem was, apparently, temptation – to which from time to time he yielded. As an early Inspector put it, 'With so much money in hand one is inclined to make local advances, but I am of the opinion that the more we curtail these at the Port the better.'

As the Siamese authorities, acting on the advice of a British financial adviser, began to develop their own policy, they took back the right of note issue, placed Siam eventually on a gold exchange standard, and set up the Siam Commercial Bank. When their bank became involved in both financial and political difficulties during World War I, the Hongkong Bank was asked to

[k] This section is based mainly on material in Group Archives, but it is also dependent on the research of Thiravet Pramuanratkarn, and readers may wish to refer to his essay, 'The Hongkong Bank in Thailand: a Case of a Pioneering Bank', in King, ed. *Eastern Banking* (London, 1983), pp. 421–34.

supply a manager, and G.H. Ardron (East in 1899), the Accountant, took on the task, staying until his retirement in the late 1920s.

Bangkok was reputedly the 'white man's grave', with mock 'final' farewells for those assigned there. In fact with cholera under control the record was relatively good; R.A. Niven was sent invalided from Bangkok to Hong Kong in 1894 where he died from complications arising from fever, and in 1912 young A. Tillbrook just returned from his first Home leave was buried there.

Exchange banking in Bangkok, 1888–1914

The Hongkong Bank had been represented in Bangkok from 1865 to 1883 by the Hanseatic firm of Pickenpack, Thies and Co. – Thies had signed the 1858 commercial treaty between Siam and the Free Hanseatic Cities of Hamburg, Bremen, and Lübeck. Subsequently, with the failure of that company in 1883, the Bank's agents were the Swiss firm of Jucker, Sigg and Co.[1] Smith's arrival was confirmed in a Head Office circular of November 3, 1888, and on December 2, the Hongkong Bank's Bangkok office was formally opened at the 'old Belgian Consulate' at a rental of $74 a month. As the Hongkong Bank's Inspector of Branches, G.E. Noble, put it, '. . . by establishing its Bangkok Agency when it did, the Bank for the first time got ahead of its main competitor, the Chartered Bank . . .' He had forgotten Iloilo.

In 1890 the Bank moved to Klong Kut Mai, between Customs Lane and the Oriental Building, a place known today as Tanam Si Phya and the site of a luxury hotel, a joint venture with the Hongkong Bank Group, and there it remained until 1977. The first building on the site had been rented for fifteen years at $200 a year initially; the lease was renewed in 1905 and the office rebuilt in 1929.

Heralding the forthcoming opening of the Hongkong Bank, the *Bangkok Times* announced, 'It is reported to be favourably regarded by the Siamese Government, who fully appreciate the benefits that this country will reap by a branch operating on a large scale here and abroad, and ready to promote financial, commercial, and friendly relations.'[39] As a former British Ambassador was to recall:

From the moment of my arrival at Bangkok in 1904 [as a language student], the Hongkong and Shanghai Bank was associated more than any similar institution, to my mind, with Siamese affairs. More than that, I regarded the Bank – as, I think, did most of us – as being the principal agent (though in the nature of things it could scarcely be

---

[1] Jucker died in 1885 and Henry Sigg carried on until he brought out Albert Berli to help liquidate the firm. Berli bought the goodwill and when Sigg died in 1889 established Berli and Co., later Berli, Jucker and Co., a firm which remained a good customer of the Hongkong Bank. It was Berli who as the Bank's merchant agent urged the establishment of a Bank agency, in much the same way that Delmege was doing in Colombo.

recognized as such officially) of H.M. Government in the United Kingdom in financial matters affecting the Far East generally.[40]

The Siamese Royal family and Government had had accounts overseas, partly with the Hongkong Bank in Singapore, since 1877. With the establishment of the Bank in Bangkok, official current accounts of the King and Palace officials of some 6 million Tcs (ticals) (=$3.56 million @5 ticals or baht=$3 Mex) were deposited, the Thai archives confirming that the Bank held His Majesty King Chulalongkorn's private account, opened in 1889 with Tcs1.6 million at 3% compounded monthly.

The Inspector's report for 1890 shows that the Bank held the accounts of the Customs, Telegraph, and Education departments, the Royal Railway Department, and the Royal Siamese Treasury – as well as the St Andrew's Society and the Women's Temperance Union, one report speculating that the last mentioned had been founded by the wives of the former.

Having counted the cash, Bank Inspectors turned their attention to overdrafts, and it is clear that when J.R.M. Smith as the new Inspector of Branches reported on Bangkok in 1901 he concluded that the popular and hospitable T.McC. Browne (East in 1882) was not being sufficiently pressing in his attempts to have these accounts paid off.

There were two basic categories: (i) the up-country trader who had to invest in overheads and traded on the Bank's funds and (ii) the foreign shopkeeper, the pharmacist perhaps, who not only needed funds to keep in business but tended to become attracted to ancillary small enterprises which he operated on insufficient capital. There was no dearth of enterprise; the scarce factor was capital, and this a local Bank Manager, especially one awash with funds, would supply (in between inspections) contrary to the principles of exchange banking. 'These advances are not sufficiently liquid to suit us . . . they would take a long time to liquidate.'

The pre-war system of security against loans has led contemporaries to compare their activities to that of pawn shops. Indeed, the Bank in Bangkok lent against jewellery, but as one Manager commented, 'If we are to do business here we must be prepared to meet specific requirements.' The Bank, however, did more than this; customers included the Anglo-Siamese Trading Company, the Bangkok Tramway Company, and the Siam Electricity Company. To these and others it provided needed accommodation, although its original temporary nature was longer-lasting than the Inspectors could approve.

As for exchange banking, in the decade preceding the establishment of the Hongkong Bank in Bangkok, there were clear signs of economic awakening with the growth of rice exports, which would expand dramatically before the end of the century, and, most important as a signal to foreigners, the approval of railway construction. The financing of either activity would be sufficient justification for a bank, while the state of the currency (despite the opening of a mint in 1860) and the accumulation of wealth reinforced the need.[41]

When the Bank opened in 1888, Siam's total foreign trade was Tcs 45.4 million, of which exports were Tcs 27 million. By 1919/20 these figures had increased to Tcs 315.7 million of which Tcs 177 million were exports, indicating an overall increase of 600%.[42] Underlying this was the great development of rice growing in central Siam, the export of tin, and the beginning of Siamese rubber growing in the South. Sugar, which had caused the Bank's first direct contact with Siam, albeit indirectly through its financial involvement in sugar companies based in Hong Kong and the visit of C.I. Barnes, proved disappointing as world prices dropped. In the period now under discussion the sugar trade was insignificant.

The impact of the change of standard

The falling price of silver led the Siamese Government to reconsider the standard of its monetary system, and as a first step the Government in 1902 closed the mint to free coinage to effect a higher exchange rate. The background to this and subsequent events may be understood in the context of area-wide reform efforts as described in Chapter 4. In Siam the exchange banks played no advisory role and the changes are considered merely for their impact on the accounts of the Bank's Bangkok branch.

With the closing of the mint the exchange banks complained, as they had in India, of being locked out. The Hongkong Bank had Tcs 8 million in deposits and Tcs 2.5 million in outstanding contracts; the difference from the old rate was 26% and the potential loss (even if the Bank accepted a compromise offer) would have been £55,000. In the protracted negotiations which followed, the Hongkong Bank had recourse to an agreement, which it had made when the Royal and official accounts were opened, fixing the rate of exchange, thus cushioning the potential loss from the monetary change. The loss was in fact eventually estimated to be £10,000.

J.R.M. Smith as Chief Manager in Hong Kong sent J.C. Nicholson (East in 1880), the Manager in Singapore, up to Bangkok to assist in the negotiations, suggesting that he did not place full confidence in Browne, whose operations he had criticized only two years previously as Inspector of Branches. Browne was in fact the spokesman for the exchange banks, and the unusual interference was both resented and ineffective.

Siam's first foreign loans[43]

The Royal Siamese Government 4½%, £1 million sterling loan of 1905
The first public overseas loan of the Siamese Government was issued in 1905 for the announced purpose of railway construction. The Government, under the advice of a British financial expert, attempted to retain a minimum Treasury balance of 22 million baht; with increased military expenditures from 1903 and already heavy railway construction costs, this balance had been drawn down. Railways were of a high priority in the unification and centralization of the Kingdom, the Government had already financed 451 kms from current revenues and the decision was therefore made to borrow abroad.

The Siamese Minister in Paris, who was in touch with his Government's adviser, Rivett-Carnac then in London, approached both Rothschild and Schröder who declined apparently on political grounds. The Siamese then turned to the banks – one British, the Hongkong Bank, and one French, Banque de l'Indo-Chine. The two banks agreed to an internationalized issue; either French or British issued bonds were to be equally good delivery in London or Paris, at 90½ (to the Siam Government) and 95½ (to the public) for 40 years repayable by 30 annual drawings after ten years. The Hongkong Bank arranged for the Chartered Bank to take a sub-participation of £75,000 at 92½. The loan was issued in London and Paris without underwriting in March 1905 and was oversubscribed; 'an immense success', wrote Addis in his diary, 'the rush of applications was enormous'.[44] Paralleling the established China loan procedures, the Prospectus announced that the loan had been 'authorized under the authority of a Royal Siamese Decree of His Majesty the King of Siam [compare role of the Imperial edict] . . . which decree has been officially communicated to the British and French Governments through their respective Legations at Bangkok'. The Prospectus provided something which a China Loan prospectus could not provide, an authoritative statement of the revenues of the Kingdom, known to have been authenticated by a foreign adviser. There is, however, no mention either of control of expenditures or of any specific security, and Addis noted in his diary that the Agreement was, in his opinion, a 'one-sided affair'.[45]

The King of Siam could command what China failed to obtain.

The actual signing of the Agreement was celebrated with a dinner at the Savoy for twenty persons including the Siamese Ambassador to Paris, Phya Suriya: total cost £100 – Addis's Scottish comment, 'wicked'.[46]

The Royal Siamese Government 4½%, £3 million sterling loan of 1907
Although the first loan was designed to replenish the Treasury, the second

loan, the $4\frac{1}{2}$%, £3 million loan of 1907, was specifically assigned for the railways, construction of which by this time totalled 579 kms.

The Germans had expressed concern that they had not been invited to participate in the 1905 loan and, in the meantime, they had become involved in the so-called 'Book Club' which was the Commercial Bank of Siam in embryo. By the time the two banks were again approached by the Siamese Government, it had received an offer made by Felix Killian of the Deutsch-Asiatische Bank for financial assistance from a German consortium; consistent with its policy of independence, however, the Government sought, but without success, for funds in Berlin, London, and Stockholm.[m]

The Hongkong Bank, who were eventually authorized to conduct the negotiations, brought in the Deutsch-Asiatische Bank as co-contractors for a £750,000 participation, sharing the balance with the Banque de l'Indo-Chine, apparently without clearing either with the French or the Siamese, or keeping their own Bangkok agency informed.

The confusion resulted from the fact that negotiations had been conducted both in Europe, through the Hongkong Bank's London Office, where A.M. Townsend brought in the Germans without consultation, and in Bangkok, where the local Agent, A.M. Bruce (East in 1887), correctly stated he was unaware of the German involvement. There was considerable discussion, during which it appeared for a time that the Siamese would not accept German participation, if only because they didn't consider it a light matter to have the King's decree changed.[n] The King's decree was in fact amended, and the Agreement, which had been previously signed on January 19, 1907, with the Hongkong Bank, the French, and the Germans as co-contractors was thus approved.[48] The terms were similar to the 1905 loan except that the Government received $93\frac{1}{4}$ and the loan was issued to the public at $97\frac{1}{2}$.

The loan was underwritten, and the Bank received a commission of $1\frac{1}{2}$% taking up £300,000 of the loan on its own account.

Due to the state of the European markets already burdened with American railway bonds and high interest rates, the loan was not a success and was only fully sold in 1911. In 1908 the Siamese Government and the DAB were in disagreement over the amount to be withdrawn from the German bank, the Government insisting on the full £750,000, the DAB releasing only £500,000.[49] The conflict perhaps reflected German-British antagonism over

[m] The approach to Stockholm is probably due to the influence of M. Waldburger, a Swedish citizen connected with the Siamese Stockholm consulate, who was probably the man responsible for the success of the 1905 loan negotiations and who had arrived in Bangkok as preparations for the second loan were underway.[47]

[n] Charles Addis, then the junior London Manager, recorded in his diary, January 15, 1907, his strong feeling that Townsend had made a 'mess of the new Siamese loan . . . it will be a pretty kettle of fish if Siam doesn't yield, all owing to T's ineptitude'.

the actual construction of the railway, but the issue was eventually resolved with the Siamese Government agreeing to buy £100,000 German Government bonds. Political issues further complicated relations, since the British had a secret treaty with Siam affecting the Southern Line, eventually leading to Siam's loss of suzerainty over Perlis, Kedah, Kelantan, and Trengganu.

Traditional Siamese foreign policy gave priority to the maintenance of its independence from any one country. In banking the original almost total dependence on the Hongkong Bank had therefore to be diluted, and in 1907 the Siamese turned to the National Provincial Bank in London. In Bangkok the French and British were balanced, but the Siamese nevertheless encouraged German and Danish involvement until the events of World War I led to Siam declaring war on the Central Powers. The Hongkong Bank continued, nevertheless, to hold the bulk of the Government's funds and to handle their exchange transactions at least through the 1920s, that is, during the tenure of the Hongkong Bank's G.H. Ardron as manager of the Siam Commercial Bank.

LYONS – THE BANK'S FIRST EUROPEAN 'SPECIAL AGENCY'[o]

The founding, 1881

As the key to the Bank's involvement in the Philippines and the Netherlands East Indies was sugar, the latter especially in trade with Hong Kong, so was silk to Lyons. In the twenty years before the Bank opened there, the silk market was moving from London, and the Lyons manufacturers were importing directly from the sources of supply in the East. The Hongkong Bank had been interested in this trade almost from the first, and its Lyons agent, Crédit Lyonnais, testified to the importance of the Bank by commenting on the loss of the agency.[p] 'The silk branch [of our business] has been profitable as long as we were the Hongkong and Shanghai BC's representative. We used to receive its silks, and [we] had rented premises for that purpose. But since that company has had the unfortunate idea of having an

---

[o] The correct present day usage is 'Lyon', but the old English spelling of the town, mentioned after all by Defoe, is 'Lyons' and has been retained. The retired French staff members of the Lyons branch inevitably use the English pronunciation with the 's'! The research on the Bank in France was undertaken by Claude Fivel-Démoret, and he contributed a paper provocatively entitled, 'The Hongkong Bank in Lyon, 1881–1954: Busy, but too Discreet?', in King, ed. *Eastern Banking*, pp. 467–516, from which the major part of this section is taken.

[p] There is unfortunately no basis for a quantified assessment, except that in July 1881, a few months before the Bank opened in Lyons, one-twelfth of the Crédit Lyonnais' commercial portfolio was created through the silk trade. The claim would suggest an almost total dependence of this bank on the Hongkong Bank for this line of business (see note 50).

agency in Lyon, we are drowning.'[50] McLean in London advised against opening; he also advised against E. Morel as the Agent. His argument was that funds could not be easily raised in Lyons, while in Paris, where the Bank's main agents were located, funds could be obtained through the Banque de France. The problem with Morel has already been discussed in Volume I. But the Hongkong Bank was again determined to be a pioneer; normally conservative, the Board were willing to chart new paths when the China/Japan trade was involved. The Hongkong Bank was the first overseas bank in New York; it was also the first British bank in Lyons and Hamburg – and in Peking and Iloilo.

The site for the Bank's Lyons office was well chosen; as a local author put it, 'This district is, *par excellence*, the silk district.'[51] The Place Tolozan is located at the bottom of the Croix Rousse Hill where the Lyons silk-weavers lived. The famous Condition des Soies (an official laboratory charged with weight and quality testing of all silk arriving in Lyons) was a couple of streets above the Bank's building. Nearby was the area occupied on both sides of the Rue de la République (leading to the Stock Exchange and the Chamber of Commerce) by the other banks and the silk houses. At a time when silk was still the dominant factor in Lyons' economic life the Bank was ideally situated to enable it to keep in touch with the latest news of the trade.

The misconduct of E. Morel had nothing to do with the actual working of the Lyons agency; François de Bovis came from Hong Kong to sort out matters, London took a stronger position on regular inspections, and with the return of Thomas Jackson to the East in 1893, de Bovis assumed control until his retirement in 1922.

From 1900 at least the Hongkong Bank was involved in negotiations with French banks over indemnity payments, railway finance, and loan consortiums; all of this passed Lyons by. When negotiations were carried on in Paris, Charles Addis came from London to conduct them. In view of the strong dislike Addis had for de Bovis (see Volume I, Chapter 15), this might suggest a personal reason for ignoring the Lyons Manager. There is, however, a business explanation. When, probably through an oversight, Lyons branch became involved with the transfer of French Boxer Indemnity funds, there was an immediate protest from the Banque de l'Indo-Chine.[q] This bank was the leading institution in the French Group; Addis came to Paris as head of the British Group. The Lyons branch was part of the Hongkong Bank as

---

[q] Exceptionally, in 1907–1908, the Hongkong Bank's Shanghai branch remitted three Boxer Indemnity payments due to France through the Bank's Lyons agency, thereby cutting out the Banque de l'Indo-Chine; that bank protested and there is no further record of Lyons' involvement.[52]

exchange bank; Addis came from London to represent the Bank as merchant bank.

Having argued this, one should in fairness compare the situation with Germany, where the Hamburg Manager, J. Brüssel, was definitely involved in loan negotiations with the DAB and related consortium banks in Berlin, but the commencement of these negotiations predated Addis's ascendancy; Brüssel's successor, F.T. Koelle (East in 1894), was not so closely involved. Addis travelled to Berlin as well.

To the list of activities in which the Lyons agency and its Manager were not engaged should be added retail banking; the agency kept no current accounts although it did accept fixed deposits.

The business of the Lyons agency

The origins of the agency were in silk. Claude Fivel-Démoret has described the financing as follows:

(i) 'Silk and Co.' of Shanghai would obtain an advance from the Hongkong Bank's Shanghai branch to buy silk. The advance was in Shanghai taels against a D/P or D/A bill on Silk & Company, Lyons (usually the parent company; it was then a case of drawing 'pig on pork', a frequent occurrence, though not the only type of transaction).

(ii *a*) The D/P bill (documents against payment) was a draft attached to the documents which were necessary to release the goods from the shipping company: bill of lading and insurance certificate.[53] With a D/P bill the Lyons house could only gain possession of the documents and consequently the silk it wanted to sell on the Lyons market against cash payment to the agency of the Hongkong Bank in Lyons. The Lyons merchant could choose not to take up the bill, and thus the Bank held the security although it ran the risk of a collapse in the market.

(ii *b*) Alternatively, the Lyons merchant could 'retire' the bill by settling it before it reached maturity.[54] He would then be allowed a discount on the amount due.

Since the agency was in fact crediting the funds represented by the bills to the accounts of the branches of the Bank which had bought or negotiated the bills, the Lyons Manager had to ensure that the cost of funds and his exchange operations was not more than offsetting his return on the interest on the bills:

It is understood that the rate allowed to the Branches is 3%, which is also the discount rate to merchants. But the true rate of selling D/P Bills to our neighbours is 3.75% quoted by all the local Banks. I am glad I resisted the temptation of raising money this expensive way, because Silk Bills are promptly retired. Six months DP Bills sold at 3.75, rebated after one month at 3%, represent a finance costing 7.5%.[55]

At a time when the official Banque de France rate of discount fluctuated between 2% and 5%, the banker's space of manoeuvre was limited, and all possibilities had to be exploited before resorting to the more expensive service of the central bank: one Banque de France inspector remarked in 1910 that the Hongkong Bank agency in Lyons 'rediscounted its portfolio, all year round, at the market rate, [and] brought it to [our] branch only when the difference between the official and the market rate was not superior to one eighth of one per cent (generally from October to July)'.[56]

(iii *a*) The D/A bill, on the other hand, allowed the documents to be surrendered simply against acceptance by the drawee. The D/A bills were 'put aside, ready for discount when settled by the Agent'.[57] This type of bill was, therefore, in normal times, of greater interest to the agency, since it was saleable on the discount market, and could thus bring in ready cash. It was also, from the merchant's point of view, rebatable.

(iii *b*) Accepting a bill to put it for sale on the money market implied that the drawee was trusted by the agency's Manager, who had to be sure of his knowledge of the merchant's affairs. Of particular importance was the apportionment of D/A vs D/P bills inside the line of credit allowed to each customer, particularly in all the 'pig on pork' cases, where drawer and drawee were the same firm or person.

Judging a customer as 'working satisfactorily; profits probably small, but business devoid of speculation', de Bovis advised the Bank's London Office (the customer was dealing with a London-based China house) that the 'risk advised' should not exceed £100,000 made of '25,000 D/A and 75,000 D/P'.[58] This kind of ratio was fairly common, the D/P bill carrying a lower interest, being safer than the D/A bill.

Detailed information was gathered by the agency about its customers and transferred to the branches in the East and to Head Office. There were general assessments of the constituent's situation, which were always linked to the state of the silk market, such as this one:

Silk has not been profitable to the importer for the past three months, whereas the first quarter had been brilliant. For the big firms, it does not signify much when they disburse their profits, and start on the same level for another half-year. But we have many impecunious importers over whom we must keep a close watch, because when they cease earning the amount of their charges, they speculate in order to right themselves, and thus be saved from death by starvation.[59]

Naturally de Bovis compiled an Opinions List which he circulated to the branches and from time to time modified the opinion or answered specific queries, for example:

Geisenheimer – Paris: but for the risky nature of his advances, I would say that he deserves a higher credit than 2¼. He owns 4 million F in his business, besides private property that may be roughly estimated at 10,000 pounds. Out of the 4 million, 3 are invested in credit to his clients, out of whom he must be getting fat commissions.[60]

In the same letter, reacting to a query from Yokohama, de Bovis stated that he was asking Lazard frères in Paris about the standing of another house specializing in the *habutai* trade.[r] The answer from the Parisian bank came a week later:

Oppenheimer: no difficulties ever; discounts his own paper on arrival of each mail, and as the Bills were drawn DA, it shows clearly that he is not overtrading and that his till is full of spare cash. Lazard frères states that he has 1 million worth of goods in his private godown.[61]

Relations with the Banque de France

From 1881 to 1884 the Lyons agency was permitted to discount directly with the Banque de France; as a result of changes in French banking regulations, this privilege was cancelled and then in 1907 renewed. Bills were drawn on Lyons mainly by the Shanghai and Yokohama branches (73%) and also by Hong Kong and Canton. From 1884 the *présentation* of the Crédit Lyonnais to the Banque de France contained bills of several banks, but the majority were those of the Hongkong Bank.[62]

During the years 1885 to 1908 the Bank was either not mentioned at all in the reports of the Banque de France or only with a brief comment: 'Big business, which has, until now, given nice results'; 'Beautiful profits'. In July 1893: 'Big gains and big losses; good credit, which is nevertheless watched by the Crédit Lyonnais and the Comptoir National d'Escompte', followed in 1894 by: 'Is regarded, on the market, as working more cautiously now, after having been too ardent.' This obviously referred to the interim period between de Bovis's two stays in Lyons.

In the years that followed, the inspectors' opinion was to become more positive; it was nothing other than a synthesis of the opinions of Lyons' main bankers and merchants who sat on the Banque de France's local board with those of the branch manager. De Bovis had built his agency's goodwill well. 'Good constituency', said the 1898 report; 'Very good credit; Silk consignments. Gives the third signature on almost all the bills of exchange drawn on Lyons' or Switzerland's silk merchants domiciled in Lyons.' (But in the same report, exactly the same thing was said about the Yokohama Specie Bank, whereas the amount of that bank's endorsements was half of the Hongkong

---

[r] The *habutai* was a special type of Japanese *pongé*, the trade which seems, according to de Bovis, to have been fairly important with Eastern Europe. He commented in a letter to Yokohama of 28 November 1913: 'There must be something rotten in the *habutai* trade. I would not be surprised if the late war in the Balkans has cost heavy losses to all those who exported *habutai* to the South East of Europe.'

Bank's total.) In 1900: 'Reserves (in Hong Kong) equal to the capital. Very important branch in Lyons; big dealings in silk.'[63]

De Bovis's pleasure at the right to a direct approach can, therefore, be understood. In 1907 he wrote:

I have at last been able to open an account with the Bank of France, in the name of the Hongkong and Shanghai Banking Corporation. At distance, it may seem a small matter, but I may assure you we shall not only gain local credit, but also obtain discounting facilities, as our endorsement is accepted *direct* [that is, without the backing of a French signature] by the Bank.[64]

In 1908, the Hongkong Bank was listed among the presenters. That year, the Banque de France inspector's report stated emphatically how *au fait* de Bovis was of the details in Lyons' trading: 'The agent in Lyon, Mr de Bovis, is an intelligent man, who seems to be most listened to in business.'[65]

Until World War I, the agency was classified in the Banque de France's inspection reports as a first-class establishment. After 1913 the Hongkong Bank ceased to be mentioned as the reports focused on other developments; the right to discount directly with the Banque de France also ceased; a French signature was again required.

The Bank, the Lyons agency, and French Indo-China

The main development in the Lyons agency's business with Indo-China occurred during the inter-war period, but the origins go to the earliest days of the Bank. A Saigon agency had been opened in 1870 primarily to finance trade between Saigon and Hong Kong, particularly in view of investments in Cochin-China's sugar plantations. In the following years the Bank built up its business and appointed merchant agents in Haiphong and Hanoi; as the Bank profited fortuitously by the establishment of agencies in both Manila and the United States in connection with finance of Philippine trade with that country, so the Bank was thus well-positioned to finance the direct trade with France and the Lyonnaise region in particular by linking up its independently established agencies in France and the East.[66]

The Lyonnais merchant community placed their first hopes in the Tonkin, before the French conquest, in relation to their quest for silk supplies. After the Sino-French War of 1884–1885 and the founding in 1887 of the colonial entity of the Union Indochinoise, the Lyons merchants for the most part gave up their attempts to develop silk production in Tonkin and turned toward, *inter alia*, cement, mining, plantations, and general trade.

Ulysse Pila, one of the Hongkong Bank's most important Lyons customers, had been represented in the East as early as 1884, and his firm was the Bank's agent in Haiphong from 1887 to the end of 1893. Sometime during the years 1884 to 1886 he had founded a Haiphong-Hong Kong steamship company;

he also persuaded the mercantile community in Lyons that Tonkin was the ideal route by which French goods might be exported to the southern Chinese provinces.[67] When he founded his Union Commerciale Indochinoise in 1904, he opened an account for it in the Hongkong Bank's Head Office. The company required increasing credit limits – up to HK$100,000 in 1906 – and these were granted on the basis of de Bovis's official 'opinion'.[s]

De Bovis held the old silkman in high esteem but had to scrutinize the business of the Union Commerciale Indochinoise as closely as any other. With other bankers in Lyons, he was worried by the fact that 'for a young concern . . . they are a good deal locked up' by too many goods bought in Tonkin and being sold too slowly. He partially succeeded in obtaining from Pila and other directors of the company a personal guarantee for the credit extension required in Hong Kong. He also approved of the decision to increase the firm's capital from Fr5.3 million to Fr8 million. He must have felt justified later in his backing of the company requirements, since the Union Commerciale developed in a very promising fashion.[68]

In the south of Indo-China, where the Bank had opened an office in Saigon in 1870, another pillar of its business in the region was developing with the growth of the Bordeaux-based house of Denis frères, and of their relations with the Bank. 'We do a steady business with them, & again send you a few bills today, although they complain that our terms are dearer than through other Banks', wrote de Bovis to H. Hewat, the Saigon Manager, in December 1905.

Denis frères was probably not the only house realizing this difference in conditions since, even after the extended facility had been granted to Ulysse Pila's Union Commerciale Indochinoise, de Bovis had to advise (Sir) John C. Peter in Head Office that they 'ought to give us a share of the outward business, which all goes to the [Banque de l'Indo-Chine]'.[69] He further advised Hong Kong to refuse to renew the agreed overdraft if there was no *quid pro quo*, and added, 'Make them sit up a little, and they will be bound to come to you.'[70]

The relationship between the Bank and Denis frères was, however, strengthened over the next few years. The company became the Bank's agent in Haiphong (1901–1922) and in Hanoi after 1907. This closeness allowed de Bovis to make a sounder evaluation of the standing of these constituents, sending to Saigon and Hong Kong usual information about the firm's capital, profits, and trading procedures. He was careful to underline his role of strict transmitter, concluding that, whatever he could say about the parent company, the credit offered to the Saigon house was 'a local affair for which the Saigon agent has to put on one side of the scales all the advantages he derives from the

---

[s] Pila was also a director of the Syndicat du Yunnan, Ltd.

advance, and the risk on the other. He can also feel the pulse of a firm which does all its business in Indochina.'[71]

By this development of a more broadly based Indo-China connection, the Hongkong Bank was able to offset the loss of its Lyons silk business as the centre moved south to Milan. The attraction of the Bank was its Far Eastern branch network to the development of which the Bank's Board of Directors had given priority; to ensure its full utilization the Board for the first time set up an overseas bank on the Continent. It was a daring and successful move marred only by the initial decision to appoint Morel as Manager.

With its Head Office in Hong Kong the Bank viewed European centres perhaps more objectively than could London; indeed, McLean, as already noted, disapproved the innovation. Thus not only did Hong Kong provide a sound base for developing a regional China bank but it also permitted an evaluation of the Bank's requirements which were less dominated by London or City preconceptions, an advantage possibly never fully analysed by the Board and certainly not foreseen at the Bank's founding.

A parallel might be drawn to the history of the Bank in Hamburg, although unlike Lyons the timing there was dictated by the Bank's concern with the potential competition of a planned German competitor, the Deutsch-Asiatische Bank. The Hongkong Bank had much earlier rejected suggestions that it withdraw from Saigon and appoint the Banque de l'Indo-Chine its agent in French Far Eastern territory; its move to Lyons was to replace its agency dependence on a great domestic joint-stock bank, Crédit Lyonnais, and undertake business directly with Metropolitan France.

The Hamburg story is instructive in its similarities, but it should be told in the context of the Bank's overall German relations in Chapter 9.

APPENDIX: A SUMMARY OF JAPANESE PUBLIC LOANS WITH A HONGKONG BANK PARTICIPATION[72]

1   1897 Imperial Japanese Government 5% Bonds for ¥43 million= £4,389,583:6s:8d.

The bonds formed part of the Imperial Japanese War Loans of 1894 and 1895 for ¥250 million of which ¥125 million, including the bonds mentioned here, had been issued at 101½. Redeemable after five years but not later than 1950. Interest and principal payable in Gold Yen or at the option of the holder in London at fixed rate of 2s:0½d per yen.

Issued by: HSBC, Chartered Bank of India, Australia and China (Chartered), Yokohama Specie Bank (YSB), Samuel and Samuel, Capital and Counties Bank (CCB).

Refinanced by No. 20.

2   1899 Imperial Japanese Government 4% Sterling Loan for £10 million.

Issued at 90 for 55 years, redeemable by drawings after ten years. Underwriting commission 2%; Hongkong Bank's share about £250,000. Railway construction, steel works, and extension of telephone service.

Issued by: HSBC, Parr's Bank (PB), Chartered, YSB.

3   1902 Imperial Japanese Government 5% Bonds for ¥50 million= £5,104,166:13s:4d.

Issued at par, redeemable at par after five years but not later than 1956. Exchange at 2s:0½d guaranteed; bonds to be inscribed at the Bank of England. Hongkong Bank's share about £200,000 and commission at ½ of 1%.

Issued by: HSBC, Baring Bros, YSB.

Refinanced by No. 20.

4   1902 Yokohama City Waterworks Public 6% Loan for ¥900,000=£91,875.

Issued at 98, principal and interest secured on revenue of waterworks and municipal funds, redeemable in 22 years by annual drawings commencing 1904.

Issued by: HSBC, CCB.

5   1902 Osaka City Harbour Constructions 6% Loan for ¥3.5 million= £357,291:12s:4d.

Issued at 99, redeemable by annual drawings from 1905 to 1981, to be paid from the sale of reclaimed land and from City taxes.

Issued by: HSBC, CCB.

6   1904 Imperial Japanese Government 6% Sterling Loan for £10 million.

Of the total, £5 million to be issued in London at 93½; HSBC underwrote £235,000 at 2% commission. £5 million to be issued in New York by Messrs Kuhn Loeb and

Co., a portion of which was actually issued in Germany. Secured by prior lien on the Customs revenue; repayable after 5 April 1907 and on or before 5 April 1911.

Issued in London by: HSBC, PB, YSB.

Refinanced by No. 13.

7   1904 Imperial Japanese Government 6% Sterling Loan (second series) for £12 million.

Of the total, £6 million issued in London at 90½; £6 million in New York by Messrs Kuhn Loeb. Secured by Customs revenue and repayable after April 1907 and before October 1911. Underwriting commission 2%.

Issued in London by: HSBC, PB, YSB.

Refinanced by No. 13.

8   1905 Imperial Japanese Government 4½% Sterling Loan for £30 million.

Of the total, £25 million issued in London at 90; £15 million underwritten in U.S.; underwriting commission 2%; HSBC's share £400,000. Secured by a first charge on the Tobacco Monopoly Revenue. Repayable at par on or after 15 February 1910, not later than 15 February 1925.

Issued in London by: HSBC, PB, YSB.

9   1905 Imperial Japanese Government 4½% Sterling Loan (second series) for £30 million.

Of the total, one-third taken by each of three syndicates, U.S., German, and London; of the London syndicate, HSBC had one-third; issued in London at 90; Hongkong Bank to underwrite £300,000 for 2% commission and tender for allotment of £150,000 on behalf of the Bank. Secured on the Tobacco Monopoly Revenue. Repayable at par between July 1910 and July 1925.

Issued in London by: HSBC, PB, YSB.

10   1905 Imperial Japanese Government 4% Sterling Loan for £50 million.

Of the total, £6.5 million issued in London at 90; repayable at par on or after 1 January 1921 and before end 1930.

Issued in London by: HSBC, PB, YSB.

11   1905 Fusan-Seoul Railway 6% interest bonds for ¥4 million.

Issued at 95½ plus ½ of 1% commission to the company which arranged the terms and subject to the signing of the Peace Treaty. Redeemable in five to seven years.

Issued by: HSBC, Baring Bros.

12   1906 City of Tokyo 5% Sterling Loan for £1.5 million.

Issued at par, repayable between 1916 and 1936 on six months' notice. Principal and interest secured on revenue specially designated; underwriting controlled by Nippon Kogyo Ginko, Tokyo; issuing commission ½ of 1%, underwriting 1½%. Loan entirely on responsibility of Nippon Kogyo Ginko (Industrial Bank of Japan). Hongkong Bank's share £20,000.

Purpose: refinancing. Proceeds to be applied to repayment of all outstanding loans (¥5,505,000) and balance to harbour works, street improvements, public works.

Issued by: HSBC, PB, YSB.

13   1907 Imperial Japanese Government 5% Sterling Loan for £23 million.

Of the total, £11.5 million issued in London at 99½; repayable on or after 12 March 1922 but not later than 1947. Underwriting commission 1½%; Hongkong Bank's share £200,000.

Purpose: refinancing. Proceeds to be applied to the redemption of the Japanese Government 6% Sterling Loans issued in London and New York in November 1904 for £10 million and £12 million. (See Nos. 6 and 7 above.)

Issued by: HSBC, PB, YSB, N.M. Rothschild and Sons.

14   1907 South Manchurian Railway Co., Ltd 5% Sterling Bonds for £4 million.

Issued at 97, repayable 10 to 25 years by drawing at par or purchase. Principal and interest secured by guarantee of the Imperial Japanese Government. Underwriting commission 2%; Hongkong Bank underwrote £112,620, applied to hold £50,000, and received a total profit of £15,000.

The South Manchurian Railway Co. was a joint-stock company created by a Japanese Imperial Government ordinance of 1906 to take over and operate the railway between Dairen and Changchun, including branch lines to Mukden and Fushun, and to develop the resources of Manchuria.

Issued by: HSBC, PB, YSB.

15   1908 Industrial Bank of Japan Ltd 5% Sterling Bonds for £2 million.

Of the total, £1 million issued in London and £1 million in France. Issued at 97, repayable 1918–1933 by drawings at par or by purchase. Principal and interest secured by guarantee of Imperial Japanese Government.

Issued by: HSBC, PB, YSB.

16   1908 South Manchurian Railway Co., Ltd 5% Sterling Bonds for £2 million.

Issued at 97½, repayable 1917–1932 at par by drawings or by purchase if below par. Principal and interest secured by guarantee of the Imperial Japanese Government. On 17 December 1908 Addis noted in his diary that it had been subscribed ten times over.

Issued by: HSBC, PB, YSB.

17   1909 City of Osaka 5% Sterling Bonds for £3,084,940.

Issued at 97, repayable between 1919 and 1939 at par on six months' notice. Principal and interest secured by general charge on the revenues of the City. Addis noted in his diary on 1 May 1909 that this loan was a 'great success'.

Issued by: HSBC, PB, YSB.

18   1909 City of Yokohama 5% Sterling Bonds for £716,500.

Issued at 98, repayable at par from 1924 to 1954 on six months' notice. Principal and interest secured by general charge on revenues of the City. Proceeds for extension of the waterworks.

Issued by: PB, HSBC, YSB.

19   1909 City of Yokohama 6% Loan for ¥648,000 (£65,000).

Purpose: for the Gas Works.

Issued by: HSBC, PB.

20   1910 Imperial Japanese Government 4% Sterling Loan for £11 million.

Issued at 95, repayable from 1 June 1920 to 1970.

Purpose: refinancing by conversion and redemption of ¥43 million 5% War Loan Bonds of 1895/96 and ¥50 million 5% Bonds of 1901–1902. See Nos. 1 and 3 above.

Issued by: HSBC, PB, YSB.

21   1911 South Manchurian Railway Co. 4½% Sterling Bonds for £6 million.

Issued at 98, repayable 1921–1936 at par by drawings or by purchase if below par. Principal and interest secured by guarantee of the Imperial Japanese Government.

Purpose: partly refinancing, repayment of £2 million notes due 1 June 1911 and partly development projects, improvement of harbour works, increase in locomotive and rolling stock, extension of electric and gas works.

Issued by: HSBC, PB, YSB.

22   1912 City of Tokyo 5% Loan for £9,175,000.

Of the total, £3,175,000 issued in London; issued at 98, repayable 1916–1952 at par by drawings or by purchase if below par. Principal and interest secured by a first charge on the annual net revenues of the electric tramways and electric lighting of the City. Redemption may be accelerated by purchase, or after 1922 by additional drawings for whole or part. Proceeds applied to purchase electric tramways and electric lighting undertakings from Tokyo Railway Co. and extension of these works.

Loan was quoted at par but underwriters had to take up 52%. The Hongkong Bank underwrote £30,000 at 1½% commission.

Issued by: HSBC, PB, YSB.

Japan and Parr's Bank, a brief note[a]

The role of Parr's Bank as lead manager in many Japanese Government loans has been explained in the context of Japan's regard for old friends. The purpose of this note is to make the connection more explicit.

The Oriental Bank Corporation had been the Japanese Government's London banker; when it failed in 1884, the Yokohama Specie Bank was appointed, and the Alliance Bank and the London Joint Stock Bank were designated as depositories. The choice of the Alliance Bank was undoubtedly influenced by the presence of Alexander Allan Shand as a manager; he had earlier served the Chartered Mercantile Bank in Yokohama and had been subsequently employed as a highly regarded adviser on banking to the Japanese Ministry of Finance, 1872–1877.[b] In 1892 the Alliance was acquired by Parr's, and its connections with Japan increased; for example, Junnosuke Inoue, later president of the Bank of Japan and Finance Minister, studied banking with Parr's in 1897. The following year Korekiyo Takahashi, then Vice-President of the Yokohama Specie Bank and, from 1899 to 1911, Vice-President of the Bank of Japan, consulted with Shand in London relative to lead managing a syndicate to issue a £10 million loan (No. 2 in the list above).

Takahashi had, as it happens, been employed as a 'boy' by the Yokohama office of the Chartered Mercantile Bank, 1866–1867, at which time Shand had been the acting manager. Although this may well have facilitated later relations, the links between Japan and Parr's Bank had been developed independently. Undoubtedly it was Shand's standing with the Japanese financial authorities which was significant throughout.

---

[a] The information in this note was provided by Professor Kanji Ishii, Faculty of Economics, University of Tokyo.
[b] Shand is thus another who left the East in mid-career for a 'Home' position, see pp. 154–55.

3

HONGKONG BANKERS, 1900–1914

I am now a member of the staff of this bank. Its interests are my interests. Psmith, the individual, ceases to exist, and there springs into being Psmith, the cog in the wheel of the [Hongkong Bank] . . .

P.G. Wodehouse, Psmith in the City[a]

In the first fourteen years of the new century the Eastern staff of the Hongkong Bank increased by more than a third, from 156 to 214 officers, and, at the outbreak of the Great War there were some 75 juniors training in the London Office, waiting for 'orders' to go East. Despite this growth there would appear to have been no major changes in personnel policy. Although some cost-of-living and housing allowance adjustments were made exceptionally in Japan, such matters as salaries, pensions, leave, passages, and the always contentious restrictions on marriage remained in place.

This chapter is, therefore, focused on the consequences of growth and, developing from this, there follows an examination of the atmosphere, especially in London Office, which marked the larger organization. Opportunities for promotion remained virtually unchanged. What was different was the size of the more important offices and the impersonal elements which this fact, despite efforts to retain the concept of the Bank as family, naturally introduced. Nowhere was this more apparent than in London Office where the growing number of juniors gaining banking experience was not so much a consequence of the requirements of London Office itself (except during the rush of loan issues and related work) but a reflection of anticipated requirements elsewhere in the East.

There are, however, two other topics which must be recorded: first, the fact of the hardened rules relative to participation in public affairs; second, the passing of the early managers. Even with this additional history, however, this

---

[a] P.G. Wodehouse, *Psmith in the City* (London, Penguin edition, 1970), p. 31. The descriptions of the 'New Asiatic Bank', and its staff refer to the Hongkong and Shanghai Bank in which Wodehouse served as a London junior in 1900–1902. The references to banking and staff in the office are considered accurate and the personalities referred to have been identified. There is, naturally, a considerable fictional content throughout the novel.

chapter remains by the nature of events to be covered primarily one dealing with London.

A policy confirmed

Both J.R.M. Smith and Newton Stabb confirmed the Board's policy that it was 'undesirable for the Bank's officers to undertake outside duties and responsibilities'.[1] James Greig, the Bank's second Chief Manager, had served briefly as a substitute on the Legislative Council in 1872 and Thomas Jackson had been nominated as the 'elected' choice of the General Chamber of Commerce, serving from 1884 to 1886, but these were exceptions. Such exceptions continued to be made when the Bank was directly affected; thus as already noted T.S. Baker was permitted to accept an appointment to the Straits Settlements Legislative Council because the currency issue was under consideration, but H.E.R. Hunter, when Manager Shanghai, was instructed he could not become a member of the Shanghai Municipal Council. Charles Addis, Sub-Manager, Shanghai, was 'advised' not to join the board of the China Mutual Life Insurance Company of Shanghai, but he was appointed a Railway Commissioner and became the Bank's representative on the board of the Shanghai–Nanking Railway; this last was a British and Chinese Corporation responsibility and the Bank was the Corporation's banker and one of its managing agents in China; Jardine Matheson was the other.[b]

In supporting the Board's position on outside appointments, Newton Stabb was reflecting in part his own predilections. Except for his brief service on the Legislative Council in 1919, he was in any case consistent (see Chapter 1).[2]

The Bank and the China Association

The Board's firm stand relative to the Shanghai Municipal Council brought them in conflict with the policy of the China Association in London; the Association was anxious for strong British representation in Shanghai and feared that the Bank's policy of refusal to permit their chief local officer, Harry Hunter, to accept a seat would be followed by other major hongs.[3] The Bank was not 'officially' represented in the Association in the sense of a selected

---

[b] Charles Addis was a member of the Hankow Municipal Council in 1896, but the Agent's responsibilities, except at the height of the season, would have allowed him the time to participate in the less demanding affairs of that Yangtze port. In all these directives from the Board there were exceptions. For example, C.H. Wilson as Manager Rangoon was on the Legislative Council (1903–1904) and the Municipal Board of the Council of the Corporation of Rangoon (1901–1904) as well as being Chairman of the Rangoon Chamber of Commerce from 1902 to 1905 inclusive.

officer receiving formal Board of Directors' nomination or endorsement but many Bank staff individually sat on key committees and at least in London probably played a restraining role in the Association's more provocative discussions. On this particular issue, however, the Bank was subjected to severe criticism.

Sir Ewen Cameron, Sir Thomas Jackson, and eventually Sir Charles Addis were all members of the general committee of the China Association and undoubtedly 'spoke for' the Bank. A.G. Stephen in Shanghai and V.A.C. Hawkins in Yokohama were local committee chairmen, and both Gershom and Murray Stewart were active in Hong Kong. Even the reluctant Newton Stabb was a member of the Hong Kong committee, at least from 1913.

Charles Addis as London Manager

The position of Charles Addis as junior Manager in London was, however, an unusual one. He rather than Townsend succeeded Cameron on the boards of the British and Chinese Corporation and the Chinese Central Railways. This it is fair to point out was consistent with Addis's own experience in Shanghai and with Board policy.

But in December 1908 Addis was invited by the Governor of the Bank of England on the recommendation of the Foreign Office to become the British Censor (or adviser) to the State Bank of Morocco. Addis's first reaction was to turn down the offer, in line with Bank policy, as being too demanding on his time, but on being informed that the post was non-executive and advisory – there was a separate board of directors for the bank – Addis consulted Sir Thomas Jackson, then the Chairman of the London Consultative Committee, who told him, 'I regard this offer as a very great compliment not only to yourself but to the Bank, and I have not the slightest hesitation in advising you to accept it.'[4] Addis wrote to his old friend from Hong Kong days, Dudley Mills, that his duties would be much like those of a censor in China.[5] The position would, moreover, involve a voyage every two years to Tangiers and, on occasion, to Paris.

The original offer came on December 16, Addis agreed on the 18th and formally accepted on the 24th; with the support of Jackson, Addis had left the Board in Hong Kong no time to make an objection.[6]

Although his efforts in the field of China finance, a subject to be considered fully in Chapters 5–8 below, were directly related to his position with the Hongkong Bank, his contribution to China and related policies had a national impact and, on the day following the opening of the Bank's new building on Gracechurch Street in October 1913 (by which time Addis was senior Manager, London), he accepted a knighthood for eminent services in connection with China finance.

Eba much astonished as she had no idea it was coming. I received a great ovation on entering Bank. Clerks stood on desks & cheered.[7]

Very curious to be addressed as 'My Lady'. It seems like a play that must shortly be over.[8]

Sir Carl Meyer, who had watched Addis's development from his position on the London Committee, wrote, 'The honour conferred on Addis is a tardy recognition of his great services for China and British interests there during the last few years. It is a fitting landmark in connection with the new premises where we had a function yesterday.'[9] Addis was knighted by King George V on November 15, 1913.

As Addis's reputation in the City grew, so did the opportunity for him to render public service. This culminated in 1918 when Addis, then but the manager of a branch of a British overseas bank, became the first 'joint-stock' banker to be elected a director of the Bank of England; the bar against directors from clearing banks would remain for another half-century.

THE PROBLEMS OF GROWTH

The impact and statistics of growth

The most significant change in the Hongkong Bank was elusive; it is usually described as 'atmosphere' and stems in part from the growth of the Bank itself. When Addis joined the Bank's London Office in 1880, he was one of fifteen juniors who spent two to three years in London before leaving for the East. When Addis worked in Hong Kong in 1885, he was one of seven juniors. His contact with the Chief Manager, even from his first year, was therefore direct and significant; he observed Jackson; he learned banking in his presence.

In 1900 there were 48 juniors in the London Office, including the newly recruited P.G. Wodehouse; the number of juniors in the Hong Kong office had reached 17 and would grow to 26 by 1914. Once back in London, the great Jackson himself had in this context receded to the impotence of a legend.

H.E. Muriel (East in 1909)[c], who joined the Bank's London Office as a junior in 1905, catches both the light and the dark.

'T.J.' was Chairman of the London Committee and sat in the small room where the Committee sat, and which was truly the sole vacant space in all that overcrowded jammed together 31 Lombard Street. Consequently when [there was] any extra work, such as sorting loan coupons, it had to be done in the Committee Room; T.J. sat there almost every day from 10:30 to 4 p.m., and we lads sat at the long table with him.

Very rightly we considered this a great honour, that we, mere specs in the Bank's microcosm, should be there cheek by jowl with the great T.J. – a legendary figure, the

---

[c] The year in parentheses following the name of an Eastern staff member signifies his seniority, that is, the year he arrived in the East on his first tour.

famous Chief Manager who according to repute had 'made the Bank' . . . to us he was a hero, a figure of romance, as well as a man of very kindly charm who spoke to us quite freely, without any pomp or ostentation almost as if we were his great-nephews.

In my mind I see him now quite vividly, as the time came for him to leave to catch his train. There was competition among us to help on his long great coat with its astrakhan collar. Sometimes he would look at the two or three or four of us and bring out cigars from his pocket, always one less cigar than our number. 'Ye must toss for them', he'd always say.[10]

This was the Jackson who, as the seniors and guests left the formal annual dinner, would be pressed for his song. 'The old man got a soft hat and a stick from somewhere, took off his coat with the Order Star, threw it on the ground and sang "The Wearin' o' the Green".' And M.W. Wood, who went East in 1911 and became Manager Vladivostok, recalls playing the accompaniment.[11]

But when Muriel reached Hong Kong, he found what he described as a 'semi-cowed atmosphere'; from friends of London days there was a 'nice to see you but we can't talk now' reception. A.B. Lowson (East in 1897), who would rise to be Manager Shanghai, complained later that he felt physically sick whenever he set foot in the Colony 'by reason of the misery he had suffered as a junior straight out from home'.[12]

This may in part at least have reflected 'homesickness'. Nevertheless the personal touch, the professional impact of a brilliant banker, supplemented by home entertainment in the early Bank offset in the mind of a young Addis the burden of the work and the consequences of Jackson's personality – 'fiery, if you like, but I don't believe in a man who has not got a temper'.[13] To some in a later generation the regime as it developed during the chief managership of J.R.M. Smith was seen as the consequence of the Sir Thomas Jackson, who, 'for all his Irish *bonhomie*, his father-figuring towards the Staff and his reputation for personal generosity, was a slave-driver who ground out the last ounce of effort from his Staff – the minimum Staff to do the maximum of work'.[14]

The large number of relatively untrained men certainly required a change in policy, but apparently the necessary discipline was unsympathetically enforced by J.C. Peter (East in 1884) who, according to Muriel, was 'cordially disliked . . . as Chief Accountant'.[15] Peter's management of the Singapore office during the years 1911 and 1920 was also reputed to be severe – and a Singapore caricature showed him leaning over his desk with the caption, 'All day and every day, Sundays and holidays included.'[16] Peter's own dedication and abilities may have made him less understanding of the changing relationships, but it was under his management that V.M. Grayburn (East in 1904) was noticed and first brought to Hong Kong where he would eventually become Chief Manager. Opinions on Peter might best be summarized by the phrase 'very strict but fair'. Even Muriel is careful to stress that under the

Jackson regime – as under Smith and Stabb – first-class bankers had been developed.

It is right to comment that Muriel, whose musical talents make it fair to refer to him both as artist and banker, was particularly sensitive to these problems, although he himself enriched both his own junior years and Tientsin and Shanghai society by his contributions as a singer and amateur actor – in these latter activities he was often teamed with M.W. Wood and the pair were known as 'Nikisch and Gerhardt'. Muriel's own career, in which he was Agent Bangkok, then Manager Calcutta, and finally headed the London Office, was highly successful. His criticisms are, therefore, particularly interesting, and it is evident from the statistics that, for whatever cause, a banking career in the East was found by many to be unsatisfactory. Many indeed dropped out in London Office – they were unsuited for banking or found the profession, even in its embryo London Office form, unpleasant; alternatively, they left to be married, or were considered unsatisfactory even by a relatively lenient London management. The wastage could be as high as 50% of any year's intake.

The statistics of dissatisfaction

Turning to other statistics, of the 84 who came East between 1885 and 1899 and who were still on the Eastern staff in 1902 when Jackson retired, more than a third left the Bank before the outbreak of the Great War in 1914. The reasons reflect the range of problems confronting the expatriate businessman, and not only in the period under study in this chapter; they are probably relevant for later periods as well. In considering the following survey, it is important to recall that those who went East did so in the context of joining a 'service' and of remaining for a full career.

In the period 1902 to 1914 the number of Bank offices increased from 24 to 31, mainly due to new agencies opened in 1910. There were also new sub-managerships and sub-accountantships established in larger offices. Nevertheless even with these developments and the considerable wastage the normal time to appointment remained thirteen to fifteen years. For those ambitious and unwilling to wait, the alternative was usually in a brokerage firm – the other great hongs, for example, Butterfield and Swire and Jardine Matheson, had their own career services based on recruitment in Britain. Thus there was a necessary loss of many capable officers; there was no alternative 'selection' system.

Some, however, returned, usually with loss of seniority. H.J. Scott (East in 1885) and W.H. Wallace (East in 1884) left the Bank during the stock market boom of 1889; they rejoined in 1892. There was however a price to pay, and not only in loss of seniority. Of Scott's readmission Mrs V.A. Caesar Hawkins wrote to Addis, 'It was a great thing for him and his family as they were in miserable straits.'[17] Wallace eventually became Manager Amoy (see below).

J.K. Tweed, who had survived the Siege of the Legations, left the Bank in 1903 to become a broker with Bissett and Co.; he was for a time an agent for the short-lived Anglo-Japanese Bank. During the rubber boom of 1910 company speculation in Shanghai made the ambitious consider the stock market, and Grayburn after six years in the East submitted his resignation to join Tweed's own firm, Shaw and Tweed, much as another potential Chief Manager, Gershom Stewart, had done during the Hong Kong stock market boom of 1890. But the 1910 boom collapsed before Grayburn's resignation was effective and he was allowed to withdraw it.

'Heart and Soul Breaking Corporation'

Marriage was still controlled by the ten-year rule, which, after several *ad hoc* exceptions had been allowed, was reinstated. Newton Stabb might write to Addis of the joys of married life: 'I only regret Effie and I did not meet before. So many years of happiness wasted. It is a great help having a wife to go home to at the end of a day's work.'[18] But two years later writing as Chief Manager, he explained to Sir Thomas Jackson that 'Marriages too early are detrimental to the service' – even when the bride was the daughter of the British Minister, Sir Claude MacDonald.[19]

Muriel records the bitterness the rule caused, noting that it was morally bad and led to drink as a release. Another solution, however, was resignation from the service of the Bank. Mrs Eba Addis visited the young wife of T.W. Ogilvy, a junior who had come East in 1895 and resigned in 1898/99 to marry early. 'Charlie and I in afternoon go out to call on little Mrs T.W. Ogilvy; he late of our Bank. Went into cotton mill to get married. Is now dismissed. Poor things, with a baby 2½ months old. She, very nice and ladylike. Going home in spring.'[20]

Marriage created its own problems even among those most dedicated to the Bank's service. This was a factor in David McLean's unwillingness to accept the Board's offer of the chief managership and of Jackson's own request to retire to London Office in 1886; it also explains McLean's need to visit Chislehurst and advise Mrs Jackson when these plans were upset. Her reaction is recorded in a letter to Charles Addis. 'It is certainly a great disappointment. We always hoped to avoid what falls to the lot of most Eastern people, being separated from husband or children, but it has come to that after all . . .'[21] Andrew Veitch's plans to retire to the English countryside (see Volume I, Chapter 15) had been delayed by a late marriage and the fall of silver; indeed his plans were never fulfilled – as Addis observed, 'There are other calls to part alas! which no mortal man resists.'[22]

Nor was the problem only with God or the East. A.M. Townsend had tired of New York and was quietly seeking a position in Britain during the 1890s.[23]

Charles Addis himself, loyal to the Hongkong Bank, had resisted the lure of a senior position in the National Bank of China or the Trust and Loan Company in 1890, but by 1896 Addis, then Agent Hankow, had initiated a savings plan which would enable him to retire to Britain by 1905 and thus avoid the 'separations contingent upon Eastern life'.[24] In this context the continuing fall of silver was a personal blow, which, Eba recorded, he took well. In 1886 his brother George, although apparently prospering in the Chartered Mercantile Bank, had for similar reasons and after seventeen years in the East seized upon the unsolicited offer of a senior post in England, the sub-managership of the Bank of Liverpool; in 1901 George died painfully of cancer and Charles Addis wrote immediately as a candidate for the vacant post. He was unsuccessful.[25]

In fact, the strains of child rearing under Eastern conditions had told on Eba Addis and the prospect of a 'family separation inherent in an Eastern career' – the Addises were thinking of the usual long separation from their children or the return of the mother with her children to Britain – was causing Addis to reconsider his career.[26]

In 1902 he turned down an offer to become Hong Kong manager of the International Banking Corporation; it would not have taken him to Britain and, barring this, his loyalty was to the Hongkong Bank.[27] Then in 1902 he bought a bungalow in the central China hill station of Kuling, 1,220 metres above Kiukiang, explaining to Mills that 'It seems like tying myself to China to buy a house, but with falling exchange and the prospect of a home billet growing more remote as I grow older, it is to that I must reconcile myself.'[28] Ironically he would return to London in 1904 on leave and would remain. Yet when the fortuitous and unsolicited London Office assignment was confirmed Addis wrote to J.R.M. Smith, the Chief Manager, 'It is impossible to turn my back on the East, where I have spent so many happy years, without a touch of regret . . .'[29] The story is revealing.

As previously noted Addis had been marked for the eventual managership of the Shanghai office but with Cameron's sudden illness and wish to retire, Jackson again intervened, this time without controversy, urging that Addis should remain in London to serve under A.M. Townsend, who would be promoted to Cameron's senior position. Addis's friend, Gershom Stewart, wrote from Hong Kong:

I have heard of your appointment as No. 2 in London with mingled feelings. From a domestic point of view it is a most joyful change and I congratulate you most heartily. To see the children grow up and be with them is after all probably the best possible way you can discharge the highest duties accorded to you here below.

From the point of view of the Hongkong and Shanghai Banking Corporation and as an Englishman I regret you are not going to 'end up' in the Far East.[30]

The social priorities of this Hong Kong stockbroker are significant; the strain of separation was of great importance in assessing the joys of life in the East. Nor was this (at least in Addis's case) merely a formal statement of pious sentiment; Addis was a family man; his interest in the development of his ever-increasing family, his wife gave him thirteen children, is fully documented in his correspondence and diaries.

The health factor

Health, surprisingly, could be a problem either way, although usually it was a factor cutting short a career in the East. When the long-serving R.H. Cook left Hiogo under a cloud in 1903 – his juniors had been speculating – he returned to England on leave and would have returned to a less important post, had not death intervened. The late marriage system placed a burden on the widow in such cases; she still had responsibilities to the children. One solution, if a son had begun training in London Office, was to send him East as soon as possible. Percy de C. Morriss, for example, had gone East in 1890 on the prompting of David McLean. His father was obviously ailing (see Volume I, p. 416); the junior's salary would be sufficient once in the East for part to be remitted Home – or at least would relieve the father of subsidizing his son's meagre pay as a London Office junior. H.R. Cook was another case. He had already been in London for three years; in 1906 he was sent East but almost immediately suffered a nervous breakdown and within six weeks had been sent Home.

This suggests another possible factor leading to wastage, the fear of immediate responsibility in the East. Wodehouse, at least, seriously records that such was his immediate expectation.[31] There were two contrary factors at work. First, the dream that once East 'natives' would do all the work while the white man sat with his feet on the desk. The second dream was the opposite: the white man would take on immediate and heavy responsibilities, the banker's version of Sanders of the River, the banking counterpart of the District Officer who managed an area larger than England.

The work was in fact tedious and hours were long; the responsibilities were sufficient for a beginner, if lacking in excitement and, in the larger branches, challenge. This point established, the next problem was one of cultural adjustment. The junior was, after all, in the East. But the Bank had no offices in the 'ulu' or up-country where contact with the 'true' East might be made; its agencies were at Treaty Ports or their equivalent. The 'cultural shock' was at least partially cushioned; there were the facilities of the cricket club (be it in Amoy or Staten Island, New York), the bachelors' mess or chummery, and the heavy work schedule. Nevertheless there were those who could not handle the change, who wished they had never come.

The continued absence of an adequate retirement policy forced *ad hoc* solutions. For those highly qualified who were found unfit to return to the East, one such solution was to recommend an appointment to the London Office, but there were obvious limits to this. In 1902 when R.M. Roe attempted to join London Office after thirteen years in the East, the Board of Directors noted sympathetically that, 'London Office deprecates filling London Office with sick men from the East.' Roe retired with a gratuity.

J.C. Nicholson's problem was different. After retiring as Manager Singapore, he was appointed Sub-Manager, London, in 1907. The Addises watched his health deteriorate from asthma – 'Nicholson up from Bexhill to lunch with me. He is better but quite reconciled now that we have put [C.W.] May in his place to go off again to Switzerland for a time. Poor chap! I fear he is fighting against fate. The climate of London is too much for him.'[32] That same year he faced his fate and returned to the East as Manager Batavia, replacing the veteran M.C. Kirkpatrick. Nicholson remained there throughout the Great War; when he retired after 41 years in the East the Board granted him a gratuity of £20,000, a relatively generous sum even in 1921.

Personnel policy was an integral part of the total societal structure. From the first the newly established Bank had determined its policies only after consulting the older exchange banks; members of the Board were familiar with standards in their own firms and would be reluctant to introduce terms more favourable in the Hongkong Bank. Business life in the East was based on certain assumptions and no single institution had reason to initiate radical changes. The Bank's Board of Directors might rightly pride themselves on relative generosity, the juniors had confirmed Jackson's reputation as a chief with the interests of the staff in mind, and the minutes of the Board are replete with individual decisions affecting, for example, pensions to elderly watchmen in Bombay and the widows of long-serving shroffs in Singapore. But the 'junior system', the marriage rules, and the other codes of behaviour were written into the British social system in the East.

One innovation should be noted. The Board resolved in 1908 to require employees when hired in England to agree to serve in the Volunteer Corps. There had been considerable debate in Hong Kong over the reluctance of the leading hongs to permit time off for such activities, but the decision was made.

Yet this was in keeping with traditional policies and values. These would not yet be changed.

Nor was there need. For while there has been a description of dissatisfaction and wastage, the net growth of the staff first noted in this chapter remains the dominant fact. The Bank retained sufficient officers for its purposes; furthermore, while it lost potentially able men, it also retained many others of at least equal qualifications. The remainder of the chapter must deal with them.

The passing of the early managers[33]

Victor Kresser had died as long before as 1883; **James Greig**, the Bank's second Chief Manager, in 1911. Their history has been told (see Volume I, Chapter 7). The Bank's third Chief Manager was Thomas Jackson; he will be considered below.

John Walter, although only an Acting Chief Manager, acted during a leave from which Jackson did not intend to return; had Walter's administration been successful he would undoubtedly have been confirmed in his post. He was first Sub-Manager London, then Manager Shanghai, Inspector, and in 1897 G.E. Noble's replacement as junior Manager with Cameron in London. In 1902 he became a member of the London Committee on the death of Noble; he retired in 1906 to make way for Sir Ewen Cameron whose health had recovered sufficiently for him to again take an active interest in the Bank's affairs. Thus despite his misfortunes as Acting Chief Manager, Walter was able to serve the Bank in the highest positions virtually until his death in 1907.

Walter had been eventually succeeded as Chief Manager by **G.E. Noble**; thereafter it was Noble who took precedence and, after serving with Cameron as a London Manager until 1897, retired for health reasons but requested a seat on the London Consultative Committee. This was agreed to by the Board with some degree of enthusiasm, but A.M. Reith wrote to Charles Addis in December 1899 that Noble was very shaky and 'an interview with him is rather a painful business'.[34] Noble died, as noted above, in 1902.

François de Bovis left the East in 1893 and remained Agent Lyons until 1922. He died in 1930.

David McLean, the Bank's first Shanghai Manager, is barely mentioned in the records after his departure from the London Consultative Committee in 1894. When McLean died in June 1908, Addis was on holiday in Scotland with his wife Eba; they attended the funeral at Alford with Allan Cameron, son of Sir Ewen Cameron and partner in the firm of Panmure Gordon and Co., and Dr Patrick Manson, McLean's brother-in-law. Charlie Beveridge, the son of McLean's first Scottish manager and who had come East to Shanghai in 1868 to serve under him, was also present. There was a special train to

Alford from Aberdeen, and Addis described the scene at the shooting estate of Littlewood above the river as it flows quickly through a gap in the hills, forested on the slopes and covered with gorse at the crests. 'Laid old David McLean to rest in the little cemetery below his place.'[35]

Sir Ewen Cameron, KCMG, left Shanghai to become joint (but junior) London Manager with Thomas Jackson; fortunately for the Bank this overly talented pair were separated and Jackson returned to Hong Kong, leaving Cameron to develop the early merchant banking operations of the Bank, to pave the way for the even greater successes of Addis in the period from 1905 to 1913. In 1902 Cameron was operated on for appendicitis, from which he apparently recovered. The doctor was privately concerned that there remained the danger of a malignant tumor, and certainly in 1905 Cameron was once again an invalid; his death was thought imminent.

From this he again recovered and, with John Walter willing to resign in his favour, was offered a seat on the London Consultative Committee. He was even able to travel to India to visit his son. The *Times* correspondent, Valentine Chirol, who travelled home on the same ship, remarked on his 'wonderful resurrection'.[36] Cameron had a relapse in 1908 and was unable to attend the Bank's First Annual London Dinner that February, but he again recovered. Attending to City affairs to the end – 'even on his sickbed devouring the City article', Sir Ewen Cameron died on December 10, 1908, at the age of 67; his funeral was in London and his ashes were buried in Inverness.[37] During his management loans to China and Japan of over £80 million were negotiated with the involvement of the Hongkong Bank; he had been awarded honours by both the Chinese and Japanese Governments.

Charles Addis wrote, 'I have lost a very dear and faithful friend of 25 years standing. What an inspiration he bequeaths of courage and cheerful patience.'[38] It was Cameron who had given Addis the chance in Peking, who had, with Jackson, watched his career during the difficult days of de Bovis's chief managership, and who had encouraged his assignment to London in 1905. The Board of Directors stated without hyperbole that 'by his death the Hongkong and Shanghai Bank loses a wise and able counsellor and one whose name will always occupy a prominent place in its history'.

As for the last years of **Sir Thomas Jackson** himself, his substantive role is little mentioned in the available records. As Chairman of a highly prestigious London Consultative Committee his influence on the Bank's successful merchant banking role, given his other City connections, must have been considerable, but it is undocumented.[d] In 1910 Jackson became the Chairman

---

[d] Jackson was on the London Committee of the North China Insurance Company and served on the boards of the London County and Westminster Bank, the Union Discount Company of London, the Royal Exchange Assurance Corporation, and the Yorkshire Penny Bank. No reference to these activities or to his later chairmanship of the Imperial Bank of Persia is found even in the comprehensive and personal collections of Sir Charles Addis.

of the Imperial Bank of Persia, and he was joined on the Board by his cousin V.A.C. Hawkins, who, for reasons of health, had resigned from the Hongkong Bank in 1908 as Manager Yokohama.

The best source for Jackson's last years, at least as far as the history of the Hongkong Bank is concerned, is the Addis diaries. In the first years of Addis's London managership there are frequent references to business encounters with Jackson: before negotiating with the Colonial Office and the Treasury relative to Board-approved policies Addis consulted him on such matters as the increase of the note issue; there were differences on which London wished to advise the Board as to whether the Bank should open in Malacca or Kuala Lumpur; Jackson wrote to J.R.M. Smith on Addis's work with the China and Japan loans. Yet there were already occasions when Jackson was described as 'flapping around'; if only he would go on vacation, Addis wrote, much work could be done. For Jackson sadly there was nothing left but work; it was too late to find other interests in his remaining years.

Certainly in 1911 Jackson was closely involved with loan affairs, as Eba Addis noted in their diary:

Long day with Americans, French and Germans over the Currency Loan. [Mrs Addis dined with them at the Savoy.] Thos Jackson and Carl Meyer the only other *British* there. Charlie [Addis] walked down the Strand into City at midnight with T.J. who remembered past years leaning on the arm of his old disciple.[39]

Jackson was also involved with the management arrangements in London. Both Jackson and Smith, for example, cabled Newton Stabb in Hong Kong advising the appointment of H.D.C. Jones as 'junior Manager' London, the appointment being 'not necessarily permanent'.[40]

Addis, who had been approached concerning the general managership of the Royal Bank of Scotland in 1910, was, just a few days after taking over as senior Manager in London, offered the chief managership of the Union of London and Smith's Bank at £5,000 or more. Jackson immediately wrote to Stabb in Hong Kong to raise Addis's salary from his £2,500 to at least £4,000; the Board responded with £4,500, and Addis remained.[41]

And yet, not surprisingly, Jackson was already fading. As early as 1905 Addis was writing, 'I see Jackson restless in his leisure and eager for an excuse to flee from his country solitude to the bustling town.'[42] This was not the answer. In 1908 when Jackson and Addis lunched at the Royal Exchange, he was not yet 70, but it seemed as if his life's mission had been fulfilled and he was waiting.

A solitary man, he clings to old friends. What a nemesis is business! When the time and opportunity for rest and leisure comes at long length it comes too late. The taste for it is vanished. There is nothing left but ennui on the one hand or to toil on unceasingly on the other. 'Nor let me die before I have begun to live.'[43]

And then again in 1915, 'Poor old Jackson! His merriment is mighty offensive at such times as these we are passing through. . . . Jackson is sadly aged and worried and restless. Poor man, I hope he will rest.'[44] Four months later, on December 21, 1915, Sir Thomas Jackson died. Sir Charles Addis wrote to the Chief Manager, (Sir) Newton Stabb, a full account.

At noon on Tuesday he was talking with his usual vivacity in my room from which he passed to his own. There he appears to have fallen asleep in his chair and to have passed peacefully away without waking. It was, for him, an enviable death, to pass, with his natural force indeed abated by age, but with his faculties undimmed, in the Bank he loved so well, surrounded by those with whom he was accustomed to go out and in as a father.

His was a commanding personality . . . tempered by a tender and playful disposition which engaged the affection of all with whom he came in contact.

Great and many were the public services he rendered. His most enduring monument, to my mind, is the standard of commercial morality which he set throughout the Far East. Nothing that was not generous, nothing mean, underhanded or tricky could abide his presence and he leaves to those that follow him a noble and inspiring example of unselfish devotion to duty.[45]

Stabb, who had last seen Jackson during Home leave in 1914, wrote a personal tribute addressed to Lady Stabb, the former Effie Townsend:

In his day, which is almost before you can remember, he was a great man. A real leader, large hearted and generous and not self-seeking. We were all glad to follow him. Latterly he became feeble and often querulous, though at times his old spirit would light up again.

It was he who welded the Staff into 'a service' and so long as he was at the helm, there was always a fine esprit de corps among the men.[46]

Sir Thomas Jackson was buried at Stansted on December 24, and in the cold and deluge of rain, a gathering of old friends said their final farewells to a man who had meant so much not only to the Hongkong Bank but to them all personally.

In recording the passing of the Bank's great Managers, there should be a pause for others. Some at least can be mentioned by name: in 1906 a Portuguese clerk, C.J. Gonsalves, whose all too brief extant diary has been quoted in Volume I, died after 42 years' service – he had been with the Bank since the beginning; the head cashier Bombay, Temooljee Pestonjee Setna, retired in 1907 at the age of 84 on full salary of Rs300, which he lived to enjoy for just six months. A gratuity was then paid to his invalid daughter. A.J. Dinez of the Shanghai staff resigned after 40 years service; he was 68 and was granted a pension of Ts110 per month. The death was recorded in 1913 of M.A. de Carvalho, who had been sent from Hong Kong to Shanghai probably in 1865. When he retired in 1879 with poor eyesight he had been described as old, but he married in 1886 and had been receiving a pension of $800 per annum ever since. The Board considered it had been generous and voted not to continue the pension to the widow; a terminal gratuity of $800 was paid instead.

In 1914 A. Perrin of the Saigon office died while on leave in France. He had joined the Bank in Saigon in 1872. As if in anticipation he had married his mistress in 1913, and the Board voted the widow a gratuity of Fr20,000.

The memories of the Bank's first days were ending at all levels. This history turns again to those presently responsible for the Bank's affairs.

Hongkong Bankers in the East

The post-Jackson settlement

When Sir Thomas Jackson retired in 1902 the Board of Directors not only selected his successor, J.R.M. Smith, but they made plans for the future. These, for various reasons, were not fulfilled. The planned career of Charles Addis, then Sub-Manager Shanghai, was probably Manager Shanghai in succession to H.M. Bevis – and after that perhaps Chief Manager. As previously recorded, Sir Ewen Cameron resigned while Addis was on leave in London, and on Jackson's urging, with Smith quite willing, Addis became junior London Manager.

This upset the hopes of the more senior J.P. Wade Gard'ner, who apparently expected to follow the sequence of A.M. Townsend and move from New York to London. He might well have done so had Addis's career stayed on course. Addis's move to London also left the Shanghai succession in doubt, a problem compounded when Bevis, on an extended leave in London in 1906, committed suicide in the Thatched House Club. Smith solved the problem by appointing H.E.R. 'Harry' Hunter as Manager Shanghai. Hunter had been brought down to Hong Kong to be Smith's Sub-Manager, much to the temporary concern of Addis, and he had then become the Inspector of Branches, a sequence which Smith himself had gone through; perhaps Hunter too was being groomed.

To summarize the points made in Chapter 1, the Board had also to deal with V.A.C. Hawkins. He had been appointed Inspector of Branches while waiting for a senior managership to open. With the death of David Jackson in 1903, Hawkins was sent to replace him in Yokohama; but the Shanghai and New York positions never opened, and he was not appointed Acting Chief Manager when Smith went on leave in 1906; Hunter was again brought down from Shanghai. Hawkins went on leave in 1907 and retired for health reasons; he joined the Board of the Imperial Bank of Persia. The former Manila Manager, H.D.C. Jones, was sent to Yokohama, and A.G. Stephen was Manager Manila.

In Hong Kong Smith had replaced Hunter as Sub-Manager with J.C.

Table 3.1 *The Hongkong and Shanghai Banking Corporation*
Long tenures as Managers which began in 1902–1913

		Number of years served
Shanghai	A. G. Stephen, 1912–1919	8
Amoy	W. H. Wallace, 1902–1912	11
Foochow	C. H. Balfour, 1905–1920	16
Hankow	H. G. Gardner, 1912–1920	9
Yokohama	R. T. Wright, 1911–1923	13
Manila	A. M. Reith, 1911–1919	9
Singapore	Sir John C. Peter, 1911–1922	12
Johore	G. W. Wood, 1913–1918	6
Batavia	J. C. Nicholson, 1909–1920	12
Calcutta	W. K. Dods, 1905–1921	18
Bombay	C. H. Wilson, 1907–1920	14
Rangoon	R. C. D. Guinness, 1911–1921	11
Hong Kong	Sir Newton J. Stabb, Sub-Manager, 1909–1910, Chief Manager, 1911–1920	12
	A. H. Barlow, Sub-Manager, 1911–1924, Chief Manager, 1924–1927	16
London	Sir Charles S. Addis, 1905–1922	17
	H. D. C. Jones, 1912–1932	21
Hamburg	F. T. Koelle, 1906–1920	15
New York	J. P. Wade Gard'ner, 1902–1919	18
San Francisco	T. S. Baker, 1912–1921	10

ª Read with Tables I.15.4 and II.10.8.
Note: certain Managers, e.g. Dods and Koelle, were Accountants in the same office immediately prior to their managership.

Peter, but Newton Stabb had been brought down from Shanghai and after a brief session as Manager Saigon, where he replaced H. Hewat (East in 1880), returned to Hong Kong to take over from Peter. Finally in 1910 Smith resigned and Stabb became Chief Manager, at which time no senior Manager (with the exception of A.M. Townsend, the senior Manager London) was where he had been expected to be when the Board made their projections eight years earlier.

Later developments
Many agencies enjoyed a continuity of managership. This is shown in Tables 15.4 (Volume I) and 10.8, which largely overlap this period. A list of those who had long tenures during the period 1902–1913 inclusive is shown in Table 3.1.

J.C. Nicholson was Manager Singapore from 1901 to 1906 and then returned to England to become Sub-Manager London. As noted elsewhere in this chapter, he returned to the East for health reasons. Nicholson was succeeded in Singapore by **T.S. Baker**, but with the final retirement of **W.H. Harries** at the age of 70, Baker went to San Francisco.

In 1902 E.H. Oxley was still in Hankow, E.G. Hillier in Peking, D.H. Mackintosh in Tientsin, C.B. Rickett in Foochow, M.C. Kirkpatrick in Batavia, T.McC Browne in Bangkok, R. Wilson in Colombo, de Bovis in Lyons and Harries in San Francisco. By 1914 of these veterans only Hillier and de Bovis were still in place.

The Bank Manager's garden, Amoy

In contrast perhaps with the lives of managers in major ports was that of the Hongkong Bank's Amoy Agent, W.H. Wallace. Born in 1861, at seventeen his participation in an orchid hunting expedition to South America began a life-long avocation. He joined the Bank's London Office in 1882, went East in 1884, resigned during the Hong Kong stock market boom in 1890, and rejoined in 1892. He won the Hong Kong tennis championship in 1901 and then was transferred to Foochow. In 1902 he was appointed Manager Amoy, where he remained until his retirement in 1913 (see Table 3.1). A contemporary commentary states that his garden, adjoining the Bank house in Amoy (where great banners in 1984 were to proclaim 'Welcome back Hongkong Bank'), was one of the 'finest in China'.[e]

Harry Hunter

H.E.R. Hunter (East in 1882) was a cousin of James and W.G. Greig (see chart of relationships in Volume III); his hostess was his sister and he was known in Shanghai as 'the Prince of Bachelors'. Fond of horse-racing he was a steward of the Shanghai Race Club. His career in the Bank brought him to the managership of Shanghai, a position of almost equal importance to that of the Chief Manager although for that reason it was, with one exception (A.G. Stephen), a terminal appointment in the East. The period of his managership involved acting as contact between Hillier in Peking and Addis in London, especially when there was any involvement in Shanghai as with the Shanghai–Nanking and the Shanghai–Hangchow railway negotiations. There was also work with international banking groups involving the Boxer Indemnity and custodianship of various Chinese Government funds. According to A.S. Henchman (East in 1903), the Bank's Shanghai Manager in the 1930s, Hunter was over-strained during the share market boom of 1910 and

---

[e] This interest in flowers was apparently in the family and when considered with his early South American experience suggests a relationship with the famous naturalist A.R. Wallace. When Sir Charles Addis retired to Frant in 1933 and sent for a consultant on roses in October 1937, he was surprised to learn he had engaged W.H. Wallace's younger brother.[47]

the subsequent collapse; he retired in 1913 and returned to London where he became a director of Hambro's Bank and the Imperial Bank of Persia.[48]

He was first referred to in the limited records of the period for his survey of the Bank's prospects in British North Borneo and in 1891 he went to Manila to assist with the Jurado case. He was Agent Bangkok in 1896, Agent Batavia in 1898, and then in 1899 Sub-Manager in Shanghai under Wade Gard'ner. His call to Hong Kong to work under Smith and his acting chief managership in 1906 have already been noted.

Hunter was undoubtedly one of the men who, following the Jackson Era, kept the Bank prosperous and maintained its role as the leading bank in the East.

E.G. Hillier

With the self-effacing J.R.M. Smith succeeded by the publicity shunning Newton Stabb, for many observers the Hongkong Bank must have been visible only through Charles Addis in London, E.G. Hillier in Peking, and Harry Hunter in Shanghai. This was the era of the China loans, of the Hongkong Bank as merchant bank, and it was reasonable that its Peking Agent should become a public figure. But in addition to his role and his ability, Hillier was blind and among foreigners he became one of the great characters of the ancient capital.

Hillier was born in 1857 the posthumous son of Charles Batten Hillier, a former Chief Magistrate of Hong Kong who died in 1856 shortly after taking up an appointment as H.M. Consul in Bangkok; his mother was the daughter of the Rev. Dr Walter H. Medhurst, a well-known Protestant missionary. A graduate of Cambridge University, where he was a member of Trinity College, Hillier was for a time tutor to Robert Buchanan Jardine; he came to the East as the secretary to the Governor of British North Borneo. He then joined Jardine Matheson in Hong Kong.[49]

As he was a student of the Chinese language Hillier's application to join the Bank in 1883 was supported by Ewen Cameron, then Manager in Shanghai, for the same reasons that the latter encouraged Charles Addis. Thus Hillier, as an exception, was never a London junior. Sent north to Tientsin in 1885, Hillier was well placed when Cameron decided to attempt to open an agency in Peking. This Hillier undertook and despite Chinese bankers' opposition managed to hold the doors open until its role was seen to be beneficial to the capital. Hillier then went on leave, and it was Addis who actually got the sub-agency fully operative. Then came the uncertain tenure of H. Hewat, who complained bitterly of life in Peking, and the door was open to either Hillier or Addis to take over again.[50]

At this point Addis made the decision to be a banker rather than a China expert; he accordingly returned to the ranks and was transferred from North China. Hillier returned to Peking and with the official opening of the agency in 1891 was appointed Agent. But in 1893 he too felt the need for decision, and he requested Wade Gard'ner, the Shanghai Manager, for a transfer to a post where he might gain more banking experience. Only the Bank's recognition of his special status – and with it an increased salary – caused him to willingly remain in what must have seemed, from a banking point of view, a backwater. But he had made a choice, the opposite of Addis's; he would be the Bank's China expert and, it is fair to say, learn banking as well.

In 1896 and 1898 he played a key role in the negotiation of the second and third Indemnity loans, and his salary was raised from $400 to $500 a month. His gratuity for the 1896 loan was, moreover, £2,000, the Peking agency was enlarged, and he was *de facto* promoted. His skilful role in the various loan negotiations will be considered in Chapters 5–8 below.

He first felt eye strain in 1896 and upon completion of the loan negotiations went to Shanghai for treatment. He was told he had lost the sight of one eye; the other was threatened with glaucoma. He left for Vienna, but Dr Fuchs told him it was too late; nevertheless he underwent a painful but unsuccessful operation in London before returning to China.[51]

Hillier was absent on leave during the Boxer Rebellion. On his return to China, he spent considerable time in Shanghai as the British representative on the International Commission of Bankers relative to the Boxer Indemnity; for this service he received the CMG in 1904. His brother Sir Walter Hillier, KCMG, sometime H.M. Consul-General in Korea, was suffering from the disease-laden dust of North China; both brothers also had glaucoma, and E.G. Hillier finally suffered virtual total blindness. In 1907, the Bank, having declined to accept his resignation, authorized instead an allowance of £100 per annum to enable Hillier to employ a private secretary.

As the *Times* obituary stated:

For the next quarter of a century all who knew him – and it may generally be said that everyone in Peking, Chinese or foreign, knew 'Hillier of the Hongkong Bank' – saw day by day a heroic struggle of the spirit against this physical handicap. For with him it was not more than a handicap. He overcame it and won his race by will power and indomitable courage.[52]

A Catholic, Hillier played the organ in the Church of St Michel in the Legation Quarter of Peking. When after the Boxer Uprising his blindness had become more severe, he was led about by a young Chinese boy, and he would come down early for dinner to play the piano. As his second wife and sometime secretary described him:

He loved to ride, his mafoo riding by his side, his pony trotting when the mafoo's pony trotted, pacing when the mafoo's pony paced. He also loved to swim, as he felt he was his own master in the sea. He learnt to type and would type out drafts for letters and agreements. He used to play on a small organ old Gregorian music. He had a keen sense of humour and possessed a trenchant wit; he also had a wonderful memory.[53]

Sir Robert Hart, the Inspector-General of the Chinese Imperial Maritime Customs, remembered him for his brilliant knowledge of the Chinese and for his attempt to create a system of braille suitable for that language.[54]

Independent in spirit he yet had many friends. One of them was Heinrich Cordes, the representative in China of the Deutsch-Asiatische Bank, with whom the Hongkong Bank was working under agreements which dated back to 1895. Cordes would take Hillier for walks in the city, a German and an Englishman. There would be a sequel.

The seniors in London

The senior posts

Ever since the arrangement whereby Cameron, working in London under Jackson, had been granted permission to refer to himself as 'Manager', there had been two London Managers, the senior being in charge and fully responsible. When Jackson returned to the East in 1893, Cameron became senior and G.E. Noble was the junior Manager. Noble retired in 1897 and the position was taken by the then Sub-Manager, John Walter, who in turn retired in 1901 to be replaced by A.M. Townsend from New York. The two London Managers, Cameron and Townsend, were brothers-in-law.

When Cameron resigned in 1905, Townsend was appointed senior Manager. It was at this time that Addis was appointed to the joint managership, an arrangement which lasted until the end of 1911 when Townsend retired. Addis was promoted to the senior post and H.D.C. Jones took the junior position. As both Managers were entitled to refer to themselves, without qualification, as 'Manager London', contemporary writers and historians have naturally been confused, especially in view of Addis's greater public exposure, even while the 'junior'.

There was, in addition, a Sub-Manager's post, usually occupied by a returned senior member of the Eastern staff, with sound technical banking qualifications. This was first held by David McLean; his successor was William Kaye; it had a great tradition for excellence, although it might be fairly said that the post when held by Cameron was, in fact, up-graded. The subsequent reestablishment of the post for Noble was a sign of expansion in the London Office. In 1900 the post was held by H.T.S. Green (East in 1884), who had had experience in the New York office of the Bank as the Accountant from 1892 to 1899; he resigned from London Office to accept a position with an American bank. When Addis began his London assignment, the Sub-

Manager was G.W. Butt, formerly Manager Singapore. He resigned (retired) in 1907 and was replaced by J.C. Nicholson, also from Singapore who, as noted above, returned to the East in 1909 on grounds of health; he found the Eastern climate more salubrious than London's. The post was then filled by J. MacLennan (East in 1883), the Agent Kobe, then on leave in Britain. He was known popularly as 'the ancient Briton' and even referred to in official correspondence as 'the ancient'.

A.M. Townsend

Townsend (East in 1870), the first London Office junior to be employed for Eastern service, had been appointed Manager New York in 1880 and remained until 1901. It had not been an entirely happy time, and he had been out of touch with the East. The Board had permitted him annual rather than five-yearly leaves; it may be that he had been able to keep in touch with London and brought unique qualifications to the London managership. Certainly his old Japanese contacts, based on his Yokohama position in 1878, became important during the negotiations for the issue of the Japanese loans on the London market.

When he first reached New York, most of the banking business with the East was financed by the American banks, but, recorded Townsend in his 1937 memoirs, as the trade increased the finance gradually came to the Hongkong Bank.

He settled with his family in Englewood, New Jersey, and commuted by train and ferry across the Hudson.

Our amah attracted a good deal of attention with her native costume and trousers, and in the local paper appeared the following note: 'The "IT" that drives the baby carriage is a "SHE".' Later on, the Amah was unwell and the Doctor got her into a New York Hospital, where, at first they hesitated about taking in a Chinese. I called at the Hospital a few days later, and found her up and in full charge of the Ward and a great favourite.[55]

The Townsends later moved to Long Island.

He recalls that on visits to Washington he stayed at the Embassy with Baron Julian Pauncefote (1828–1902), the first British representative in the United States to rank as Ambassador. Pauncefote had been Attorney-General in Hong Kong in the early days of the Bank and had advised on its organization and ordinance of incorporation.

As Manager New York Townsend would appear to have employed 'New York Office Juniors', some of whom presumably left the Hongkong Bank for other banking positions in America. There were two exceptions: the first was Newton Stabb, a Newfoundlander; the second was A.G. Kellogg (East in

1906), an American citizen. Both of them resigned in New York and rejoined the London Office as juniors in the normal way.

Given this background and aside from his Japanese interests, Townsend appears to have accepted J.R.M. Smith's decision that Addis was to take over Cameron's primarily merchant banking role. He was overshadowed in the correspondence and Bank records by Addis, whose role outside the Bank would naturally have this consequence.

When Townsend retired at the end of 1911 he was invited to Hong Kong and, like Addis ten years later, made as it were a triumphal circumnavigation of the globe, being especially welcomed in Hong Kong, where his daughter Effie was the wife of Newton Stabb, the Bank's Chief Manager, and Japan, where Townsend's role in Japanese overseas finance brought him contacts with the senior financial statesmen and an audience with the Emperor who bestowed on him the Order of the Rising Sun.

When I arrived at the palace (in evening dress) I was ushered by two powdered foreign footmen in silk stockings, into the State Drawing Room, where I was received by the Prime Minister, a charming man, who spoke English perfectly and told me that his wife was at the time at Chicago attending some Woman's Conference. He shewed me the reception room and explained the procedure in the presentation to the Emperor. The Emperor would be standing at the head of the room with a general on each side of him – and as we approached, he and another Minister would walk on each side of me, and we would bow three times as we walked up the room.

The Emperor would shake hands with me and make a short speech, thanking me for my services (which he would interpret to me). I would then reply (which he would interpret to the Emperor). The Emperor would then again shake hands with me, and we would retire, walking backwards and bowing once.[56]

On the world tour he visited Manila and travelled north on the railway the Bank had done much to finance. Crossing America he returned briefly to New York and then to London where he became involved in the controversy as to whether he should be a member of the London Consultative Committee. In fact there had been some difficulty relative to J.R.M. Smith's membership, presumably on the grounds that Smith knew nothing about London and therefore could provide no expert input to the Committee's deliberations. This dispute had been settled in Smith's favour in 1911.

By this time Addis had shown a certain weariness or perhaps impatience with Townsend, who is sometimes referred to as 'Uncle' Townsend in the diaries, and the retired senior London Manager did not go on the Committee until 1916, after the death of Jackson. Addis was certainly one of those opposed to Townsend's membership; as the latter was the Chief Manager's father-in-law, the 'snub' may have affected relationships between Stabb and Addis and subsequent developments should be read with this possibility in mind.

Addis and the London Office

When in 1905 Addis settled with his family at 6a Primrose Hill, he began a London residence which would last until his retirement as Chairman of the London Consultative Committee in 1933.[57] In the more than 28 years, that is, until he was 70, that Addis worked in the City, he had grown in stature; he had become a 'power' in the City. Having first developed an expertise through China finance and a knowledge of the working of the Chinese Government, by providing expert and concise advice as required by the Foreign Office, the Colonial Office, and the Treasury, he then became increasingly intimate with the senior staff members of the Bank of England, and his merchant banking responsibilities placed him in contact with the leading personalities of the City – the bankers, brokers, and international financial agents.

He was so little known beyond the range of experts that his name seldom appears in the histories and, where he is mentioned, his position or background is usually described inaccurately. Perhaps this is why his advice was much in demand; he gave it and let others stand the glare of publicity. Not that he was a power behind any throne; he gave his advice openly; it is all recorded. But he never stepped into the political arena as a direct participant. He remained a banker, albeit one who by the 1920s was outgrowing the Hongkong Bank and its Eastern orientation.

In the years from 1905 to 1914, however, Addis was very much a Hongkong Banker.

In his diary Addis records that on March 20, 1906, 'Our good and faithful Peter left us to return to China with the Geary Gardners. An honest faithful modest lad. We all liked him. He wept bitterly at parting.'[58] In September 1907 there is an entry, 'Nana, our old Chinese nurse came to see the children. She is a faithful old soul.'[59] And on another occasion, Eba Addis notes that she called on 'Miss Denby', the young lady Addis knew a generation ago in Peking. 'Miss Denby' was by then a widow, Mrs Wilkes, and was accompanied by her son. She was 'a sweet charming white-haired woman of about 50. The ideal friendship revived after a generation.'[60]

The personal links with the East remained for a time, but were breaking one by one. Addis would return only on his retirement, but the contemporary experts in the East would say that by then he was out of touch.

This perhaps is the key to the role of the Hongkong Bank's London Office. Senior Managers returned to important positions in London but, unlike other Eastern bankers, they were not returning to Head Office. If they were senior and experienced, they could give strong advice to Hong Kong, even as McLean had done, as Jackson and Smith were to do, but the decisions were made in the East. There was no countermanding the man in the field on the basis of an expertise some ten years out of date – this would plague the managers of the Mercantile Bank; the Hongkong Bankers, the management in Hong Kong, may have had other problems, but they could listen to Addis, to Townsend, and to other seniors in London; they would then make their own decisions.

London Office had, however, other roles to play in the life of the Hongkong Bank.

The Office, and to some extent Addis's private home, became at times a social centre, but one in which valuable discussions were held and important business friendships renewed. It was to Addis's home that the future president of the Chinese Republic, Sun Yat-sen, came to seek funds for his planned new government; here also those Hongkong Bankers coming and going on leave passed through, and Addis recorded his opinions as their careers progressed. Here too the members of various financial reform committees argued the potentials of China's currency proposals, or financiers from Europe met to attempt the complex compromises which could be put formally at the next day's sessions and thus keep alive the concept of coordinated finance of China's requirements.

Charles Addis and his wife Eba could watch their own family grow up, with all the successes and failures which a large family are bound to have; they could also see the problems of separation of those going East, telling the young wife of her husband's death in Batavia, visiting a dying colleague, G.W. Butt, with a cancerous tongue and larynx removed and death not far away, betting a bottle of claret that he would survive.[61]

And there was always the Bank, with its routine work, its spectacular successes in Eastern loan issues, the excitement of the day of issue – with the Bank rugger team holding back the crowd, the quiet walks back to the City in the evening with TJ, the quick trip across the Channel to Paris, Berlin, and back to Paris as key negotiations seemed to be falling apart, and then the quiet of a Scottish vacation, of riding in the park, of walking with the children and coming home across London to be present when the children had their nursery tea.

The Addises also entertained from time to time the young London juniors in their home. There were, furthermore, what were at first the annual Bank 'smokers', informal gatherings with champagne and oysters in the City. Perhaps reflecting the formalization of London Office, or perhaps the growing recognition by the London Managers that the Bank should play a greater social role as a British overseas bank in the City of London – offsetting perhaps the fact that this was not Head Office the annual 'smoker' in 1908 became the First Annual Dinner. There would be seven before the outbreak of the Great War.

The First Annual Dinner was indeed a major social event. Held at the

Trocadero on Shaftesbury Avenue there was provision for 121 guests (@ 21s:1d=£127+52 cigars and sundries for a total of £137:15s) who had been formally invited by 'The London Committee and Managers'. Sir Thomas Jackson was in the chair, Charles Addis proposed the toast to the guests, and the Chinese Minister, H.E. Li Ching-fang (1855–1934), nephew and adopted son of Li Hung-chang, made the formal reply. Carl Meyer of the London Consultative Committee and chairman of the Pekin Syndicate proposed 'the Staff', and A.M. Townsend (for the London staff) and V.A.C. Hawkins (for the Eastern staff) made the replies.

If the Bank had convinced the authorities that it could act directly in the City despite the overseas location of Head Office, it now set about to prove its ability in a social role. The entertainment for this first dinner included songs sung by H.E. Muriel, but he left for the East shortly afterwards and there was no in-house replacement; the entertainment became professional.[62]

The second dinner had as the guests of honour the Japanese Ambassador, H.E. Enjiro Yamaza, and Sir Robert Hart, with Byron Brenan proposing a toast to the Chairman, A.M. Townsend. Henry Keswick, W.M. Blackie (of the London Home staff), and H.E.R. Hunter were among the speakers. It was perhaps at the third dinner, in December 1909, that there was a historic note; Sir Thomas Sutherland, the man who more than any other could claim to be the 'founder' of the Hongkong and Shanghae Banking Company, Ltd, gave his memories of those hectic weeks in which he beat the proposed Bank of China representative to the capital resources of Hong Kong (see Volume I, Chapter 2).[63] The formal reply by the guests was given by Count Mitsui, another historical comment, for the Bank had long been closely involved in the overseas financing of the key Japanese trading and manufacturing empire he represented.

The guests included those most closely involved in the Eastern affairs of the Hongkong Bank, especially visitors from the East. These were gatherings which rivalled the annual dinners of the China Association, but they were particularly marked because, despite the array of notables, they remained primarily focused on the affairs of the Bank and were attended by staff assigned to London or visiting on leave. It was at these functions that the Bank was spoken to, that Addis launched his trial balloon on university education, and that the Rev. George Owen, Professor of Chinese at King's College, urged the study of the Chinese language – matters to be considered in detail below.

9, Gracechurch Street

The Bank was outgrowing its leased quarters at 31, Lombard Street. All descriptions suggest it was chaotic and cramped, and the Board of Directors agreed that freehold property should be sought and developed. This too was right for the Bank's London image; as the long-established exchange bank became more prominent in Eastern merchant banking, it was seen to need greater space and seen also to have the resources (and resourcefulness) to acquire it. Behind the scenes, it is true, the Bank learned once again that it had been in violation of its ordinance, but that story has been told in Chapter 1.

The site eventually chosen was an area of 12,000 square feet, approachable from four sides, from Gracechurch Street (it was No. 9), Corbet Court, Bell Yard and St Michael's Alley, giving it, the *Banker* asserted, 'one of the largest spaces, on one floor, devoted to banking in the City of London'. The architect was W. Campbell Jones.

A banking hall of unusual loftiness has been erected, which will take the whole of the working staff of the Bank which has usually to come in contact with the public. The walls and columns of this hall are all faced with marble of soft hues, and the woodwork generally is in Cuban mahogany. At the far end from the main entrance in Grace-church Street a staircase gives access to a suite of rooms for the use of the London Committee, which is virtually the London directorate of the Bank. These rooms are lined with Italian walnut, handsomely carved. The managers' rooms are situated just beyond the staircase, and they are almost completely panelled with a very handsome wood, known as the Australian silky oak, which, we believe, has been used for this purpose for the first time in London. The lighting of the Bank is greatly assisted by three glass domes, in addition to the windows.

The building is what is known as a steel-framed structure, that is to say, the skeleton is framed up with girders and stanchions and then closed with stones and brick. This form of construction was specially necessary on this site since the building had to be recessed back on each story in order to avoid interfering with the light of neighbouring buildings. In addition to the banking hall the bank will occupy two basements, and the rest of the floors above will be let as offices, excepting the top floor, which will contain a luncheon club for the Bank staff. In the basement there are extensive strong-rooms, with walls of great strength, fitted by Chubb and Co., and no pains or expense have been spared to make the building as up-to-date and as complete as any structure of the kind in the City of London. Special attention has been devoted to ventilation, the air being continuously ozonized by means of an elaborate plant, and thus the staleness of atmosphere which often characterizes large buildings of this kind is avoided.[64]

Almost as if it were a conscious supplement, the Bank's new sports pavilion was opened with a speech by Addis on June 14, 1913. On October 22, his new building on Gracechurch Street was completed and the Bank celebrated with an At Home which some 200 persons attended for the cold collation and 60 for tea. Among the guests was the Chinese Minister, Liu Yu-lin, and the London manager of the Yokohama Specie Bank, K. Tatsumi.

In 1915 Addis discovered that the Church had a right of way by the Bank's windows and the negotiations to have it stopped were lengthy. Finally the Bank agreed to make the church graveyard into a public garden at a cost of £284:16s:1d, and the problem was ended.[65]

In the new building there was room not only for expansion but for ancillary activities. On the Luncheon Club, there is more to relate in the sections that follow, but when old Hongkong Bankers refer to the Bank in London, they refer to 9, Gracechurch Street. For those that saw it, and it survived as the Group's London headquarters until the early 1970s, it epitomized the visual conception of a City bank. Although Wodehouse wrote of the earlier Lombard Street office, the story can be easily transferred in the imagination to Gracechurch Street; the grandness of the halls matched the seeming grandness of the senior Managers as they passed before the eyes of the London Office juniors – once they had their 'orders' they could go East, once East they could work for 30 years, and then perhaps return to play at last the leading role in the scene they were then witnessing.

And it is to these juniors that this history now must turn.

THE JUNIORS AND LONDON OFFICE – A FIRST APPROACH

'The Boys Bank of London'

The London juniors – recruitment
The story may be apocryphal but it catches one mood of London Office.

A customer annoyed at some incompetence and complaining to anyone willing to listen, angrily asks Henry, the dignified Bank messenger, 'Look at the way this Pass Book has been written up! Do you call this a Bank?' To which the messenger responds, 'No, Sir, this is an institution for learning young gentlemen to become bank clerks.'[66] And it was said that, whereas elsewhere there were bankers pretending to be gentlemen, in the London Office of the Hongkong Bank there were only gentlemen pretending to be bankers.

This makes no allowance for the young Scots. They however were accounted for by the so-called 'porridge trap'. The agents of Eastern banks would, it was alleged, dig large pits on the altogether uninhabited moors of Scotland, place a bowl of porridge therein, and thus trap the native youths who roamed wild in search of food. Once secured (no pun intended) they were shipped down to London and trained as bankers.

In fact those joining the Hongkong Bank for Eastern service were supposed to be properly introduced, have served in some other relevant establishment for one to two years, and be selected as the result of an interview and written examination. But by common testimony the introduction was not difficult to secure, the interview was perfunctory, and the written examination designed to give the management an excuse for turning down a candidate without offending his referee. A final judgement on the role of the written examination is difficult; those retired staff members we interviewed had all passed. The prior work actually performed, with the exception of the Scottish candidates who worked in Scottish banks, was so elementary that it served little purpose in itself (except perhaps as a test of maturity). Little had changed since A.M. Townsend attended for his interview in the first years of the Bank – or, indeed, since Anthony Trollope applied to join the civil service.

Thus there were congregated in the crowded office of 31, Lombard Street a large number of young men, innocent of purpose, leavened by a London staff whose ability to train was erratic, and headed by three or four Managers returned from the East who kept aloof and whose very passage through the banking halls was marked with reverent or irreverent awe (depending on the mood) as they walked grandly to and from mysterious appointments.

There is little wonder then that the impatient dropped out and those without self-discipline were asked to leave. There were those, possibly the majority, with genuine though probably baffled interest and pride in the Hongkong Bank, the pride of the new boy in public school who, though totally at sea, associates immediately if confusedly with the traditions and purposes of the institution to which from the first day he most certainly belongs. These faithful nevertheless search for something familiar, something by which to orient themselves; the Hongkong Bank juniors found it not only in the fact that those about them were in similar circumstances, that the hierarchy was similar to that which they had left behind in school – masters, senior boys, junior boys, staff – but particularly they found that which they almost all had in common – sports.

In the formal interview the young man was asked if he played games; what else could the old experienced banker from the East ask the youngster who knew nothing about banking or the East? The Mercantile Bank was smaller and would have trouble putting a good side in the field; they turned to swimming. But the Hongkong Bank, at least until the acquisition of the soccer playing British Bank of the Middle East in 1960, developed two good rugger teams and its New Beckenham sports grounds had facilities for cricket, tennis, and squash. It was during these pre-Great War years that the role of sports developed, it was during these years, as the junior staff increased, that such a development was needed.

Even as the new Bank building on Gracechurch Street was being completed in 1913, the Board in Hong Kong authorized a new Athletic Club pavilion, which would serve not only as a focus for athletics but also as a social centre for those juniors who took lodgings, partly for this reason, in the Beckenham area. V.M. Grayburn was first noticed as a determined captain of rugger, responsible for initiating the Bank Sports Day despite official apathy; it became a major event in the Bank's social year. Before going East in 1904 Grayburn sought Sir Thomas Jackson's support for funds to purchase a

Championship Cup; Jackson came up with the grand sum of £70. After Grayburn's day the sports continued to flourish and the Bank boasted international players.

To be accurate, however, not all the juniors came from British public schools or the banks of Scotland. One came from Staten Island, New York. In 1900 A.M. Townsend as Manager of the Bank's New York agency received an application for employment as clerk from a young American school-leaver, A.G. Kellogg; there being no vacancy, Townsend turned him down. On the following Monday morning, however, Kellogg showed up for work, informing Townsend that he would come without salary until a vacancy was available. This took Townsend aback but, admiring his approach, he employed the youngster. When Townsend became a London Manager in 1902 he recommended Kellogg, who, as E.M. Bishop had done from Calcutta office, joined the Foreign staff through the now mandatory process of serving as a London junior. Kellogg ventured to the City in 1903, went East in 1906, and was eventually appointed Manager New York in 1937; he retired in 1949 after 50 years' service with the Hongkong Bank.

Life in London Office – the standing orders

> The practice of throwing pellets of paper about the office must be discontinued.
> 13 July 1893.[67]

Problems began at 0940 hours – it was difficult to get juniors to arrive on time and at this point, ten minutes after the official office hours began, the sign-in book was removed by one of the messengers and taken to the Accountant. Latecomers had to report; frequent offenders had their annual increment reduced or cancelled.

Both Grayburn and Henchman, the latter to become the Shanghai Manager during Grayburn's chief managership, suffered the penalty for excessive late arrivals; the list of defaulters suggests, however, that there was little correlation between daily on-time arrival at the London Office and excellence in exchange banking. Perhaps the rules did more to encourage initiative, to devise stratagems for avoiding being reported – hold on somehow to the sign-in book, for example – or work out schedules which would permit departure from 'digs' on a train leaving say four minutes later. These devices became part of the folklore of Hongkong Bankers.

The first notice relative to late arrival is dated January 1886, it was repeated in December 1887, November 1900, July 1901, November 1905, and January 1919. A similar need for repetition may be observed over the prohibition against smoking during office hours; the rule led to juniors taking longer over tea breaks, lurking in corridors, sitting in the basement – all for a smoke. 'Owing to the liability to contract blood-poisoning through the habit of putting pins into the mouth which have been used to fasten documents together, especially documents from the East, the Staff are warned against the practice.' (January 15, 1902)[68]

More serious were the indications that some juniors were dangerously in debt, for which the only solution was a discharge from the Bank's service. Underlying too many of the circulars was the suggestion of lack of discipline – 'the increased lack of *carefulness and sense of responsibility*' (July 1907), 'attention of the foreign staff is drawn to the lack of discipline in the office generally and to the rowdyism which is so prevalent after hours' (March 1912), '. . . to the increased number of complaints . . . regarding mistakes made in connexion with the transfer of funds from the East, the posting of payments and cheques to wrong accounts . . .' (August 1919).[69]

H.E. Muriel put the whole matter succinctly when he wrote, 'I entered London office in Lombard Street in 1905 from the Westminster Bank; the change from a formal ordered strict regime to the undergraduate atmosphere of the Hongkong Bank was very pleasant though rather startling . . . about half of us were reasonably serious over our work . . .'[70] The statistics bear him out.

There were other, more routine circulars: the reading of newspapers during office hours was forbidden; the need to spread out the two or three-week annual holidays led to July, August, and September being reserved for more senior officers; the need to complete routine work within office hours was stressed and an extra payment for refreshments or meals was made only for overtime authorized on balance nights or for other special assignments.

Finally, there were repeated reminders that a junior destined for Eastern service who, for whatever reason – behaviour, competence, health – was ineligible when 'orders' came would be summarily dismissed with six months' pay. Transfer to the Home staff was not a solution for those who, though competent, were for example debarred from Eastern service through failing the medical examination or wishing to marry; transfers did occur, but they were exceptions.

The juniors saw the authors of these Standing Orders, the department heads and managers, as Dickensian characters, probably not far removed from the caricatures in Wodehouse. The most comprehensive set of comments comes from F.E. Nicholl who was in London Office from 1909 to 1913. A sampling reveals the following:

The managers: Sir Thomas Jackson. T.J. to everyone . . . In daily attendance. A magnificent man of great charm. He was kindly to juniors and always avoided fuss. Faithful to the square bowler.

A.M. Townsend. A venerable figure with snow white hair and pink complexion enhanced by white moustache and a tuft under the lip.

C.S. Addis. Possessed of a commanding presence and outstanding qualities.

H.D.C. Jones. A bulky man with a genial if erratic manner and was known as Jumpy Jones.

John MacLennan. Sub-Manager. He was called 'the Ancient Briton' and one could imagine him looking well in a sheepskin armed with a club. A kindly soul.

Home staff (dates are those of joining the Bank): W.S. Edwardson (1885). 'The Barber' in charge of securities. A florid manner and given to washing his hands with invisible soap.

H.C. Carruthers (1886). 'The Flea'. Very short with grey beard.

W.F. Spalding (1905). A £2 a week stenographer who by intense study and application became an authority on Far Eastern Exchange and was the author of several textbooks.

H.L. Rowett (1873). 'Uncle'. A Dickens character in frock coat and silk hat with a wide brim. Suffered from senile decay and was almost reduced to tears if thwarted. Titular head of Share Department because no one had the heart to turn him off.

K.L. Gordon (1889). Actual head of the Share Department and originally on Eastern staff but he did not go East. Bosom pal of Gershom Stewart, M.P., who came in for a chat with Gordon almost every day.

S. Broadbent (1886). 'The Skipper'. No. 2 in Share Department. Given to sudden ejaculations, for example, 'Rumjohn, will the night soon pass?'

A. 'Sandy' Moncur (1890). The one member of the Home staff whom the juniors revered. A choleric Scot with a rasping tongue but a grand instructor of the young and a splendid fellow.

J.S. Davies (1887). Stiff and formal but a great rugger enthusiast.

G.O.T. Hawkins (1906). Associated with Saturday morning shopping at Leadenhall Market, invariably returning and showing his purchase with the remark, 'There's a fine piece of fish for you.'

Charles. White mutton chop whiskers.

William. Brother of Charles [both feature in *Psmith in the City*]. An ex-railway signalman who used to tap messages at tea time with his spoon on the cup.

Henry. Bearded like the pard and a slight stammer. A specialist in growing roses.

Alfred (fat) and George (thin) brokers men.

And there were Frank, Fred, Percy (the last mentioned in charge of the tea room), Tom (in charge of poste restante letters and well-versed in the movements of the Bank's overseas constituents). Albert and Sydney were office boys.[71]

Of Spalding there will be more to tell in the inter-war period, but his importance is correctly stated.

The Luncheon Club

In today's City of luncheon vouchers or company dining facilities the problem of proper eating on a junior's salary is one of dietary rather than financial concern, but it was a serious matter at the turn of the century. Writing in 1954 P.G. Wodehouse tempered his recollection of two enjoyable years with the Hongkong Bank by remarking, '... but I can still remember my dismay when I realized on the first morning that all I would be able to afford in the way of lunch was a roll and butter and a cup of coffee. I had come straight from school, where lunch was a solid meal.'[72]

The founding of the Luncheon Club in 1913, that is, with the opening of the new Bank building at 9, Gracechurch Street, though authorized by the Board, is attributed to the concern of the then senior Manager, Sir Charles Addis. Although tea had been available in the Lombard Street office, lack of space had prevented implementation of any larger scheme. The need arose from the fact that juniors were paid so meagre a monthly stipend that they were tempted to economize on meals. Addis himself when a junior had suffered from what one doctor diagnosed as symptoms of 'starvation' when he virtually collapsed in the street during one of his routine walks home, despite the fact that he had already borrowed from relatives to supplement his salary.[73] Consistent with the traditional reluctance to raise the basic salary, the London management devised the Club 'in the interests of the staff'.

In the circular announcing the management's decision, the staff were informed that 15s:0d per month (messengers 2s:6d) would be deducted from their salary in advance; the scheme was apparently compulsory. In return the Bank would provide free of cost to the Club (i) the kitchen and lunch room, (ii) gas, (iii) 5s:0d per member per month to the funds of the Club, (iv) waiters for the first year as it was expected that the Club's own funds could afford this once it was in full operation.

The result of this cooperative funding would be a lunch consisting of joint, two vegetables, sweet, bread, butter, *and* cheese – except on Saturday. (Many years later, in 1941, an elderly Sir Charles would note in his diary that the exigencies of war had led to cheese being counted as a meat dish.[74]) Mineral water and beer were at 1d a glass. The specimen menu for Monday was roast leg of mutton and rice pudding, and the combinations on other days were equally certain to bring back memories, happy or otherwise, of boarding school. On Friday, before the custard and stewed prunes, there was fish, but this the circular assured the members was not compulsory – an alternative joint would be provided.

The Club was to be managed by a committee of four, of whom two would be appointed by the Bank, one by the Home staff, and one by the Eastern staff. There is no statement as to whether the chairman, who was a Bank appointee, would have a casting vote.

'The Managers take this opportunity of stating that no afternoon tea will be served in the Bank after leaving [Lombard Street].'[75]

The Wodehouse version[f]

During his two years with the Hongkong Bank, P.G. Wodehouse was already

[f] The legitimacy of testing the realities against the Wodehouse version is confirmed by the use of oral history interviews covering the inter-war period. There is an underlying unity in the entire

contributing paragraphs for the 'By the Way' column in the London *Globe* and experimenting with other writing projects. His progress from department to department in the Bank yielded him little in the way of banking information, but he nevertheless caught an atmosphere which, as described in his *Psmith in the City*, has been certified as authentic by retirees who were in London as late as 1930.[g]

The fall of silver adversely affected the fortunes of the Wodehouse family, going up to the Varsity was no longer practical, and P.G. Wodehouse, whose father having served in Hong Kong as a magistrate would be known to senior management, went, apparently without previous commercial experience, directly into the Hongkong Bank. Thus in the novel Psmith's friend Mike Jackson is confronted by his father:

> 'I understand perfectly how keen you are to go to Cambridge, and I wouldn't stand in the way for a minute, if I could help it. . . . I'm just as anxious to see you get your Blue as you are to get it. . . . I can't afford to send you to Cambridge. I won't go into details which you would not understand; but I've lost a very large sum of money since I saw you last.' . . .
>
> During his absence a vacancy had been got for him in that flourishing institution, the [Hongkong Bank]; and he was to enter upon his duties, whatever they might be, on the Tuesday of the following week. It was short notice, but banks have a habit of swallowing their victims rather abruptly.[76]

After describing the soulless experience of securing 'digs' near Dulwich, where Wodehouse attended public school, he has Mike Jackson report for his first morning at the Bank.

> As he stood near the doorway, one or two panting figures rushed up the steps and flung themselves at a large book which stood on the counter near the door. Mike was to come to know this book well. In it, if you were an *employé* of the [Hongkong Bank], you had to inscribe your name every morning. It was removed at ten sharp to the accountant's room, and if you reached the bank a certain number of times in the year too late to sign, bang went your bonus.[77]

Mike then reports to the 'Manager'.

> 'Jackson? Ah, yes. You have joined the staff?'
>
> Mike rather liked this way of putting it. It lent a certain dignity to the proceedings, making him feel like some important person for whose services there had been strenuous competition. He seemed to see the bank's directors being reassured by the chairman. ('I'm happy to say, gentlemen, that our profits for the year are £3,000,006-2-2½ – (cheers) – and' – impressively – 'that we have finally succeeded in inducing Mr.

1900–1940 period. For an amusing and instructive essay on this theme, see Christopher Cook, 'The Hongkong and Shanghai Banking Corporation on Lombard Street', in King, ed. *Eastern Banking* (London, 1983), pp. 193–203.

[g] Allowance must be made for (i) hyperbole, (ii) the eccentric and not altogether satisfactory character of Psmith, (iii) the changes made for the purposes of the novel, e.g. the name of the bank, the fact that the Head Office was in London, that the 'manager' of the novel is probably the 'Accountant' responsible for juniors, etc., and (iv) for 'Cambridge' read 'Oxford'. The messengers and department heads can, however, be positively identified.

Mike Jackson – (sensation) – to – er – in fact, to join the staff!' (Frantic cheers, in which the chairman joined.)
  'Yes,' he said.[78]

One of the first duties of any junior was the postage desk. Jackson undertook the routine and tedious task of stamping and entering the letters in the appropriate book. Wodehouse switches to the humour of ridicule as the department head, Rossiter, moves in to see what Jackson and Psmith are actually accomplishing and is verbally overwhelmed by Psmith.

'I tell you, Comrade Rossiter, that you have got hold of a good man. You and I together, not forgetting Comrade Jackson, the pet of the Smart Set, will toil early and late till we boost up this Postage Department into a shining model of what a Postage Department should be. What this is, at present, I do not exactly know. However. Excursion trains will be run from distant shires to see this Postage Department. American visitors to London will do it before going on to the Tower . . .'[79]

On the actual act of posting the letters, Psmith comments, ' "Ah, so you put the little chaps in there, do you? . . . You seem to have grasped your duties with admirable promptitude. It is the same with me. I fancy we are both born men of Commerce." '[80]

But for Psmith as for Wodehouse, who would write later that he always considered the 'Postage Department' had been his spiritual home, this was a premature judgement. On leaving the Bank Psmith said – as Wodehouse perhaps would like to have said to the 'manager' – ' "... how much Comrade Jackson and I have enjoyed our stay in the bank. The insight it has given us into your masterly handling of the intricate mechanism of the office has been a treat we would not have missed. But our place is elsewhere." '[81]

These extracts, with others from the same source, describe one legitimate reaction to London Office; there were others to be considered below. But before leaving Wodehouse as Hongkong Banker it is only fair to recount in brief a true episode which Wodehouse has told in full elsewhere and to note his comment that '. . . the fact that [the Bank] survived me and is still going strong shows the stuff it was made of'.[82]

The particular event recounted was Wodehouse's unthinking decision to write a suddenly inspired story onto the front page of a new ledger and then, realizing the enormity of this offense, compound it by carefully cutting out the page with a sharp knife. A missing page in a ledger is always a traumatic matter in a banking institution.

A few mornings later the stillness of the bank was shattered by a sudden yell of triumph such as the Brazilian wild cat gives when leaping on his prey. It was the Head Cashier [actually G.W. Moore of the London Office staff] discovering the absence of the page, and the reason he yelled was that he was feuding with the stationers and for weeks had been trying to catch them out in some misdemeanor. He was at the telephone in two strides, asking them if they called themselves stationers.

They said they did, and asked him what made him dubious on that point.

He then touched off his bombshell, accusing them of having delivered an imperfect ledger, a ledger with the front page missing.

This brought the boss stationer around in person, calling heaven to witness that when the book had left his hands it had been all that a ledger should be, if not more so, the sort of ledger that goes down in legend and song.

'The front page is missing,' said the cashier.

'Somebody must have cut it out.'

'Absurd! Nobody but an imbecile would cut out the front page of a ledger.'

'Then,' said the stationer, 'you must have an imbecile in your department. Have you?'

'Why, yes,' he admitted, for he was a fairminded man. 'There is P.G. Wodehouse.'

'Weak in the head, is he, this Wodehouse?'

'The best judges have always thought so.'

'Then send for him and question him narrowly,' said the stationer.

This was done. They got me under the lights and grilled me, and I had to come clean.

The story ought to end with my being fired and cast into outer darkness where there was wailing and gnashing of teeth, but actually all that happened was that I became the recipient of a number of home truths, among which the accusation that I had about as much intelligence as a jellyfish figured largely. But as I knew this already, the sting was not deep. It was only a matter of days before all was quiet on the Cash front. Which shows what hearts of gold bank authorities had in those days. It was a pleasure to be associated with them.[83]

The cashier 'was at the telephone in two strides'. Hongkong Bankers recall that a specially employed operator always answered the instrument with 'I am the Hongkong and Shanghai Bank'. The Bank was, in fact, one of the first City institutions to be connected, and this, as the use of the telephone became more common, provoked a standing order still relevant to that particular innovation:

Members of the Staff will please note that the telephones are to be used for the Bank's business only and not privately unless under special circumstances.

This particularly refers to Junior members of the staff. [1907][84]

The telephone and the wireless which followed constituted what Charles Addis saw as a revolution in communications, a revolution moreover which required a response from commerce, and some sixty years later the Bank did in fact respond. Nevertheless, the above description of life in the London Office is one-sided; it requires examination and consideration of the factors which provoked Addis to premature recommendations designed to modify the 'junior system'.

LONDON OFFICE – A SECOND APPROACH

The 'Junior System' – a critical analysis

The issue of non-professionalism

The incompetence of British performance in the Boer War provoked a brief period of reexamination of non-professionalism; criticisms were made and reforms proposed as the target shifted from the British army officer to members of other services with similar systems, including the overseas banks.

In Tientsin the Bank's Agent H. Hewat's comment was not surprising – 'From what we have seen and are daily seeing of the British officer here, all gold braid and swagger, and no brains, we can easily understand the blunders that have been made in South Africa.'[85]

In Shanghai Charles Addis was shocked when asked by a young officer the name of the well-known 'Soochow Creek'; Addis told him a German would have known not only its name but its capacity for naval warfare. Indeed, non-professionalism was a disputed factor in explaining the gains the Germans were making in the Far Eastern trade (see Part III to this volume). Addis was particularly concerned with the role of the 'mess' system on the attitudes and capabilities of the military service; from this he was led inevitably to a consideration of the Bank's mess system and from that to the role and training of juniors, particularly Hongkong Bank juniors. He was also led to wonder 'how much the British passion for sport has to answer for', and he concluded by noting that all this must be changed, 'But how?'[86]

In 1900 Murray Stewart resigned from the Hongkong Bank after some ten years in the East. To Addis he confided that he had been four years in the [Hong Kong] Peak Mess; it had been good discipline perhaps but there had been too much drinking and too little thinking. He commented on the British dislike of ideas as such – there was a lack of professional interest and pride (as opposed to 'silly social pride'), and he made the direct link between attitudes in the military and the Hongkong Bank mess. 'It is the same all round. The atmosphere in British communities stifles study. The little fright the Boer War gave us . . .' had been dissipated.[87]

A rationale of the system

There were many reasons why reform of the junior system was untimely; like the terms of service themselves, the system was locked into the social structure and could not be changed piecemeal. But there were other considerations, the most important of which was simply that the system was to some extent appropriate for the majority of the tasks to be performed. For all the jokes about London Office, veterans of the Bank's service recalled that considerable work was in fact accomplished; Wodehouse – and others like him – neither understanding its purpose at the time nor willing to wait until much had become clear, was not in a position to evaluate the consequences of the routine jobs he and his colleagues were required to perform. When the Bank faced the labour-intensive responsibility of issuing public loans, the staff were not only up to the task but often surprised the City with their efficiency.

The fact is that future bank managers began as clerks, or, to put it more dynamically, their first tasks were identical to those performed by career clerks. The difference lay in the fact that, from the first day, they were marked for Eastern service and promotion. Thus their qualification for promotion depended on what insight they gained from their clerical assignments and/or what informal instruction, what hints at implications were given them by their immediate supervisors. A junior who showed interest might be told quietly of the secrets of exchange rate calculations, a junior on current accounts asking whether an overdraft should be permitted might be subjected to a barrage of questions relative to his knowledge of the account, questions designed to instruct him in the principles of personal credit.

There remained several difficulties, of which the conflict between the need to have routine tasks performed by the 'British' staff overseas and the need to recruit men who could eventually be promoted to manage agencies, or the Bank itself, is particularly relevant here. The conflicting requirements were resolved by recruiting from a 'type' or 'class', recognizing that the need in the managerial ranks was relatively limited and so letting a natural selection take place; this resulted in wastage en route and to an excessive number of juniors in the London Office. This last was accentuated at times by erratic scheduling of requirements in the East for new men, and the consequent idle moments and discipline problems in London Office were thereby compounded.

If the London experience had shaped a banker's attitudes throughout his career, it would have been a matter of more serious concern. The record does not support any such development; either the discipline of the Hong Kong office or the immediate responsibilities faced by a young man in a smaller agency were sufficient to ensure in the great majority a sense of purpose. London for the Hongkong Bank junior was limbo; he was working, yes; formal instruction in banking was not at the time an alternative; thus the junior saw himself as simply waiting to go East.

One consequence to note, however, is that the Manager in the East, faced with some error perpetrated in London Office, might recall his youth and ascribe to London many of the exaggerated attitudes which, though legitimate fun in *Psmith in the City*, were not an accurate reflection of the actual situation. But however reasonable, there exists an approach to London Office which seems to find its origins at least in part to reminiscences mistaken for realities.[h]

---

[h] The 1919 circular critical of London Office operations (note 69) should be considered in the context of the immediate post-war situation – new staff recently released from military service and the reaction to civilian life.

As for the 'mess system' narrowly defined, the references are inevitably to the Bank's Hong Kong Peak Mess. In almost all other cities a 'mess' or 'chummery' referred to a small self-composed group of juniors, not all necessarily from the Hongkong Bank, and with luck these groups, being matters of individual decision, would be composed of compatible personalities. One could live alone; the prevalence of the mess was the consequence of the cost of living alone and the low level of salaries commensurate, one should add in fairness, with the simple tasks the juniors were then performing. The London Office juniors lived in digs, either alone or with one colleague. The social life revolved around the Pavilion at the New Beckenham sports ground and was thus more flexible. Criticism of the system would appear justified, but the adverse impact of the type referred to in the immediate post-Boer War period was minimal as far as the Hongkong Banker was concerned – except perhaps in Hong Kong.

The majority of Hongkong Bankers would probably not accept this contemporary criticism of the system as valid. The 'mess' was part of the team training, of the total socialization process; it was part of belonging to the Bank. Nor was this making a virtue of what was certainly a necessity; the Bank's post World War II planning has been purposely designed to ensure the continued existence of the Peak Mess at Cloudlands.

As a postscript, these comments from George Addis, by then in Liverpool, provide a basic contrast:

My own idea is that so long as a fellow is young and unencumbered and has got to do office work, he is better off and more comfortable doing it abroad than at home. But as one gets older, I think one gets a little tired of Eastern life . . .[88]

A home bank is a terrible place for an ordinary fellow to spend his life in – no hope of anything but a constant struggle to keep one's head above water.[89]

A remaining objection

But even accepting that the Wodehouse/public school image of the Bank junior was exaggerated, there remained a problem: the ambitious could not appear too ambitious; a strong and forceful character, a Grayburn, could show leadership from the first, but such a man was an exception. The team spirit, the impact of the majority, was overwhelming; what Addis had achieved self-taught when the Bank was smaller had become impossible by the 1900s. Indeed, Addis had been fortunate in his sponsorship and assignments; Gershom Stewart had resigned despite Thomas Jackson's high opinion of his potential. There simply wasn't the promotion available for him at the time his maturity required it.

Addis and the attempt to 'up-grade' the juniors

While he was on Home leave in 1899–1900 Charles Addis matriculated as an undergraduate at Edinburgh University and read economics under Professor John Shield Nicholson.[90] Thus Addis returned to the path his father, the Rev. Thomas Addis, had hoped for him. In Charles's adolescence the discipline imposed had been too rigorous; he had rebelled and turned to commerce.

In the 1920s Sir Charles Addis would take part in debates on the return to pre-war parity and other banking and currency issues, and although his career never required the full qualifications of a professional economist, his background, training, and his further informal studies prepared him for a policy role in the national and international banking scene. None more than Addis knew that such scholarly attainments were not necessarily appreciated by senior management – or perhaps by one's own contemporaries. Nevertheless Addis as a Manager of the London Office would encourage the recruitment of university graduates and pursue his plan to encourage the study of the Chinese language as part of the training of self-selected juniors.

In both endeavours he would fail, but for somewhat different though allied reasons. A consideration of Addis's efforts will assist in understanding the Bank's basic personnel problems and policy during the period almost, one is tempted to suggest, to the mid-1970s.

The recruitment and performance of university graduates[i]
(Sir) Michael W. Turner (East in 1930) and G.P. Stubbs (East in 1947) were graduates of Oxford University, the former became Chief Manager and the latter Manager London Office. These with E.G. Hillier (referred to above) and J. Hall (East in 1919), who became Agent Penang, would seem to exhaust the early list of university graduates who actually went East in the service of the Hongkong Bank. While the list is hardly long enough to permit generalization, it remains true that those who went East did well; there was nothing contradictory about being both a university graduate and a banker. The list is, however, short enough to permit the conclusion that Addis's scheme for general university recruitment was unsuccessful. Why?

Charles Addis launched his proposal to recruit university graduates in his speech at the Third Annual London Bank Dinner in 1909. His critique of the

---

[i] This section must be read against the context of the long-lasting British tradition of providing 'professional' education 'on-the-job', restricting formal education to that provided by extramural courses with examinations provided by the relevant professional organization, and the reserving of university places for limited scholarly purposes – and sports. (On this last point, see, for example, the speech of the fictional Mike Jackson's father quoted on p. 179.)

existing system is startling in its candour – and he was speaking before an audience consisting mainly of London juniors:

I confess, for my part, I have no patience with those laudators of times past, of the so-called *practical system* of mercantile education, which consists in snatching a lad from school at a tender age, and plunging him during the most impressionable years of his life – between 15 and 20 – in the mechanical routine of an office. Can you imagine anything more deadening to the mind and spirit of a future captain of industry? I say these old rule-of-thumb methods will no longer suffice. Men will be compelled to recognise that commerce is becoming, has become, a science in which none can hope to excel but he who has mastered its laws.[91]

Addis saw the university-trained entrant as a potentially successful competitor to the highly trained Continental banker, a position which, it is fair to remark, remains one not fully accepted today with reference to banking generally. On the other hand Addis admitted that the university course was not necessarily suited for business – both sides had much to learn about each other. 'What a boon to the nation it would be if business affairs were conducted with more of the analytic and reflective power of the universities and if university affairs were conducted with more of the prompt and practical methods of business.'[92] The nature of the university course had led many to conclude that the university offered nothing that would prepare a young man for the 'drudgery of business'. To this Addis had a significant response:

Can you point me to any profession, any science, any art, in which drudgery is not the price of mastery? And am I to be told that the liberal education considered indispensable in the one case is to be regarded as of no value, nay, even as a positive hindrance in the other? I refuse to believe it. Believe me, the nature of drudgery is everywhere pretty much the same, and everywhere it yields up half its tedium to an intelligent attempt to discover the meaning which underlies and explains it.[93]

At this point Addis began, certainly without realizing it, to undermine the practicality of his proposal to recruit university graduates. He concluded his argument by asking:

Can anyone doubt that given two men of equal capacity, the advantage will lie with him whose faculties have been the better trained? His three or four extra years at the university will not have been lost. Sooner or later he will overtake the start gained by his contemporary, who has gone straight from school to the office desk, and, in the end, he will gain enormously when in the higher branches of his profession he has to tackle practical problems in the light of principles acquired in the schools.[94]

To return to earth, it is quite clear that Addis was not proposing to give the university graduate any seniority – 'sooner or later he will overtake . . .' Enter the Bank then with a B.A. at the age of say 23, remain two years in London (or four in the depression), go East at the age of 25–27, and, under the worst scenario, receive permission to marry at the age of 37. An unattractive prospect.

The graduate was to spend a full tour in the London Office. Would many be willing at the age of 23 to relive their adolescence and interpret the life, à la Wodehouse, in public schoolboy terms? Addis's expectation was that such a graduate would, while performing the drudgery, think deep thoughts about the meaning of things, and that this would cause him to be quickly promoted once in the East. Such a development would be possible only if (i) a majority of Managers had Addis's preference for graduates, or at least had no prejudice against them, (ii) there were no effective protests from non-graduates, and (iii) the university graduate was demonstrably shown to be particularly able from the beginning. None of these were likely, the first least of all. H.D.C. Jones, the junior London Manager from 1912, would himself prove to be the counter to Addis.

One aspect of the problem, financing a university education, seems not to have been considered, although it was the determining factor in Wodehouse's career. In recent comprehensive interviews (1979–1982) of inter-war recruits in which the focus was on banking, the fact of family inability to pay for a university education after the burden of public school fees was referred to with sufficient frequency to suggest that any plan which did not take this into account was likely to fail. If in particular cases family financial inability were not absolute, the burden might be related by interviewees to their prospects. On a cost/benefit basis, was it worthwhile straining the family resources for a university education which Bank candidates were advised was irrelevant?

On this last point, Addis expected that the universities would respond to the challenge. The first positive reaction was in fact the Bachelor of Commerce degree, and Addis would assist through membership on the appropriate University of London committee; the Hongkong Bank would contribute funds to further the experiment – but even though the course had highly placed defenders, the Bank and the graduates themselves professed themselves unconvinced.

The Hongkong Bank was an exchange bank. Its top Managers were operators on the exchange. Exchange operators, it was said, were born not made. If these statements are open to challenge, they were not successfully challenged in the period under discussion.

Addis did, however, secure two or three graduates. His diary for November 20, 1911, notes, 'Young [H.R.] Otty, the Bank Cambridge recruit at tea. A fine young fellow.'[95] But Otty never went East. F.E. Nicoll (who entered the Bank in 1909, went East in 1913 and was Manager Bombay in 1940) recalled that the only graduate joining with his own group found banking a dreary business and left to become a lecturer for the Society for the Prevention of Cruelty to Children. 'So far as I recollect the only graduate of my time to survive and join the Eastern staff was James Hall.'[96]

Hall, who had been a senior wrangler at Cambridge, was caught by both wars; his service in the Great War prevented his going East until 1919 and he was interned during the Pacific War. Under the circumstances he had a respectable career, but he became Agent only in 1946 and retired from Penang in 1951. Nevertheless Hall is remembered by juniors who worked under him for just those reasons that Addis anticipated. In 1937 Sir Vandeleur Grayburn had sent him down to Saigon to teach exchange accounting to the Manager; post-war, J.W.L. Howard (East in 1946) compared his first two Agents, W. Cardiff Murray and James Hall, who were, he found 'extremely knowledgeable men on banking matters and able to impart' their knowledge to juniors. 'James Hall was much more of an academic and went rather by the book', which, Howard explained, meant that from Hall he received a fair grounding in theory as well as practice.[97] M.G. Carruthers (East in 1937), though less appreciative, confirmed Howard's view:

You'd be working away like mad hoping to be able to get off at five o'clock because you'd got a game of tennis and [Hall] would come out and plonk down in front of you some mathematical conundrum . . . I was absolutely no good at it. John Howard was quite good, but then it meant that he was off doing nothing for the next half hour while he worked it out, so you had to do his work too.[98]

The information cited may be deficient; there were possibly graduates who joined London and then left for the war and who, for one reason or another, did not return to the Bank, but the overall picture is unchanged.

Chinese language study

Very few Hongkong Bankers had a working knowledge of the Chinese language; Addis estimated that in 1908 only 5% of the 170–180 Eastern staff had any familiarity with an Oriental language, and there were sound reasons why this would be so.

The difficulty as Addis saw it was the burden of learning banking *and* Chinese at a time when 'a young man should be building up a strong constitution for life in the East', that is, by participating in the program down at the Bank's sports grounds in New Beckenham.[99] This is a recurring and interesting theme and even Addis was ambivalent on the value of sports.

Ewen Cameron, with Jackson supporting, had as Shanghai Manager seen the need for Chinese-speaking Bank officers, especially in the north. The Bank had arranged Chinese classes in London, encouraged Addis, and assigned Hillier to Peking. Despite some moderate interest and success, the Bank's efforts fell short of a 'program'. Although Addis himself was not wholly convinced of the practicality of his proposals, and he was certainly critical of the classical orientation of the early classes under Professor Douglas, he nevertheless submitted to Cameron, then London Manager, a 'plan of study'.

The plan had as essential elements the commencement of Chinese language study in England, the passing of examinations with financial inducements, and further study in Peking or Nanking – half on the Bank's time, half on the junior's time. The scheme ran parallel to that devised by the Imperial Maritime Customs and was similar to that on the books of (but not always implemented by) other Eastern banks for the study of Indian languages.

In 1904 when Addis submitted his proposals there were only twelve members of the Eastern staff, 7% of the total 163, actually serving in offices where Chinese was the language of the local population. With the growth of the Bank's North China business and the sending of representatives to Manchuria, this number had doubled by 1914; there were then 24 of a total 214 on the Eastern staff actually in Mandarin-speaking areas; this is still only 12%. Even then the compradore and a few of the merchants might prefer Shanghainese or southern dialects.

After the establishment of the China Association School of Practical Chinese in 1900, reinforced by the return from the East of Sir Walter Hillier, brother of E.G. Hillier, instruction took on a more commercial orientation.[100] The Bank did attempt to assign those who had done well in classes in London to Peking where, under E.G. Hillier's guidance, they could continue their studies on a more practical basis, but the teaching of the language was still encumbered by old-style methods.

Addis's own 1904 scheme was revised by a Head Office program in 1909 and is shown on page 195. Only H.E. Blunt (East in 1906) would appear to have completed the full program as there outlined, but his career ended in the Great War and he did not live to prove the program's usefulness to the Bank.

A Bank junior contemplating the investment of his time, especially once he had reached the East, had to consider the ever-present question of the impact of Chinese language knowledge on his career as a banker. Or he had to decide to become, frankly, a Chinese language specialist. Addis envisioned Bank staff capable of checking the Chinese interpreters during negotiations; to achieve this level of proficiency and keep up with even the fairly simple banking tasks assigned first-tour juniors could be difficult in a small service. The problem increased with seniority, and a study of the career paths of those with some proficiency in Chinese forces the conclusion that the exigencies of the service would within the first ten years require the officer to be assigned outside the 'Mandarin'-speaking area, and probably outside China. The conclusion can be tested by outlining career histories.

R.E. Sedgewick (East in 1904) after more than a year in Shanghai was sent to Peking where he passed his second-year examination in Chinese. He left Peking in 1910 and, although he remained throughout his career in China, he spent all but three years in non-Mandarin-speaking ports, retiring as Agent Foochow in 1934.

In contrast, **H.E. Blunt** (East in 1906) was assigned to and remained in Peking; in 1913 he actually passed the interpretorial examination in Chinese, for which he received a gratuity of £100 (see p. 195). He left China in 1914 and died on active service. **D.A. Johnston** (East in 1910) remained in Mandarin areas until 1928; he was acting Sub-Agent in Peking and Tsingtau, but his career prospects were ended when the Peking compradore absconded with a loss to the Bank of $1.4 million, for which he was held to have been responsible (see Volume III). Johnston completed his service in Lyons in 1946 having served during World War II in London Office. **L.H. Hitchcock** (East in 1910) served only until 1914 in Hankow, he joined the Forces and on return to the Bank's service eventually became Sub-Agent in Haiphong; he did not return to a China post until 1937 when he was appointed Agent Amoy, from where he retired in early 1941. He was reported to be qualified in Siamese but was never assigned to Bangkok.

A.S. Baskett (East in 1912) was assigned first to Tsingtau and then to Tientsin, both Mandarin-speaking; his name is not on the Eastern staff list after 1914. **C. Farnworth** (East in 1915) had five years in Peking and Harbin, but the balance of his career was in Malaya/Singapore and Manila, in which last port he was Manager and so caught by the 1941 war and interned. He retired in 1946. And finally **F.E. Beatty** (East in 1909) served for his first ten years in Malacca and Yokohama; he was then assigned to Hankow for two years. His career ended sadly in 1929 when, concerned with certain Shanghai losses incurred on his responsibility as Accountant, he was lost overboard en route home via Canada.

These appear to be the only Chinese language students of this period who went beyond a few elementary classes in London, but an interpretation is complicated by the fact that promotion would depend on their qualifications as bankers, and early performance reports were mixed.

There were therefore juniors on the Hongkong Bank staff who indeed studied Chinese and who earned certificates of proficiency, having passed examinations supervised by the British Legation in Peking. But those who judged the needs solely with reference to banking concluded correctly that language study was neither a necessary nor always a useful career step.

Thus the scheme as one designed to equip the Bank with its own in-service linguists qualified to deal with customers or check interpreters did not gain the necessary momentum; those that studied Chinese were few and these suffered varied fortunes. As George Addis had warned his younger brother relative to the latter's own career, the Chinese pidgin was not necessarily the best ticket.[101] Addis had in fact accepted demotion rather than continue as a

'China [language] expert'; the Bank's public school recruits could list German and/or French (of an unspecified standard) or even colloquial Spanish, and the records show several who had learned Malay and Hindustani, but if Addis wanted China linguists sufficient to fully staff the Bank's China branches, then he needed to prove its career value and/or to recruit the type of man who preferred to attend university, and such a man, once through the Varsity, usually decided against banking as a career.

The Bank had been founded, *inter alia*, to end the compradoric system. The Board and the management remained as firmly convinced in the 1900s as in 1864 that the compradore was a burden on trade. But even in this matter Addis could not guarantee success; he would not argue that a thorough knowledge of Chinese by Bank officers would *in itself* enable foreign firms to dispense with the compradore. The ideal for which Addis appeared to be groping was a direct relationship in the Chinese language between banker and customer backed by the expert local market knowledge of a Chinese manager. 'It is of little use to be able to read the name on a Chinese bill of exchange unless you can tell what these names stand for, the capital, the credit, the probity of drawer and endorser.'[102]

In the end the direct relationship would be effected in the English language, supplemented by the appointment of Chinese managers with executive authority. Local advisers, whatever their title, performed the functions Addis foresaw as a necessary backing for a foreign banker. Only when the Bank was ready for such developments in the late 1950s could the compradoric system be ended.

Thus Addis testifying before the Parliamentary Committee on Oriental Studies in London was able to further a project to create a School of Oriental and African Studies in the University of London, where his papers and diaries now rest; he was not able to convince his own Hongkong Bank that Chinese language study should be given the priority he sought; yet it is fair to note that the Bank had perhaps the best record to date of language study encouragement.

This contrasts with, for example, the subsequent experience of the Swire Group, which (i) recruited from universities and (ii) successfully encouraged the study of Chinese, both the official language and dialects. But then Swire juniors went up-country as sugar merchants; their contacts with the Chinese were more diverse; they *required* the language. And, ironically, Addis's Chinese language proposals for the Hongkong Bank were sent to Swire's and formed the basis of their program.[103]

The exchange banker, however, was tied to his office in a foreign concession. As Hankow Manager A.M. Reith (East in 1888) put it in a flash of inspiration after eighteen years in the East, 'Did it ever strike you that we are confined in compounds in China more or less?'[104] The Bank's customers did not use the official language for business, and the compradoric system did not encourage direct contact – except with Westernized Chinese businessmen and political figures who, in that case, spoke English, French, and/or German.

The language problem was seen by the Bank primarily in terms of Chinese. In the British territories the young bankers followed the example of their contemporaries, except perhaps that Hongkong Bankers did not attempt formal study in India where they were in any case considered 'birds of passage'. The obvious reason for the focus on Chinese was the importance of China to the Bank, but Chinese was also classified – not without reason – as a 'difficult language' requiring special facilities and inducements for its study. Japanese too was considered 'difficult', but there would appear to have been no formal facilities for its study. Nevertheless, two men became proficient and their career data are relevant in the general context of this section.

J.H. Lind, the son of the long-serving G.M. Lind of London Office, passed with a distinction in Japanese and served a high proportion of his career in Yokohama. Lind went East in 1901, serving first in Manila where he had the encounter with the American patriot related in Chapter 2; he was transferred to Yokohama in 1905 where he achieved proficiency in Japanese, remaining in Yokohama until 1922 by which time he had become Accountant. But his further career, except for a few months in Nagasaki in 1927, was first in Chefoo and then Ipoh; his final assignment was to Hamburg. His banking career could not be maintained in a single country, nor for that matter was his knowledge of the language evidence (one way or the other) that he possessed banking qualifications necessary for the Bank's chief representative in Japan.

S. Wheeler, who came East in 1900, was reported to be able to speak Japanese; he was assigned in Yokohama or Kobe from 1900 to 1906, but on his return from leave he was sent to Shanghai where he remained (with one year in Amoy) until his death as Sub-Accountant in 1918.

Conflicting priorities

Health was, as previously noted, perceived as a problem even by Addis. While in London a young man was supposed to be 'building up a strong constitution for life in the East' through participation in sports.[105] And in this context, and again forcing a significant modification to the Wodehouse image, Addis as noted above, confessed to see the problem in the context of learning Chinese *and* banking at the same time. For the latter juniors were encouraged to attend special lectures and to prepare for the Institute of Bankers Examination, usually Part I, although some more ambitious undertook Part II as well. 'With a view to promoting the efficiency of the Staff' the Board of Directors sanctioned a gratuity of £10 for those passing either part of the examination.[106] At times indeed success in Part I was made a condition for being sent East, but on this policy varied.

A balanced view

Life for juniors in the London Office was in part a reflection of the junior, his understanding and purpose. Wodehouse confessed to failure to grasp the principles of the tasks assigned; others found them humdrum and left the Bank. But some, moving from department to department, taking advantage of informal instruction, enjoying the games and the 'feel' of the Bank, went East and prospered without the benefit of either a university education or knowledge of Chinese. Such a man was F.E. Nicoll and the complex of views expressed in the previous sections requires interpretation through the more balanced view which he presents.

Life in London Office was very pleasant and had, for the foreign staff, a care-free atmosphere reminiscent of school days. The hours were reasonable, 9:30 to 5, but monthly balance night in current accounts meant dinner in town, either at the Blue Anchor or the George & Gate. When I was in Outward Bills one or two of us made it the rule to have a big lunch at the Ship & Turtle on Fridays (mail day) to sustain us until 8 or 9. On occasions the mail was not ready until after 8 when it had to be taken to Charing Cross and posted on the boat train connecting with the Brindisi–Port Said service. Other occasions for overtime were prior to the issue of new Chinese or Japanese Government Loans, which entailed a good deal of work in dealing with applications, preparing letters of allotment, and subsequently sorting out the bonds . . .

I started work in the Coupon Department which dealt with the payment of interest on Chinese and Japanese bonds. It was a deadly job and I was glad when I was transferred to the Securities Department. There I remained nearly a year and subsequently I served in Current Accounts, Outward Bills and Inward Progressives, the latter being another soul-destroying job.

A few of the foreign staff were students at the Institute of Bankers and two or three took Chinese lessons. I remember attending a series of lectures on Banking by Sir John Paget, K.C. but otherwise my colleagues and I had no instruction in Banking or Exchange and we entered on a career in the Far East with no qualifications beyond what we had picked up in the course of our three or four years in London Office . . .

There was always one junior allocated to Lyons Agency and one to Hamburg . . .

The Bank had its playing field at Beckenham but the pavilion accommodation was primitive compared with modern ideas. The standard of rugger was high and in my time there were two International and a few county players. I remember the indignation when Mr Addis gave orders at the end of the 1910/11 season that the then jerseys of yellow with a black dragon must be abandoned and replaced by red and white jerseys. It was felt that the susceptibilities of the Chinese Republic would be offended by the flaunting of the Imperial dragon on the playing fields of London.

No. 31 Lombard Street [where the Bank had remained for 41 years] was a gloomy office with a narrow passageway from the entrance door to the Manager's rooms at the end. On the left were Current Accounts, Cash, Fixed Deposits, Drafts, Accountants Room, Share Department and Securities. On the right: Outward Bills, Inward Bills,

Coupons, Telegrams with the Correspondence Room (the only one with daylight) at the back. Upstairs on the 3rd floor were the London Committee Room the Books Department and Inward Progressives. There were no women in the establishment either as clerks, stenographers or cleaners.[107]

The basic recruitment policy of the Hongkong Bank set the limits to the flexibility of staff development. The stress on social background and introduction, the concept, that is, of a proper 'type' for Eastern banking, dictated with exceptions the possibilities of deviation from the norm. Those London juniors within these parameters did not automatically remain to become bankers – P.G. Wodehouse left to write, Bernard Leach to develop a creative pottery, and by way of parallel the Chartered Bank's (Sir) James A.H. Murray to compile and edit a dictionary of the English language.[108]

Nor were those who stayed the course necessarily stereotypes. J. Waddell (East in 1905) was highly respected as an organist, R.P. Thursfield (East in 1905) wrote poetry, F.T. Koelle preached sermons in Batavia's Anglican church and established a mission to the aborigines of Ceylon, A.G. Stephen was noted as a literary and musical authority, H.E. Muriel was a singer and actor, G.W. Wood a pianist, W.H. Wallace an authority on gardening, and in the outports Hongkong Bankers with less noted artistic talents contributed to the amateur theatricals, musical comedies, and general cultural life – some developed individual characteristics (later juniors would prefer the term 'eccentricities') which were marked and commented on in the small foreign communities.

But there were limits. Addis tested them; neither the Bank nor the commercial world were as yet ready for his innovations. The London system as developed by David McLean and Thomas Jackson was to continue in operation for many years to come. By 1914 Grayburn and Henchman were in the East and Arthur Morse, Chairman and Chief Manager 1941–1952, was already an experienced London junior. Fifty years later, after the Bank's centenary, Sir Arthur would remember that he had heard Sir Thomas Sutherland speak of the Bank's founding.[109]

The continuity was assured; the succession was in place.

APPENDIX: THE STUDY OF THE
CHINESE LANGUAGE[j]

A scheme to encourage members of the staff to study Chinese language (incorporating Mr Addis's scheme of November 18, 1904, and Head Office scheme of June 1, 1909).

Study in London:
1 Selected officers to study in London at King's College.
2 Books to be supplied and fees paid by the Bank.
3 Course of two years of four hours a week. Students to be allowed to leave the office at 4 o'clock instead of 5 o'clock two days a week.
4 A cash bonus of £15 (£20) to students on passing first (second) exam.

Study in China:
1 Selected officers to work in the Peking Office of the Bank and to be allowed time to study.
2 Books to be supplied and teachers to be paid by the Bank.
3 A bonus of £50 (£100) to be earned by passing the 1st year's (second year's) standard examination.
4 The student can then be transferred to some of the other offices of the Bank in China where he can continue his studies.
5 After three years' service at other offices a student may take the Interpretorial examination on passing which he will receive a cash payment of £100 and earn a bonus of £100.
6 The £250 given as Bonus to be placed as earned on Fixed Deposit with London Office; the amount plus accrued interest to become the property of every student on his completing 6 years' service after passing the examination for a qualified interpreter . . .
7 The examinations to be on the lines of and similar to those laid down for HBM Consular Service.

Source: abridged from FO 371/640, ff. 116–17.

---

[j] At no time would Addis, whose concern was Continental (especially German) competition, appear to have referred to the Japanese efforts in training China-oriented businessmen, specifically the Tōa Dōbun Shoin in Shanghai. Addis's focus was on a more relevant university degree coupled with employer-financed Chinese language training. The former would lead eventually to the London University Bachelor of Commerce degree, the latter, a concern shared with others, was a factor in the development of the School of Oriental and African Studies – the British were not totally unresponsive, but their efforts were not matched by suitable changes in the recruitment policy or the social and management structure of China-coast firms. The Japanese, however, pioneered the full 'area studies' approach as part of a national program in China. For an initial study (in English) and bibliography, see Douglas R. Reynolds, 'Chinese Area Studies in Prewar China: Japan's Tōa Dōbun Shoin in Shanghai, 1900–1945', *Journal of Asian Studies* 45:945–70 (1986).

4

THE HONGKONG BANK'S ROLE IN CURRENCY AND BANKING REFORMS

Currency questions are so involved that one is naturally diffident about expressing decided views, and I can assure you the present occasion is no exception to the rule.

J.R.M. Smith, Chief Manager, the Hongkong Bank, 1910

I have no axe to grind in this matter. I am here to watch over the interests of the Singapore Chamber of Commerce and the merchants of Singapore. The bankers of Singapore are quite able to look after themselves. All I want, Sir, is to see the Government adopt a sound Currency Note system, and I will do everything in my power to assist them to that end. But, on the other hand, Sir, I will do everything in my power to frustrate them from adopting any unsound system.

Hon. T.S. Baker, Manager, the Hongkong Bank, Singapore, in the Straits Settlements Legislative Council, 1908

Coinage is the prerogative of the Sovereign; a sound coinage, a usable medium of exchange, is basic to sound government. A government may succeed for a time to regulate a full-bodied coinage within the nation, city-state, or Empire; in the long run – despite the efforts expended in this basic function of government and for a complex of factors – insuperable problems seem inevitably to arise. Nevertheless, the first focus of reform is usually on measures designed to make the existing 'full-bodied' coinage system more rational, more workable.

When this proves impossible or should more radical reform suggest itself, the question of the standard arises.

The maintenance of a sound silver coinage in the East defied the experts. In China and the offshore trading centre of Hong Kong, this goal remained the main focus of currency reform throughout the period covered by this volume; the question of a change of standard, from silver to gold, was indeed discussed, but problems of implementation were seen as overwhelming despite the depreciation of and fluctuations in the gold price of silver. In the more practical aspects of the currency reform question the Hongkong Bank had much to contribute, particularly in Hong Kong.

As silver depreciated those countries which looked to Europe and after 1893, with the closing of the mint to free coinage, also to India tended to seek a solution through a change of the monetary standard accompanied by a controlled currency, both coin and note. The Philippines became oriented to the United States but otherwise looked to a similar solution. The process of these changes was complex and the developments were not wholly foreseen, causing from time to time losses or gains which appeared to be the consequence of Government intervention. In these matters the Hongkong Bank played a role; in Singapore the Manager was a member of the Legislative Council, in London the Bank made representations to the Colonial Office and Treasury, in China the Bank dealt with the local money changers, with officials, and with the Consular bodies in the several ports, and in Hong Kong the Bank's advice and assistance were constantly in demand.

This chapter is not intended as a monetary history of the East. Rather it is a selective description of or a series of case studies in the role the Hongkong Bank – and Hongkong Bankers – played in improving, as they saw it, the monetary environment in which they worked. There was a certain degree of special pleading involved, but the Bank advised disinterestedly; after all, as T.S. Baker told his fellow legislators, 'I am convinced that the more the Government bungle and blunder over their currency affairs, the more it will rebound to the advantage of the banks, and especially to the advantage of the foreign banks.'[1]

Foreign advisers saw the elimination of the tael, for example, as fundamental in any Chinese currency reform; the Hongkong Bank supported this, although it earned a commission each time there was even a local transfer between dollar and tael-denominated funds.

The exchange banks performed varied functions, some consistent with the theoretical principles on which they claimed to operate, others less so – although not necessarily for this reason unsound or unwise. Their capacity was however limited, their contact with the local market often tenuous and undertaken through agencies which would not themselves survive political or monetary reforms. There was little the exchange banks could do to reform the native banking systems *per se*, but they could and did provide working examples of an alternative system of modern commercial banks; they could and did offer advice as to how such banks might best be established.

The form in which the pressure for a modern bank developed was not standard throughout the East. In Japan the move was part of an overall program, and the Hongkong Bank was the model for a Japanese exchange bank, the Yokohama Specie Bank, and not for the banking system. In China the first impetus came from compradores, Chinese merchants, and officials familiar with Western business practices; in the Philippines there were other colonial pressures and eventually a political/business movement to gain full control of the banking system.

Most common was the feeling that the territory needed a 'national bank', a bank with predominantly local interests to handle Government funds and to earn the profits which they saw going to overseas banks, to be staffed by local officers, and to be 'more receptive' to local requirements than was supposed possible for the exchange banks with their overseas shareholders. The Hongkong Bank could hardly argue with this; it was itself founded in Hong Kong for precisely this last reason. The Hongkong Bank, however, soon established itself in ports where it served local banking requirements but on so marginal a basis that Government business was essential if the agency were to remain feasible. A move to found a local 'national' bank was, therefore, a competitive threat. The Hongkong Bank's primary concern was to defend itself and other exchange banks against officially sponsored competition in the exchange business; but the Bank was capable of taking a long-run view and on occasion supported or assisted the authorities in their requirements.

Underlying the Hongkong Bank's cooperation was the basic assumption that as a bank whose profits depended on turnover – and turnover depended on trade – any measure which promoted and facilitated trade would, despite increased competition, be to the Bank's long-run benefit. There was not a 'lump of business' to be monopolized.[2] There were economies needing development; the Bank did not have the resources to develop them – although it was legitimate to assist the country to find them through public loan issues. It was an article of faith that in these economies there was the potential of increasing business which, even if shared, would lead to improved returns for the Bank and for its constituents in both East and West.

PROBLEMS WITH THE CURRENCY

China

By 1865 when the Hongkong Bank was established the pattern of the Late Ch'ing monetary system had been set in the Treaty Ports and no effective reform or simplification was achieved until the abolition of the tael as a unit of account and the establishment of a national dollar in 1932.[a]

For the purposes of this section the mediums of exchange for domestic transactions were dollar coins and monetary sycee; the copper sector is not considered.

---

[a] A description of this system is found in Volume I, Chapter 1.

During the period through 1918 the various authorities from time to time attempted local *ad hoc* reforms; from 1902 to 1911 there was at the same time an on-going consideration of total monetary reform, that is, of both the coinage and the standard. This latter climaxed in the abortive 1911 Currency Reform Loan, which eventually became the Reorganization Loan of 1913 and as such is considered in Chapter 8. The proposals put forward by the Chinese Government in 1911 dealt only with the medium of exchange and to this extent will be covered briefly below.

Ad hoc *reform*

The dollar system was at first dependent on supplies of dollar coins from Mexico, the form and continuation of which were in doubt. The coins once in China were usually defaced by chopping. The obvious reform was for a locally minted dollar which would by law and practice escape chopping. But this had to wait for a sufficiently strong centralized national Government; in the meantime relief was found first in the Japanese silver yen and then in 1894 in the British dollar, 416 grains of 900 millesimal fineness; in the promotion of both the Hongkong Bank was active.[3]

Sycee, or monetary silver, was, for purposes of economic analysis, a form of coin, but one peculiarly susceptible of debasement. This difference from the theoretical standard could be noted by the special markings stamped by the *kung-ku*, the public assay office. Should this office fail, as it did in Tientsin (see below), the value of the local tael unit of account would eventually fall against other taels, and, unless action were taken, holders of the debased sycee could face substantial losses. The Bank's local Manager took a very active role in the Tientsin affair.

The substitute for both dollar coin and sycee was the banknote, but there the Hongkong Bank was limited by its charter – it could not issue notes in excess of its paid-up capital. When an 'excess' issue was permitted, the requirement of 100% reserve discouraged note issue, and the Bank's issue in China itself was never substantial. Notes were with few exceptions denominated in the local dollar unit of account; tael notes were attempted but taels were usually used when making payment for large amounts.

There was, however, no Chinese prohibition against the Bank issuing banknotes in China. Operating under extraterritorial conditions, the Bank was, therefore, subject only to the terms of its charter which controlled the size of its issue and, indirectly, the place of issue. Treasury control on this last depended upon the implementation of the traditional difference between a branch and an agency, that only the former could issue notes. After 1889 when the Bank's status outside Hong Kong had been clarified by ordinance, the Bank's own *ad hoc* custom of referring to certain potentially important offices as 'agencies' could have interfered with their note-issuing ability, as, for example, in Tientsin and Peking. After the Great War the Bank took steps to rectify the situation, but plans for new issues were in fact abandoned in response to changed banking and political developments.

There is no record that, before the years of the 'excess' note issue, the Bank had priorities as to the location of its issue; the assumption must be, therefore, that the relatively small China issue – 12% of the total, compared to 52% for Hong Kong and 34% for the Straits – was the response to demand (see Volume I, Table 11.1). Business of a kind suitable for banknotes could in the smaller Treaty Ports be handled by 'chits', which, incidentally, avoided stamp duty; to some extent this must have been true also in Shanghai, where the 1889 circulation of Hongkong Bank banknotes was less than in Penang.

With the enactment of regulations for the 'excess' note issue requiring a 100% backing, there was little encouragement for the Bank to issue additional banknotes unless they passed at an 'adequate' premium over silver. The definition of 'adequate' varied with the Bank's estimate of the silver market and its ability to control the market for Hong Kong currency. The Bank could not expect to have such an influence on the Shanghai exchanges, and, therefore, after 1900 the Bank did give Hong Kong a priority for its note issue; the Straits issue was being withdrawn in response to Government policy there.

There is evidence, however, that the Bank had made no final decision to abandon the possibilities of a China note issue; for example, it pressed hard for the right to issue notes in Dairen, but its attempts to obtain the necessary Japanese permission were blocked, despite British diplomatic intervention.[4]

In the 1920s and before the establishment of a Nationalist Government there remained thoughts of a larger network of Bank offices with note-issuing potential. There is, however, no evidence as to the use the Bank would actually have made of any new authorizations; the fact is, it made little use of those it already possessed.

What was needed in Shanghai, as elsewhere in China, was reform in the system of small payments, but this in the early years of the present century created new problems – the over-production of subsidiary coins and hence their depreciation in terms of the dollar unit of account and the uncontrolled issue of native banknotes with insufficient backing. The Hongkong Bank joined in general representations as to the dangers inherent in the situation, but there was little chance of effective national reform despite an Imperial Edict in 1909.[5]

In the south redemption of Kwangtung Government notes by a new issue was attempted by the newly refinanced Bank of China, but the operation was flawed by attempts of that bank to discourage redemption of the new issue. The resulting general distrust led to an attempt to obtain silver dollars. The

Hongkong Bank and the Deutsch-Asiatische Bank were accused of buying up large parcels of old notes and attempting to force the Bank of China to redeem them in silver dollars, a charge which the former denied and which ran counter to the Bank's proclaimed desire to see a soundly based banknote issue available in south China.[6]

The process of providing a sound paper currency which could be redeemed in silver was in fact interrupted by a complex of factors in which the Hongkong Bank was involved. The fact that the notes were not legal tender and not accepted by the Chinese Government for certain purposes, as, for example, levies against indemnity payments, led to periodic financial disruption and reassessment of the usefulness of banknotes.

In 1912 some foreigners were advocating reform in Shanghai only, a plan which A.M. Townsend, then on the general committee of the China Association in London, considered to be impractical.[7] In 1915 however the Shanghai Branch of the China Association, on the initiative of A.G. Stephen, then the Hongkong Bank Manager, commissioned Stephen himself to draw up a report on the viability of a Shanghai token copper coinage, possibly to be minted in Bombay, for circulation at first in the International Settlement. The possibility of the scheme being defeated by counterfeits Stephen dismissed by the assertion, which, to the extent true, reflects a sad necessity, 'All Chinese are coinage experts.'[8]

The problems remained until the forced acceptance of Chinese Government banknotes as legal tender in the reforms of 1936, by which time the Hongkong Bank's China banknote issue was negligible.

Tientsin – a case study

The standard fineness of the monetary silver of Tientsin, that is the fineness on which monetary calculations were based, was 992 (parts in 1000). In Shanghai the sycee in circulation was not necessarily of a standard fineness, but the difference was marked on the 'shoe' and passed current as marked; in Tientsin, there was no such consistent system, but the shoes came from official money shops, and their fineness was apparently the responsibility of the appropriate guild. As long as the person receiving the silver was, however, satisfied that the sycee was standard, it passed as such. In this it resembled the more usual form of coin which would be accepted at its face value so long as no one suspected it had been debased or tampered with.

What happened in 1909 in Tientsin was that (i) the sycee had in fact been debased, sometimes to 880, without notice but had passed current until (ii) the Haikwan Bank, the official Chinese bank which received payment for Maritime Customs duties, demanded a supplementary payment to bring the actual silver content of the sycee presented up to par. The exchange between the Tientsin monetary tael and the Haikwan tael in which duties were assessed was Tientsin Ts105 = HkTs100, assuming the sycee tendered was on a 992 basis.[9] This rate would naturally not hold good against depreciated or incorrectly marked sycee, but for a long period the Haikwan Bank did not protest; when it did, the foreign banks objected.

The basis for the protest was the same as for a conventional coin. A coin usually circulates at a slight premium over its intrinsic value, a premium necessary to cover the expense of minting. The premium can exist because of the convenience of handling – the intrinsic value of the coin should not need to be questioned at the time of payment or it is failing to serve its function as a coin – there would be no advantage over payment in bullion. But acceptance of a coin assumes that the Government or other authority is ultimately responsible (except for obvious carelessness in dealing with counterfeits) for the reliability of the coinage.

The foreign merchant community in Tientsin now took just this position. Monetary sycee had been accepted after the equivalent of a coinage process, the making of the silver into an alloy in a traditional shape (the 'shoe') and marking that shape with an official notification which implied the actual silver content and therefore the intrinsic value of the silver alloy (monetary silver or sycee).

After negotiations in which the Bank played a leading role, it was agreed in 1910 that the cost of bringing the debased sycee up to par should be borne by the Chinese Chamber of Commerce and that an official assaying office would be established under Chinese jurisdiction.[10] In the course of the negotiations the Shanghai branch of the Hongkong Bank wrote to D.H. Mackintosh, the Tientsin Manager, reminding him of a Shanghai precedent. When in 1906 a shipment of sycee to Japan turned out, exceptionally, to be below standard, claims were accepted by the *kung-ku*, or official assayer. The Shanghai *kung-ku* was financed by local guilds and bankers and his appointment confirmed by the Taotai.[11]

The Currency Reform Loan of 1911

Under the provisions of Article II of the Mackay Treaty of 1902 China agreed to 'take the necessary steps to provide for a uniform national coinage which should be legal tender in payment of all duties, taxes and other obligations throughout the Empire by British as well as Chinese subjects'.[12]

Sir James Mackay's report on this problem was based in large part on a memorandum by Charles Addis, then Sub-Manager Shanghai, which had been written at the former's request. The main objectives were a uniform coinage based on a standard, full-bodied coin, the necessary establishment of regional mints under national control, a national Government bank, the abolition of sycee as a means of payment and the tael as a unit of account, and the advice of a foreign expert.

In early 1903 Addis was sounded as to his willingness to serve as the expert, but he declined, although he continued to be consulted informally by, among others, E.G. Hillier, then in Shanghai having been seconded as British representative with the international Commission of Bankers.[13]

The assessment of anything as complex and unlikely as reform of the Chinese monetary system required an economist with Eastern experience, and Professor Jeremiah W. Jenks of Cornell, whose main academic qualifications were based on his recent assessments of monetary problems in the East, including those of the Philippines, was commissioned to draw up a scheme which he determined should involve the establishment of a gold standard based on a loan of £4 million.

The Chinese in fact reversed the scheme, determined to establish a uniform silver currency and then, perhaps, move to a gold standard. But despite what the Foreign Office saw as the serious view the Chinese Government took towards the problem of currency reform, there was naturally considerable wavering on so complex a subject. At one time, in 1905, an Imperial edict decreed a uniform coin on the basis of the Kuping or Treasury tael, a scheme which came under the reasoned criticism of E.G. Hillier, the Bank's Peking Agent, and his views were transmitted to the Foreign Office.[14]

In 1910, by the time the Chinese Government's currency proposals were in a form requiring foreign financial assistance, the Hongkong Bank was the British Group of a Four Power Groups Inter-Bank Agreement, also known as the China Consortium, comprising in addition the Deutsch-Asiatische Bank, the Banque de l'Indo-Chine, and the American Group represented by J.P. Morgan and Co., Kuhn, Loeb and Co., First National Bank, and National City Bank – all of New York. In fact the Chinese first offered a $Gold 50 million loan to the American Group, but diplomatic negotiation led to the offer being turned over for consideration by the Four Power Groups (see Part II below). The loan was negotiated by the Groups at Brussels in March 1911 as the 5% Currency Reform Gold Loan for £10 million.[15]

In the course of negotiations the Currency Loan was joined with an industrial loan for Manchurian development. Since the Manchurian revenues were pledged as part of the security, the French felt it necessary to clear actual expenditures with the Russians. Thus from the first the matter of currency reform became involved with international politics, confusing even further a particularly complex matter. The two sections of the proposed £10 million loan were to be divided with £2.5 million for industrial development and £7 million for currency reform, and it was presumably noticed at the time that this did not add up. Nevertheless the Brussels Agreement was successfully presented to the Chinese on April 15, 1911, with Hillier signing for the Hongkong Bank.[16] The currency sector of the loan was to be paid out on the basis of firm proposals from the Chinese as agreed to by a Committee of Experts appointed by the participating banks. The consideration of such proposals was, accordingly, the next step in the proceedings. The Committee, which was headed by Professor Jenks for the American Group and included Sir David Barbour, Bernhard Dernburg, and A. de Foville, met with the local Peking representatives of the banks, E.G. Hillier of the Hongkong Bank, H. Cordes, René Saint Pierre, and Willard Straight, and with Ch'en Chin-t'ao, the Vice-President of the Ta-Ch'ing Bank and chairman of the Currency Committee of the Board of Finance in Peking, as the principal Chinese representative at the discussions.

The proceedings were marred by the resentment of the Chinese Government that the judgement of a foreign group should be a prerequisite for a loan dealing with China's internal monetary affairs. Dr Ch'en was present, in fact, almost in secret, and considerable time had to be spent working out a formula which would be sufficiently ambiguous as to give the report of the expert committee credibility while convincing the Chinese that it had not actually existed as such.[17]

As the Currency Loan did not come into effect in the form then negotiated, the detailed provisions do not concern this history. It is nevertheless useful to note that the Chinese envisaged incorporating into any relevant edict the right to set a limit to the number of full-bodied coins to be minted. The foreign experts pointed out that unless the mints were open to the free coinage of silver, China could not be said to be on a silver standard, or, more properly, the measures proposed in the report before the Committee would not result in China's retaining the silver standard. To this Dr Ch'en replied that the Government had not yet decided between the merits of a silver or gold standard for China and, if the latter were decided on, China would have to be able to restrict the silver coinage – as in the Philippines.[18]

Throughout the discussions, which were reported to the Inter-Bank Group in full, it is clear that despite the political impediments Dr Ch'en was extremely helpful and frank. Nevertheless Charles Addis's assessment as provided to the Foreign Office is essentially fair: 'I cannot say that it is a satisfactory document. You may search in vain for what I think we might reasonably have expected from a committee of such eminence . . .'[19]

Despite this apparent set-back the Inter-Bank Group met in Berlin on September 23, 1911, and, with Addis then junior London Manager representing the Hongkong Bank, surprisingly came to an agreement which basically gave the Chinese a free hand in the expenditure of the loan funds as far as currency reform was concerned. The meeting also recommended the appointment, subsequently accepted by the Chinese, of Dr G. Vissering, the experienced and prestigious president of the Java Bank – and thus as a Dutch citizen representing a 'neutral' country – as the financial adviser.[20]

But time was running out. The conference continued over October 10, 1911. If the Double Tenth passed unnoticed in Berlin, it did not in China.

By January 1912 the Peking representatives of the banks had composed a memorandum which took note of developments and recognized that the Agreement would have to be in whole or part renegotiated – it evolved eventually into the Reorganization Loan of 1913 (see Chapter 8).[21] The last of the Ch'ing emperors, the six-year old P'u-i, abdicated the Dragon Throne effective February 17, 1912. In the interim the banks permitted advances against the eventual signing, but the monies thus borrowed were needed urgently to keep the Government afloat and currency reform was a luxury which was once again postponed.

Hong Kong

When the Bank was established in 1865 the focus of monetary reform was on the full-bodied legal tender coin, the Mexican dollar. Banknotes were but a substitute; demand deposits were not reckoned as part of the money supply. The status of Hong Kong as a Crown Colony meant, in a sense, that what was economically but a port of China, a small part of a larger economy, it was, as far as political determination of its monetary system, part of the British Empire. While officials in London were aware of the anomaly, they were prepared to deviate from colonial practice, if at all, only after lengthy discussion during which the residents of Hong Kong had to find, if they could, their own remedy.

To a growing extent they found this in bank money – both banknotes and demand deposits.

Selecting the legal tender coins

Much was written on the inadequate 'supply' of coins. To the extent that this was a complaint about the amount of monetary silver available for payments in Hong Kong, it was a comment on the balance of payments on the Colony's current account and the relative value of silver; it was a comment as to whether silver in any form was being imported in the quantities required. But usually the term 'supply' in this particular context referred to the supply of coins in sufficiently good shape to pass as coins and not simply as a weight of silver of a given fineness. The problem had arisen due to the Chinese practice of chopping or otherwise tampering with the silver coinage.

The first solution which had suggested itself was the establishment of a mint in Hong Kong, but, as described in Volume I, this depended on silver being brought to the mint and on users absorbing the cost of minting. As conditions were not appropriate, the mint was closed and the machinery moved to Japan where the Hongkong Bank's Agent, A.M. Townsend, assisted the Japanese with the supply of bullion and the introduction of the Japanese equivalent to the Mexican dollar, the 'yen'.[22]

In March 1877 members of the Chinese community of Hong Kong stated the problem concisely in a 'no-nonsense' petition, 'praying the Government of their goodness to settle the currency question, and to issue a proclamation ordering a reform to be made, for the benefit of the people concerned'.[23]

The Hong Kong bank managers then attempted to persuade the Government to declare the American trade dollar and the Japanese yen a legal tender in Hong Kong but were opposed on the latter by the General Chamber of Commerce. The history of the former coin is found in Volume I; the Japanese yen was refused on the grounds that (i) too few coins had been minted and (ii) the Japanese authorities did not as yet seem to understand coinage principles, there having been both a 'yen' and a 'trade yen', a surprising comment in view of the Treasury's own failure to solve colonial monetary problems and of their willingness to sanction the yen's legal tender status in the Straits Settlements. The yen was officially accepted in Canton and passed current in other Chinese cities.[24] In a sense this was ironic because the recent history of the Mexican dollar, reflecting internal problems in Mexico, had been one of uncertainty.

In 1877 a special committee of the Chamber of Commerce, of which Thomas Jackson was a member, did petition the Government for a British dollar to be minted in India. The committee urged that the closing of the Hong Kong mint had been premature – they engaged in no recriminations, but the Hongkong Bank had made an offer, then refused, by which the mint could have been kept open (see Volume I, Chapter 5).[25] However the cost factor thwarted this reform once more.

The next concerted action was triggered by the fear of a Mexican export tax on their dollars and by the fall in silver in 1893 which led to the closing of the Indian mints to free coinage of silver. The first proposals, endorsed by the Hongkong Bank, were to grant legal tender status to the Japanese yen, but shortly afterwards Japan herself began reconsidering her standard and the future of the silver yen was becoming increasingly uncertain – it was in fact demonetized in 1900.[26]

The British dollar
This led to a second set of proposals for the coinage of a British dollar coin,

both for Hong Kong (and China) and the Straits. The relevant Straits Settlements authorities had in 1893 rejected for the time being any prospect of leaving the silver standard, and the British dollar was consequently authorized for both colonies by an Order in Council of February 1895 which specified a fineness of 900 and a standard weight of 416 grains, the same specifications as for the Mexican dollar.[27]

After a survey by a Colonial Office committee – before which Ewen Cameron testified – it was agreed between the Hongkong Bank and the Chartered Bank that they would support the minting of such a coin by the Indian mints at a minimum level of five million coins a year at 1% seigniorage, and both banks entered into a contract for delivery of the new British dollar – G.E. Noble signing for the Hongkong Bank with G.H. Townsend, the Bank's Bombay Manager, authorized to negotiate the details in India.[28]

There were expectations, as previously noted, that the coin would circulate in China, and indeed it was Sir James Mackay in 1905 who called the attention of the British Government to the fact that the coin was then little seen. This puts a focus on the special circumstances which made the British dollar coin an initial but, in a sense, reluctant success.[29]

The 1894 date for the initial negotiations relative to the British dollar suggests the closing of the Indian mints to free coinage of rupees, which in turn suggests a potentially idle mint and thus explains the willingness of the authorities to undertake a 'foreign' coinage at the low seigniorage of 1%. Even then the negotiations which followed the signing of the contract introduced surprising elements which forced the Chartered Bank's manager to protest on behalf of both the Chartered and Hongkong Banks. The Bombay mint was undertaking the task on a narrow profit margin and was insisting on conditions, including a longer-than-expected delivery time, which undermined the prospects for the success of the coin.[30]

One positive development was noted. The Hong Kong Government had assumed that special legislation would have to be introduced to prevent chopping of the new British dollar coin, but Thomas Jackson, writing as the Bank's Chief Manager, urged that this was unnecessary and the coin was consequently admitted as legal tender by tale or count. The custom of chopping was, Jackson reported, dying out, especially, one might add, when clean dollars were at the high premium they then commanded.[31]

Although the initial difficulties were eventually overcome and expenses of the coinage fully covered by the 1% seigniorage, the circumstances had been particular and when the Indian mints were again needed for Indian coinage the banks, facing the demand for an arbitrary seigniorage of 2%, let the agreement lapse in June 1903. The need for a dollar coin, however, remained.[32]

In 1905 the Hongkong Bank reopened negotiations with the Indian mints, but it then became clear the mints were unable, at least for a period, to undertake additional commissions.[33] Consequently in early 1906 the Hong-kong Bank's San Francisco Agent, W.H. Harries, began abortive negotiations by correspondence with the 'Comision de Cambios y Moneda' in Mexico City for the coinage of a Mexican trade dollar especially for the Eastern trade; the Mexican demand for up to $2\frac{1}{4}\%$ seigniorage, although on a downward sliding scale, opened up the question of renegotiation with the Indian mints and there was even discussion of reestablishing the Hong Kong mint.[34] At the same time J.R.M. Smith was assuring Governor Nathan of Hong Kong that Harries had been reminded that 'as a British Bank it is for us in the interests of British trade and prestige in China to push the British Dollar and to see that it is not handicapped in cost of minting as compared with its rival the Mexican'.[35]

Thus while Harries was attempting to bring down the Mexican costs, Smith was trying to play the nationality card to bring down the Indian seigniorage to 1%, arguing on the basis of British prestige in China. Given the problems of maintaining a coinage, such largely irrelevant issues were particularly unfortunate.

In any case the importance of China was overwhelming and despite continued consideration of proposed solutions to the coinage problem, in effect the Colony waited for developments in China before committing itself. As the Foreign Office memorandum on the renegotiations concluded:

> It looks therefore as if the British dollar will disappear gradually from China, and that any efforts we may attempt to prevent this would be more fruitful if made in the direction of inducing the Chinese Government to give effect to Article II of the Mackay Treaty of 1902 by introducing a uniform system of coinage into China, thereby removing the need either for a Mexican or a British dollar.[36]

All this became reflected in the statistics of banknotes in circulation, a story that has already been considered in the context of the Bank's relations with Government. The one-dollar banknote issue as a separate problem has also been considered.

Sufficient to add here that by 1913 and given the Treasury decision that an increased banknote issue was preferable to a Government note issue (see discussion below), the Chartered Bank's note issuing capabilities in Hong Kong had been increased by supplemental charter and reallocation from other branches, and new legislation had restored the right of the Mercantile Bank of India, Ltd, to a Hong Kong note issue, including an 'excess' issue in a declared emergency.[b]

---

[b]   In the Mercantile Bank Note Issue Ordinance, No. 65 of 1911, Article 6 permits an excess issue against 100% backing in silver dollars when the Governor-in-Council certifies the existence of a temporary emergency. The Chartered Bank obtained permission from the Treasury on three

The curious case of the premium

And yet after all this the Hong Kong dollar unit of account was still quoted at a premium over its theoretical silver value.

Under such circumstances it was natural that there should be considerable discussion concerning a Hong Kong Government note issue, and indeed, legislation was discussed in Council.[38] Expert opinion was however unanimous in supposing that a Government note issue would be ineffective in solving the current problem and would create its own additional problems. A Government note issue was not expected of itself to correct the premium, as this was seen as the consequence of trade factors, quite possibly disturbances in South China since 1905 had resulted in Overseas Chinese remittances remaining and being banked in Hong Kong, building up idle funds. This view was supported by statistics showing a fall in imports into the region.

A Government note issue would be expensive and the Government did not have the staff or expertise to handle the details. This could have eventually been overcome, the Hongkong Bank even inviting the Government to send observers to see how the note issue was handled.

Finally, critics noted that if, as was being considered, the Government were to invest part of the currency reserve in gold securities, it would be running a considerable exchange risk.[39]

The Hongkong Bank's advice was sought, provoking the careful comment by J.R.M. Smith quoted at the head of this chapter.[40]

In the end it was the China dimension that made the Government reconsider; in other territories the issue was at least for a single Colony and its British-controlled hinterland; in Hong Kong the success of a currency depended on an intimate knowledge of the China trade such as only the exchange banks possessed.

The Treasury's R.G. Hawtrey, who minuted at length on the subject, was concerned that if there were no limit to the Hongkong Bank's note issue it could circulate throughout China and, should there be a credit crisis, the whole weight of the loss of confidence would fall on the monetary facilities of Hong Kong. Secondly, the Chinese Government was still in the process of developing its own plans for monetary reform. This, therefore, was once again an inopportune time for the Government to take over.[41]

The Government contented itself, therefore, with attempting to improve the subsidiary coinage and prevent the circulation of foreign and Chinese banknotes.

The failure to reform the Hong Kong currency had put Hong Kong *de facto*

---

occasions between 1905 and 1913 to 're-allocate' its note issue to allow for a larger circulation in Hong Kong.[37]

onto an arbitrary standard, which, while not unrelated to silver, could and did fluctuate in reference to supply and demand factors independently of the theoretical limitations imposed by the silver import/export points. Such a phenomenon was not unusual in monetary history and had in fact been alluded to in Adam Smith's *Wealth of Nations* in relation to the notes of the Bank of Amsterdam.

The first prerequisite for such development to succeed would be for the legal tender coin, when available, to be unaccepted at par in the normal course of trade. This happened in Hong Kong; payments had perforce to be made in bank money. And since (i) the banks alone decided whether to increase their note issue and (ii) with a 100% silver backing required for the marginal issue plus a 1% tax, it did not always suit the banks to do so, the value of the Hong Kong dollar was effectively divorced from that of the value of the accepted silver content of the legal tender coin. Even J.R.M. Smith recognized that, given the then state of the Colony's finances, there was no point in raising the question of repealing the 1% tax, although there are indications the Colonial Office would have been sympathetic under other circumstances.[42]

A debt in Hong Kong expressed in terms of the Hong Kong unit of account could no longer be satisfied by payment in legal tender at par; it could only be satisfied by payment of banknotes or cheques on a current account at par.

Such a situation could in theory be corrected by arbitrage; those who had the coin could pay in at par (as by law was required) and draw out notes at a premium, buy more coins and so repeat the process, making a profit on each turn.

This proved impractical because the Hongkong Bank, and presumably the other exchange banks, would only receive coins to the credit of an account at par on the understanding that payouts from such accounts would also be in coin.[c] Thus the banks did not violate the legal tender laws. However, this policy prevented the customer from benefiting from the potential of arbitrage, and, if he did draw out his funds in coins, he found that shopkeepers and other merchants would only accept them at a discount. He could let the matter become the subject of legal action – so could those tendering and facing refusal of the recently minted Susan B. Anthony U.S. dollars in a more modern example of legal tender rejection. He could on the other hand simply

---

[c] Recently in Hong Kong (1982) large denomination U.S. notes were passing at a slight premium in the market over small denomination notes. The Bank reacted to protect itself from a customer paying in small denomination notes to the credit of U.S. dollar accounts, withdrawing large ones, selling them in the market for small notes to a marginally larger value, paying these in and repeating the process. The Hongkong Bank paid out only in small-denomination U.S. dollar bills to its U.S. dollar savings account customers, for example, unless their passbook indicated they had at some time paid in large denomination U.S. dollar bills.

conform to the mercantile custom of Hong Kong, an alternative he learned it wise to pursue.[43]

The Commander of British Forces in Hong Kong urged the Governor to 'pass a law'. The Governor declined to do so.[44]

Unsatisfactory as the situation might appear to Government, Treasury Chest operations did not force a change. In London Sir Charles Addis protested against the Paymaster paying in dollar coins and demanding unqualified credit at par. His protest was successful; the Paymaster was instructed to conform to mercantile practice in Hong Kong.[45]

This then was the situation through 1918.

There was naturally considerable concern in Britain over the situation. For a silver standard currency exchange rate to vary from par within limits set by insurance, freight, etc., the import/export points, was understood, but for the exchange to vary as between legal tender coin and bank money and for the latter to be standard was not. The main public concern derived from the problem of determining the rate at which to pay British soldiers and others entitled to a certain specified sterling amount. The problem of the Paymaster was complicated by the Treasury's policy towards the one-dollar note issue of the Hongkong Bank. Soldiers entitled to sums not multiples of five had to be paid in five-dollar notes plus dollar coins as there were insufficient one-dollar notes for the purpose, but as the dollar coins passed current at a discount the soldier considered himself cheated and, apparently, said so.[46]

A Parliamentary Committee was established to discover 'the mode of issuing the Dollar in the East'; the concern of members was to ensure that the Treasury paid out the sums authorized while at the same time meeting the rights and requirements of the soldiers, who could not be expected to understand such esoteric matters. The real problem was that on the contrary some soldiers at least fully understood, and the protests arose when, in order to prevent them from engaging in profitable arbitrage, they were forbidden, for example, to purchase postal orders in amounts exceeding their salary plus 50% of allowances![47]

Sir Charles Addis's testimony on these subjects is masterful; he recommended acceptance of the reality of Hong Kong mercantile practice and, *inter alia*, payment of the troops at the TT rate on Hong Kong.[48]

The Hong Kong exchange rate and the Bank

But what was the TT rate and how was it determined?

The official Hong Kong exchange rate was set at 9:00 a.m. by the Chief Manager of the Hongkong and Shanghai Banking Corporation. The foreign staff 'junior' responsible for cables notified him of the closing price of silver in the London market, the officer in charge of 'books' had brought him up to date on the Bank's currency position, and with these considerations in mind the Chief Manager set the basic rate from which all other rates could be derived by formulas.[49]

This rate was based on bank money, that is, the rate, Hong Kong on London, assumed the purchaser of sterling would pay in Hong Kong banknotes (or have his current account debited); if he paid in silver dollars he would require a special rate, which the Bank stated in December 1914, for example, would be as much as 10% lower.[50]

During Jackson's time the practice developed of posting the rate outside the Chief Manager's door and ringing a bell. The brokers then ran off to the other banks with the 'official' rate, determined on the sole responsibility of the Hongkong Bank's Chief Manager.

This, it should be noted, was also the pattern in Shanghai where silver rather than notes was and would remain the basis of the exchanges until 1936. That a foreign bank should set the 'official' rate has been misunderstood in a political context; a further explanation relating to the practice in Hong Kong may be helpful in placing the Manager's 'power' in context.

If the Manager set the 'correct' rate, business would be transacted at that rate; if it were the 'wrong' rate, the other banks would buy against the Hongkong Bank and force it to change the rate to its serious loss. The Bank acted as a market leader, to be followed only under the right conditions, and there was no compulsion to accept the Hongkong Bank's decision. If a bank had a particular temporary position which it wished to correct, it might do business at a rate entirely of its own choosing.

Addis was especially concerned to stress that the rate was determined without collusion; it was one man's estimate of the correct rate, a man who had, moreover, the resources to maintain it – for a time.[51] But all this partly begs the question as to what was the 'correct' rate – how did the Chief Manager determine what he thought would be accepted in the market?

The principle involved is simple: the correct rate is one which will clear the market, or, to put it another way, cause the supply of Hong Kong dollars offered on the market in purchase of sterling to equal the demand for Hong Kong dollars of those willing to purchase them with sterling. Although Newton Stabb – in a 'private memorandum' for the use of Governor May in explaining to the Secretary of State the reasons for the continued premium on notes – put this at first in terms of the balance of trade, he later added 'invisibles', including remittances of Overseas Chinese; he might also have added the demand and supply of the Bank's own resources, or short-term movement of funds, being used to lay in funds or unload funds in anticipation of changes in the balance of payments.

The volume of the trade of South China which is financed through Hong Kong is very large and runs into many millions of sterling per annum. Apart from the export of silk and other produce from Canton against which merchants sell Bills, there is an enormous amount of money remitted from America, Philippines, Java, Siam, and Straits Settlements by Chinese to South China all financed through this Colony – this money represents savings and is also sent in payment of exports from ports in South China for use of Chinese abroad. Such remittances, which from a banking point of view have the same effect on exchange as exports, always increase at a lower level of exchange, and we find that we get more on one side of our book than we can cover, the consequence being that exchange is automatically forced up until a change takes place, that is, either drawings from abroad on Hong Kong fall away or a demand for remittances from Hong Kong to gold countries arises sufficient to cover the operations on the other side of the book. The exchange banking business of the Colony is almost entirely buying and selling gold in some form, and exchange is influenced accordingly – if the greater volume is on the buying side the tendency is for exchange to advance and vice versa.[52]

For 'gold' read 'currencies on a gold standard'; in practice this meant mainly sterling.

Stabb's experience was that the exchange market adjusts quickly, in part because the market forces are highly responsive to small changes in the exchange rate. His analysis deals with immediate short-run factors; it does not consider, for example, the development of new export industries when the exchange remains low for a considerable period of time, an argument advanced by Thomas Jackson and others in support of China remaining on a silver standard. This will be considered below.

At the time of writing, that is in June 1915, Stabb reported that at the current rates, which were at a $6\frac{3}{4}$% premium over the silver par of exchange, it was easier for the Bank 'to buy than to sell gold', suggesting that there was pressure for the rate to go up further, increasing the premium which so worried the Colonial Office. The situation would be altered, Stabb warned, only by an advance in the price of silver which would eliminate the premium for a time, or by an increase in the demand for imports into China, thus increasing the demand for gold which would in turn tend to cause the exchange rate to fall towards silver parity.

At this point Stabb turned to the key question: why, in view of the premium, did the Bank not increase the note issue until parity were restored?

It is not quite clear what procedure is intended to increase the note issue, but assume that the Bank agreed to accept silver and pay out notes until all requirements were met at a decreasing premium; this would tend to equate notes with silver and so lower the exchange to the silver parity. Stabb stated that this was in effect 'to depress the exchange artificially and the volume of business on one side would soon cause a reaction. We could not continue to receive silver dollars which could be imported at say 1s:8$\frac{1}{4}$d at par with notes the purchasing power of which was considerably higher.' In other words the lower exchange effected in this way would increase the amount of Hong Kong dollars demanded in the market and tend to drive the rate up again, all the while the Bank would be continuing to pay out notes at par; it would be the very arbitrage transaction which the Bank had been careful to prevent.

But Stabb had another and related problem: 'By Government regulation the Bank is required to deposit dollar for dollar the equivalent of every additional note which we issue, and we have to reckon with the fact that some day these notes will come back leaving us with a mass of silver which might – and probably would – involve us in heavy loss.'[53]

As the Bank was then operating, when a merchant financed imports, he paid in dollar notes and the Bank paid sterling to his order in London by TT. The Bank's holdings of silver remained unchanged. 'Our note circulation,' Stabb explained, 'has dropped about $10 millions at times without a dollar leaving us.'[54]

Or, he might have added, the Bank's silver position was determined by the Chief Manager to some extent independently of the balance of its exchange operations. Its pay-out of sterling, a decline in assets, was offset by the pay-in of a banknote, a decline in demand liabilities; it was not offset by the gain of an asset or covered by the movement through sale of silver bullion. Bullion movements were determined by the Chief Manager on the basis of further criteria, as for example, the demand for coinage in countries where silver coins were the medium of exchange even where the monetary system was based on gold, for example, India.

Subsidiary coinage

The dollar coins circulating in China came from overseas and until the very last years of the Ch'ing dynasty, there was no effective coinage of the dollar in China itself. There was also no subsidiary coin in the dollar system. The Chinese used copper 'cash' for small payments, a full-bodied copper coin passing current because of its intrinsic value, round in shape, with a square hole in the middle to permit stringing in sub-sets which passed current at one hundred *'ch'ien'* units of account or in ten sub-sets passing at 1,000, theoretically equivalent to one tael of sycee. In fact the copper coins varied in value to their silver equivalent according to the price of silver as expressed in copper – and other factors.[55]

There were many variants to this system, which was complex, costly, and labour-intensive, since the stringing of the cash alone was a skilled task requiring an ability to detect spurious coins and to arrange a combination of full-weight and defective coins such that the string of cash would be accepted as current in the market. Little wonder therefore that the first 'reform', occurring as early as the 1890s, was the coining of a modern-style minted copper cash and in the early 1900s the attempted replacement of a copper coin from the 'cash' system by a silver subsidiary coin in the dollar system.

With the establishment of modern mints the Chinese provincial authorities also undertook to coin subsidiary silver coins. By definition these contained less than the proportionate amount of silver, that is ten ten-cent silver coins contained less silver than a standard British dollar or Mexican dollar. It was profitable, therefore, to produce as many subsidiary coins as the market would take at par, but there was always the temptation to over-produce. The minting of an excessive number of subsidiary coins, which were not legal tender for unlimited amounts, would remain profitable so long as the discount was less in value than the difference between the value of the silver in the dollar and the value in the subsidiary coins nominally totalling a dollar.

The effect of the over-production of subsidiary coins was to require say eleven ten-cent coins in payment of a dollar unit of account or, as it came to be known, *ta-yin* or 'big-silver'; however if a price were quoted in *hsiao-yin* or 'small-silver', then it could be settled by tender of subsidiary coins at par. The 'reform' had introduced yet another complication into the system.[56]

In 1905 71 million twenty-cent pieces were minted in Canton, dollars being melted down to provide the silver, and one-dollar notes being overstamped that they were redeemable only in twenty-cent coins. Thus *hsiao-yin* was becoming effectively the actual currency of the Liang-Kwang provinces.[57]

The official mind in Hong Kong naturally rebelled against such developments, even though the use of small coins was practically confined to the Chinese sector of the population and economy. As long as only Hong Kong subsidiary coins were involved, the Government could prevent excessive supplies and therefore maintain them at par; the Government could not, despite putting $46.8 million worth of subsidiary coins into circulation between 1883 and 1906, always ensure an adequate supply, and in consequence coins minted in Kwangtung began to circulate, the supply of which the Government could not control. Just as their minting was profitable to the provincial mint authorities, so their import into Hong Kong was profitable to small traders; it was overdone, and subsidiary coins, both Kwangtung and Hong Kong, depreciated. Public transport companies, which had to accept payment in subsidiary coins, objected to finding them accepted by the banks only at a discount, and in 1906 the Government was forced not only to take steps to ensure the supply of its own subsidiary coinage but also to attempt to prevent the import and circulation of Kwangtung coinage. This last in reality involved attempting to convince the Kwangtung authorities that they should cease for the time being the minting of subsidiary coins.

Once again the Hongkong Bank became involved. J.R.M. Smith as the

Hongkong Bank's Chief Manager instructed the Sub-Manager J.C. Peter to discuss the problem with mint authorities in Canton and report. Peter, with the assistance of the British Consul-General, R.W. Mansfield, met with the Taotai, two Chinese officials of the mint, and one of the Board of Reorganization. The problem, as with the Indian mints in 1894, was excess capacity and the need to keep a trained staff employed, but, as Peter saw it, the existence of the mint and the revenue shortages of the Government combined to create the temptation to over-produce. 'One of the Chinese had a brilliant idea that the Government should buy up as much of the subsidiary coinage as possible in the open market, and store it till contraction brought it back to par, but he was immediately asked by his colleagues where he expected the money to come from to carry through such a scheme.'[58] Peter concluded his memorandum by noting that the Consul-General 'afterwards most hospitably entertained us all to lunch'.[59]

The problem was a continuing one.

Currency and payments problems in the Philippines

The currency question first presented itself to the American authorities in a form which has plagued commanders in the field from time immemorial – as a payments problem; that is, the Government intended to pay specific sums to its officers, men, and civil servants, when the recipients dealt with the banks they in some mysterious way seemed to 'lose out' to the inevitable 'gain' of the banks. The *Manila Times* stated that Philippine currency was –

an extremely mixed-up affair, so mixed up that it constituted the study of a lifetime, and various people who devoted their lives to the study of it used to make money of it at the expense of the people whose time was otherwise occupied . . . at all times and under all circumstances the banks, exchange brokers, and a few clever Chinese and others managed to juggle with the fluctuations in change and currency legislation so as to score always.[60]

There were many money changers who wished that this were true.

There were such practical problems as: assume that an American soldier tenders a nickel in U.S. currency to pay for a two centavo tram ride, what change does he get? The answer to this might well depend on factors irrelevant to monetary history, but there are a few observations, based on memorandums submitted by the Bank's Managers H.D.C. Jones in Manila and A.M. Townsend in New York, which are helpful in view of the Hongkong Bank's subsequent position on currency reform.

The Bank encouraged the authorities to regard these specific incidents of manifest confusion not as aberrations caused by tricky banks but rather as evidence of a basic defect in the monetary system of the Philippines, a system which consequently needed overall, not piecemeal, correction.

The monetary system of the Philippines was based on the use of a silver coinage, but the Spanish authorities had not been certain whether to allow the peso unit of account to be silver, gold, or fiat based.

If a country determines to use a silver coin but is not to be on a silver standard, then the value of the coin in terms of the unit of account must be separated from its intrinsic value as silver. If the Government can enforce its laws, this goal can be achieved by declaring a specific silver coin to be sole legal tender and then controlling its supply.

The Spanish authorities in the Philippine Islands declared the Mexican dollar legal tender, with the tender of one dollar Mex satisfying a debt of one peso unit of account. When silver depreciated, the authorities decided that they did not wish the currency, the peso, to depreciate. The solution was to legislate against the import of more Mexican dollars, thus limiting their supply. The Spanish Government considered the Philippine unit of account to be – or wished it to be – related to a gold standard and were attempting the equivalent of the Indian 'closing' of the mints to free coinage. Unfortunately, they put these import restrictions into effect before they were in a position to provide the Islands with a specifically minted coin of their own, although they did contract with the Hongkong Bank for the import of silver for this purpose.

The measures taken to achieve the Spanish policy had two defects, one immediate and one potential: (i) the authorities were unable to prevent the smuggling of Mexican dollar coins, which thus had a lower value in the Philippines, reflected in the fact that the exchange rate was usually such that the Hongkong dollar was at a premium over the Philippine unit by the cost of smuggling; the Hongkong Bank had consistently obtained smuggled Mexican dollars in the export season and seen these same coins leave the country in the 'dull' periods and (ii) the Mexican dollar, the actual legal tender coin of the Islands, might not, and in 1900 did not, move with the value of silver even on open markets. The uncertain position of the authorities and the undefined nature of the standard was further accentuated by the demonetization of Mexican dollars in Spain, which prevented the development of a system similar to that which existed in the first years of the American administration.

With the coming of the Americans the U.S. dollar silver coin circulated with the Mexican dollar; both were called 'dollars' yet the former, referred to as a 'dollar gold', had twice the value of the latter in terms of the peso unit of account, although containing less silver, because it could be exchanged *in the United States* at par with the gold-based currency there. Thus there were gold-based and silver-based silver coins both called 'dollars' circulating side by side with par rates declared arbitrarily (as far as the Manila market was concerned) by U.S. Government paymasters.

In 1899, to restore a measure of reality and order to the system, General

Greene, acting for General Merritt, granted permission to the two British banks, the Chartered Bank and the Hongkong Bank, to import silver Mexican dollars legally to an unlimited amount. The attempts since 1878 to give the silver Mexican dollar a unique value in the Philippines by prohibiting its import and all plans to replace these coins eventually with a special (Spanish) Philippine coin were for the time being abandoned.

The break in the two standards had by General Greene's action become clear cut, although not necessarily understood; currency reform, when it came, would in consequence be simpler to justify or at least to explain.

Should the American authorities decide to place the Philippines on a gold standard, the Hongkong Bank would be permitted to cover itself, as H.D.C. Jones explained it, to the extent that the Bank supplied Mexican dollars to the troops for 'gold', to that extent it would be allowed to replace them, that is, import an amount of Mexican dollars equal to the amount of gold purchased.

The result of this operation, had it been successful, would have been (i) to minimize the cost to the American soldier of exchanging 'gold' coins and other means of payment for Mexican dollars and (ii) to legalize and recognize the existence in the Philippines of two distinct standards, one 'gold' based on the monetary system of the United States, the other not silver (as some probably expected) but Mexican dollars.

By relating the second standard to the Mexican dollar, however, the agreement with the banks did not achieve the purpose of minimizing fluctuations in the exchange rate between the two standards.

Unfortunately for the authorities, between 1899 and 1900 the gold price of silver rose some 12% but the Mexican dollar itself rose to a premium in terms of its silver content by as much as 8% in terms of currency taels on the Shanghai market. The first years of the American administration coincided with unusual silver and currency fluctuations which were in part a consequence of changes in the Mexican balance of payments but more proximately in the increased demand for silver to pay for the military and related expenses arising from the Boxer Uprising in China.

The Hongkong Bank's role in providing silver and silver coins where they were most in demand, that is where the price was highest, overrode its attempts to assist the Philippine authorities in providing stability in the internal exchanges. Despite all the efforts made on his behalf, the soldier found the U.S. dollar depreciating in the country he had done much to conquer, and his superiors, those responsible for his pay, sought someone to blame. The two foreign banks came first to mind, but a spirited defence was made by the Canadian Bank of Commerce as New York agents for the Chartered Bank, and their explanation was accepted by L.J. Gage, Secretary of the Treasury.[61]

To General Arthur MacArthur (MacArthur, *père*), referring to the British banks as official depositories under the circumstances prevailing in 1900, the system seemed designed to 'furnish foreign banks gratuitously funds for speculation in opposition to the interest of the United States', but Gage responded sharply:

General MacArthur seems to think that the higher price of Mexicans at the bank is due to the perversity and greed of the bank, but finds its excuse in the disturbances in the movement of money caused by Chinese troubles. I am more inclined to believe that the banks are giving no new exhibition of sordidness, but that they themselves are the necessary victims of the unfavourable influences occasioned by the Chinese war. They are obliged to adjust themselves and their actions to the influence of movements they cannot control and I do not see why General MacArthur is not subject to the same rule of commercial necessity.[62]

This was all quite complex. As far as the American administration was concerned the problem arose from its own publication of fixed par rates at which payments would be made in Mexican dollars to local creditors and for local wages and contracts, only to find that, on payment, the gold sum agreed would not equal the silver amount promised or expected. The pay of American soldiers was in terms of U.S. dollars – as the British soldier's pay was denominated in sterling, and the problem of both British and American paymasters was to pay out in the local currency of Hong Kong and the Philippines respectively an amount not only equivalent to the legal entitlement but also in a form which would be accepted as such by soldiers fully aware of their rights.

Soldiers had the right to be paid in U.S. coin and suggestions that they be paid in silver Mexicans were turned down not only on principle but also for more practical reasons; a soldier's weekly pay would then weigh more than 60 rounds of ammunition (presumably for rifles rather than artillery), a lieutenant's 29 pounds, and a colonel's about 73 pounds, although certain Treasury storage facilities could be made available.

A soldier paid in 'gold', that is in U.S. silver coins, would take his pay to a bank, expecting say two Mexican dollars for every one 'gold' dollar, only to receive less; alternatively he might hand in the gold dollars and request credit in the U.S. only to find that the banks would charge a commission or refuse to credit his U.S. account at par; or again the customer might hand over Mexican dollars expecting say half the number of gold dollars in the U.S., only to find that this transaction was subject to an exchange rate which fluctuated.

In brief, U.S. funds outside the United States could not be handled at par; non-U.S. legal tender silver coins were an item of trade, the value of which fluctuated according to market forces not at all times directly related to the value of silver.

In addition to background memorandums and the import – and export – of

Mexicans, the Hongkong Bank made two further practical interventions, (i) recommendations as to how funds might be laid down in the Philippines by the American authorities and paid out economically by the banks and (ii) recommendations as to the appropriate form of currency for the long run. The latter will be considered in the following section.

Townsend summed up the position of the Hongkong Bank in an explanatory letter to Elihu Root, the Secretary of War, by asserting, 'It is our business to provide funds to meet all requirements in that part of the world.'[63] His proposal had been to place credits at the disposal of disbursement officers in the Philippines enabling them to draw bills on U.S. sub-treasuries in San Francisco or New York, negotiable with the Hongkong Bank in Manila, which branch would pay out an equivalence in Mexican dollars. Officers commenting on the proposal asked (i) whether the Bank would always have sufficient Mexican dollars on hand and (ii) whether the Bank would continue the operation if the exchanges turned against them. The Paymaster General of the United States Army took the quite reasonable position that he would not like to be responsible for the approval of any plan which could lead to a failure in the payment of troops in the Philippines.

Funds were actually being laid down in Manila by the export of legal tender coin from the United States by transport, an expensive and time-consuming operation. As long as the Hongkong Bank could provide funds faster and cheaper, Townsend's proposal was acceptable, but American military officials were concerned as to whether they could depend upon it. They had overlooked the margins which the cost of the present methods provided; they failed to recognize, as Townsend reminded the Secretary of War, that the Bank would provide funds without limit at the rate of exchange prevailing at the time of the transaction, that is, at a rate which would probably be determined in large part by the operation itself and, therefore, likely to make the provision of funds profitable to both the Bank and the authorities. The entire cost, including profit, was built into the exchange rate; as Townsend stressed, there would be no other cost in the form of commission, interest, etc.

The Bank's proposal was for the provision of Mexican dollars, the currency of the country. The military authorities were still opposed to payment of troops in other than gold currency, which the Hongkong Bank would also provide but at a 2% discount, which was more, the authorities claimed, than the cost of shipping the coins by transport as presently undertaken.

These discussions, although inconclusive, were useful in setting the stage for eventual monetary reform. All possibilities would seem to have been discussed and the majority of them tested. In cases where, for whatever reason, a payment could be made faster and more cheaply in U.S. 'gold' coin, it would seem that the U.S. authorities could handle it without the intervention of the banks; where payment could be made in Mexican dollars, there is evidence that Townsend's proposal was in fact operated. But these pragmatic solutions still left the recipient of 'gold' coin wishing (i) to remit to the U.S. or (ii) to obtain Mexican dollars dependent on the rates quoted by the two British banks and these remained, therefore, subject to popular or uninformed criticism.

CHANGING THE STANDARD

The catch phrase was 'stability of exchange'. Trade would enrich the world; anything which hindered trade was detrimental to the growth of civilization, fluctuating exchange rates hindered trade, therefore all nations must accept a single monetary standard. So much was clear to Jackson's contemporaries. And by 1900 with the villain identified as silver, all were agreed that the basis for that single standard must be gold – all except a few diehard bimetallists who were still campaigning for William Jennings Bryan. And the Chinese.

Having considered the matter under foreign pressure at least since the Boxer Uprising, the Chinese were, as noted above, still uncertain in 1911. At a 1902 debate in the China Association Thomas Jackson had few doubts. With all the countries about her going on gold, China should remain on silver and reap the competitive advantage of a low exchange. He ruled out the alternative of a silver currency and a gold standard since (i) it would require a standard coin which the autonomy of the various provincial mints would not permit and (ii) the necessary restriction of the coinage could not be achieved as it had been in the Philippines.[64]

The Straits were on the balance geographically, ethnically, and economically. Those who looked to India and westwards urged a form of gold standard; those who looked to the East and north to China urged retention of silver. Meanwhile the currency difficulties of the Philippines forced the American administration into an immediate consideration of monetary problems. They opted for a gold link. The Netherlands East Indies linked with the guilder in Europe, the Straits moved towards gold, and Siam followed.

And Hong Kong? The discussion was only tentative, but there was discussion. Nevertheless the principle was obvious. Hong Kong must have the same currency as South China, it must stay on silver. Nominally Hong Kong did stay on silver, but in fact, as noted above, it was on an arbitrary standard based on the bank money of the exchange banks. That was close to the ideal and fully understood in the Canton Delta region.

Except in Hong Kong, where the Hongkong Bank dominated the monetary system, the Bank played either a passive, accepting role, or else acted as advisers, usually advocating the *status quo*, that is, retention of the silver standard. Exceptionally, in Ceylon the Bank's Manager urged the coining of a separate Ceylon rupee, but that story is marginal to the great monetary developments stimulated by the fall of silver and effected between 1893 and 1914.

A significant Bank role may be observed in the Straits Settlements, where the Manager, T.S. Baker, represented the Chamber of Commerce on the Legislative Council, and the Philippines where the Bank, as a long-established institution, was first subject to criticism for its working of the currency system and the exchanges and then, when the problem was seen to be structural, as an adviser to the Commission sent to consider money and banking questions. As a postscript, the Bank's comments in Ceylon are noted.

The Hongkong Bank and Philippine monetary reform

The task of reporting on the Philippine monetary and banking system and making recommendations for reform was assigned to Charles A. Conant, whose report was submitted on November 25, 1901. In the report an interview with the Hongkong Bank's acting Manila Manager, W. Adams Oram was appended.[65] With reference to the monetary standard and currency Conant had three realistic alternatives: (i) a gold standard with the coins of the United States, (ii) a silver standard with the Mexican dollar or some other coin, or (iii) a gold standard with a special Philippine silver coin. The Hongkong Bank advised a silver standard, Conant chose and the United States adopted the third alternative.

The time was not particularly auspicious for anyone arguing in favour of a silver standard, especially if based on the use of the Mexican dollar, but the arguments usually advanced were of two kinds (a) the decline in the gold price of silver was advantageous to exporting economies and to their per capita real income and (b) the use of a silver coin put the Philippines on the same standard as the rest of the Far East (except Japan) and so facilitated trade.

Conant argued successfully that (a) was not supported by the facts available and that (b) was not sufficiently important to outweigh the disadvantages observed in practice.

This brought him to consideration of a gold standard and the use of American coins. As was often the case in argumentation at this time, the currency was planned to be understood by the 'native' and his level of comprehension, despite considerable evidence to the contrary, was not ranked particularly high. Conant considered that the ordinary Filipino might find it difficult to accept that a coin, for example, a U.S. silver dollar, weighing slightly less than a Mexican dollar, was worth twice the value of a Mexican dollar simply because it could ultimately be used in the United States to buy a gold coin which would be intrinsically worth two Mexican dollars. Without in any way denigrating the intelligence of the ordinary barrio resident (or history student), Conant's concern would seem to have been well-founded.

This left him with alternative (iii), that is, a unit of account, which was to be called the 'peso', two of which would denominate a value equivalent to that denominated by one U.S. dollar unit of account. The 'peso' unit of account would be represented by a specially designed peso coin, later known as the 'conant peso', with a silver content slightly less than that of a Mexican dollar, which coin would then be demonetized. Debts expressed in dollars Mex would be carried at a one-to-one ratio as peso debts; the par value of the peso would be maintained at a 2:1 ratio with the U.S. dollar by means of an exchange fund, and actual market rates would fluctuate between limits set by the commission charged by the Treasury for transfer of funds between the Islands and the United States.

Conant urged the supplementary use of a paper currency and in passing commented favourably on the solvency of the Spanish-Filipino Bank with existing note-issuing privileges, but he was aware that the Hongkong Bank was not then interested in participating in any local issue since their authorized note issue had been fully utilized and any additional issue had to be covered by a 100% deposit of current coin in equivalent value. This position the Hongkong Bank reiterated at various times in the American period.

Monetary reform

The position of the Hongkong Bank with respect to monetary reform was based on the conclusion that the Indian and Japanese monetary changes had not been as successful as expected and that the Philippine trade with the rest of Asia outweighed any other consideration. Putting aside the fact, which the Bank could obviously not have foreseen, that Siam and the Straits Settlements were soon to leave the silver standard, that Indo-China and the Netherlands East Indies would be linked with the mother country, and that even China would eventually abandon silver, the Hongkong Bank's argument made the assumption concerning the importance of intra-regional trade. Whatever validity that might have had was overcome when the Philippines eventually was granted tariff preferences within the U.S. protectionist system.

The Hongkong Bank's views are, perhaps, better put by Oram himself and, as he also explains the Bank's general position in the Philippines, deserves to be considered *in extenso*. The interview with Conant ranges from general currency and banking policy to comments on specific grievances with their possible remedy.[66]

Oram viewed the existing situation as intolerable as the Hongkong Bank was, like the other banks, required to open accounts either in U.S. gold dollar units of account or in Mexican dollar units of account and – as in Shanghai with its dollar or tael accounts – customers found it difficult to accept that they must either withdraw in terms of the same unit of account or accept the fact that they were involved in an exchange transaction. If a customer deposited 100 Mexican dollars in a Mexican dollar account, were he subsequently to ask to have this account debited with 100 dollar units of account and request payment in Mexican dollars, he would receive 100 Mexican dollar coins, but if he requested payment in U.S. dollars or 'gold' coins, he would receive not 50 (at the par rate), but some other amount depending on the rate of exchange.

Oram's preference was for 'a sound silver dollar as being the least liable to disturb trade and best suited to the requirements of the country in general'. And, while he could not overcome the objection that a silver standard was liable to fluctuations, he was able to show that Japan had had difficulties and that the exchange of countries on the gold standard also suffered instability. Oram stated further that the special problems created by circulation of the Mexican dollar could be overcome by coining a special Filipino dollar of the same weight and fineness, the supply of which could be managed by the Government. The British dollar and its ready acceptance was an obvious parallel.

Given the possibility of a gold standard, which Oram disapproved, he nevertheless felt that Filipinos would quickly learn the value of the American silver coins and did not accept this as one of the long-run defects of the proposed system. But his preference was for a special silver coin, in effect a token silver coin, worth a peso ($=\frac{1}{2}$ U.S. dollar).

As for banknotes, Oram stated that they were needed in greater quantities and, provided they were secured by special funds and by shareholder liability, as with the Hongkong Bank, he had no objection to American banks issuing them in the Philippines. He added that the Hongkong Bank had at present no wish to issue banknotes in the Philippines but would appreciate legislation which would reserve it the right to do so. This was a recommendation not accepted. Aware of the seasonal demands for cash, Oram hoped that the introduction of banknotes would lessen the need for the movement, the import and then export, of physical coin. In this expectation he was undoubtedly correct.

The Bank's operations and its advice on reform

Oram described the nature of the Hongkong Bank's exchange operations to the Conant Commission in the hope of answering general criticism.

First, he stressed that all charges were in the rate of exchange and that the Bank's profit from any exchange transaction came in the margin between the buying and selling rate; secondly, he was able to demonstrate that what some customers were calling 'commission' were charges for collecting cheques, *inter alia*, interest covering the period the cheques were in transit and thus remained unpaid, the period during which the Hongkong Bank was out of funds. To prove the point, Oram noted that this charge was not made for Government cheques because the Government minimized the time element by cabling New York to pay into the Hongkong Bank's agency there – a low cost method of laying down funds in Manila.

At this point Oram noted that gold was leaving the country. This suggested that the Mexican dollar was slightly overvalued at 50 cents gold, and thus the export of gold was inevitable, an illustration of the problems of a bimetallic currency system and a further cause for the introduction of a token silver peso with a maintained ratio to a gold unit of account in a system where the actual gold coin did not itself circulate.

Two weeks later Charles A. Conant was writing from Hong Kong:

[I] had a conference yesterday with Sir Thomas Jackson, Chief Manager of the Hongkong and Shanghai Bank, and he entertained me today at a nice lunch at which Mr T[homas] H[enderson] Whitehead, manager of the Chartered Bank of India, Australia and China was present.[d] Both gentlemen, while inclined to prefer the continuance of the Mexican currency system in the Philippines, admit that the system of a gold standard with a token coin of silver is perfectly practicable and would tend to attract capital to the islands by affording certainty as to the monetary future. They were not disposed to put any obstacles in the way of the execution of American policy in the Philippines.[67]

While the Hongkong Bank had once again offered conservative advice, both Oram on the scene and Jackson at Head Office had the ability to adjust to alternatives, and both recognized the need to cooperate with the authorities of the country in which the Hongkong Bank operated.

Postscript in America

The Conant Report was submitted to the U.S. Senate and in February 1902, the Hongkong Bank's New York Agent, A.M. Townsend, testified before the Senate Committee on the Philippine Currency with Senators Lodge, Aldrich, and Allison present. Townsend made a strong plea for a full-bodied silver coin standard with a Philippine dollar to be coined on principles similar to those of the British dollar. In this he was in communication with Francis B. Forbes, whose own memorandums on the same subject were read to the Committee. Townsend commented, 'Mr Gage no doubt made a very good Secretary of the Treasury, but he was a very unresponsive man, and talking to him was like talking to an icicle.'[68]

This was to be Townsend's last American appearance, for in April he left to

[d] Whitehead was a member of the Hong Kong Legislative Council and later became a joint manager of the Chartered Bank in London.

become the junior Manager in London – 'very sorry to part with so many good friends here, but it will be pleasant to have a settled home in England after so many years wandering'. His wanderings had begun in 1866, for Townsend had been one of the Bank's first two London juniors.

Forbes was also in communication with Sir Ewen Cameron, the Bank's senior London Manager. Nor was the effort to stress the need for a silver standard confined to the Hongkong Bank; J. Howard Gwyther of the Chartered Bank and their agents, the Canadian Bank of Commerce, strongly supported a silver standard. However the Chartered were having second thoughts, for, as their London manager W.A. Main wrote to their New York agents,

We instructed Mr [T.H.] Whitehead during his recent visit to America, in his interviews with Government Officials and others, to advocate the maintenance of a Silver Currency in the Philippines. Recent sinister reports regarding the future of the Silver Market may lead us to reconsider the matter. We refer to the attempt by Mr Rockefeller and others to create a corner in Silver and force the price to a figure to suit their operations altogether irrespective of the want of those countries whose currency follows the fortunes of that metal . . . [69]

In January 1903 the Chartered Bank was contemplating the change-over to the gold standard and was urging, in conjunction with the Hongkong and Shanghai Bank, transitional provisions including payment of debts. The tide had turned and in the end the United States adopted a gold standard for the Philippines with a peso unit of account and with a peso silver coin of weight less than a Mexican dollar as the standard of payment.

Currency reform in the Straits Settlements

The Straits Settlements Government correctly interpreted post-1874 colonial currency policy to favour the replacement of banknotes by a Government note issue, as indeed was done in both Mauritius and Ceylon. However it had been the exchange banks and not the Government who had underwritten the Oriental Bank's issue when that bank failed in Singapore, and the complications created by the circulation in the Malay States and the influence of the China trade with the influx of Japanese yen, Mexican dollars, and, eventually, the British dollar introduced complications which delayed the inevitable, with the exchange banks for a time successfully urging the retention of their own note issue.[70]

As the Governor querulously observed, the Colonial Office seemed rather to be fostering the power of the banks, their issues had increased significantly rather than been replaced since 1874, and he continually pressed for a Government note issue.[71] Events eventually played into the Government's hands since the Hongkong Bank, faced with increased preference for its notes over dollar coins in Hong Kong and South China, issued notes in excess of its capital. This seemed to the Governor, Sir Alexander Swettenham, an opportunity to pillory the Bank, but the Colonial Office and the Bank together recognized the need for an 'excess' issue, which both at first thought would be temporary, until the Straits initiated their note issue and the exchange banks had withdrawn their issue.

Although there were delays even after the passage of the 1899 Straits Ordinance setting up the Government's issue, the principle had been established, and by 1903 when silver had fallen to a pre-1914 low, the question had become not one of the currency but of the standard.

The controversy of the standard was basically between those who were oriented to silver-using China and those who, concerned primarily with the growing export trade in tin and rubber, looked to markets in Europe. Not surprisingly, therefore, G.W. Butt of the Hongkong Bank expressed his Bank's disapproval of a gold standard, while the Chartered Bank approved, subject to certain conditions.[72]

The change of standard would affect the demand for the 'extraordinarily successful and opportune' British dollar – for the introduction of which Governor Swettenham acknowledged a debt of gratitude to the Chartered and Hongkong and Shanghai Banks – and consequently the contractual arrangements of the two banks might be infringed. The Government asked whether the banks would be willing to waive any damages, but as the Hongkong Bank was opposed to the change of standard, its answer was clearly negative. The Chartered Bank asked for time to readjust.[e]

The Hongkong Bank's role was throughout in support of the *status quo*, although it contributed to the success both of the existing system and, when that was changed, of the innovations. First, as already noted, the Bank opposed a Government issue; secondly, with the Chartered Bank it contracted for and thus made possible the enhancement of the supply of dollars through the minting of the British dollar in India. When a Government note issue became inevitable, the Bank did not attempt to use the right to an 'excess' issue to thwart this development; rather it concentrated its issue in Hong Kong.

Most of those who had assumed that a low exchange would benefit the export trade had agreed by 1903 that the rate was now too low, and the stage was set for a series of measures which eventually put the Straits Settlements, and with them the Malay States, on a gold exchange standard. The Straits Government determined to raise the exchange rate by coining a special Straits

[e] Naturally, as the Hongkong Bank did not see the change of standard as an advantage to the community, it would not consider forgoing any contractual rights.[73]

dollar coin, withdrawing other dollars, including the British dollar in which the Hongkong Bank had an interest – and then limiting the supply of the standard coin.[74]

The Hongkong Bank, still concerned with obtaining supplies of British dollars, saw in these projected changes an opportunity of mutual benefit and expressed its willingness to provide the Straits Government with the Bank's bar silver then awaiting coining at the Indian mints in exchange for British dollars which the Government would be withdrawing from circulation in the Straits. Since there was a waiting period at the mint, this exchange would speed both the minting of the new Straits dollar and the Bank's possession of new British dollars.[75]

Although in 1905 the Board of the Hongkong Bank had confirmed its opinion that it was 'undesirable for the Bank's officers to undertake outside duties and responsibilities', in January 1907 it sanctioned the Bank's Singapore Manager, T.S. Baker, accepting the nomination of the Chamber of Commerce for appointment to the Straits Legislative Council 'in view of the present condition of the Straits currency'.

The Straits Government did not from the first plan a reform which had as a clearly seen goal the establishment of a classic currency board, sterling exchange standard. In 1906 the Governor implemented provisions of the new currency ordinance, No. 3 of 1905, by setting the limits at which the dollar could be bought and sold for sterling so that the exchange rates would effectively move only between the theoretical gold import and export points, with 2s:4d as par, and, by making the sovereign legal tender at the rate of 7=Straits$60, put the currency on a gold specie standard. The rise in the gold price of silver which Jackson had foreseen on several occasions endangered the token Straits dollar, since its silver content approached the melting point; this forced a recoinage with a smaller silver content – a technical problem which was well understood.

The main problem being deliberated in 1907–1909, when Baker was on the Legislative Council, was the way in which the 1906 rate would be maintained, and the debate was characterized by the opposition of the unofficial members, led by Baker, to any suggestion that the Government or its currency commissioners should become involved in discretionary exchange operations. To a point Baker cooperated closely with the Colony's able Treasurer, J.O. Anthonisz, sitting with him on various council committees, but they broke *inter alia* over the question of the location of the gold reserve, with the Government urging it be in London and with Baker and the other unofficials demanding it be retained in Singapore.[76] The unofficials were in fact urging a full gold standard; the Government was advocating a more practical and less costly gold exchange standard.

The Government had its way, but only against the unanimous opposition of the unofficial members of the Legislative Council. The problem was that the outspoken and self-assured Baker, while able to cite specific events and interpret them narrowly in the context of the Bank's business, was unable to conceptualize a new system and reinterpret his experiences in these terms. On several matters he was inconsistent and Governor Anderson showed himself capable of entering the debate on technical points to considerable effect. Anthonisz was in control throughout.[77]

Underlying Baker's mistrust of change were undoubtedly an awareness of what can go wrong when untried schemes are first implemented and the traditional position of the exchange banker that nothing must interfere with the banks' control of exchange operations – and the profits to be derived therefrom. The link with sterling was no longer a matter for debate; it had been decided. The measures then being taken were to rationalize that link and ensure the stability of exchange – with Europe – which both bankers and merchants claimed was desirable for trade.

Baker's contribution was to present forcefully all the opposing arguments and to win on several technical points which led eventually to a more efficient operation of a system concerning which he retained serious reservations. But it was a banker's input and valuable for that.

Ceylon and the Currency Commission of 1902

After the complexities of the Straits currency reform, the problems confronting Ceylon appear deceptively simple, especially since the main changes came in the 1930s when local leaders wished to stress Ceylon's separate identity.

Following the currency decisions of 1894 which affected both India and Ceylon, the ordinary means of payment in Ceylon at the turn of the century were Ceylon Government currency notes and Indian silver rupees, the intrinsic value of which had been separated from their value in sterling exchange since the closing of the Indian mints to the free coinage of silver. By law the notes could be redeemed on demand for rupee coin and much local trade between southern India and Ceylon was still conducted in specie, with the result that an unusual demand for placing such funds in India could lead to a drain of coin from Ceylon and, indeed, since the currency notes had to be backed 50% in legal tender coin, could force a contraction of the money supply under inconvenient circumstances.

In his testimony before the commission the Hongkong Bank's Manager, Robert Wilson, urged the minting of a separate Ceylon rupee coin, identical in weight and fineness to the Indian coin and passing as legal tender with the latter coin.[78] Presumably he felt that such a Ceylon coin would become more and more accepted and that the Indian coin would then be used primarily to settle trade balances between say Colombo and Madras. The demand for the Indian rupee would then, however, be determined by factors separate from those determining demand for the Ceylon rupee, and there is question as to whether they could long have continued to circulate at par. This would, in effect, have separated the currencies of two territories closely linked in the economic sense, and Joseph Chamberlain, then Secretary of State for the Colonies, confirmed that the currency of Ceylon must conform to that of India.

Wilson also agreed that the Hongkong Bank would cooperate with the Government in the initial stages or with alternative schemes, including financing the export of gold to India and the import of silver rupees, should a separate coinage for Ceylon not be approved. His expertise on the role of the Mexican dollar (as opposed to the newer British dollars) in the Treaty Ports was also called upon.

Within the Bank Wilson had a reputation for caution, but his testimony before the commission suggests an ability for independent thinking which, while politically premature, anticipated many of the changes which occurred in the Ceylon currency in the long period to independence.

THE HONGKONG BANK AND BANKING DEVELOPMENTS

The long-established exchange banks, including the Hongkong Bank, secured British and British-colonial Government business by tender. The Hongkong Bank was, after its initial period of uncertainty, inevitably successful in Hong Kong and China; in other ports it shared the business, which was both a source of funds and, through the related exchange transactions, a source of profit.

Not surprisingly these banks viewed officially sponsored competition with concern, but it was apparent that Governments, once their operations had reached a certain level, would wish to establish a bank as far as possible under local ownership, if not directly under the State, which would be more responsive to local requirements. To the extent that this latter was not a statement of political belief rather than economic analysis, it states the fear that exchange banks, operating as they did in several territories, would allocate their resources on an overall corporation basis without regard to the welfare of a particular territory – as interpreted by the Government of that territory. The Hongkong Bank was seen as 'local' in this sense as far as Hong Kong was concerned, but elsewhere it too was sometimes under suspicion by local authorities.

This pressure for a local bank to handle Government business, referred to in Chapter 2 in the context of Siam and the Siam Commercial Bank, will be considered in more detail below. There have also been references to the Imperial Bank of China, and in 1902 (Sir) Robert E. Bredon and F.E. Taylor, both of the Imperial Maritime Customs and at the time with the Treaty and Tariff Revision Commission, sought the advice of Charles Addis about a 'Chinese National Bank'.[f]

Japan developed her own banking system and the exchange banks never occupied a favoured position from which they had subsequently to be dislodged.

Perhaps the earliest example of the problem arose in India.

The banking system of British India extends back to the period when many theorists and practical men considered it unsound for a single commercial institution to be engaged in both the issue of banknotes and exchange operations.[80] For this and other related reasons Indian banking developed with the state-sponsored Presidency Banks, which issued notes but did not engage in exchange operations, and the exchange banks, which undertook the reverse. Indeed, the Hongkong Bank itself was modelled after the Presidency Banks, but the provisions of its prospectus which implied it would not engage in exchange were effective only until the Bank opened for business in early 1865. It is not surprising therefore that by 1900 the Presidency Banks had grown restless under a restriction few still considered valid.

But another element had entered into the discussion – established interests. The position of the exchange banks can be best appreciated by the frequent restatement of the principle that their profits derived from turnover and that these depended primarily on the finance of trade which in turn is but another way of stating the overriding importance of exchange operations to the exchange banks. Anything which threatened this aspect of their operations was then likely to meet with their united opposition.

In 1900 the Indian Government entertained the proposal of combining the three Presidency Banks into an 'Imperial Bank of India' (now the State Bank of India) – and permitting it limited but direct access to the London market. The opposition to this 'combined' bank was based partly on the rather exaggerated expectations concerning its potential role in economic development and the implied criticism of the exchange banks, but the immediate threat was the potential development of an exchange business through the new overseas access which would be permitted. Accordingly the exchange banks of Calcutta memorialized the Governor-General, Lord Curzon, with an address which by exaggerating their role left them open to attack by the Government.

---

[f] Addis's wife, Eba, commented, 'How they sap his brains and cover themselves with the honour!'.[79]

The memorial was signed for the Hongkong Bank by its Calcutta Manager, P.E. Cameron.[81]

The limitations under which the Imperial Bank operated were challenged subsequently, and in 1914 Sir Charles Addis refused to take the traditional exchange bank position, arguing that the development of India through the competition of the new bank in all fields would result in a growth of trade in which all could participate. At that stage the Hongkong Bank did not join in the joint protest of the Indian exchange banks.[82]

These themes were more fully developed in the 1930s; they reached their obvious conclusion with the final preparations for independence of the territories post World War II. In consequence the exchange banks had to reassess and readjust their roles.

The Hongkong Bank's role in Korea, Siam, and the Philippines is documented and provides case studies as detailed below.

The Bank and Korea

The Hongkong Bank had by 1897 designated Messrs Holme, Ringer and Co. their agents in Chemulpo (Inchon), Korea. In 1899 the company opened in Seoul and represented the Bank as agents in the capital. This arrangement would appear to have stood until 1910 when the company closed in Seoul, stating as a reason that Korean Government contracts were now concluded in Tokyo. The Bank transferred its business to W.D. Townsend of Townsend and Co., an arrangement which lasted to 1924.

Business was very limited; as a Japanese report of 1900 stated, it included negotiations of bills and small advances, settlement of which was considered part of the business of the Nagasaki branch, and the report concluded that the Bank's agency did not appear to contribute to the development of the financial institutions of the peninsula.[83]

Correspondence relative to the change of agents in 1910 indicates, however, that Ringer and Co. operated some current accounts on behalf of the Nagasaki branch, transactions taking place without exchange costs as if they had occurred in Japan. This practice ceased with the transfer, but the new agent was authorized to accept funds for fixed deposit in Nagasaki without commission. Otherwise business remained confined to the sale of drafts and TTs on various branches of the Bank, the purchase of missionary and consular drafts, and bills under first class letters of credit or documentary credits authorized by the Bank at a commission of $\frac{1}{8}$ of 1%, and transactions for the convenience of travellers. There was a Chinese compradore for Chinese business, although a note of 1916 states there were only two Cantonese in Chemulpo.

In 1916 the Korean operations were transferred to the supervision of the Yokohama branch of the Bank. As they were mainly in connection with Shanghai business, the Yokohama and Shanghai branches shared the costs of the operation.

As early as 1895 the British representative in Korea – (Sir) John N. Jordan, who was succeeding W.C. Hillier as Consul-General in Seoul – was urging the Bank to set up an agency. At the same time John McLeavy Brown, 'strange, lonely, clever, unlovable, friendless, undaunted figure of a man', who was the Chief Commissioner of Customs, a Korean service under the supervision of Sir Robert Hart, was seeking financial advice on the setting up of a national bank to thwart Russian ambitions. Charles Addis, the Bank's Hankow Agent, was at that time on leave in Japan and he was ordered to Korea to advise Brown on the banking issue.

Addis, as noted in connection with his assessment of the Tsingtau agency, based his recommendations on commercial factors, and, after six 'delightful weeks' concluded that although there was great potential in Korea, the time to establish a Bank-staffed agency had not yet arrived, that there was only one British merchant, Holme, Ringer and Co., that the Japanese had already set up branches of their First National Bank in Fusan, Chemulpo, and Seoul in response to the developing economic relations between the two countries, and that the Russians were in the process of considering a similar move. There would be little left for the Hongkong Bank in the face of this 'formidable competition'; the compromise, as noted above, was the appointment of Holme, Ringer and Co.[84]

On the question of the central bank, the main theme of this section, Addis was pessimistic, mainly on account of the political atmosphere and, therefore, the need to operate the Bank with foreigners, a foreign manager, and all the expense and complications this would entail.[85]

After several sessions with Korean bankers, it was clear that they were seeking capital for a central bank, could not obtain it from the Government, and were looking overseas, but would not be able to afford a properly qualified foreign adviser. Nevertheless Addis did work on a set of appropriate regulations and sent a full report to Wade Gard'ner, the Bank's Manager in Shanghai.

Later it became clear that the timing of this mission had been dictated by McLeavy Brown's fear that Russian moves were endangering Korean political integrity and that a strong British presence would be in the country's interests.[86] Addis's general approach to such matters was, however, to suppose that any economic development was beneficial not only to the country tendering it and to the recipient, but also to other trading nations who would find new opportunities opening up. Addis was reluctant to take into account the danger of special spheres of interest which were contiguous with national boundaries. He, like the Hongkong Bank, thrived in a world of equal economic opportunity and of free trade.

Addis left Korea in early November 1896 – not a moment too soon. He and his wife had failed to bring winter clothing with them. They were accompanied by W.C. Hillier, whose assistance to Addis in his Peking days was noted in Volume I, Chapter 14.[87] W.C. Hillier would retire from the Consular Service to become Professor of Chinese in King's College, University of London, from 1904 to 1908, and to teach Chinese to those among the Hongkong Bank's London Office juniors who volunteered.

Later Addis was to complain that some in Hong Kong chose to consider his report too 'literary', part of a quiet campaign to have him labelled as 'clever . . . very; but I mean not really a banker . . .'[88]

Banking reform in the Philippines

The exchange banks had dominated the pre-American Philippines and had operated virtually in terms only of their charters of incorporation – which were in fairness comprehensive and designed for the purpose – although subject to interpretation by Spanish law as implemented in the Islands. Even without the example of the Mendezona loans before them, this would not have suited the new American administrators or the Comptroller of the Currency in Washington. 'Reform' in American banking terms meant 'regulation', and the Hongkong Bank was to learn to face it. Fortunately 'regulation' implies reporting, and the results are preserved in the U.S. National Archives.

In his interview with the Bank's Manila Manager, W. Adams Oram, Charles A. Conant made it clear he wished to introduce American standards and American systems of control but without the limitations prevailing in certain states, referring especially to the restrictions on branch banking. Interestingly, he saw the Hongkong Bank as well as the Chartered Bank as 'British' and, although he met with Jackson in Hong Kong, he talked of London head offices. Conant's concern with the power of the financial interests was typically American, and he saw American commerce likely to be frustrated by the British banks.

Conant's solution, however, was not the restriction of non-American banks but the encouragement of new American institutions in competition. Writing of the Hongkong Bank, the Chartered Bank, and the Spanish-Filipino Bank he stated:

All these banks have abundant capital, are prudently conducted and are entirely safe in their character and management. The two English branch banks have behind their obligations in the Philippines the great resources of the parent banks . . . It is recommended that full power be given to the government of the Philippine Islands to make general regulations governing banking, in harmony with the laws of Congress, which shall apply to the foreign banks as well as to those of the United States and the Philippines. While many complaints are made against the foreign banks in respect to their charges and methods of doing business, these are conditions which are less likely to be influenced for good by the direct action of the government than by the effective competition of the American banks if they are given sufficient power to establish branches and to issue circulating notes.[89]

There were questions on related topics – the note issue and regulation.

'As a banker located here', Conant asked, 'you have no objection to the establishment of American banks here and to their issuing notes?' Oram's not unsurprising reply, given all the circumstances, was 'None whatever.'[90]

But on the question as to what kind of supervision he considered necessary by the United States over banks, Oram did not give quite so welcome an answer. 'It is not the custom in Great Britain or her colonies', he declared, 'for banks to be inspected, and we do not see the necessity for it here.'[g]

He was particularly concerned to stress that while the annual statements of an entire bank might be published, the Hongkong Bank did not wish the accounts of the Manila branch (or indeed one assumes of any single branch) to be published separately. In this he was to be disappointed. But Oram's position was that bank inspection and reporting were suitable only for purposes of determining solvency, but this, as the Bank was soon to discover, was not a particularly limiting condition.

The Hongkong Bank had apparently been unaware of the Spanish law requiring 25% of its demand liabilities to be covered by coin, but Oram stated the Bank always operated with this degree of liquidity as a minimum – although previous reports writing of Manila banks in general had suggested otherwise, but without being specific as to which bank or for how long a period.

Oram specifically welcomed the idea of American mortgage banks and, by extension, other specialist banks dealing with the finance of the agricultural sector; exchange banks wished to finance trade and keep their funds as liquid as possible. The history of the Hongkong Bank in the American period

---

[g] In view of the supervisory responsibilities implied of the British Treasury and Colonial authorities in the Hongkong Bank's charter, this may seem at first glance an extraordinary statement, but it will be recalled that except for the note issue and matters relating to the Bank's holding of Government funds, the authorities refrained from all acts which suggested to the Bank's customers any Government responsibility. Even the perfunctory publication of accounts was undertaken in a way to minimize Government involvement. A classic reference is found in Treasury correspondence with the Colonial Office 1884.[91]

Another example of the retreat from supervision would be the reaction of the Hong Kong Government and the Colonial Office to the discovery in 1910 that the Bank had failed to notify the Governor when planning purchase of land with an annual value exceeding the amount specified in the charter, see discussion in Chapter 1.

suggests, however, that an exchange bank could not keep its money in the port and wait for the produce to arrive; it was financing merchants and agents who, whatever the legal terms might be, involved the Bank in crop finance and loans secured by mortgages.[92]

These and related problems were to develop over the years to the period of independence.

The Bank and the Siam Commercial Bank

The Siamese Government was advised by its own appointed experts, whose advice it did not necessarily follow, and the Hongkong Bank appears to have played a purely consultative role, mainly in London. Official British correspondence interestingly refers to consulting the Hongkong Bank's 'directors in London', a confusion which was to persist even after the retirement of Sir Charles Addis in the early 1930s. The events did, however, affect the Hongkong Bank's operations and position in Bangkok.

The Hongkong Bank had introduced banknotes into Siam in 1889 with the permission of the Siamese authorities. The latter accepted the idea on an experimental basis; typically they took over the note issue in 1902 when they had seen its usefulness – despite the limited circulation of the notes – and learned the principles involved.

From 1906 to 1914 there were problems in the Siamese banking sector related to the German management of the Siam Commercial Bank and its possible transformation into a Siamese Government bank. The situation was complicated by the fact that the bank's compradore was also involved as the 'manager' of the local-style Chino-Siam Bank. When this latter bank came into difficulties in 1913 the compradore/manager was accused of defalcation. This endangered the Siam Commercial Bank's position, but the defalcation of other compradores, including the Hongkong Bank's, made it impossible for the latter to take advantage of the situation.

The Siamese obviously wanted their own Government bank; the transformation of the Siam Commercial Bank in which the Privy Purse was heavily invested was, until the banking crisis of 1913, the simplest solution. The British Government was concerned with German influence, the Hongkong Bank with the loss of both deposits and exchange business – but primarily the latter; consequently the British were attempting to work out a counter proposal which would please the Siamese and the exchange banks, while excluding the Germans. This ruled out encouraging the establishment of yet another British bank to play a role similar to that expected of, for example, the Imperial Bank of Persia. The eventual outcome – after considerable consultation by the Foreign Office with Charles Addis in London – was the appointment of a banking expert, W.B. Hunter, a former treasurer of the Bank of Madras, who could be depended upon to advise the Siamese on the establishment of a new bank *without exchange privileges*, in the Indian Government tradition.[93]

The involvement of the Privy Purse at the time of crisis made it impossible, however, to change the status of the Siam Commercial Bank, which thus remained under German influence until 1917 when, with the declaration of war by Siam and the secondment of the Hongkong Bank's G.H. Ardron to its managership, German influence ceased and the bank prospered.

By 1914 the nations had made their choice of standard, but the presence of a large silver coinage in India, the Straits, Siam, and the Philippines as well as in the silver standard countries was to prove a source of almost continual disruption in the world silver markets during and immediately after the Great War. In the amelioration of the problems this created the Hongkong Bank played a significant banking role, and the story will be told later in this history.

The Bank was beginning in this pre-war period to be sought for advice. Charles Addis, exceptionally, became British censor for the Bank of Morocco; Bank staff were prominent in the China Association; governors and the Foreign Office wrote specific queries concerning specific problems. Throughout the Bank played a constructive role; its officers were not always right and it was not, except in Hong Kong, predominant. But it had become respected and its comments on matters of currency and banking were no longer dismissed in summary Treasury minutes. Thus in yet another way the Hongkong Bank had come of age.

Yet it is true that the Bank's greatest impact in this period was a consequence of its China experience and its role in the China loans. This is the subject of Part II.

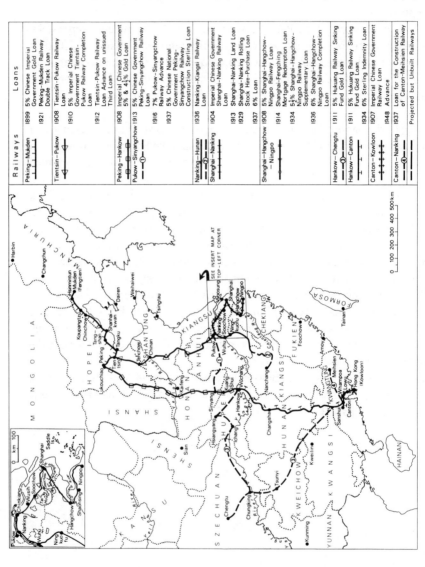

Railways	Loans
Peking–Mukden	
1899	5% Chinese Imperial Government Gold Loan
1921	Peking–Mukden Railway Double Track Loan
Tientsin–Pukow	
1908	Tientsin–Pukow Railway Loan
1910	5% Imperial Chinese Government Tientsin–Pukow Railway Completion Loan
1912	Tientsin–Pukow Railway Loan Advance on unissued Third Loan
Peking–Hankow	
1908	Imperial Chinese Government 5% & 4½% Gold Loan
Pukow–Sinyangchow 1913	5% Chinese Government Peking–Sinyangchow Railway Loan
1916	7% Pukow–Sinyangchow Railway Advance
1937	5% Chinese National Government Peking–Sinyangchow Railway Construction Sterling Loan
Nanking–Hunan 1936	Nanking–Kiangsi Railway Loan
Shanghai–Nanking 1904	Imperial Chinese Government Shanghai–Nanking Railway Loan
1913	Shanghai–Nanking Land Loan
1929	Shanghai–Nanking Rolling Stock Hire-Purchase Loan
1937	6% Loan
Shanghai–Hangchow–Ningpo 1908	5% Shanghai–Hangchow–Ningpo Railway Loan
1914	Shanghai–Fengching Mortgage Redemption Loan
1934	5½% Shanghai–Hangchow–Ningpo Railway Supplementary Loan
1936	6% Shanghai–Hangchow–Ningpo Railway Completion Loan
Hankow–Chengtu 1911	5% Hukuang Railway Sinking Fund Gold Loan
Hankow–Canton 1911	5% Hukuang Railway Sinking Fund Gold Loan
1934	6% Sterling Indemnity Loan
Canton–Kowloon 1907	Imperial Chinese Government Railway Loan
1948	Advance
Canton–Nanking 1937	Loan for the Construction of Canton–Meihsien Railway
	Projected but Unbuilt Railways

2 China: Principal railways with which the Hongkong Bank was financially involved

238

Part II

THE HONGKONG BANK AS MERCHANT BANK, CHINA, 1895–1914

I have accepted this invitation not merely to show that I am just as alive as Western statesmen are to the importance of keeping on good terms with the accumulated capital (loud laughter), but more especially in recognition of the most important services rendered in the past by the [Hongkong] Bank to the Chinese Government (cheers) at times when its managers and directors did show that they had broader views and more far-reaching aims than men usually have. (cheers) The loyal supporters or patronizers of the Bank in the years of plenty can count upon the loyal support of the Bank in times of scarcity, embarrassment and need. (cheers) This very spirit which I have just now eulogized has raised the Hongkong and Shanghai Banking Corporation to its leading position in the Far East.

Li Hung-chang at the London Banker's Dinner, 1896

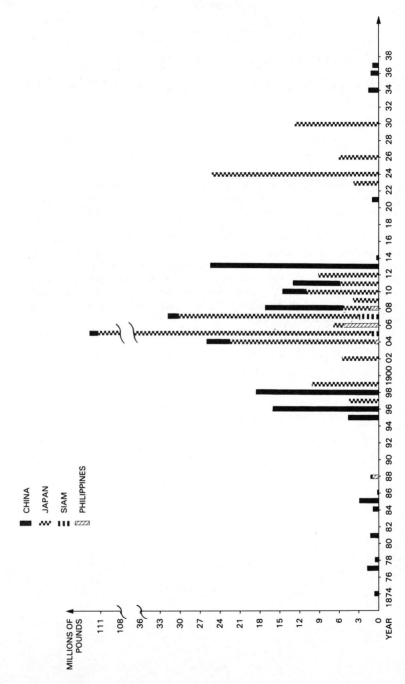

Figure 8 Nominal value of public loans in which the Hongkong Bank participated, in sterling, 1874–1938

240

After 1895 a defeated China, her 'self-strengthening policy' proved a failure, turned first to reform and then, inevitably in the frustration generated by floods and famines and by the threatening pressure of the Powers, to reaction in the bloody climax of the Boxer Uprising. Views from the West have historically vacillated between sympathy for the Chinese masses, inheriting a culture with social values which had absorbed so many varied enrichments but now seemingly unable to cope with the needs of modernization, and despair at the presumed inefficiency, corruption, and incompetence of her leaders – appearing all the worse in the context of the sentimentalism which China has always evoked.

The weakness of China came at a time when the issues of war and peace were world-wide in the balance. The commercial ability of the Hanseatic merchant was now given a new aggressiveness by the assertiveness of the German Empire. The dangers of French imperialism in the South, and the outreach of the Russian Empire across Siberia and down into Manchuria came into conflict with the assumed position of the British, the newly perceived interests of Japan, and the opportunistic and erratic response of the United States to the appeal to 'take up the white man's burden'.

With these imperial developments Britain was unconsciously perhaps in sympathy. There had been a rediscovered rationale for Empire, for protection (or 'fair trade'), and exclusiveness; but this could be admitted only at the cost of losing the rationale of her position in China. Were not the Treaties negotiated in the concept of world free trade, was not extraterritoriality a temporary provision until the universality of equal relations was understood, enacted, and enforced by a China brought at last into the comity of nations, and were not the tariffs a concession either to revenue requirements or to the less developed understanding of a civilization as yet unblessed by steam power or political economists?

Thus Britain expressed her reaction to developments in the context of free trade and open doors but moved to protect her interests in what at times appeared to contemporaries as the imminent breakup of China, if not into separate territories at least into spheres of influence. Her loss in relative influence in China, quantified by the decline in the percentage of the China trade, was seen by many British merchants not as a warning that the competitive advantages, which were the underlying basis for trading patterns, were adjusting, but rather as evidence of some sinister political influence depriving Britain of the fruits of a system Britain had first advised and espoused.

In fact Britain's Far Eastern position was threatened both by 'legitimate' economic forces and by political pressure. Britain was ill-equipped by tradition to counter the former by positive action, and her merchants were eager to shift focus to the latter.

By the mid-1890s the Hongkong Bank, the local regional bank, had become the most important financial institution in the East. In all this its role would therefore be significant and, not surprisingly, controversial. As a bank in the traditions of free trade and equal opportunity, the Hongkong Bank continued to serve the traditional requirements of a multi-national constituency, its shareholders continuing to elect, for example, German merchants as directors, ensuring the continued patronage of their growing business. As the bank which had served Governments – the Hongkong Bank had the British Treasury Chest business in China and it acted on occasion as the financial agent of the Chinese Government – the Hongkong Bank's role in the East made it a prominent actor in the drama of concessions, railway, and other development finance. This latter role in a world of contesting Powers and China's Rights Recovery Movement was, as noted, controversial; it was often misunderstood.

The relationship which developed between the Hongkong Bank and the British authorities was imperfect, first because the Bank was in fact two banks: a commercial and exchange bank oriented from the twin centres of Hong Kong and Shanghai and a merchant bank of increasing political influence operating with a consultative committee of financial experts in the City of London. How these 'two banks' were reconciled is a theme to be developed below, but they were never in conflict. The Hongkong Bank was, nevertheless, perceived by imperialists and jingoists to be pursuing self-contradictory policies and was consequently subject to severe but undeserved criticism.

This then is the period in which the Hongkong Bank came 'Home' out of the East as the representative of British financial interests, but, contrary to all precedent, stayed firmly in the East as a regional bank serving a multi-national and multi-cultural constituency. The latter was neither surprising nor particularly spectacular (see Volume I, Chapter 13 and Volume II, Chapter 1); the Bank continued its growth, increased its capital by a rights issue, and expanded its operations cautiously with commercial advantage and shareholder interests its primary concern.

The Bank in London had had modest beginnings, its branch on Lombard Street designed at first as the European base for its trade finance, advised by a committee of banking and merchant experts who were its contact with the City. Beyond expectation the 'China bank', teamed with Panmure Gordon and directed by shrewd managers with China experience, had proved capable of managing a series of loans to the Imperial Government of China (see Volume I, Chapter 14); the Hongkong Bank had established a position and reputation. Nevertheless, through early 1895 the Bank's largest loan had been £3 million; in that key year China needed £65 million simply to pay Japan the price of her victory; finance for modernization lay beyond that.

For a few exciting months the Hongkong Bank attempted, as it had done before, to act alone. The First Indemnity Loan was lost to a Russian–French syndicate and the Hongkong Bank turned at last to seek banking and other commercial alliances without political commitment. The first was the purely financial agreement of July 1895, subsequently revised, with the Deutsch-Asiatische Bank. This was followed in 1898 by the joint promotion with Jardine, Matheson and Co. of what was intended to be a broadly based British syndicate to compete with foreign counterparts in the international scramble for railway and mining concessions in China; the company, the British and Chinese Corporation, Ltd (B&CC), was successfully floated, but, despite the apparently broad base of its support, it soon became associated almost entirely with the two promoting companies and managing agents in China, the Bank and Jardine's.

Whatever the promoters' original intentions the B&CC can best be understood as a formal extension of the *ad hoc* agreements made in the 1880s by Ewen Cameron, then the Bank's Manager in Shanghai, with J.J. Keswick of Jardine's; significantly, the B&CC was conceived by Cameron as the Bank's London Manager and by William Keswick of Matheson and Co., formerly Jardine's taipan on the China coast.

Ineffective in its efforts to establish a framework for a British cooperative investment front in China, the B&CC immediately faced the competition of other British groups, particularly the Pekin Syndicate and the Yangtze Valley Syndicate. Where the syndicates were actually seeking the same or similar concessions, the Foreign Office faced the dilemma of choice without an established basis in the context of British economic policy for making such a choice. The Foreign Office's position was made more difficult by the complex secondary relations the various syndicates had with French and Belgian interests, which were at the same time negotiating on their own behalf for China concessions, on occasion with the support of their Governments.

As far as British competition was concerned, the problem was at least partially resolved in 1903 and 1905 by agreements among the syndicates to form the Chinese Central Railways, Ltd (CCR). Even this combination would be challenged as inadequately representative, but the resources and broad representation of the three syndicates as combined were sufficiently apparent to facilitate the unenviable decisions of a Foreign Office which, while still preferring a policy of 'keeping the ring', was nevertheless required to intervene on behalf of British commercial interests if these were to receive consideration by a Chinese Government under pressure from the several Powers. The Foreign Office's task would have been simpler had there been a single agreed British commercial representation in China, but to the extent that the B&CC and CCR were dominant and the remaining separate

Table II.1 *China: public loans issued through foreign banks*
other than the Hongkong Bank[a]
1895–1914

Title	Managed by	Amount (millions)	Years	Issued to public at
1895				
4% Gold Loan	Franco-Russian Syndicate	Fcs 400	36	–
1898				
5% Loan Contract Luhan Railway	Société d'Étude de Chemins de fer en Chine	Fcs 112.5	–	–
1902				
CIG 5% Gold Loan (Shansi Railway)	Banque Russo-Asiatique	Fcs 40	30	96½
1903				
CIG 5% Gold Loan (Pienlo Railway)[b]	Banque Belge pour l'Étranger	Fcs 25	20	–
1905				
CIG 5% Gold Loan (Honan Railway) Taokow–Chinghua	Pekin Syndicate	£0.8	30	87½
Supp. Loan to comp. Luhan Railway	Société d'Étude de Chemins de fer en Chine	Fcs 12.5	–	–
1907				
CIG 5% Gold Loan (Pienlo Railway)	Banque Belge pour l'Étranger	Fcs 16	20	–
1907/09				
Japanese 5% Loan (Hsinmintun–Mukden)	South Manchurian Railway Company	Yen 0.32	18	93
1909				
Kirin–Changchun Railway	South Manchurian Railway Company	Yen 2.15	–	93
1911				
CIG 5% Railway Loan	Yokohama Specie Bank	Yen 10	25	97½
1912				
CRG 5% Gold Loan	Banque Sino-Belge	Fcs 25	–	97
CRG 5% Gold Loan	G. Birch Crisp and Co.	£10	–	–
1912/13				
CRG 5% Gold Loan (Lunghai Railway)	Banque Belge pour l'Étranger	£10	30	91

Table II.1 – *cont.*

Title	Managed by	Amount (millions)	Years	Issued to public at
1914				
CRG 5% Industrial Gold Loan	Banque Industrielle de Chine	Fcs 150	50	–
CRG Railway 5% Gold (Shasi–Shingyi Railway)	Pauling and Co. Ltd	£10	–	–
Hankow Improvement Loan (5% Gold Loan)	Samuel and Co. Ltd	£10	–	100
CRG 5% Gold Loan Ching–Yu Railway	Banque Industrielle de Chine	Fcs 600	50	–

[a] For Hongkong Bank loans see tables in Chapters 5–8.
[b] The Pienlo Railway is also known as the Kaifengfu–Honanfu Railway.
CIG Chinese Imperial Government.
CRG Government of the Republic of China.

syndicates, the Syndicat du Yunnan, Ltd, for example, not in direct competition – or, better yet, to the extent they had already been designated by the Chinese as the preferred British firms – official British support could be reconciled with traditional policy.

The Hongkong Bank had become the British Government's banker in China and Japan through competitive bidding; it was successful primarily because it offered the highest interest rate on Government accounts. The Hongkong Bank also had superior facilities for handling Government business; the two factors were closely related. Similarly the Hongkong Bank, the B&CC, and/or the CCR so frequently received official support in their negotiations with the Chinese not because they had been arbitrarily selected by the British Government as the official instruments of economic policy in the East but because, by the standards of 'keeping the ring', they were for objectively formulated reasons the most suitable organizations as determined in each particular instance.

Where this was not the case, the Foreign Office and the Legation in Peking supported other British interests, Pauling and Co., Pritchard Morgan, the Eastern Extension Company, and the Pekin Syndicate – these syndicates did not necessarily raise their funds through the Hongkong Bank. Furthermore, the Foreign Office welcomed the possibility of a new syndicate, for example, David Sassoon and Co. and Erlanger interests (1904), if only this would relieve them of their dependence on the Hongkong Bank and the B&CC (see Table II.1).[1]

In the purely financial field, however, the Hongkong Bank was reluctant to enter into any domestic relationship. The Foreign Office was frustrated;

criticized for supporting a single bank, it nevertheless had no real alternative. Although there were political complaints relative to the Hongkong Bank's apparent 'monopoly of support', this was not, at least in the simple form stated, Government policy. The complaining institutions were not capable of wholly replacing the Bank; their motivation was varied. Some, like Pauling and Co. were legitimately frustrated, some believed that the B&CC could not perform the tasks assigned and that they could do at least as well, still others sought 'participation', or what the Hongkong Bank chose to describe as the right to share, without risk or expense, the profits resulting from costly negotiations undertaken by the Bank.

As long as the Government's support of the Hongkong Bank could be defended as being based more or less on project by project decisions, the Bank was able to resist pressure to form a 'British Group' composed of banks other than itself. With the development of an international consortium from 1909 the Bank's position became increasingly untenable. The leading financial institutions of France, Germany, Russia, Japan, and the United States had in one way or another each organized a national financial 'Group' interested in China; the corresponding British Group was simply and exclusively the Hongkong Bank. The Foreign Office could not break into this international relationship which they had encouraged, particularly since the Hongkong Bank had played such a key role in its development and done so on a purely commercial basis. And yet the Foreign Office was criticized for supporting the Hongkong Bank under circumstances which potential competitors, journalist scaremongers, and others chose to describe as an officially created 'monopoly position'.

The pressure on the Hongkong Bank to broaden the British Group was thus logical and irresistible, and in 1912 the change was made. There would be a truly British Group which the Government could support, but typically execution of the policy was flawed. The initial terms offered the Chartered Bank of India, Australia and China would be refused, leading to renewed difficulties (Chapter 8). This is not surprising; there would always be outsiders and British industrial interests refused to combine for purposes of China contracts. Even the French Group, apparently disciplined to fulfil Government policy, faced competition from the Banque Industrielle de Chine and the Berthelot interests in and after 1913, a development further complicating the Hongkong Bank's position.

The British Government still drew back from *de jure* exclusive support of the enlarged and more representative British Group; the Government was nevertheless forced close to such a position in reality. The multi-national Groups were a consortium which had been apparently accepted by the Chinese Government as agents for the issue of a series of reorganization loans expected to total £60 million. This would exhaust China's credit-worthiness and pre-empt the possibility of any further sound lending. To support these loans on a 'project basis', that is, temporarily, was, given the peculiar circumstances in China at the time, tantamount to a grant of 'exclusive' support for a considerable period.

The Foreign Office made several attempts to resolve this contradiction. To meet the general deterioration of the Groups' control over suppliers' credits and other small loans, the Foreign Office obtained the exclusion of 'industrial loans' from the international agreements and thus from the area of its own exclusive support to the British Group. Since financial loans can be disguised as industrial loans, this exclusion further undermined the effectiveness of the Consortium.

The Foreign Office also wavered as to whether the Government had agreed to support the British Group for the first loan of the series (the only one in fact issued, the £25 million Reorganization Loan of 1913) or for the whole series. The Foreign Office went further; it accepted that the British financial institutions comprising a rival Anglo-Belgian syndicate and represented by the Eastern Bank were legitimate candidates for British official support in lieu of the Hongkong Bank (and the Six-Power Groups Consortium). Only when China first chose the 'Six-Power Groups' and only when the Hongkong Bank as part of that Consortium had actually advanced funds against the eventual issue of the first Reorganization Loan did the Foreign Office grant the 'British Group' its 'exclusive' if temporary support.

The Hongkong Bank would have preferred to operate without the necessity of Government support, but when the Legation had secured an opening for British economic involvement, the Bank had to respond through the Legation. Or, alternatively, where the Bank and its associates had secured Chinese patronage, the Chinese sought confirmation through the Legation that this would be acceptable as the British participation. Such relationships forced the Bank into increasingly intimate discussions with the Legation in Peking and the Foreign Office in London. The conflicting objectives of the two parties required continuous negotiation and mutual consideration; each influenced the other's policies.

The initial Hongkong Bank agreement with the Deutsch-Asiatische Bank in 1895 and its subsequent amendments were carefully noted as agreements between banking companies and not between Governments, although consultations with the respective Governments had been undertaken by each party. This increasingly controversial British/German banking relationship would continue; it would also be the basis of a series of attacks on the Hongkong Bank by those who considered war with Germany to be inevitable. These attacks were ineffective in influencing British Government decisions relative to support for the Bank, partly because the Foreign Office considered the accusations ill-informed or inaccurate and partly because the basis of the Foreign Office's relations with the Bank was their objective assessment of the specific business involved on the Bank's position and requirements as a private-sector business rather than on its 'foreign policy'.

Notwithstanding the Hongkong Bank's a-political pretensions, it was inevitably involved in international banking relations which could not avoid comment by the Foreign Office and which indeed required Foreign Office approval for their successful implementation. Agreements reached by the Bank on 'purely' commercial matters affected overall British interests, both political and economic, in China. Should the Bank come to an arrangement inimical to British commercial interests, for example, the Foreign Office could reply to critics that the matter was purely a concern of the private sector, but the issue would continue to be debated at the political level. Should the B&CC concede a major construction contract to a foreign syndicate, the Foreign Secretary could argue in Parliament that the matter was private, but he would be unconvincing. Nothing relative to British involvement of economic significance in China could be safely effected without its passing through the Legation, whether the Bank and Legation wished it or not. And once the Legation was required to support the Bank's representations, it was in a position to negotiate also with the Bank to amend or withdraw. This very fact of procedure in China suggested to both the Bank and the British Government that prior consultation would be sound; from this to mutual influence was a small step.

The effectiveness of the Hongkong Bank's influence on British commercial policy in China was in part a consequence of the competence of the Bank's chief London negotiator, Charles Addis, and its Peking representative, E.G. Hillier, and in part a result of the strong international position the Hongkong Bank had created for itself, a position which could not be ignored or denied by the British Government without international repercussions and policy inconsistency.

Addis began his training in Chinese affairs as Acting Agent in Peking in 1885. Despite, or perhaps because of, his determination to remain a banker rather than a 'China expert', he became responsible as Sub-Manager Shanghai for railway negotiations with Sheng Hsuan-huai at least by the late 1890s, and when he was assigned fortuitously as the junior London Manager in 1905 he succeeded the experienced Cameron as the Manager responsible for European negotiations relative to China. His influence can be understood in the context of his concisely written memorandums, in his precis of negotiations with the French and German Groups, and in his forthright defence of a sound China-lending program as he saw it. His ultimate knighthood and appointment as a director of the Bank of England are measures of the esteem with which he was held by the Government and the City, independent of his status as an employee of the Hongkong Bank.

In Peking Hillier was the only banker to head a major foreign bank – the other bank managers were, as Hillier's successor would be, seconded from their national diplomatic services.[2] His personal achievements are described elsewhere in this history, but the Hongkong Bank's success in Peking was more a consequence of Hillier's capabilities than of equivocal if necessary Legation representation with the Imperial authorities.

Indeed it was the Hongkong Bank's strong position not only in Peking but throughout China and the East which proved the foundation on which all else was built – including its problems. As with Jardine's its expertise was so all-inclusive, its coverage so complete that neither firm could understand the arguments or the fairness of demands for 'broadening' their British base. In 1908 the French Minister to Peking, C. Bapst, wrote to the Ministry of Foreign Affairs in Paris to account for a certain British success which he attributed –

... secondé par les deux splendides institutions que possèdent en Chine nos voisins d'Outre-Manche, la Hongkong and Shanghai Bank et la British and Chinese Corporation. Il y a, en effet, dans ces deux institutions britanniques une puissance matérielle et morale assez forte pour que, dirigée avec esprit de suite vers un but déterminé, elle impose respect aux Chinois et réussisse à vaincre leurs répugnances.[3]

Alexandre Conty, as the new French Ambassador, would have different and more nationalistic thoughts, but the above fairly represents the respect with which the Hongkong Bank – and the B&CC – were generally held, despite strongly expressed views that, from time to time and despite explanatory circumstances, the B&CC was insufficiently aggressive in the exploitation of its concessions.

The Bank's increasingly important international position began with the July 1895 Agreement with the Deutsch-Asiatische Bank. After the Boxer Uprising the Powers turned to the exploitation of their individual concessions granted in the heady years between 1896 and 1900. They were to find conditions changed or changing. First, the granting of a concession was not equivalent to an agreement relative to the actual terms under which the concession might be developed. During the resulting delays a second factor developed – the Chinese reluctance to accept foreign management or conditions relative to funds provided for development projects. The third factor was the logical climax of a growing sense of Chinese nationalism, the Rights Recovery Movement, the practical consequences of which were the repurchase, often through new external loans, of rights previously granted by concession.

The ultimate consequence of these Chinese policy trends – as far as the Hongkong Bank was concerned – was the undermining of the Bank's role in the British and Chinese Corporation. The latter assumed 'concessions', that is, the Chinese would commission the B&CC to build the railway and, at the same time, find finance for that building. The B&CC would assign Jardine's to handle the former part of the task, the Hongkong Bank to perform the latter. If, however, the Chinese were to build the railway themselves, they needed only finance. To this need the Hongkong Bank could address itself directly.

These problems did not arise immediately nor were they at first in so absolute a form. More urgent were the international problems created by the existence of concessions and conflicting spheres of interest which were not consistently recognized either by China or the Powers and they were subject to renegotiation and modification. Nor were they always suitable for the purposes intended. The railway from Tientsin to the Yangtze at Pukow, for example, would cross from North China through the German sphere of Shantung into the English sphere of the Yangtze Valley. There was furthermore the distinction between the political reality of a concession and the economic reality of its exploitation; the political Power might not have the resources; the financial support for, say, Russian accomplishments in the East would come through French and Belgian capital markets.

The extent that these diverse pressures in the context of a politically weak central authority did not result in the 'break up' of China was due in part at least to the recognition by the Powers that no foreign authority could rule China nor would any Power be permitted to do so, and that the preservation of a central authority was necessary for the continued recognition of concessions and other agreements made. The impact of railway politics at the provincial level, however, would encourage the *de facto* decentralization of power once the fabric of traditional Chinese authority, the imperial dynasty in Peking, had been discarded.

A more positive factor was the surprising consequence of foreign cooperation at the time of the Boxer Uprising on the measures taken to ensure continuity of government and on the subsequent protocols which, while they burdened China with an unnecessarily high indemnity, encouraged China in the development of a central executive authority based on Peking more closely resembling the Western nation-state structure than had the traditional Ch'ing councils and boards. The very administration of Boxer Indemnity funds brought the bankers onto an international commission sitting at Shanghai; the concept of Western cooperation, which by 1914 had become strained and abused by the competitive and increasingly nationalistic attitudes of the Peking ministers themselves – often degenerating into unseemly squabbles –

nevertheless existed. It was an atmosphere receptive to the Hongkong Bank's, and Addis's, concept of cooperative international financing of China's requirements.

Once the Bank had recognized that it could not stand alone, it was as constructive in international finance cooperation as it was reluctant to respond to demands that its one bank 'British Group' be enlarged. The essence of the Hongkong Bank's post-Boxer China policy was to minimize the dangers to China's sovereignty by encouraging the cooperation of comprehensive and exclusive national financial groups which would control lending to China and so protect her from the pressures which threatened her political integrity. The policy was suspected in Europe because the Bank was British; it was criticized by China and in Britain – by China because it ran counter to the traditional Chinese policy of preventing an alliance of barbarians, in Britain because the Groups no matter how 'comprehensive' in scope remained exclusive, the British Group most of all.

To the experienced Addis the responsibility of the Hongkong Bank to China and to the bondholders, for whom the Bank or the B&CC/CCR were often trustees, was to maintain the credit of China. The Bank proved itself in paying out interest to the public on occasion before the Chinese Government had placed the necessary funds with the Bank. Key to the success of the China loans was the Hongkong Bank's ability to ensure an orderly market through underwriting; the City had confidence in the Bank's China expertise.

The alternative to a continuous, responsible body to whom both China and bondholders could turn was the costly meddling of adventurers, the 'in and out' tactics of temporary financial groupings which would dissolve once a loan had been issued or which, having won a concession on the basis of competitive bidding, would be unable to meet the terms agreed. This last would lead under conditions of extrality to renegotiation through the Legation and added costs for China.

By pressing a consistent policy on wavering international financial groups, by continuous consultation with the British Foreign Office, and by unquestionably sound management under Sir Charles Addis, the Hongkong Bank became the leader of the international China Consortium, and the lead manager in the Consortium's loans, its London Office the clearing house for Consortium affairs, and its London Manager a virtual managing director/ executive secretary of the Consortium. Meanwhile the Bank's Head Office remained in Hong Kong where the Board and Chief Manager, apparently approving but passive, kept the finances on 'an even keel', aware that their Bank had become the centre of international finance for China and that, in the East, their Peking and Shanghai Managers were responsible not only for the financial negotiations and the carrying out of complex monetary movements connected with the loans but also for vast development projects in conjunction with the Princely Hong of Jardine Matheson through the British and Chinese Corporation.

The Bank had made itself virtually indispensable.

Britain was still attempting to limit its policy to 'keeping the ring'; the Foreign Office did not, therefore, need an 'instrument'. The British Government remained responsible, however, for conducting foreign relations with the purpose of protecting the interests of British subjects; in China this meant ensuring that the demands of other Powers did not deprive British interests of opportunity. This in turn required on occasion positive action; a concession granted by China through Government intervention would then be exploited by a private sector company. The Government was involved; it could not avoid some responsibility for the consequences.

The consequent international financial operations resulted in British subjects being involved in agreements which passed through the Legation and which, under extrality, might eventually be disputed before British courts. Furthermore, British subjects were buying bonds, guaranteed by the Imperial Chinese Government, in the open market. If these obligations were not met, the Foreign Office might be forced as a consequence of domestic political pressures to intervene to protect the bondholders.

The problem would be minimized by redefining the 'ring', that is, by attempting to set minimal conditions for those who entered the ring and to maintain the rules by which the game was played. This policy suggested first, the encouragement of the Hongkong Bank and its associates, and secondly, the minimization of the risk by insisting on the inclusion in concession and/or financial agreements of appropriate performance 'controls' on the borrowers, on China and its official subsidiary authorized entities. The Legation could not itself descend into the arena of detailed commercial negotiations for what was, from the British point of view, a private-sector operation.

Here the Foreign Office and the Hongkong Bank once again had a coincidence of goals – they would differ on specific terms, but this could be negotiated between the Bank/B&CC/CCR and the British authorities both in Peking and London. Adventurers, anxious to close a deal, would object to official interference; their hope of success lay in underbidding the Hongkong Bank on terms (including the degree of control) offered the Chinese. The Hongkong Bank's long-term interests required responsible terms, but without Legation support for such mutually desired provisions, the adventurer might succeed.

All these factors led, as previously noted, to the development of close relations between the Hongkong Bank and the British authorities. There were limits, however, beyond which the Bank could not successfully go even to meet British Government wishes. There was international competition and there were the policies of the borrower to consider. For any British/Bank policy to be successful, the Chinese had to be willing to accept the terms offered by the Bank and/or its associates; without this no relationship between the Bank and the British Government would be relevant. This essential qualification brought the Bank and Government back into cooperation; only through the Hongkong Bank developed international Consortium could competition in fact be minimized and the Chinese encouraged to accept conditions which safeguarded the bondholders.

All factors pointed to a lasting relationship between the Bank and Government; yet it was this 'lasting' relationship which could not be accepted as official policy in the British context. To the extent there appeared such a relationship *de facto*, the British Government came under attack from potential rivals or would-be 'sharers' of the Bank's position.

The Foreign Office and Legation most certainly considered the problem of apparently continuous support for the Bank, but what organization provided a viable alternative?[4] Was it possible for the British authorities to undermine the international position the Hongkong Bank had established for itself – and, therefore, for British interests? There being no practical or politically sound alternative, the Foreign Office returned to the Bank, but often at a price. The Bank, having obtained for itself international financial influence, had to act within limits agreed by the Government.

The situation was short of ideal and when counsels were divided resulted in confusion. When, for example, the Foreign Office and Legation pressed the Bank – in the case of the 5–4½% Gold Loan of 1908 for Luhan Railway rights recovery – to accept the Chinese terms, which were without adequate safeguards, the Bank eventually capitulated, throwing the ultimate responsibility for shareholder protection to the British Government – a responsibility which was not specifically acknowledged (see Chapter 7).

The Bank's overwhelming position in the East and the logic of official support rendered in London and Peking could not be questioned. There was, however, a surprising point of attack. The sole member of the British Group, the Hongkong Bank, was charged (with increasing frequency and improbable detail) with not being really British – it was German, or if not German then it was under German policy control with a majority of German shareholders. This was untrue, but as a merchant bank the Hongkong Bank had made an agreement with the Deutsch-Asiatische Bank, as a commercial bank there were German directors; the combination was too much for the simple minded. Both Government and the Bank proceeded virtually as if unaffected.

In consequence the relationship between the British Government and the Hongkong Bank has been seen in history as if the latter were in some sense a 'chosen instrument' which the Government tenaciously retained to the disadvantage of a great queue of qualified 'true-British' alternatives. The scaremongers, the propagandists, and the adventurers had done their work well.

To return to the Bank itself: the Hongkong Bank's international policies ran along two tracks: an international expansion (i) of the B&CC/CCR concept and (ii) of the Hongkong Bank/DAB relationship.

The Chinese Central Railways was itself reorganized in 1905 to differentiate between the original participants, now referred to as the 'British Group', defined as the British and Chinese Corporation, the Pekin Syndicate, and the Yangtze Valley Company on the one hand and Belgian and French Groups on the other. The French Group, which included the Banque de l'Indo-Chine and the Régie Générale de Chemins de Fer, was overwhelmingly the more important of the two. The reorganized CCR retained its British status by the casting vote of a British chairman.

The next development might be seen as the industrial counterpart to the 1895 financial agreement between the Hongkong Bank and the DAB. In July 1909 an agreement was signed between the British and Chinese Corporation, the CCR (including French and Belgian interests), the Deutsch-Chinesische Eisenbahn-Gesellschaft and, in its separate capacity representing a French syndicate of companies interested in China, the Banque de l'Indo-Chine. The French participation in the CCR had not been an altogether satisfactory solution to the problem of Anglo-French cooperation, since, as the French Ministry of Foreign Affairs put it, the British appeared to treat with the French as shareholders rather than with France as a Power, hence the further and separate French inclusion in the 1909 Agreement.[5] This was extended to include an American Group in November 1910.

However, the effectiveness of this line of development – the distinction was not in any case always clear-cut – was minimized when Chinese resistance to 'concession-type' construction projects became effective.

On the financial track, the extension of the 1895 Hongkong Bank/DAB Agreement was in one sense another consequence of the complex negotiations leading up to the 1911 Hukuang Railways Loan agreement. The adherence of the Banque de l'Indo-Chine to the agreement created three national Groups which covered the three major capital markets of Europe. At this point Charles Addis would have stopped; the Americans, for whom shares had been reserved in the Chinese Central Railways, had proved uninterested and the financial coverage was now complete. In 1910 however President Taft insisted on participation of the United States in the finance of the Hukuang Railways, and an American Group joined both the 'industrial' agreement (as noted above) and the financial Groups.

The financial Groups are usually referred to by the accurate but clumsy designation 'Four Power Groups', later Six and then Five Power Groups (or Sextuple/Quintuple) as national participation changed. Others have referred to the Groups as a 'Consortium', consistent with the official designation of the post-Great War national Groups as the 'New China Consortium'. 'Consortium' will be used in this history to refer collectively to the composite of the Groups bound at any one time by the inter-bank or inter-Group agreements. The more clumsy 'Four Power Groups Consortium' etc. will be used when this more specific term seems appropriate.

The existence of the Groups did not imply participation by each member or each Group in any particular transaction. The effective Groups and their member Groups might, for a particular project, be referred to therefore as the 'syndicate' (with the Hongkong Bank as lead manager), and contemporary literature (and this history) uses this terminology.

Post-Boxer development was seen by the Powers as dependent on a reorganization of the Chinese Government and economy – especially, with reference to the currency. To the extent this concerned the Bank, currency reform was considered in Chapter 4, and it was there stated that the Bank became involved as part of the Consortium with the American-planned loan for currency reform and Manchurian development – an unhappy combination.

Several threads now lead to an appreciation of the Hongkong Bank's involvement in the planned reorganization loans to the Chinese Government, plans for which matured on the eve of the revolution which effectively forced the abdication of the last emperor of the Ch'ing dynasty. The rationale which brought the Bank and the DAB together in 1895 in an agreement designed primarily for such administrative loans was now particularly relevant. In the meantime the agreement as modified had been expanded to include French and American Groups; between 1911 and the signing of the loan the Consortium would be joined by Japan and Russia. As these latter two countries could not provide the capital required from their own markets, their participation was seen correctly as political and it was thus opposed by Charles Addis as the representative of the Hongkong Bank. In the end political pressures forced the British Group's acquiescence.

Before the first Reorganization Loan was made in 1913 the American Group had withdrawn from the syndicate, but its undertakings relative to previous Consortium operations remained unchanged.

These events are crucial in the economic history of China. They are part of the history of the Hongkong and Shanghai Banking Corporation because the Bank played throughout a leading role. The leadership was provided by Charles Addis, and it was fitting, as noted in Chapter 3, that the Bank's new building on Gracechurch Street and Addis's knighthood should follow the successful completion of the China railway loans – and precede the less well-conceived Reorganization Loan of 1913.

Addis was never wholly successful. His banking Consortium was joined by Powers whose interests were mainly political. He was never successful in having his British Group recognized on a long-term or comprehensive basis as the sole representative of British capital in China. He was awarded exclusive support only when by the nature of the transaction support had for the time and for that purpose to be exclusive – and even then the Bank paid a price (a reasonable price it is fair to conclude in retrospect) in the broadening of the British Group.

This is a history of the Hongkong Bank, not of China's railway and political development nor even of its finance. Indeed for a history of the Hongkong Bank many details can be omitted; many of the railways discussed in such detail in railway and political histories were never built; the agreements relative to chief engineers, controls, and vital national interests soon became wholly irrelevant.

Key lines were, however, constructed and the principal issues were therefore of relevance. In the four chapters which follow the focus is on the role of the Hongkong Bank and, especially after 1904, with particular reference to the role of Charles Addis, in that period of Chinese history which has often been referred to as the 'Period of Imperialism'. The Bank, however, was anxious to remain clear of political entanglements; it wished only to act as the agents of China in obtaining the funds necessary for its development and self-determined reform. In the period 1895 to 1914 it was impossible to act without political support and the Bank, often frustrated, had to accept the limitations this implied.

In Chapter 5 the story is told to 1900 and the outbreak of the Boxer Uprising; the chapter covers the Bank's initial defeat and subsequent successes in the context of its new agreement with the DAB on the indemnity loans. There follow the first railway negotiations, the founding of the B&CC, and the impact of competitors. The Boxer Uprising requires a pause, and the story is continued in Chapter 6 with the financial consequences of the Uprising as they affected the Bank. At the same time the Bank took up once more the developmental tasks abandoned temporarily in 1900.

The Chinese reacted; the Rights Recovery Movement and the role of Young China are referred to in Chapter 7. Nevertheless development with foreign funds continued. After the Hukuang Railways Loan of 1911 the focus is on the Reorganization Loan of 1913, but this is only part of the story of the Bank's financial involvement in China in the last years before the Great War.

The story of the Reorganization Loan also reflects the limitations of the Bank's ability to control events given the basic premises of British economic policy; Chapter 8 recounts the challenge to the Bank's role in China as perceived by Addis and accepted, reluctantly at times, by the Foreign Office.

While the Bank moved on the world stage, it was also involved in smaller crises and to place the major story in perspective certain of these are considered at appropriate points.

In 1914 the Powers turned on themselves and the consequences to the Bank are told in Part III of this volume.

5

DEFEAT, INDEMNITY, AND RAILWAYS, 1895–1900

[Make] every effort facilitate matters for Chinese Government in order to secure future loans.

1894 cable to Hongkong Bank, Tientsin

A preliminary survey, 1895–1914

The defeat of the Chinese Empire by the Japanese in 1895 had an immediate impact on foreign and, therefore, banking relations, but China itself remained apparently incapable of change. The success of foreign arms surprised and, in a sense, caused concern to the very Powers which had been impatient of China's slow acceptance of modernization. The territorial interests of France, Germany, Russia, and Japan as contrasted with the primarily economic priorities of the other Powers provoked rivalries and implied dangers to which only a credible Chinese central authority could respond. Thus China policy seemed often to be characterized on the one hand by opportunistic struggles for exclusive rights, spheres of influence, and concessions but on the other by a partial recognition that any benefits gained could be secured only by the eventual confirmation of a China strengthened and modernized.

Both policies were unacceptable to the Chinese conservatives, and the Boxer Uprising of 1900 more than the arbitrary ending of the 100-days reform of 1898 expressed Chinese frustrations. Both policies were equally unacceptable to the nationalists and anti-Manchu revolutionaries, whose temporary success in 1911 is another bench-mark, as important for financial as for political history.

Despite such opposition, foreign influence, whether forced or encouraged by those Chinese willing to accept 'modernization' sufficient for survival, had a significant impact and yet, appearances notwithstanding, remained surprisingly under Chinese control.

The Hongkong Bank had been the agent of the Chinese Government in loan negotiations since the mid-1870s, but the relationship was never

258

exclusive. There is evidence that the Bank handled official exchange and overseas banking operations on various official accounts. Several cables to the Bank's negotiating base in Tientsin during the Sino-Japanese War stress the desire to obtain some exclusive agency, but in this the Bank failed; the Chinese wished always to keep their options open. Nevertheless the Bank declined Japanese business as it would 'prejudice' them with the Chinese, and the opinion wired to Tientsin expressed a widely held view – 'HSBC having special Chinese connection can attempt what others cannot . . .'[1]

The Hongkong Bank was also the British Government's banker in China, although this 'Treasury Chest' operation was mainly routine, based on the Bank's higher bid for the business; there was no question of policy status.

Thus on the eve of the 'Period of Imperialism' the Hongkong Bank had the advantages of experience and contacts but enjoyed no exclusive privilege.

Indeed the Bank was willing to proceed as before and at first claimed it needed neither official support nor special consideration. But the times had changed; the size of China's financial operations, the growth of national rivalries, the consequent sponsorship by European Governments of particular banks in relation to China activities, and the development of activities requiring Government support or approval brought the Hongkong Bank eventually into the mainstream of British and international financial developments, not all of which would receive the approval of history.

The Bank's experience with the First Indemnity Loan of 1895 would be sufficient to convince management that conditions and, therefore, operating procedures had changed. The need for combination and agreement on railway development also required more than a purely financial approach. These lessons were quickly learnt.

Then came the Boxer Uprising and the consequent financial demands of the Powers. Here the Bank as the British Government's banker became intimately involved as adviser, negotiator, banker – and, to an extent, beneficiary in the long years and tedious negotiations relative to the Boxer Indemnity. As the burden of the Japanese indemnity of 1895 had hindered sound investment in modernization at the end of the nineteenth century, so this new wearing down of China's credit, consequent on imposition of a new indemnity, endangered those railway and mining projects so close to European hearts. The Hongkong Bank, however, played a key role both in the initial financing of the projects and in China's Rights Recovery Movement, thus in this latter stage enabling China to regain control of her railway development.

Given China's straitened financial circumstances, the limited room for manoeuvre forced a degree of international cooperation. Charles Addis as London Manager of the Hongkong Bank, who headed the British Group and who as such was 'head' of the China Consortium, led the Bank's efforts which climaxed in the controversial first (and only) Reorganization Loan of 1913.

The China Consortium, however much they were responsible for the modification of foreign pressure, however much they preserved China's credit-worthiness, were strongly resented by the merchant-gentry of the provinces and by Young China, the returned students and those who were nationalist in the sense that they judged Chinese foreign relations in the context of nation-state principles. The Consortium appeared to confront the Government with a unified body of financiers frustrating China's traditional policy of ensuring foreign competition, of dividing the barbarians. China failed to acknowledge the significance of recent developments – several countries had by themselves sufficient power to force unequal terms on China, consequently the combination was designed as one of self-restraint by the Powers; it no longer exploited, on the contrary it rationalized the offers of finance.

The complex financial history of the period in part reflects the desire of China to free itself from the restraints imposed, despite their only partial effectiveness, by the Consortium and by other combinations. It also reflects the constraints placed on the international banks, including the Hongkong Bank, who had now to undertake their operations in the context of national policies with which they might or might not agree. For the Hongkong Bank particularly – and, in fairness, for the British Foreign Office – this was a high price to pay. The Bank had played its role alone; it would have preferred to continue alone.

The Hongkong Bank, based as it was in Hong Kong and Shanghai, played a role in China which was not confined to major operations emanating from London. Certainly Charles Addis in London became a financier of international reputation, and the London Office, as already suggested, looked as much to its own Consultative Committee, the Foreign Office, and the City as it did to Head Office in Hong Kong – but this reflected sound procedure rather than a fundamental split or indication of a power struggle within the Bank. The ability of London Office to use London contacts and respond to London requirements negated the arguments of those outside the Bank who anticipated the 'necessity' of a London directorate and head office.

While Addis moved between the Foreign Office, Paris, and Berlin, while in 1898 the Bank joined with Jardine, Matheson and Co. in the British and Chinese Corporation (B&CC) and became involved in 1903/04 with the Pekin Syndicate in the establishment through the B&CC of the Chinese Central Railways, the Chief Manager and his Board of Directors in Hong Kong evaluated the Bank's situation on a global basis, continuing close

relations with the Viceroy in Canton and participating directly in the requirements of the Treaty Port economies.

Even the Hong Kong Government, anxious for the Canton–Kowloon
Railway, became directly involved in Chinese finance, and the Hongkong
Bank advised and assisted them. The Bank's role in China was on many fronts
– from banking crises in Shanghai to leadership in international syndicates.

The Bank thus served at least two masters whose interests China, to the
extent its leaders thought in such terms, would consider incompatible. That
the Bank was from time to time outspoken in support of China's interests – as
in the question of the exchange rate at which the Boxer Indemnity payments
were to be calculated – might be thought evidence of the Bank's China
orientation, but as the exchange rate controversy arose in a matter which
China would condemn in its entirety, the Bank naturally received little credit.
The Bank was nevertheless a China bank and its overall policy was based on
the success of a progressive and prosperous China.

The Hongkong Bank remained, however, a corporation owned by private
shareholders, whose shares were quoted on the Hong Kong, Shanghai, and
London stock markets. The proprietors, a third master, might have little
direct influence on the Bank's policy – provided it were successful, but this is a
significant limitation, a reminder that the Bank operated under normal
constraints which could never for long be lost sight of.

The Bank's role in China was directed by names which are well-known in
the history of the Bank. By 1895 David McLean had retired both from the
Bank and, during the debacle of the Trust and Loan Company and its
reorganization as a competing bank, from the London Committee. His place
as London Manager had been taken by Ewen Cameron, soon to be knighted
for his services in connection with China finance. Cameron was assisted by
G.E. Noble and John Walter.

By 1905 Cameron had been forced to retire but with recovered health
continued in an advisory role; Walter had died. The new team comprised
A.M. Townsend and Charles Addis, with the latter very much in control of
China affairs, overshadowing his titular chief and, on the former's retirement
at the end of 1911, replacing him. Addis was assisted by Murray Stewart, the
younger brother of Gershom Stewart. Although both Stewarts had earlier
resigned from the Bank, Murray was brought back to assist Addis in
Consortium affairs and played an important role as secretary and confidant in
the negotiations.

In China the scene of negotiations was shared by Tientsin with Shanghai
and, growing in importance, Peking. Addis's immediate contact was E.G.
Hillier, the Bank's Peking Agent. Communication passed, often through

Foreign Office channels, between them via the Shanghai office. As Peking developed into a national capital in the executive sense, the Tientsin office, which for so long had developed sound relations with Li Hung-chang, had now served its main purpose; it would reassert itself during the Boxer troubles and it remained important for exchange banking and for relations with the administration of China's national railways and with new industries.

As Addis met bankers and statesmen in the capitals of Europe, so Hillier mastered his own small world of Peking, establishing key sources within the Chinese bureaucracy, maintaining daily contact with the British Legation, and enjoying difficult relations with sometimes rival, sometimes cooperating representatives of other banks, usually those who formed part of the China Consortium and the several syndicates with which the Hongkong Bank was involved.

The Tientsin compradore, Wu Mao-ting, had close ties to the bureaucracy and kept the Bank informed through his assistants. His relatives served the Bank in Peking. When rumours of the Emperor's death reached Shanghai during the Empress Dowager's *coup d'état* of September 1898, Peking office was able to reassure the Bank by cable to Tientsin on the 26th that 'Wu Jim Pah saw the Emperor in good health yesterday noon. Have no reason to believe he is dead since.' The additional comment – 'No cause for anxiety political situation' – was more debatable.

Successive Shanghai Managers, H.M. Bevis, H.E.R. Hunter, and A.G. Stephen, were familiar with China's position and requirements. In Tientsin, still key for northern railway and mining developments, there was also the expertise of D.H. Mackintosh; South China operations were directed from Hong Kong rather than from the Bank's small and late-established Canton agency. In Hong Kong the China expertise is more difficult to identify; Jackson and Smith were primarily interested in exchange; Stabb was positively disinterested in 'political banking'. In 1874 James Greig had gone to Foochow to ensure the success of the Hongkong Bank's first China loan; thereafter the Chief Manager remained in Hong Kong. De Bovis went to Canton in the 1880s and other Sub-Managers followed him, but contact with the Canton Viceroy would seem to have been maintained chiefly through the compradores, with negotiations in Hong Kong.

The Bank's China expertise, sound and significant as it was, touched a limited number of the top management only (see Chapter 3). Other important officers of the Bank were in Japan, the Philippines, India, and elsewhere. Below this level China affairs were reflected in coupons to be paid, drafts to be prepared, and other routine tasks performed, indistinguishable in the routine of banking. In consequence the young Chinese businessmen and the new officials, schooled, many of them overseas, in the principles of nationalism, did not see in the Hongkong Bank a China bank working in China's interests, but a foreign bank staffed by capable and honest men no doubt, but men whose lives were Treaty Port lives and whose knowledge of the East was restricted by the demands of the office routine and social obligations within the foreign community. On his return to China as British Minister in 1906, Sir John Jordan sensed the new atmosphere created by Young China and took note of it; so to a degree did the Bank, but, with ledgers that had to be written up, the Manager his own exchange operator, and the compradore system all-pervasive, there were limitations.

This new generation of Chinese naturally judged the Bank in the context of China's existing foreign relations. To them the Hongkong Bank was the agent of British 'imperialism', the financial instrument by which the imperialists obtained the benefits of 'disadvantageous' economic agreements; it was a Bank staffed by apparently uninterested Britishers into whose homes they were never invited, whose clubs they could not join, and with whom they could not even transact business except, as they saw it, through the compradore.

This emotional reaction was not always modified when the nationalists needed the Bank and used it or when the Bank could be seen objectively to be acting in China's interests. There was underlying the reaction a political factor which prevented cool analysis of costs and benefits.

The Hongkong Bank, while admitting its duty to shareholders and its status as a British bank, considered its role sympathetic to China and its interventions designed to further China's interests. If the Bank had a self-image it was as a 'China bank'. It prided itself on its Chinese constituents, was convinced that its international role was beneficial to China, and believed sincerely that the development of the trade which it did so much to finance was in the interests of the Chinese, as well as of the British and the Germans.

Some part of the contemporary misunderstandings and the judgement of later commentators rests on lack of knowledge of technical banking practices. There has been criticism, for example, of the rates of interest on the publicly issued Government loans; indeed, judged in the late 1930s against the then prevailing rate on U.S. Treasury bills, the rates can be seen to have been higher. The China orientation of some critics may blind them to the forces which the banks serving China had to contend with in the European capital markets; the terms of loans were not set arbitrarily by the banks, but reflected their almost day-by-day assessments of the several world capital markets and hence the terms necessary for the successful issue of each particular loan in London, Paris, and Berlin.

The concessions which force obtained and the banks financed were seen by European political apologists as unfortunate necessities in the light of China's refusal to join the comity of nations as an equal. The firm belief prevailed that this refusal was temporary; hence the foreign role was temporary, preserving China's integrity until more progressive leaders would take over in the spirit of the Rights Recovery Movement. Like all theories of 'tutelage', including that of the Kuomintang, the end of tutelage is in the future and those who suggest the time is now are resented.

The Hongkong Bank, which had no interest in European expansionist policies, was convinced its actions served China's long-run interests. Exclusive privileges granted to the Powers undermined the Hongkong Bank's ability to finance the China trade on an a-political basis. The Bank was, like Britain, the leader in economic relations with China; like Britain the Bank had a rational basis for advocating a *status quo*; the Bank and the Foreign Office would therefore have a basis for cooperation. At the same time the Bank would protect its position by taking the initiative to participate in the trade brought about by the growing German presence.

The Bank could not deny, however, either the need for modernization in China or its own role as part of the European presence on the China coast. Not surprisingly the Bank expressed its views and participated in the giving of advice, often unsolicited and unwelcome, to China. In the period 1895–1914 the Hongkong Bank was therefore too often stereotyped and associated uncritically with the contemporary system of which it was necessarily a part – indeed, a leading actor.

In the account which follows the problems raised in this introduction will be seen in the context of the specific loan, the specific event within the international system as it existed and in which both China and the Hongkong Bank had then to operate.

FINANCING THE JAPANESE INDEMNITY[2]

The first indemnity loan, 1895[3]

In the 21 years between 1874 and 1895 the Hongkong Bank acted on behalf of China for a total of £12 million in publicly issued loans (see Volume I, Table 14.2), of which the largest was the £3 million 6% Gold Loan of 1895. In April 1895 the Chinese signed the Treaty of Shimonoseki, which called *inter alia* for payment of an indemnity to Japan of Kuping Ts200 million (approx. £32 million) and the cession of the Liaotung Peninsula. In May, under pressure from Russia, France, and Germany – the Triple Intervention – the Japanese gave up the Liaotung Peninsula in return for a further Ts30 million. As Japan retained certain privileges until the indemnity was paid, it was to China's advantage that payment should be made as quickly as possible, and before the end of April China was known to be seeking a £40 million loan.

An early payment was also to the advantage of the Powers, especially Russia, as only on payment would the Japanese surrender certain interim privileges detrimental to other foreign, especially Russian, interests.

As early as November 1894 the Bank had considered the possibility of an indemnity payable in gold should China be defeated; exceptionally, physical gold would be required and actually shipped for a likely switch by Japan onto the gold standard, and the Bank warned branches to watch their positions, retaining gold balances in anticipation of the impact on silver.

Sir Robert Hart, the Inspector General of China's Imperial Maritime Customs, also anticipated that a large indemnity would be one consequence of defeat, and on April 8, 1895, had cabled London to enquire if the Hongkong Bank were interested in responsibility for the public issue of a £60 million loan – £3 million to disband the Chinese army, £15 million towards the Liaotung retrocession and the first indemnity payment, and £42 million for the later payments and expected administrative expenses – the total sum, in excess of the amount required for the indemnity alone, reflects the state of Chinese finances and the need for funds for other purposes. Hart still hoped to meet Chinese wishes by issuing at par.[4]

The Hongkong Bank reacted favourably, asserting that it could raise the £15 million towards the first two items and would consult with others in relation to the total requirements. In fact, Cameron instructed the Bank's Hamburg Agent, Julius Brüssel, to negotiate with Adolph von Hansemann of the Disconto-Gesellschaft in the latter's role as effective leader of both the Deutsch-Asiatische Bank (DAB) and the Konsortium für Asiatische Geschäfte (KfAG). The Hongkong Bank also proposed inclusion of the Crédit Lyonnais and the Banque de Paris et des Pays Bas.

At first glance all this might seem familiar. Hart, who would be finally entrusted with China's loan negotiations, had turned to the Customs' own bankers, the Hongkong Bank, which had, after all, the experience. The Bank in turn offered to share the issue with the German interests as it had in 1885, although admittedly with a difference. The Bank now sensed it would need assistance and this time took the initiative.

In fact, nothing was the same.

Previous loans had not endangered China's international position nor brought into question the adequacy of the purely financial security offered; the loans had not been of sufficient importance to require political assurances beyond the sanction of an Imperial edict. Nor previously had the Hongkong Bank found it *necessary* to approach others; the Bank had acted alone.

Not that the Bank had been without competition prior to 1895, but the experience of the Hongkong Bank, its immediate presence in China, and the superiority of London as a capital market had been factors effectively enabling it to outmanoeuvre its rivals on business grounds. With the British Minister 'holding the ring' this had usually proved sufficient.

The Hongkong Bank's initial 1895 negotiations were for the formation of an international syndicate for an all-inclusive indemnity loan to include participation from the banks of three Powers, England, France, and Germany. Russia had not been included; the Bank thought in financial, not political, terms, and Russia had no capital market of its own. These efforts had from the first been hampered by the intervention of other loan and concession seekers who, had their activities been publicly known, might have destroyed the remaining elements in China's financial image, reducing it through indiscriminate and uncoordinated borrowing to the chaotic financial status of a South American country – to a position, that is, in which previous borrowing could only be repaid by new borrowing. But this too was an old complaint.

The new factors began to reveal themselves when in May the German syndicate was advised by their Government to break off negotiations with the Hongkong Bank in view of a possible international loan under the sponsorship of Russian, French, and German banks backed by their respective governments.

These Powers had always taken a political approach to economic relations; but now there was a difference – they were in a position to be effective.

China considered England had let her down, had stood aside while, on the contrary, French, German, and Russian diplomatic representations had been responsible for the reluctant Japanese retrocession of the Liaotung Peninsula; these Powers now claimed their reward which included, in addition to the right to float the necessary indemnity loan, political concessions in Manchuria and Yunnan and international control of the Imperial Maritime Customs. The demands were not unrelated, the control of the Customs being a direct consequence of the heavy dependence of the success of the loan on the security of the Customs revenues. Overall the situation threatened both the basis on which economic relations were conducted with the Imperial Government and the territorial integrity of the Empire.

The Hongkong Bank, despite its past record, was seen by the Chinese as a British bank, and was consequently out of favour. The Bank was later to be offered merely a participation in the proposed tri-partite loan and that by courtesy of the three Powers, but Ewen Cameron rejected the subordinate position and warned the Foreign Office of the threat to Chinese control of their own Maritime Customs.

Meanwhile the Hongkong Bank, frustrated by the DAB's withdrawal, nevertheless attempted to form a syndicate through Paris, reporting on May 11 the likelihood of a successful loan at 6%. Despite fears that the Bank would be unsuccessful in the face of positive opposition from the French and

German Governments, the Foreign Office, almost to the end, was anxious to let Cameron attempt to arrange a rival loan but without British Government interference or public endorsement.

There was, however, a second line of approach developing within the British Government which the Prime Minister, Lord Rosebery, in consultation with Lord Rothschild grew to favour. Assuming that a financial victory in the matter of the indemnity loan would anger the three Powers to the detriment of China, Rosebery argued that the Hongkong Bank should be encouraged to work with Rothschild's for an international consortium under conditions which would preserve the existing system of Customs control, including an English succession on the retirement of Sir Robert Hart, the Inspector-General. Thus under all plans some foreign interference in China's administrative discretion was envisaged, potentially weakening the influence of Hart whose role could henceforth be seen – by those Chinese and others unfriendly to the system – primarily as protecting British rather than Chinese interests.

Cameron learned of this new British approach to China loans indirectly through Panmure Gordon, the Bank's stockbroker. The Foreign Office confirmed the position, warning him that 'in face of the opposition of the French and German Governments it would be a serious task to carry the [Cameron/Hart] plan through and that a failure would have the worst consequences'.[5] Cameron rejected these overtures; he remained convinced that the Bank would be successful in (i) obtaining a commission from the Chinese to issue the loan – consistent with the traditional role of the Bank, seemingly confirmed by the original approach of Hart, (ii) including a 'simple engagement in the contract for the maintenance of the European customs', and then (iii) obtaining the participation of German and French interests.

On May 13 a Foreign Office memorandum, reflecting the views of Lord Rosebery, wished Cameron success in terms which suggested doubt:

I think I had better . . . tell [Cameron] that if the Bank can manage the loan on the lines they wish [£15 million immediately, and two later advances] we shall think they have done remarkably well. But that we cannot take any part in the negotiations, as we should arouse international jealousies which would smash the whole transaction, and the Government would rather only hear of it as an accomplished fact. Perhaps I might say that *privately* I shall be glad to hear from him, and to give him any information I can.[6]

But all was not coordinated among the three Powers, for while both Russian and German interests at one time were attempting separately to secure loans of £8 million equivalent, the Russians were also pressing China for acceptance of a Russian Government-guaranteed loan, reportedly between £8 and £16 million and with exclusively French (that is, without German) financial support, the political implications of which were serious. At the same time the Germans and French were reported anxious to contract a second and larger loan which would include funds for development capital purchases, with the condition that expenditure be made in the lending countries only. The situation contained all the elements Britain had so long attempted to avoid: exclusive development contracts, interference in the Maritime Customs, and politicization of loans. There is little wonder that Cameron refused to participate or that Rosebery tentatively wished the Hongkong Bank success.

At this point, May 19, Cameron turned back to the British Government and linked the events in China not simply to the Hongkong Bank but to the whole question of the British position. Not only would the Bank itself lose its pre-eminence among its foreign competitors in China, but:

> a great blow would be dealt to British interests for which an issue of part of the loan in the London market would in no way compensate . . . It is therefore my humble opinion that England should make a firm stand at the present juncture and not give up the position we have won and justly hold in China.[7]

The following day Cameron, facing the reality of a potential £50 million loan, made three queries of the Foreign Office which marked the changed position of China loan operations and was an acknowledgement of the need for an official Government role: (i) Cameron wished confirmation that the British Government would not compromise on the question of Customs control, that is, international control was to be ruled out if the Bank's case were not to be weakened, (ii) he asked whether there was an objection to his approaching a French financial group requesting them to drop the demand for international control of the Customs, and (iii) he asked whether Her Majesty's Government would 'recognize and support' the Hongkong and Shanghai Bank as the representative of British interests in China for the negotiation of the loan.[8]

There were already rumours, at first discounted, that the Russians were attempting to place a loan of their own in Peking, thus breaking the Triple Entente. Since the Russians had approached Rothschild frères in Paris, who had in turn contacted N.M. Rothschild and Sons in London, the Foreign Office was undoubtedly aware of developments, including the possibility of piecemeal lending with Russian political involvement. In this atmosphere the risk of a Hongkong Bank failure became even more serious; indeed the Bank's request for official recognition was virtually an admission of the difficulties. Lord Rosebery with Lord Kimberley, the Foreign Secretary, again turned to Lord Rothschild, cabling Peking at the latter's suggestion to see if the Chinese would authorize a British attempt to put together an international consortium. Meanwhile Lord Rothschild, who had all along been sceptical of the ability of the Hongkong Bank to negotiate a £15 million loan in the face of antagonism from France and Germany, reopened contacts with von Hansemann in Berlin.

This was all on the 20th, the day Cameron was to return for the answer to his three questions.

When Cameron called at the Foreign Office on the evening of May 20, he was told of the almost overnight reversal.

> ... the pressure of other Governments on China had become so strong and it was so clearly essential that the loan should be brought out as one transaction that we have been compelled to get the assistance of the Rothschilds in preventing anything being done to prejudice British interests ... We think that in their own interest and in British interests it would be best for the Bank to ally themselves with the Rothschilds.[9]

The Hongkong Bank's London reputation had been based on its ability to issue loans through Panmure Gordon without the intervention of the great City merchant banks, and David McLean had earlier recommended rejecting the leadership pretensions of both Baring's and Rothschild's.

The apparently sudden change of position on the part of the Foreign Office appeared inexplicable – either that or Cameron refrained (as some French observers did not) from commenting on the family connection between Rosebery and Rothschild. Rosebery's position can, however, be more easily explained. The Hongkong Bank had indeed surprised the City in its ability to manage China loan issues, but the amounts had been small. Neither Rosebery nor Rothschild could be expected to have foreseen the Bank's ability to handle the major loans it would soon be managing.

Nor must the ultimate goal be lost sight of. Major British interests were united in their wish to support a syndicate which could provide China with the funds to pay off the entire indemnity with a minimum of delay and with no political conditions.

Cameron's reply to the Foreign Office nevertheless reflected his indignation. Placing the Bank's recent statements in the context of the previous thirty years of China experience, he wrote to Kimberley:

> ... your Lordship may assume that a Bank in the position we hold would not lightly volunteer to undertake a business it could not carry out ... Now, after having helped to maintain British commercial supremacy in China for so long, and against such powerful competition, I am sure your Lordship can understand the dismay with which I heard yesterday that we were about to be deprived of the position we had gained for our Country and for ourselves – and that through the action of our own Government.[10]

The following day, May 22, Cameron capitulated. He had little choice; perhaps on reflection he recognized the problems.[11]

The British Government was now able to make its own position known. On the same day as Cameron's letter was received, the Foreign Office sent a memorandum to the German Government – and to others – stating their great interest in the loan, and especially their concern that China's security not be wasted in the confusion, a discreet reference to the question of the internationalization of the Maritime Customs. The memorandum added that the loan could not be raised without the London market and therefore proposed that the loan be shared by all the Powers equally, and that perhaps some great financial house (they later suggested what had already been decided, the London and Paris Rothschilds), could organize an international syndicate. The German Foreign Minister on receiving the British proposal is reported to have exclaimed, 'When the other Powers have settled the political side, England wants to exploit the financial side!'[12]

By June all were clear that the Russians were in fact negotiating on their own but on the basis of Russian-guaranteed French capital participation, and the indignation in Germany had the eventual consequence of breaking the Triple Entente and bringing the Hongkong Bank and the Deutsch-Asiatische Bank into an agreement to be signed on July 27, 1895. The Chinese Government was by now having hesitations, but Russian pressure was strong and the Chinese declared they could not break the preliminary agreement, a claim interpreted by German Secretary of State von Holstein as 'perhaps an excuse for those mandarins who had been bribed by the Russians'.[a] If so, there was an obvious solution – outbid the Russians: 'Rothschild could do that for us,' he wrote. 'What else is the fellow [*Kerl*] good for?'[13]

The Russian deadline for Chinese acceptance of an indemnity loan was June 17, but the issue of the Russian guarantee of the loan and the political implications delayed the Chinese decision. Between June 17 and July 6, the date the loan was in fact signed in St Petersburg, Rothschild attempted to direct coordinated negotiations to secure a £16 million loan for the Anglo-German Group, to snatch victory from the Russians at the last moment.

Rothschild asked von Hansemann to instruct the DAB in China to cooperate with the Hongkong Bank and to allow the British bank to do as much of the negotiating as possible as it was on good terms with the Chinese. He added (although this was not a part of the original proposal), both Groups would sign the final loan contract. Now it was in their common interest to cooperate and not compete, and, he warned, despite his attempts to stop them, the Hongkong Bank was very inclined to negotiate alone.[14]

These instructions were confirmed by Rothschild directly to the Hongkong Bank's Peking Agent, E.G. Hillier, but he took care to put the matter in the correct sequence – a *German* syndicate had offered a 5% loan of £16 million and was willing that the British should participate and take a lead in the

---

[a] The assumption that Chinese officials were bribed is common to many despatches from or about operations in Peking. Specific references can be found in Group Archives, but proof is not easily obtained. The relevant point is that, often without conclusive evidence, bribery and corruption were assumed and policy determined on this basis.

negotiations.[15] Thus on June 20 Hillier approached the DAB with the approval of the British Minister, who had just been assured by the Tsungli Yamen that the Chinese would not accept a loan dependent on a Russian guarantee and the political concession this implied.[16]

Although the path appeared still open, the Chinese were not yet prepared to deal with the British, and rumours reached London that the Germans in Peking were planning to extend an £8 million loan on their own account. In fact the German Minister, Baron von Schenck, made an official visit to Prince Kung, President of the Tsungli Yamen, and informed him that the German Group were willing to lend the Chinese Government £8 million, but that they preferred to make an offer of £16 million along with the British Group. Prince Kung who again acknowledged Germany's service to China, claimed that this offer was new to him, and that he preferred to close first with the German Group alone.[17]

On June 26, Rothschild cabled von Hansemann urgently at the request of the Hongkong Bank concerning a report by the Chinese Government that the German Group had closed an £8 million loan with them. Rothschild would not believe the report, but the Bank still wanted confirmation.[18] The Chinese were indeed urging the DAB to close this loan with them alone, perhaps in an attempt to avert a union of the German and English markets, but the DAB insisted they would only close together with the Hongkong Bank.

Meanwhile the Russians and the Chinese were continuing negotiations while Rothschild pressed urgently ahead. On his advice the Hongkong Bank again sent Julius Brüssel, the Bank's Hamburg Manager, to Berlin to talk to von Hansemann. Indeed, the next day, July 2, Rehders, the DAB's negotiator in Peking, was instructed as follows: the two banks were to seek a £16 million agreement at 5% and 94 net. Although the two Peking representatives were to negotiate on equal terms, Rothschild once more insisted that Hillier was to take the lead in consultation with Rehders, because 'otherwise', the Hongkong Bank had argued – apparently convincingly – 'we are certain the influence we have in Peking cannot be fully exercised'.[19]

Rothschild added that they were not to allow the Russians to get a prior lien on the Customs for the proposed 'partial loan'. This would result in there being insufficient security remaining for the further loans necessary to repay the indemnity in full. Instead the British and German negotiators were instructed to determine the full amount that China needed and make an offer for the full amount.

Rehders and the German Minister in Peking reacted angrily to the suggestion that the British negotiator, Hillier of the Hongkong Bank, should take the lead in the negotiations.[20] They argued that the Tsungli Yamen were prepared to close an £8 million loan agreement with the Germans alone, and yet the Germans were supposed to give precedence to the British, something which the German Minister in Peking considered unacceptable under any circumstances. However, Rehders was told that the instructions stood despite his protests; he was reassured that in the final agreement the two banks would be on an equal footing.

Sir Nicholas O'Conor, the British Minister in Peking, was only instructed to join his German colleague in supporting the combined Hongkong Bank/DAB negotiations just before the Russian loan was closed.[21] The Hongkong Bank had been warned by the Foreign Office that Britain's position in China was too weak politically to permit effective intervention – a last minute touch of realism which confirmed the wisdom of the Rosebery–Rothschild approach.

Despite these desperate last minute negotiations by the Anglo-German Group, on July 6 the Russian-sponsored syndicate successfully concluded negotiations for the First Indemnity Loan, the Chinese Imperial Government 4% Gold Loan of 1895, taking the loan firm for the nominal amount of Francs 400 million or Gold Roubles 100 million (=£15.8 million). The prize had slipped by the Hongkong Bank and the new era of politicized loans had been confirmed.

The immediate consequence – the Hongkong Bank/Deutsch-Asiatische Bank Agreement

Agreements wrested from a reluctant China had in the past been matters for mutual congratulation. Under the 'most favoured nation' clause the benefits were passed to all the Treaty Powers. The Hongkong Bank's Shanghai Sub-Manager, Charles Addis, judged the Russian success in this context, explaining the loan as a simple desire to rid China of Japanese exclusive privileges as quickly as possible and to open Manchuria, assuming equal rights.[22] He failed to appreciate that the Russian loan, by failing to cover the entire indemnity, delayed the evacuation of the Japanese; furthermore, the new privileges Russia secured were of an exclusive character. The Russians had not obtained all their objectives; the Imperial Maritime Customs (IMC) was not internationalized, but China agreed not to accept any further loan for a further six months.

Related understandings, however, led to Chinese-Russian cooperation in the founding of the Russo-Chinese Bank and the concession for the Chinese Eastern Railway under Russian management. Indeed, the Russian success stimulated the other Powers to seek similar exclusive privileges in the form of concessions or spheres of influence, forcing State and foreign policy involvement in every major loan negotiation, subjecting China to intolerable pressures which were somewhat modified by the formation from 1909 of an international consortium in the image of the Hongkong Bank's frustrated plan of 1895.

The more immediate consequence of the Russian loan was the urgent need for China to negotiate further indemnity loans. To retain some form of credibility with the third of the Entente Powers, China offered the next loan to the Germans; they, in turn, felt bitter at being abandoned by Russia and France and were prepared to confirm their relations with Britain, that is, with the Hongkong Bank; at the same time Britain was placing diplomatic pressure on China to ensure British participation in the subsequent indemnity loan(s). The logic of the Anglo-German position was that a loan offered to Germany for political reasons would have to be shared with Britain for economic reasons, provided the representative banks cooperated.

The course of negotiations was, however, far from direct. China was a sovereign power, albeit in defeat; the violent protests of O'Conor, the British Minister, caused his recall, while the pressures of the French Minister, A. Gérard, were counter-productive; China would not agree to foreign control of the Maritime Customs. A British-German offer would be China's only viable alternative to complete financial domination and consequent political subservience to Russia in the Northeast and France in the Southwest, linked perhaps by a Peking–Canton railway which they would build and control.

The Hongkong Bank had earlier stated its reluctance to consider participation in a second indemnity loan on the grounds of the inadequacy of the security, a lien on the Customs revenues, which would now be subordinate to Russian claims. However, once the Russian loan was signed, the Bank changed its position.

Franz Urbig, the new Tientsin manager of the DAB, recognized that the success of any negotiations for a second indemnity loan would depend on a formal agreement between his bank and the Hongkong Bank, but one made not in China but at a 'higher level', by which he meant 'Europe' despite the fact that his own head office was *de jure* in Shanghai and that of the Hongkong Bank was *de jure* and *de facto* in Hong Kong.

In July 1895 representatives of the proprietor financial institutions of the Deutsch-Asiatische Bank, led by A. von Hansemann, and the Hongkong and Shanghai Banking Corporation, represented by Julius Brüssel, met in Berlin to discuss an arrangement for sharing Chinese loan business. The consequent agreement of July 27, *which was an agreement between two banks and not between two Governments*, stipulated that all future Chinese Government or Government-guaranteed loans and advances would be split equally between the two banks on behalf of the interests, 'Groups', they represented, although the contracts would be made without joint responsibility.[b] Non-guaranteed financial operations with railway and other companies would be dealt with on a case by case basis; smaller deals were not covered.[23]

Under the agreement the two banks would observe complete parity in negotiation, in the actual business, and in signing. There was an explicit understanding that the German Group would allow the Hongkong Bank to lead in the negotiations – on a mutually agreed course. It was further stipulated, in recognition of Rothschild's role (through von Hansemann) in bringing about this alliance, that if the Hongkong Bank needed help in placing a loan in London, the Bank would turn to N.M. Rothschild and Sons first; it was also agreed that the Hamburg Branch of the Hongkong Bank could accept subscriptions on behalf of the German Group.[24]

Interestingly, the agreement does not appear to have been brought before the Hongkong Bank's Board of Directors. It was signed in Berlin by J. Brüssel and A. von Hansemann and stipulated that the DAB was to deal with the London Office of the Bank.

There were two difficulties, one of short-term, the other of longer-term importance.

There is an early reference to the agreement in a letter from Carlowitz and Co. to the German Minister in Peking concerning a Krupp loan, which the 'Disconto-Gesellschaft', in fact the DAB, was offering to split 50/50 with the Hongkong Bank.[c] Carlowitz, whose Hong Kong firm was not as yet represented on the Hongkong Bank's Board of Directors, speculated that this was an attempt by the German Foreign Ministry (Auswärtiges Amt, AA) to establish an Anglo-German alliance to counterbalance the Franco-Russian alliance, and that they would have had nothing against the participation of 'this London bank', if it had not done the 'dumb thing' in telegraphing the details of the agreement to its branch in Tientsin. There the Hongkong Bank Manager, D.H. Mackintosh, had told his compradore and 'principal' director of the Imperial Railways of North China, Wu Mao-ting, about it. Despite working for the Hongkong Bank, Wu, who was alleged to be anti-German, attempted unsuccessfully to use his great influence to obstruct the project. This, however was a misconception and was denied by Mackintosh.[25]

[b] The German financial institutions as listed in the agreement were: The Direction der Disconto-Gesellschaft, S. Bleichröder, the Deutsche Bank, the Berliner Handelsgesellschaft, the Bank für Handel und Industrie, Robert Warschauer and Co., Mendelssohn & Co., the Dresdner Bank, the A. Schaaffhausen'sche Bankverein, Born & Busse (all of Berlin), Jacob S.H. Stern in Frankfurt am Main, Sal. Oppenheim, Jr & Co., Cologne, the Norddeutsche Bank in Hamburg, and the Deutsch-Asiatische Bank in Shanghai. The Hongkong Bank represented only itself.

[c] Due to von Hansemann's leading position in the German consortiums until his death in 1903, business offered to the DAB or the KfAG is often referred to as being offered to the Disconto-Gesellschaft.

More important was the immediately observed difference between the British and German signatories to the agreement. The Hongkong Bank was just that – one bank; the DAB was a consortium bank representing virtually all German financial houses with interests in China. Indeed, the latter's composition changed when interests changed. Thus the DAB could speak for Germany, but the Hongkong Bank had rivals, at times placing the Foreign Office in the unenviable position of supporting one British private company against the interests of others.

In the DAB's opinion the Hongkong Bank was under an obligation to try to form some kind of union with its financial competitors, a view the Hongkong Bank never willingly accepted.[26] The DAB's constituents also had close connections with German industry; the Hongkong Bank would attempt to remedy its own isolation through promotion of the British and Chinese Corporation (B&CC) in 1898.

The Hongkong Bank/DAB partnership was never an easy one, even before it became subject to politically inspired criticism. The DAB was interested in the finance of long-term German investment; the Hongkong Bank was concerned primarily with finance; even its participation in the B&CC involved a potential conflict of interest. On the other hand the Hongkong Bank was able to retain its share of German trade finance and to retain the loyalty of its German trading constituents despite its competition at the trade finance level with the 'German bank', with the DAB.

The second indemnity loan, 1896[27]

The negotiations
At first glance China's decision to accept the offer of the Anglo-German syndicate would seem an obvious outcome of the disappointments and contentions of the negotiations for the first indemnity loan. In fact, the course of events was far from certain. The Russian agreement required the Chinese to forgo any further foreign borrowing for six months and the actual negotiations continued amid hard bargaining until March 1896, when the Chinese closed with the Hongkong Bank and the DAB having won significantly more favourable terms than originally offered.

China needed the funds, but there were many who sought to lend; it is little wonder that this and similar experiences convinced the Chinese of the wisdom of maintaining competition and so set them against the foreign combinations which reached their ultimate form in the international China Consortium, 1909 to 1946.

The burden of keeping the Anglo-German offer before the Chinese rested with the Germans, but the final breakthrough came when the Chinese placed the matter in the hands of Sir Robert Hart and Hillier acted decisively in accepting terms which, while providing minimal benefits to the lending banks, would nevertheless ensure the assignment to float the loan.

The actual negotiations reflect the inherent conflict between the Power with the political advantage, in this case Germany, and the Power with access to the finance, Britain in the London capital market. The Germans were torn between the desire to close the loan on their own and their recognition that, if they tried to do so, it would be a smaller loan inadequate to meet the current Chinese indemnity obligations. The Chinese were consciously divisive in their tactics, but in view of the recently signed Hongkong Bank/DAB agreement there was little real chance of separating the two banks.

With such views, the German Minister, Baron von Schenck, agreed. He admitted that it had been in the German interest to go along with the English as they had thus been able to place a much larger loan, and that only with the support of the English did German finance show the 'decisiveness' necessary to close a loan in China.[28] A more nationalistic opinion was expressed by the official German interpreter, Otto Franke (J.N. Jordan was the British interpreter). Franke accepted at face value the Chinese assurances that they would prefer to deal with the Germans alone, concluded that without what seemed to him to be inexplicable German support the Hongkong Bank would have been unsuccessful, but failed to consider the question of Germany's ability to raise the funds required.[29] These views reflect the early spirit of competition in Peking which would later frustrate effective international cooperation in China on the eve of the Great War.

While the Germans in Peking questioned the new relationships with the Hongkong Bank on nationalistic grounds, Sir Robert Hart was concerned, as Rosebery and Rothschild had been concerned, with the Hongkong Bank's ability to manage a larger loan. The Bank was confident of its ability; in the end this confidence proved justified, but those responsible for the sound management of China's overseas borrowing were right to be sceptical. Hart's comments on the Bank, however, show that his concern was at least partly based on misinformation relative to banking practices; accordingly, he 'dithered'.

On the one hand Hart wished to deal with the Bank directly in order to avoid political interference; presumably for this reason he was critical of its agreement with the DAB although, in apparent contradiction, Hart too was convinced that, given the political situation in Peking, the Hongkong Bank did not have any chance alone. His main criticism of the Bank in the 1895/96 negotiations was its insistence on demanding what Hart considered 'high charges', including underwriting fees, which he thought a larger bank could dispense with. The Hongkong Bank was, in his view of the moment, 'provincial'. Hart was always in favour of 'simple' agreements, but then he found the Hongkong Bank's approach too simple, perhaps unprofessional, although Hart himself had no qualifications for making the judgement. At one point he appeared to favour a loan from the Bank of England through the Hongkong Bank, but this was turned down by the former, and it was in any case a proposal based on a misunderstanding.

In the end Hart returned to the Hongkong Bank, his preference for the Bank being based on his overriding consideration of China's interests which, in terms of the Imperial Maritime Customs, meant non-interference. For this second indemnity loan Hart would be the arbiter and the Hongkong Bank his choice.

The initial struggle for the second indemnity loan was in the hands of the German representatives, von Schenck, the German Minister, and Franz Urbig for the DAB, as the Chinese had as late as October 1895 expressly excluded a participation by and even more the leadership of the Hongkong Bank.[30] They even denied that Hart had been authorized to contact the Bank, restating their position in favour of the countries which had intervened on China's behalf.[31] In November the Hongkong Bank became suspicious, and Brüssel informed von Hansemann that von Schenck was negotiating a separate German loan.[32] However that may be, von Schenck introduced Hillier to the Tsungli Yamen as the joint-negotiator for the two groups on November 12. The Chinese had failed to divide the two banks; the Hongkong Bank was again in the competition.[33]

Meanwhile the Russians with French financial support were not only attempting to offer the necessary funds for a second loan at a rate which would undercut the Anglo-German offer, they were also, according to Hart, threatening to buy out the Hongkong Bank's 1895 loan, and thus would be in a position to commandeer the Customs. There were other offers, and the situation was complicated by such diverse matters as the French position in Madagascar, the extent of Russian development financing through the German markets, which placed a limit on their anti-German activities, and the state of the London capital market.

In November 1895, the Hongkong Bank and the DAB made a joint offer involving two series totalling £16 million. The interest rate was not to be more than 5%. The capital was repayable in 36 years, with a sinking fund of 1.04345% per annum. The Chinese were to agree not to take any further loans for six months, and the loan was to have a prior lien over all future loans secured on the revenues of the Maritime Customs. The price to the public was not to be less than 95, and the charges of 4% were to be paid by the Chinese.

The banks' commission was fixed at a flat $1\frac{1}{2}$%, and any savings in placing the loan on the market were to go to the Chinese; this would compare with the final terms of $98\frac{3}{4}$ to the public and 94 to the Chinese, see below.[34]

The Chinese then attempted to improve the Anglo-German terms – a three-point improvement as it turned out – while entertaining or encouraging other offers. That the Chinese were successful was due partly to an improvement in the capital markets and partly to the pressures placed on the Hongkong Bank by Hart and others to sacrifice the commission and modify the 4% charges.

On December 17, 1895, Hillier wrote to Cameron that he had met with the Tsungli Yamen on the 15th with the representatives of the German Group. The Chinese claimed that the conditions being offered were too harsh, which Hillier maintained was not the case, as they had been based on the current quotations of earlier Chinese loans on the markets and included compensation for the deterioration of the security. Hillier wrote that it had been a mistake to offer the Chinese their best terms right at the beginning, as 'a Chinaman cannot bear to clinch a bargain without having squeezed out some small concession'. Now he felt that the banks should try to rearrange the terms so as to make them look better and thereby save 'face' for the Chinese negotiators before the Emperor.[35]

Towards the end of December, the National Bank of China had been invited by Chinese officials to make an offer on the basis of 5% and 93 to the Chinese.[d] The National Bank would not have had the necessary access to the capital markets, but in any case the Hongkong Bank convinced them not to make the offer in exchange for a participation in the hoped-for Hongkong Bank loan.[36]

In January 1896 Hillier wired that there was now no real competition and the Chinese were only holding out hoping to get better terms or squeeze. He proposed offering a $\frac{1}{2}$ of 1% commission to the Tsungli Yamen as a way to end the delay. This would decrease the banks' commission to 1%, and Hillier saw no way of amending this as it was already too late to change the rates.[37]

This concession did not prove sufficient, however, and two days later Hillier proposed setting a one-week deadline within which the Chinese must agree or negotiations could only be reopened on different conditions. But this deadline too passed without any response, and now the banks had to decide whether or not to reopen negotiations on the same terms.

In February 1896, improved conditions on the European markets allowed the banks to offer considerably better terms.[38] Still the deadlock continued for

---

[d] The foreign-style, London-incorporated National Bank of China, established in 1891, was a private-sector bank originally promoted by Russell and Co.; it probably had a preponderance of Chinese shareholders (see Volume I, Chapter 12).

several weeks as it was not possible to decide on what terms to reopen negotiations. On February 17 the Chinese seemed willing to reopen on the same terms as before, but at the same time their Minister in Berlin had been looking for better terms in France, and Hillier and Urbig, the banks' negotiators in Peking, were becoming afraid of a possible French–American coalition.

On February 21, 1896, Hart suggested that all charges would have to be reduced by two-thirds and the issue price fixed at 98; he warned in a telegram: 'underwriting greed killing goose'.[39] His concern was partially due to apparently favourable French offers, which however did not state the charges.

Although the French were now negotiating seriously, their market could not easily absorb a second loan, and they were not willing to attempt it without another guarantee by some Power, presumably Russia. They also sought to bring about some reorganization of the Maritime Customs' control in their favour. The French even approached both the Hongkong Bank and the DAB to suggest dividing the loan three ways. Von Hansemann refused to consider sharing a Chinese loan with the French, and the two Groups suspected that Russia was behind the offer – Russian agents were again negotiating in Paris.[40] The Anglo-German Group had an advantage in that the German and English markets could handle the new loan without the French, but the French alone could not place a second loan.

The Chinese again asked the National Bank of China to make an offer. As of February 24 that bank considered the best terms possible in London were 5% and 95, while the Hongkong Bank and DAB were only willing to offer 5% and 91½. On March 3 the banks raised the commission to the Tsungli Yamen to 1%, cutting their own to ½ of 1%. On the 5th, the Russians agreed to support the French in a loan not to exceed 200 million francs, only half what the Anglo-German Group was offering. The Foreign Office and the German Foreign Ministry wrote strongly to Peking, warning the Chinese of French designs on the Imperial Maritime Customs, while Hart again urged the Anglo-German Group that their 'ridiculous' charges were making the loan impossible.

The German Legation in Peking reported on March 7 that the Tsungli Yamen, fearing French designs, had placed the loan negotiations in Hart's hands.[41] This they saw as a clear mandate to deal with the Hongkong Bank and its ally the DAB, and in fact the drama was over – Hart and Hillier had acted with competence and determination and the matter was actually closed on the day of the German despatch.

March 6 had been the crucial day.

Hart had returned to Peking aware of the French threat and the cause of the Anglo-German impasse; he had approached the Tsungli Yamen with a warning of French intentions and had been 'badly received', but the French Minister Gérard followed him and so angered the Chinese that they reconsidered Hart's warning.

That evening the responsible Chinese Ministers put the matter in Hart's hands.

Some time on the 6th Hart had reminded the German Minister that the Chinese were looking for the 'cheapest money' regardless of political conditions and repeated his fears that they would get this from the French now that the Russians had agreed to back them.[42] Von Schenck informed him that the banks would 'allow' a reduction of charges to 3% if essential.

With this new concession, Hart was ready.

As to our £16,000,000 Loan, it only came into my hands at eight o'clock on the evening of the 6th of March, and, as H'kong Bank and German Bank had withdrawn their offer (or themselves, which in the eyes of the Yamen came to the same thing) over a month before and the French Legation was manipulating the business to the exclusion of all others, *I was free to take it wherever I pleased.* I decided to give the refusal to the Anglo-German Syndicate and so offered it to Hillier and Schenck at 9 a.m. on the morning of the 7th, and they very speedily assented: and I had the preliminary understanding signed [by Hillier and Urbig] and in my pocket before tiffin time! All has gone well since and we'll sign the definitive contract tomorrow – a Chinese '*lucky*' day. Tell Cameron this and say Hillier has acted very smartly and courageously in the matter: the H'kong Bank would have lost the business had he not done so.[43]

Indeed Hillier had acted so courageously and the Chinese so persistently that the Hongkong Bank expected difficulty in placing the loan under the terms agreed. On March 14 an Imperial edict authorized the loan on the conditions in the preliminary agreement, on March 17 the syndicate in Europe agreed to the terms, and on the 23rd the definitive agreement was signed.

The conditions of the final agreement were no longer very attractive to the issuing banks, and indeed the loan could not be placed without the support of the Bank of England and the Prussian state bank, the Königliche Seehandlung. The latter gave its approval on the 14th, but the Bank of England was not willing to give its support without conditions. On the 21st the Tsungli Yamen, at the request of the Hongkong Bank, urged the British Government to press the Bank of England to support the issue as a political concession, and the Bank of England finally agreed to inscribe the bonds against ¼ of 1% charges on the condition that the issue price to the public did not exceed 98¾.

The terms

China, defeated and 'humiliated', had shown itself still the master. But there was a price. The loan was secured on the already encumbered Maritime Customs revenue, hence the additional condition:

The administration of the Imperial Maritime Customs of China shall continue
as at present constituted during the currency of this [36-year] loan.[e]

Chinese administration of the Imperial Maritime Customs had been
preserved but under the terms stated in a loan agreement receiving Imperial
sanction transmitted through the Tsungli Yamen, thus making it an international commitment. Non-interference in the Customs may be considered as
'interference' when it is incorporated in such a document. China could not be
pressured into permitting international control without violating a Treaty;
China was thus protected. On the other hand, as China was to discover in
1906, neither could China itself change the administration of the IMC
without violating the agreement it had signed (see Chapter 6).

For those who gave first priority to the territorial integrity of China and the
actual sovereignty of its Government, the Anglo-German loan was a signal
victory. And the phrase 'as at present constituted' would turn out, in the
context of current political realities, to be a very flexible concept indeed.

The Hongkong Bank too had paid a price.

It was now associated by agreement with a German bank representing a
national syndicate; it had recognized its inability to operate alone on behalf of
China in a politically competitive Europe; it had accepted the tutelage of the
Foreign Office. These lessons and associations would prove useful if the Bank
learned to manage them, but management is a relative concept, and, if the
Bank as merchant bank was no longer its own master, nor, for that matter, was
the Foreign Office. Yet the Hongkong Bank had this satisfaction: despite the
pressures to subordinate its operations to Rothschild's during the unsuccessful first indemnity loan negotiations, it had been able to free itself while
retaining good relations; it was still the recognized China bank in Britain.

The Chinese Imperial Government 5% Sterling Loan of 1896 for £16
million and dated April 1 was, in fact, the second indemnity loan; it provided
China with the funds required to meet payments until May 8, 1898. The
second indemnity payment was due on May 8, 1896, and totalled £8,225,245;
this plus the interest and payment for the expenses of Japanese occupying
troops at Weihaiwei accounted for a total of £8.5 million; the third indemnity
payment, due the following year, would on the same assumptions account for a
further £2.9 million.

The 1896 loan was issued in two series for £10 and £6 million respectively;
the annual interest of £800,000 and the yearly sinking fund of £166,952 were
to be paid to the Hongkong Bank and the DAB in monthly instalments of

[e] In the draft preliminary agreement this sentence was prefixed by the clause, 'The Imperial
Government of China hereby undertakes that . . .' This was deleted. The statement stands for
itself and is not made a political undertaking of the Imperial Government.[44]

sufficient Shanghai sycee to permit remittance to Europe of a sum equivalent to £80,579:6s:8d at a rate of exchange to be settled on the day the sum was due.

The question of the rate would prove a matter of serious contention later; at the time, this provision, while questioned, appeared routine – exchange banks were understood to handle their own exchange operations. 'Fixing' the rate is not to be considered an arbitrary decision of the Bank; there were objective reference points. The rate was quoted by the Bank to the Chinese; it could be discussed; it was not effective until accepted by the Chinese. Hart summarized the discussion thus:

Bank would like a fixed rate 0.025 below the rate of the day, but Yamen objects: I say 'The rate of the day must rule, hand Bank approximate amount in silver to turn into gold, and square up afterwards. Bank, as agent, will do its best for you!' And Yamen seems disposed to agree to this.[45]

But, given the terms of the agreement, it is fair to note that China's room for manoeuvre was limited.

The syndicate took the loan firm at 94, and thus the loan netted the Chinese Government £15,040,000, with charges and commission paid. The loan was issued at 98¾ and the first tranche of £10 million rose to a 2.5% premium being some 100% over-subscribed; the second tranche of £6 million, issued in September, was 50% under-subscribed due to the fear of dear money and political disturbances. Net profits to the Hongkong Bank after all charges but excluding underwriting commission on the loan were £130,415 (=0.87% of net) but were not fully appropriated to the Profit and Loss Account for 1896 (see Volume I, Chapter 13).

Bonuses were paid to those involved: Ewen Cameron as London Manager received £2,000, as did Hillier in Peking; Brüssel in Hamburg received £1,500 and there were lesser sums to G.E. Noble, John Walter, and G.H. Burnett, with gratuities being awarded by Cameron on the authority of the Board to the London and Hamburg staffs. The rationale of these grants is never stated; the smaller awards can be explained virtually in terms of overtime and/or more intensive work requirements. The larger sums, which for the time carried considerable purchasing power, may have represented a differential to cover the routine pay of a deposit bank manager and the fees expected by key partners in the leading City merchant banks. Certainly a request from Brüssel in Hamburg for a higher salary had been put off by the Board with a reminder that a loan-bonus would soon be paid.

A memoir of Hillier

The new agreement between the Hongkong Bank and the Deutsch-Asiatische Bank had won them the second indemnity loan; but the agreement was nevertheless the product of a necessity which neither bank fully accepted. The Hongkong Bank had been independent and wished to remain so; the Germans had placed themselves in a strong political position, and even though betrayed by their Russian and French partners did not enjoy taking second place to the British. Otto Franke felt that the British, Hillier, kept trying to push the Germans into a subordinate position; Urbig however claimed he was always able to recognize and counter these British tactics.

Two years later when Franz Urbig had returned to negotiate the Shanghai–Nanking Railway Loan with the Hongkong Bank, he had an interview with the great Viceroy Li Hung-chang and was reminded of these earlier events.

LI: Two years ago you closed a loan at 5% for 100 million taels. What kind of 'costs' did you have to sustain in Peking during the negotiations?
URBIG: That you'd have to ask Hillier of the Hongkong Bank as he kept the books in Peking that time.
LI: Hillier? But he's blind.
URBIG: That doesn't matter. Even a blind man can pay money.
LI: Do people in your country believe that someone who cannot see also has a dark soul?
URBIG: No. I know people who can see well, but still seem to have dark souls.[46]

Urbig then explains why he quoted this conversation:

When Li spoke of the soul of a blind man, I couldn't help thinking about how shortly before the 1896 Loan Agreement was signed, an almost blind man [Hillier] made the attempt – luckily it was discovered in time – to alter the wording of a paragraph which had been gone over in great detail to the advantage of his party's interests.[47]

The partial blindness (which grew worse with the years) came upon Hillier during the negotiations for the second indemnity loan. As his widow, Eleanor Hillier, told the story:

While studying carefully all the characters in the Chinese version of the Loan Agreement, he felt a great strain on his eyes and found that he had lost the sight of one eye. Directly the loan was floated he left for Shanghai . . . he was told by a specialist that he had glaucoma in the other eye.[48]

The consequences of this have already been related.

The third indemnity loan, 1898[49]

Between July 1896 and March 1898, when the third indemnity loan was signed with the Anglo-German Group, the price of silver had fallen 16% further eroding China's credit-worthiness and making more difficult negotiations which on the one hand would provide sufficient for a final indemnity payment and on the other would preserve China's administrative integrity. (See Volume I, Table 13.1.)

The intensity of the negotiations was a measure of their importance. The Japanese, who in the end took back a portion of the issue, needed the gold funds to complete their monetary reform without interruption to industrial development; the Chinese recognized that under the Treaty of Shimonoseki, if the final payment were made in 1898, previous interest payments would be counted as capital and other benefits would accrue; the Russians and the French saw the possibility of wringing further concessions; Germany, in the midst of involvement with Shantung, needed a political victory; while the British recognized the dangers to China and the importance to their own interests of the *status quo*.

As G.N. (later Marquess) Curzon, then Under-Secretary of State for Foreign Affairs, quite simply expressed the British position in Parliament, 'I accept the contention that this country enjoys a preponderant interest in China. That indeed is one of the commonplaces of modern politics and history, which it is needless to demonstrate or to endorse.'[50]

The obvious solution to meet China's needs and frustrate political pressures was for the Hongkong Bank to once more act as agent for the Imperial Government. The Bank was, however, still linked by the 1895 Agreement to the Deutsch-Asiatische Bank and had to offer its partner equal participation in any government loan. The eventual solution this time, given Germany's aggressive action in Shantung, was for the Hongkong Bank to conduct the negotiations and present the DAB with a *fait accompli*, thus achieving the primary goal – accomplishment of a non-political loan which met the financial requirements of the Chinese Government.

There were British political objectives. They would be expressed in the two declarations of February 1898 (see below), but these were in the end kept separate from the loan and the related Bank-conducted negotiations. The Hongkong Bank had for a time regained its independence.

The negotiations

The first step was indeed an approach to the Hongkong Bank by Viceroy Li Hung-chang in February 1897, apparently for the purpose of meeting all further indemnity payments when the May 1897 tranche became due. Li also approached the German consulate, thereby setting the new German Minister, Baron Edmund von Heyking, on an independent course claiming (i) that the agreement between the Hongkong Bank and the DAB was not binding on the Governments and (ii) that the Chinese had approached only the Germans.

Von Heyking had to be brought into line, principally by von Hansemann. The agreement was indeed between banks, but, since the DAB represented all German financial institutions interested in China, Germany would in the end have to turn to that bank for implementation of any arrangement, thus bringing it within the terms of the inter-bank agreement. On the second claim von Heyking was of course mistaken; the Chinese had as usual approached more than one potential lender. This left the Germans facing the fact that the British would be involved and that they would have the support of the Hongkong Bank 'whose capital strength and outstanding information service had a dominating position [in Peking]'.[51] The network founded by Addis and Hillier in the mid-1880s had obviously been expanded.

Sir Claude MacDonald, the British Minister, actually informed the Tsungli Yamen that the two Groups would now be negotiating together. On March 16 Li Hung-chang, attempting the now familiar divisive tactics, informed the Germans he was opposed to a Hongkong Bank participation in this loan and was later behind many of the wild counterschemes which were to obstruct the negotiations.

Li, in an effort to deal solely with the Germans, in fact provided a necessary breakthrough on the question of security; he offered the Germans the land tax as supplementary security, but as he had also made the same offer to the British Minister and also promised that the proceeds of the loan would be held in London until they were transferred to the Japanese (as a guarantee that they would not be used for any other purposes), he only succeeded in making the Hongkong Bank/DAB joint offer feasible.[52]

The British and German Groups had become involved in mutual discussions concerning (i) the lack of suitable Chinese security and (ii) the way in which additional revenue could be designated as security for the loan. The attraction of the Imperial Maritime Customs was the fact of its administration by foreigners in the Chinese service, consequently any such discussion would focus on discovering ways to bring further revenue administration under the IMC; but this in turn made the capture of the IMC an even more attractive prize to the Powers. Ewen Cameron recognized the problem, but he wrote to Brüssel for von Hansemann's information that he considered such questions outside the sphere of banks and that their resolution would in any case delay the conclusion of a loan which China urgently required.

The weakness, at the British end, of the Hongkong Bank–DAB agreement was now to be revealed. In Britain the Hongkong Bank stood alone; consequently it was possible for two rival groups to enter into competition: one, the Wilson Group, backed by Seligman Brothers, and the other, the Hooley–Jamieson Syndicate, which was interested in railway concessions; both sought the assignment of politically unacceptable revenues; both failed from lack of actual financial support. Viceroy Li Hung-chang was particularly involved with the latter, and when it failed he turned ineffectually to Jardine Matheson.

Hart, watching again from the sidelines and annoyed with certain unrelated activities of the Hongkong Bank, wisely chose not to intervene; he noted, however, that Li was reluctant to return to the Hongkong Bank – it had apparently become a matter of 'face'.

At the same time the Germans were confronted with competition and/or offers of participation by Russian, French, and Belgian interests. They remained in the end bound by the DAB's agreement with the Hongkong Bank, and the Russians approached China alone, making a favourable financial offer coupled with intolerable political conditions.

The Chinese Government eventually turned to Britain.

In December 1897 Cameron recognized the danger to British interests implied in the Russian offer and recommended a Bank of England loan through the Hongkong Bank with a British Government guarantee or statement of protection to bondholders. In the speech, partly quoted above, Lord Curzon explained, after the event:

> We were asked to make a loan. We did not in the first place offer to do it of our own accord. The initiative was taken not by us, but by the Chinese Government, but when the request came to the Government from China, the Government decided not merely that they were better qualified to lend the money than any others, but that in the interests of commercial expansion, which we have also had in view, and in the interest of sound finance, the assistance was what might very properly be given. The Government offered to give assistance of a loan of £16,000,000 [£12 million was in fact offered by MacDonald on January 8, 1898] in terms which, it cannot be denied, were of the most advantageous kind.[53]

But the conditions, reasonable enough in the context of British policy, aroused the immediate opposition of France (the provision of a railway from Burma to the Yangtze) and Russia (the insistence that Talienwan [Dalny or Dairen] be opened as a Treaty Port). The British Government also insisted on the control of the additional revenue from the customs, salt, and likin, the abolition of likin at the treaty ports, and the promise not to alienate territory in the Yangtze Valley to any foreign Power. Pritchard Morgan, a radical MP with China interests, later claimed credit for the underlying proposal – but without the controversial conditions.

Although agreement was reached between the Chinese and MacDonald on January 19, by the end of January 1898 the Chinese declared that they were under Russian political pressure and would no longer accept either the British or the Russian proposals.

The next delay was caused by a Chinese plan to raise the funds by a domestic loan. There was no possibility, however, that such a loan could produce the necessary funds, certainly not by the May deadline, nor could China expect to obtain a six-month extension as hoped from Japan; thus by February 21 the Chinese had turned again to the Hongkong Bank; Sir Robert Hart on behalf of the Imperial Chinese Government and E.G. Hillier for the Hongkong and Shanghai Banking Corporation signed a preliminary agree-

12 The negotiators.
E. Guy Hillier, Manager Peking (1891–1924); Sir Ewen Cameron, Senior
London Manager (1889–1905); A. M. Townsend, London Manager (1901–1911).

13 The negotiators.
Sir Charles Addis, 1913. London Manager (1905–1921);
Chairman, London Consultative Committee (1922–1933).

14 H. E. Li Hung-chang at T'ang-shan on the completion of the Tientsin,
T'ang-ku, and T'ang-shan Line (from *Railway Magazine*).

Rail-Way Station, Tientsin.(N.China) 　　　天津停車場

15 Tientsin station during the Boxer Troubles (from the collection of Jeffrey Richards).

16 Shanghai station and offices, the Shanghai–Nanking Railway (from *Railway Magazine*).

17 A £20 bond of the 1913 Chinese Government Reorganization Loan
for £25 million.

18 The Peking office, 1912, presumably at some time other than 10:47.
This was 'the Bank where the wild time grows'.

19 London office, 9 Gracechurch Street.

20 London office, interior.
Down the central corridor the senior managers, watched by ambitious 'juniors', strode, cigar in hand, after a full bankers' luncheon.

ment for what was to become the Chinese Imperial Government $4\frac{1}{2}$% Gold Loan of 1898 for £16 million.

Final stages and terms

On January 4, 1898, China assented to German demands for a 99-year lease on Kiaochow Bay (including Tsingtau) and special rights in Shantung. These concessions originated in the reaction to an anti-German incident in November 1897 and feelings in Peking precluded German participation in the final loan negotiations, the successful conclusion of which, even von Heyking had to admit, was due essentially to Hillier – Sir Claude MacDonald, for all the credit he was receiving, had no more to do with it 'than with the creation of the world'.[54] Indeed, Curzon's intervention in Parliament had made the Hong-kong Bank's commercial negotiations appear as mere political intrigue.[55] It would endanger the loan even after the final agreement was signed.[f]

As usual in such negotiations, the final stages were fast moving. On February 3 the Chinese formally broke off negotiations with Britain; the following day the British Premier and Foreign Secretary, Lord Salisbury, confirmed the situation in a cable to O'Conor, then British Minister in St Petersburg:

> The Chinese Government has been warned by Russia that their acceptance of a loan guaranteed by Great Britain will entail an interruption in the friendly relations existing between the two Empires. In consequence of the minatory attitude assumed by Russia, the Chinese have been obliged to come to a decision not to take a loan from either the Russian Government or that of Her Majesty, and the British Minister at Peking has been informed accordingly.[57]

The Chinese Government had not actually objected to the British conditions *per se* and subsequently agreed that the IMC would remain under the control of a British subject as long as British trade predominated. This was confirmed on February 10.[58] On the following day the Chinese confirmed British requirements relative to non-alienation of areas within the Yangtze Valley.[59]

MacDonald, regardless of his role in the actual loan, had cleared the path for any negotiations with the Hongkong Bank to proceed on entirely financial criteria, and shortly after promulgation of the declarations on the IMC and the Yangtze Valley, the Tsungli Yamen approached the Bank through Hart.

In the preliminary agreement signed with E.G. Hillier on February 19 and confirmed by the banks on February 25, China agreed to the assignment of Ts5 million of additional revenue as security, but, presumably as a conse-

---

[f] Sir Michael Hicks-Beach, Chancellor of the Exchequer, was opposed to the loan and consequently to Ewen Cameron's requests for British Government intervention. 'I think it time that communications from Mr Cameron should be discouraged. . . . Cannot you stop this man [knighted in 1900] from pestering us with his proposals?' he wrote the Premier, Lord Salisbury. For these objections he had little if any sustained support in the cabinet.[56]

quence of the declaration of intent regarding the future of the IMC, the loan agreement did not question China's right to retain control of the IMC; the agreement required only that the task of administering the sources of the additional Ts5 million security be assigned to that department. Thus, as far as the Hongkong Bank was concerned, the revenue question was merely one related to the need for security to successfully float a public loan under difficult circumstances; the political questions had been resolved. This was vitally important to a beleaguered China and alone justified the commercial terms on which such a loan had to be undertaken.

Hart himself hoped that the security arrangements, which included IMC control of likin and other internal taxes, would provide an opportunity for reform of the system but noted that the Tsungli Yamen's undertaking, 'contrary to the advice of all financial officials', was based on their assessment of Hart as a person. Hart therefore remained in Peking – 'I am ashamed to run off when they are in such difficulties.'[60] In fact Hart had to approach the matter carefully and it was some years before the IMC exercised real control over the new funds.

Given the state of the capital markets, concern with the political situation, and fears for the future of silver and China's capacity to repay, the terms of the loan were not surprisingly unfavourable – $4\frac{1}{2}$% at 83, to be issued to the public at 90, and to run for 45 years, until 1943.

But there were still to be anxious moments.

The preliminary agreement had been signed with the Hongkong Bank only; however under the 1895 Agreement the Hongkong Bank had now to offer a 50% share to the Germans. Von Heyking formed the impression that the British were anxious for German participation and urged that conditions be set, the renunciation, for example, of British claims to equal treatment in Shantung. But when Brüssel wrote to von Hansemann on February 21, he made it clear that the Germans had until noon the next day to signify their willingness to participate; the terms were not to be modified and no political conditions were to be introduced. Hart's London Office Manager Campbell cabled Peking, 'Germans take half share. They had to take or leave it, and jumped at it. Important prepare final agreement forthwith as delay may be dangerous.'[61]

The French Government then called a meeting of the major French credit institutions and suggested that they demand an equal share in all aspects of the new loan, including the right to co-sign. All of them, except the Crédit Lyonnais, agreed to the proposal, which was to be forwarded by the Comptoir National d'Escompte.[62] The French threatened to take Hainan Island as a reprisal. In any case when news of this intervention was forwarded to Berlin, it served to confirm the need for haste.

The loan was in fact signed on March 1, 1898, by the Hongkong Bank and the Deutsch-Asiatische Bank in Peking.

The prospectus became a matter of dispute, the German Government insisting on the insertion of a clause stating that on payment of the indemnity made possible by the loan, Japan would evacuate Weihaiwei. Cameron informed the Japanese Legation in London (see below) that he had objected to the DAB on the grounds that this would appear to make the banks responsible for an action of the Japanese Government. The Hongkong Bank was again insisting on standing clear of political action. This was a commercial loan, and the Germans eventually agreed to submit the prospectus as it stood for approval by the Hamburg Börse.

The next problem was the response of the investing public.

The negotiators' awareness of this problem is reflected in the definitive agreement by, *inter alia*, (i) the provision that China shall contract no further loan for a period of twelve months (except through the contracting banks), (ii) the reinsertion of the clause, deliberately omitted (see above) in the 1896 indemnity loan, 'The Chinese Imperial Government undertake that . . .' in connection with the essential provision 'the Chinese Imperial Maritime Customs service shall remain as at present constituted during the currency of the loan' – and China waived the right to early redemption or conversion – and (iii) the designation of the required use of the funds borrowed, the payment, that is, of the balance of the indemnity due the Japanese Imperial Government.

Confidence, however, was shaken at a crucial moment by a 'financial panic' in London caused, according to E.G. Hillier (March 9, 1898), by an exaggerated report published in *The Times* and written by their Peking correspondent G.E. Morrison about the form in which Russian demands on China had been expressed.[63] Equally unfortunate were Curzon's comments on the Anglo-German loan, referred to above, which reintroduced the nationalistic factor in an operation requiring an international acceptance.

The subscription list was opened on March 22 and closed the following day, but only £1,460,000 of the £8 million British tranche was actually subscribed; the German tranche fared better.

The *Statist* commented that 'the confidence in the Hongkong and Shanghai Bank shown by the underwriters is a great compliment to that Bank and proves that it has a very powerful following in the City', but in the end the underwriters had to take up 75% of the London issue and the price fell from 90 to 88 immediately.[64] Hart had urged the Bank, once it had agreed on a contract price of 83, to issue below 90, in the expectation of receiving further commissions from the Chinese Government; his arguments assumed however that the Bank 'made' 7% on the transaction – he made no allowance for expenses.[65] For sounder reasons a lower issue price might have been wise, but the effect of Morrison's cable to *The Times* could not have been foreseen.

As agreed, £12 million of the £13.28 million net proceeds became available in London on May 6, sufficient after transfer to the Chinese Minister in London to permit him to make the indemnity payment of £11,008,857:16s:9d (plus £1 million for the additional Weihaiwei expenses) due on May 8 – the cheque for this amount drawn by the Hongkong Bank on the Bank of England was reputedly, up to that date, the largest ever written.[66]

At the end of the half year the Hongkong Bank itself was holding £25,000 of the loan at the depreciated price of 88½ – and holdings of the 7% Silver Loan of 1894, the 6% Gold Loan of 1895, and the 5% Sterling Loan of 1896 had similarly depreciated. An exact calculation of 'profit', which the Board of Directors recorded as £220,971 net (=1.4% of nominal), is therefore subject to definitional problems. Nevertheless, the Board of Directors again awarded gratuities to Cameron £3,000, Hillier £2,500, Brüssel £1,500, and £1,000 to A.M. Bruce, who had taken charge in Peking during Hillier's absence and remained as No. 2 – as well as the usual minor gratuities.

The Hongkong Bank had put up a bold front, but the fact is Cameron was aware of the difficulties of placement. Therefore from early February he was in communication with Takaaki Kato, then Japanese Minister in London (and later Prime Minister), in an effort to obtain a Japanese commitment to purchase (virtually 'underwrite') up to £4 million of the loan at 2% under issue price, which was equivalent to the commission for the actual underwriters, should the public fail to subscribe to the entire issue.[67]

At the outset these communications were kept secret both from the DAB and from the Chinese; the loan was, as noted above, still in danger.

When German participation was endangered by the attempt to include the Weihaiwei evacuation clause, the Japanese agreed to purchase bonds up to a nominal value of £6 million. The Hongkong Bank, despite its public assurances that it could float the entire £16 million, had become both realistic and concerned. However, the DAB and the Börse accepted the prospectus, and the Japanese eventually asked to take a minimum of £2 million even before the results of the public subscription were made known; the Hongkong Bank agreed to a pre-allocation allotment of bonds with a nominal value of £500,000. Finally on March 25 Cameron informed the Japanese Legation that under the terms of their agreement and following the public subscription he had decided to allot £2 million at a cost of £1,760,000 to the Japanese Government, which the latter accepted as inclusive of the £500,000 previously allotted.

The Japanese evacuated Weihaiwei, but on March 6 Britain took over the port for as long 'as Port Arthur remains in the occupation of Russia'. Russia leased the Liaotung Peninsula for 25 years on March 27, and the French leased Kwangchowan in April. In June the British also extended the area of the Colony of Hong Kong by a 99-year lease on a section of the mainland and neighbouring islands to be known as the 'New Territories'.

Meanwhile efforts were continuing to develop China's railways, although the first step, the gaining of concessions, seemed likely to divide the Empire into spheres of influence despite China's successful efforts to minimize encroachment on her sovereignty in the process of negotiations for the three indemnity loans.

To these efforts of the Chinese Government the Hongkong Bank had contributed.

The Bank was not dependent on any concession-seeking, home-based syndicate; although these loan operations had been based on London, Cameron best of all knew the Bank's strength lay in its Eastern constituency and that its influence, dependent always on the goodwill of China, was primarily in its commercial position as an exchange and merchant bank.

The Hongkong Bank's proper motivation was the interests of its proprietors broadly defined; this included development of trade and the modernization of China, but the Bank attempted to prevent its pursuit of these ends reaching the arena of international politics. In the second and third indemnity loans the Bank had been largely successful. The political objectives urged by senior officers of the Bank, by these bankers as British subjects, on behalf of a British banking institution had, to the extent they were adopted by the British Government, been negotiated through British diplomatic channels in the normal course of international relations; the issue of the indemnity loans by the Hongkong Bank had been undertaken as separate commercial operations.

The net proceeds of the three indemnity loans to Japan was something over £43 million.[68] From this China suffered, and the consequent financial and political weakness did nothing to further the hopes for modernization; her credit-worthiness was shaken and, except for the brief 100 days of reform (June 11–September 21, 1898), the question of political change was once again in abeyance. The Powers forced China to the edge of desperation; the events of the next two years would push her over – into the Boxer Uprising.

THE FIRST RAILWAY CONCESSIONS AND LOANS

THE FRAMEWORK

The time for railways had come. In 1894 there had been only 312 kms of railway in China, by 1903 when post-Boxer construction began total kilometres were some 4,330. On the eve of the Great War China had 9,680 kms of railways.[69]

In the years 1895–1898 no less than twenty concessions covering 10,000 kilometres were granted by a defeated China. After years of promises, of false expectations, the Chinese had apparently been forced to yield.

Twenty years later less than half these lines had been built.[70]

There were many reasons why this should be so. The years immediately following China's 1895 defeat confirmed previous Chinese conservative opinion that railways could not be separated from foreign interference and even domination. Among the first major railway concessions were those to Russia in the Northeast, to France in Yunnan, and to Germany in Shantung – all involved loss of political rights and threatened the integrity of China. This provoked Chinese reaction against both railways and foreigners. These developments served as a warning to foreigners of the questionable durability of the privileges they had won from China. In consequence there developed a greater foreign willingness to accept a sphere of interest system which was not wholly exclusive, one perhaps compatible with an 'open door' policy. To achieve a less exclusive and more flexible 'spheres' policy, the Powers had to negotiate endlessly not only with the Chinese but also among themselves, establishing a series of agreements which not only covered the development of each railway but also considered the allocation of each section of the line, each appointment to the administration, each placement of contracts.

In time these early arrangements fell into place and matters were sufficiently ordered to permit the formation of long-term syndicates; by 1909 the first of a series of syndicates under the auspices of the China Consortium was being negotiated; China faced a consortium of Powers, each represented by a 'Group' having some degree of Government support. As this confrontation was unacceptable to China, the China Consortium, which in one form or another survived until its formal disbandment in 1946, was, after 1914, either attacked, circumvented, or ignored – and yet a case can be made in its defence.

All this took time. The negotiations for the Shanghai–Nanking line, running through prosperous territory and potentially profitable, had begun at least by 1894, a preliminary financial agreement was signed in 1898, the final agreement in 1903, but the railway was not actually in operation until 1908 and a final loan to recover expenses for land purchase not negotiated until 1913. The Boxer Uprising and the subsequent concern with yet another indemnity delayed progress. When a final railway agreement was reached, capital markets might not be receptive, political conditions both in China and among the Powers might have changed, and renegotiation become necessary. The key trunk line from Peking to Canton was not completed until the 1930s, the missing link of the Shanghai–Hangchow–Ningpo Railway was not constructed until 1937 – only to be destroyed weeks later in the face of a Japanese military advance. Other lines, including those for which concessions were granted in the years 1897–1899, were never built until after the 1949 revolution.

There are several approaches to a history of railway finance, even when the focus, as in this history, is on the contribution of a single foreign bank, the Hongkong and Shanghai Banking Corporation. Considering the matter chronologically, the years from 1895 to the Boxer Uprising of 1900 were the years of the major concessions, during which rights were granted to the Powers, or directly to syndicates accepted by the Powers, for the total construction and management of a railway, the 'concessioned lines', and for other related economic or even political rights.

As the granting of the concessions was not necessarily the end of the matter and as specific agreements had to be made within the context of the concession, a second period is introduced. The immediate post-Boxer years to say 1908 (see Chapter 6) defined a period of rationalization. Certain concessions were implemented, others were rearranged, some construction was undertaken.

The third period (see Chapter 7) overlapped with the second, say from 1905 to 1911 and was marked by increasing nationalism which impacted on the railways in two ways: first, the Chinese pressed for purely financial loans, that is, for funds to construct railways themselves; and, second, they sought funds to recover rights signed away in earlier concessions.

From 1914 to 1928 limited new mileage was constructed, but major foreign financing was not available and lines previously profitable were run down during the Warlord period. During the Nanking Decade, that is, to the Japanese Incident of 1937, defaulted or non-performing loans were renegotiated, new construction planned and new funds raised. The Pacific War saw a further deterioration in the railways, and from 1945 to 1949 most discussion focused on debt collection rather than reconstruction.

This outline suggests a more thematic approach to the consideration of Chinese railway finance prior to 1914. The actual construction of railways by foreign contracts required the alliance of financial institutions with construction companies and the acknowledgement of such a syndicate by their own Government, the latter being urged either to assign a concession already won or to seek a concession from the Chinese Government, thus providing the political cover. This approach is evident in the history of the Hongkong Bank, which in 1898 was one of the two promoters of the British and Chinese Corporation (B&CC).

The need for Government support encouraged the syndicates to come to terms with competitors, and the Hongkong Bank reached accommodation with the Pekin Syndicate and the Yangtze Valley Company by the formation of the Chinese Central Railways Company (CCR) in 1903/04. The failure of any Power to achieve the total concession system which the Government or private sector considered suitable led to international competition and then, as Chinese resistance mounted, to a framework of international cooperation within which reallocation of rights could be made prior to confrontation with the Chinese. The Hongkong Bank found it necessary (i) to adjust its agreement with the DAB in 1898 and 1905, (ii) to agree to French and Belgian participation in the CCR in 1905, (iii) to encourage and then lead a consortium of national 'Groups' (from 1909), and (iv) to broaden the basis of its own financial support in Britain by opening the British Group, hitherto consisting of the Hongkong Bank alone, to other interested banks (1912, see Chapter 9).

These developments had to take account, however, of yet another theme – control of loan disbursements and control of the railway itself. The earlier loans, for example the £3.25 million 1904 loan for the construction of the Shanghai–Nanking Railway, were made under the terms of a concession for complete construction and management, and the public were asked to subscribe to the loan on this understanding – they would also be entitled to profit sharing. This system had been the rationale behind such combinations as the British and Chinese Corporation, in which the financial agent, the Hongkong Bank, associated with the merchant agent, Jardine, Matheson and Co. The 1904 Shanghai–Nanking Railway Loan was in fact contracted by the B&CC, who were trustees for the bondholders and responsible to them for the satisfactory performance of the tasks listed in the prospectus. The role of British enterprise, the degree of foreign control in the project would affect the terms on which the loan could be issued to the public.

Reacting to Chinese pressure operating on the delicate international agreements which were designed to prevent the success of just such Chinese pressure, the various syndicates modified their terms of control and the role, if any were permitted, of the contracting company. This is a theme particularly clearly developed in the initial competition for the Hukuang Railways Loan (signed in 1911), during which the Chinese were successful in inducing competitive syndicates to withdraw offers based on the stricter control terms found in the agreement for the Canton–Kowloon Railway (1907) in favour of the less severe terms of the Tientsin–Pukow Railway Agreement (1908). At the same time the Chinese sought and obtained a purely financial loan to recover concession rights in the Luhan Railway from Peking to Hankow (1908, see Chapter 7). In this way such combinations as the B&CC lost some of their relevance, and control issues became less important to lenders than the basic question of sovereign risk.

In the period from the Nationalist Revolution of 1911 to the Great War, the focus, given the state of Chinese national and provincial finances, was of necessity on administrative loans. At the same time nationalistic pressures in Europe became more intense, and the system of international cooperation among the Powers, by then seeming secure in the highly developed framework designed in large measure by Sir Charles Addis as the London Manager of the Hongkong Bank, was in fact threatened with collapse. China seemed ready once again for intensive railway development and a new period of competition was beginning with construction advances made for purely Chinese railway construction against public loans as yet unissued.

These themes do not apply however to concessions which came within exclusive spheres – the Russians and the Japanese in Manchuria, the French to a lesser extent in Yunnan. Their history is separate, although the Hongkong Bank, for historical reasons, was permitted to retain its financial role (1899) in the Tientsin–Mukden line, despite its extension north of the Great Wall.

For the present chapter the discussion is confined to the period of the initial concessions, the founding of the B&CC, and the first public railway loan. The loan, which was concluded in 1899, was the climax of a series of financial operations in which the Bank had been involved since the very first years of the Chinese Imperial Railways; these preceded both the granting of concessions and the formal, joint operations typified by the B&CC, both of which can be dated in 1898. The three topics are considered separately, but it is important to remember that they overlap.

The British and Chinese Corporation[g]

The founding and initial subscribers

The British and Chinese Corporation was incorporated in London on May 24, 1898, with a capital of £250,000 in 2,500 shares of £100 (of which £5 was paid up) for the purpose of carrying out public works and undertakings and acquiring rights in China and for the financing thereof.[h] To achieve these ends Article 3 required the company to enter into agreements with both Jardine, Matheson and Co. and the Hongkong and Shanghai Banking Corporation, who were to act jointly as the B&CC's managing agents in China and who were each entitled to nominate one member of the Board of Directors. The provisions of Article 3 were approved by subscribers.

[g] In 1979 the Hongkong Bank confirmed its holding of 61% of the voting equity of the British and Chinese Corporation, Ltd. The company was listed in testimony before a sub-committee of the U.S. House of Representatives as 'dormant'; it became a private company in 1982.[71]

[h] Further capital was paid up in 1902 and 1904; in 1907 the £100 shares were split 10:1 and the consequent £10 shares were £5 paid up.

The Hongkong Bank was designated bankers to the B&CC. The first Board consisted of William Keswick as chairman, Ewen Cameron for the Hongkong Bank, Sir Auckland Colvin, and Charles Colin Macrae.[72]

The only early reference to the Corporation in the minutes of the Bank's Board of Directors is in connection with the signing of the preliminary agreement for the Shanghai–Nanking line, when on May 21 the Board were informed that the Bank with Jardine Matheson had acted for a powerful London syndicate. The Hongkong Bank's own investment in the B&CC was in the form of 190 shares held in the joint names of Ewen Cameron and E.F. Duncanson, the latter a member of the Bank's London Committee. Similarly Jardine interests can be detected in the 190 shares in the name of William Keswick.

The timing of the B&CC's incorporation suggests that it was formed in connection with the concessions (see below) being obtained for British interests by the British Minister, Sir Claude MacDonald, from the Chinese. The lone position of the Hongkong Bank compared to the more comprehensive representation around the DAB (the KfAG) and the Banque de l'Indo-Chine, prompted the Bank to seek a broader base of support while keeping control of the financial aspects expected from exploitation of the new China concessions. This is confirmed by Cameron, who wrote to the Foreign Office in April 1898 that he foresaw the formation of a 'strong representative and influential syndicate' for the purposes subsequently outlined in the B&CC prospectus.

Cameron and Keswick were apparently successful. The B&CC was formed with a wide range of shareholder support. The two promoting companies together held 380 shares representing only 15% of the subscribed capital; the rest was subscribed for by friends of the promoting companies, individual capitalists, and major investment interests.

In the first category were officers and retired staff of the Bank, men like Julius Brüssel, J.P. Wade Gard'ner, Thomas Jackson, John Walter, Ewen Cameron (in his personal capacity), and David McLean; among the Bank's friends were the founder, Sir Thomas Sutherland, a London Committee member, E.F. Duncanson, and former directors of the Bank – Adolf von André and F.D. Sassoon. Even if it were fair to assume that these shares would be voted to support the Bank – and in the case of Sassoon and possibly others, this was by no means certain – and if the further assumption were made that Jardine's friends held a similar stake in the B&CC, still by the most generous of definitions the two promoting companies could count on only 30% of the votes.

So prominent were the B&CC's agents and bankers in the China field that the very presence of other interests has been ignored in the literature. This omission has led to the belief that the Hongkong Bank and Jardine's comprised the B&CC and were somehow selected by the British Government as the latter's instrument in the execution of China policy. These are not valid comments on the early purpose of the B&CC and the role it was intended to play on its foundation in 1898.

Lord Rothschild, for example, subscribed to 100 shares. He was also a shareholder in the several Yangtze Valley companies (see below) and in the Pekin Syndicate; he at least quite obviously did not expect the B&CC to be the Government's sole chosen instrument, but rather to be one of several key syndicates developed for the purposes of British investment in China. Other financial interests were represented by the initial shareholdings (in parenthesis) of Baring Bros (100), Ernest Cassel (50), Henry Gibbs (50), E.A. Hambro (100), Henry Oppenheim (30), Louis Samuel Montagu (50), Pauling and Co. (30), Sir Marcus Samuel (10), and Edward Elias Sassoon (50). There were in total some 94 shareholders and those in the categories listed would seem to account for approximately one-half of the shares, the others being even further distributed in small holdings.

Nor did these representatives of financial interests abandon the corporation. On the contrary, the list expanded: Baron Émile Erlanger became a shareholder in 1899; by 1905 the list would include Calouste S. Goulbenkian and even the great Chinese railway official Sheng Hsuan-huai (100) himself – listed under his literary name, Tzu-yi. By 1909 T.H. Whitehead of the Chartered Bank and Carl Meyer, joined later by Émile Francqui (formerly Belgian Consul in Hankow, then with the Banque d'Outremer), the Banque d'Outremer in its own name, and the Clydesdale Bank, were among the several new subscribers; the Goulbenkian interest had increased significantly. The Jardine and Hongkong Bank percentage, narrowly defined to include only shares owned in the names of the senior partners of the former and the joint London Managers of the latter, remained unchanged.

The first subscribers, it might be argued, may have been brought in to cover the otherwise unacceptable decision of the Government to grant exclusive patronage to Jardine's and the Bank, but this is improbable. First, neither Rothschild nor the other financial leaders who subscribed were likely either to agree to an action so contrary to their interests or to be duped into subscription; second, several subscribers were known to be genuinely interested in China investment, especially Pauling and Co., a company which would be much frustrated over the next fifteen years in its efforts to secure China contracts and would be involved in efforts to develop opposition syndicates; third, the Government was not granting exclusive patronage – it also recognized the legitimate interests of the Pekin Syndicate and the Yangtze Valley companies; and fourth, new subscribers representing new financial interests with a China orientation are found on the lists at least through the early 1920s.

The Government in 1898 may well have hoped for a single representative of British capital, especially if there were competition for the same concession; this is evidenced by the encouragement given to the cooperation which led in 1903 to the formation of the Chinese Central Railways. It was in anticipation of this cooperation that the chairman of the Pekin Syndicate, Carl Meyer, who had long been closely connected with N.M. Rothschild and Sons and had been secretary to Lord Rothschild himself, became a member of the Hongkong Bank's London Committee in 1899.

The B&CC and the Hongkong Bank

The Memorandum of Association was signed in May 1898 and the B&CC was registered on May 24. The Memorandum contained a sub-clause [3(r)] stating that one of the purposes of the corporation was to enter into the two agreements mentioned in the Articles of Association. This referred to management agreements with Jardine, Matheson and Co. and with the Hongkong and Shanghai Banking Corporation – they would be the B&CC's joint managing agents in China; Matheson and Co. would provide for the secretary's office in London.

The agreement with the Hongkong Bank was dated June 30, 1898, and called for the Bank (i) to act as managers in China in conjunction with Jardine, Matheson and Co., and (ii) 'to be the Bankers of the Company and all public issues of capital and securities made by the Company . . . shall be issued by and through the Bank unless the Bank shall otherwise agree in writing'. (par. 2) The agreement would be effective for twenty years, the company to pay a mutually agreed remuneration and also commission on any public issue; the usual banking charges (except in relation to public issues) would be paid.

During the period of the agreement the Bank was entitled to nominate a director of the B&CC, who would not then be subject to rotation. Ewen Cameron was the first such director; he was succeeded by Charles Addis in 1905. Addis continued as the Bank's nominee until 1933 when he was replaced by O.J. Barnes, the London Manager; Addis was then elected in his own right, resigning from the Board only in 1944.

The agreement was renewed in revised form and remained effective until the Hongkong Bank acquired a majority of the shares in the virtually dormant company in the 1950s.

The B&CC and the 1898 concessions

The initial performance of the B&CC was highly encouraging; this would lead to later problems when early expectations were not satisfactorily fulfilled.

The B&CC did not begin its China negotiations *de novo* in 1898. The B&CC must be placed in historical context: (i) it was the institutionalized successor to the informal arrangements made in Shanghai in the 1880s between Ewen Cameron and J.J. Keswick of Jardine's (see Volume I, Chapter 14), and, as the British rough counterpart to the KfAG, (ii) it was the beneficiary of negotiations carried out by the Hongkong Bank in cooperation with the DAB under the auspices of the 1895 Agreement. When, therefore, the British Legation in Peking obtained assurances from the Chinese Government that British interests would be preferred on specified projects, these were projects already under negotiation with China by the Bank and/or Jardine's. The relationship was formalized and strengthened by the formation of the B&CC, and the Government recognized the corporation's existing interests.

At the corporation's annual meeting in November 1899, a report was presented noting (i) the issue of the Northern Railway Loan for £2.3 million and the option on the Nanpiao Coalfield concession granted by the Northern Railway Administration, (ii) that surveys had been made on the route of the Shanghai–Soochow–Nanking Railway, (iii) a preliminary contract had been obtained and a survey completed of the Canton–Kowloon Railway, (iv) a new line under contract from Pukow to Sinyang, a cross-country connection of some 480 kms, (v) the Hankow–Canton Railway – an agreement with the American China Development Company (ACDC) to 'offer each to the other opportunities of participating in business', and (vi) the signing of a preliminary agreement in May 1899 covering the financing and construction of the Tientsin–Pukow Railway (or, as it was then known, Tientsin–Chinkiang) and signed jointly by (a) the DAB and (b) the Hongkong Bank and Jardine Matheson as joint agents for the British and Chinese Corporation, the two Groups being then referred to as the 'syndicate'.

The agreement with the American China Development Company, formalized in February 1899, was, however, denounced in 1901 by the ACDC when that company came under control of Belgian interests, that is, of the Compagnie Internationale d'Orient; the B&CC assumed that the change of national direction had not affected the validity of the concession and decided against invoking Foreign Office intervention.[73] The Hukuang Railways Loan of 1911 covered only the border south to the Kwangtung Provincial line.

Despite these last modifications, the B&CC had not exaggerated its prospects, although the time span was certainly greater than either the directors or, probably, the shareholders anticipated. The £2.3 million loan was issued in 1899, a loan for the Shanghai–Nanking Railway in 1904 and 1907, for the Canton–Kowloon Railway in 1907, for the Tientsin–Pukow Railway in 1908/09, and for the Pukow–Sinyang line an advance was made in 1913 against a preliminary agreement.

Although the B&CC would be criticized for its apparent unwillingness to move quickly in the post-Boxer period, in 1900 the corporation negotiated the purchase of the 'Gwendoline (Unsan) Gold Mine' concession in Korea and on this basis the following year, in association with one of the two vendors, Eastern Pioneer Company, established the British and Korean Corporation, Limited (B&KC), with a capital of £390,000 divided into 280,000 ordinary and 110,000 preferred shares of £1 each, fully paid up by mid-1903. The other vendor, Gwendoline and William Pritchard Morgan, was paid 10,000 shares. The B&CC's investment totalled £25,000 in preferred shares and the corporation was accordingly entitled to nominate four of the eight directors; the Yangtze Valley Corporation held 10,000 shares. Neither Cameron nor his successor, Charles Addis, were directly involved, but the B&CC's Keswick was Chairman. The B&KC went into receivership in 1907 and was wound up in 1914.[74]

Despite this eventual misadventure, the Hongkong Bank may be excused for supposing that it had been the partner in laying a sound foundation for British long-term development finance not only in China but also in Korea.

The B&CC, its support, and its critics

The developments, reported by the B&CC's chairman in 1899 and which will be considered in their appropriate chronological sequence, were inherited from the efforts of the Bank and Jardine's; these two corporations provided the investment opportunities, the British Government obtained the necessary political agreement from the Chinese, and the shareholders provided the capital to permit the B&CC to function. The funds for developing the approved projects would be obtained from public bond issues managed by the Hongkong Bank and, it was assumed, the DAB. The B&CC's income would arise, therefore, from the interest differentials in funds obtained from the Bank and advanced to China, from commissions as detailed in the agreements with China within the terms of the concession, and on income from corporation investments. Shareholders would benefit from dividends, from anticipated capital gains, but also from their own participation in the placing and underwriting of the bond issues of the B&CC and/or from contracts awarded for construction financed through the corporation.

The role of the major financial subscribers relative to the public issue of railway and other concessional bonds was vital to the success of the B&CC, but the initiatives which led to the issue would be associated with the corporation's agents in China, the Bank and Jardine's, hence the assumption in the popular press that the two China companies *were* the B&CC. Similarly, the overwhelming presence of the Bank and Jardine's in China made it likely, but by no means inevitable, that it was their preliminary negotiations which led to the British concession or that, alternatively, they were the only syndicate both qualified and prepared to take up the concession; therefore the assignment of that concession to the B&CC was neither an arbitrary act of Government nor part of a discretionary policy for which the B&CC had been arbitrarily selected as the instrument.

The opposition to the B&CC in Britain became vocal over the years and was based on a complex of factors at different levels. First, there was the straightforward opposition of competing British syndicates; second, the political objection that the corporation was not exploiting its concessions with sufficient despatch; third, there was the objection of 'monopoly'.

The first two objections are self-explanatory and will be examined on a case-by-case basis as the story develops. The third requires definition.

China was not a major destination of British overseas investment flows; given the initial support for the B&CC and the Government's encouragement for a single British syndicate active in international competition, the predominance of the B&CC was not in itself the target; the criticism was directed at the position of the B&CC's agents in China, the Hongkong Bank and Jardine, Matheson and Co.

The Bank in the B&CC was criticized first on the same grounds as was the Bank as the sole member of the British Group in the China Consortium – it was the sole bank of issue. Second, with the growing impact of China's Rights Recovery Movement, some saw the Bank faced with a conflict of interest. As long as the Bank could issue a loan it would receive a commission; there was therefore reason for it to abandon the B&CC whose interests it was pledged by the agreement cited above to promote and further.

Jardine's was criticized for contracting for supplies through companies for which it was agent or in ways which seemed more related to the company's other interests than to those of the B&CC. These objections were made by those who felt aggrieved or, in the case of the Bank, by those who had other and political factors in mind. Pauling and Co. would, for example, be particularly critical and would encourage rival syndicates. In 1908/09 the role of the B&CC and in particular its relations with the Bank were brought to a point of crisis by J.O.P. Bland, China representative for both the B&CC and the Chinese Central Railways, in the context of the loan negotiations for the Luhan line redemption and the Hukuang Railways.

The B&CC was also criticized in China as being expensive, but negotiations usually reduced the charges and the Chinese were, in any case, attempting to bypass such syndicates as the B&CC, consistent with the principles of Rights Recovery. This too will be considered as the policy evolves, especially from 1905.

Undisputed is the fact that the role of the Hongkong Bank in the British and Chinese Corporation would be of great significance in its history in the period to 1914. The role of the B&CC during the revival of railway interest in the mid-1930s is a subject for Volume III, and the decline of the company's fortunes thereafter, including the Bank's buy-out of ordinary shareholders, is a subject for Volume IV. The B&CC would remain a problem of the Bank to the present time.

Two rival syndicates

This section is limited to a brief account of the origins of the Pekin Syndicate and the Yangtze Valley Company, both of which later became associated with the B&CC through the Chinese Central Railways. Other syndicates are referred to in the account of various negotiations.

The Pekin Syndicate was intended as an Anglo-Italian venture; it was in fact promoted in 1897 and the main Shansi and Honan mining and railway concessions obtained in 1898 by Angelo Luzzatti, an engineer and nephew of the highly respected Treasury minister, Luigi Luzzatti. From the first, however, financial support came from British capital with South African connections and with interlocking interests in the Yangtze Valley Company. There were George Cawston, a founder of the British South Africa Company, Edmund Davis with Belgian and African connections, and, the syndicate's chairman, Carl Meyer, who provided a direct link to Rothschild's – he had formerly been secretary to Lord Rothschild. Meyer also had South African interests as chairman of the London committee of De Beers Consolidated Mining Corporation and associate of Cecil Rhodes; he was a director of the National Bank of Egypt and of several mining companies with interests in Burma and Siam. The Syndicate obtained its China expertise from George Jamieson, formerly commercial officer in the Shanghai Consulate-General; also involved were James G.H. Glass (engineer) and Robert Miller (Indian interests).

During the crucial 1898 negotiations Luzzatti, the Pekin Syndicate's agent-general, received reluctant support in Peking from both Sir Claude Macdonald and the Italian chargé d'affaires Salvago Raggi, but his unique personal success was due to contacts through Ma Chien-chung to Shansi and Honan officials, to Li Hung-chang, and to the court. When, however, Italian financial interests failed to subscribe, the Syndicate, despite the agreed employment of Italian engineers in China and American, especially Morgan, investment, became for a time virtually a British operation.[i]

In 1900 the Hongkong Bank, as agents, managed the ill-timed issue of

i For the Syndicate's own story see *A Few Facts concerning the Pekin Syndicate* and for Italian references 'Le memorie de Salvago Raggi' and the study by Giorgio Borsa (pp. 43–44), listed in the Bibliography; Ma Chien-chung's relations with the Bank are told in Volume I, pp. 519–20; the intricate corporate interrelationships are described in G. Kurgan-van Hentenryk, cited; other references are in the end note.[75]

900,000 shares in the Syndicate's Shansi concession; Boxer disturbances forced the underwriters to take up the bulk of the issue. Carl Meyer had meanwhile become a member of the Hongkong Bank's London Committee; any rivalry was with the B&CC, not with the Bank, nevertheless relationships which would facilitate later cooperation – including the role of Jamieson as managing director of the B&CC – had been established.

Like the B&CC the Pekin Syndicate would be criticized for its apparent slowness in exploiting concessions obtained in China. Continental share-holders were to become particularly dissatisfied with the progress of the company, eventually forcing the resignation of the 'London' directors.

The Yangtze Valley Company was founded in 1901 as the successor to the Upper Yangtze Valley Syndicate and the Yangtze Valley Syndicate, founded in June and October of 1899 respectively. Luzzatti and the Pekin Syndicate were shareholders in the former, Earl Grey in the latter. These companies and their successors were generally active; in 1900 for example the Yangtze Valley Syndicate came to an agreement with the proprietors (including Sir Thomas Jackson) of the Hongkong Tramways, Ltd, to form a company to complete the building of the lines authorized by the Hongkong Tramways Ordinance (1883), thus accounting, eventually, for the direct presence of a Belgian interest. The Belgian Compagnie Internationale d'Orient (CIO) had through Edouard Thys been in contact with the Yangtze Valley Company relative to acquiring a block of shares in the Chinese Engineering and Mining Company – both were involved in the complex affairs of the Kaiping mines; the Yangtze Valley Company had a greater interest in the Yunnan concession of the Syndicat du Yunnan, Ltd, in the Societé d'exploitation de Ling-nam, the Singapore Electric Tramways, etc. In 1903 the CIO acquired 500 deferred shares out of 60,150 issued by the Yangtze Company and became active participants in its affairs, including its joining in the British Group of the Chinese Central Railways.[76]

THE RAILWAYS

The Tientsin–Mukden Railway

Almost from the opening of its Tientsin agency in 1881 the Hongkong Bank had been involved with the development projects of Viceroy Li Hung-chang. From time to time the Board of Directors had authorized the granting of modest overdrafts, up to Ts300,000, on the security of the seal of the provincial Treasurer. As the rail lines connecting the Kaiping mines devel-oped into an embryo railway, the Chinese authorities attempted to raise funds by a public issue and/or by borrowing from the Hongkong Bank, which had become the company's banker. Under various names and administrations the initial line had reached Shanhaikwan in one direction and the outskirts of Peking at Lukouchiao (the Marco Polo Bridge) in the other. In 1894 the Hongkong Bank's compradore, Wu Mao-ting, had become the managing director of the Imperial Railways of North China, and between 1894 and 1897 the Hongkong Bank had advanced approximately Kuping Ts1.3 million in five separate transactions. Other advances totalling an equal amount had been made by Jardine Matheson, the Deutsch-Asiatische Bank, and the Russo-Chinese Bank.[77]

Wu's administration of the railways had been both vigorous and honest, but he was unable to withstand the political changes of 1898. In that year Hu Yü-fen, brother-in-law of Wu Mao-ting and notorious in Russian sources as a 'known henchman of the Hongkong Bank', was administrator-general of the Imperial Railways of North China.[78] Hu and E.G. Hillier, the latter on behalf of the Hongkong Bank as representing a 'British syndicate', the British and Chinese Corporation, concluded a preliminary agreement on June 7, 1898, for a gold loan of Ts16 million to finance (i) the redemption of existing loans and (ii) the extension of the railway.

The agreement was finalized in October authorizing the Chinese Imperial Railways 5% Gold Loan issued in 1899 for £2.3 million; it was underwritten by the British and Chinese Corporation and issued on the security of the railway at 97 for a period of 45 years. The contract price to the Chinese was 90, but the offer was not firm and a poor market forced the Bank to issue at 89. The brokerage fee to the Hongkong Bank was set at 2%. These terms, which had originally been more favourable to the Chinese, reflected a fall in the bond market; nevertheless, when offered to the public in February 1899 the loan was ten times over-subscribed – a sign perhaps of the national prestige interest rather than sober commercial judgement since the loan would soon be quoted at a discount.

The Hongkong Bank was further involved in the railway through Wu Mao-ting, who remained a director of the railway; he and his fellow directors were concerned at the appointment of the director of the Chinese Engineering and Mining Company to work in association with Hu Yü-fen. Wu and Hu both urged the Bank to protest, and efforts were made to ensure proper management, but this sort of intervention, whether in the Bank's name or as agents of the B&CC, pushed the Bank dangerously close to becoming a continental-style 'banque d'affairs', a role for which it was neither prepared nor staffed.[79]

In 1886 the Bank had been involved in the management problems of the China Merchants' Steam Navigation Company, and the Shanghai Manager, Ewen Cameron, had agreed to waive certain provisions of the Bank's 1885 loan (see Volume I, Chapter 14) provided that the company retain the services of H.B. Morse, an American, seconded from the IMC. But Chinese officials did not accept this form of intervention easily; Morse resigned under pressure.[80] The same type of drama was unfolding in Tientsin in 1899–1900.

A.M. Bruce (East in 1887) was seconded to the Imperial Railways to establish an accounting system, but, as he wrote to E.G. Hillier in Peking, he was frustrated at every turn. His futile attempts to prevent diversion of loan monies, the chaos of the accounts, the lack of interest of the staff were all indications that China was not prepared to reform its practices to make real development possible. Meanwhile the new director, Chang Yen-mao, was simultaneously attempting Bruce's removal and memorializing the Throne relative to alleged misconduct by Hu and his 'close-relative', Wu Mao-ting.[81]

Despite the long-standing connection the Hongkong Bank had enjoyed with the railway, the loan agreement became a matter of immediate political contention. The Germans, possibly through G. Detring of the IMC, were suspected of undermining sound control provisions for the northern railways in the hope of delaying construction and diverting traffic to Tsingtau. The Russians were also a source of concern. The loan agreement dealt after all with a railway extending north of the Great Wall into the Northeast Provinces, where Chinese undertakings to Russia had given the latter prior rights over any concession to a foreign syndicate. The loan, it is true, was Chinese Government-guaranteed but was made to a Chinese railway which was Government-owned; the loan was not guaranteed by any foreign power nor did the floating of the loan constitute foreign control much less turn the railway into a British line. The sole purpose of the loan was commercial – to permit further construction. Thus it would seem to fall outside the Russo-Chinese arrangements.

The Hongkong Bank's agreement did, however, require China to retain in their employ a British engineer – Claude William Kinder (1852–1936) had been employed by the railway from its establishment – and provided for a mortgage on the line which contained the impractical provision that, in the event of non-payment, the line would become forfeit, presumably as the possession of a British company.

In accordance with the agreement of 1895, the Hongkong Bank offered a 50% participation to the DAB, which was declined in view of the political controversy that had been aroused. The German consortium behind the DAB had investment interests in Russia and were not anxious to become involved in a British-Russian spheres of interest controversy.

Strong Russian objections remained but were ineffective. In April 1899 the British and Russians agreed on recognition of respective spheres of interest, the Yangtze Valley and Manchuria, but the Hongkong Bank's loan agreement was specifically excluded; it would be permitted to stand.[82] The Chinese confirmed Russian privileges in an exchange of notes on June 1, and made further concessions to meet Russian demands, but the basic rights contained in the Bank's agreement were not affected.

Construction on the extensions began in 1900, but there would be destruction and further international discord during and after the Boxer Uprising. Russian attempts to seize and hold the line were frustrated.

The Shanghai–Nanking Railway and the 'spheres of interest' agreement

As early as 1894 Charles Addis, then the Bank's Shanghai Sub-Manager, was negotiating with Sheng Hsuan-huai on the subject of a railway from Shanghai to Nanking. At the same time Jardine Matheson were independently of and unknown to the Bank involved in discussions which may be considered the 'original negotiations' as far as later developments are concerned. Jardine's had then advised its London friends, Matheson and Co., to seek the cooperation of Rothschild's or some other merchant bank in view of the Hongkong Bank's agreement to share Government-guaranteed loans with the DAB.[83]

In 1897 von Hansemann of the DAB in fact proposed a plan whereby the Shanghai–Nanking line would be financed by the Hongkong Bank-DAB syndicate in accordance with their 1895 Agreement, and in October 1897 he sent a plan to Julius Brüssel at the Hongkong Bank in Hamburg to be forwarded to Ewen Cameron in London.

The Hongkong Bank however was non-committal, merely notifying the DAB of the receipt of their letters. Von Hansemann took this to mean 'tacit acceptance'.[84] Accordingly, Franz Urbig and E.G. Hillier met in Shanghai and agreed between them that the DAB should lead the negotiations, as the Hongkong Bank had led in the negotiations for the two indemnity loans. The Germans proposed, and the British did not expressly reject, that the line should be built and administered by a German registered, Deutsch-Chinesische Eisenbahn-Gesellschaft to be founded especially for this railway and with equal participation.

In March 1898, Cameron went to Berlin to discuss the question with von Hansemann. At the end of their discussions, Cameron declared that the Hongkong Bank wanted to suspend the 1895 Agreement with regard to this particular railway. As the meeting became the subject of much empassioned debate and as it is not clear what was actually said, it is perhaps more useful to outline the issues than detail the lengthy exchanges between Cameron and von Hansemann, the latter at one point taking the position that his personal integrity had been questioned.

Although Britain and Germany never came to an agreement over the

Yangtze Region, China had acknowledged a British interest in her note of February 11, 1898, and it was clear that a railway built by a German company with a German name would be politically unacceptable. Furthermore the German position relative to railway construction in Shantung was as yet unclear; the KfAG declared itself willing to permit the Hongkong Bank to participate in accordance with the 1895 Agreement, but the German Government's policy revealed itself in opposition with the formation of two independent consortiums, the Adelssyndikat and the Industriesyndikat, especially designed for railway and mining development in Shantung, but with, for the most part, the same participants as in the KfAG.

There would thus appear *de facto* to be two claims to special 'interest', German in Shantung, British in the potentially more remunerative Yangtze Valley. Accordingly Cameron's solution was to offer German participation in a British company involved in the Yangtze in return for the Hongkong Bank's financial participation in German railway concessions in Shantung, a solution which, in view of the prior understanding of Urbig and Hillier, appeared to German Secretary of State von Bülow to be a flagrant violation of the 'Open Door'.[j]

In a sense the Shantung question was irrelevant since the DAB/KfAG were never awarded the railway concessions in that province and therefore could not share them with the Hongkong Bank. Considering the problem as between banks alone, the breakdown in the 1895 Agreement, which resulted in the temporary exclusion of railway projects from its automatic provisions, came as a result of the Hongkong Bank's reaction to German attitudes relative to Shantung and perhaps also in the anticipation of the status of the Yangtze Valley as a British sphere of interest. Indeed, Cameron may be said to have precipitated British involvement by his request for British Foreign Office support in April 1898.

In early May 1898 the Chinese Government accepted the British position relative to the Yangtze Valley, and Sheng Hsuan-huai, then the director-general of Chinese Imperial Railway Administration, began final negotiations with Jardine Matheson which were concluded on May 13, but in the name of both Jardine Matheson and the Hongkong Bank acting as agents for a 'British syndicate'. The 'British syndicate', the British and Chinese Corporation, was incorporated only eleven days later.

At this point Rothschild invited von Hansemann to London. Von Hansemann's reaction reflected personal and national sensitivities; he declined the

---

[j] As Cameron himself put it, 'The proposed line between Shanghai, Soochow, and Nanking will . . . run through one of the richest and most populous districts in China. It will help to open up the country, and as the line is sure to prove remunerative, it will also stimulate similar enterprises in other directions greatly to the advantage of British trade.'[85]

invitation claiming that after the DAB had undertaken preliminary negotiations the Shanghai–Nanking project had been taken over by Jardine
Matheson while the Hongkong Bank persisted in misunderstanding the
Shantung situation. Cameron did nothing to ease the situation by claiming,
inter alia, that the Germans were responsible for the breakdown of the 1895
Agreement; von Hansemann charged that Cameron's memo contained
statements he considered a personal insult and demanded a formal apology.

Even the German Ambassador in London, von Hatzfeldt, thought this an
over-reaction and urged von Hansemann that Cameron had not intended to
be insulting, adding, 'Cameron is an uncut diamond, lacking manners, but
wholly honest in business matters.'[86] Eventually Cameron responded, 'I am
grieved to think anything I have said should have given von Hansemann the
impression that I consider his conduct in the matter anything but absolutely
straightforward and most honourable,' adding that he was interested in
returning to the understanding which had existed before the Groups decided
to work independently on railway projects.

Rothschild immediately forwarded this 'apology' to von Hansemann.[87]

Von Hansemann finally went to London in the beginning of September
1898 for discussions with the Hongkong Bank in the offices of Lord
Rothschild. The British Group was represented by William Keswick –
formerly Chairman of the Hongkong Bank (1880/81) and partner in
Matheson and Co. and Jardine, Matheson and Co. – for the British and
Chinese Corporation, and Ewen Cameron and Julius Brüssel for the Hongkong and Shanghai Banking Corporation. This was not to be purely a meeting
between private banking groups; both the British and the German Governments were interested that an agreement should result from these negotiations, and both sent representatives.

The DAB received very little from the negotiations, except possibly
confirmation that the British no longer claimed that the Yangtze Valley
included all of China up to and including Tientsin, as the Germans chose to
interpret Prime Minister A.J. Balfour. The new agreement of September
1898 merely defined for the two banks the respective 'spheres of interest': for
the DAB, Shantung and the valley of the Yellow River, and for the Hongkong
Bank the Yangtze Valley.[88] There were some exceptions, especially those in
connection with the Tientsin–Pukow line (see below).

The agreement, despite the presence of officials, remained one solely
between the two banking Groups. Von Hansemann indeed proposed and it
was agreed that 'it is desirable for the British and German Governments to
agree about the sphere of interest of the two countries regarding the railway
constructions in China, and to mutually support the interest of either
country'.[89] Since, however, the two Governments had not agreed, the meeting

was in the position of attempting to pre-empt their role; the two banks succeeded only in setting the terms for themselves.

Von Hansemann proposed the main division 'regarding the British and German spheres of interest' which, for the reason stated, had to be qualified by adding, 'for applications for Railway Concessions in China'. The terms were as stated above. Von Hansemann knew that he was in a weak position; the Hongkong Bank (and the British Government) objected to the Shantung situation – as perhaps did the DAB, but the DAB was powerless in view of the position taken by its own Government.

Although the meeting brought the two Groups back together once more, the Germans were at a political disadvantage.

In December 1899 von Hansemann wrote to Reichskanzler von Bülow trying to convince him that it was in German interests that the German Government reach an agreement with the British on 'spheres of interest' along the lines of the September 1898 Agreement between the banks. *De facto* Germany was already bound by the agreement, as there were no financial groups in Germany able to build in the Yangtze independently of the DAB and KfAG – the creation of 'straw men' to circumvent such agreements, though often mentioned, was never really a viable solution, except, as in the case of Shantung, the Government already had the political situation under control. On the other hand, von Hansemann pointed out, there were other British groups – he had in mind specifically the Pekin Syndicate – which, if the agreement remained merely a private one between the banks, could seek projects in Shantung with the support of the British Foreign Office. Von Hansemann recognized that the German Foreign Ministry did not want to give over the whole Yangtze in exchange for the relatively unimportant Shantung region and the Yellow River, however he felt that the Ministry should recognize that this had already been done.[90]

The British Government recognized the agreement; the German Government did not.

The cause of the dispute and consequent agreement, the Shanghai–Nanking Railway, was not built for another ten years. The British opened negotiations again in 1903 but only in March 1908 was the line finally ready for traffic.

The Tientsin–Pukow Railway[91]

A railway from the important northern city of Tientsin, with connections both to the capital and to the Northeast Provinces, connecting to the Yangtze River first at Chinkiang and then, on the decision of the British and Chinese Corporation (B&CC), to Pukow opposite Nanking, and so, via the Shanghai–

Nanking line to the great International Settlement of Shanghai, was obviously a railway of economic and strategic importance.

The main series of negotiations for the reconstruction of this line began as early as 1895 under German auspices. Carlowitz and Co. took the lead for the Berliner Handelsgesellschaft, presumably also on behalf of their associates in the KfAG.

In accordance with the banks' 1895 Agreement, 50% of the expected operation was to be offered to the Hongkong Bank, but when the German involvement became known the Bank's compradore, Wu Mao-ting, attempted, unsuccessfully in the end, to block it.

The course of these negotiations was also complicated by (i) the invitation to the Russians and French to become involved through the Russo-Chinese Bank, (ii) the concession granted by the Imperial authority to Yung Wing (Yale '54), a naturalized American, who received ineffectual American diplomatic support, and (iii) the impact of the German arrangements in Shantung.[92]

The first faded in importance as the Russians, anxious to protect their rights in Manchuria, were reluctant to become involved in any controversy with Britain over a railway into the Yangtze Valley. They were, on the other hand, unwilling to support Britain; there was an overlap of German financial interests in the DAB consortium and the Russo-Chinese Bank.

Yung Wing appeared to the Germans as primarily a nuisance to be bribed – 'to use the methods which the Hongkong Bank or the Russo-Chinese Bank normally use' was the way the German Minister Baron von Heyking put it – but the problem partially solved itself when in October 1898 Yung Wing was forced to flee Peking for political reasons.[k] The concession, however, remained; J.P. Wade Gard'ner, the Hongkong Bank's Shanghai Manager, urged the Foreign Office to buy it out, and representations were made by the Anglo-American interests behind Yung Wing to obtain British support. This, on the decision of the Foreign Office, was denied – not because of any prior commitment to the Hongkong Bank but because the proposed routing, designed to avoid Shantung, interfered with the Pekin Syndicate's proposed Pukow–Sinyang concession. Finally, the Chinese cancelled Yung Wing's Anglo-American concession.

There remained the Shantung problem.

[k] Von Heyking explained, without sound foundation, that the Hongkong Bank received only 'slack' (*schlaffe*) support from the British Legation, but kept a whole troop of Chinese spies and secret agents, who gave the Bank all sorts of information and also conducted negotiations with Chinese ministers. This, he added, is very expensive, but the Hongkong Bank 'does not scrimp in these matters'. A less dramatic explanation would be that its Tientsin compradore by marriage and through his Peking associate was well connected and was himself appointed to a high Chinese position with access to the official world, and naturally had contacts which he used as information sources. These were supplemented by E.G. Hillier's own extensive official contacts.[93]

The most economical route from Tientsin to Pukow ran through Shantung via the provincial city of Tsinan, a junction with the German-planned railway to Tsingtau. A third of the line was north of the province; a third to the south, but the German Government insisted that the section running through Shantung should remain a German railway, although the whole line might be coordinated as to management and run as one enterprise: (i) the capital for the two 'normal' sections was to be raised jointly, (ii) the northern third from Tientsin to Shantung was to be built and equipped and worked by the German Group, (iii) the southern third from Shantung to the terminus on the Yangtze was for the British Group, and (iv) when completed the entire line to be worked for joint account. These provisions were consistent with the 1898 spheres of interest agreement between the Hongkong Bank and the DAB.

In August 1898, that is, during the period the 1895 Agreement was inoperative with regard to railway contracts, the Hongkong Bank approached the Chinese with the support of the British Minister, Sir Claude MacDonald, who was responding to British public pressure not to let the line fall into the hands of the Germans.

Once the spheres of interest agreement was signed by the banks in early September, joint negotiations over the Tientsin–Pukow line were again possible, but the German insistence on its 'rights' in Shantung delayed agreement; the Tsungli Yamen nevertheless responded positively in December 1898. Eventually, in April 1899 the Germans modified their position; the railway would be Chinese throughout but the German syndicate would be responsible for construction of the northern two-thirds of the line. Meanwhile the Hongkong Bank and the B&CC were meeting potential British competition from the Yangtze Syndicate (see above), the DAB was advised by the German Foreign Ministry to ignore the threat, and the British Foreign Office informed the representative of the Syndicate that it could not support two syndicates for the same project and that the Anglo-German Group had already been promised support.

As the German Government had not officially recognized the 1898 spheres of interest agreement, the British Minister, Claude MacDonald, urged the Hongkong Bank to insert a clause into the proposed Tientsin–Pukow draft agreement referring to the 'spheres'. His purpose was to use the railway agreement as a vehicle for stating the general application of the spheres of interest concept for all British companies. The German Minister, von Heyking, who violently disapproved of the 1898 Agreement, successfully insisted that the DAB delete the clause, arguing correctly that it merely involved the two banks and not the Governments.[94]

Two further problems were to develop: the form of the Imperial Government guarantee and the nationality of the directors. Neither was satisfactorily

Table 5.1 *The Hongkong and Shanghai Banking Corporation
China: public loans, 1896–1900*

Title	Purpose	Amount (£ millions)	Terms (i)	(ii)	(iii)	(iv)
CIG 5% Sterling						
Loan of 1896	indemnity	16.0			36	DAB
of which:						
tranche 1 (March)		(10.0)	92^f	98$\frac{3}{4}$		
tranche 2		(6.0)	92^a	98$\frac{3}{4}$		
CIG 4$\frac{1}{2}$% Gold						
Loan of 1898	indemnity	16.0	83^f	90	45	DAB
CIR 5% Gold	Tientsin–					
Loan of 1899	Mukden					
	Railway	2.3	89^b	97	45	B&CC

(i) contract price to Chinese. (ii) price issued to public.
(iii) number of years.   (iv) with whom or for whom issued.
CIG Chinese Imperial Government; CIR Chinese Imperial Railways.

DAB Deutsch-Asiatische Bank; B&CC British and Chinese Corporation.
^{a} First tranche firm; second tranche could be but was not at a different price.
^{b} Contract price 90, but in an unfavourable market may lower to 88.
^{f} Firm.

solved, the DAB being anxious to conclude the preliminary agreement thus
securing the contract, leaving outstanding matters to be solved later. The
B&CC resisted but bowed to an ultimatum to accept or withdraw.[95]

The preliminary agreement was signed on the evening of May 18, 1899, but
various attempts to start negotiations for a final agreement were delayed by the
Boxer Uprising and the matter of the Tientsin–Pukow line was not formally
reopened until 1902.

As far as the Hongkong Bank was concerned, the outcome of the Battle of the
Concessions was promising, but by 1900 despite general agreements, little
specific had been accomplished – with the one exception of the 1899 loan.
When the Siege of the Legations was raised, priorities were on reestablishing
the position of both the Chinese Government and the Powers. These are the
first matters to consider in Chapter 6. The further story of railway development must be postponed.

6

BOXERS, INDEMNITY, AND RAILWAYS, 1900–1908

Support the Ch'ing; destroy the foreigner!
a Boxer slogan

THE BOXER UPRISING

The Boxers and the Siege of the Legations

For the Hongkong Bank the year 1898 was a year of success. The Bank's reserves then were equal to its capital, the third indemnity loan was signed, and there had been significant progress in railway finance. But in China there were signs of trouble – for those who could read them. Even Eba Addis, the wife of the Bank's Shanghai Sub-Manager, caught the sense of excitement: September 25, 'K'ang Yu-wei on board "Chungking" with us yesterday. We witnessed his escape in the launch. Great excitement over affairs here.' The next day was the Hong Kong and Shanghai cricket match and a half-holiday. Then, after noting that 'Charlie very busy, loan business – long telegrams at all hours', Eba Addis recorded an ominous note for October 10: 'Empress Dowager [Tz'u-hsi] in power. Daily Imperial Edicts reversing all reforms.'[1] The hundred days were over.

There was a saying, 'Keep the dykes low, keep the channels deep', but as the great Yellow River flows towards the North China plain it carries with it huge quantities of silt, which, as the river slows, settles on the river bed, and the dykes are built higher to contain the flood.

Western Shantung was one of the most densely populated areas of China, and it was here in that same eventful year of 1898 when Germany seized Kiaochow and the British occupied Weihaiwei that the Yellow River, China's Sorrow, burst its banks. Those lands not rendered useless by the water suffered from drought, and there was famine.

The Imperial Government was helpless to prevent disaster. The repair of dykes was left to villagers whose homes and crops lay beneath the waters. To many of them the famine and drought seemed both evidence that the Ch'ing rulers had lost the Mandate of Heaven and brought a curse about by the presence of hated foreigners. It was in this context that the Boxers made their first recorded appearance.

Related to the Eight Trigrams Society, they were known as I-ho ch'üan, literally, 'righteous and harmonious fists', and were first regarded as yet another secret society, a band of wandering, near-starved peasant bandits, who attempted to rally the people with the cry, 'Overthrow the Ch'ing, destroy the foreigner.' But their history was unique among Chinese secret societies: first, their anti-government attitudes were to disappear and be replaced by an extravagant loyalty to the dynasty – 'Support the Ch'ing, destroy the foreigner' – and second, they were for a brief astonishing period to storm out of provincial obscurity into Peking and into the limelight of world history. Then they vanished, leaving in their aftermath massacre, chaos, destruction – and a large indemnity.

At first the Boxers were suppressed, but in March 1899 and in the context of increasing anti-foreign reaction, Yü-hsien, newly appointed Governor of Shantung, took a different course and, when his dismissal was successfully obtained by foreign pressure, returned to Peking to advocate the cause of the Boxers. The stronger measures of the new Governor, Yüan Shih-k'ai, drove the Boxers, who were already attacking missionaries and the 'secondary devils', the converts, into the home province of Chihli and closer to the capital. On May 17, 1900, 65 converts were murdered 145 kms north of Peking; on May 28 the Boxers made their first attack on the railways, and by June 10 when the anti-foreign Prince Tüan was appointed President of the Tsungli Yamen the Boxers were loose in the capital.

The same day the British Admiral, Sir Edward Seymour, with 2,000 naval troops set out for the capital to supplement the already increased Legation guards. He never reached Peking. Within 25 miles of the capital he was forced back by a combination of Boxers and, significantly, Imperial troops to a Tientsin in chaos. Meanwhile in Peking itself a Japanese diplomat and the German Ambassador, Baron von Ketteler, had been assassinated, and the Siege of the Legations had begun. But with the capture of the Taku forts on June 17 by allied forces, the way to Tientsin had been reopened and eventual military supremacy ensured, although the Chinese responded to the event by declaring war on all the foreign Powers.[2]

Three days after the siege had begun Sir Robert Hart, who remained throughout in communication with the Yamen, sent a message to Tientsin: 'Foreign community besieged in the Legation. Situation desperate. Make haste.'[3]

On July 16 London's *Daily Mail* published a false and gruesome report of the final fall of the Legations and the massacre of the diplomatic corps, their wives, and their children. The Legations and the Pei T'ang Cathedral were in fact relieved by the Allied Relief Expedition on August 14, 1900, in some confusion of command and not before heavy loss of life.

If the Boxers' initial success depended on anti-foreign reaction in Shantung, so its later development was a consequence of the desperation felt in the conservative bureaucracy smarting not only from defeat and concession but also from what they saw as the foreign-inspired reform movement. And yet, during the siege and for reasons never convincingly explained, the Chinese with numerical and military superiority failed to push home the attack. Certainly there was early disillusion with the Boxers, but opposition to the anti-foreign policy was rewarded with death; after the failure of this policy, many conservative leaders were either executed or ordered to commit suicide.

Foreigners in Peking had felt insecure before, particularly at the beginning of the Sino-Japanese War. Later, in 1898 Hillier wrote to the British Minister with a report from the Hongkong Bank's compradore, Wu Mao-ting:

The common talk of the streets last night was a certain remark said to have fallen from one of the members of the Council [Chün-chi Ch'u] that advantage should be taken of the present opportunity, when there is only a handful of foreigners here, to exterminate the lot and burn the legations . . . Of course we have heard this sort of thing before, but, in view of current events, you might think it well to bring the matter to the notice of the [Tsungli] Yamen.[4]

Hillier ascribed the idea to either Jung-lu, who succeeded Wu Mao-ting's respected friend Wang Wen-shao as Viceroy of Chihli, or Kang-i, both of whom were close to the Empress Dowager and active in the Boxer Uprising. The cause had long been there, and 'a single spark can start a prairie fire'; but the Uprising of 1900 failed and the consequences were severe. Imperial China would never be the same.

Indeed, by late 1900 there were 45,000 foreign troops in North China, the Empress Dowager was on 'western tour' in Sian, and the Boxers were dispersed. The Allies, who had only recently (and somewhat reluctantly) accepted the American formulation of the 'Open Door', were now faced with a dilemma. While Russia might intensify her privileges in Manchuria and France in Yunnan, the Powers, always disunited, held back from attempting an unrealistic policy of dismembering China. Ruling the highly civilized, anti-foreign Chinese could prove a task more complex than the division of Africa. Thus the victors, while demanding vengeance, the promise of specific reforms, and an indemnity which was eventually set at £67.5 million, preserved the dynasty and the integrity of the Empire.

At another level this realistic decision could be foreseen. The Boxer Uprising and the consequent declaration of war against the Powers was never effective in all key areas of China nor obeyed by all provincial leaders. With these latter the Powers maintained a continuity of effective contact, and when the Court ordered Li Hung-chang, then Governor General of the Liang-kwang provinces, and I-k'uang (better known as Prince Ch'ing) to negotiate with the Powers, they were in a position to respond effectively.

In the financial sector the Powers were at first preoccupied with setting the indemnity, a task followed by a series of renegotiations, pricking of consciences, and *ad hoc* decisions on indemnity remission or the beneficial use of funds received. As the situation returned to normal, the Powers and/or the banks then returned to consideration of the preliminary railway and mining agreements and their finalization. In the process they were to learn that a China restored, though defeated, was still capable of exercising the rights of a sovereign power and that despite acceptance of development in principle the preliminaries remained long and complex. Indeed, in the end railways and mining concessions were an important factor in developments leading to the Revolution of 1911.

The Hongkong Bank in Peking and Tientsin, 1900–1901

The Hongkong Bank's Agent in Peking, E.G. Hillier, was on leave when the Boxers, supported by regular Chinese forces, began the Siege of the Legations in June 1900. The Peking agency was in the charge of J.K. Tweed, a young man who had come East only in 1894; he was assisted by A.D. Brent (East in 1897). Both had some knowledge of the Chinese language and had been first assigned to Peking to improve on their elementary studies in London. They had handled the routine banking business while Hillier had been primarily concerned with loan negotiations.

The Bank's Peking office had burned down some two months before the Uprising. When the troubles began Tweed decided to move the cash into the safer British Legation compound, a cart was hired, and while Tweed whipped on the camel, Brent ran along behind and picked up the dollars or bullion that fell out of holes made by snipers' bullets.

Throughout the siege Sir Claude MacDonald, who had had military experience, gave guarded leadership to forces of the several nationalities – careful not to offend diplomatic sensibilities. In his report he cited Tweed of the Hongkong Bank as one of the 'indefatigable' captains and organizers of the fire brigade. Tragically the Hanlin Academy library was burned, but this caused danger to the Legation and again Tweed and a companion came to the rescue. Tweed, manning the barricades and showing what MacDonald described as military aptitude, was appointed one of the Minister's special orderly officers.[5]

A graphic account of the siege was written by A.D. Brent for Reuters. By chance his mother had been visiting him in Peking, and she too endured the siege; like many of the ladies, Brent reported, she bore up well in the crisis but suffered a relapse shortly thereafter.[6] After the raising of the siege Brent was sent with the Bank's mail to Shanghai where he arrived at the Manager's office in his tattered Volunteer uniform with a month-old beard and still carrying a rifle. A keen amateur actor he later concluded that this was the most spectacular entrance of his career.

J.K. Tweed, however, had already reopened the Peking office for business. The Chubb safe and most of the cash had survived, and one of his first tasks was to consider the request for an advance for Prince Ch'ing, who was penniless – the Prince, whom the Empress Dowager had appointed to negotiate with the Allied Powers, had first applied to Sir Robert Hart, who referred him to the Hongkong Bank where his application was successful.

When Hillier returned, he wrote to the Chubb safe company to congratulate them on a product which had first withstood a fire and then the Boxers with the contents undisturbed.[7]

But the siege took its toll. Addis, who had been on leave in Scotland at the time of the Uprising, observed later, 'How the Peking siege operations, or rather experiences, have deteriorated people.'[8] The Board of Directors had awarded £750 and £500 to Tweed and Brent respectively, and their personal losses were met under the terms of the indemnity. There had been a farewell party for Tweed in Shanghai with a 'loving cup' in memory of the Peking siege on his departure for leave in 1902, but he apparently resigned the following year to become a broker in Shanghai and was eventually associated with the Anglo-Japanese Bank; the German-speaking Brent rose to be post-war Manager in Hamburg. The Board also noted that losses had been minimized due to the assistance of an overseer by the name of Turner, and he was granted Ts500.

By 1901 the branch was operating normally, and Shanghai shipped sycee valued at Ts3 million. A junior, D. Forbes (East in 1895) from the Shanghai office, accompanied the bullock carts and later, at the invitation of the compradore and from a special vantage point, watched the return of the Court. The Bank's premises were rebuilt in 1902 and the piece of land on which the German Post Office had stood was given to the Bank for the extension of its site in exchange for another lot given to the German Legation for use as their barracks. It was on the tower of this new building that the clock, which the Board of Directors had authorized in 1899 to meet an admitted public need, proved so inaccurate that the witty were heard referring to 'the Bank where the wild time grows'.[a]

In Tientsin the experienced Agent, D.H. Mackintosh, was on leave, and

---

[a] The witty apparently had their own moments of inaccuracy.

H. Hewat, who spent most of his senior career in Saigon, had been assigned as a replacement – he had had both Tientsin and Peking experience and was familiar with the language. His account of events during the hostilities confirms the generally held adverse views of the conduct of the various components of the Allied forces.

The Russians [he wrote to H.E.R. Hunter, then Sub-Manager Shanghai] are shooting down every Chinaman they can get hold of, and I am sure if my Chinese staff returned, they would all be shot on landing at Tangku [at the mouth of the Pei Ho].

The French have proved themselves generally useless, all they think of is eating . . .

Hewat added:

It is the first time that any of us has seen the British Officer on the war path and we never want to meet him again. His great inferiority to the German and American Officers is most conspicuous. No wonder the soldiers are thieves when they see their officers doing the same thing.

From what we have seen of the British Officer here, all gold braid and swagger, and no brains, we can easily understand the blunders that have been made in South Africa.[9]

Hewat also had the opportunity of watching the destruction, possibly due to 'incendiarism', of various properties, including half the fleet of the Taku Tug and Lighter Company, some of which held goods which were security against Hongkong Bank advances. The Agent's main banking concern however was to ensure that the British army paymasters did not deposit coin in the Bank at the Bank's risk; the army should either post its own guard on the Bank or accept the full risk. Once the security in the Bank was assured, Hewat became concerned with the problem of transit from Tangku.

Short of staff in the absence of Chinese assistants, some of whom were cut off in the native city, the Bank could not open and maturing bills were extended. The need to take the native city, where the business of Tientsin was based would, Hewat feared, endanger the commercial importance of the Treaty Port itself. But in the event recovery was relatively fast.

The military operations Hewat witnessed, however, confirmed his negative view of the European troops and of the confusion of the top command. The Bank itself was shelled and suffered considerable damage, but the building proved not to be beyond repair. The Tientsin staff, who had their individual war experiences, were rewarded with a bonus equivalent to six months' pay.

When Brent returned to Tientsin, he found the agency remitting small sums for the troops of various nations, the Indians suspicious, the British complaining of the usual commission, and the Italians demanding sterling. To give the staff a rest, Hewat closed the office for the Chinese New Year Holiday; the *Peking and Tientsin Times* objected, and Brent wrote a letter signed 'Over-worked Bank Clerk' in which he noted that customers have to recognize 'that the Bank is neither a philanthropic institution nor a systematic swindling institution'.[10]

The loyal Viceroys – the Customs and a loan

The main hope of foreigners in China was that the 'madness' would be confined to the North. The China Association in London was urged by Sir Ewen Cameron, a member of its General Committee, to support a policy in favour of those Viceroys who were attempting to maintain order. The British approach as generally incorporated into Government policy was to retain relations with provincial authorities until the siege in Peking was raised and negotiations with the central Government representatives could be reopened. The British were concerned that the Uprising would afford certain Powers an opportunity for consolidating their concessions in defiance of the 'open door' and of China's rights.

The administration of the IMC

One immediate problem was the administration of the Imperial Maritime Customs, which was the basis of security for, *inter alia*, the indemnity loans. There were proposals in Shanghai for a joint foreign commission, which the Hongkong Bank's Manager, Wade Gard'ner, cabled London Office to oppose. The Nanking Viceroy, Liu K'un-i, had in fact appointed F.E. Taylor of the IMC as 'officiating temporary Inspector General', and Gard'ner was asking Cameron's approval for accepting Taylor's signature. But the long-term concern was that, if the functioning Chinese authorities were overruled and a foreign appointee or a temporary foreign committee of control were once established, Chinese control, and therefore its acceptance of the Imperial Maritime Customs as a Chinese department, would be permanently undermined, while the status of Sir Robert Hart, should he survive the siege, would be equivocal.[11]

A British loan to the Hukuang Viceroy

A more dramatic case of provincial support arose in Hankow where the Viceroy of the Hukuang provinces, Chang Chih-tung, requested funds through the Hongkong Bank for the payment of his troops, claiming that without this he would . . .

suffer serious loss of influence not only with them but with his subordinate officials . . . I am to suggest that the matter may most conveniently be arranged by communication with the Hongkong and Shanghai Bank, through whom the Viceroy is endeavouring to obtain the money. But delay is becoming dangerous.[12]

The Bank felt unable to lend the amount on its own account. The loan would not be marketable, and the Bank was not prepared to lock up its funds. In any case, a standing Imperial edict had warned potential lenders to provincial authorities that such loans would stand 'on their own merits'. Unless approved by an edict communicated by the Tsungli Yamen, a loan would lack a central Government guarantee and, therefore, would not rank as a 'sovereign risk' loan.

On the urgent advice of the Shanghai Consul-General, the Foreign Office with the concurrence of the Treasury agreed to lend the Viceroy of Wuchang, that is, the Hukuang Viceroy, Chang Chih-tung, £75,000 for ten years at 4½%, through the Hongkong and Shanghai Bank, the British Government's bankers in China. The British Government agreed, that is, to guarantee the advance of the funds by the Bank; of the 4½% interest, the Bank would retain 3% interest and a ¼ of 1% commission annually during the life of the loan; the balance would be paid over to the British Treasury as a 'sinking fund'.

Cameron apparently was not particularly pleased with the terms being offered by the Government, and Sir Michael Hicks-Beach, the Chancellor of the Exchequer, threatened that if the Bank did not fall into line the loan would be placed elsewhere with a consequent loss of prestige to the Bank.

The problem of the lock-up of funds was, however, a real one, and it was circumvented by permitting the Bank to use the loan (with its British Government guarantee) as an 'approved security' against the note issue, thus releasing marketable securities of equal value. With this agreed – at the expense of consistency with reference to Treasury policy on banknote security – Cameron approved the operation.

During the week of negotiations the Viceroy received offers from German and Belgian Groups, conditional on industrial or other concessions. The German Government in Berlin, however, scouted the idea of lending to the authorities of a country with which Germany was at war.[13] However tentative or unauthorized, the other offers were a factor in the decision of the British negotiators in Hankow, E.G. Hillier from the Bank and acting Consul-General E.H. Fraser, to close quickly.

The actual loan agreement of August 28, 1900, was between (i) Chang Chih-tung as Viceroy of the Hukuang provinces binding his successors in office and (ii) E.G. Hillier for the Hongkong Bank acting for the Government of Great Britain. The agreement was also signed by the acting British Consul-General in Hankow (Fraser).

As the Treasury were quick to notice, Hillier had agreed, on behalf of the British Government, to accept security considerably less attractive than anticipated by the preliminary communications from the Shanghai Consul-General Pelham L. Warren. The Hongkong Bank as representing the bondholders of previous loans secured on Hukuang revenues had faced questions of precedence, and there existed a complex of internal Chinese financial arrangements which Hillier thought it unwise to unravel and revise in a time of emergency. As he put it in a comprehensive memorandum:

(i) that the amount at stake was small, and offered insufficient inducement for the introduction of further fiscal innovations in the province;
(ii) that such innovation might jeopardise the popularity of the Viceroy in his province, a consideration which must be allowed special weight under the present disturbed conditions;
(iii) that a German offer, on less onerous conditions, was being pressed on the Viceroy [but see above].[14]

Although Chang Chih-tung had represented that he needed the funds urgently, he was unwilling to simply sign the agreement as presented by Hillier. Everything was ready for his signature on August 25, but the agreement was actually signed on the 29th, after three days of manoeuvring in which the Viceroy suggested that only his representative sign the agreement and that he not be asked to account for the use of the funds.

But [as Hillier wrote to Sir Ewen Cameron] the points were, of course, merely a matter of face and, after all the trouble we had taken, we were naturally annoyed at the old man haggling over such trivialities in times like the present . . . It was just a little bluff on the part of the old gentleman and I am sure he thought none the worse of us for meeting it with the same game: at any rate he was exceedingly friendly the next morning and raised no more points, and thanked both Fraser and myself several times for the trouble we had taken and for the fair way in which he had been treated . . .
Chang [Chih-tung] impressed me favourably. He is a hale, cheerful little old man, with a frank manner, and a full white beard that would do credit to an European. He carries his responsibilities lightly, and shows no sign of the great strain he must have gone through lately.
It is difficult to realise that it is this little man who, by sheer force of character, has kept his provinces quiet through the present dangerous troubles and, if he pulls them through without a revolution, will certainly deserve well of the British Government.[15]

On reconsideration the British Government decided to ask an appropriation from Parliament and, after one year, to repay the Hongkong Bank the amount advanced. There was some question as to the fee to the Bank for managing and servicing the loan, but the original $\frac{1}{4}$ of 1% from the gross interest payable by China was confirmed. The Bank continued to service the loan throughout its life, but it received back the funds it had advanced, plus 3% interest for one year and, in turn, had to redeposit acceptable, marketable securities against its note issue.

This was the first time that the Government had used the Bank as agents to make a political loan. The Bank's original objection had, however, been financial, not political; both the risk and the lock-up of funds were unacceptable. The guarantee and the release of marketable securities solved these objections – at the cost of a lower interest rate – and the Bank advanced the funds; under these revised circumstances the Bank would have been willing to hold the loan to maturity.

The Boxer Indemnity

I am sure it is of vital importance that the burden of the indemnity should be as light as possible.

Sir Ewen Cameron to Foreign Office

The Protocol of 1901[16]

The Protocol which formally restored normal relations with China was signed in September 1901 and required, *inter alia*, the payment by China of an indemnity of HkTs450 million or £67.5 million equivalent at the specified exchange rate of 3s:od per tael.[b] Since China could not, given her credit position, borrow this on the market, the Powers agreed to advance the sum at 4%, a rate considerably under market, thereby effectively decreasing the present capital value of the indemnity. Moreover, since the debt was payable to each country severally and independently, the policy adopted by the Powers also made possible remission on a country-by-country basis at such times as conscience overcame baser emotions. The end result was the total actually paid by China for the purpose originally intended, the indemnity, being *de facto* drastically reduced.

The wording of the Protocol gave rise to a controversy as to whether the Boxer Indemnity was a gold or a silver liability. Although the Protocol stated clearly in Article VI (a): 'These four hundred and fifty millions constitute a *gold debt* . . .' and continued, 'This sum *in gold* shall bear interest at 4 per cent per annum' all the schedules were worked out as if the payments were to be made in silver, and accordingly the Shanghai Taotai, who had responsibility for actually effecting the payments, insisted on paying in Shanghai taels in accordance with the amortization schedule published with the Protocol (emphasis added).[17]

The Protocol was in this respect poorly drafted; 'ambiguous' was the favourite but inaccurate term used. If the indemnity had been paid immediately with the rate fixed at 3s:od per tael, the sum paid would have been HkTs450 million; if the Chinese had been able to borrow on the market they would have borrowed HkTs450 million. As they paid over time and as the indemnity was expressly stated as being a gold liability, the exchange risk was China's. Similarly, had they borrowed on the market to permit a single

[b] In the arguments as to whether the indemnity was a silver or gold liability of China, the term 'Protocol tael' was used. A Protocol tael expressed a value equivalent to three shillings sterling, and was thus a gold unit of account: a debt of 100 Protocol taels would thus be the same as 300 shillings or £15 sterling.

payment, the exchange risk would also have been China's, but there was no question of China's being able to borrow such a sum in silver either in China or overseas.

The purpose of stating the exchange rates in the Protocol was not to determine the question of total payment by the Chinese, but rather the relative allocation among the claimant Powers. The annexed amortization schedule was, therefore, effective only if the exchange rate remained unchanged. Silver, however, depreciated; the Powers demanded payment in Shanghai in silver at the lower exchange rates, and China's agent refused, insisting on the rates listed (for an entirely different purpose) in the 1901 Protocol.

Although several inconsistencies in the Protocol and subsequent actions and statements could be itemized, the operative provisions of the Protocol cited above took precedence, despite the representations of Hillier as British delegate to the Commission of Bankers (see below) that the exchange rate used for certain purposes in the Protocol ought to be interpreted as a statement that the liability was in silver. His calculation showed that for the payment of July 2, 1902, a difference of some 24% was involved.[18]

As silver was falling the dispute was seen inevitably as a question of the burden on China. Since no one could be expected to predict (nor did anyone in fact predict correctly) the future course of the exchanges through the 1940s, the arguments were misdirected. The question was simply who should bear the risk. The Powers were in principle requiring a payment from China to meet certain obligations; the British Treasury at least would require cover and would see no reason to accept a risk which was not theirs to bear.

In fact, the risk worked both ways. The price of silver, on which the exchanges were based, was in China's favour during part of 1904–1907, 1912–1914, and from 1915–1926. Although various indemnity remissions make precise calculations difficult, on the assumption that effective repayment ceased about 1922, the gold payment requirement actually worked in China's favour, despite the disadvantage due to the fall of silver while the controversy was taking place, that is, between 1901 and 1904. With the second fall of silver to 1931 and on the assumption that the Boxer Indemnity were repaid in full through 1940 with the heavier payments scheduled later, the gold payment requirement would have worked against China.[c]

---

[c] If the payments are taken as given in the Protocol and added as simple annual amounts converted at the average exchange for the year as given by the IMC, the relative figures are: (i) if payments ended through remission and otherwise in 1922, China would have paid in principal and interest a total Ts443.7 million if the Indemnity had been a silver obligation, but only Ts404.7 million as it was a gold obligation; (ii) if payments were ended in 1940 without any remissions, the position would have been reversed – Ts1,803.0 million as a gold obligation but only Ts1,006.7 million had it been a silver obligation. The results of this exercise in arithmetic would hold under more sophisticated assumptions.

The argument was settled by an exchange of notes on July 2, 1905, in which China admitted the indemnity was a gold liability and agreed to compound past shortfalls by a payment of 8 million Protocol taels equivalent to £1.2 million. Anticipating that the actions of the Shanghai Taotai would have to be repudiated, the Chinese Government had earlier in the year turned to the Hongkong and Shanghai Bank, and the latter, in conjunction with the Deutsch-Asiatische Bank, was already prepared; the two banks raised a £1 million loan by a public issue in London and Berlin.

The role of the Hongkong Bank

As the bank undertaking Treasury Chest business in China, the Hongkong Bank was designated a 'custodian bank' to receive the proceeds of that proportion of the indemnity payable to Great Britain; until the 1905 agreement referred to above, the Hongkong Bank also undertook the exchange thus required, although after this period the Chinese were free to seek open tenders. As the sums were due monthly from China but remitted on a semi-annual basis, the Hongkong Bank was instructed to credit the account of the Treasury Chest in the interim periods; since the Bank paid interest on Treasury accounts and after 1905 on Chinese balances, the benefit to the Bank depended on its ability to utilize funds held temporarily. The cash/assets ratios (see Table 1.6) indicate that the Bank on occasion had difficulty placing its funds profitably; the balance would have to be worked out in considerable detail, but the impression at the time was that the availability of funds strengthened the Bank's competitive position and was an overall advantage.

The Protocol provided for the establishment in Shanghai of a Commission of Bankers, composed of delegates from the Powers signing the Protocol and on which the British delegate was E.G. Hillier, the Peking Agent of the Hongkong Bank. When the Chartered Bank of India, Australia and China requested permission to participate as a custodian bank, the request was refused by the Foreign Office on the grounds that the Hongkong Bank was providing Hillier (and, which was not stated, the Bank continued to pay his salary), but that if exchange were opened to tender, the Chartered Bank could participate.[19]

The Commission of Bankers met in January 1902 and immediately became involved in an argument as to whether English or French should be the official language.[20] Although this set the tone, there were more significant differences.

First was the problem of the exchange rate. The Protocol called for semi-annual payments in Shanghai of silver equivalent to the gold payments due the Powers, but this amount depended on (i) the exchange rate on London selected as effective and (ii) the calculation of the Continental cross-rates. On both these points Hillier was at odds with the other commissioners.

The 'official' rate for TT, Shanghai on London, was that quoted by the Hongkong Bank, but, as Hillier cogently argued, this was not 'official' in the sense suggested by the use of the term on say the Paris Bourse; it was merely the rate at which the largest bank opened; it had no other status. Hillier not only advocated open tender but he also urged that a Chinese representative, who would have the right to object to what he considered an unfavourable rate, be present at the proceedings. Hillier was a Hongkong Banker, but he was looking after the long-term rather than the short-term interests of the Bank whose continued growth depended on its China business. He was also representing Great Britain. His efforts, often theoretically sound but operationally impractical, reflected his inexperience in ordinary exchange banking. But he was motivated by a desire for fairness to China within the terms of the Protocol.

Hillier's recommendations were rejected by the Commission. In fairness to them, it was also Sir Ewen Cameron's view that, because of the narrowness of the market, China would not necessarily benefit from open tender. His own recommendation was a compromise:

My suggestion is, in fact, that the original recommendation of the Commission for the settlement of exchange might be adopted with perfect fairness to the Chinese and all concerned, provided that the amount were at the same time put up to tender, in order that the Chinese might have the advantage of any better rates that might be offering on the market.[21]

Hillier corresponded on these matters with Cameron in London and not with the Head Office in Hong Kong.

On the question of cross-rates, both Hillier and Brüssel, who had been consulted, were opposed to the inclusion of a charge or commission (which would be payable by China) on the grounds that all rates were quoted inclusive of such charges in the first place. Again, Hillier appears to have been defeated, and again Cameron advised that, for technical reasons, a minimum commission was fair to both China and the Continental Powers.

A second difference arose as to whether the Chinese, required to pay monthly for obligations due semi-annually, should be granted interest on those deposits. Hillier felt that this was reasonable, although not required by the Protocol, but he could not accept the 4% urged by the Shanghai Taotai; 4% was the rate granted by the Hongkong Bank on twelve month deposits, hence Hillier suggested 2%. The willingness of banks to grant this interest depended, however, on the terms under which they held the funds on behalf of their Governments rather than necessarily on their concern for the highest possible return on the operation.

At one point, pending other decisions, the American commissioner suggested as a temporary compromise placing all indemnity funds in a neutral bank, specifically, the Chartered Bank of India, Australia and China, to which Hillier agreed. The proposal was rejected by the other commissioners on the grounds that the Chartered Bank, while not a designated 'custodian bank', was British and thus not neutral. It was an indication of the changed times that distinctions were made in terms of nationality rather than individual identity.

For a period the funds were divided equally, but as the International Banking Corporation (today's Citibank) had no Treasury, it kept its account and its share of the indemnity funds with the Hongkong Bank.[22]

All this was being done so that eventually claims against the Chinese Government for losses during the Boxer Uprising might be paid. These, in the British case, were assessed by the Claims Commissioner and actually paid on the order of Hillier from funds on deposit in the Hongkong Bank.[23] The claims were paid without interest, causing some dissatisfaction, but, as Hillier pointed out, the delay in payment, during which the exchanges fell, was an advantage to the large majority of claimants whose actual losses were in silver, since their claims had been transferred into sterling at 3s:0d and paid in Shanghai taels at say 2s:4d or lower.[24]

Hillier himself claimed expenses roughly equivalent to £1 per diem from the British Government, which sum the Hongkong Bank debited to the indemnity account.[25] He returned to Peking in 1902 and was awarded the CMG for his services. He was succeeded as British delegate by H.M. Bevis, Shanghai Manager of the Hongkong Bank, and, although this was not _ex officio_, the Foreign Office continued the practice of appointing the Bank's Shanghai Manager. When H.E.R. Hunter was Acting Chief Manager in Hong Kong in 1906, his temporary replacement, W. Adams Oram, was appointed delegate.[26]

The Gold Loan of 1905

The solution of the various controversies surrounding payment and transfer of the Boxer Indemnity was delayed by the mutual suspicion of the Powers, by the misunderstanding of China as to the denomination of the liability, and by real technical problems of the kind represented in the previous discussion.

In 1905 however when China agreed that the indemnity was a gold liability, the Powers accepted China's request for 4% interest on the monthly prepayments and China's right to a competitive determination of the exchange rate, although this latter was complicated by the existence of three optional methods of calculation and payment at the discretion of each Power.[27]

China, which had been paying only on a silver basis, had now to meet the difference plus interest due to the fall in exchange. This amounted to an agreed eight million Protocol taels and, as noted, China had in anticipation turned to the Hongkong Bank. Late in 1904 the Chinese Government had sought a loan of £1 million, the stated purpose being payment of indemnity due, ostensibly in anticipation of an adverse ruling on the denomination question, but probably to cover expenses involved in the suppression of provincial revolts. Control of end-use is difficult; money is fungible.

The loan was negotiated by E.G. Hillier with Chao Erh-hsün, a Chinese bannerman and at the time the acting Minister of Finance; the final agreement called for a contract price of 91, 5% interest on the nominal amount, and a twenty-year repayment schedule. The Hongkong Bank agreed to forego the ¼ of 1% commission usually charged for the expenses of loan servicing 'in consideration of the special object of this loan', which was not, however, specified in the agreement. The loan was issued to the public at 97 without underwriting by the two banks in London and Hamburg respectively and was over-subscribed. The Hongkong Bank was allotted £50,000, of which it immediately sold £20,000 at a 3% premium.[28]

Sir Robert Hart did not like the loan – although he bought £5,000 worth – as he feared that China's continued willingness to borrow might stem not so much from knowledge of her ability to repay as the feeling that 'they'll soon burst and run amuck!'[29] China took a different turn, but in the meantime the loan proved the beginning of another lengthy controversy, fuelled largely by the anti-German Peking correspondent of *The Times*, G.E. Morrison.[30]

Although the preliminary agreement had been signed without reference to German participation, under the provisions of the Hongkong Bank/DAB Agreement of 1895 the Hongkong Bank offered the DAB a 50% participation, which the latter accepted. The Chinese, however, would not at first permit the loan to be signed jointly, and the Hongkong Bank refused to permit German participation in the servicing of the loan. The first objection was met by permitting both banks to sign, but stipulating that the Hongkong Bank alone was the contractor and that the DAB was signing only to acknowledge compliance with the terms of the agreement.[31]

The second objection was more difficult. The domicile of the loan was, for the first time, Peking, where the DAB had no branch. Then too the servicing of the loan was to come from the Shansi likin through the 'Peking Oktroi' funds, at that time deposited in the Hongkong Bank. If there were a joint loan service, the Bank would lose part of the funds to the DAB, while the Chinese would have to pay for their transfer to Shanghai. In the end the Hongkong Bank kept the servicing for itself. The DAB opened a branch in Peking.

Hillier's position in Peking placed the Hongkong Bank at a negotiating advantage, as the Bank had insisted from the first. In this case Hillier and Chao were old associates, and the DAB negotiator, H. Cordes, had as yet developed no position from which to bargain.

Under these circumstances it is not surprising that Hillier was annoyed at being instructed from London to share the loan with Cordes – for these matters can become personal. Unfortunately Hillier was indiscreet enough to let Morrison know of his annoyance, and this was immediately translated into a statement of national patriotism consistent with Morrison's hostile position relative to Germany. When Morrison's cable critical of the 1895 Agreement was sent for Hillier's comments by the German Minister in Peking, Baron Mumm von Schwarzenstein, Hillier wrote that he was sorry Morrison was dragging the two banks into a (political) discussion which did not interest them. The Hongkong Bank's senior London Manager, A.M. Townsend, had apparently written a letter commending the cooperativeness the DAB board in Berlin had shown in the negotiations.[32]

Morrison's ostensible point was what he chose to see as the one-sidedness of the 1895 Agreement; his actual belief, which he held with an increasing conviction, was that Germany and Britain were headed for war and that any concession to the former bordered on the traitorous. In his correspondence he claimed that 'all the best Englishmen in China' denounce the Hongkong Bank/DAB Agreement; this generalization was supplemented by quoting without context the alleged and apparently supportive comments of important people, including Sir Thomas Jackson, the Chief Manager of the Hongkong Bank. His attempt to explain this so-called German 'domination' by noting the German representation on the Bank's Board of Directors – 'the Hong-kong Bank is largely German unfortunately' – has been considered in an earlier chapter; the explanation was based on a total misconception as to how the Hongkong Bank operated.[33]

Morrison was immediately rebuffed by the *London and China Express*, which he consequently dismissed as dependent on the 'Jardine Matheson ring' – although characteristically he would shortly praise Henry Keswick, the firm's Shanghai taipan, for, he claimed, expressing disapproval of the Bank's 1895 Agreement.[34] The offending newspaper had commented: 'There is no abler managed institution than the Hongkong Bank, and if it has not terminated this agreement, there must be excellent reasons for not doing so . . .' Noting the success of the 1896 and 1898 indemnity loans, the editor continued, 'Where it is a matter of business and not of politics, we must trust the acumen of the men who manage the Hongkong and Shanghai Banking Corporation.'[35]

The *Times* City editor, however, was in another department, and, allegedly at the insistence of Lord Rothschild, he published, in the same edition as Morrison's Peking cable, that 'well-informed City circles' considered his criticism of 'one-sidedness' to be inaccurate; Morrison's evidence had proved only that negotiations had been left in the Hongkong Bank's hands – to the advantage of the British.[36]

The source of the counter-article may have been the Hongkong Bank's acting junior London Office Manager, Charles S. Addis, who on February 5 had an interview with Valentine Chirol, the *Times* foreign editor and former Berlin correspondent.[d] Addis records that Chirol promised to publish a reply to Morrison.[37] The German press responded to Morrison's attack indirectly by quoting other British newspapers which were less sensational and, possibly, more accurate. But underlying it all was the fact that Morrison had a mission.

The Hongkong Bank/DAB Agreement was in fact revised in October 1905, but for reasons unconnected with the Gold Loan or with the anti-German attacks on the Bank.

Silver loans in 1905

The following month E.G. Hillier informed the Legation of a plan he had discussed with senior officials in Peking for a 'Chinese National Loan', to be issued in silver on the general guarantee of the Chinese Government for a trial amount of Kuping Ts10 million, at 7% and 90, for 31 years. Hillier estimated that a par loan could be floated at 8%, but that the arrangement he proposed offered the attraction to subscribers of the gain to be obtained by holders of bonds selected for early redemption.

The scheme had the support of the Hongkong Bank's Head Office; the loan was in silver and domestic; Hong Kong and not London had been consulted. It was an attempt to make China less dependent on foreign finance and the political consequences inevitably connected therewith; it was a timely attempt, but there would appear to have been no definitive Chinese reaction.[38]

Almost unnoticed was the Hongkong Bank's 1905 silver loan, authorized by an Imperial edict, of Ts300,000 to the Foochow Tartar-General for three years at 7% on the profits of the new mint at Pagoda Anchorage. Such security tempted mint officials to over-produce profitable subsidiary coins, as noted in Chapter 4 above.

While international operations naturally hold the main attention, the continuing regional and local activities of the Bank in support of the Chinese economy were nevertheless of considerable cumulative importance.

The problems created by the Boxer Protocol of 1901 were to last at least until the 1930s; even after remission and the redirection of Boxer Indemnity

---

[d] Sir Ewen Cameron, seriously ill, was on the verge of resigning; A.M. Townsend was then promoted to senior Manager and Addis cancelled his return passage to Shanghai and took up his new appointment as junior London Manager on February 28.

Funds, including an allocation to the University of Hong Kong, the Bank was involved. It will be a recurring theme in the chapters which follow.

RAILWAYS AND THEIR FINANCE, 1900–1908[39]

THE INSTITUTIONAL SETTING

The Sino-Japanese War brought about a peace the opportunities of which were minimized by the imposition of a heavy indemnity and by the competitive efforts of the Powers to ensure their role in developments which the Chinese had been hindered from either resisting or financing themselves.

The Boxer Protocol established a peace of desperation.

The Powers again rendered it difficult for China to finance its own development at just that time when local gentry provincialism and anti-Manchu nationalism were combined with the traditional exclusiveness of the Imperial authorities to seek, and too often fail to obtain, that domestic support which would permit the development of railways and other resources without recourse to foreign financial assistance and the foreign political involvement which this entailed.

The Allied efforts in the Boxer Uprising were sufficient to confirm mutual suspicions and antagonisms. But the strength of Chinese resistance combined with the weakness of her political institutions forced the foreign Powers into a complex of national and international syndicates which, after several years of formulation, eventually developed into consortiums which protected themselves and China from the worst excesses of political pressure and concession seeking.

The Hongkong Bank and its associates

The Hongkong and Shanghai Banking Corporation remained a private-sector oriented institution, but it too operated under typical post-Boxer constraints.

As a China bank, rather than a specially formed representative of home-based national interests, the Hongkong Bank had both advantages and disadvantages: as for the former her branch network, confined though it was, gave the Bank a legitimate, working, and profitable banking presence in key Treaty Ports and in Peking; the Bank's experience and information networks, both dependent, but not exclusively dependent, on the compradores and their political and up-country contacts, gave the Bank prior warning of developments and an ability to negotiate with reference to past successes and favours; the Bank's long-standing role as the British Government's banker, a role resting solely on objective banking considerations, gave the Bank credibility as the British Government faced the necessity of a more active and supportive role for British enterprise in China.

Anxious to play a leading role in the finance of China's Government and railways, the Hongkong Bank had in 1895 come to an agreement with the Deutsch-Asiatische Bank (DAB), thus linking itself to German interests at a time when the French had joined with the Russians in the Russo-Chinese Bank. This step in the international scene was followed in 1898 by a formalization of a long-standing but not wholly satisfactory arrangement with Jardine, Matheson and Co. by the establishment of the British and Chinese Corporation (B&CC). The promised powerful British syndicate did not, despite its nominally broad base, solve the problem of the Bank's isolation; the Bank remained exposed to competition within Britain.

Meanwhile as noted in Chapter 5 another British syndicate, the Pekin Syndicate, had been successful in obtaining mining and railway concessions north of the Yangtze. Its chairman, Carl Meyer, had been brought onto the London Consultative Committee of the Hongkong Bank in 1899 and there was discussion of an amalgamation of the B&CC and the Pekin Syndicate. Instead, the two companies formed the Chinese Central Railways (CCR), Ltd.[40]

The founding of the Chinese Central Railways, Ltd

The CCR was registered on January 7, 1904, with a nominal capital of £100,000 in 100,000 shares of £1 each, of which 50,000 were allotted for cash on a 50/50 basis between the two founding companies (directors' qualifying shares excluded) and 4s:0d paid up on allotment. The initial directors were William Keswick, Ewen Cameron, James Glass, and C.C. Macrae from the B&CC, and Carl Meyer and Robert Miller from the Pekin Syndicate.[41] The interest of the Hongkong Bank came through its equity investment in the B&CC.

The advantage of this new arrangement was that the founding companies could assign certain operations to the CCR while keeping others for their own development; the Pekin Syndicate, for example, kept its exclusive rights to the Honan Railway, then already under construction. The area of operation of the CCR could be described as being limited by Shantung in the north, the Yangtze to the south, the sea to the east, and the western border of Szechuan to the west. The B&CC transferred by sale their rights and/or negotiations for the Tientsin–Pukow, the Pukow–Sinyang, and the Sinyang/Hankow–Szechuan (Chengtu) railways to the CCR, while keeping the rights to activities north of Shantung and south of the Yangtze. The Pekin Syndicate kept certain mining concessions, but agreed not to seek new railway concessions in the agreed area – except in the name of the CCR. The Hongkong Bank were bankers for the B&CC and the CCR, and for some activities of the Pekin Syndicate.[e]

The catalyst for this merger of interests had been the Foreign Office, which was primarily motivated by the need to reach agreement on a British application for the Szechuan Railway concession, but the Foreign Office was also sceptical of the B&CC's ability to exploit concessions already obtained, concerned over adverse public reaction to the B&CC's apparent unwillingness to take action, and worried over French competition. A letter from Campbell in the Foreign Office to Sir Ernest Satow, the British Minister in Peking, was particularly blunt – and enlightening:

> ... if our railway via the Han river is to take 15 years to build (and if in the hands of Keswick and Co. this may be extended to 150) ... the French may be found in possession and they are really keen about it. ... So we called a meeting at which Lord Percy presided, and Cameron, Keswick [then chairman of the B&CC], and Carl Meyer attended. ... I put it pretty straight to them. If we get the concession can you get the money, otherwise it's no use wasting our time and that of the minister and public funds in telegraphing. They thought they could, *for a light line.*[42]

This initial concern with French competition turned, however, to thoughts of cooperation. This development would take another eighteen months.

The impact of French competition

Conflicting interests with the French, particularly over the line to Chengtu from the Hankow–Sinyang area, threatened to check negotiations with the Chinese authorities. The French had approached the Chinese Central Railways and then in July 1905 the French Government had confirmed to the Foreign Office that any construction of a railway from Yunnanfu, the end of the line from Indo-China, would be entrusted to the Chinese Central Railways, if reconstituted. The basis for solving this problem lay in the French-British Declaration of 1896 providing, *inter alia,* that 'all commercial and other privileges and advantages conceded in the two Chinese provinces of

---

[e] By an agreement of February 19, 1904, the CCR was specifically assigned the benefits of (i) the preliminary agreement, January 6, 1899, between Jardine's, the Hongkong Bank, and the Imperial Chinese Railway Administration for the construction and working of a railway from Pukow to Sinyang and (ii) the preliminary agreement of May 18, 1899, between the Imperial Government of China and the DAB jointly with the Hongkong Bank and on behalf of Jardine's as joint agents for the B&CC for the construction and working of a railway from Tientsin to the Yangtze. Note should also be taken of the promises made by Prince Ch'ing to the British Chargé d'Affaires (Townley) in July 1903, as confirmed by an exchange of notes between Satow and Ch'ing in September 1903, for (a) the Hankow to Szechuan line for the Pekin Syndicate and B&CC jointly, reserving participation for American capital (if Chinese capital were not forthcoming), (b) the prior right of the Pekin Syndicate to construct a line from Pukow to Yen Cheng on the Luhan Railway south of the Yellow River, and (c) a further priority, added by a separate Chinese undertaking in 1903, that British capital should construct the Kaifeng–Yangtze line, if required.

Yunnan and Szechuan either to Great Britain or France . . . shall, as far as rests with them, be extended and rendered common to both Powers and to their nationals and dependents . . .'[43]

French efforts to secure British cooperation were reported to Sir Ewen Cameron by E.G. Hillier from Peking and in London by Carl Meyer as early as mid-1903, but the Foreign Office was not ready to advocate joining with the French; instead, as noted above, they urged action by the British Group. There was however a fundamental weakness in the British position – the reluctance of British investors to invest in Chinese railway bonds; except for investment in gilt-edged securities, the London capital market was not receptive. Despite 'stagging' and investment based on national enthusiasm, there had been difficulties even in the period 1898–1899, before the problems created by the Boer War and the revulsion to Chinese ventures apparent in the reaction to the Boxer Uprising. As a first step the Hongkong Bank was quite willing to cooperate with the Banque de l'Indo-Chine in negotiations which eventually culminated in the Royal Siamese Government $4\frac{1}{2}$% £1 million Sterling Loan of 1905 (see Chapter 2).[44]

By early 1905 Foreign Office attitudes had changed, partly due to the failure of American interests to respond to any invitation to participate in the Szechuan line and partly in recognition of the poor support the market had received in connection with the Shanghai–Nanking Railway, which many thought was likely to be the most remunerative line in China. There followed a series of meetings which led to the significant reorganization of the Chinese Central Railways finalized in October 1905. Several related agreements were involved, creating deferred shares, allocating shares among the several Groups, determining the method of voting for directors, and agreeing to Belgian terms relative to their rights in any Szechuan railway. At the conclusion there were three national Groups, the British, the French, and the Belgian. There had also been an addition to the British Group, the Yangtze Valley Company, but the British voting rights remained with the B&CC and the Pekin Syndicate. The major new voting interest was in the French Group, consisting of the Banque de l'Indo-Chine, the Comptoir Nationale d'Escompte de Paris, the Société Générale, the Régie Générale de Chemins de Fer, and Messieurs N.J. and S. Bardac, all represented at the negotiations by Stanislaus Simon.[f]

As the basic Anglo-Continental voting equality had to be maintained, the

---

[f] Before the end of 1905, the French Group had been augmented by the Banque Impériale Ottomane, the Société Française d'Explorations Minières en Chine, G. van Brock, the Société Générale de Crédit Industriel, the Banque de l'Union Parisienne, the Banque de Paris et des Pays Bas, and the Banque Française pour le Commerce et l'Industrie. The financial backing of the British Group remained, as before, confined to a single bank – the Hongkong and Shanghai Banking Corporation.[45]

allocation of shares had to be made in consideration of both profit-sharing and voting in different proportions. The processes involved were tortuous.

The restructuring of the Chinese Central Railways, 1905
The capital of the CCR was increased to £101,000 by the creation of 1,000 deferred shares of £1 each, entitling the holders to receive one-half of the profits of each year after the ordinary shares had received in dividends a sum equal to the amount paid up; deferred shares also carried residual rights on the winding-up of the company. The crucial decision was that each deferred share entitled the holder to 100 votes and the appointment of directors as follows: shares numbered 1 to 550, nine British directors; 551–1,000, nine French directors.

The agreements made provision for Belgian financial interests: the Compagnie Internationale d'Orient (CIO) with its interlocking and varied China investments, for example, Société des Mines du Luhan, Crédit Foncier d'Extrême-Orient, Cie des Tramways des Éclairage de Tientsin, and the Hongkong Tramways.[46] This and other decisions involved a reallocation of the British Group's original 50,000 ordinary shares as follows: 5,000 were transferred to the Belgian Group (from the B&CC and Pekin Syndicate equally) and a further 7,500 were held for an American Group, which in fact never materialized. The allocation of British shares to the Belgian Group was in consideration of a discharge of its claims to the projected Szechuan Railway. The tentative American allocation was eventually divided, with 2,500 going to the French Group and 5,000 being retained by the British Group.

The previously unallocated 50,000 ordinary shares were then assigned to the French Group, of which 7,500 were for the CIO and the Banque d'Outremer. The Belgian Group agreed that 2,500 of their shares were to be made over by the CIO to the Yangtze Valley Company (in which Archibald Little of Chungking was active), in consideration for which latter transfer the Yangtze Valley Company agreed that the chairmen of the B&CC and the Pekin Syndicate should be its attorneys for voting purposes.

The Belgians were then allotted 80 deferred shares, which would have entitled them to 100 votes per share for 'British' directors. The Belgians agreed, however, to have these shares held in trust by the B&CC and the Pekin Syndicate, who then voted them in their own interests. The Yangtze Valley Company was assigned twenty deferred shares under the same conditions.

The resulting distribution is shown in Table 6.1.

The Continental participants had to accept the expanded CCR thus created as a British company registered in England, holding its general meetings in London. The British Group held 45% of the ordinary shares, the French Group 45% and the Belgians 10%; of the 'deferred shares' their

Table 6.1 *The Chinese Central Railways, Ltd*
Capital restructing, 1905

	Shares		Votes
	Ordinary	Deferred[a]	
British Group	45,000	450[c]	100,000[c]
French Group	45,000	450	90,000
Belgian Group	10,000	100[b]	10,000
Total	100,000	1,000	200,000

[a] Each deferred share entitled the holder to 100 votes.
[b] Voting rights assigned to the British Group.
[c] Including assigned Belgian votes.

voting rights were assigned as follows: the B&CC/Pekin Syndicate directors of the British Group held 550 (450 of their own and the 100 assigned by the Belgians and the Yangtze Valley Company) and the French Group 450; each ordinary share entitled the shareholder to one vote. It can be seen from Table 6.1 that the consequence of this last provision was to give the French and Belgian Groups together an equal strength with the B&CC/Pekin Syndicate.

By agreement the chairman of the CCR had, however, to be British; with the voting rights of the Yangtze Valley Company's and Belgian Group's deferred shares assigned to the B&CC and the Pekin Syndicate, his election was bound to be from among the directors elected by the B&CC/CCR. The British-controlled members of the British Group consequently retained the ultimate control of the company through the chairman's casting vote.

The specificity of the agreements was designed to maintain the basic Anglo-French entente subject to this final casting vote of the chairman. To achieve this and yet to provide for the participation of Belgian interests which extended potentially into the British Group through their holdings in the Yangtze Valley Company required the degree of complexity outlined above. These nice adjustments faced a weak link – the Pekin Syndicate.

The Pekin Syndicate had obtained mining concessions but had been unsuccessful or unfortunate, both politically and technically, in their exploitation. At a shareholders' meeting in 1907 a letter from Angelo Luzzatti, one of the Syndicate's promoters, was read; it reflected the discouragement of the Continental investors, but little practical could be effected. Indeed, action was delayed while a full reorganization of the company's complex capital structure was carried out. With a temporary improvement in share prices, many British shareholders sold out; French and general Continental influence increased in the Pekin Syndicate and the consequent shareholders' revolt led to the ousting of Sir Carl Meyer and his associates. This in turn made Meyer's presence as a director of the CCR inappropriate, but the problem of selecting replacements satisfactory to both the new Pekin Syndicate board and the CCR resulted in an impasse reflecting the increasingly intractable differences between the various national/commercial interests on the eve of the Great War.[47]

The impact on the Hongkong Bank

The Hongkong Bank, through its shares in the B&CC and the latter's domination of the CCR and through its own agreement with the DAB, was now linked separately to the rival Continental financial Powers, to Belgium, France, and Germany. The conflicting interests which this situation created came to a head in the negotiations for the Hukuang Railways in 1909, leading eventually to the Three-Power Group, subsequently the Four-Power Group, which concluded the negotiations in 1911.

Almost coincident with these developments, which related mainly to railway projects, was the belief that China would at some time require a major loan. The Banque de l'Indo-Chine, which had replaced the Russo-Asiatic Bank as representative of major French financial interests in China, approached the Hongkong Bank as early as 1906 with an offer to participate in a £20 million equivalent loan they were proposing to make to the central Government.[48] The approach proved premature, but it would prove another factor in the development of the cooperation of the national banking Groups.

A significant consequence of this trend towards cooperation was that differences between the major Groups forming the Consortium would be resolved by conferences in Berlin, Paris, and London and the results presented to the Chinese Government. Whatever reservations the Chinese might legitimately have, this proved preferable to the former practice of pressing on the Chinese authorities – provincial viceroys exposed to local and other disparate influences or the Imperial Government primarily concerned with balancing political rivalries – the various demands of this or that concession seeker from this or that importunate Power.

The three Groups were eventually joined by the Americans (for a time), the Russians, and the Japanese. Their controversial and final pre-war accomplishment would be the Reorganization Loan of 1913 (Chapter 8).

The Groups were composed of banks and as such the Hongkong Bank was the 'head', indeed the only member, of the British Group; its representative represented British Group interests, those of the Hongkong Bank. In contrast, although the DAB was also the only German bank, it was itself owned by several key banking institutions, and its representative was in a sense their representative. Behind the DAB's member banks were the KfAG and its member firms; similarly, it might be argued, behind the Hongkong Bank were the B&CC and the CCR, but the British financial sector involvement remained narrowly based, despite the potential support of the institutions and interests represented on the B&CC, including Baring's and, especially, Rothschild's.

Whatever the Hongkong Bank's position was in Britain, its representative nevertheless was on an equal footing with the heads of the more broadly based Continental Groups. Indeed, the Hongkong Bank's representative was the chairman of the meetings of the several national Groups, of the Consortium as composed from time to time, and the Consortium secretariat operated from the Bank's London office.

Until his retirement in February 1905 Sir Ewen Cameron as senior London Manager of the Hongkong Bank was the undoubted leader in British China finance. He was succeeded as senior Manager by A.M. Townsend, but his position on the boards of the B&CC and the CCR was taken not by Townsend but by the new junior London Manager, Charles Addis, whose experience in China loans extended back to 1884 when he had been Agent of the Bank's Peking sub-agency and had continued while he was Sub-Manager in Shanghai until his Home leave in 1904. Then too Addis had been a Railway Commissioner representing the Bank on the board of the Shanghai–Nanking Railway. In his diary are notes of meetings with the chief engineer and

At 5 a Railway meeting at Sheng's [Hsuan-huai] house. Sat for an hour in a stifling Chinese room, no punkahs & lots of flies. It was like the old days when Alford and I used to meet with Sheng to discuss the preliminary agreement. That was in 1894. It is a sickening job.[49]

When Townsend retired at the end of 1911, Addis as the new senior Manager kept his primary interest in the Bank's international operations.

The evolution of the Hongkong Bank's involvement with European interests may be summarized: 1895, the Bank and the DAB, modified in 1898 and 1905; 1905, the joining of British, French, and Belgian interests, the last mentioned dropping out as an independent factor until say 1911. After a period of competition the DAB would be brought into the Anglo-French cooperative sphere and the China Consortium would become a real factor from 1909 with the first formal consequence in 1911.

In this Consortium the Hongkong Bank played its major international role. Such was the personality and authority of Charles Addis, the reputation of the Bank he represented, and the major role of Britain in China, that he came to be more than a chairman; he was the acknowledged leader of the Consortium. Knighted in 1912 Sir Charles remained the Consortium's inspiration in the years beyond his retirement, first from the Hongkong Bank in 1922 and then in 1933 from the Bank's London Consultative Committee he had chaired for so many years.

The Hongkong Bank and the Foreign Office

The directors of the Hongkong Bank were responsible to the shareholders for a high level of performance for the Bank as a commercial operation. A bank is nevertheless a service institution, and, just as managers of small branches would provide financing and advice to traders, so the senior managers related to major customers – including Governments. This does not suggest that the interests of banks and their customers are always coincident or that, even if both understand the underlying principles of each other's operations, they should in consequence be always in agreement.

It is not surprising, therefore, that the record of the Hongkong Bank's relations with the Governments it served, especially the British and Chinese Governments, should be uneven. The Bank's Board of Directors provided little leadership in the field of merchant banking; the Chief Managers, Jackson, Smith, and Stabb, were their own exchange operators, and there was little time to direct the complex strategy of railway finance in a China under diplomatic pressure. The leadership came instead from Sir Ewen Cameron in London where there were two Managers, from Charles Addis in Shanghai where as the Sub-Manager he had the time to consider such matters – then from Addis in London, J.D. Smart in Shanghai, and from E.G. Hillier, alone in Peking where he had this primary function. Tientsin office provided Hillier's service back-up, otherwise he came to be in direct communication with London.

The Hongkong Bank's policy with regard to railway finance was therefore the policy worked out by Cameron, and then Addis, in London. They negotiated on the one hand with the City and Continental financial interests and on the other with the Foreign Office, whose support they might need to confirm the Bank's status with Chinese authorities pressed by other Powers to accord concessions.

The close relations which built up between the British Government and the Hongkong Bank were not the result of a conscious selection of the Bank as the 'instrument of British financial policy in China'. As for the official support the Bank received for its non-official operations, this evolved as required by China's internal policy and international position; it was subject to the trend of British foreign policy, which might from time to time be out of phase with the policy of the Bank, subject as it was to an entirely different set of factors, including the state of the capital markets. British official support for concessioned lines would change in the face of growing Chinese opposition. This would affect the B&CC and therefore the Bank as agent of the B&CC more than it would the Bank itself.

This is relevant in considering, for example, the relationship of the B&CC's

representative in China, J.O.P. Bland, with the Legation, and his frustration at finding the Minister and his Chinese Secretary not fully supportive of each specific term in agreements being negotiated. Under the circumstances Bland did not feel obligated to take the Legation fully into his confidence. As he wrote to Addis in the latter's capacity as a B&CC director, 'I am entirely in favour of frankness and loyalty to our Legation but my first duty is to the Corporation . . .'[50] Understandably the Legation officials had reciprocal views.

Consideration of the Hongkong Bank's position through the distorting glass of the B&CC requires caution; Hillier's relations with the Legation, given his great sensitivity to the changing scene, were apparently on a sounder footing. Nevertheless, Bland's comment is suggestive and useful.

There was, however, another factor in the Bank's relationship with the Foreign Office which from time to time caused problems – the 1895 Hongkong Bank/DAB Agreement.

In 1905, for example, Chang Chih-tung's policy of railway redemption, of recovery of concessions and other rights previously granted, provided an opportunity for a British loan, eventually the £1.1 million Hong Kong Government Loan of 1905, which would once again create a favourable basis for seeking the Viceroy's assistance in the complex negotiations then recommencing over construction and finance of the Hankow–Canton Railway. In connection with the proposed loan, the British Minister, Sir Ernest Satow, opposed the Hong Kong Governor's advice to seek the assistance of the Hongkong Bank; Satow feared the international complications arising from the Bank's German connection; he suggested instead that the Chartered Bank of India, Australia and China might be considered.[51]

News of this exchange, which was secret, reached the Hongkong Bank's London Manager A.M. Townsend, who questioned the Foreign Office as to whether the German agreement was endangering the continuation of official support for the Bank; he offered to wait upon the proper official the following day. Townsend was assured that Satow's concern must be read as affecting this operation only; the Foreign Office 'desired that our relations with the (DAB) should continue, in the future as they had been in the past, to be of the best'.[52]

Nevertheless, the matter was not so easily resolved. In connection with a £3 million related transaction, Townsend wrote to the Foreign Office on July 20, 1905:

It would appear that while the British Minister declines to give any information to Mr Hillier, the German Minister on the other hand is taking a most active interest in the matter, and the Agent of the Deutsch-Asiatische Bank is urging Mr Hillier to cooperate with him, in terms of our German agreement.

I shall be very much obliged if you can assist me in sending some reply that will make the situation easier for us.[53]

The Foreign Office and Townsend resolved this particular incident by referring the matter to the B&CC which, Townsend claimed, was not bound by the agreement.[g]

This set other problems in motion; the DAB remained outside the agreement and, free to act on its own, did in fact act alone; the Hukuang negotiations resolved these conflicts.

The actual developments in Hankow and the amendment of the agreement between the banks will be considered below, but here it is important to note (i) that the Hankow Consul-General informed both the Hongkong Bank *and the Chartered Bank* that British financiers would be given first option on the £3 million loan; this is consistent with the conclusion that the British Government had no 'chosen financial instrument' in China and (ii) that the agreement with the DAB, being reconsidered after ten years, was in fact revised later in the year, although not perhaps in ways directly relevant to the problems considered here.[55]

Neither the Bank nor the Foreign Office took their relationship for granted.

Two illustrative cases

Bank loans should only be made against adequate security; the adequacy depends in part on the legal system and on interpretation. Thus when in mid-1906 the Szechuan provincial authorities approached the Hongkong Bank for a loan, without the authority of an Imperial edict, to replenish provincial funds exhausted in the suppression of a rebellion, A.M. Townsend asked the Foreign Office whether, in view of the 1891 Chinese disclaimer of central Government responsibility for repayment of such unapproved provincial borrowing, the British Government would take cognizance of such a loan, whether, that is:

H.M.'s Government would be prepared to instruct the British Minister to record his official recognition to the loan as a legal and binding obligation by the Szechuan provincial government to the Bank, and, in the case of need, to support the claim of the Bank upon the government and revenue of that province for reimbursement under the terms of the contract.[56]

The reply was equivocal.

---

[g] Townsend's statement contradicts the memorandum of A. von Hansemann, dated March 10, 1903, accepted by the Hongkong Bank and communicated by Cameron to the Foreign Office, which stated that the two banks were bound by the agreement even if they were only acting as agents for the loan in question. However, the Foreign Office was writing that the Hongkong Bank issued the B&CC's loans but otherwise had no connection with them – a misleading description of the very close relationship between the two companies.[54]

... if the Viceroy of Szechuan gives His Majesty's Consul General at Chengtu an official assurance that the loan will be duly and punctually repaid ... that officer will be instructed to use his best endeavours in case of default to secure repayment.

It must, however, be clearly understood that no guarantee on the part of His Majesty's Government, either of principal or interest, is implied.[57]

In contrast the Hongkong Bank's Ts500,000 (Hankow *yang-li* sycee) loan to Ch'en K'uei-lung, the Hukuang Viceroy, in 1909, was authorized by an edict, and was routinely registered with the British diplomatic representative in Hankow as a matter of record.[58]

In both cases the Hongkong Bank was operating within a system developed by the relevant national authorities, and the support it received was consistent with the policies and agreements of both nations. That support was not in any sense exclusive.

Foreign policy and the requirements for public loans
Public loans had to be presented to potential subscribers in an acceptable form; consequently certain provisions were a virtual necessity in loan agreements, including evidence of compliance with Chinese regulations such as were necessary to ensure official recognition of the obligation; this in turn led to the need for the Bank to be able to assure subscribers that the British Government had taken cognizance of the Chinese Government's obligation and would assist in enforcing the contract should that prove necessary.

The Foreign Office was then in a position to control, modify, or direct the terms of a transaction. Before 1895 both parties would have been anxious to avoid such a relationship.

Dependence on Government was not sought by the Bank, and it had some unfortunate consequences. In the pursuit of foreign policy goals, the British diplomatic and consular officers in China and the Foreign Office in London undertook their own negotiations, often unknown to or contrary to the wishes of the Hongkong Bank, leading to arrangements with which the Bank had then to conform, or modify by negotiation, if it wished Government support.

Aware of this chain of consequences, the Bank, particularly Addis in London, attempted to influence Government policy. There was an interchange in which both parties had strengths: the Bank had the means to finance railways, it had the ability to present its plans successfully to the Chinese authorities; it did not have the ability to counter political pressure from other Powers or to present its financial proposals to the London market without political guarantees; the Foreign Office had the diplomatic authority and established relationship with China, but it could not itself undertake the development opportunities the British ministers had opened up for British enterprise.

The British Government, having provided the opportunity for its citizens, had then to wait for a British Group to negotiate within the range their diplomacy had set. Or alternatively, the initiative could come from a British Group, which would then seek such Government support as was necessary to complete the commercial arrangements successfully. The close relationship with the Hongkong Bank grew from the fact that the Bank, and by that expression is included in discussions of finance the B&CC and the CCR, was usually, from its size and connections in China and from Hillier's contacts and ability, the most credible candidate for support.

As the Hongkong Bank had forged for itself international links in China for sound commercial reasons, so the Foreign Office recognized from diplomatic experience that successful British participation in railway development in China involved international agreement and cooperation. The inter-bank Group agreements and, eventually, the China Consortium were the climax for both the Bank and the British Government, but they came to this goal by different paths, negotiating at different levels, and not necessarily on identical terms. These terms had to be adjusted by discussion between the Bank in London, represented by Charles Addis, and the Foreign Office, and between the Bank in Peking, represented by E.G. Hillier, and the British Minister in China's capital.

The contradictions of successful policy

Once having achieved this roughly common goal the Government faced a policy contradiction. The Foreign Office had never given its exclusive support to the Hongkong Bank or any other British institution except on a project-by-project basis, and then only as the need for such support became accepted by the Foreign Office. This Ewen Cameron had learned from his experience with the Tientsin–Mukden railway agreement in 1898–1899. Diplomacy set the framework, the private syndicate obtained at least preliminary acceptance by the Chinese and appeared credible to the British authorities, and the latter then gave the minimum recognition required under the circumstances for the success of the enterprise.

Having manoeuvred the interested Groups into an international consortium with the Hongkong Bank's Sir Charles Addis as chairman and the secretariat in the Bank's London office, the British Government had either to insist on the British Group becoming, like the German Group, all encompassing, or somehow disengage itself from its own policy of encouraging international economic cooperation in China. This cooperation had virtually come to be equivalent not simply of exclusive support for a single project but continued exclusive long-term support of the Hongkong Bank against other

British companies. The Consortium was, after all, intended to continue from project-to-project; the scene had changed.

Although great stress has been placed on the leadership and initiative of Cameron, Addis, and Hillier, there is no question but that in the end the Chief Manager operated under the direction of the Board which understood and controlled the activities of the Bank in the interests of the Bank as seen from Hong Kong. This could be easily forgotten in the Foreign Office and among others dealing with the Bank, not only by Addis in his somewhat independent later years (see Volume III); a letter from the Banque de l'Indo-Chine referring to some agreement made with Addis expresses the expectation that Addis will no doubt bring the matter to the attention of the Bank's Hong Kong 'branch'.

The task now is to test these thoughts against the history of negotiations for key railway finance in China from the Protocol of 1901 to the revolution of 1911.

The Bank's German connection and the modification of the 1895 Agreement

The Hongkong Bank, unlike the Imperial Bank of Persia, was not, and did not try to become, a state bank; it was merely well-known, experienced, and proven. But, just as the Bank was not the automatic or pre-selected choice of the Foreign Office, so it was not always a favourite either with the Tsungli Yamen (and its successor the Wai-wu Pu) or with the relevant provincial authority. Much depended on the nature of recent contacts in other matters.

One objection to the Hongkong Bank from the Chinese viewpoint – as indeed from the Foreign Office's and Legation's earlier viewpoint (see above) – was its association with banks of other nationalities. In the £1 million 1905 Gold Loan, for example, the Chinese, who thought they had been negotiating with the Hongkong Bank alone, found themselves in a deal in which the Deutsch-Asiatische Bank was inextricably involved.

When in 1906 the Chinese made tentative proposals to the British Legation for a major loan for general trunk-line financing, the Minister was asked to nominate an independent British financier and asked to keep the matter secret at that stage from the Hongkong Bank with whom the Chinese were unwilling to deal direct because of its involvement with other countries. The Foreign Office contacted Sir Ernest Cassel and then informed the Wai-wu Pu that they had found a willing 'independent financier' whom they did not at that point name. There was certainly no suggestion of any obligation to the Hongkong Bank on either side, merely the recognition that the Bank would be interested and should be 'kept in the background' for possible later use.[59]

Given China's need to balance the demands of the several Powers for concessions and her traditional policy of preventing importunate barbarians from uniting, an element of distrust of the Bank can easily be understood. This factor was also present in the complexities of the Hukuang Railways negotiations to be considered in Chapter 7.

Many of the proposals and counter-proposals, some urging the involvement of the Bank, others insisting on its exclusion, never moved past the initial stages; many proved to be negotiations being carried on in parallel, perhaps by other officials, directly with the Bank; still others were resolved without reference to the Bank's foreign entanglements. Nevertheless the problem of the German relationship was insufficient to cause the Bank in 1905, despite the scaremongering of such writers as Morrison of *The Times* or the misunderstandings involved with China in the 1905 Gold Loan and with the Foreign Office in relation to the Hong Kong Government Loan to the Hukuang Viceroy (see above), to seek its cancellation; only minor amendments were made in the ten year old agreement after the reconsideration in 1905.[h]

The Hongkong Bank's Head Office cabled Addis instructions on August 31, 1905, to leave immediately for Berlin to revise the 1895 Agreement. As the 'German syndicate people' were 'out of town' Addis postponed the trip until October.[60] Before leaving Addis consulted with the Foreign Office as well as with Sir Thomas Jackson and Carl Meyer.

Addis accompanied by F.T. Koelle, then the Manager of the Hongkong Bank's Hamburg Branch following Brüssel's resignation in August, met with Franz Urbig of the DAB at the Hotel Metropole in Brussels on October 4 to discuss the 1895 Agreement. Urbig had replaced von Hansemann (d. 1903). The changes Addis proposed were actually consistent with the procedure the Bank had used earlier in the year.

Addis, while stating that the Hongkong Bank had no complaints concerning the past application of the agreement, proposed modifications the Bank considered appropriate in the changed situation in China. International rivalry had intensified since 1895 and Germany's diplomatic position had been weakened by its seizure of Kiaochow, its extreme attitude during the Boxer Uprising, and, ironically, the economic insignificance of its Shantung adventure.

The purpose of the agreement continued to be in furtherance of their mutual interests in China, to share equally any business obtained, and to avoid

---

[h] On the term 'Hukuang Viceroy': there was a Viceroy of the two provinces of Hupei and Hunan, referred to as the Hukuang provinces; hence the 'Hukuang Viceroy'. His capital was in the central China complex of Hanyang, Wuchang, and Hankow, and he is also referred to by one (or both) of the last two names. Even if consistency were maintained in the text, confusion could exist; the sources vary.

unnecessary competition. In effect the only business undertaken had been the two indemnity loans and the 1905 loan, railways being considered on a case-by-case basis. As the Chinese were, as Addis put it, suspicious of joint negotiations, the Bank proposed that business coming within the scope of the agreement:

> . . . may be entertained and negotiations entered upon by either Bank alone, with or without notice to its partner; and should it appear in the course of such negotiations that the conditions imposed upon the business preclude joint negotiation and/or joint signature by the two Banks . . . the negotiating Bank may conclude and sign the agreement under negotiation, his partner being entitled to all rights of participation under the Agreement . . . other than those implied by joint negotiation and joint signature.[61]

Both parties were to endeavour to negotiate jointly, but if this were not possible, an additional clause would be added to the signed agreement permitting the other bank to share *inter alia* in the loan servicing (as the DAB did not in the 1905 loan) – this was at the insistence of the DAB – and was to include authority for obtaining an official quotation on their respective markets.[62]

The problem was on the one hand the prestige or 'face' involved in actual participation in the negotiations and on the other the disinclination of the Chinese to negotiate jointly with the representatives of more than one bank unless such a procedure were openly agreed. The amendment would, however, achieve little since the agreement did not remain secret and the Chinese were aware that to deal with the Hongkong Bank on matters within the scope of the agreement meant that at some time they would find themselves also in a public relationship with the DAB.

If anything, the 'visibility' of the Hongkong Bank would be enhanced; if the amendment were advantageous to any party, that party would be the Hong-kong Bank. In any case Addis noted happily in his diary, 'Outcome of the negotiations much approved by TJ', and Addis reported accordingly to the Foreign Office.[63]

The Hongkong Bank and Chinese railway policy

The Chinese had stated long before the Sino-Japanese War that when the time came to develop railways, they would do the task themselves. Even Sir Robert Hart had been optimistic that the Chinese would raise the necessary funds internally; he was confident the surplus was there.[64] But when the time came, China was unable to raise the funds domestically. Nevertheless the Chinese preferred to finance, engineer, and manage their own railway construction. They were more successful in obtaining control of management than of finance, but foreign finance usually meant an attempt to impose some form of control or foreign supervision, the degree of which was open to negotiation – and dispute.

Owing to the inability of China to obtain domestic financing and the need to raise funds in the international capital markets in the context of the generally poor foreign image of Chinese administrative practices and fiscal account-ability, a certain degree of foreign control had, at first, to be proved in the prospectus. Observers – historians and Chinese patriots – have since detailed the criminal activities of certain foreigners in connection with the railways; they have in this context questioned the validity of the adverse contemporary judgement on relative Chinese integrity. The popular feeling against Chinese practices, however, had a reality in the market and if the loan were to be subscribed at an acceptable price, some foreign control measures, however difficult to enforce, however unrealistic, were considered essential by banks with long-term interests in China.

This does not, however, provide an answer as to the necessary degree of that control; the Chinese wished as little as possible, but since this might result in a loan under-subscribed at a cost to the issuing banks and underwriters, the banks negotiated for the greater control they considered necessary – although in this, as will be noted below, the banks and the contracting corporations they represented might well differ in opinion. The categories under discussion were, *inter alia*, (i) the security – was the line to be mortgaged, (ii) the financial control – how was the use of the loan proceeds to be monitored, how were the accounts to be controlled and audited, (iii) the appointment of the chief engineer – what were his responsibilities, to whom did he report, and who controlled his dismissal. And on this last, the Groups argued among them-selves and with the Chinese on the nationality of the foreign chief engineer, who, it was assumed, would direct purchases to his own nationals and, especially important to the French, would encourage Chinese employees to speak his language.

The easier terms, those involving less control, came to be characterized as the so-called 'Tientsin–Pukow (T–P) terms' representing the aspirations of the Young China Party for a Chinese constructed and administered railway system. The first agreement consciously meeting these requirements was, by definition, the Tientsin–Pukow Railway Agreement of 1908 as accepted by E.G. Hillier of the Hongkong Bank, acting temporarily for the B&CC; the tighter controls actually favoured by the B&CC's representative in China, J.O.P. Bland, were referred to as the 'Canton–Kowloon (C–K) terms'.[i] When

---

[i] In essence the differences were as follows: (i) control of construction on C–K terms, the chief engineer with limited executive power was appointed by the Bank, removable by China; T–P terms, only consulting powers, appointed by China with Bank's approval, removable by China, (ii) control of expenditure, C–K terms, requisitions authorized by Bank's agent, funds from loan

Bland subsequently rejected 'Tientsin–Pukow terms' for the Hukuang lines, the Chinese turned to the DAB, setting in motion a chain of events not fully resolved until the agreements of 1911. As the negotiations for the principal rail lines prove, the Chinese retained a surprisingly broad area of manoeuvrability throughout this period of their reputed political weakness.

With reference to those railways organized under foreign management, there developed the increasingly strongly based Rights Recovery Movement in China, and the Hongkong Bank was among the financial organizations which financed recovery of foreign railways for the central Chinese administration.

Meanwhile there was developing within China a serious argument over the overall organization of the railways. Was this to be a national enterprise, or was it to be at least in part a series of projects sponsored by provincial leaders and the local gentry? The role of the gentry was one of the unresolved questions causing the growing unrest which eventually overthrew the dynasty, but it was also a factor which delayed and confused the issue of railway development, as, for example, in the matter of the progress of the Yueh–Han line north from Canton or the construction of the Shanghai–Hangchow–Ningpo line.

In brief, all aspects of railway development were subject to negotiation on the basis of principles which were themselves in dispute. Once these matters were resolved sufficiently to draw up preliminary agreements, sudden shifts in market rates, political allegiances, or international power relationships could upset commercial arrangements and cause time-consuming recourse to political authorities both in China and in Europe and America.

It is in this context of unresolved and conflicting interests that the following sections must be understood; it is for this reason that they must, in a history primarily concerned with a single institution, be selective and abbreviated.

The Hongkong Bank did not always negotiate in its own name but as agent for the British and Chinese Corporation or the Chinese Central Railways, and the roles of Hillier for the Bank and J.O.P. Bland for the B&CC or CCR were not always coordinated, with Bland complaining, as had von Hansemann of the DAB earlier, that Hillier often moved ahead on his own. The Bank was not itself directly involved in the construction aspects of the railways, but to the extent that the terms in the prospectus dealing with technical matters affected the marketability of the loan, the Bank was interested; nor was it always possible to separate the financial interests of the Bank from the overall concerns of the B&CC or the CCR.

---

proceeds transferred from London for deposit in Bank; T–P terms, expenditures subject to audit only, (iii) control of receipts, C–K terms, British accountant-in-chief participated in management, banking of earnings with the Bank; T–P terms, annual report of receipts only.[65]

THE PRINCIPAL RAILWAY NEGOTIATIONS

The position in 1905/06 and general comments

The year 1905 was a bench-mark. After the Boxer Protocol, the preliminary agreements were taken up one by one for finalization, but, with the exception of the Shanghai–Nanking line, the main breakthrough occurred in 1907/08, following which the focus was on the complex Hukuang negotiations, which continued into 1911 and which will be covered in Chapter 7.

By the end of 1905 the parties were in place. The Boxer Indemnity controversy had been settled by the Gold Loan of 1905, the Pekin Syndicate signed an agreement with China covering rights recovery in the Taokow–Chinghau line, the Hongkong Bank/DAB Agreement of 1905 was amended, the French and Belgians had been brought into the Chinese Central Railways, and the American syndicate had apparently given up its Hankow–Canton concession, the redemption financing arrangements for which had been concluded with the Government of Hong Kong.

Japan had defeated the Russian Empire, and the implications of that would be quickly realized.

On the Chinese side Sheng Hsuan-huai had been replaced by the able, American-educated T'ang Shao-yi as Director-General of Railways. Charles Addis wrote to J.O.P. Bland, the B&CC's representative in China, 'T'ang does not love the English. Why should he? He has no reason to. But he has brains and that is half the battle. He will not, like a stupid man, let his feelings blind him to his country's, which is his own, interest. [Sir John] Jordan knows him well and likes him.'[66]

In 1905, with the exception of the Pekin Syndicate's loan, which involved Lloyds Bank and the Imperial Bank of China, no loans covering the finance of railway construction were completed. It was rather a year in which the Chinese and the foreigners reorganized and rethought the railway question, the former in the context of Rights Recovery, the latter in the hope of renewed negotiations to complete the promises of 1898/99. As Charles Addis expressed it to his confidant Dudley Mills,

Our railway negotiations for the Tientsin–[Pukow] (Anglo-German), the Szechuan (Anglo-French), the Shanghai–Nanking, the [Shanghai–Hangchow]–Ningpo, Hankow–Canton and Canton–Kowloon lines are all suspended. Why? Well, I believe it is because the territorial integrity of China having been guaranteed by the Anglo-Japanese Treaty, China is determined to make her railways her own and can no longer be squeezed into doing what she does not want to do by threats of territorial aggression. All negotiations are hung up for a year and in this I think the Chinese government is wise. They want time to take breath amid the shouting of the railway touts, to examine the schemes they keep pressing on them and a break to see to what extent native capital is available for native railway enterprise.[67]

The Customs decree

The successful financing of China's railway development was dependent on the security offered, and, although the revenues supervised by the Imperial Maritime Customs had been fully pledged for past loans, foreign confidence in China's credit generally and in new offerings especially would, it was assumed, be undermined if the integrity of the IMC were questioned.

China's rights in the question had been modified by (i) those clauses of the 1896 and 1898 indemnity loans which provided that during their life the 'administration of the (IMC) shall remain as at present constituted' and (ii) the 1898 declaration on the British nationality of the Inspector-General.

In May 1906, virtually on the eve of Sir Robert Hart's intended retirement, an Imperial edict ordered the IMC, which through Hart had reported only to the Tsungli Yamen or its successor the Wai-wu Pu, to be subordinate to two commissioners, T'ieh Liang, President of the Hu Pu (Board of Revenue), and T'ang Shao-yi, Vice-President of the Wai-wu Pu. There was no explanation, but foreign fears seemed confirmed when in July the Chinese established the Shui-wu Ch'u, or Revenue Council, which departmentalized the change.[68]

Charles Addis in London immediately asked the Foreign Office for an explanation.[69]

The Hongkong Bank's Peking Agent, E.G. Hillier, cabled his concern. He probably over-reacted: to him this appeared a potentially major change which would have an impact on British prestige, adversely affect the price of China securities on the London market, and possibly result in the removal of Customs funds from the Hongkong Bank.[70] In August when Hillier was on leave in Dorset he again wrote to Addis discussing what steps ought to be taken; meanwhile the China Association and *The Times* offered forceful advice, and questions were asked in Parliament.[71]

The reaction of the British Legation, however, was tempered by the knowledge that the edict had been issued on the advice of T'ang Shao-yi, whose ability was respected; events had made him both popular and powerful. Furthermore, the Canton–Kowloon Railway negotiations had been moved to Peking and the Chargé d'Affaires, L.D. Carnegie, supposed, correctly, that T'ang would be the chief Chinese negotiator.[72]

A touch of reality was contained in Hart's forthright letter to the Hongkong Bank's acting Peking Agent, H.G. Gardner.[73] Hart had never had patience with the complex provisions in the loan agreements for 'security', and he began by repeating his long-standing position – an edict alone is sufficient security; it pledges the resources of the Empire. Thus for Hart all else was superfluous window-dressing. Loans secured on the Customs were not necessarily repaid from Customs revenues, nor were Customs revenues handled in any way by the IMC, subtle points which tended to be forgotten.

Prince Ch'ing had assured the Legation that the relevant terms of the 1896 and 1898 loan agreements and declaration would be observed. All further representations by the Legation would be interference in China's internal affairs and counter-productive. Hart recognized this. Is the Maritime Customs, he asked Gardner, a Chinese department or a bondholders' trustee? If the latter then it will exist only so long as it is forced on China by foreign power; if the former then the more subordinate it is, the less the Legations interfere, the longer it will survive to serve China.[74]

Hart did recognize the change would have an impact on the morale of the service and that unfortunate changes might be made.

The Foreign Office was frustrated and uncertain. Then on August 17 Charles Addis called, left a brief but concise memorandum, and within 24 hours instructions consistent with Addis's advice had been cabled Carnegie, the chargé d'affaires in Peking. Restating policies which could not be pursued, Addis had recommended simply that Hart should be persuaded to postpone his retirement; with Hart still in control, adverse policies were less likely. The passage of time would clarify the situation. 'In this way, and in this way only,' Addis concluded, 'the situation may yet be saved.'[75]

Three days later Carnegie in Peking was strongly advised by cable to visit Peitaiho, the north China seaside resort where Hart was resting.[76]

Hart agreed to postpone retirement.

The general and immediate concern ended when T'ang in an interview with Hart instructed him to issue a circular to the Customs staff assuring them of continuity. T'ang is reported as commenting, 'Yes: China for the Chinese is a thing that must be recognized, but also *it must not be exaggerated.*'[77] Young China had made its point; to go further would be to undermine China's credit position. Possibly the reaction had been stronger than T'ang Shao-yi himself had expected. In any case Hart remained in China, the IMC operated virtually as before, but subordinate to a new department as the Chinese intended, and China was ready to negotiate the outstanding railway agreements.

The agreements – general terms
In the following sections, the focus is on the conditions peculiar to each particular railway, with special reference to those relevant to the Hongkong Bank and its associated companies, the British and Chinese Corporation and the Chinese Central Railways.

The four Hongkong Bank loans described below carried a nominal interest of 5% and a length of 30 years and contained a clause stating the conditions, usually including a $2\frac{1}{2}$% premium, under which the loan could be prepaid (see Table 6.2).

IMC-supervised revenues were fully committed and thus no longer available as security for new loans. This had been an immediately acceptable form of security recognized by the foreign investor, although Hart was correct in considering that the matter was, after all, one of sovereign risk. Another obvious security was a mortgage on the railway line, but this proved increasingly unacceptable to a China newly awakened to protest its rights and concerned with the possibility of foreign control of its railways and the lands adjacent to them. Another security was the assignment of the earnings of the line, but in foreign eyes this would be less valuable if financial control was assigned to the Chinese administrators.

In consequence, each loan agreement sets forth a list of miscellaneous revenues on which the loan is secured, and this the potential investor could accept or not, presumably relying in the end on the Legation's recognition of the loan as having been authorized by edict according to the laws of China, making it, once again, a sovereign risk loan.

The accounts which follow vary in length reflecting the importance of the railway to the history of the Hongkong Bank rather than to the history of China, of the foreign Powers, or even of railways. Lines within the concessions granted to Russia and/or Japan in the Northeast, although an integral part of the history of China, were guaranteed by Japan or instruments of Japan, and have been listed, therefore, in Chapter 2.

There is a logic to following the negotiations for a single line through at least to the agreement. Nevertheless, each negotiation impinged on the others, and their inter-relationship should be kept in mind.

Tientsin–Mukden

The first post-Boxer Uprising task was to detach the Russians from the Tientsin–Mukden Railway and check their removal of its property, material pledged as security to the bondholders to whom the Hongkong Bank remained responsible. Hillier as early as October 1900 had written of the confusion on the line and the restoration attempts within the Great Wall by German and Russian military authorities.[78]

The early administration of the line from Peking to Shanhaikwan, that is, within the Wall, fell to the British Military authorities, and the turn over to the Chinese Civil Administration was effected by an agreement on April 29, 1902.[79]

The two Chinese administrators, Yuan Shih-k'ai and Hu Yü-fen then undertook an 'additional agreement', in consultation with the British Minister, Sir Ernest Satow, for the administration of the railway 'in the interests of the Chinese public revenue and of the British bondholders'. This contained control arrangements, which, although of benefit to the bondholders and of use as a precedent for future Bank and B&CC negotiations, should have been a matter for negotiation with the B&CC and of no concern to the British Minister. The agreement to incorporate into the Northern Railways Administration, as part of the security for the 1898 B&CC loan, lines built by the military authorities was, on the other hand, a benefit which only the political authority could have bestowed.

Shanghai–Nanking

The preliminary agreement for the Shanghai–Nanking line had been signed, after international discussions described in Chapter 5, in May 1898. Negotiations between the British and Chinese Corporation, represented by Byron Brenan, former British Consul-General in Shanghai, and the Director-General of the Imperial Railway Administration, Sheng Hsuan-huai, began in 1902 and the loan agreement was signed in July 1903.

The new negotiations confirmed Chinese determination to retain as far as possible full control over their railways, and the resulting delays were ascribed by Sheng to Brenan's 'artful bickering'.[80] Sheng attempted to improve the terms of the 1898 agreement by reference to the Sino-American Agreements of 1898 and 1900 covering the Hankow–Canton Railway; in this he was only partially successful. Brenan, while making concessions to Chinese sovereignty, kept control in British hands and secured remuneration for the administrative and construction supervision services of the B&CC through a 5% commission on material purchased; the Hongkong Bank would receive a commission for servicing the loan equivalent to $\frac{1}{4}$ of 1% on the interest and principal as repaid; and there was included a profit-sharing clause which assigned 20% of the net profits of the line to the B&CC for their disposition in favour of the bondholders.

In places where the Hongkong Bank had no agency, the final agreement, which was signed by the Bank (H.M. Bevis) as agent for the B&CC, called for the use of banking facilities provided by the Sheng-promoted Imperial Bank of China, for which the Hongkong Bank's retired Tientsin Manager A.W. Maitland had become the first foreign chief executive, 'it being the intention of the British and Chinese Corporation to utilize the Imperial Bank as much as practicable for facilitating the movement of Funds'. The agreement also referred to the purchase of Chinese products where appropriate. The loan was to include funds for the purchase of the already rebuilt Shanghai–Woosung line.[81]

The terms were a first but still unsatisfactory post-Boxer step towards the attainment of Chinese objectives.

Of the total loan amount of £3,250,000 authorized on the primary security of the railway and its property, £2,250,000 was issued in July 1904 at 5% and 97½ with a low fixed contract price of 90, reflecting the risk taken in a poor market. The underwriters took £750,000 firm, leaving for the public £1.5 million of which the Hongkong Bank took £100,000 firm and underwrote a further £175,000. The Hongkong Bank's 'profit' (undefined) as shown in the semi-annual unpublished accounts was $243,000 or approximately 1.1% of the nominal value of the loan as issued (@ an exchange of 2s:0d).

Despite open Foreign Office suport, the public took up only £550,000 of the bonds, an apparently devastating comment on investors' interest in China railway loans.[82] London Office had cabled Tientsin to hurry the final stages of the negotiations; Cameron was aware that £3 million of Cape of Good Hope bonds would be issued on July 1 at 3½% and 95; there was also the immediate prospect of an issue of Brazilian bonds with a nominal value of £4 million, but the Shanghai–Nanking Agreement was not signed until July 9. On the actual days subscriptions for these were open, London Office reported a 'general depression' on the Stock Exchange.[83]

The reluctance of the London capital market overshadowed subsequent negotiations and, as already noted, encouraged various forms of international cooperation, including the participation of French and Belgian interests in the CCR. Whatever the temporary Stock Exchange problem had been, the bonds had gone to a discount of 2⅞% and were quoted below 97½ for several months.

This first issue was not expected to cover the entire cost of construction, and the opportunity for local Chinese finance existed throughout these operations. It was not, however, sufficiently forthcoming; consequently political pressure for retrocession of the line was ineffective and a further tranche of the agreed 1904 loan was issued in January 1907 for £650,000 at 5% and par, with a favourable contract price of 95½ firm.

The price to the Chinese has caused comment in the histories, but it was not, as Bland expressed his concern in a personal letter to Addis, a reckless gamble. The loan was to be issued at par in a favourable market and underwritten; even then Addis admitted the 4½ point differential, which left no room for error, was possible only if the underwriting were done at 1%; the underwriting syndicate was operating on a 2% basis and Addis accordingly committed the Hongkong Bank to underwrite the entire tranche at 1% and it was on this basis that the Board of the B&CC accepted the price. In fact, the Bank's willingness caused the underwriters to rethink, and they first lowered their commission to 1½% and then to 1% to meet the Bank.[84]

But, Bland asked (in personal correspondence), why if the Bank were willing to work on a 1% commission should an underwriting syndicate be brought in at all? To this Addis responded that the Hongkong Bank had drawn together a number of companies which underwrote everything offered, the good with the bad; the Bank could not withhold the profitable issues and expect this syndicate to help in difficult times. This was especially true after the underwriters had been forced, in view of the public disinterest, to take up some 63% of the 1904 tranche.[85]

In fact, the 1907 tranche was heavily over-subscribed, but the B&CC's 'profit' was only £6,500, which Addis stated was 'insufficient to cover the Loan's share of the corporation's general expenses'.[86] Too late T'ang Shao-yi cabled Addis through Bland for an option on £100,000 for Chinese subscribers; the loan had been issued and the Bank itself held only £25,000.[87]

The line was opened for through traffic in April 1908 and a working agreement determined. Further financing of £150,000 to recover the cost of land purchases was required in 1913 and the new 6% bonds were purchased for public issue by the B&CC at 92.[88]

A digression – the Tientsin Gas and Electric Company

While these grand operations emanating from Peking and executed in London were capturing world attention, the Hongkong Bank continued to operate normally from its offices in the East and Head Office in Hong Kong. On June 2, 1904, for example, D.H. Mackintosh, the Tientsin Manager, wired Shanghai for permission to underwrite the flotation of 7% debentures of the Tientsin Gas and Electric Company, total issue, Ts80,000. The company had a capital of Ts2.5 lacs and was operating under a fifteen-year contract with the British Municipal Council. The underwriting commission was 2½% and Mackintosh required an immediate answer.

The reply, which would seem to have been modelled on an Imperial rescript, was – act at your discretion.[89]

A 1909 Bank inspector's report suggests that, despite all warnings to Bank Managers not to lock up funds, relationships in a small community can set the pace. The company was not as yet on its feet and with an apparently 'permanent' overdraft of Ts25,000, the Inspector, W. Adams Oram, noted, somewhat impractically, his preference for a further 'covering' debenture issue. Risk capital from a transient foreign community is understandably difficult to obtain, but 'temporary' accommodation from an exchange bank for long-run requirements is unsound. Nevertheless the leading bank often had little choice.

Canton–Kowloon (Chinese section)

When hereafter China constructs a railway to the boundary of the Kowloon territory under British control, arrangements shall be discussed.

Convention of June 9, 1898.[90]

The Shanghai–Nanking line touched key British interests in the Yangtze Valley, but the Canton–Kowloon line was seen as vital to the prosperity and usefulness of the British Crown Colony of Hong Kong. Delay in any railway negotiation could be expected to provoke criticism from imperialist correspondents in Peking and business representatives in Shanghai but to this would be added for the Kowloon line pressures from the Governor of Hong Kong, from the Colony's China Association, and from all those concerned with the Empire, however narrowly defined. This impatience was matched by the opposition on the Chinese side, especially from the always anti-foreign Cantonese, now reinforced by the support of the Liang-Kwang Viceroy, by their own business interests in local railways, by the interposition of extraneous issues, and by the relationship of the Hankow–Canton Railway and the talked-of deep water port at Whampoa near Canton as a possible terminus for the major trunk line.

The Deutsch-Asiatische Bank was not involved in the Canton–Kowloon line.

The first official reference to the Canton–Kowloon Railway is in the 'Convention respecting an extension of the Hong Kong territory' by means of a 99-year lease to expire in 1997. The reference was formalized the same year as one of the five concessioned railways demanded by Sir Claude MacDonald, and in 1899 Sheng Hsuan-huai signed a preliminary agreement for the line with the British and Chinese Corporation. Then progress was checked by the Boer War and the Boxer Uprising.

The final agreement was signed in Peking on March 7, 1907, by J.O.P. Bland for the British and Chinese Corporation, H.G. Gardner, acting Agent Peking, for the Hongkong and Shanghai Banking Corporation, and by T'ang Shao-yi, who had replaced Sheng Hsuan-huai as Director-General of Railways in late 1905, for the Wai-wu Pu.[91]

Addis reported that the money market was in a good position to take the issue, and the Imperial Chinese Railways, Canton–Kowloon Railway loan of £1.5 million, was issued at 5% and par, with a contract price of 94; subscriptions were closed on April 30 and the loan was over-subscribed, the Hongkong Bank being allotted £59,000 on its own account, with an underwriting interest in £199,000. Plans had been approved for setting aside £750,000 for local Chinese subscription with the Viceroy to accept this allotment at the underwriter's price, but, as with most such local finance schemes, this was not taken up.

The loan was for what became known in Hong Kong as the 'Chinese section', that is from Canton to Shumchun/Lowu on the border of the 'New Territories'; the remaining 35 kms of line was financed as a Hong Kong Government Railway. Construction on the Chinese sector began in August

1907 and the railway was completed in 1911. Due to competition from river steamers, the line was not profitable and disputes prevented it from being linked with the line running north from Canton until new agreements were reached in 1934 (see Volume III).

The 'British Section', the line from Tsim Sha Tsui (Kowloon) to the Chinese Border at Lowu, was constructed separately by the Government of Hong Kong and financed by Government borrowing on the London market under the authority of Ordinance No. 11 of 1905, thus avoiding any direct involvement by the Hongkong Bank (see Chapter 7).

A review of the Hongkong Bank's other activities

The first half of 1907 was, according to the minutes of the Board of Directors, a busy time for the Bank. In addition to the Canton–Kowloon Railway loan the Bank had participated in the issue of the £23 million 5% Japanese Government Sterling Loan at 99½ and was in April in the process of increasing the Bank's capital by $2.5 million.

In May the Bank was involved with the Crown Agents for the 4% Colonies Loan of £5 million at 99, underwriting £200,000 and having to take up £89,500. Also in May the Bank underwrote Shanghai Club debentures worth Ts275,000 to permit the construction of the new building which would house, so it would be claimed, the longest bar in the world.

Funds had been allocated to the relief of staff in the San Francisco earthquake; to compensate for his blindness Hillier was voted £100 per annum to enable him to employ a secretary; and the Government of Hong Kong obtained the Bank's agreement to the moving of various statues of the royal family around Statue Square, the Bank taking the opportunity to confirm that its assignment of its property between the Head Office building and the sea as a public open space remained discretionary with the Board.

There were frauds in Batavia, Sourabaya, Shanghai, and Singapore; in Penang a compromise was reached over sums owing by the compradore.

Railways were but one concern of the Hongkong Bank.

The course of negotiations

Strategically the great north–south trunk line from Peking to Canton, and on to Hong Kong, was of the greatest importance, cutting across the Yangtze Valley at Hankow and affecting British interests in the South. In 1898 only Jardine, Matheson and Co. among British firms was qualified to make a practical bid for the concession, but they had expressed caution on the economics of trunk lines, and, in any case, the prize slipped away. This story will be told in Chapter 7. Its present relevance is that if the line were under non-British control and if the Chinese were financed to develop Whampoa as a deep-water port, Hong Kong might be bypassed. Although a deep-water port was not economically feasible and the bypassing of Hong Kong was never a practical issue since *inter alia* it assumed the development of a supporting, Canton-focused railway network which could neither be financed nor constructed, it was nevertheless an issue which could arouse emotions and force a priority consideration for the Canton–Kowloon line.

The B&CC, however, gave post-Boxer priority, with Foreign Office approval, to the Shanghai–Nanking line. The unfavourable state of the capital market in London, the China-wide involvement of the B&CC, and the Corporation's shortage of top personnel capable of negotiating with the Chinese and the Legation in cases where preliminary agreements were being challenged clause by clause were, however, factors bound to cause delays. The Corporation was in consequence severely criticized by the China Association and others impatient for the 'opening of China' and development of the markets of the interior.

Nor was China prepared nor her Government staffed to give priority to a multiplicity of complex railway negotiations. The plea was one railway at a time, and each railway required time. It was not that potential investors were impatient. They were if anything only marginally interested. There were those, however, with a private vision of a China opened, and for diverse reasons they pressed their Home Governments for action and blamed the banks and syndicates for inaction, disregarding both political and economic realities.

The Hongkong Bank offered only on-the-job banking training to its junior staff, the Bank's Chinese language program had not been developed, and men at the second level, Accountant or, in larger offices, Sub-Manager, were usually required for routine tasks. Cameron, Addis, and Hillier grew in the job as the loans grew; they could depend on support from the Tientsin Manager, on occasion from his Accountant, and from the Shanghai Sub-Manager, but that was all. This situation was not peculiar to the Bank; it was typical of British firms in the East at least until the late 1950s. Consequently all the others involved in development financing in post-Boxer China were brought in – Byron Brenan, J.O.P. Bland, George Jamieson, and S.F. Mayers in China, and Murray Stewart in London for the Hongkong Bank.[j]

Local Hongkong Bank Managers were in contact, usually through the compradore, with the key officials and served these officials with considerable

---

[j] B. Brenan (B&CC), George Jamieson (Pekin Syndicate and B&CC), and S.F. Mayers (successor to Bland) had been taken from the Consular service, Bland (B&CC and CCR) had been private secretary to Sir Robert Hart, secretary to the Shanghai Municipal Council and a journalist, while Murray Stewart was a former Eastern staff member of the Hongkong Bank, who had left to join his brother in a Hong Kong brokerage firm.

flexibility and expertise, but in this section the focus is on matters which came ultimately for judgement in the City.

J.R.M. Smith as Chief Manager of the Hongkong Bank held discussions in January 1904 with the Officer Administering the Government, F.H. May, suggesting a loan guaranteed on the London market in the tradition of Indian railway loans, and although this was accepted by May, a Colonial Office minute suggests that the idea was not well received in London. Underlying London's concern was (i) the actual feasibility of the railway, given the possibility of a 'rising' of the local population of the area and (ii) the state of the Hong Kong Government's finances which would neither permit an annual contingent liability of the estimated $429,000 required nor yet permit the Government to guarantee a loan on the London market.[92]

In May 1904 came word that the Shanghai–Nanking Railway negotiations were in their final stages, and F.H. May cabled:

I venture to urge that pressure should be brought upon the British and Chinese Corporation to make similar arrangements for the Canton–Hong Kong railway. The Chamber of Commerce and China Association have both recently urged upon me the necessity of demanding that the corporation should either utilize or resign its concession.[93]

The Colonial Office continued its pressure on the B&CC, eventually stating that the Government considered the matter to be 'one of urgency and trusts that it may receive very early attention'; a copy of the letter was given to the newly appointed Governor, Sir Matthew Nathan.

When Nathan arrived in Hong Kong in July he referred in his first speech before the Legislative Council to the Canton–Kowloon Railway which he said he wished to see completed during his term of office.[k] Nor, given the problems involved, is it surprising that some three months later there had been no report of progress. The China Association, Hong Kong branch, was again urging action.[94]

In November the Committee of the China Association in London minuted new-found wisdom in two important but related points: (i) the delays were due to the Chinese rather than the B&CC, thus giving a respite to that much criticized organization and (ii) Sir Thomas Jackson's rather shrewd observation that 'the Chinese want to build their own railways and should be allowed to do so'. To this last the response of the Committee was, 'Yes, if they will.'[95]

The Canton Viceroy, Ts'en Ch'un-hsüan, had no intention of accepting a preliminary agreement negotiated without local approval in 1899, and while the negotiations centred in Canton little progress was made, despite direct

[k] Sir Matthew Nathan left Hong Kong in April 1907, less than two months after the agreement had been signed in Peking and before construction started; Sir Frederick Lugard was Governor when the railway opened in 1911.

communications between Governor Nathan and the Viceroy. Ts'en had led troops to the rescue of Peking during the Boxer Uprising, had accompanied the Court on its Western tour, and had became a favourite of the Empress Dowager; he was an opponent of Yuan Shih-k'ai, who was involved in northern railway negotiations.

In effect, the Canton Viceroy unilaterally attempted to cancel the preliminary agreement and undertake the entire financing and construction of the line from Canton to the Shumchun/Lowu border point from Chinese resources.[96] Only when an Imperial edict transferred the problem to Peking could progress be made; in the capital an agreement was eventually negotiated with the Wai-wu Pu, represented by T'ang Shao-yi.

Governor Nathan meanwhile pursued an active policy. He prepared both for the possibility that, if negotiations with the B&CC should fail, the corporation would indeed resign their concession and that the Chinese would then be faced with the task of financing the construction of their own railway. Nathan had already made £1.1 million available to Chang Chih-tung, the Wuchang Viceroy, to enable him to buy out the existing concessional rights on the Canton–Hankow line (see Chapter 7). He was unsuccessful, however, in obtaining any official Chinese admission of a connection between the assistance to Chang and an agreement relative to the construction on the Canton–Kowloon Railway.

The Hong Kong Government loan to the Viceroy had been financed by borrowing without formal authority short-term funds from the Crown Agents at Bank (of England) rate, and Nathan needed legislative authority to cover his financial position. Taking advantage of this, he obtained authority (Ordinance No. 11 of 1905) to borrow £2 million, of which £400,000 was to enable the Canton Viceroy, in the context of the real possibility that the B&CC negotiations would break down, to begin construction of a purely Chinese line towards Hong Kong.[1]

These financial manoeuvres were a way of bypassing the need to finance through the Hongkong Bank. The Crown Agents had provided Hong Kong with the initial funds on a short-term basis; with the ordinance as the ultimate security, the Governor then considered ways of replacing this borrowing with long-term funds, either by the sale of Government stock, or, ironically, as a last resort, through an overdraft from the Hongkong Bank at the usual Government rate.[98]

This is an example of British Imperial finances in disarray. As a Colonial Office minute commented, 'This is a curious position – here is a question

---

[1] The £2 million was composed of the following sums: £1.1 million as a loan to the Wuchang Viceroy, £0.5 million to construct the British section of the Canton–Kowloon Railway, and £0.4 million to assist the Canton Viceroy.[97]

which may be one of considerable importance from an Imperial point of view in which the Imperial Govt declines to intervene or accept any risk, but asks Hong Kong to do it for them.'[99]

The cancellation of the American concession and the prospect of a British-controlled line from the Yangtze to Canton, by seeming to eliminate the 'red-herring' of Whampoa, gave new encouragement to the negotiations, the role of the B&CC was again questioned, and completion of financial arrangements for the 'British sector' of the railway put further pressure on the British negotiators, who by this time had become convinced that the Canton Viceroy could not be moved. Considerable goodwill had been gained in Hankow, but an exchange between the Viceroy in Canton and the Governor of Hong Kong in December/January showed that the two were as far apart as ever.[100]

As T'ang Shao-yi, the Wai-wu Pu appointed negotiator, summarized developments:

> The Viceroy Ts'en [Ch'un-hsüan] held, however, that local conditions had changed, and desired to change the modus operandi to that adopted in the case of the Northern Railway Loan.
> The Corporation argued that the existing understanding must be adhered to, and, as neither side would give way, it was not until half a year had elapsed in fruitless discussions that an Edict was issued in the fifth month of this year [June–July 1906], commanding that negotiations with the Corporation should be taken up by the Wai-wu Pu.[101]

In fact T'ang had had a difficult time; despite his support from Yuan Shih-k'ai (or perhaps because of it) the criticism from Canton combined with that of reactionary elements in Peking almost neutralized him at just the moment when Addis, recognizing that the success of the second tranche of the Nanking–Shanghai loan and the conditions of the market made this the best time to issue, was pressing Bland, the B&CC representative in Peking, for a conclusion.[102] Fortunately, Carnegie and the Legation had handled the saga of the Customs edict calmly and T'ang had not been alienated; he was thus willing to persevere on the Canton–Kowloon loan.

The terms of the Canton–Kowloon Agreement

Pursuant to the Imperial edict of 1906 the final negotiations were held in Peking; at the formal meetings there were four Chinese representatives headed by T'ang Shao-yi, with two representing the Viceroy of the Liang-Kwang provinces, and the secretary of the Wai-wu Pu. J.O.P. Bland represented the British and Chinese Corporation.

At the conclusion of the negotiations the Canton Viceroy remained dissatisfied with the terms of the agreement, but after the signing his objections were countered by T'ang Shao-yi, who listed one by one how he had improved on both the Shanghai–Nanking and the Northern Railway terms. T'ang noted particularly (i) the elimination of profit-sharing with bondholders, (ii) the commutation of the syndicate's 5% commission for services and administration to a fixed sum of £35,000, and (iii) the lowering of the premium required for early redemption from 20% (Northern Railways) to 2½%. He also touched on the contract price, referred to confusingly in contemporary documents as the 'issuing price' or 'price of issue', and on the method of calculating the rate of exchange.[103] On these two last mentioned points, more should be said.

The price. The Canton–Kowloon Agreement assumed that the loan would be issued at par with a contract price of 94. The price to the public reflected the state of Chinese finances, the position of other Chinese issues in the market, and the condition of the London capital market (and the Bank rate) at the time of issue, not at the time of negotiation. The price which the syndicate expected to issue to the public affected the contract price, that is, the price to the Chinese. The difference between the issue and contract prices, or 'points', was affected by such factors as the expected cost of underwriting and, important in the Canton–Kowloon negotiations, the risk, whether, that is, the syndicate were taking the loan firm.

As for the first category, Addis estimated that at least four points were necessary just to meet fixed obligations: underwriting 1½%, Bank's commission 1%, Panmure Gordon (the Bank's brokers) ½ of 1%; stamps ½ of 1%, brokerage ¼ of 1% and printing ¼ of 1%. If, as in early loans, the underwriting were 2%, then the number of points necessary to cover fixed obligations could rise to six overall.

As for the second category, when the corporation took the loan firm, a risk element was involved and this would be reflected in the number of points required; the Shanghai–Nanking Agreement specifically states, 'any profit or loss in selling these bonds to the public shall be borne by or go to the Corporation'.[104]

T'ang pointed out that the contract price for the Northern lines (and the Shanghai–Nanking) was 90 but according to the logic of the above argument it does not follow, as T'ang inferred in his letter to Viceroy Ts'en, that the 94 rate was *a priori* 'exceptionally favourable' relative to 90; there was *inter alia* a new risk factor to be evaluated.[105]

The negotiations had continued for many months and, therefore, various prices had been named in the several drafts, each price reflecting the situation at the time. In the last stages the Hongkong Bank through Bland was urging 93, firm for 30 days; the Chinese insisted upon 96, the rate mentioned in T'ang's memorial.

The earlier talk of a higher contract price was based on factors which changed to China's disadvantage: (i) the Bank rate rose to 6%, (ii) the premium on China railway bonds already in the market dropped with prices falling from 103 to 100$\frac{3}{4}$, over two points, and Bland estimated that the new issue could be made only at approximately 99$\frac{1}{2}$–100, and consequently a contract price of 96 to the Chinese was an 'impossibility'.[106]

Under these circumstances 94 would seem, as T'ang urged the Viceroy to believe, a good price, but there was another factor involved; in view of market uncertainties and T'ang's successful pressing for a better price, the syndicate had withdrawn their agreement to take the loan firm. The figure of 94 depended upon there being a six-point differential, that actual issue to the public would be at par; if the market improved to permit an issue of 101, to use the illustration actually in the agreement, the contract price would be raised to 95.[m]

Was this gain of a point against additional risk an advantage to China? The answer would depend upon an evaluation of an overall 'underwriting policy' for China – had one existed; in the present case the one-point gain was probably in China's favour.

Rate of exchange and the position of the servicing bank. The Shanghai–Nanking Agreement stated that the Hongkong Bank should be the servicing agent for the loan, receiving $\frac{1}{4}$ of 1% commission on the amounts of interest and capital repaid from time to time. The funds were to be delivered in Shanghai sycee to the Bank in Shanghai and the exchange into sterling was to be settled with the Bank 'on the said date of payment at the rate fixed at the time of settlement'.

In the exchange of notes of July 1905 resolving questions relative to the Boxer Indemnity, it was agreed that 'China may obtain bills and telegraphic transfers as best suits her interests at any place and at any bank at the lowest price or by public tender...', and it was natural that to the Chinese negotiators for the Canton–Kowloon Railway this apparently improved term should be incorporated into the railway loan agreements.[108] The indemnity had special features which made such conditions reasonable; the railway loans were different and the Bank was quick to provide the explanation for this.

Bland's first response to the Chinese demand for the right to undertake exchange without restriction was to remind T'ang Shao-yi that as the Hongkong Bank was to service the loan, the effect of the proposed revision

---

[m] The Shanghai–Hangchow–Ningpo Loan of March 6, 1908, issued to the public at 99, provided for a contract price of 93$\frac{1}{2}$. Not all B&CC negotiated loans carried a six point differential; this example is purely illustrative. Indeed, it was agreed that any need for additional funds would be met by a further issue with a 5$\frac{1}{2}$ point differential, see Art. 15.[107]

could be to create 'artificial competition to the Bank's disadvantage'. The agreement as then drafted required the Bank to operate at 'the most favourable rates' and, Bland added, 'His Excellency would no doubt recognise the fact that its established reputation for fair dealing was sufficient guarantee that such rates would be given in the future as in the past.'[109]

On this matter the Hongkong Bank, which had conceded much in the course of the negotiations, stood firm.

As has been said of exchange banks generally, their profits came from turnover; their interest in such operations as public loan issues came from the continued business, both direct and indirect, that these would encourage. But there were specific factors involved. The Chief Manager, J.R.M. Smith, was reported as having insisted on the Hongkong Bank's handling the exchange; the issues are, moreover, fully explained by Charles Addis in a letter to the Foreign Office:

> In practice this [freedom to settle exchange when and with whom the Chinese please] would result not in fair competition, to which no objection could be taken, but in a quasi-monopoly to the continental bankers. They would be free to compete or not as it happened to suit them, with the result that the Hongkong Bank would be left with the exchange whenever it happened to be unfavourable. As the Bank is responsible for the service of the loan, we have no option in the matter; we are always obliged to remit at the rate of the day, whether it happens to suit us or not.
>
> It is not contended that the Chinese would fail to receive the market rate, but apparently the suspicion is entertained that the rate may be 'pulled' by the Bank in anticipation of an instalment falling due.[110]

His solution, which was ultimately accepted, was to concede to the Chinese the option to settle the rate of exchange at any time within six months prior to the date of payment of each instalment. 'Even if it were possible for the Bank to tamper with the rate for one day, it cannot be seriously argued that it could continue to do so every day for six months. Further than that we cannot go . . . it is impossible for us to give way.'[111] The Bank also agreed that, if China had *bona fide* gold funds available, defined as gold funds not resulting from a transfer made especially for this purpose, they were free to use them to make payments of principal and interest.

The Foreign Office authorized Jordan to support Addis's proposal.[112]

The exchange question has been seen as a political issue, but indeed there was nothing else the Hongkong Bank could do. Addis was aware of the precedent involved. All loan servicing when taken together would be a significant factor in the Shanghai exchange market, and the Bank which had ultimate responsibility for the transfer had to know where it stood. Under other terms in the agreement it had to be prepared to provide the exchange, and, if it were so prepared by a special positioning of its funds, it could not afford to be suddenly deprived of the business to meet the peculiar convenience of a competing bank. In a more nearly perfect and much larger market, these problems would not have been so important.

A misunderstanding may arise from the often-repeated statement that the Hongkong Bank set the 'official rate' in Shanghai and could therefore set an arbitrary exchange for the loan servicing. As noted previously, the Bank's so-called 'official rate' was merely the opening quotation of an admitted 'price leader'. The rate at which the Hongkong Bank or any bank would undertake to handle a major transfer was a matter for negotiation.[113]

On April 26, 1907, as Sir Ewen Cameron lay dying at his home in London, Charles Addis reported in his diary: 'Canton–Kowloon loan issued today. An instant success. That and our dispatch in getting the whole business put through in a couple of days has created a profound impression in the City and at the Colonial Office.'[114]

Tientsin–Pukow[115]

The preliminary agreement for the 1,085 km Tientsin–Pukow Railway was signed in 1899, the final agreement in January 1908, and the first or £3 million tranche of the £5 million loan to cover part of the cost of the line was issued in London (£1.11 million) and Berlin (£1.89 million) as the Imperial Chinese Government 5% Tientsin–Pukow Railway Loan at $98\frac{3}{4}$ with a contract price of 93 firm. Addis had intended to issue at 99, which with a ten shilling bonus coupon was equivalent to $98\frac{1}{2}$ net, but last minute market changes made this too risky; the Canton–Kowloon loan had just dropped to ($100\frac{3}{4}$ as quoted but after allowing for accrued interest =) $99\frac{1}{5}$. Addis then set $98\frac{3}{4}$ as the offer price to the public, but amended the instalments in the schedule to achieve a net price of $98\frac{1}{2}$, identical to that quoted for the German issue, as previously intended.[116]

Subscriptions were to be made through the Hongkong Bank as agents for the Chinese Central Railways and the Deutsch-Asiatische Bank; the closing date was March 31, 1908. The Hongkong Bank underwrote £80,000 at 1% commission and purchased £63,000 for the Bank's account. The minutes record a profit of £12,000. Describing this operation to Bland, Addis describes the care taken over the prospectus; it went through seventeen proofs. He also noted that Scottish insurance companies 'were particularly useful'.[117]

The issue was a success and rose immediately to a $\frac{3}{8}$ of 1% premium. An exchange between London and Tientsin illustrates the usual 'stagging' involved. At least some offices of the Bank were given advance notice of an issue; officers and possibly the compradore were invited to 'underwrite' the issue, subject to availability; there would also be an offer to the Chinese Government on underwriting terms; in the case of the first tranche of the Tientsin–Pukow loan, Tientsin was to inform the Government that they had been pre-allotted £260,000. The Bank's Tientsin staff requested £10,000, keeping £2,000 'for investment'; accordingly, on April 2 London cabled, 'Have allotted you £5,000 have sold £3,000 at ⅜% premium.'[118]

The balance of the loan was issued in June 1909 at par; as the agreement guaranteed the syndicate 5½ points, the Chinese received 94½.

Consistent with the Rights Recovery Movement and provincial interest in railways, the balance of the finance required was sought from Chinese sources, but only £250,000 was pledged and this was not paid-up, forcing the provincial Government to take up the bonds by borrowing at 7% from a German bank, presumably the DAB in Tsinan, the junction city for their line to Tsingtau.[119]

Accordingly the Groups involved in the original loan negotiated a 'Supplementary Loan' for £4.8 million of which £3 million (£1.11 million in London) was issued in September 1910 at 100½; the contract price, stipulated to be 5½ points below the price to the public, was thus 95; two advances against the balance were subsequently made by the DAB for a total of £89,000 and one from the CCR for £300,000.[120]

Early post-Boxer negotiations
The negotiations were reopened in January 1902 on German initiative and British acquiescence, but progress was slow and it soon became clear that British interest, due to the state of the London market, was minimal.[121] Indeed it was only in 1907 that serious consideration was given by the British authorities to furthering the activities of J.O.P. Bland, the appointed agent of the B&CC and the CCR, in the Tientsin–Pukow negotiations. The course of negotiations illustrates the whole range of problems confronting railway development in China.

The early delays were due partly to capital market problems in London and partly to the changes in corporate structure as the B&CC founded the Chinese Central Railways to include the smaller but rival Pekin Syndicate and then to expand to include the French and Belgian Groups. During this period both the Germans and the British considered and then rejected proposals to deal singly with the Chinese who were opposed to joint negotiations throughout. One fear entertained by both the British and the Chinese was that the Germans, having completed their line to Tsinan, where it would connect to the German-owned railway to Tsingtau, would not continue their portion south to the junction with the less profitable British southern third of the through route from Tientsin to Pukow.

Important as these factors were at the time, they did not feature in the final negotiations.

On completion of its reorganization and the assignment by the B&CC of the Tientsin–Pukow line to the CCR, the latter was in a position to deal directly with the DAB, but by 1905 the Chinese, heartened perhaps by the Japanese-British Alliance's guarantee of Chinese territorial integrity and pressed on the one hand by a conservative reaction and on the other by nationalists anxious to build the railways under Chinese control, successfully checked virtually all progress on foreign-financed railway negotiations. Interestingly, despite Bland's fears, the Chinese do not appear to have objected to the replacement of the B&CC by the CCR, despite the different national composition of the latter.[122]

In the final two years certain of the issues were clarified.

British interests were anxious to complete negotiations on the Canton–Kowloon, the Shanghai–Hangchow–Ningpo, and the Shanghai–Nanking lines, all of which, being wholly British concessions, took priority in British planning over the Tientsin–Pukow line which was two-thirds German, and in which the French, being shareholders in the Chinese Central Railways, shared an interest in the remaining one-third. At the same time British diplomatic support in Peking was hesitant due to a reevaluation of the policy which had won the concessions in the 'scramble' of 1898.

In 1907 the Chinese shifted the scene of the negotiations temporarily from Peking to the joint managership of two viceroys, Chang Chih-tung and Yuan Shih-k'ai, who, Bland assumed, would be unlikely to agree together on any issue and must, therefore, be seen as a delaying tactic. The Chinese authorities then made an attempt to cancel the concession on the grounds that the CCR and the DAB had done nothing to begin construction. In April 1907 Sir John Jordan, the British Minister, was authorized to cooperate with his German counterpart in pressing for the signing of an agreement, and, after strong representations by the German Minister on behalf of himself and Jordan, the negotiations were continued in Peking.[123]

In a sense these diplomatic manoeuvres were undertaken without coordination or even, perhaps, without regard for the position of the corporation's representative in the field. The Germans for their part had long since given up their demand for sovereign possession of the line in Shantung and were now prepared to retrocede their rights on other Shantung lines once the Tientsin–Pukow Agreement was signed. But the British had problems, both in China and at home.

The British Minister and the Foreign Office held back from full support of the Tientsin–Pukow line because, *inter alia*, they wished the entirely British Shanghai–Ningpo Railway Agreement signed at the same time. Progress on the latter was delayed by an internal struggle between the Yuan Shih-k'ai party and an opposition led by Sheng Hsuan-huai with the support of the 'Young China Party' and the Chekiang local gentry; withdrawing pressure for a signature on that railway agreement would be considered, the Foreign Office supposed, a victory for Sheng, and the Foreign Office wished to give support to Yuan. In this view the Hongkong Bank, as represented by Addis, concurred.[124]

Bland was apparently not fully informed of the complex political situation; there were different counsels in London and Peking. Bland saw only that an important project was being delayed. As the representative of the CCR, he was determined to expedite the matter and he proceeded with a singleness of purpose which, while successful in this instance, would lead to disaster in the Hukuang negotiations later.

Organizational and operational difficulties – the B&CC, the Bank, and Jardine's
The problems lay in the conflicting interests of those comprising the Chinese Central Railways, particularly in the long-term role of a major shareholder, the B&CC; this in turn affected the Hongkong Bank's position.

The B&CC was a public company based in London dependent for its success on management by two different organizations based in China. With the exception of J.O.P. Bland it had, virtually, no staff of its own; in China Bland had to work in cooperation with the B&CC's 'joint managers', one from the Hongkong Bank and one from Jardine's, or through 'agents' whose primary loyalty was to the Bank (as in the case of Hillier) or to Jardine's. Bland's growing disaffection would be yet another element in the problems confronting the boards of the B&CC and the CCR.

The B&CC board appears to have lacked a continuity of interest and, as William Keswick grew older, came in fact to be dominated first by the personality of Cameron and then by Addis. Bland confided for a time in Addis, but Addis received separate advice from Hillier and from City and other sources. He had to compromise with the other interests represented on the B&CC board – and on the CCR board when that corporation was involved; he consequently developed his policy independent of and in disagreement with Bland. Unfortunately, given the personality of Bland, suspicions and a breakdown in relationships would soon develop. (See the discussion of the controversy in Chapter 7.)

The confusion caused by these complex channels of responsibility and apparent conflicts of interest, which led to publicly criticized delays and eventual recriminations, was exacerbated by the strong personalities involved. Indeed, perception was not necessarily reality, and in the confusion legitimate differences of opinion could become suspect, lack of clear lines of authority meant that policy too often had to be modified 'behind the scenes'. The B&CC and to an even greater extent the CCR had been established 'at the top' by those in London, without, in the case of the Hongkong Bank, any note in the minutes of the Board of Directors. Those normally in charge in the field, the management of the Bank and the senior partners of Jardine, Matheson and Co., found themselves servicing a company about which they knew little, over which they had no effective control and whose interests, relative to their own, they found it difficult to give priority.

The alliance between the Bank and Jardine, Matheson and Co., which was the basis of the B&CC and hence, from the Bank's point of view, of the CCR, was again subject to the strains which had operated during the more informal arrangements between Cameron and Keswick in the 1880s. The interests of the Bank and of Jardine's were not the same. The position the Bank held in China was and would be compatible with that nation's sovereign integrity; the position of the B&CC, some argued, was not. Bland for the B&CC (and CCR) argued in contradiction to this view; 'concession lines' in the purely contractual sense did not constitute an infringement of sovereign rights and therefore the B&CC had a legitimate role in China as a leading representative of British development interests; the B&CC was misunderstood and criticized, often unfairly, for delays for which it was not responsible.

It was a danger of the British position in China that the occasional concession-seeker, investor, or syndicate representing some British interest other than the B&CC and CCR, approaching the Legation for sponsorship, too often proved either ill-timed or flawed. Nor was there a system by which these new contenders, if legitimate, could, as did interested firms in Germany, join the leading national China syndicate. Neither the B&CC nor the CCR ever had a long-term commitment of exclusive British official support in China, but under the circumstances, and as a matter of fact, major projects had of necessity to wait until these organizations and the Hongkong Bank were ready, or considered the market ready, to proceed.

Both the Bank and Jardine's had built strong and independent reputations for themselves in China. They both considered the maintenance of their respective positions more important than supporting the B&CC at the cost of losing their own identity or independence of action.

Bland expressed the Bank's position in the extreme form he attributed, probably unjustly, to E.G. Hillier: the Hongkong Bank was only interested in the loan – once the loan was made, the use of the funds and the success of the purpose for which the loan was made were not the Bank's concern.[125] If the loan were suitably secured and, if the project failed, the loan would nevertheless be repaid, provided that, in the case of dispute, British diplomatic intervention were successful.

This view can be put more charitably (as far as the Hongkong Bank's position is concerned) and probably more accurately by examining Bland's equally personal analysis of Jardine's position.

The 1898/99-style concessions, in which China agreed to permit foreign syndicates to develop and operate her railways and mines and to finance the initial stages from public loan issues through these same syndicates, were representative of a discredited policy which China was steadily reversing. From this it seemed to follow that companies such as the B&CC which were formed to exploit these concessions were also or soon would be without purpose and would consequently depart from China.

For such financial institutions as the Hongkong Bank, this argument continues, there was still room, for just so long as China could not raise her financial requirements internally. Even then, as the example of the Yokohama Specie Bank would suggest, a foreign bank's role would be limited to one of permitted participation (see Chapter 4).

In practice, Bland had to admit that Hillier was not opposed to the inclusion in the loan agreement of minimal control provisions which, by making the success of the project more likely, were designed to encourage subscription to the bond issue. At this point the argument (i) is one of what controls are necessary and appropriate and/or (ii) descends to personalities.[126]

Bland also had harsh comments for Jardine Matheson; he saw himself as the representative of something separate from both the Bank and Jardine's, that is, he was the representative of the B&CC. In the context of the long history of Bank/Jardine cooperation, this was a dangerous position to take. To the extent that the B&CC was already involved in long-run responsibilities, Bland's focus on the Corporation, who were after all his employers, was sound. Bland agreed that forced political concessions verged on the immoral, but he pointed out that 'concessions' in the normal sense were found in every nation and that China might well prefer to have certain of its development projects handled by a foreign company, Pauling and Co. in particular; for financial reasons China might find such a decision necessary. In any case, the role of the B&CC was, in his view, far from over.

At this point some sense of balance must be restored. The problems of the B&CC reflected the real problems of China operations; they had to be discussed and resolved somewhere and for better or for worse they were resolved through the medium of the B&CC. The delays, so often ascribed to the Corporation and, by those with inside knowledge, to the stormy conflicts which characterized its board meetings, were in fact delays inherent in the complexity of the tasks being undertaken, usually a result of forces outside the control of the B&CC.

But to return to Bland.

If in attempting a careful balance between the conflicting interests he represented, directly or indirectly, Bland were to be incautious, too personal, or too contentious, or if he by taking a strong position on controls made negotiation with the Chinese more difficult, his removal would be a virtual necessity. With Addis dominating the Bank's policy as well as the boards of both the B&CC and the CCR, Bland would soon be in difficulties, but that would come after completion of the Tientsin–Pukow Agreement.

These considerations had an immediate impact on the negotiations.

The concluding negotiations

In the summer of 1907 when Bland returned briefly to London, he left H. Cordes of the DAB to represent the CCR. This decision was countermanded by the CCR board at the request of the Peking Legation, writing through the Foreign Office, and the board accordingly appointed E.G. Hillier, which in turn met with the outspoken disapproval of Bland because of what Bland saw as Hillier's exclusively pro-Hongkong Bank approach.[127]

While Bland was absent, Hillier and Cordes, both ascribing responsibility to the other, made concessions to the Chinese which seriously weakened the foreign management control of the railway. The DAB cited this as an example of Hillier's '*Eigenmächtigkeit*' (arbitrary authority); Sir John Jordan complained of Cordes's indifference; but to Bland, who found the concessions impossible to reverse, this was typical of Hillier.[128] Hillier's and Cordes's decisions reflected the realities of the changing situation in China, and Bland would have been wise to recognize this. Indeed, Addis had previously warned Bland that after a full consideration of the latter's views, 'You should clearly understand that Hillier possesses the entire confidence of the [B&CC] Board, and you and Cordes [of the DAB] will be well advised in all your negotiations to treat him with complete frankness and to be guided by his advice.'[129]

At the other extreme, the Chinese representative, Liang Tun-yen, Acting Junior Vice-President of the Wai-wu Pu, objected to Bland replacing Hillier on the former's return from leave, but Sir John Jordan persuaded him that at this late stage the principal negotiator should not be changed.[130]

The final agreement, the so-called 'Tientsin–Pukow terms', gave up key management provisions which Bland had but recently and with difficulty confirmed in the November 1907 Canton–Kowloon Railway Agreement; the Tientsin–Pukow Agreement came closer to meeting the Chinese goal of total control of its own railways; it weakened the position of those who, like Bland, felt that the success of railway development depended, at least for the time being, on foreign fiscal, technical, and administrative leadership.

Specifically, Hillier and Cordes agreed to give up the requirement that the two appointed foreign engineers-in-chief (one British and one German) should have control over funds; furthermore there was to be no foreign accountant, but a copy of the accounts would be kept in England and be open for inspection. A Foreign Office minute states: 'No foreign control over the funds is risky, but apparently it was that or nothing.'[131]

Addis in London was more positive:

For better or worse the decision has been taken and we are entering upon a new era in railway agreements which, by stripping them of control and responsibility for construction, reduces them nearly to the level of pure finance, but not quite. In my opinion – I give it for what it is worth – such a development had become inevitable and I believe that, given the right kind of Engineer, the direction of the railway, both during and after construction, may still, in practice, be retained by the foreign syndicates to such an extent as to safeguard efficiently the rights of the bondholders.

As regards the future I do not think the Chinese will be able to dispense with the services of the B&CC in developing their railways for a long time to come.[132]

This attitude is consistent with the ultimate German evaluation of Hillier's action; although still not admitting joint responsibility, Cordes agreed that Hillier had conceded key demands made by Chang Chih-tung in July 1907 only when he recognized that the Chinese were unlikely otherwise to conclude the Tientsin–Pukow Agreement.[133]

Hillier's action set the stage for the disputes which would develop during the Hukuang Railways negotiations (see Chapter 7); it was a reflection of a more realistic position being taken by the Hongkong Bank, by Addis and Hillier. Nevertheless the weakness of the organizational structure of which the Hongkong Bank was a key part had been revealed. The B&CC was represented in China by joint managers, with Bland as the agent of the Corporation reporting back to London, providing a further rationale for the bypass of the Bank's Head Office in Hong Kong. Bland was to seek the advice and agreement of the Corporation's China managers, but these, he claimed, withheld support and by retaining a primary loyalty to their respective firms were in conflict with the agent of a corporation which was a public company, not simply the Bank and Jardine's in their often uncomfortable cooperation.

The Germans, who had little regard for either the organization or funding of the B&CC, alternated between frustration and anger at the British behaviour. Bland, who was concurrently a *Times* correspondent and might be characterized as anti-German, felt strongly that, although regretting the 1895 Bank/DAB Agreement, it existed; therefore, the only honourable course was to pursue the Tientsin–Pukow negotiations to a successful conclusion regardless of the percentage of German participation – and at one point he joined the Germans in complaining of lack of British diplomatic support; he was labelled pro-German for his pains.[134]

Meanwhile Charles Addis and Carl Meyer held a final conference with their German counterparts at the office of the Disconto-Gesellschaft in

Berlin on November 30 and December 1, at which latter, Addis records, 'I was again invited to address (the fourteen German representatives present) and succeeded in carrying all our points.'[135] Any further delay would be in China.

In the last days before the signing, the German Minister continued to press Jordan for action in Peking and in London the German Ambassador wrote to the Foreign Office. The German syndicate however suddenly began delaying tactics as their market turned weak, at one point asking for a postponement. For the British the position was reversed: in Peking Jordan continued to seek time to secure an agreement on the Soochow–Ningpo Railway concession, while in London Addis saw his market slipping away and pleaded urgency.[136]

In the end Jordan succumbed; Addis threatened his DAB associates that, if they did not accept immediately, the whole project would be delayed until after the 'Shanghai–Ningpo' agreement; accordingly after all the delays and recriminations the Tientsin–Pukow Railway Agreement was signed on January 13, 1908, and the related loans and related advances successfully issued. As Morrison expressed it in a cable to *The Times*,

The final agreement shows how Chinese diplomacy has succeeded in altering the conditions of the preliminary contract of May 18, 1899. The Chinese recognize that such favourable terms have never been obtained before, nor such a clear admission of China's claim to control her railways without foreign interference.[137]

The Foreign Office and Addis for the Hongkong Bank in London, Jordan and Hillier in Peking would accept the judgement favourably. Bland remained concerned.

The Soochow–Ningpo, or as the name was finalized, the Shanghai–Hangchow–Ningpo Railway Loan Agreement, was subsequently signed in March 1908 (see below). Nothing, except possibly time and goodwill, had been lost.

The British envisaged a coordinated Chinese railway system of which the concessioned lines would form an initial nucleus. The great trunk route from Shanghai to Peking and the Northeast provinces had now been negotiated, but even when the separate lines had been completed gaps in the smooth functioning of the system would remain. Not until 1933, with the completion of the train ferry link across the Yangtze, for example, would the wagon-lits of the famous Blue Train pass through from Shanghai to Peking.

Shanghai–Hangchow–Ningpo

The negotiations relative to the 320 km railway from Shanghai to Ningpo were among the most contentious in the so-called 'Age of Imperialism'. The opposition of provincial gentry and officials, in part reflecting anti-Manchu sentiment, made the final signing of any agreement doubtful; hence the desire of Jordan to connect it to the Tientsin–Pukow negotiations where greater diplomatic pressure could be exerted. The loan, when issued in 1908, was not needed, and the line was constructed from Shanghai to Hangchow and south to Zakow (but excluding the bridge across the Chientang River) and from Ningpo to Pokwan by provincial companies without the use of the funds borrowed. These remained in the Hongkong Bank drawing 5% interest. The Hongkong Bank did later assist in the completion of the line by participating in the financing of the link between Zakow and Pokwan in 1936, including the costly Chientang River bridge.

The through line was completed in 1937; a few days later the Chinese blew up the bridge as the Japanese advanced.[138]

The Imperial Chinese Government 5% Shanghai–Hangchow–Ningpo Railway Loan for £1.5 million was issued by the British and Chinese Corporation in March 1908 at 99 with a contract price calculated by a differential of $5\frac{1}{2}$ points, that is, $93\frac{1}{2}$.[139] The loan was three times over-subscribed, the Bank was allotted £100,000, and the Hongkong Board minutes recorded a profit to the Bank of £16,000.

In the last days of the negotiations for the Canton–Kowloon Railway T'ang Shao-yi had referred to his transfer to the newly established Board of Communications and Posts, the Yu-ch'uan Pu. The Shanghai–Hangchow–Ningpo loan was the first in which this new Board, together with the Wai-wu Pu, was a contracting party.

The loan agreement contained certain unusual features which can best be explained in their historical context. The right to finance a line from Soochow to Ningpo was demanded by Britain in 1898, and a preliminary agreement was signed the same year. As with several other such concessions, nothing was done until several years after the Boxer Protocol had been signed. In this case Sheng Hsuan-huai wrote to the B&CC in 1903 warning them that if action were not taken, their concession would be granted to provincial companies. Receiving no response, Sheng actively encouraged the formation of gentry-financed companies to undertake construction of the line; the British, however, when aware of these developments claimed that the 'cancellation' of the concession was unilateral and pressed for loan negotiations despite the fact that in this particular case funds had been raised and construction begun.[140]

The loan agreement was originally designed for negotiation on Shanghai–Nanking terms, the line being considered, as Addis instructed Bland in 1906, an integral part of the Shanghai–Nanking system.[141] But all parties recognized that, under the circumstances, these were too severe, and discussions developed on so-called 'Tientsin–Pukow' terms. The line itself was redesignated to run from Shanghai rather than Soochow and its route was redrawn, both changes reflecting *faits accompli*. The security of the loan involved no question of mortgage of the line, and there was no provision whereby control could be obtained by the B&CC. Approval was, however, given for the appointment by the Chinese management of a British chief engineer.

The provincial gentry were placated by being assured of their continuing role; the central authorities were exonerated by invoking the contractual nature of the preliminary agreement which China, under the circumstances, could not renounce. Nevertheless, as late as December 1907, Li Ching-fang, the Chinese Minister in London, was warning William Keswick, still chairman of the B&CC, that there would be a boycott of the British in Shanghai if the agreement were pressed.[142]

Concluding comments

The agreement of March 1908 marked the end of one period of China's post-1895 financial relations. It was the last British loan concluded on the basis of the concessions of 1898, and it represented Britain's concern for its interests in the Yangtze Valley in a period when the 'break up of China' or the scramble for concessions or the need to ensure recognition of a sphere of interest were matters which dominated foreign policy towards China.

On the Chinese side, the terms of the agreement, once accepting the fact that the loan ought not to have been made on any terms, marked the culmination of an evolutionary process whereby the Chinese had been able to insist on increasingly favourable terms by way of management and construction control.

If this evolution is not seen in the financial terms, the reason lies with the condition of the London market whose willingness to accept China railway loans did not improve, the failure of Chinese gentry themselves to invest in the issue as hoped, and the lessening of the control provisions which offset any chance of optimism in the market.

This loan did not mark the end of foreign lending to China. A new era of international cooperation in 'China proper' was developing with the Hongkong Bank/DAB Agreement, the B&CC and the CCR acting as the nucleus. Although Germany had given up some of her pretensions in Shantung and the position of France in Yunnan had stabilized, the defeat of Russia in 1905 had not brought the Open Door to Manchuria; Japan had taken Russia's favoured position, as the Hongkong Bank, seeking to operate commercially in the Northeast provinces, would soon discover.

One of the unfortunate effects of a history which must, perforce, focus on railway finance, is that a major activity is made to appear one which is unpopular to all concerned. The Chinese did not wish to construct railways which would be foreign-financed or under foreign control; the London market was not anxious to finance them; the provincial gentry on the one hand deprecated foreign finance but were unwilling, with minor exceptions, to become seriously and effectively involved in the financing themselves. All sides would appear to have been driven on by a competitive fear that some advantage might otherwise accrue to another Power or party.

The Foreign Office negotiated for concessions in the 1898 scramble which, while meeting with the approval of the Bank, Jardine Matheson, and no doubt other British interests in the general political sense, did not assure their immediate exploitation. Even when immediate action was taken, as in the case of the Northern Railways Loan of 1899, the Hongkong Bank had to seek from a reluctant Foreign Office even further action, that is, a virtual guarantee.

To many British observers the delays in taking advantage of the opportunities power politics had apparently secured appeared a mark almost of ingratitude. The main criticism fell on the B&CC, which with the Pekin Syndicate was the only major contender for the actual development of the concessions. They confirmed the Foreign Office's diplomacy, but this did not in itself place them in a position to proceed. The concessions did not ensure Chinese compliance and the preliminary agreements contained a clause referring to changed local conditions, a clause which was fully exploited by the Chinese during the subsequent negotiations. Meanwhile efforts to share the financial burden with foreign groups were regarded in the context of the popular rivalry as virtual treachery.

The question must then arise, was anyone in favour of railway construction?

Many wanted to utilize the railways after they had been built. But that is not the same thing.

There were those in favour of the actual construction process – those employed in the operations, the engineers, foreign accountants-in-chief, and men like J.O.P. Bland. Manufacturing interests were hopeful of construction contracts, and to an extent they were behind the national-oriented approach. But their determination to obtain the contracts when actually available is another controversial topic in the history of foreign enterprise in China.

The China Association pressed for the maintenance of 'British rights' in China in general terms and particularly in the matter of the Canton–Kowloon Railway. To the China Association any delay, whether caused by a recalcitrant viceroy or a hesitant syndicate, was a target for criticism. They were more concerned with the development of trade in general, with the ending of impediments to such trade, especially internal transit taxes, and the railways were one way in which trade could indeed be developed. To advocate this, to wish for it, to argue that it is all in the interests of China were popular positions, perhaps at times even reasonable; but to finance it, that was more difficult.

Difficult or not, it was done. And in the period to 1911 more would indeed be accomplished, but China's railway network would not again receive positive or priority attention until the Nanking Decade; it would not be significantly developed until after 1949.

The Hongkong and Shanghai Banking Corporation was the financial agent of the British and Chinese Corporation and the Chinese Central Railways. The Bank's position favoured competition; if the possibility of a railway existed, the concession ought either to be open to competition or be reserved for British involvement; once that had been determined, the Hongkong Bank was anxious to undertake the tasks related to the financing – the negotiation of the loan agreement (or a substantial role therein), the issue and service of the loan, and the consequent ordinary exchange banking business. These were its legitimate concerns, but in the period 1895–1914 these could not be achieved by dealing only at the banking level.

The Hongkong Bank thus became involved in all aspects of the railway problem, including, through its membership on the boards of the B&CC and the CCR, the non-financial terms of the several agreements. This role was enhanced by the positive characters of Ewen Cameron and his successor Charles Addis; through them the Hongkong Bank developed the skills which eventually resulted in the Bank's playing a leading role in the international Consortium.

This is a subject for the following chapter.

Table 6.2 *The Hongkong and Shanghai Banking Corporation*
China: principal loans, 1900–1908
(discussed in Chapter 6)

Title and/or purpose		Nominal amount (£ millions)	(i)	(ii)	Terms (iii)	(iv) for/with
4½% Loan to the Wuchang Viceroy 1900	provincial payments	0.75			10^d	UK Govt
ICG 5% Gold Loan of 1905	indemnity	1.0	91^f	97	20	DAB
ICG 5% Shanghai–Nanking Railway Loan of 1904: authorized		3.25			50	B&CC
1st tranche	(July 1904)	(2.25)	90^f	97½		
2nd tranche	(Jan. 1907)	(0.65)	95½^f	par		
ICG 5% Railway Loan of 1907	Canton–Kowloon Railway	1.5	94	par	30	B&CC
ICG 5% Tientsin–Pukow Railway Loan of 1908		5.0			30	CCR DAB
1st tranche	(March 1908)	(3.0)^a	93^f	98¾^b		
2nd tranche	(June 1909)	(2.0)^c	94½	par		
ICG 5% Sterling Loan of 1908 for the Shanghai–Hangchow–Ningpo Railway		1.5	93½	99	30	B&CC

and: Foochow Ts300,000 silver loan of 1905; Szechuan silver loan of 1906; the Hukuang Viceroy's Ts500,000 silver loan of 1909
(i) contract price to Chinese   (ii) price issued to public
(iii) length in years   (iv) with whom or for whom issued
ICG Imperial Chinese Government; CCR Chinese Central Railways
DAB Deutsch-Asiatische Bank; B&CC British and Chinese Corporation.

^{a} Of which £1.11 million in London and £1.89 million in Berlin.
^{b} 98½ net, see text.
^{c} Of which £740,000 in London and £1.26 million in Berlin.
^{d} Taken over by the British Government after one year.
^{f} Firm.

7

RAILWAYS – RIGHTS RECOVERY, FINANCE, AND THE CONSORTIUM, 1905–1911

All railways built by Russia . . . shall be at the sole expense of Russia and the regulations and building thereof shall be solely on the Russian system, with which China has nothing to do.

Cassini Convention, 1896

The construction and control of the railway lines shall be entirely and exclusively vested in the Imperial Chinese Government.

Hukuang Imperial Government Railways Agreement, 1911

RIGHTS RECOVERY

By early 1911 major pre-war foreign financing arrangements for China's railways had been virtually completed. The previous chapter focused on those lines which still envisaged some foreign control. The Chinese preference for purely financial loans, loans designed and advertised for railway construction but in fact divorced from any specific control of the railway by the lending banks or the agency companies (the B&CC for example), forced the banking Groups to retreat step-by-step to the terms of the Hukuang Railways Loan Agreement of 1911.

This chapter is focused on China's great north–south trunk line from Peking to Hankow (the Luhan line) and from Hankow to Canton. In the finance of these railways the Hongkong and Shanghai Banking Corporation played an international role. This role has been considered in many histories, and from many points of view. Here it is told as part of a business history of a bank, a public company, a corporation in the private sector owned by and responsible to shareholders in the East and in Europe. This is the story of the Hongkong Bank as a merchant bank, its activities directed from London by Charles Addis, who, growing in stature with the Bank itself, would become while still the junior of the Bank's two London Managers, a financial authority in the City.

The 'concessions' in their extreme form, involving, *inter alia*, territorial jurisdiction, applied to the Russian railways in the Northeast, the French to Kunming, and the Germans from Tsingtau in Shantung. Less harsh, but wholly unacceptable to China, were the terms of the preliminary agreements for the 'concessioned' lines of 1898/99, but these terms were, in the event, modified during the post-Boxer negotiations, during China's 'period of submission' – perhaps the most misnamed epoch, at least as far as the present topics are concerned, in the history of the Chinese Empire.

The change from 'Canton–Kowloon (C–K) terms' to 'Tientsin–Pukow (T–P) terms' had occurred in 1908; the trend had been reinforced by the Shanghai–Hanchow–Ningpo Railway Loan, and, as many had foreseen, there would be no turning back. Although non-comparable, the Rights Recovery loans of 1906 and 1908, to be discussed in this chapter, were seen by the Chinese as supportive of their argument that the banks could lend without controls; the public would subscribe to bonds issued on this basis. Thus after two years of negotiations the Four Power Groups of the China Consortium -- the Hongkong Bank, the Deutsch-Asiatische Bank, the Banque de l'Indo-Chine and the American Group headed by J.P. Morgan and Co. – capitulated to Chinese demands. The Hukuang Railways Loan would be raised on terms which gave the Chinese virtually full control of the funds.

Foreign opposition to these trends was only partly self-interested. There was a not unreasonable concern that without proper supervision the funds might be diverted or the engineering might be inferior. As a consequence in case of default the security, which no longer was related to the railway itself but was stated as a miscellaneous list of provincial revenues, could lead to foreign interference and/or pressures on the already unstable links between the central and provincial authorities. These, some thought, could destroy the Government.

And, at the end of it all, China would still be without the railway.

As this is virtually what happened, although for a more complex set of reasons, the concern of men in the field, J.O.P. Bland for the B&CC and CCR, for example, cannot be dismissed by vilification.

Just as Bland cannot be dismissed by the simple label of 'imperialist', those accused of accepting 'pure finance', including Charles Addis of the Hong-kong Bank, cannot be dismissed as irresponsible, of advocating the position – 'let China borrow, the consequences are hers alone'. Addis and his Continental colleagues attempted to protect the bondholders by (i) insisting on normal financial control provisions and (ii) a continuing assessment of China's capabilities, which later critics might consider to have been optimistic. The bankers gave up control with misgivings and only under a complex of pressures including interference by their own Governments, on whom Addis consequently laid the responsibility.

Indeed, given practical political and legal considerations, the responsibilities which had been incurred by the B&CC or CCR and indirectly by the Hongkong Bank under stricter terms were incompatible with the actual control they could exercise. The Bank was in an especially weak position: it negotiated and signed the loan agreements as the agent of the B&CC or CCR; as agent it was not legally a party to the agreements and therefore could not withhold disbursement of funds properly requisitioned by the Chinese management on the grounds that they had not fulfilled certain undertakings made with the principals, the B&CC or CCR, despite 'known' misappropriations.[1] The position of the principals was only slightly stronger.

By moving closer to a purely financial agreement, the focus moved to the banks as opposed to the agency syndicates, the B&CC or the CCR. Bland professed in moments of annoyance with the Bank to see no future for either of the latter two corporations, but in this he was unduly pessimistic as they could and did remain agents for the import of foreign materials purchased from the loan funds. Nevertheless their role was muted and, for contractors who hoped to work through the syndicate, this was a fateful setback. Pauling and Co., backed by Belgian banking interests, came to an understanding with the B&CC in 1907 in connection with the Hukuang Railways; by 1909 when the purely financial trend of the negotiations became apparent, the agreement was determined with recriminations.[2]

On the other hand, for countries, such as Japan, which had no capital market for external financing, the ability to compete for the supply of material which another country was financing had a special appeal.

The move also affected the Hongkong Bank's relations with German and French financial syndicates. In 1898 the Hongkong Bank and the DAB declaration with respect to recognition of spheres of interest (or preference) had been agreed and was in addition recommended to the respective Governments. The declaration referred to railway construction concessions of which finance was but a part; if the Hongkong Bank were to negotiate financial loans simply to provide funds to the Imperial Chinese Government to construct its own railways, the 1898 arrangement, which the German Government had never recognized and which the DAB declared ineffective in 1903, was also irrelevant; the 1895 Agreement (as revised in 1905) would be the only effective agreement. The DAB therefore remained eligible to share with the Hongkong Bank any guaranteed loan with the central or provincial authorities negotiated by the Hongkong Bank, even a loan ultimately designed to finance railway construction, the Canton–Hankow Railway for example. This last mentioned railway was in the British sphere of interest, and the British authorities, especially the Government of Hong Kong, wished to ensure that a loan would not involve German participation, even if it were only a financial participation.

The ability of the Bank to hide behind the front of the B&CC and thus avoid the consequences of the 1895 Agreement was open to question. Sir John Jordan wrote, 'The B&CC is the Hongkong Bank under another name.' On the other hand Charles Addis and the Foreign Office maintained the wholly untenable though legally correct position that the Bank, although agent for B&CC and CCR loans, was entirely separate from and unrelated to these two corporations.

If a financial loan were signed by the Bank as principal, as appeared possible in connection with the Canton–Hankow line, these sophistries would become irrelevant.

Nevertheless the potential for confusion and argument did not end here. In 1905 the Hong Kong Government made a £1.1 million loan to the Wuchang (Hukuang) Viceroy. Had it, as originally considered, first borrowed the funds from the Hongkong Bank, would the Bank have been in violation of its 1895 undertaking?

These interesting developments put pressure on the Bank to renounce the 1895 declaration after the year's required notice; this the Bank resisted, despite vilification by the *Times* correspondent, G.E Morrison.[3] At this point another development became apparent and superseded the relatively simple question of the Hongkong Bank's relations with the Deutsch-Asiatische Bank.

If railway financing were to be undertaken on the basis of the security of the line or if interest and capital repayment were to come from the income of the railway, there would be a built-in control as to the amount of Chinese borrowing. If the railways were concessioned, that is built and managed by a foreign syndicate to whom the lines were mortgaged, the use of the funds lent by the bondholders could be monitored and protected, and China's credit further enhanced. From this it followed that, if Chinese borrowing were to be rationalized and so limited, each Power became interested in the share assigned its own nationals. Certain Governments had, however, a double motive: (i) economic benefit to their own nationals and (ii) indirect support for foreign policy goals. This latter could lead to 'concessions' in the full political sense, that is, to exclusive privileges, which, while not unrelated to the whole 'concession' problem and seen as such by the Chinese Government, are not under discussion in this chapter.

If railway financing were to be unrelated to the railway except by statements of intent and if loans ostensibly for the construction of railways were to carry with them no responsibility to bondholders for the completion of the line, the potential for lending becomes dangerously unlimited. The loans, that is, become sovereign risk loans, and merchant bankers have shown (and continue to show) themselves to be incapable of a sensible appraisal of sovereign risk; promoters without a long-term China interest could float the loan and then renounce further responsibility.

In the field of China finance and in the period after 1907 the Powers became increasingly aware that lending for railway development without control made such lending open to competition from any group who had, or thought they had, funds available. The pressures on China's disorganized financial system, the opportunity for ill-advised borrowing, and the undoubted loss of control of foreign borrowing which would result could lead to default and financial chaos. The danger of consequent political intervention in the case of default would be real.

The counter to overlending in small-scale agriculture is 'supervised credit'; the equivalent for China railways was, at the least, Canton–Kowloon terms (see Chapter 6). With these abandoned as unacceptable, with great Power financial rivalry apparent, the ultimate financial collapse of China might be forestalled by cooperation through bank inter-group agreements, that is, the formation of a consortium.

The immediate impact of, for example, a German group free to compete anywhere in China was confusion; the ultimate solution was the membership of the Six Power Groups in a China Consortium.

Such a system required, as earlier suggested, a long-term Government commitment to the national Group. This in turn put pressure on the Hongkong Bank to form a British Group which was as representative as possible. The Bank, however, finding itself second to Parr's Bank as the financier of the Japan loans, had no intention of losing its position as the leader in China finance. In any case, its position was not, in one sense, as exceptional as it appeared. Other Groups might consist of more than a single bank, but in each case there was a single lead bank which undertook responsibility for the negotiations and obtained the remuneration appropriate to a lead bank (see Table 8.1).[4] Behind them, however, as members of the national Group or as companies less formally associated, were the institutions interested in China.

The problem was that the Hongkong Bank did not occupy a similar position in England. It had not been created for the purpose of negotiating on behalf of other institutions as, for example, had the DAB; nor was there an acceptable relationship with other banks as in the case of France. The Hongkong Bank therefore opposed an enlarged Group composed of banks which, the Bank argued, would share the profits of issue without sharing in the negotiations in China, negotiations which, as was well known, only the Bank could undertake.

The Bank had the support of underwriters, including clearing banks and City merchant banks, and its capabilities were nation-wide; thus its base was broader than at first appeared. In 1912, and in the face of Foreign Office insistence, its unique position could no longer be maintained, and the Hongkong Bank accepted other banks into the British Group.

If the British Group were once expanded, it still could not encompass all who wished (or thought they wished) to be involved in investment in China. Thus came the vexed problem of separating financial from industrial loans, a subject which was not settled until 1913 (see Chapter 8).

On the international front the Hongkong Bank was similarly careful, objecting to the adherence of Japan (the Yokohama Specie Bank) and Russia (the Russo-Asiatic Bank) to the inter-bank agreements and thus to the China Consortium on the grounds that their funds would have to come from the London or Paris markets; the Japanese and Russians were thus making no contribution but were diluting the profits and placing themselves advantageously to bid for construction requirements – and to enhance their general political position.

Underlying all this were developments in China: (i) the increased interest of local gentry in railway promotion through private-sector, provincial railway companies and the increasingly outspoken gentry opposition to both foreign financing and control and central Government control and (ii) the inability of either central or provincial promoters to obtain adequate funds either within China or from overseas Chinese.

These developments as they affected the Hongkong and Shanghai Bank are best seen through (i) the railway recovery loans of 1905 and 1908 and (ii) the 1911 loan for the Hukuang Railways. These dealt mainly with the main trunk line from Peking to Canton, although the Szechuan (Hankow–Ichang–Chengtu) line was also involved. There were other railway deals being negotiated contemporaneously, but the main developments can be seen in terms of this single route, divided at Hankow into the Peking–Hankow and the Canton–Hankow railways.

The key junction was at Hankow, until 1906 the seat of Chang Chih-tung. From here part of the drama was acted out between provincial railway interests and the central authorities, as represented by the policies of the Minister of Posts and Communications, Sheng Hsuan-huai, and here in 1911 was the outbreak that signalled the revolution.

THE CANTON–HANKOW LINE

The American China Development Company

In the 1898 scramble for concessions, Sheng Hsuan-huai, then Director-General of the Imperial Railway Administration, signed a preliminary agreement for the Canton–Hankow Railway with the American China Development Company which was subsequently incorporated in New Jersey as the China Development Company (ACDC). The same year the British and Chinese Corporation were awarded the Canton–Kowloon concession, but the British were disappointed that the link with the Upper Yangtze, which they considered within their sphere of 'preference', should fall into foreign hands. By 1899 the B&CC had concluded an agreement with the ACDC by which each would be able to share in business obtained by the other, but, with the outbreak of the Boer War, British markets were no longer receptive to China railway investment, the agreement was cancelled, and B&CC involvement ended.

However, by 1900 Belgian interests, including Léopold II, had secured a strong foothold in the ACDC. Despite American concern, the Belgians continued their investment in the company, and the King brought in his friend J.P. Morgan, who became heavily involved in its affairs.[5] Nevertheless, the Belgian role in the company, which was greater than appearances made it, was sufficient for Sheng, supported by Chang Chih-tung, to consider the company in violation of its agreement not to alienate the shares to citizens of other nations. A further complaint was that no loan had been floated and no construction undertaken, although this was also a complaint against other syndicates on other lines.

Sheng Hsuan-huai did not wish to move against the American company, but Chang Chih-tung, who was under pressure from local gentry and the advocates of Rights Recovery, first wished to cancel and then decided to redeem the concession; he knew that the Belgian interests in the Peking–Hankow line had French capital behind them and he feared that a Belgian line to Canton would mean French domination of the entire route, linking with Russia in the north. In the end the Viceroy, Chang, prevailed; J.P. Morgan had bought out the Belgian interests, now Chang would buy out Morgan.

The Hong Kong Government Loan of 1905

Those [gentry] who advocate [redemption of the line] do not have the money, and those who have the money do not concern themselves with it. We definitely cannot rely on the efforts of the gentry, yet government resources are extremely limited . . .

Chang Chih-tung[6]

The Hongkong Bank's initial interest in the Hankow–Canton line was through its role in the B&CC. The latter's attempt to obtain a concession for construction of the line was frustrated when in 1898 the concession was granted to the ACDC; an agreement was then signed accepting B&CC participation. When Belgian interests replaced American control of the ACDC the agreement with the B&CC was terminated. Renewed hopes for British involvement came when the Belgian syndicate failed to begin construction and the Chinese objected in any case to the change of nationality of the owners. The Bank hoped to participate in raising the funds necessary for the Viceroy, Chang Chih-tung, to buy out the ACDC, but the Bank's agreement with the DAB made British authorities unwilling to deal with the Bank, which was accordingly bypassed. Ironically, in the end the Bank had to become involved both in Hankow and in London.

The realities of Rights Recovery

After lengthy negotiations both within his own region and in Kwangtung, and it was as Canton Viceroy that his realistic assessment quoted above was made, Chang Chih-tung recognized the need to obtain funds (i) to buy out the ACDC and (ii) to construct the railways within the Hukuang provinces; he also recognized that this would require a foreign loan. This section deals with the former problem. Although there was much discussion of a £3 million loan for construction in which the Hongkong Bank showed a continuing interest, nothing materialized; these negotiations may nevertheless be considered one of the origins of the move towards the Hukuang Railways Loan of 1911.

While Chang and Sheng were considering the problems created by the Belgian intrusion and subsequent American take-over of the Canton–Hankow concession, the Government of Hong Kong was frustrated by the slow pace of negotiations over the Canton–Kowloon Railway, a line which, as noted in Chapter 6, was seen as vital to the interests of the Colony and, indeed, as an extension of the Canton–Hankow line. Aware of Chang's need for funds, the Governor of the British Colony initiated a plan whereby the Government of Hong Kong would lend the funds required for redemption in return, he hoped, for guarantees relative to the Canton–Kowloon line.[7]

The model for such a loan agreement would be the Hongkong Bank's 1900 contract with the Wuchang (Hukuang) Viceroy.[8] The 1900 loan, however, had been funded by the British Government through the Hongkong Bank; the Hong Kong Government's first proposal for the redemption loan included a provision that it should be funded by a Hongkong Bank overdraft through the Hong Kong Government.

That the Hong Kong Government should have been directly involved was a consequence of (i) the absence of any centralized British imperial financial facility and (ii) the declaration of 1895 whereby the Hongkong Bank would have had to share any loan with the Deutsch-Asiatische Bank.[9] The DAB in any case suspected the Hongkong Bank's financial involvement and accused it of attempting to bypass their agreement. In the end the Hong Kong Government had to borrow the funds from the Crown Agents in London (at Bank rate) and cover subsequently by special legislation, Ordinance No. 11 of 1905, authorizing a loan for redemption of the Hankow–Canton line concession and for construction of the British sector of the railway from Kowloon to the border of the New Territories at Lowu. The Crown Agents had temporarily and without security assigned for the use of the Hong Kong Government funds deposited with them which belonged to other colonies, who might, as the Crown Agents reasonably pointed out, require their use at any time.[10]

The loan agreement between the Hong Kong Government and the Wuchang Viceroy, signed on September 9, 1905, was for £1.1 million at 4½% amortized by ten equal payments of £110,000. The agreement, which specified the purpose of the loan in some detail, made no mention of the Canton–Kowloon Railway; Chang Chih-tung had successfully resisted every attempt to connect the two problems.

The Viceroy did, however, write a letter to the British Hankow Consul-General, E.H. Fraser, on the same day the loan was signed undertaking that (i) if a foreign loan were negotiated for the construction of the Canton–Hankow line or any other railway in Hunan or Hupei provinces, which would include sections of the line to Szechuan, British financiers would be given the first option at equal rates and (ii) if funds were in fact borrowed through British financiers and imported materials and equipment were required, British goods would be given priority if provided at competitive prices. The letter (the 'Fraser Note') was later declared by the Chinese Government to have been an 'addendum' to the loan agreement, from which it would follow that its effect would cease with the repayment of the loan.[11]

The Hongkong Bank's advance of £400,000
The Hongkong Bank had not, however, been completely cut out. In the long-term the Viceroy's letter provided a potential for future involvement of the B&CC, but in the short-run the Bank would be called upon for emergency assistance.

The Viceroy's redemption agreement with the ACDC had been signed on June 7, 1905, but shareholder ratification came only on August 29 and required that $Gold 2 million of the total $6.75 million agreed compensation should be paid on or before September 7, that is, two days before the Hongkong Government's £1.1 million loan agreement could be signed. To be able to make the necessary initial instalment, Chang first attempted to speed the negotiations, but a breakdown in telegraphic communication prevented Fraser from signing in time. Chang had therefore to turn to the Hongkong and Shanghai Bank in Hankow.[12]

The Bank, which had been closely watching all the negotiations, was prepared to advance £400,000 against the security of the revenues of the Provincial Currency Office and to remit this sum to New York in time to make the required payment to the ACDC by the September 7 deadline. The Hong Kong Government Loan Agreement was consequently revised to take this transaction into account; the agreement called for delivery of £400,000 equivalent in sycee to Chang Chih-tung in Hankow to enable him to repay the Hongkong Bank; the balance of £700,000 was to be made available to the Chinese Minister in New York to repay the balance of the compensation due the ACDC.[13]

The Bank's loan agreement with the Wuchang Viceroy, Chang Chih-tung, called for repayment in Hankow sycee in Hankow; the Hong Kong Government therefore called on the Crown Agents to remit, through the Hongkong Bank, the equivalent amount to Chang in Hankow for repayment to the Hongkong Bank.

The Foreign Office shrewdly suggested to the Crown Agents, however, that although the transfer of such an amount could prove costly it was highly likely that the Bank, whose London Office had already laid down the £400,000 equivalent in New York on account of the Shanghai branch, did not in fact wish to take repayment in Hankow. Furthermore, the Foreign Office suggested, since the Bank might someday benefit from the Fraser Note, A.M. Townsend, the London Manager, might be persuaded to be accommodating on the rate.[14]

This indeed proved to be the case. Townsend grumbled, but in the end admitted that as the transfer to New York had been accomplished by debiting Shanghai branch's account with London Office, the Crown Agents could therefore actually pay the £400,000 due Chang in Hankow by deposit in London. The sum would then reinstate the Shanghai branch balance, and no exchange was involved.

As noted in Chapter 6, Townsend was concerned, as much for the future as the present, at the way in which this transaction had been kept away from the Bank by the British and Chinese Governments. The Foreign Office was reassuring, and the problem never again arose in this particular form. On the other hand French and German representations charged that the loan was actually from the Bank, but again the Foreign Office could, with a clear conscience, insist that the Bank's role had been limited to the advance of the £400,000, which advance had been almost immediately repaid.[15]

The Hong Kong Government, meanwhile, made arrangements with the Crown Agents to raise funds in the London capital market to cover the £1.1 million made available to Chang, for the finance of the Canton–Kowloon Railway (British section), and a residual amount to assist the Canton Viceroy to begin construction of the Chinese section should negotiations with the B&CC break down. As indicated in Chapter 6, the B&CC was successful.[16] In London there is evidence that the Hongkong Bank subscribed to the Crown Agents loan in the normal course of business.

In consequence of the Hong Kong Government loan, Chang was able to regain control of the Canton–Hankow line and he was free to turn the construction and the financing over to Chinese companies. He had not in fact solved all problems relative to Belgian interests nor had he extinguished the American interest in the line; President Roosevelt protested and President Taft would later intervene when it became clear that foreign and not Chinese financial resources were to be involved. The former problem was solved by the Chinese; the American concern would lead in 1910 to a consortium of Four Power Groups, a subject to be considered below.

THE PEKING–HANKOW (LUHAN) LINE[a]

The loans and advances of 1908

Although the British Minister, Sir Claude MacDonald, had hoped for British involvement in the Peking–Hankow line as early as 1898, the concession had been awarded to the Belgian Société d'Étude de Chemins de fer en Chine. The line was constructed and had proved profitable. The loan agreement provided for redemption by China any time after September 1, 1907, and, in accordance with declared Chinese policy, Chang Chih-tung and T'ang Shao-yi among others sought funds to enable the redemption at an early date. Despite setting aside part of the net profits of the line and a loan from the Hu Pu (Ministry of Finance) to the Yu-ch'uan Pu (Ministry of Posts and

---

[a] The Peking–Hankow line is often referred to as the 'Luhan' Railway, a name derived from the usual Chinese practice of taking the two first characters of the railway's terminal cities. A problem for those unfamiliar with China arises when an unexpected name is used instead of one which to the foreigner would seem more obvious, 'Yüeh–Han' or (Yüet–Han) for Canton–Hankow; in the case of the Peking–Hankow line, 'Lu' refers to Lu-kou-ch'iao; the railway originally began there at the Marco Polo Bridge rather than in Peking itself; 'Yüeh' (Cantonese: Yüet) refers to Kwangtung and Kwangsi provinces. 'Hukuang' is the name of an old province which included Hupei and Hunan provinces and was accordingly used, as in Hukuang Railways, to designate these two provinces, then under the jurisdiction of Viceroy Chang Chih-tung at Wuchang/Hankow.

Communications), it became obvious to the Chinese ministries concerned that China would require another loan from the foreign banks.

On October 8, 1908, an agreement was reached between the Yu-ch'uan Pu and the Banque de l'Indo-Chine and the Hongkong and Shanghai Bank for the Imperial Chinese Government Gold Loan of 1908 for £5 million sterling at 5%–$4\frac{1}{2}$%, for 30 years, with a contract price of 94 and a servicing commission of $\frac{1}{5}$ of 1% (as opposed to the usual $\frac{1}{4}$ of 1%) of each sum paid in principal and interest. The agreement made no reference to the Peking–Hankow line *per se* but asserted that 80% of the funds would be used 'to complete the redemption of certain railway loans', a provision which could only relate to the railway in question. The change from 5% to $4\frac{1}{2}$% was to come after fifteen years. The loan was issued at 98.[17]

At the same time a domestic 7% (plus profit participation) Peking–Hankow Railway redemption loan for $10 million was authorized, although the bonds had both to be underwritten and a large block purchased by the Hongkong Bank.[18] Further blocks were subsequently sold in Europe through, *inter alia*, the London City and Midland Bank, Ltd, and Messrs Dunn, Fischer and Co.[b]

Despite these loans the Chinese claimed that they had insufficient funds to effect the redemption on schedule. Accordingly the Chiao-t'ung Bank (Bank of Communications), Shanghai, obtained an advance of Ts3 million at 7% per annum from the Hongkong Bank; the Ministry then approached the other participating banks, plus the Deutsch-Asiatische and Yokohama Specie banks, for further advances of Shanghai Ts3.9 million or a total of Ts6.9 million or £762,000 equivalent, all for three months on the security of the balance of £1 million of the Anglo-French loan described above. The proceeds of the Hongkong Bank advance were to be remitted the same day on a TT basis to Paris at the rate of Ts1 = Fr2.39 and held to the order of the Chiao-t'ung Bank.[20]

The Chinese problem was to pay £5 million by December 10, 1908; the 80% of the loan at 94 which had been set aside for this purpose equalled £3.76 million. Despite claims that they could meet this deficit of £1.24 million (= Ts10.5 million) from funds already available to the Ministry of Posts and Communications, in fact the sum had to be met almost entirely by borrowing from various departments of the central Government, and a balance had remained, which had to come from foreign banks. The $10 million internal loan was raised to repay the advances.

[b] The sale of these bonds brought into question the status of the loan as an 'Imperial' loan, one sanctioned by Imperial edict communicated by the Wai-wu Pu to the British Legation in Peking. Addis kept the Foreign Office in touch with Hongkong Bank opinion, and the Stock Exchange committee refused a quotation until the loan's status was established.[19]

I am unaware [wrote Sir John Jordan] of any advantages which this complicated method of raising money may possess for China, and can only judge from the fact that the transaction is considered highly lucrative by the banks concerned that the borrowers have chosen a costly way out of their difficulties.[21]

The course of negotiations

The 1908 gold loan involved factors which were key to Young China's policy and had a marked influence on future loan negotiations. That China's intention was Rights Recovery was fully understood from the first; nevertheless the CCR expected that while China wanted overall control and elimination of extraneous provisions, some vestiges of foreign management and/or financial control would remain in the interests of the bondholders and of the Chinese who, the negotiators thought, would need such provisions to ensure the continued profitability of the line.

As it became increasingly clear that China would not agree to a loan on terms which gave the CCR any appropriate role, the negotiations moved into a purely financial sphere handled by the Hongkong Bank and the Banque de l'Indo-Chine. The loan was no longer related, *de jure*, to the railway; it was purely sovereign risk and financial. The foreign lenders had abandoned their control requirements, admittedly for a fully operating and profitable line; a precedent, nevertheless, was seen by the Chinese as having been created.

Whether a CCR operation or a purely financial loan, the Hongkong Bank was equally involved. The switch from the CCR to the Hongkong Bank could be seen as an 'abandonment' of the CCR by the Bank. Or worse: it could be seen as an abandonment of principle. To lend without controls suggested irresponsibility. The argument did not develop during the Luhan line negotiations. These would all be matters of serious concern subsequently.

Developments on the Chinese side were not clean-cut; their financial operations were tortuous and expensive. Young China understood the policy they were attempting to execute, but they had to operate within a confused fiscal system. This gave the foreign lenders some hope that their services, which could cover the entire operation with one relatively cheap loan, would still be required, even within a new context.

On the foreign side the negotiations revealed that the development of national Groups and their various combinations, for example the CCR and the Consortium, had not eliminated competition. No Government appeared willing to grant exclusive support, *de facto*, to any Group not fully comprehensive; forming such a group became a goal of policy. Groups were accordingly expanded, but they never became all-embracing; competition would remain.

From the CCR to the Hongkong Bank

Despite the efforts to rationalize foreign lending in China through the Hongkong Bank/DAB declaration of 1895, the subsequent railway 'spheres of interest' declaration of 1898, and the expansion of the Chinese Central Railways to include French and Belgian interests, there was still intense competition. The negotiations for the 1908 Peking–Hankow redemption loan illustrate this and suggest how the Chinese were able to force the purely financial loan on the reluctant foreign lenders.

Although German interests, as represented by the DAB, were very much involved in rival negotiations relative to the construction of the Canton–Hankow line, they refused an interest in the redemption of the northern trunk line to which they were entitled by virtue of the 1905 Agreement, ostensibly on the grounds of unattractive security but more probably because of the condition of the German capital market at the time.

The Belgians, however, well aware of Chinese redemption policy, attempted to offset their loss of profit-sharing rights in the Peking–Hankow line at least partially by making their own offer for a redemption loan, the terms of which would enable the Belgians to retain some vestigial management and/or other control during the life of the loan.

The French Government indicated that in view of the majority French financial investment in the Société d'Étude de Chemins de fer en Chine, the controlling Belgian company, they would support any proposal that company might have to retain control of the Luhan line.[22] This position was effectively modified, however, by the French Government's attitude in a totally unrelated dispute with the Belgians over taxation – French capital had been moving to Belgium to escape taxation – and the Bourse was effectively closed for the time to Belgian finance.[23] Consequently, in July 1908 the Société Générale de Belgique, which was one of the major Belgian investors in the Société d'Étude, formed a solely Belgian company, the Société Belge de Chemins de fer en Chine. This new company, in association with Schröder and Co., the London merchant bankers, was then prepared to challenge from the City of London itself any offers from the Chinese Central Railways (CCR), for whom the Hongkong Bank was the bank of issue.[24]

Both the Belgians and the British entered the competition in the expectation that the terms reached with the Chinese would include some control of railway operation and of the finance made available, presumably on a basis no worse than 'Tientsin–Pukow terms', during the period of the loan. The Chinese, represented by T'ang Shao-yi, rejected all such approaches; a purely financial loan was required.

In March 1908, the CCR board wired Bland, their Peking representative (shared with the B&CC), that a Belgian syndicate appeared to be negotiating successfully and instructing him to see 'if it were possible to secure the business for the Chinese Central Railways'. Bland informed the CCR board that such action would be 'injudicious' and merely informed the Chinese, albeit on several occasions, of the offer; for this failure to act decisively he received Addis's personal criticism. The CCR again wired Bland on April 4; Bland continued to inform the Chinese of the willingness of the company to enter into negotiations 'if required'.

As Addis explained to Bland on May 1,

> It was not considered safe to leave the matter in this state and accordingly Hillier was asked to see what could be done by way of an international loan, acting on behalf of the Hongkong Bank in conjunction with the French and German groups. The CCR were of course advised when this was done, and naturally the consent of the Continental groups was obtained.[25]

The Hongkong Bank had discovered the involvement of Schröders and also of a possible Belgian relationship with Martin's Bank; it had accordingly sent an urgent message to E.G. Hillier in Peking to negotiate on the best terms available. To Bland this appeared both a personal betrayal and a jettisoning of the Chinese Central Railways and granting terms incompatible with the principles he, in apparent agreement with the CCR's Board of Directors, espoused as the CCR's representative in China.

The situation in Peking was the consequence of confused lines of communication and failure to keep representatives fully informed of international developments and thereby protected against sudden turns of events or unexpected actions by colleagues; for Bland there was a lack of official instructions directly from the CCR board; when they came, they were equivocal.[26] Bland was not the only one left the victim of apparently conflicting responsibilities; Maurice Casenave of the Banque de l'Indo-Chine was similarly confused, and the French Minister C. Bapst was pro-Belgian at a time when French policy made his position untenable.[27]

Bland communicated his concern to the Legation and the relevant correspondence was copied to the Foreign Office, with a covering letter from Sir John Jordan who appeared in the unwonted role of adjudicator.[28] His conclusion appears justified: 'I would suggest that this could perhaps be remedied by more explicit instructions from the Bank and the Companies to their agents, who, I am certain, are performing their duties under difficult circumstances with complete loyalty to their principals and French associates.'[29]

A frustrated Bland eventually chose to see Addis's instructions to Hillier as evidence of a basic conflict of interest between the Bank and the B&CC/CCR. Addis as Manager of the Hongkong Bank in London had acted against the interests of the CCR on whose board he sat as an influential, if not the most influential, director. Similarly in Peking, Bland saw Hillier as Agent of the Hongkong Bank working against Bland, the agent of the B&CC/CCR, whose interests the Bank was by agreement bound to support. These only slightly veiled accusations Addis denied. The course was set for confrontation.

Bland came to England during the summer but failed to resolve the outstanding issues either of principle or of personality. He returned to China embittered and, for the first time, hostile to Addis.

'Young China' sets the pace

What in fact had happened?

As the Belgians were then working through the Société Belge de Chemins de fer en Chine without French participation, the Banque de l'Indo-Chine was free to cooperate with the Hongkong Bank. Addis and Stanislaus Simon (of the French bank) had come to an agreement in February 1908 that the finance and related construction contracts for the trunk line would be shared equally – the British taking priority in the south, the French in the north, that is, from Peking to Hankow.[30] The refusal of the Chinese to accept any but purely financial terms for the Luhan line was, therefore, a more serious blow to French than to British interests, and the Hongkong Bank's 'take-over' from the CCR was not, under these circumstances, considered by the latter as a particularly serious development.

In Peking Hillier, who faced problems similar to those which had delayed Bland, had been quick to accept the French interest and on instructions from Addis accordingly negotiated in conjunction with Casenave of the Banque de l'Indo-Chine. Hillier thereby both enhanced the chances of success by forestalling other competitive offers from French financial sources and, when Chinese refusal to consider any form of control became apparent, countered in advance any objections the French interests on the CCR might otherwise have had.[31]

As for the Anglo-Belgian syndicate, Schröder's, although anxious to gain a foothold in China finance, was not willing to compete with the increasingly unprofitable terms being negotiated primarily by Hillier on behalf of the Anglo-French syndicate, which thus in the end prevailed – but at a sacrifice. As Casenave cabled the Banque de l'Indo-Chine:

J'ai fait remarquer que le projet
1. Implique participation Allemande;
2. Ne stipule rien en ce qui constitue le personnel Français;
3. En ce qui concerne l'utilisation du surplus à de nouveau chemins de fer, engage l'avenir dans de mauvaises conditions.[32]

The Hongkong Bank regretted the lack of control and did not give up easily.

As late as July they were demanding the appointment of a European engineer and auditor.[33] Bland was not alone in his concern. The main consideration was, however, that, unless the Foreign Office and Legation were to strongly support the requirement for financial control, this condition could not be pressed without the real danger that the loan would go elsewhere. Such support was impractical, the loan was agreed on a purely financial basis, the consequences of which were all foreseen.[34]

Even with approval in principle from London and Paris, there would remain, however, anxious moments. The proposal of the Hongkong Bank made in August 1908 for a loan at 95 and 5% proved unacceptable to the French who, due to French stamp tax requirements, considered that they required a margin of seven or eight points. Accordingly, the Bank reopened negotiations at 93.[35] The Chinese continued to negotiate with, *inter alia*, the Belgians throughout, but Casenave obtained from Paris, and Hillier received identical instructions from Addis in London, a last-minute authority to accept, if necessary, the Chinese counter-proposal of an increased contract price of 94 fixed but with a 5–4½% interest rate. This provisional acceptance of the Chinese terms was leaked to the Chinese and, naturally, any hope for a settlement at 93 had to be abandoned.[36] The loan was in fact issued with only four points, that is, at 94, suggesting the intensity of the competition, the strength of the Chinese bargaining position, and the willingness of the two banks to meet the Chinese terms despite the narrow margin for profit afforded them.

At this point it became clear that the Chinese would not, under any circumstances, permit the loan to specify in precise terms that its main purpose was the redemption of the Luhan line. This refusal was both baffling and serious, the latter since the success of the loan depended on stating its purpose clearly in the prospectus. The compromise was the use of the phrase 'certain railway loans' which could, in fact, only relate to the Luhan line.[37] Explanations for the Chinese position include concern for Belgian susceptibilities and a general unwillingness to appear subject to the orders of foreign financiers.

In the end, the negotiations, which had been tentatively based on a sum of £7 million (to include new railway development), were closed for a loan of £5 million at 94 with interest at 5%–4½% with the other conditions noted above.[38]

The actual issue of the £5 million redemption loan was not without drama. On the day the agreement was signed in Peking, Austria annexed Bosnia-Herzegovina, and Addis could not find underwriters. The issue was postponed, but Addis insisted on action, and, on his advice, it was eventually issued on October 13; by closing time at 3 p.m. on the 14th it had been 'amply covered'. Perhaps the most fulsome praise for Addis's behaviour came in a copy of a letter from Sir Thomas Jackson to the Bank's Chief Manager, J.R.M. Smith – Addis recorded in his diary, 'TJ made me blush at the eulogistic terms . . . he says but for my determination and pluck [the loan] would never have been floated. So there!'[39]

THE HUKUANG RAILWAYS

In 1905 the Hong Kong Government left the Hongkong Bank to one side while it completed negotiations for redemption of the ACDC concession; in the redemption of the Luhan line, the terms were set by the intensity of the competition and the Hongkong Bank accepted the consequences. But as the Hukuang Loan negotiations continued over the years, the Bank, represented by Charles Addis, assumed the leadership and formed an international consortium which was to continue, with varying membership and effectiveness, until 1946. This time the Hongkong Bank played a determining role.

The Consortium with which the Bank was associated was comprised of banking Groups representing the major financial interests concerned with China investment in each particular country; national participation varied over the years. The Groups were not in themselves 'official', nor did they represent their Governments. They operated, however, in a context which had been at least partially established by the Governments, who, in return, set limits beyond which support could not be expected.

Thus, relative to the Hukuang negotiations, in 1905 the British Government through Fraser, its Hankow Consul-General, had obtained assurances that preference would be given on equal terms to (a) British capital and (b) British material. This preference was for 'British' not for the Hongkong Bank (the Chartered Bank were informed of the Fraser Note at the time of its execution), not for B&CC or CCR capital. Therefore, it was not a right which the Bank or Corporation could bargain away without Government permission.

If the Hongkong Bank or its associates wished to sign a loan agreement with the Chinese authorities, it had to ensure (i) that Chinese regulations were complied with – obtaining the sanction of an edict, for example – and (ii) that the British Government would register the agreement and undertake to make representations on behalf of the lenders in case of default. Any unusual conditions, or, more likely, lack of usual conditions would lead to an enquiry by the Bank at the Legation or Foreign Office as to the likelihood of support, as, for example, in the case of the Szechuan Loan referred to in Chapter 6. Failing agreement with these officials, the loan or project might have to be dropped or at least reconsidered; the risk would be excessive. Some, Birch Crisp for example, took the risk (see Chapter 8), but most did not.

The necessity of obtaining official agreement however placed the Bank's policy subject to British foreign policy.

A loan agreement, especially one involving the finance of a railway, contains detailed statements of the obligations of both parties. If these are not acted on, legal action can be taken; this was not, however, a procedure particularly useful in Ch'ing China. The alternative was representation to the Legation or Foreign Office, and, as this necessity was anticipated, diplomatic officials became concerned with virtually every detail of a loan agreement.[c]

The Hongkong Bank, and others in a similar position, being subject to the applicable provisions of their country's policy, attempted to change that policy where they disagreed, or improve it where their expertise made this relevant. Similarly, officials kept in touch with the bankers; they too had reports to write and recommendations to make. Often these originated with expertise from the private sector, as the Addis diaries frequently record.

Commercial negotiations could not be entirely separated from foreign policy, especially where arrangements involved political sanction and affected British policy in other fields.

The task of negotiating China loans became more difficult when these inter-relations between the Bank and the British Foreign Office had to be squared with the positions of foreign financial Groups who were, in turn, in a similar position *vis-à-vis* their own Governments. And beyond all this, once the Consortium Groups were in agreement, were the Chinese authorities with their own particular requirements.

The complexity of the problem made any success at first glance unlikely. The delicate balance established among the Groups could be offset by

---

[c] As a single example of something the Legation would have preferred to avoid, the following may be helpful. The March 6, 1908, Shanghai–Ningpo Railway Agreement, Art. 17, stated, '... the Yu-ch'uan Pu or its duly appointed Managing Director, will select and appoint a British Chief Engineer ... [who] will be under the orders of the Managing Director ...' On October 20, 1908, W. Keswick, as chairman of the B&CC, wrote to the Foreign Office:

> ... beyond the nominal appointment of a Managing Director and an Engineer-in-Chief, no progress has been made to giving effect to the terms of the Loan Agreement.
>
> Taotai Shih Chao Tseng [Shih Chao-chi or Alfred Sze] poses as the Managing Director, but we cannot satisfy ourselves that he really holds any authority from Peking, and, while the Chekiang Railway Company has accepted him somewhat under protest, and treat him as an inferior, the Kiangsu Railway Company has so far refused to recognize him at all ...
>
> Mr Foord's Agreement [as Engineer-in-Chief] has not yet been signed, and, although the Chekiang Railway Company appears prepared to accept him, it does so more in the light of a Consulting Engineer than an Engineer-in-chief ... The Kiangsu Railway Company has, so far, not taken any notice of Mr Foord.[40]

Keswick's hope was that Sir Edward Grey would be pleased to communicate with Sir John Jordan in Peking.

Jordan later recommended that the Hongkong Bank withhold further funds; the lawyers advised that the Bank having signed as agent had no standing (see above) and could not withhold funds.

There were at least bureaucratic advantages to a simple financial loan.[41]

unexpected competition from a firm or individual not covered by the Group, undoing months of negotiation. Hence the continued efforts by Group member banks to obtain exclusive Government support.

Charles Addis provided the essential leadership. While not always in agreement with those responsible for foreign policy in Britain, he had the confidence of the Foreign Office, of his Manager, A.M. Townsend, in London, and of J.R.M. Smith and later Newton Stabb, the Chief Managers in Hong Kong. By his determination, his concise expression of the issues, and his unparalleled experience, he carried (or forced) his colleagues into support, sometimes standing alone, stubborn but unyielding – and, at times, successful.

FROM RIGHTS RECOVERY TO THE THREE POWER GROUPS CONSORTIUM

The main line of the events which comprise the subject of this section begins with the fact of the redemption of the Luhan line and the terms of the British preference granted in the Chang/Fraser understanding, the Fraser Note, by the Viceroy Chang Chih-tung in connection with the Hong Kong Government loan of £1.1 million. The story proceeds to the proposed establishment of an Anglo-French company, modelled after the Chinese Central Railways (CCR) but specifically designed for the exploitation of the Canton–Hankow line, to the request of the German Group to join with the Anglo-French Groups, to the tentative beginning of a cooperative approach temporarily frustrated by independent German action and which ended with the fiasco of the apparent German success in early 1909 – an event which hastened the creation of the Three Power Groups Consortium in July.[42]

The first stage of the Hukuang Railways negotiations may be said to have begun with the redemption by the Chinese in 1905 of the rights granted to the China Development Company (ACDC). Although certain aspects of this 'redemption' were challenged on wholly false premises by Belgium, the consequences were only temporary in their impact. Other delays arose from the confusion of approaches, the persistent unwillingness of Chang Chih-tung to entertain any proposal involving the French, and the pressures of the Japanese who were then particularly involved in industrial developments in the region. In the history of the Hongkong Bank the detailed pursuit of these matters, which E.G. Hillier at one point described as something of a comic opera, would not be particularly helpful.[43]

Later sections will describe the negotiations under the Three Power Groups Consortium, the last-minute demand by President Taft for American involvement, and the influence of the Luhan terms on the move from concession to final approach, with the final compromise by which the Hongkong Bank's Charles Addis justified the lack of those controls the Powers and the banks had hitherto deemed essential – the responsibility of Government in the event of default.

At the height of its success as a leading international bank, the Hongkong Bank became more enmeshed in British Government policy and constrained by the increasingly political atmosphere of Consortium negotiations. The policies pursued by the Bank and the Consortium had become too important to be left solely to the discretion of bankers. This Charles Addis of the Hongkong Bank, along with many of his associates, accepted.

The establishment of the Anglo-French position

The first step was an agreement signed in London on October 18, 1906, by Addis for the B&CC and S. Simon for the French Group – the Banque de l'Indo-Chine, the Comptoir National d'Escompte de Paris, the Société Générale, the Régie Générale des Chemins de fer, the Banque de Paris et des Pays-Bas, and Messrs N.J. and S. Bardac. The agreement envisaged project type loans for railway construction and management, and, with special reference to the Canton–Hankow line, with controls not less strict than those in the Canton–Kowloon Railway Agreement.

The second stage was a new memorandum of agreement between Addis and S. Simon for the French Group, February 24, 1908, in response to an urgent cable from J.O.P. Bland in Peking (i) warning that Chang Chih-tung would never close on the terms involving recognition of the French role as stipulated by the French Government and (ii) advising that German competition was present. Bland was thereupon authorized to negotiate on behalf of the B&CC alone, an additional clause to be added later acknowledging French participation. At the same time the British and French might negotiate together relative to the Peking–Hankow (or Luhan) line, the French to take precedence as to management etc. in the north and the British, in terms of the Fraser Note, in the south.

As Addis would recognize formally in early 1909 the Chinese were not prepared to deal in terms of railway 'concessions'. The demands of the Chinese, represented by Chang Chih-tung, by then a Grand Councillor in Peking and director-general of both sections of the Peking–Canton trunk line, were for conditions with minimal specified controls, and to this neither the French Group nor the B&CC were as yet willing to agree; nor, had they done so, would they have been supported by their Governments, as Addis was later to point out.

Chang, for example, did not wish the loan prospectus to state specifically that the loan was for the Hankow–Canton line; it was simply to refer to 'industrial undertakings'. Besides the problem which such vagueness would arouse in itself, since nothing specific was mentioned, there was the obvious implication that no control would be permitted. The context of these discussions, therefore, foreshadowed the provision of the 1908 Luhan line redemption loan. The French and British Groups were, however, still adhering to the policy of requiring Canton–Kowloon (C–K) terms for any loan for construction of a new line and their representatives in China were so instructed.

In an interview with Chang Chih-tung in December 1908, J.O.P. Bland argued cogently on the need for a project-type loan in the interests of all parties, contrasting the redemption of a working line with the construction of a new line. On some points Chang agreed, but he rested on the political issue; the gentry and people would not accept a 'concessioned railway', a loan with controls, or a project loan. What they sought was simply financial assistance through a foreign public issue on the security of the Imperial Chinese Government.

In the last months of 1908 the pressures on Chang Chih-tung had been mounting, provincial gentry in the Hukuang provinces had proved unable either to raise sufficient funds or to undertake significant construction – although the gentry would possibly disagree – and the only question which interested foreigners were considering was to which foreign syndicate the loan would be granted.

Addis had argued – in much the same terms as Bland expounded to Chang – that the Hongkong Bank and the French Group had accepted the 1908, 5–$4\frac{1}{2}$% £5 million Gold Loan for redemption of the Luhan line on purely financial terms as an exceptional case. The line was operating; the Chinese were merely exercising their rights under the original agreement to buy out the concessionaires. As many had predicted, however, the Chinese considered this a precedent rather than an exception; they were certainly expecting a loan for construction on terms no worse than those in the Tientsin–Pukow agreement. The B&CC and the CCR had both had unfortunate experiences with the loose control provisions on the Tientsin–Pukow and Shanghai–Hangchow–Ningpo lines, and they were standing firm on the provisions of the Anglo-French agreement. Both sides had hardened their positions.

The B&CC failed to take sufficient notice of the fact that German experience on the northern sector of the Tientsin–Pukow line had been very different; the Germans would not have the same objections to T–P terms.

The German intervention

On January 13, 1909, the DAB asked the Hongkong Bank officially whether a share of the Canton–Hankow loan would be offered to the DAB.[44] Addis's initial response was that this line was, by the terms of the 1898 Hongkong Bank/DAB declaration, in the British sphere. Accordingly, he hoped the Germans would not press for inclusion.[45]

The Germans implied surprise that the Hongkong Bank thought the 1898 Agreement was in effect, but added that, even if it were, it was irrelevant. The agreement referred to railway concessions; what was contemplated with reference to the Hankow–Canton line was railway finance. The DAB concluded with the threat that if they were not offered a share of the financing, they would be free to negotiate separately on the basis of an offer already made by the Chinese authorities.[46]

The Hongkong Bank was not, at this point, its own master. The Canton–Hankow line, or that portion of it in the Hukuang provinces then being considered, involved a preference for British goods granted by the Chinese to the British Government, not to the Bank. The Bank could not negotiate away the right offered through its own Government. Yet the DAB agreement of 1895 existed; the Bank had refused to renounce it.

Charles Addis was now aware that the Berlin capital market had improved and that the German threat was real; he alerted the Foreign Office to the possibility of Germany's successfully negotiating for the Canton–Hankow loan and thereby depriving the British of the advantages promised in the Fraser Note. The French were bound by their previous agreements to accept the British position; the Germans were not.

The Foreign Office concluded that the main issue was the preservation of the advantages contained in the Fraser Note. Their proposal was to keep the finance British through the B&CC, but to permit that corporation to share with the French and, if necessary, the German Groups at a subordinate level. Having shared so much, the time would then be appropriate to refer to the more important condition of British preference in matters of supply.[47]

Addis proposed, and his plan was accepted by the B&CC, that in fact the negotiations with the Chinese should be carried out in the name of the Hongkong and Shanghai Bank as a wholly financial transaction, to be shared as such with the French and German Groups, the profits to the Hongkong Bank then being passed back, less commission, to the B&CC. As the agreement would be signed by the Hongkong Bank alone, the finance would appear British and in this way the advantages in the Fraser Note would remain untouched when it came to Chinese purchases for construction.[48] As Addis noted later, 'It must be admitted that the scheme, as proposed, offered but a slender chance of success, but no other had been suggested and for want of a better it was decided to give it a trial.'[49]

The British Group, that is, the Hongkong Bank, accordingly approached the French Group, that is, the Banque de l'Indo-Chine, and received agreement in principle on January 21; on the following day the Germans were informed accordingly. During the subsequent negotiations with the French in Paris, January 25–27, the basis of an agreement was worked out: all parties would have been bound to accept C–K terms, to share the loan equally, and:

... as regards construction, the Banque de l'Indo-Chine and the Deutsch-Asiatische Bank, recognizing the predominance of the British interest, agree to abstain from any action likely to prejudice the preferential rights of the British Group to the appointment of Engineers and to the supply of material in virtue of the Anglo-Chinese Agreement of 1905.[50]

But the French Government at this point reversed the French Group's position relative to the Canton–Hankow line, arguing that, while there was no objection to an agreement for sharing railway loans, that is an Anglo-German–French '*entente générale*', they would not agree to German participation in the Canton–Hankow line *ad hoc*.

As a matter of courtesy Addis proceeded to Berlin on January 28 and informed the German Group of the French position, adding an expression of regret on behalf of the British Group. This angered the French who protested to the British through their Ambassador in London; Addis was given an opportunity to respond and the Foreign Office rejected the French complaint. Addis had described the British Group's position as one of 'reluctant acquiescence', which Sir Edward Grey, the British Foreign Secretary, in a private letter to Sir Francis Bertie, the British Ambassador in Paris, described as 'a correct definition of our attitude'.[51] The course of negotiations relative to the Canton–Hankow line moved on unaffected by this exchange.

The German response to the French refusal was to assert their independence of action while promising that 'no bid would be made except upon terms at which they would be prepared to finance the whole loan themselves'.[52] Nevertheless, the situation had dramatically changed; it was recognized that the Germans would accept T–P terms and that they could finance any consequent financial agreement. The Anglo-French position had been dangerously undermined. Bland in Peking would have to exercise the greatest of negotiating caution. This he would fail to do.

The British Group now felt it essential to establish an Anglo-French-German understanding which was, essentially, an extension of the Hongkong Bank/DAB declaration of 1895 to include the Banque de l'Indo-Chine but to substitute the B&CC for the Hongkong Bank. To achieve this Addis recognized and the Foreign Office accepted that the advantages under the Fraser Note would have to be formally given up.[53]

Negotiations were initiated in Paris on this basis. On February 27 the British and French agreed; Addis then moved to Berlin.[54] After difficult negotiations, the Germans showing themselves 'un peu brutal', on March 1 the Disconto-Gesellschaft on behalf of the German Group signed a Protocol which (i) extended the Hongkong Bank/DAB Agreement of 1895 relative to railway loans to cover the French Group, thus creating a Three Power Groups Consortium, and to include in the British Group the B&CC and the Chinese Central Railways and (ii) confirmed that negotiations would always be undertaken on the minimum basis of Canton–Kowloon terms.[d]

The Protocol was, as noted, signed; it was not, however, ratified.

Addis returned to Paris and obtained the French signatures; he then returned to London where the boards of the B&CC and the CCR confirmed the agreement. Everything was now completed except ratification, and Addis accordingly requested the Germans to suspend their independent Canton–Hankow negotiations then underway in Peking – or to at least modify their offer by withdrawing T–P terms.

At a sacrifice of the Fraser Note the Hongkong Bank had obtained support for a policy which had led, apparently, to an entente relative to the Canton–Hankow line. The policy of adequate control would seem to have won the approval of Addis's associates and, Addis assumed, of their Governments. Then all was to fall apart.

The German delegates, Schröder and Erich, had at first undertaken to withdraw their offer of T–P terms and to send appropriate instructions by cable to Peking. The cable was never sent; the other members of the KfAG refused their assent, and the negotiations were reopened. When Addis was informed of this by cable from Berlin on March 3, he confirmed to the DAB that Bland had already rejected T–P terms on behalf of the Consortium. Addis then repeated his request that the DAB do the same. Under pressure from the German Foreign Ministry the DAB on behalf of the KfAG refused.[55]

Instead, the Germans subsequently stated that, if successful, they would offer to share the loan with the British and French Groups.[56] As the basis of the loan would presumably be T–P terms, such action would negate the entire

[d] As defined in the Anglo-French-German Protocol, Canton–Kowloon (C–K) terms included:
  (i) Appointment of the (Chief) Engineer to be approved by the lenders.
  (ii) Commission to be shared between the three Groups as may be arranged hereafter.
  (iii) The British preference having been abandoned, an endeavour would be made to substitute a preference to the 'lenders', the Chinese retaining, within these limits, the right to purchase railway material in the open market.

purpose of the Protocol. 'What', Addis asked in a personal letter, 'can you do with men like that?'[57]

'Not honourable according to our ideas,' was Addis's final verdict.[58]

But there was a reason for the German position.

Events in Peking and their impact in Europe

In Peking the DAB representative, Heinrich Cordes, had continued to discuss the Canton–Hankow Railway loan with Chang Chih-tung on T–P terms, while J.O.P. Bland, thinking that his position was secure, stood firmly for the C–K terms which Chang had so often refused. Unwisely Bland also refused to inform Chang of the financial terms of the loan, thereby making comparison impossible and technically violating the terms of the 1905 Fraser Note. Grand Councillor Chang Chih-tung was himself under pressure from the Yu-ch'uan Pu (Ministry of Posts and Communications), who resented his interference in railway matters.[59]

The issues were clearly defined.

Preference had been given under the terms of the Fraser Note to Britain; the British authorities accepted that the B&CC had already shown interest in the Canton–Hankow line and were ready to negotiate with the Chinese. Accordingly the Chinese were informed that the Legation supported the B&CC. The B&CC's experience led them to negotiate on the basis of the more stringent C–K terms and in this they were joined by the French. Their position was made obligatory by their respective Governments who were opposed to terms which, lacking adequate control, might later involve the Legations in lengthy disputes with the Chinese authorities. The Germans, excluded from the negotiations, independently offered the easier T–P terms, but then signed a protocol with the British and French agreeing to negotiate on C–K terms. This protocol was not ratified; the German offer of easier terms stood.

Only China's understanding with Britain that a British firm would receive preferential treatment on an equal-terms basis now stood in the way of China's acceptance of the more favourable German offer.

Chang Chih-tung's task was to force British admission of the position or, alternatively, force the B&CC to offer 'equal terms', that is, T–P terms. The weak point was Bland. He had not correctly assessed the situation and was unaware that his principals in London might shift their position. He was also ill-advised in his approach to negotiating with China's elder statesman.

On February 13, 1909, Bland fell into the trap. According to Chang Chih-tung, J.O.P. Bland left an interview 'in a fit of temper' with the remark, 'without the chief engineer's signing [for all expenditures] he would refuse to undertake the loan. If there is another Power that wanted to undertake it, then China could go ahead and settle with that Power.'[60]

This is precisely what Chang Chih-tung would attempt, but first the record must be clear. On February 20, confident that he could obtain the terms he wished from the DAB, Chang sent Bland through Liang Tun-yen, the President of the Wai-wu Pu (the Minister of Foreign Affairs), what amounted to an ultimatum: (i) the chief engineer would not be allowed to sign for the purchase of materials or other expenditures, (ii) T–P terms, and (iii) settlement in two days. Bland's response was delayed but his cable to London on March 3 made it clear he still thought C–K terms possible in the absence of competition if all stood firm. Liang was later to refer to the statement as a threat to make a 'corner against the Chinese' in the European money markets from which Chang was merely 'making his escape'.[61] Bland concluded his cable by asking for telegraphic instructions as quickly as possible, but no record has been found in the Foreign Office files of further communication from London.[62]

On March 6 Bland refused on behalf of the B&CC any agreement on Tientsin–Pukow terms; he then asked for a further day to reconsider. On the evening of the 7th, the Chinese having heard nothing further from Bland, intensified the pace of their negotiations with the Germans. Jordan wired the Foreign Office that the Germans might now accept on T–P terms 'at any moment'.[63]

News that a preliminary agreement with the DAB for finance of the Canton–Hankow Railway on T–P terms had been actually signed in Peking reached London on March 8, only a week after the Protocol agreeing to C–K terms had been signed by the Germans in Berlin. Eba Addis put the matter in human terms by noting in the diary, 'Telegrams from three different sources told him [Charles Addis] of it, but he still thinks there must be some mistake. It would be too mean – & then they have accepted the invitation to a grand dinner at the Carlton on Friday.'

The following day there was some relief. Although Cordes had signed the preliminary agreement, the Deutsch-Asiatische Bank in Berlin had not as yet confirmed his signature.

Bland was blamed in the contemporary press for bungling the negotiations and questions were asked in Parliament. Having been involved in the difficulties which followed the Tientsin–Pukow and the Shanghai–Ningpo agreements, Bland had strong views on control. As the representative of the B&CC he saw their survival at stake.

To put these criticisms in their proper context: Bland was not acting on his own; he was standing on the Canton–Kowloon terms, including control, and these terms had been endorsed by Addis and agreed, Bland had reason to believe, among the British, French, and German Groups.

But Bland had failed to reassess the changing situation; he had discounted the German factor; for this reason, perhaps, he did not successfully communicate to his principals the seriousness of Chang's 'ultimatum'. His fault was not his insistence on C–K terms but his handling of the negotiation process; he had fallen into Chang's trap and the British position had been destroyed on Bland's responsibility.

Addis's later summary of Bland's action, following his subsequent recall by the B&CC board in May 1909 as *persona non grata* in China, was particularly harsh, but it touched the key elements of the fatal decision:

Who is to blame? I say Bland. The order to refuse the T–P terms was not ours. It was the order of our own government, aye in concert with the French government, but to interpret that order in such a way as to provoke a rupture of negotiations indicates an ineptitude, an elementary inacquaintance with the very meaning of oriental negotiations which is hard to understand. I ascribe his blunder to his pinning his faith, rashly and mistakenly, to a mistaken interpretation of the obligation of the Chinese government under the Fraser Agreement, to a totally mistaken idea of the ability of the Germans to finance the loan, and to an impetuous and not too conciliatory manner.[64]

The position at this point was that British interests had apparently lost whatever advantage might have been obtained from the Hong Kong Government's £1.1 million loan and the Fraser Note of 1905. The agreement with the DAB on T–P terms confirmed Bland's fear that China would never again agree to control, thereby, in the view of Bland and many others, leaving the B&CC without a role. Furthermore, nothing could at this stage be corrected by expression of 'right'; it is true that Liang, as the President of the Wai-wu Pu, had promised to inform Jordan before the Chinese approached a non-British lender, but to Jordan's protest the Chinese replied that Bland had first refused terms which the Germans had then accepted, the B&CC had been put forward as the only British syndicate, and hence China's undertaking to Britain had been fulfilled.[65]

The Germans too appeared in an unassailable position. They had asked to participate in the Anglo-French syndicate for this project but had been refused. They had warned of the inapplicability of the 1898 spheres of interest agreement. They had then only accepted the Chinese offer when they learned that J.O.P. Bland, on behalf of the Anglo-French syndicate, had refused the terms offered.

Or put more brutally, the poorly executed though well-intended action of the B&CC representative had damaged not only the B&CC's, and through them the Hongkong Bank's, prospects but those of all British firms who might otherwise have participated in the railway's construction. Here, indeed, was a clear example of why consultation with the Foreign Office by banks and syndicates had become a necessity. Bland had in fact consulted; the events were therefore also illustrative of the need for proper lines of communication and full coordination between the syndicates and their Governments, a coordination rendered difficult by the reluctance of both parties to become too dependent on each other.

In all this Bland had been but an agent; the issues were more important. Bland was, however, articulate and respected. He could be a persistent though, as it turned out, ineffective adversary. But he was a person to reckon with.

In Europe the B&CC and their French associates, the various foreign ministries and the DAB had to consider a course of action based on the existing situation and long-term expectations.

Addis urged the Foreign Office to protest the course of events to Berlin, but Sir Edward Grey was correct in pointing out that up to this point the Foreign Office had made no comment on the affair and there was consequently nothing on which to base something as serious as a formal protest.

There was, however, as Addis saw, an opportunity and a way out. The opportunity remained only so long as the DAB refrained from confirming Cordes's signature. As for the way out, there was a weak link in the German argument: by signing the Protocol the DAB had already agreed in principle that they would not negotiate on terms less severe than C–K, yet their success in the Canton–Hankow negotiations had depended on their accepting the easier T–P terms. The only possible justifications were (i) a failure of communication with Cordes in Peking or (ii) the legalistic quibble that the Protocol, although signed, had not been ratified. Addis knew that in fact the Germans had communicated positively with Peking, but here was a public excuse available and the matter could be remedied by the Germans withdrawing the still unconfirmed agreement; if they pleaded the quibble, they must be shown that the Hongkong Bank at least did not accept this as appropriate behaviour.

The German-Chinese agreement had not been confirmed; it must be withdrawn.

The Three Power Groups Consortium – initial negotiations

The question of German withdrawal

The Berlin cable, dated March 9, formally notifying Addis of the German success stated:

As in accordance with our telegraphic correspondence Friday, Saturday last week [March 5–6], we could not instruct Cordes to withdraw from negotiations. The latter telegraphs that the Chinese Government has accepted an offer made by us for Deutsch-Chinesische Eisenbahn-Gesellschaft for £3,000,000 sterling 5% loan at 95 in terms Tientsin–Pukow final agreement for construction of Hankow–Canton railway. Bearing in mind that on your side preferential rights are claimed for this line, we think that the Chinese Government has accepted only for the purpose of trying to get better conditions from you. Will discuss matter on Friday [March 12], having reserved eventual participation of English and French groups.[66]

At the Friday meeting with William Keswick in the Chair, Charles Addis, representing the British and Chinese Corporation, took a firm position.[e] In the context of the Protocol, Addis argued, the British and French Groups had undertaken not to do business on T–P terms and consequently refused business they would otherwise have had; the Germans, by breaking the agreement, obtained business which they would not have had. By so doing, Addis continued, they had, however unwittingly, inflicted loss and detriment to the other signatories and, as honourable men, he looked to them to rectify their error.[67]

The German position, however technically valid, was weak in a long-term European political context; they hesitated, agreeing not to upset the *status quo* until the final inter-group agreement was signed and calling for diplomatic assistance in Peking to adjust the situation.

The meeting concluded on the 13th with the signing of a memorandum of agreement, stressing equality, including the Canton–Hankow line – and thus requiring the withdrawal of the German offer. The memorandum also laid stress on three minimum control conditions: (i) appointment of the Engineer-in-Chief by the lenders (with a British engineer for the Canton–Hankow line), (ii) proceeds of the loan to be under the control of the lenders until actually required for construction on certification of the Engineer-in-Chief, and (iii) provision for proper account keeping and financial control under the direction of a Chief Accountant to be approved by the lenders.[68]

On March 17 the DAB instructed Cordes by cable not to sign the final agreement, but, as the Foreign Office noted, the cable did not instruct him to cease negotiations or maintain the *status quo*.[69] The situation was still tense.

The German position was clarified on March 20 with the request for two separate agreements: (i) between the banks, the Hongkong Bank, the DAB, and the Banque de l'Indo-Chine, providing for the sharing of all loans on the model of the 1895 Agreement and (ii) between the interested corporations, the B&CC, the CCR, the Deutsch-Chinesische Eisenbahn-Gesellschaft, and a railway syndicate to be formed by the French for railway loans and advances only. The Germans insisted on the abolition of any reference to spheres of interest, but, at the same time, argued that Shantung must be excluded from

---

[e] Meyer and Jamieson were present for the CCR; Simon and Ullmann represented the French and Erich and Rehders the Germans.

the agreement. The Foreign Office, working on the pragmatic basis that no British firm would wish to build a railway in Shantung, decided not to oppose the Germans simply on a matter of principle.[70] However, the Germans made the implementation of any new agreements dependent on the DAB's current preliminary agreement with China on the Canton–Hankow line being successfully renegotiated to include the control provisions which had been accepted in the Protocol, that is, C–K terms.[71]

On this basis Addis informed the Foreign Office that negotiations could reopen.[72] With the draft of the final agreement prepared, Addis scheduled a meeting in Paris for April 2.[73] A banquet was scheduled for the same evening; the delegates would then move to Brussels, where the Belgians were involved through the French, and there would be a second banquet.

On March 26, however, the German Group informed Addis that they could no longer withdraw from the preliminary Peking agreement. Repeated cables from the *Times* correspondent, G.E. Morrison, reinforced by alleged statements of the B&CC representative, J.O.P. Bland, predicted that the Germans would withdraw under pressure due to their inability to float the loan without British assistance. This made actual withdrawal now appear as confirmation of Morrison's claim that the Germans could not meet the terms of their agreements.

These allegations Bland denied by cable; Addis claimed he could not find in *The Times* the alleged messages from Morrison. Urbig then sent Addis a copy of a German newspaper which reprinted the *Times* report. Apparently the German Minister, Baron von Rex, had been pressing Cordes to conclude the agreement contrary to policy in Europe; after considerable exchanges of urgent cables etc., the *status quo* was nevertheless maintained.[74]

The role of Charles Addis

Despite this altercation the negotiations were in fact resumed in Paris on April 2 as scheduled and, with S. Simon of the Banque de l'Indo-Chine in the Chair, the British Group pressed for a formal German withdrawal of their Peking offer; the Germans once again refused. They offered instead their previous proposal, to attempt to amend the terms to accord with the Protocol. But, they warned, should the Chinese prove unwilling, they would sign the loan agreement.

The thrust of the Anglo-French argument as presented by Addis remained unchanged: (i) the B&CC had been negotiating to obtain C–K terms but were always free to adjust should they choose to do so, (ii) the Anglo-French Groups and the German Group then signed a Protocol requiring negotiations on C–K terms, thus tying the hands of the B&CC negotiator, (iii) the Chinese refused C–K terms as offered by Bland for the B&CC (and French Group),

(iv) the British then 'withdrew', (v) the DAB, having just been party to the Protocol, when approached after the B&CC withdrawal, nevertheless continued to negotiate on terms which by the Protocol they should have refused, actually signing an agreement and picking up business which, under the restraint of the Protocol, the British had just refused. This, it seemed to Addis, was 'unfair'.

The banquet was held on schedule (Moussigny 1863), and the conference resumed on Saturday, April 3, with Franz Urbig urging that the impossible Canton–Hankow question be shelved and the *entente générale* be considered.[75]

The French responded simply, 'Tout depend sur M. Addis . . . where he goes, we will follow.' And they very loyally did so.

Accordingly Urbig came to Addis and put the matter bluntly. Was Addis really prepared, merely to have the satisfaction of proving himself in the right to sacrifice the two finest railways in China and £22 million of loans?[f] The French were ready to agree, so were Addis's colleagues.

Addis replied, 'Whatever my colleagues might be prepared to do for the sake of expediency, I will not give way.' But typical of Addis, if he made such a statement he had a potential solution in mind. If the Germans could not withdraw their offer, what if the Chinese were induced to withdraw? Urbig took the point; this way Germany would not, as Rehders had expressed it, 'speaking in the Chinese manner', lose face.[76]

Although not reflected clearly in the formal proceedings, this was in fact the basis for the continued negotiations. At the conclusion of the meeting on April 3, however, no immediate solution was in sight.

Franz Urbig at one point threw up his hands, at another he claimed to have misunderstood the term 'withdraw' assuming that the British had refused a Chinese offer and had withdrawn completely any interest in the affair, an assumption made possible (though not credible) by the way Bland had handled the negotiations. But it was the timing that told against the Germans. Urbig then outlined the long association of the Hongkong Bank and the DAB claiming that they had always been loyal. This provoked the following exchange:

ADDIS: . . . And I am sure you will agree, Mr Urbig, that I have never used one word to indicate that there was bad faith . . .

URBIG: Well, I don't know! You have used some words such as "unfair", and so on . . . [laughing][77]

The situation might be described as grim. Addis, on behalf of the British and French Groups, concluded the meeting by reading the following protest:

The British and the French Groups beg to place on record their deep regret at the

---

[f] The £22 million refers to all possible loans for all possible lines radiating from Hankow; it was never a practical figure.

decision arrived at by the German Group, in consequence of which they are unable to continue these negotiations any longer, but having laid down the principle that some reasonable measure of control over the expenditure of the loan funds is absolutely necessary as a safeguard to the European bondholders – they have no alternative but to part company with their German friends. They wish also to state that they now hold themselves at liberty to take whatever steps they may deem necessary in their own interests, relieved of any obligation under the Protocol.[78]

The hope which Addis entertained for his private proposal to Urbig was reinforced when he learned that, despite these adverse developments, by April 5 at least the Germans had still not confirmed Cordes's signature. Addis commented, 'While there's life there's hope!'

Similarly at the Foreign Office Addis's optimism, based on Urbig's privately expressed but obvious desire to come to an agreement, was linked closely to Sir Edward Grey's previous proposal (on which Addis's position had been partly based) to protest to Peking on the basis of the 1905 Fraser Note and the failure of the Chinese to notify the British Minister of their decision to turn to a non-British syndicate; Grey's and Addis's ultimate intention was to encourage the Chinese to 'kick out' the Germans, the latter thus 'saving face'.[79]

Holding firm

Addis feared that the Foreign Office was weakening and Grey, on the eve of his departure for Northumberland, suggested capitulation, by accepting the offered participation in the German loan on T–P terms. Addis recorded, '*I will not* give in.'[80] Grey might be Foreign Minister but Addis was responsible for the commercial interests of the Hongkong Bank; he knew that the B&CC would be trustees for the bondholders.[81]

At this point the negotiations in Europe were broken off temporarily. There were two separate issues: (i) the survival of the concept of an *entente générale* and the inclusion of the Canton–Hankow/Hankow–Szechuan or Hukuang loan within its framework – this was the issue between the Anglo-French Groups and the German Group and (ii) the actual terms of future railway agreements: as a minimum, financial control through the Chief Engineer or the auditor in a form which would permit the Bank to refuse to pay out funds in the absence of the engineer's/auditor's favourable recommendation. This was the issue with the Chinese.[82] The April meetings had shown that general agreement on the minimum terms required could probably be reached, once the difficult position of the still pending German preliminary agreement on a Canton–Hankow loan could be resolved.

Negotiations were in fact resumed in May, and Addis received Sir Edward Grey's authority to make the best arrangements he could with the Germans.[83]

In Peking it had become clear that the Chinese would not deal with the B&CC, partly perhaps because of Bland's methods but partly because the corporation was linked with the concept of a railway 'concession'. Furthermore, Sir John Jordan was aware that the DAB also preferred to deal with the Hongkong Bank. Accordingly the negotiations were switched to the Bank, as indeed Addis had originally proposed. In making this change Addis noted that the transaction would nevertheless be for the account of the B&CC.[84] E.G. Hillier then replaced J.O.P. Bland as the responsible negotiator in the capital.

Addis, however, may have underestimated the force and nature of the opposition to the British position both in China and in Germany. As the British Minister, Sir John Jordan, put the situation privately to Sir Edward Grey, 'Hongkong and Shanghai Bank seem too inclined to ignore political side of this matter in their anxiety to conclude financial bargain.'[85]

Chang Chih-tung's traditional policy was opposition to combinations of foreign powers, but with Britain claiming a priority of interest in the Yangtze Valley, the intervention of a foreign power which might break this claim appeared desirable, even if this were brought about by a temporary alliance. A Three Power Groups Consortium for the Canton–Hankow Railway would break the British monopoly by bringing in France and Germany; it had been to forestall such a development that the Hong Kong Government had in 1905 lent the Wuchang Viceroy £1.1 million.

On the German side, Count Fürstenburg was opposed to the view that the '*entente générale*' was necessarily beneficial for the Konsortium für Asiatische Geschäfte (KfAG). 'Now is the time to get out of the British embrace,' he had urged.[86] His advice was to close first with the Chinese and then deal with the British and French in terms of a general agreement. The formal position of the German Foreign Office was that they could not advise the DAB to withdraw the offending Canton–Hankow Railway loan offer, a fact of which Addis was aware and which governed his dealings with Urbig and his colleagues.[87]

In early May Addis was writing that, as time went by, the force of the opposition to the German loan was weakening in both France and Britain.

The British Minister has ratted . . . Grey has ratted. The B & C Chairman has ratted. Hillier has ratted. In fact I believe [Sir F.] Campbell, the permanent undersecretary, and I are the only two stalwarts left. To one and all I answer, 'I will not give in. If you want to rat, you must get somebody else to do it, for I will not.'[88]

Addis omitted to record that S. Simon and Ullmann of the French Group remained firm.[89]

The Powers had virtually accepted that they could not require China to agree to terms which were contrary to their firmly held policy. If the loan were to be made at all, the Groups must compromise.

Addis's and the Hongkong Bank's position assumed that, if the Groups stood firm and if their Governments supported them, the Chinese would eventually accept C–K terms. Behind this was Addis's firm conviction that C–K terms were advantageous to the Chinese; the terms would ensure the construction and management of the railway under the lowest cost conditions. Addis was also convinced that C–K terms were the minimum a potential trustee could sign. His position was not eccentric; in signing the Protocol the three Groups had acknowledged their validity. Bland's fault had not been in his insistence on C–K terms but on his conduct of the negotiations.

Addis was standing firm waiting for favourable developments in China. In this he was, it seemed at first, rewarded for his patience.

The British protests in Peking were at length successful in dissuading the Chinese from insisting that the Germans close the Canton–Hankow Railway Agreement (on T–P terms) with them, and on May 13, following a partial breakthrough and preliminary agreement in the negotiations between Hillier/ Cordes and the Chinese in Peking on both the Canton–Hankow and the Hankow–Szechuan lines, the European negotiations could be resumed in Berlin.[90]

The Berlin meetings of May 1909

The exclusive support issue
At this crucial point a long-suppressed issue had to be considered.

All parties wished for a general agreement on China loans, but the agreement (or agreements if the German two-tier system were approved) had always been designed for signature by firms in the private sector. Indeed this had long been the pattern, but whereas in 1895, 1898, 1905, and 1907 the agreements had been made without continuous reference to the Foreign Office and sustained diplomatic advice and had been for limited purposes, it was clear that a general agreement of the kind Addis and his European colleagues now envisaged was comprehensive and long term and would be fully effective only if the national Groups had exclusive Government support. Such support was the more likely the more comprehensive was the coverage of each national Group.

The British Group could not be described as comprehensive; the Bank could not guarantee to the French and German Groups that other British firms – for example, the Chartered Bank, Pauling and Co., or Samuel and Co., despite their shareholding in the B&CC – or British adventurers and concession-hunters would not receive Foreign Office support and, being outside any general agreement, be free to operate on any terms which suited them.

This was not a new problem. Indeed, the B&CC had joined with the Pekin Syndicate and the Yangtze Valley Company to rationalize their competition by the formation of the Chinese Central Railways, Ltd; they were thus able to obtain Foreign Office support for their immediate projects. The present negotiations, involving diplomatic intervention at the highest level, seemed perhaps an appropriate time for the Foreign Office to insert a word of warning – the Hongkong Bank should not promise more in Berlin than it could in the end deliver.

Grey therefore warned Addis that he could expect exclusive support for the British Group only for the two lines under negotiation, Canton–Hankow and Hankow–Szechuan. He concluded the interview with some long-standing advice:

I suggested to Mr Addis that the difficulty of affording support to a particular group in this country would be, in a great measure, removed if it were possible for the principal firms of financiers and contractors of good standing interested in business in the Far East to amalgamate. The French and German groups at present negotiating with the Hongkong and Shanghai Bank, were, I pointed out, formed of a combination of financial firms, and in the same way the firms of Armstrong and Vickers, Maxim have combined for certain undertakings in Japan.[91]

Unless, that is, the Hongkong Bank were to broaden its British base of support, all these negotiations and all this overhead of inter-bank agreements were in reality (and from the British standpoint) relevant to only two lines. The DAB realized this as a latent weakness of the Hongkong Bank's position and from time to time expressed concern. As it took some two more years to close the loan for the lines then under consideration, the DAB's concern and the Foreign Office advice were premature; in 1912 the advice would have to be given again, and in 1912 the Hongkong Bank agreed.

Addis as negotiator

It was with this caution that Charles Addis of the Hongkong Bank left for Berlin where he once again played a prominent role, perhaps even dominated the proceedings.

They began in a tense atmosphere and little progress was apparently made the first day. The German Government would not yield, and Addis sent a warning cable to the Foreign Office in London.[92] At the formal banquet there was a 'great gathering and magnificent with personal decorations, but an air of constraint hung upon the scene which was extremely distressing'. Addis continued:

I was the last to speak and from the hush it seemed that the English pronouncement was awaited with curiosity and even anxiety. Happily I had what I can only regard as an inspiration. Dropping the official tone entirely I began by saying that I hoped I might be pardoned if I referred to the painful and distressing illness that had deprived us of the presence that evening of their chairman . . .[93]

Addis had broken the ice, and the changed atmosphere permitted that informal negotiation which is often essential to a successful conference.

The delegates agreed in principle to a two-tier *entente générale*; they also concluded a specific agreement calling for a £5.5 million loan for the Canton–Hankow line on C–K terms, including (i) an English engineer for the whole Canton–Hankow line, (ii) a German engineer limited to east of Ichang, the Hupei section of the Szechuan (Hankow–Chengtu) line, and (iii) waiver of the German demand to supply all the material for the line east of Ichang. The agreement was initialled by all three Groups on June 2.[94]

The outcome of this operation was reported to the Kaiser by Reichskanzler von Bülow as an achievement by German finance; the British monopoly in the Yangtze Valley had been broken.[95] There was a similar reaction in China.

The reaction in China

The Powers having arrived at this tri-partite accord, the results had to be presented to and accepted by the Chinese, who refused to deal with the B&CC. In part this was said to be due to what the Chinese referred to as the 'extravagance' of the corporation, referring mainly to the cost of the Shanghai–Nanking line and not, the Foreign Office noted, to any suggestion of irregularity.[96] The impracticality of the B&CC withdrawing from China, given its already heavy commitments, and the cost of forming a similar corporation with but a different name led both Addis and Hillier to resist. Addis even cabled Head Office in Hong Kong, but they made no contribution. The Bank offered to request the B&CC to withdraw Bland, and although Chang Chih-tung at first stressed the need for the B&CC itself to withdraw, in the end it was clear that the attack was on Bland personally.[97]

The crisis was resolved by June 6. The Bank would sign the agreement and the B&CC would be permitted the agency for purchases, 'on the other hand, Mr Hillier gave an undertaking that the Corporation would no longer be represented by J.O.P. Bland' and that, furthermore, he would not be subsequently reinstated.[98] As Jordan commented to Sir Edward Grey:

Chang himself, it may be mentioned, dictated the terms of this arrangement, and showed a strong personal bias against Mr. Bland. It was a clear case of either sacrificing Mr. Bland or the interests of the Corporation, and your instructions left me in no doubt as to which of the two alternatives we should accept.[99]

Although the Hukuang Loan was now a matter fully agreed upon by the British, German, and French Groups and by the Chinese, the loan was not in fact signed because at this point the United States in the formidable shape of President William Howard Taft, former Governor–General of the Philippine Islands, intervened. Although this became an immediate topic of debate, the French prevailed on their colleagues in Britain and Germany to attend to the inter-group agreements and formalize the *entente générale* first. Perhaps this was just as well because by the end of June the Russians were asking to know why the Russo-Asiatic Bank was being excluded – Grey's subsequent response that this was a matter among private banks, to whom the Russians might wish to apply, did not end the matter.[100]

The entente générale

On July 2, 1909, preliminary problems had been solved and a full-scale meeting was scheduled for London on July 7.

The two basic agreements which formed the *entente générale* were (i) an agreement relative to railway loans between the British and Chinese Corporation, Ltd, the Chinese Central Railways, Ltd, the Banque de l'Indo-Chine, and the Chinesische Eisenbahn-Gesellschaft and (ii) the inter-bank Group agreement between the Hongkong and Shanghai Banking Corporation, the Banque de l'Indo-Chine, and the Deutsch-Asiatische Bank. The French and German organizations represented the same range of firms in both agreements.

The first agreement was based on equality, minimum acceptable control terms, and the basis for deciding on the nationality of Chief Engineers and other key personnel to be appointed in each railway agreement. The second, which involved the Hongkong Bank directly, was in form an extension of the 1895 Hongkong Bank/DAB Agreement to include the Banque de l'Indo-Chine – the original 1895 Agreement, however, remained separate and in force.

The situation in mid-1909

The position of the Hongkong Bank

The initialling of a Hukuang loan agreement and the signing of the two memorandums of agreement concluded the first stage of the internationalization of foreign lending to China and appeared to mark the success of the Hongkong Bank's policy as interpreted and conducted by Charles Addis. On the other hand nothing had as yet been signed with China, and that country's Government, however beset with dynastic problems in Peking, gentry intransigence in the provinces, and growing anti-Manchu nationalism throughout the Empire, was able to keep the foreigners at bay, even dictating the virtual expulsion of one of the best known British industrial representatives and journalists, J.O.P. Bland, on the ostensible grounds of what amounted to 'disrespect'.

The *entente générale*, involving British, French, and German Groups, was exclusive or comprehensive depending on whether it was regarded as having a political or a financial objective. It was intended to have the latter and in fact covered the relevant capital markets of the world.

Even before the signing, however, the Russians and Americans were making enquiries; at the national level the British Foreign Secretary was warning the Hongkong Bank that they would receive no guaranteed exclusive support beyond the two lines then being negotiated. Under the 'open door' policy there seemed to be no resting point between the rejected spheres of interest, the once-feared 'break up of China', and total cartelization of foreign lending to China. If the latter were ever achieved, the Chinese would not accept it, and there would always be sufficient interests outside any practical network of firms which were actually party to the international agreement to provide the Chinese the basis and indeed the encouragement for disruption.

The Hongkong Bank's position was particularly exposed. Its dominance in China finance rested on the firmest of grounds – long experience and expertise, head office location, Peking contacts, sound commercial contacts, a world-wide network to finance China requirements, appropriate contacts in the City of London, firm international relations especially with the Deutsch-Asiatische Bank, and genuine concern for the economic welfare and development of China.

Nevertheless, by 1909 the Bank's merchant-banking and diplomatic expertise was dangerously thin. Head Office would seem to have played little part in the proceedings, the Board of Directors even less. All had once been delegated to Sir Thomas Jackson but he was now in London, and the focus of the Foreign Office was on the London branch. Sir Ewen Cameron had died, A.M. Townsend, the senior Manager, played a minimal role; in Hamburg Julius Brüssel, whose expertise was utilized in early negotiations with the DAB in Berlin, had died, and F.T. Koelle, whatever his abilities as Manager Hamburg, was never used for quasi-diplomatic negotiations in the same way.

As the French delegation has been quoted as saying, 'Tout depend sur M. Addis.' This was true in London with one modification – Addis had the London Consultative Committee and he sat on the boards of the B&CC and CCR; he was not entirely alone. In Peking there was E.G. Hillier; Bland had not only gone, he had become a bitter opponent. With S.F. Mayers, Bland's replacement recruited from the Foreign Service, Addis would find a highly qualified B&CC associate, but that was all. Certainly Addis could, as previously noted, depend on highly competent backup from the Hongkong Bank in Tientsin and Shanghai, but the conceptual leadership and execution were all in his hands. There would be a reaction in the 1920s, but for the present this summarizes the Bank's internal position.

Not only was Addis the Bank's sole negotiator in London, he also carried the normal burden of the co-managership of London Office; he personally signed a high proportion of the thousands of bonds the Bank issued as agents for the Imperial Chinese Government.[101] In 1912, it is true, he became the senior Manager and so was more the master of his time, but he was then associated with H.D.C. Jones with whom he found it difficult to work. Even in twentieth-century London 'mail day' remained as it had been for over a hundred years, a day full of details requiring immediate attention.

Addis once wrote of his ideal manager – one freed from routine and with time to think; Addis found time to think, possibly on his walk home for late 'nursery' tea with his family at Primrose Hill, but not until his retirement from the Bank in 1922 would he escape the routine.

Exclusive support reconsidered

Sir Edward Grey used the opportunity of his reply to the Russian Ambassador relative to the Russian membership in the Consortium to restate the official British Government relationship with the Hongkong Bank: 'His Majesty's Government . . . are, as regards future business as to which no engagements have yet been entered into, under no obligation to support the Hongkong and Shanghai Bank should other British firms wish to compete and should the Chinese Government choose to employ them.'[102]

This followed Grey's pre-meeting warning to Addis and Sir John Jordan's comments in support of Grey's position. Jordan's arguments in opposition to continued exclusive support for a single financial group or firm are not echoes of the traditional nineteenth-century reluctance of the diplomat to become involved in the sordid transactions of commerce – an attitude which was not, as noted earlier in this history, in any case universal. Jordan had seen the practical problem of refusing to assist otherwise eligible British firms and he recognized that a combine having Government support might depend heavily on Government intervention rather than careful and competitive negotiation.

On the other hand Jordan did recognize that the organization of a British Group as comprehensive as the French or German was impractical. This did not prevent the Hongkong Bank from being subjected to criticism for not having formed one.

These were not theoretical discussions. In March 1909 the Foreign Office took note of Pauling and Co.'s negotiations with Émile Erlanger and Co. and several Belgian firms, including the Société Belge de Chemins de fer en Chine and the Société Générale de Belgique; in May 1909, Pauling and Co. had come to an agreement with China on a survey of the Kweilin–Chuangchow Railway, in October they reached an agreement with the American Group in relation to the Chinchow–Aigun Railway; in 1910 Dunn, Fischer and Co. were involved in the purchase of bonds of the 7% Peking–Hankow Railway Redemption Loan referred to above; in 1912 the Chinese Engineering and Mining Company, the Jackson International Financial Syndicate, and G. Birch Crisp and Co. loans were perhaps the main 'other British' involvements to have reached a stage sufficient for listing in, for example, MacMurray's collection (see Table II.1).[103]

Many of the loans listed in Table 7.1 (p. 451) received sympathetic reception at the Legation; the Crisp loan, however, will receive further consideration in relation to the 1913 Reorganization Loan (see Chapter 8).

The list confirms on the one hand that there was potential competition for the 'British Group' defined as the Hongkong Bank in association with the B&CC and the CCR, and on the other that it was limited. Later, when operations expanded further, the Hongkong Bank would be required as a prerequisite to further Foreign Office support to accept additional banks into the British Group, but the Bank, led by Addis, continued to dominate the field. The Foreign Office did not object in principle to supporting the Bank and its associates on a case-by-case basis, and at this for the time being the matter rested.

ADDIS, HILLIER, AND BLAND – THE CONTROVERSY PERSONALIZED

The Hongkong Bank's relations with its two associated companies, the British and Chinese Corporation and the Chinese Central Railways, were considered in Chapter 6. However the climax of dissension came in mid-1909 after a year of increasing acrimony in a form which focused on the differing views and personalities of Charles Addis, E.G. Hillier, and J.O.P. Bland. In an effort to clarify the issues it may, paradoxically, be helpful to reconsider the controversy in the context of the interrelationships between these three principal participants in the key events.

The events outlined

J.O.P. Bland, former secretary to Sir Robert Hart and to the Shanghai Municipal Council, was Charles Addis's choice for B&CC 'Representative in China' with the duty, *inter alia*, of protecting the Corporation's interests there. He was appointed in October 1905. This was a new post. In 1903 Byron Brenan had visited China as the Corporation's agent to attempt to counter criticism that the delays in concluding agreements under the pre-Boxer concessions had been caused by inaction on the part of the B&CC. By 1905, however, the complexities of the negotiations required an officer employed by the Corporation and reporting directly to London to be permanently in China. On Addis's recommendation Bland was asked and in June 1906 agreed to act concurrently as the representative of the CCR.

Throughout the period from 1905 to mid-1908 the unofficial correspondence between Addis and Bland suggests a harmonious working relationship and complete exchange of views. By December 1907, however, Bland was reporting his difficulties in dealing with E.G. Hillier, the Hongkong Bank's Peking Agent. In May 1908, with the revelation that for the redemption of the Luhan Railway the Chinese might obtain a purely financial loan negotiated by Hillier on behalf of the Bank, Bland introduced his first criticism of basic B&CC policy. As his relations with Hillier deteriorated, Bland was by June criticizing the role of the Hongkong Bank and thus, indirectly, of Addis.[104] Addis, sensing that there were implications of conflict of interest, consequently turned over the correspondence to George Jamieson, the newly appointed managing director, for an official response; Bland returned Home on leave but his discussion with the board only tended to 'embitter' the relations between the Bank and the B&CC – and between Addis and Bland.[105] The latter had expected Addis to rationalize the role of Hillier in the context of the Bank/B&CC management agreement of 1898, but Addis held out no promises.

Having failed to resolve his concerns and, more serious perhaps, having failed to talk out the issues fully with Addis, Bland wrote a long letter while still in London, following it up with further correspondence from Peking, all of which was critical of the role of the Hongkong Bank and expressing concern for the future of the B&CC under what he chose to see as a policy of purely financial loans. After this the easy exchange between Addis and Bland, the talking out of lines of action through 'semi-official' or 'private' correspondence between a trusted director and the man in the field, the very basis of Bland's working practice, ceased entirely.[106]

The independent negotiating role of Hillier in Peking and the growing lack of communication between Hillier and Bland set the two at cross purposes. Addis had failed to resolve the conflict nor was he able to offer cautionary advice. Thus when Chang Chih-tung expressed his displeasure with Bland and allegedly refused to deal with the B&CC while Bland remained, Hillier reported the position to the board and the board in May 1909 peremptorily and without enquiry recalled and effectively dismissed Bland. For this Bland blamed Addis and, as noted in Addis's diaries, took opportunities to express his 'hatred'.[107]

Bland threatened to sue the board for wrongful dismissal and for refusal to provide him with a letter containing what he considered a 'clean bill of health';

the threat never materialized. He left the B&CC further embittered and became associated with the by then rival interests of Pauling and Co., maintaining a correspondence with Lord ffrench, Pauling and Co.'s Peking representative, in terms which revealed the depth of his personal feelings against Addis and his enmity to the Hongkong Bank. In 1910 Bland, as a B&CC shareholder, moved for the winding up of the company; he received no support at the annual meeting.[108] Addis had attempted a purely personal letter, 'Now that I hope all cause for friction between us is removed . . .', but November 1909 was too soon; Bland did not respond.[109] Only in the 1930s was there the beginning of a forgiving.

Undoubtedly the course of events was influenced by Bland's personality – certainly the documentation is influenced by his tendency to write lengthy, defensive letters. As Addis once observed, 'You cannot stop Bland writing', and at some point he was bound to go too far in his advocacy, to impute blame in a form unacceptable to the very careful Addis. Similarly Bland's public character would conflict with Hillier's reserved and cautious approach. But this only suggests that a biography of Bland would be both useful and of literary interest. For a history of the Hongkong Bank, however, the importance of the Addis/Hillier/Bland controversy lies in the heavily documented criticism of the role the Bank and its London and Peking agents played in the history of railway development in China. The Bland papers provide a virtual review of the issues considered in the last several chapters. Not surprisingly, Bland's comments focus on the roles of Addis and Hillier. Bland was in infrequent touch with Harry Hunter, the Shanghai Manager, and he quotes second-hand the views of J.R.M. Smith, the Chief Manager; Bland would appear not to have even mentioned A.M. Townsend, Addis's titular superior in London.[110]

Bland's preconceptions and the reality

The minimal paid-up capital of the B&CC (see Chapter 5) suggested that the corporation did not intend itself to finance and build railways and other public works in China. This conclusion was reinforced by the fact that Bland was virtually the only executive of the corporation. Jamieson, as managing director, was the only other senior officer, and he was particularly conscious of the extra-corporation forces at work. In China, however, Bland appeared conscious only of the B&CC and his responsibility to protect its interests and, since it was a public company, the interests of the outside shareholders. From his lonely position he conceived his own vision of the B&CC as the sole agency (with the CCR by arrangement) of British railway development interests in China. The lack of corporation overheads was a deficiency remedied, as he interpreted it, by the general management agreements, signed by Jardine, Matheson and Co. and the Hongkong Bank. In the sphere of the corporation's interests, Bland concluded, their senior officers in China must give priority to B&CC affairs, they should work with and through him in furtherance of the corporation's projects. Anything less was treachery.

Unfortunately this was not and could not be the position taken by the B&CC's joint managers in China, the Hongkong Bank and Jardine Matheson. Bland had read too much into the 1898 agreements, which he interpreted as self-denying, binding contracts whereby Jardine's and the Bank would forgo their own advantages in the B&CC's sphere of interest and act entirely on behalf of a corporation about which their China officers knew little and consequently tended on occasion to see as a rival. The Bank agreement stated (par. 3), as Bland so often repeated, 'The Bank shall at all times use its best efforts to promote and further the interests of the [B&CC] and shall at all times and in all respects act subject to the directions and instructions and within the powers and authorities from time to time delegated to it by the Board of Directors of the Company.'[111] The context however would suggest that the Bank was committed to this policy in its previously described role as 'Bankers of the Company' when called upon to act in this capacity. There was nothing to suggest that the Bank, which would be, after all, bankers to the Pekin Syndicate and other potential B&CC rivals in China, was to dedicate itself exclusively to the interests of the B&CC in all matters relative to railway loans to China. Furthermore, the agreement spoke of acting with Jardine, Matheson and Co. in China. This level of cooperation never came about, despite the specific assumptions in Bland's first instructions, described below. In fact Bland came first into conflict with Jardine Matheson in Shanghai; his conflict with the Bank came later.

Bland also had a preconception of how foreign-financed railway construction in China must be organized; he considered a 'concession' essential. By 'concession' Bland did not mean the political concession of the pre-Boxer type; he referred to agreements whereby the financing and the construction would be conjoined, with a construction contract an essential element of the total package. This, indeed, is what a construction firm of the standing of Pauling and Co. expected; this is why they had become shareholders in the B&CC.

Ideally, therefore, Bland saw all British-financed railway construction in China as the responsibility of the B&CC (or CCR), with whom the Chinese would sign a comprehensive agreement. The B&CC would secure the necessary finance through a publicly issued loan managed by the Hongkong Bank. The loan would be well received precisely because the use of funds would be fully controlled. The corporation would accordingly place the construction contract with a contractor of proven ability, for example, with

Pauling and Co. The contractors might then purchase their imported materials through Jardine, Matheson and Co., but that was not certain and it was far down the chain of events.

If the Chinese wanted efficient, economical, and timely railway construction, Bland's position was sound. If the Chinese, whatever their wishes, had no alternative to a 'concession' (in this restricted sense), Bland's position was practical. If there were no non-British rivals, the contracts would be undertaken by British enterprise. Bland recognized that this would not always be the case, but he was certain the terms of the Fraser Note ensured that the Canton–Hankow (Yueh–Han) line at least would be 'British'.

Unfortunately political considerations dominated Chinese thinking. 'Rights Recovery' was recognized by many foreigners as a legitimate expression of national sovereignty, although exaggerated, but there were other factors at work undermining Bland's position. First, there were factions in Court anxious for financial loans with their potential of misappropriation – or, failing purely financial loans, then project loans with minimal controls and consequently no construction contracts. Then there were real political threats from provincial gentry, threats which might take the form of demands for local development of railways but which also had anti-dynastic, anti-Manchu overtones from the beginning.

Unfortunately, too, the Chinese did have alternatives; the competition to lend was at times intense. Addis at Home was aware of this; Bland in Peking was aware of many bluffs. He was not always able to detect a real change in the competitive situation.

Bland's initial problems

Even the B&CC's China administrative arrangements did not work out as planned. Bland, whose home was in Shanghai, intended to base his operations there. Had he done so, he might have made better contact with both Jardine's and the Bank. His initial instructions from the B&CC board envisaged an office in Jardine's Shanghai headquarters and a virtual committee of three – the Bank and Jardine taipans and Bland, that is, the two 'managers' in China with the representative in China – to give effect to the 1898 agreement.[112] His instructions to 'watch and promote the Corporation's interests' were to be 'in cooperation with its joint Managers in China'.[113] But such cooperation was never achieved, and it could be argued that without it the 1898 agreement and Bland's instructions were rendered virtually ineffective. In the absence of the appropriate developments in China Bland's only real communication with the B&CC was his weekly letter to the board. Having failed to establish the necessary relationship with the Shanghai managers, Bland assumed he could substitute Hillier for the Bank in Peking while also dealing with David

Landale for Jardine's in Shanghai, but this was totally outside the spirit of his instructions.

This was not Bland's fault. From the first Bland's work involved negotiations at the capital and almost all his correspondence is datelined Peking, where he needed to deal with two prima donnas – G.E. Morrison, who would resent Bland's writing for *The Times* from Peking, and E.G. Hillier whose methods of secretive negotiation and his wide range of official contacts seemed threatened by Bland's intrusion.

Bland was not unaware of the problems. He recognized that Jardine's in China and Matheson's in London were, regardless of the actual legal connection, separate and their interests not always seen as identical by the Shanghai taipan. B&CC-earned commissions went to London; Shanghai, however, had done the work. Jardine's David Landale made it clear to Bland that 'we must look after ourselves'; he was not undertaking the negotiations to pass on the benefits to companies new to China – and he had Pauling and Co. in mind.[114] The Bank, he said, was taken care of; there was little in the business for Jardine's. Bland, despite the failure of the initial administrative plans, was reasonably successful in handling Landale, but it can hardly be said that he and Jardine's worked closely together.

With the Bank and therefore with Hillier Bland at first had no policy controversy. Indeed, there was a weakness in this, for Bland was corresponding on confidential B&CC matters with only one of the several B&CC directors, Charles Addis of the Hongkong Bank. The B&CC board had reports of this and were critical. When Bland broke with Addis, he was, as already described, without an informal source of information and encouragement; he had no one with whom to discuss his problems. He conjured up conspiracy and turned on his former friend. But in the first years both Addis and Hillier, supported by the British Legation and in concert with Bland, viewed with sincere concern any 'purely financial' railway loan.

Bland was certainly instructed to negotiate with the Chinese on the basis of C–K terms, but somehow, as Bland saw it, negotiations would be shifted to Hillier and the terms would be weakened. That there were sound reasons for the changes is now admitted, but Bland began to see them in terms of the willingness of the bankers to give in too soon, thus ensuring their own profits by sacrificing the B&CC's interests. He was convinced that the Chinese did not have alternative sources of finance and that all should stand firm; when Addis did not, he felt personally betrayed.

The impact of the Luhan Railway redemption negotiations
The break came first as a result of the changing course of the Luhan line redemption negotiations which, in the end, were on a purely financial basis.

The impact of this apparent volte-face in London was reinforced by the course of negotiations for the Canton–Hankow Railway Loan. Bland was not only concerned with the move away from controls and the loss of business for the B&CC, he was more immediately baffled by the unwillingness of Hillier to confide totally in him, his refusal to act or even to formally acknowledge his role as a joint manager for the B&CC, a position which, in fairness to Hillier, was actually Hunter's in Shanghai.

Bland, however, was in Peking and Hillier appeared secretive. Bland appealed to Addis; Addis supported Hillier. As this seemed unreasonable to Bland, he provided further arguments in support of his complaints until finally in June 1908 he decided to place the matter officially before the board of directors.

The focus nevertheless remained on Addis for several reasons: (i) Bland considered Addis his friend who could, if he would, resolve all problems satisfactorily, (ii) Addis alone of the B&CC directors appears to have maintained a continuous interest in its affairs, to have been, until the appointment of Jamieson, the virtual 'managing director', (iii) it was Addis's role which by mid-1908 appeared to Bland to be subject to a conflict of interest, and (iv) in the end it was Addis who obtained the approval of the B&CC and CCR boards for the more flexible policy which Bland saw as the ruin of the two corporations and of sound railway finance in China.

Addis was in fact challenged on two fronts. First, Bland charged that Hillier was working against B&CC policy on instructions the nature of which he refused to reveal but which apparently emanated from Addis and the Bank; second, Pauling's attempted to preempt Addis's policy by obtaining the agreement of the B&CC board to terms which would favour Pauling and Co. in the event of the B&CC's obtaining an actual railway agreement with the Chinese authorities.

Addis successfully resisted both challenges.

The position of Pauling and Co.

Peking was a city of intrigue and Bland seemed to revel in it. There were the tortuous negotiations with the Chinese, the challenge of Hillier and his mysterious instructions from the Bank, the rumours of Addis's secret trips to France and contradictory reports on their outcome, local discussions over reported leaks from the B&CC boardroom, the apparent jealousy of Morrison and the competition to gain the ear of the *Times* editors in London, the role of Japanese intrigue with Chang Chih-tung and the role of the Yokohama Specie Bank; there was the policy struggle within the Legation which various interests tried to influence, and there was the presence of Pauling and Co.

always hopeful of the construction contracts they were so well prepared to handle but which had so far eluded them.

In the summer of 1908 Lord ffrench, Pauling and Co.'s Peking representative, wrote from Peking that Hillier had modified his position; the news was passed on by Pauling's in London to Bland, who was then urging his own policy position before the B&CC board. Hillier, who had seemed reconciled to purely financial transactions, had reportedly opened up a new line of argument. Although he had accepted the prevailing view that once the Chinese had won T–P terms they would never return to C–K terms, he now saw an alternative to pure finance – Hillier apparently was prepared to accept the concept of the construction contract.[115] This solution would make *all* terms irrelevant during the construction period; a foreign company would undertake the work, no doubt using Chinese materials and experts when available, but totally responsible to the Chinese and/or to the B&CC for the completed work. And Pauling and Co. was on the scene and prepared to accept such contracts – they had a record of having constructed 3,566 miles of railway in Britain, Africa, and in the Argentine Republic; they had already been asked to undertake survey work for Chang Chih-tung and other railway officials.

That Bland was already intriguing against both the Bank and Addis is clear from his role relative to Pauling's. With the fact of Hillier's new policy preference assumed proven, the time appeared ripe for those supportive of Pauling's potential role to put pressure on the B&CC board to (i) repudiate the alleged Hongkong Bank willingness to finance China on its own, (ii) to accept the contract concept, and (iii) to enter into closer relations with Pauling's – closer that is than the rather vague general understanding of mutual concern which had been signed in 1907. Bland actually dictated the draft of the letter which the firm, in a version revised by Baron Émile d'Erlanger, whose financial interests were behind Pauling's, eventually addressed to William Keswick, the Chairman of the B&CC. The letter contained a request that Pauling's be invited to present their case at the next board meeting. To confirm any arrangement made, Bland was expected to assist d'Erlanger in obtaining a seat on the B&CC board.[116]

Although Hillier on behalf of the Bank was already negotiating the Luhan Redemption Loan on financial terms which would not even refer to the actual railway and although Pauling was not actually invited to a board meeting, negotiations between Pauling's and the B&CC continued, and Bland was kept informed. From Peking Morrison was actively criticizing the Bank in *The Times*, Pauling's were forming a construction group with French interests, and the other members of the B&CC board were reportedly not unfavourable to

Pauling's overtures. The basic principle contained in Pauling's formal offer of October 14, 1908, was one of mutual, contractual preference, that is, if the B&CC should obtain an appropriate agreement with the Chinese, Pauling's would, other factors being equal, be offered the construction contract; alternatively, if Pauling's obtained the agreement, they would place the financing through the B&CC.

The Pauling offer was considered in November against what was reported to Bland as Addis's 'vehement and energetic protest', but F. Rutherford Harris, Bland's informant, expressed the expectation that Bland in cooperation with ffrench would bring about the same state of relations as if the 'offer' had been accepted by the board.[117] In reply Bland, who had already effectively broken completely with Addis, wrote a letter critical of the latter and incautious in its partisanship for Pauling's – 'incautious' because leaks are not necessarily the monopoly of one side.[118]

Addis would eventually be successful in having the board insist on Pauling's withdrawal of its offer and related correspondence; there was a consequent reversion to the general and ineffective terms of the 1907 understanding. But Addis would not find the task easy. Other members of the board saw some reason in Bland's arguments; a close relationship with an established contractor of high repute would be sound. Pauling's were themselves however prepared to seek railway agreements direct, although they promised to pass back, under appropriate circumstances, the financing to the B&CC; if the B&CC were threatened by the independent action of the Bank would they not be equally threatened by the competition of Pauling's and their French friends – the 'industrials', as Bland called them?

Whether the members of the board reflected on these terms is not recorded. Indeed, in December the B&CC board appeared willing to enter into some closer arrangement with Pauling's provided finance were left entirely to the B&CC. On January 14 Pauling's attempted to 'interpret' this new arrangement in their favour, but by this time Addis was regaining control and the B&CC rejected the interpretation. Then Pauling's made a tactical error. Depending on information of Addis's secret trip to Paris wired by ffrench from Peking, they attacked the 'financial policy now being attempted by Mr Addis of the Hongkong & Shanghai Bank' and revealed the extent of the cooperative efforts between ffrench and Bland in Peking. As Addis put it in his diary, 'My mission to Paris has been wired from London by some traitor [fellow director C.C. Macrae, Addis was later to discover].'[119] Worse still, Addis's efforts to obtain French agreement to German participation in the Canton–Hankow loan had been undermined; it was the beginning of the long road to the Hukuang Railways Loan of 1911 with German and eventually American participation.

To return to the current issue, however, Pauling's letter claimed that they virtually had Chang Chih-tung's agreement for construction of the Canton–Hankow line but that Addis's actions would result in a financial loan the construction benefits of which might go to German or Japanese firms. Pauling's informed the B&CC that they were complaining to the Foreign Office.[120] The barbarians were once again being successfully 'managed' and divided.

On February 18, 1909, Keswick and Baron d'Erlanger discussed the outstanding issues and on the following day d'Erlanger met with Charles Addis. No agreement could be reached. Keswick wrote to insist that all recent arrangements made for closer cooperation be cancelled. His stated reason was precisely the threat of the combined 'industrials'.[121] Before the end of February the outline of Addis's B&CC board-approved plan to abandon the apparently ephemeral advantages of the Fraser Note and bring in the Germans had received the approval of both the Foreign Office and the Colonial Office.[122] But the Germans themselves had not yet accepted; Bland's instructions to negotiate in Peking on C–K terms still stood.

The Hongkong Bank and the 1898 managerial agreement

In the matter of the Luhan negotiations Bland had returned to Peking from Hankow in May 1908 to learn that Hillier, acting on instructions from the Hongkong Bank, was negotiating a redemption loan on purely financial terms while, at the same time, Bland's instructions from the CCR board to obtain some control terms remained unchanged. The eventual explanation from the CCR board was that the Bank had been led to take this measure as a result of Bland's own communications, which cast doubt on the possibility of securing the loan on a control basis. Hillier, however, had been given discretionary not absolute instructions; the Hongkong Bank, that is, Addis, 'would prefer that the business should go to the Chinese Central Railways'. And the board added:

To this extent therefore it would seem that Mr Hillier had discretionary power to cooperate with you and Mr Casenave [of the Banque de l'Indo-Chine] to endeavour to strengthen your hands, and if he acted otherwise, though my Directors may regret it, they are bound to assume that it was not without good reason.[123]

Bland's well-founded argument was, however, that such interference weakened his position.

Bland suspected that behind this explanation was the Hongkong Bank's concept of its position in China despite the terms of the 1898 managerial agreement as interpreted by Bland. As if in confirmation of this Bland received a semi-official letter from George Jamieson, who was also a director of the CCR and who was writing on CCR stationery. Addis, he said, 'maintained that in any case the Bank has the perfect right to take whatever steps it thinks proper in its own interest'.[124] That this was, as stated, unsatisfactory to the CCR was made clear to Bland over the months of December and January, but, while reserving the Bank's position, Addis continued to hold that 'Railway Loans are the business of the British & Chinese Corporation and the Chinese Central Railways' – new railway negotiations relative to the Szechuan Railway tended to confirm this.

But the difficulty [Jamieson wrote] is with the British public – money is a drug in the market and likely to be so for some time. The British public are grabbing at fresh issues and Chinese Loans in particular, and what Addis is afraid of is that if they tell the Chinese plump down that they will do no more loans on the basis of the Anglo-French [Luhan] Redemption Loan, the Chinese may say very well, we will go elsewhere, and he has reason to think – or says so at least – that there are in fact 2 or 3 London Houses in the field.[125]

Jamieson implied doubt as to the reality of Addis's claims; Bland was even more sceptical.

Sir John Jordan to whom both Hillier and Bland appealed from time to time was also critical of the Hongkong Bank's handling of B&CC affairs.

The Hongkong and Shanghai Banking Corporation on the other hand should clearly define its position with regard to the Corporation [B&CC] and not expose itself to the charge of inconsistency in acting in the matter of loans sometimes through the Corporation and at other times in its own name, as its interests may happen to dictate.[126]

He presumably thought this a self-evident comment since he offered no explanation or defence, and he added that the two corporations often acted as if they were rivals rather than cooperating ventures. The Bland/Hillier disagreement had become obvious in Peking.

Addis could rejoin first, by agreeing with Jordan that consistency was desirable if possible, and second, by suggesting that the changes were due to the changing terms of the proposed loan or the sentiments of the Chinese or, as in the case where German involvement was not desired by the Foreign Office, at the request of the British Government. Where such a change acted to the advantage of the Bank and the detriment of the B&CC, the Hongkong Bank offered to pass back the profits. The purpose of the Bank's joining with Jardine's to form the B&CC had been participation where appropriate; the Bank's policy was not as erratic or as self-centred as Jordan (or Bland) chose to see it.

All this missed the point. Addis had earlier, in July 1908, when the conflict of interest issue had first been raised and in response to demands on the board that the Bank's position be defined, stated his and the Bank's interpretation of the 1898 Agreement in his usual clear terms.

As it was clearly the intention of all parties when the Agreement between the Hongkong & Shanghai Banking Corporation and the British & Chinese Corporation was entered into that such Agreement was for a specific class of business namely: – The Financing of Public Works such as Railways &c. accompanied by conditions of supervision and supply of material, the Bank considers itself bound to assist and further the interests of the Company in that class of business so long as the Chinese are prepared to accept these conditions.

Apart from that the Bank does not consider itself bound in any way to limit its freedom in negotiating financial loans with the Chinese Government for any purpose whatever provided it does not include the financing of construction of Public works accompanied by conditions of supervision and supply of material.[127]

He might have added that, as the agreement was never specifically ratified by the Bank's Board of Directors in Hong Kong, there could be no question of its having been intended as a limitation on the Bank's freedom of operation beyond the actual wording of which Addis had given a reasonable interpretation.

The Addis memorandum did not go unchallenged. Macrae presented his own at the July 30 meeting of the board; it was based on information from Bland and assumed the potential success of current negotiations on terms which would include controls. As Eba Addis put it in the common diary, 'Yesterday Charlie had a very trying meeting of the CCR & B&CC. He found himself alone & had to fight "standing with his back to the wall". It left him sore and a good deal hurt. But brave heart he alters not a word of his opinion of right.'[128]

One controversial proviso in the Addis memorandum, as Macrae had noted, was the clause 'so long as the Chinese are prepared to accept these conditions', since Bland would argue that this was circular reasoning. The Chinese would not accept these conditions if the Bank and others could be expected to offer purely financial terms. This in turn rested on a matter of fact as to the actual situation in Peking, and the situation could change rapidly – as Addis implied in his talks with Jamieson and as Bland was to find out in May 1909.

The B&CC board and Bland

Despite these disputes the B&CC board declined to exercise its option to determine Bland's contract after the initial three years; the contract instead was formally confirmed for the remaining two years. Bland was later to accuse Addis of having opposed this move; Addis strongly denied the charge.[129]

Bland, now apparently 'safe' until March 1911, left London for Peking in October 1908, but close relations with Hillier were not reestablished, intimate discussions were continuing with Pauling and Co., and the old policy disputes remained. Hillier, in fact, denied officially that he was the 'manager' in the sense indicated by the Bank/B&CC Agreement, thus undermining Bland's criticism of his lack of 'openness' by refusing to play the role Bland had assigned him.[130] Throughout all this, Bland was, it is true, involved in the many less important disputes with various railway authorities in China – disputes which, arising as they did from past agreements including those with C–K terms or better, might have suggested the futility of controls even when agreed by the Chinese. He was also in contact with the Legation, whose unwilling involvement in commercial controversies and overall concern with diplomatic relations with China, rather than the peculiar interests of the B&CC and CCR, alternately encouraged and frustrated him.

The Bank's position having been accepted by the board, the offending letters from Pauling and Co. having been withdrawn, and the situation in Peking remaining unsatisfactory, Bland's position had in consequence become particularly exposed, and the board now turned to take cognizance of his continuing 'opposition' from Peking.

This was particularly clear in Bland's negotiations relative to the Canton–Hankow Railway loan – which eventually became the Hukuang Railways Loan of 1911. Bland was aware of the German threat but he depended on the terms of the Fraser Note; Addis in London was aware that the Fraser Note would not protect the B&CC against German willingness to accept T–P terms. Bland's solution was to press directly for a settlement with Chang Chih-tung on C–K terms using the Fraser Note as the basis for Legation support; Addis sought to obtain German willingness to support the demand for C–K terms by bringing them into the Anglo-French understanding, but at the price of German participation.

Addis's approach seemed to Bland a negation of the position won by the use of 'Hong Kong Government funds' in the 1905 loan. It was a two-fold betrayal – of British national interests and of the B&CC. Once the Chinese obtained T–P or easier terms, the role of the B&CC in China was, in Bland's opinion, ended. The funds obtained would be wasted and the B&CC would have nothing left but its duties as a trustee to existing bondholders for an extended and unprofitable period.

On the broader issues of China's modernization and economic development, Bland's position was one which had been endorsed and shared by the Hongkong Bank, the B&CC, and the Legation; it was to be abandoned in London only with reluctance in the face of Chinese opposition and the realities of the competition which Bland, depending, as has been stated, on the Fraser Note, tended to dangerously underestimate.

On the narrower issue of the B&CC's future, Bland was only partially correct. He was right in foreseeing the problem of trusteeship, the reason indeed for the corporation's existence today; he was correct in seeing that ordinary shareholders could not be expected to support such a corporation over the years, the reason for the Hongkong Bank buying up the shares of outside shareholders in the 1950s (see Volume IV), but he was mistaken in supposing that the B&CC had no future role in Chinese railway development. Bland might define anything short of C–K terms as 'purely financial', but in reality the terms of the eventual Hukuang Loan did include a role for the B&CC. Furthermore, the list of subsequent railway promotions by the B&CC are proof that Bland was mistaken (see also Volume III).

Although Bland would later protest that he had been merely following board instructions in his negotiation policy, the dissatisfaction of the board was formally expressed to Bland in a letter pointedly from the chairman, William Keswick, dated March 26, 1909. It began ominously, 'For some time past the Board have been conscious that in some respects you and they have not been acting in entire sympathy, and that more especially your policy and procedure in regard to the Hankow Canton Railway Loan have not represented the views of the Corporation.'[131] Bland's own summary of the points made is to be preferred for its brevity.

Blame is imputed to me on five grounds, viz.
1. For having subordinated all considerations to enthusiasm for 'construction by contract', under the auspices of Pauling & Co.
2. For having failed to diagnose the situation correctly and to realise the importance and possible results of German influence; at the same time exaggerating the influence of the Japanese.
3. For having broken off negotiations with the Chinese by declining point blank to quote for Tientsin Pukou Railway terms.
4. For endeavouring to thwart the Board of Directors in any policy which did not provide for 'construction by contract' under the delusion that the result must necessarily involve loans without control.
5. For having contributed to the publicity given to the affairs of the Shanghai Hangchow Ningpo Railway.[132]

Bland naturally but inadvisedly defended himself point by point, but this is not the reply that was wanted nor would it meet Bland's needs. His defence was at times weak, particularly in the case of his too intimate relations with Lord ffrench in Peking and with Pauling and Co. in general. Indeed he would appear to have realized this in a letter to Rutherford Harris deprecating his role and stressing his underlying loyalty to the B&CC.[133] It was not, however, the details of the accusations which needed countering, but Bland's overall approach, and that, he could hardly deny after his several policy letters to the board, had been in opposition to what had become the B&CC's general policy. There was no purpose in quoting communications from the board in which the preference for controls and contracts was stated; this all agreed on.

'Preference' was not in dispute. Bland's conduct and judgement overall was in dispute. Keswick had been arguing policy and attitudes; Bland made a lawyer's reply. This was the last effort at conciliation.

Recall and dismissal

Bland did not change course. Bland was not an ordinary corporation employee. He was a figure in his own right in the foreign community of China; he was a correspondent of *The Times*. His reaction to his increasingly untenable position was not to adjust but to argue more forcefully against what he conceived to be unwise, unpatriotic policies and to attack those he considered responsible for them. Meanwhile in Peking he would carry out instructions, which still remained generally favourable to his concept of sound railway finance, as forcefully as possible – but without careful and continuous reassessment of the situation.

By May, as it happened, the Chinese were too well aware of alternatives to accept Bland's insistence on C–K or indeed any significant control measures. A very courteous but highly legalistic exchange of letters between Chang Chih-tung and Fraser, reinterpreting the famous 'Note', had made this quite clear.[134] On May 26 Bland was informed by Hillier that a Chinese representing Chang Chih-tung had stated that Chang objected to the corporation acting as agents for the supply of materials and that his objection was based, to some extent, upon Bland's not being *persona grata* with Chang Chih-tung. Hillier had then wired to London recommending that the Bank replace the corporation as the negotiator. Bland demanded an explanation, denying that there had been any unpleasantness between Chang Chih-tung and himself.[135] Bland cabled London immediately. In reply he was informed that the B&CC and CCR 'sympathize with you in position which has arisen and regret probable necessity to change our representative – think it desirable you come home at once bearing in mind probably not return. Leave Robertson [Bland's assistant] act under direction Hillier. Inform Hillier.'[136]

In a last minute effort to ascertain the facts relative to events immediately preceding Hillier's moves, Bland wrote to him as 'Joint Manager' demanding, in the terms of the 1898 Agreement, that all relevant correspondence be shown him.[137] Since Hillier had formally denied he was a joint manager, nothing was forthcoming. As Bland later protested, no effort was made through enquiry to the Chinese or through the Legation to determine the truth or to argue for his retention. Not only had he been personally betrayed, but, as Bland subsequently interpreted the events, the corporations had been betrayed – by Charles Addis of the Hongkong Bank.

Addis had agreed that the profits of the Canton–Hankow Loan would be paid back to the B&CC, and the Hongkong Bank and Hillier, on Addis's recommendation and with the approval of the B&CC board, took over the negotiations. Before Bland left Peking, however, Hillier was able to inform him that the preliminary agreement with Chang had been initialled and included a provision that the purchase of materials from abroad for the construction of the Hunan–Hopei section of the Hankow–Canton line would be given to a company nominated by 'this Bank' and approved by the railway Director General. This was accompanied by an understanding securing that the nomination of the B&CC would not be objected to.[138] Addis had protested to the Foreign Office, Bland had been removed, and Chang had given way.[139] The B&CC board recorded a formal vote of thanks to Addis on the conclusion of the successful *entente* negotiations and Hillier had been recommended (although unsuccessfully due to the political implications in Peking) for a knighthood.[140]

None of this would satisfy Bland. Indeed, all this seemed to mark the potential destruction of the corporation whose interests he had been sent to China to represent and he wrote one last memo from Peking in criticism of the Bank and the new era, 'long foreseen', of purely financial loans.[141] Once again Bland entered into correspondence with a single director, this time it was C.C. Macrae in whom he had found a sympathetic but relatively ineffective supporter.

Bland returned to England and attended a board meeting on July 19. As Addis recorded it, 'He was full of venom & threatens action for damages for wrongful dismissal, loss of reputation &c. Bluff! Discussion was clearly useless.'[142] And Addis noted the nature of the letter written him. It was brief:

Dear Sir,
   The Board regrets that in the present position of affairs in China it is impossible to employ you usefully as the Corporation's Representative there. It therefore proposes to give you leave for the present at home and to pay your salary as it accrues under your Agreement.[143]

It was signed by William Keswick as chairman. The CCR Agreement with the B&CC by which Bland served both corporations had already been determined.

As Bland noted, Keswick's letter omitted a verbal provision that he not return to China while the contract was in force.[144] Despite the terms of the letter, this remained a condition; Bland found it unacceptable. After considerable correspondence, a 'Terms of Arrangement' was agreed whereby the contract between Bland and the corporation was 'determined by mutual consent'. Bland received salary due in two instalments with the only stipulation that he not enter into employment or give advice to a rival concern.[145] He was free to return to China and to his role as *Times* correspondent. But he failed to obtain any statement in praise of his services; Addis and Keswick were reportedly agreed that this was rendered superfluous since the 'Arrangement' was by mutual consent. It was a bitter blow and Bland felt he had evidence that the decision was not unanimous. Nor was Bland permitted to meet with the board to discuss the issues under debate; instead he was granted an interview with the chairman.

Bland was, however, permitted one victory. In December he wrote from Shanghai that, in response to a memorial from the Yu-ch'uan Pu, he had been awarded the Order of the Double Dragon.[146]

After leaving the corporation Bland as correspondent, author, and lecturer continued to advocate his own policy, arguing on the futility of lending to China without adequate controls, on the futility of the continued existence of the B&CC, and on the betrayal of British interests by the Hongkong Bank through its role in forming the various inter-bank Groups which were to be known, in general, as the China Consortium. Experience with the handling of funds by the various railway administrations in China supported Bland's concern, but the financiers were aware of the problem without his destructive advocacy. Encouraged by the Legations, they accepted the new situation in China. Nevertheless, they attempted to retain minimal controls, surrendering their position only when no other course was possible.

The investing public apparently supported the revised policy; China bond issues were accepted by the market. The path remained open for European finance of China's requirements on China's terms. The Hongkong Bank's leadership under Charles Addis had been confirmed in this most testing controversy; the B&CC and the CCR would survive, but Bland had been effectively destroyed as an influential voice in China finance. For the bankers and the investing public it was an act of faith in China which China would later, on grounds untenable, denounce.

THE AMERICAN INTERVENTION

The initial reaction

On May 23, 1910, the railway loan agreement reached in London in July 1909 was expanded and revised to meet the peremptory demands of President Taft and to accommodate the membership of the American Group; in consequence the Three Power Groups Agreement was replaced by a Four Power Groups Agreement for the Hukuang Railways loan, which had not as yet been finalized. In the preceding sections a detailed, though still quite incomplete, record was given of the Hongkong Bank's role in the changing organizational structure of Chinese development finance. This was sufficient to indicate the importance of that role and of the dominant personality of Charles Addis who conducted the negotiations in Europe on behalf of the Bank, the B&CC, and, to a lesser extent, the CCR.

In the years which followed Addis continued to play the same role and to exert increasing influence as he moved beyond the confines of the Hongkong Bank to other senior financial responsibilities. Therefore, in what follows, the selective process has been greater and only the main outline of events is recorded.

The American intervention is important in itself; Taft sent a direct message to the Chinese regent, Prince Ch'ing, thereby circumventing diplomatic procedure and exerting personal pressure as the American Chief of State on the Chinese Empire; it was a virtually unprecedented act of 'imperialism' which upset existing relationships and, although based on the most legalistic of claims, American participation was accepted by China.[147]

After initial resistance based on his assessment of the weakness of the American financial claim to participate, Charles Addis wrote to the Foreign Office that, in view of the Secretary of State's position, further opposition would be pointless. The British delegates accepted American participation and would urge its acceptance upon their French and German colleagues.[148]

Previously, however, the Bank had received an apparently purely commercial, almost casual, enquiry from the International Banking Corporation and had turned it down – along with many similar offers. It would be reasonable to suppose that the Hongkong Bank, having just concluded (successfully, it thought) lengthy and costly negotiations, would as a commercial enterprise welcome neither the delays likely to follow from admitting a new participant nor the further diminution of the net profits accruing to the Hongkong Bank and its associates.

To write of a 'British reaction' to the sudden American interests is misleading. The reaction of the British Government, responsible for overall relations with China, and the reaction of the commercial firms engaged in this particular negotiation would not necessarily be the same. The Hongkong Bank had earlier invited American participation at the formation of the Chinese Central Railways and had reserved shares for an American Group. The offer was not taken up; the American financial houses were not interested. The new American interest arose from the promptings of President Taft and came at a particularly inopportune moment as far as the Hukuang Railway negotiations were concerned.

The Hongkong Bank's apparent rejection of the American participation, that is, its initial reaction to the IBC's approach, would cause the Bank considerable trouble; it would be used as 'evidence' of German influence in the Bank.

The Hongkong Bank and The Times – *the German bogey*

There is some evidence that the Americans were encouraged in Peking by J.O.P. Bland. Bland had let his displeasure be known before leaving the capital.

On the eve of his forced departure from China, Bland announced before Liang Tun-yen – much to the latter's surprise – 'I have been kicked out of this job, but I will do my best to make the business a failure.'[149] Bland 'leaked' to the French chargé d'affaires, and most probably to his other contacts in the Chinese capital, his version of events, stressing the pro-German obligations of the Hongkong Bank and Addis's role in allegedly undermining the B&CC. This information was forwarded with critical comments to the Foreign Ministry in Paris under the title 'Attitude de M. Addis dans les affaires en Chine'.[150] Bland, who throughout his time with the B&CC in China had remained a correspondent for *The Times*, returned to London with V. Chirol, foreign editor of *The Times*, who had just completed a visit to Japan in an attempt to justify his pro-Japanese approach to the threatened shut out of other Powers (including China) from Manchuria.

Shortly after the Bland/Chirol trip across Siberia *The Times* opened a new attack on the Hongkong Bank based on its alleged pro-German and anti-American position on the Hukuang loan question. Under a headline, 'The Hongkong Bank/Accused of being under German influence' was a Reuters 'telegram' published in the *Peking and Tientsin Times*, abstracting from a (London) *Times* telegram which itself had originated in Peking:

London, July 24th. The *Times* correspondent in Peking [G.E. Morrison] states that the Prince Regent summoned the whole staff of the Wai-wu Pu and showed considerable anxiety in consequence of a telegram from President Taft (directly to the Regent) which in friendly but unmistakable terms emphasised the fact that American claims to the rights of participation in the Hankow Railway loan are due directly to the intrigues of the Deutsch-Asiatische Bank whose influence over the Hongkong and Shanghai Banking Corporation, Ltd, is injurious to British interests.

The *Times* correspondent at Peking states that many Englishmen in Peking are of opinion that the British Government should bring pressure to bear upon the Hongkong and Shanghai Banking Corporation, Ltd, to force it to dissociate itself from German intrigues.[151]

Hillier immediately wrote to Addis,

When the Reuter was read to me I was stunned, literally as by a blow from behind. It seemed to me incredible that Morrison, my intimate personal friend for 12 years, without warning, without even giving me an opportunity of correcting his facts, which are wrong, should have deliberately attacked my good name, and that of my Bank, by such a cowardly libel.[152]

Both Hillier and Heinrich Cordes had separately written to Morrison to ask who was responsible – surprisingly in view of Morrison's known bias, but possibly because the information was so contrary to the facts it did not occur to either that Morrison himself had concocted the story. When Hillier found out, he told Morrison, 'It is a blow dealt at me from behind by a friend . . . I can neither forgive nor forget this.'[153]

Morrison's reply to Hillier exposed the whole basis of his reporting. 'Conscience,' he wrote, 'compelled me to do it. . . . We are close to war with Germany. War with Germany is inevitable.' Morrison concluded by expressing his admiration for the Hongkong Bank and his multitude of friends therein, '. . . but I would rather see your bank wiped out of existence than that it should be the means even unintentionally of assisting Germany to cause misunderstanding between us and the Americans'.[154]

The Times, that is, Chirol, refused to print a retraction, except over the Hongkong Bank's (or Addis's) signature, and Hillier's strong denunciation in Peking was refused transmission by the Reuters 'junior' then in charge of the news agency's Peking office, at least in the form submitted. Specifically the telegram as sent omitted Hillier's comment, 'General opinion regards charges of intrigue made against the DA Bank is wholly imaginary, and the publication of the telegram at the present juncture is strongly condemned.'[155]

As Morrison saw it, at stake here was the question of whose ally America would be in the coming war with Germany. America wanted to participate in the Hukuang loans. If Germany could convince America that the hesitation in admitting her to the Consortium was due to the Hongkong Bank, it would be one success for German intrigues, presumably world-wide, designed, so Morrison thought, to alienate the two English-speaking nations. With so much at stake the *Times* Peking correspondent could not wait to check his facts.[156]

On the refusal of the Americans to accept any compromise to their claims as proposed by the Consortium, Baron von Rex, the German Minister in Peking, expressed the view that there was 'no doubt but what this was due to Bland'.[157] The Germans saw British intrigue at work, Morrison and Chirol saw Bland's work in danger of being undone, and the Hongkong Bank was indicted – at least that is one interpretation which, while not inconsistent with the facts, is not wholly supported by them. It must be rejected.

The Chirol/Morrison correspondence expands the story to include William Koch [de Gooreynd], a British subject, one of Addis's 'cosmopolitan Jewish' friends and a partner of Panmure Gordon and Co., who as a partner of Messrs Koch and Speyer had supported Sir Edgar Speyer as head of one of the groups which the previous year had attempted to take over *The Times* – their purpose, according to Chirol, was to make it into a pro-German newspaper.[158]

But, Chirol reassured Morrison, he had been to the Foreign Office and countered Addis (who had been, in Chirol's words, 'lying throughout like a Cretan'), and the Bank would in consequence be receiving less support from Government from then on. The particular 'lie' cited by Chirol was Addis's assertion that the British Group had never rejected an application by the 'American' (presumably 'International') Banking Corporation for participation in the 'combine'. Addis, however, reaffirmed his assertion in a comprehensive letter to the Foreign Office, making clear that the IBC's approach had not stated any relationship to an official American Group, which was eventually represented by the Morgans.[159]

A month later Chirol took up the attack on the Hongkong Bank once again with a private letter to the Foreign Secretary, this time alleging that the Hongkong Bank had, contrary to information it had given the Foreign Office, encouraged German participation in the Hukuang Loan and then forced this view on the French. A Foreign Office memo was drawn up to refute this allegation, noting that Addis had all the time kept the department fully informed; it was submitted to Sir Francis Campbell with the comment, 'I think the enclosed memo sufficiently answers the point raised by Mr Chirol.'[160] This lack of appreciation inspired Chirol's criticism of the Foreign Office '*qua* department'.[161]

Chirol and Addis, as it happened, would both be knighted, in 1912 and 1913 respectively, and Government support for the Hongkong Bank continued subject to the limitations of long-standing policy. Chirol, considering the damage his articles were to do to British interests in China and the encouragement his pro-Japanese articles gave to those who tolerated Japanese policies in Manchuria, was knighted for services rendered in another direction – India.

It was an incredible interlude of vilification and conspiracy by men purporting to be responsible journalists.

Hillier, in a quieter mood, replied point by point, exonerating Cordes of any 'intrigue'. The American chargé d'affaires declared Cordes's actions to have been totally upright.[162] The German Legation reported to Berlin that Morrison had backed down, blaming his 'telegram' on the urgings of Bland and Chirol and asking to be relieved of his post on *The Times*, although he agreed to remain until Bland returned, presumably to relieve him. If true this probably reflected Morrison's continuing disapproval of Chirol's pro-Japanese policy rather than any remorse over his false report on the Hongkong Bank. The German Minister commented that this possible change of Bland for Morrison was unlikely to be a step forward for Anglo-German relations in China for, he wrote, although, 'Morrison is certainly not pro-German, he has a certain amount of personal uprightness, which is totally lacking in Bland.'[163]

THE FOUR POWER GROUPS CONSORTIUM AND THE HUKUANG LOAN OF 1911

Meanwhile complex negotiations with the American Group, which had begun on July 7, some two weeks before Morrison's famous 'telegram', had been continuing through J.P. Morgan and Co. and their representatives Morgan, Grenfell and Co. in London and Warburg and Co. in Hamburg.

On October 4, 1909, China's elder statesman, Grand Councillor Chang Chih-tung died. In his final memorial to the Throne he regretted having been unable to conclude the Hukuang Railways loan; the task was passed on to the Yu-ch'uan Pu (Ministry of Posts and Communications) and continued at an erratic pace until the signature of the Four Powers to a preliminary agreement on May 24, 1910. The Americans had not at that time been formally admitted to the Consortium; this was delayed until November 11, 1910, with the signing of two agreements paralleling those which had created the Three Power Groups Consortium in 1909. The actual loan agreement was not signed with the Chinese until May 20, 1911, over a month after the Groups had signed the Currency Reform Sinking Fund Gold Loan of 1911. This latter loan was never actually sanctioned by an Imperial edict; it was subsumed in the Reorganization Loan of 1913.

The terms of the Hukuang Railways Loan[164]

The Imperial Chinese Government 5% Hukuang Railways Sinking Fund Gold Loan of 1911 for £6 million at 95 (fixed) for 40 years was issued to the public at 100½ without underwriting. The Hongkong Bank bought £50,000 on its own account and the Board of Directors noted that the 'profit' of issue was £15,000. If the purposes of the loan were not achieved with the sum mentioned, a further £4 million could be raised on the same terms by the same banks. Signatories to the agreement were (i) for the Chinese, Sheng Hsuan-huai, then President of the Yu-ch'uan Pu and (ii) for the lenders, the Hongkong and Shanghai Banking Corporation (E.G. Hillier), the Deutsch-Asiatische Bank (H. Cordes), the Banque de l'Indo-Chine (R. Saint Pierre and M. Casenave), and the American Group – Messrs J.P. Morgan and Co., Messrs Kuhn, Loeb and Co., the First National Bank, and the National City Bank (both of New York City and now merged into Citibank) represented by Willard Straight. The depository bank in China for the American Group was the International Banking Corporation (now a subsidiary of Citicorp).

The purposes of the Hukuang Railways loan were (i) redemption of as yet unredeemed Gold Bonds with a par value of $Gold 2,222,000 issued by the American China Development Company (ACDC) and (ii) construction of a

Government main line (a) of 900 kms from Wuchang, the capital of Hupei, through Yo-chou and Changsha, the capital of Hunan, to a point in the District of Yi-chang-hsien in the Prefecture of Ch'en-chou on the southern boundary of Hunan, where it would connect with the Kwangtung section being built north from Canton, (b) of 600 kms from Kuang-shui, Hupei, connecting there with the Peking–Hankow line, to Ichang, and (c) of 900 kms from Ichang to Kuei-chou-fu in Szechuan, the Hupei section of the Szechuan–Hankow Railway.

This was not a purely financial loan; the terms agreed were T–P. It had been over two years since these were rejected by Bland in accordance with the then Hongkong Bank and B&CC policy.

The provisions included the method of handling and transfer of funds. First, funds would be deposited as received in Europe or America and held at 3% interest per annum; transfers from Europe to China were to be made on the order of the Ministry, the Yu-ch'uan Pu, in equal amounts from each bank but not to exceed a total of £200,000 in any one week. Exchange would be handled through the signatory banks. The deposit of these funds in China was to be shared 50% with the signatory banks and 50% with Chinese depository banks – the Chiao-t'ung Bank, the Ta-Ch'ing Government Bank, or others designated by the Ministry.[g] Amounts sufficient for one month's construction had, however, to be deposited in the construction account of the signatory bank appropriate for the section of the line involved; funds for the Hankow–Canton line, for example, would be deposited with the Hongkong Bank.

These terms solved several problems. First, the banks had to pay interest on idle balances; second, although the exchange was confined to the signatory banks, the loan agreement prevented a single, large transaction and the Ministry could decide when and in what amounts to transfer funds; the exchange banks were protected against being caught unprepared by the maximum amount permitted per week. The monopoly of the lending banks was further eroded by providing for funds in China to be held in part by Chinese banks, the final transfer to the signatory banks being for current operational purposes.

On the vexed question of control, as noted above, T–P terms were effective, with the sole management of the railway being in the hands of a Chinese director-general. The Engineer-in-Chief, although appointed by the

[g] The supposed mandatory deposit of Chinese funds with foreign banks has been the subject of frequent, if misplaced, criticism of the Powers in this period. By any objective standard Chinese banks were insufficiently capitalized to be safely entrusted with public funds and even the above concession had, in view of the need to reorganize the two banks specifically named in the Hukuang agreement, to be repealed by the Minister of Communications in March 1913.[165] The Chinese authorities were well aware of the problem; this is not the only instance of the use of foreign banks being proposed by the Chinese themselves in times of crisis.

Chinese, could be objected to by the relevant bank (and each bank was involved with designated sections of each line) during the period of construction; thereafter and during the life of the loan, foreign nationals had to be appointed but the approval of the banks was no longer necessary.

Consistent with this approach, the security of the railway was not the line itself, rather it was the by then more usual list of designated revenues, including likin. As the Powers were attempting to encourage China to abandon likin as a form of taxation, it being considered a serious impediment to trade, an alternative security was designated.

Once again one might ask the purpose of these lists, the risk being clearly sovereign. One answer would be that, in the absence of comprehensive fiscal statistics for the Empire, a listing of tax revenues not previously designated indicated to the prospective bondholder that there were such revenues collected in China and thus, provided there was a will to repay, the resources for repayment might well exist.

Each section of the railway had an appointed agent: for Hongkong Bank lines this was the British and Chinese Corporation. The agents had costly duties to perform, including assessment of bids and inspection, and in consideration for this they were entitled to 5% commission on the purchase of foreign materials. Even on T–P terms the B&CC did in fact have an agreed role.

The significance of certain of these provisions was considered by the parties concerned in the final negotiations in April–May 1911 and will be discussed in the relevant section below.

The course of negotiations

As this loan does not differ radically from previous loans on T–P terms and is certainly consistent with the trend in China finance, the question which obviously arises is, what took so long?

The agreement is in fact deceptively simple. Each section of the line was in fact the subject of lengthy discussion in an atmosphere which was not always one of mutual trust. The profitability of the loan to the participating banks was based on the relative share of the total financing, and as this was to be in equal shares, it was not in itself the source of contention.

The total national profitability depended on how each line or section of line was 'assigned' to each participating national Group. The national Group was given certain privileges on the 'assigned' line, for example, approval of the 'engineer-in-chief', who had to be a national of the specified country, and the agency for foreign purchases. The related bank also held the operating funds for the 'assigned' line, although this was probably not particularly remunerative provided the Chinese management kept a tight control on the timing of expenditures.

This explains the interest of all the Governments concerned, even if the accepted role of Government policy in the private sector were limited. No Government can permit private commercial interests to take quasi-diplomatic action – which is how commercial arrangements with the Chinese Government might be regarded and which would affect other citizens, perhaps adversely.

All this was complicated by national prestige and the particular interest President Taft took in the affair. Since each Group entered the negotiations with prior claims and commitments from the Chinese authorities, not all of which were compatible, a considerable amount of trading was involved. By mid-September 1909 Addis had become so confused that he informed the Foreign Office he would urge a meeting with the French and Germans to 'clear the air' and 'let us know where we stand'.[166]

In discussing the lines virtually mile-by-mile, Addis was firm in retaining the Hongkong Bank's interest in the Canton–Hankow line. The main problem was on the apportionment of the Hankow–Szechuan line and, since the CCR was interested, the board considered whether to divide the line with reference to the Belgian-Franco-British composition of that company. This Addis opposed; it was one company and British registered and must be treated as such, despite the presence on its board of French and Belgian interests.[167]

Early in January 1910 it was clear that the controversy over shares in the Hankow–Szechuan line had spilled over into discussions relative to the otherwise unrelated Chinchow–Aigun line, with the B&CC asking for compensatory mileage there to offset sacrifices in central China. Rumours of this reached Berlin and the DAB approached the Hongkong Bank for a participation.[168] This affair is not however cited for full discussion but as an example of the problems arising from the unexpected American intervention in a matter which had already been and for some time would continue to be the subject of lengthy international negotiations, all of which, in one way or another, touched the Hongkong Bank and were handled there by Charles Addis.[h]

At a different level the negotiations were disturbed by the increasingly hostile reaction of provincial gentry. As with the Shanghai–Hangchow–Ningpo line, gentry opposition was partly at least based on the existence of provincial private railway companies, which the foreign financed line would

---

[h] Indeed, his letters are so pervasive in the files and almost all on Hongkong Bank stationery that it is difficult to understand how his role has been so little noted and indeed his identity treated as a mystery by historians whose accounts of events are otherwise most helpful. Addis's impact on the Foreign Office, and on the representatives of other Groups, rests on the concise style and clear reasoning which characterize his letters and memorandums. Or, in the words of a Foreign Office minute of April 19, 1910, 'Mr Addis's letter is, as usual, excellent.'[169]

supersede, and partly on anti-foreignism in general; it was also a manifestation of provincialism and anti-Manchu, pro-Han chauvinism. Several of the tracts circulated by the various 'patriotic' groups and gentry were translated by the Legation and consular officers; they are unfortunately quite inaccurate as to financial arrangements, but their appeal is at a different level and nonetheless effective both with the Chinese masses and with some contemporary historians.

As Sir John Jordan observed, 'The great emphasis which was placed on the political aspect of Chinese railway loans in *The Times* and other leading organs of the British press has had its effect in China.' A Foreign Office minute summed up department opinion thus: 'There can I think be little doubt but that the misguided opinions formed by Mr Chirol during a short residence in China have done harm.'[170]

Provincial efforts to begin construction by private companies, especially the Hupei Railway Company, were given an Imperial sanction and accordingly protested in identic notes by the Ministers representing the Four Groups.[171] The British Legation saw these developments as evidence for the need to press forward with the Hukuang negotiations; this view was reinforced by the fact that, despite the protest, provincial railway company plans moved ahead. As usual, however, construction progress was hindered by the failure of the local company to raise the capital required.[172]

The British Government followed these provincial developments carefully, and their concern was shared by the Hongkong Bank, but not all the Groups assessed them with equal concern. The Germans, for example, feared that the Hongkong Bank was using the excuse of gentry opposition as a way to separate out the Canton–Hankow line for their later sole exploitation.[173] The British experience with the Shanghai–Hangchow–Ningpo line had, however, brought them into contact with Chekiang gentry with railway ambitions. The poor performance of those local companies led British and other foreign opinion to discount the importance of the Hupei protests relative to railways *per se*.[174]

The Hukuang negotiations were to continue at their slow pace, touching in the process practically every railway issue which concerned the Powers. For example, on April 13, 1910, a question was asked in Parliament:

... whether it is the fact that an agreement or understanding between Great Britain and Germany regarding German interests in the Shantung Peninsula and the British interests in the Yangtse was last year, on the demand of Germany, considered obsolete or ineffective; and whether, in consequence, Germany successfully claimed a right to participate in the Hankow–Canton railway project.[175]

To this and to subsequent questions by Earl Winterton, the Under-Secretary of State for Foreign Affairs, T. McKinnon Wood, replied for the

Government, (i) the 1898 Agreement was not between Governments but between two financial Groups made with the cognizance and approval of the British Government but never approved by the German Government (see Chapter 5), (ii) the German Group contended that the agreement related to the 'concession for the building of railways by foreigners' not to 'loans for railways', and (iii) it had not been considered advisable to contest the German interpretation, which would only have led to keen competition between the different Groups. The third point oversimplifies the facts.[176]

Addis, who had still been in China at the time the 1898 joint Hongkong Bank/DAB declaration was negotiated, informed the Foreign Office, with some exaggeration, that the 'agreement' is, 'I believe, a figment of the imagination' being only an agreement to recommend to the Governments certain spheres, which the German Government never accepted. The Hongkong Bank, the B&CC, and the DAB had intended it should be Government policy, and they had themselves tended to act, or think in terms of the agreement, as if it were effective, at least until 1903 when von Hansemann for the DAB attempted to denounce it. Again in 1909 in the case of the Canton–Hankow line Addis had written of the British 'interest' in the line and suggested that the Germans restrain themselves, referring to the 1898 'agreement', but the DAB had reminded the Hongkong Bank either of von Hansemann's denunciation or of the differentiation noted above. All this had been superseded in any case by the July 1909 Three Power Groups Consortium inter-bank Agreement.[177]

On May 11 Charles Addis of the Hongkong Bank and S. Simon of the Banque de l'Indo-Chine signed a memorandum of agreement prepared by Addis and covering the engineering sections of the Hankow–Szechuan (or Chengtu) Railway, thus opening the way for a full-scale agreement, which was signed by the Groups – with Morgan, Grenfell and Co. representing the American Group – in Paris on May 24, 1910.[178] Addis particularly drew the attention of the Foreign Office to the fact that the British Group had been awarded the engineer-in-chief for the entire Canton–Hankow line, a result 'more favourable than at one time might have been expected, and they hope it may be so regarded by the Secretary of State'.[179]

But despite what Addis referred to as the prompt (August) and apparently encouraging response of the Chinese Government, the signing of a loan with the Chinese was still nearly a year away.[180]

By October 1910 the negotiations had received a setback, with the Chinese repudiating the standing of the 1909 Agreement on the grounds that it had not been approved by the Hu Pu (Ministry of Finance) or by the Throne; thus it was a basis for discussion only.[181] Behind this was the real concern the

Imperial officials felt for provincial protest, to which they had given some encouragement.

However, under diplomatic pressure, which was consistent and increasing in the latter months of 1910, the Chinese began detailed negotiations. One concern was the Chingmen–Hanyang branch line, the rights to which the central authorities had given, contrary to preliminary agreements with the Groups, to the Hupeh (Yangtze Provinces) Provincial Company, a local Chinese company. The Groups were now requested to give up these rights. This the Peking representatives of the Consortium banks recommended. Their reason was pragmatic; delay might encourage rival foreign syndicates, which were already beginning to form, but it is fair to state that the bankers by now also recognized that a real political problem existed. As usual, the difficulty with making such a concession was that it required readjustment of rights and privileges within and among the Four Groups. That too could, but in this case surprisingly did not, cause delays.[182]

While the Governor of Hunan informed Peking that his province would not accept foreign loans, the provincial governor of Kansu, in contrast, had approached the Hongkong Bank and Hillier with major railway loan proposals involving construction into the western provinces, and in December 1910 a meeting of the Four Power Groups Consortium bank managers had been held in Peking under Hillier's leadership. But the grand schemes discussed were not destined to be developed further, and it was Hukuang and not Kansu that then was the primary concern of the Groups.[183]

The combination of political pressure, the ability of the Groups to settle, after lengthy wrangling, their own differences, and the eventual compromises which the Groups were willing to accept in order to close the loan, led eventually to the signing of the key agreements with the Chinese in May 1911.

The final terms – a discussion

The controlling factors

The Consortium banks' representatives in Peking were urging immediate closing of the Hukuang loan, virtually on Chinese terms. Their recommendations, based on concern for provincial opposition and the fear of European-American competition by rival syndicates, were accepted by the British, French, German, and American Foreign Ministers, but Addis held out. 'I may say at once, frankly, that to myself these arguments are not convincing.'[184]

Addis considered the provincial threat exaggerated. In this he was incorrect; he was in no position to make such a judgement and he throughout expressed his willingness, on behalf of the Hongkong and Shanghai Bank, to be ruled by the unanimous views of the Foreign Ministers on this subject. On the other hand he was probably correct in supposing the threat of foreign competition was not immediate, although even the hint of such could be used by the Chinese as a pretext for further delay.

Addis's main contribution at this point was to focus on the technical issues involved, as they had arisen in two previous sessions with the Chinese Government.

When the Ministers were received in audience by Prince Ch'ing on April 5, they had argued for retaining intact all provisions of the draft agreement as drawn up and agreed by the Groups; the Government's spokesman, the President of the Yu-ch'uan Pu, Sheng Hsuan-huai, successfully convinced the Ministers to withdraw the demand for inclusion of the controversial Chingmen–Hanyang branch line; the other points at issue Sheng still claimed were technical, would not be understood by the Ministers, and should only be discussed with the bankers.[185]

The Ministers had gone to see Prince Ch'ing but they and the bankers faced the still formidable, 67-year-old Sheng Hsuan-huai. Jordan wrote of him:

> [He is] in frail health, the last survivor of the Li Hung-chang school of statesmanship and intellectually is quite the equal of his great prototype. Shrewd, clever, and utterly unscrupulous, he has come into contact during his long and chequered career with foreigners of all classes and has established a reputation for successful business capacity of which the telegraph administration and the Hanyang Ironworks are the two chief monuments.[186]

The Ministers accepted Sheng's verdict, and Jordan reported on Sheng's overwhelming ability as a negotiator. Accordingly, the Peking representatives of the four banks met with Sheng on April 7 to consider the agreement article by article.

The lenders wished to ensure the control of the loan funds, that is, their availability for the purposes for which the loan was granted. The Chinese insisted that (i) the funds retained in Europe should only be sufficient for purchases in gold currencies, (ii) that the balance must be transferred to China as and when the Yu-ch'uan Pu decided, (iii) 50% of those funds should be held by designated Chinese banks, and that (iv) although the proposed 3% rate of interest on gold deposits in Europe was satisfactory, a higher rate was required for silver deposits – the exchange banks were then offering 2% on current account, and the Chinese insisted that some proportion must be permitted to be placed on a fixed deposit basis.

The question of exchange – reexamined once more

The Groups' objections to these demands were not unrelated. The lending banks retained the obligation to undertake the necessary exchange operations.

There were reports, which were not referred to at the meeting, that Chinese officials were speculating on the exchange; such activities in large amounts could act to the detriment of the exchange banks and thus arose the need to limit the amounts transferable in any one week. An 'excessive transfer' to China, defined as one in excess of silver requirements, possibly as a speculation, might have to be reversed to meet gold obligations in Europe at a possible exchange loss. The potential problems were numerous.[187]

The exchange banks depended on deposits to cover exchange operations; the deposit provisions of the Chinese demands were, therefore, another unsettling element to which the Shanghai and Hong Kong offices of the Hongkong Bank particularly objected.[188]

The control of funds – deposits in Chinese banks

As for deposits in designated Chinese banks, Sheng stated frankly that this was in part a consequence of the low rate of interest on silver deposits offered by the foreign banks; the bankers understood that this was a provision intended to bring the Chinese authorities a higher rate of interest – and the short-term use of funds for non-railway purposes – but with attendant risks. The risks were dismissed by Sheng on the grounds that the Chinese banks listed were Government banks in the process of a management reorganization and were guaranteed by the Government.[189]

Furthermore, as Jordan pointed out to Hillier, the Hongkong Bank was known by Sheng to have undertaken several loans to provincial authorities the proceeds of which passed from their control by transfer to Chinese banks.[i] Jordan had made a good debating point, but the circumstances were different; the risks the Hongkong Bank took with provincial loan funds were their own; Addis was concerned with funds made available by public subscription for Imperial Chinese Government bonds.

As for the actual railway construction provisions, the bankers were successful in retaining the agency commission at 5% provided, as Sheng demanded, they paid the cost of inspection. The banks were, not surprisingly, unable to reestablish Canton–Kowloon terms; they succeeded only in improving the reporting procedures.

Behind all this was the experience of the CCR with the southern section of the Tientsin–Pukow Railway and of the B&CC with the Shanghai–Hangchow–Ningpo line.

Capitulation

Addis, as noted above, remained unconvinced. His solution was, therefore, to recognize and accept the respective spheres of responsibility of the Hongkong

---

[i] Examples would be the loans of Ts3 million each being negotiated in early 1911, in equal shares with the DAB and the Banque de l'Indo-Chine, to the Canton and Nanking Viceroys.[190]

Bank on the one hand and the British Government on the other. The British Minister in Peking and the Foreign Office in London, in concert with the other lending Powers, considered the terms acceptable; then, wrote Addis, the Government must support the banks should this be proven, at some future time, to have been an incorrect political assessment. In a cable to Hillier, Addis, as chairman, spoke for the Four Groups:

> Although not convinced, four groups do not feel justified in resisting strong and unanimous recommendation of the four Ministers. You are, therefore, authorized agree . . . In taking this step contrary to their opinion, groups are relying upon four Ministers supply, in case of need, such diplomatic pressure as may be necessary to counteract loss of control involved by this concession made in deference to opinion of Ministers.[191]

The Hongkong Bank and/or the B&CC were trustees for the loan issues. Here they were in effect saying that they could not be responsible for the control of funds because of terms insisted on by the Foreign Ministers. In the event of problems, the responsibility was with the several Governments. This suggests a decision on the part of the Foreign Office effecting a radical change of policy, but such a conclusion is in fact unjustified; the Consortium merely stated their view. There is no evidence of the British Government's admitting a specific responsibility for the fortunes of the bondholders.

Nevertheless, if there were any suggestion of official responsibility, the argument for official involvement in commercial negotiations became stronger. By first strengthening and then protecting their commercial position the Consortium banks had provided a justification for Government interference in their affairs. Charles Addis would henceforth become even more involved with policy at the national level; national policy now affected the Hongkong Bank directly. And yet, after all this, the position of the bondholder was weakened; his trustee had no control, they had even declared themselves not responsible, but his Government, while bearing some responsibility for the situation, had not specifically agreed to replace the trustee.

The Governments had placed themselves in an impossible position – short-term and long-term – a position they had long sought to avoid. As for the short-term, the Ministers had become directly involved in the terms of a loan contrary to the expressed views of the responsible banks. In the future they would become even more involved in areas which, especially for the British, had been beyond the declared policy of 'holding the ring' and contrary to all traditions. In the long-term they would be subject to the political pressures of bondholders at times when foreign policy priorities would force an abandonment of the bondholders and their rights.

In the context of these obvious disadvantages, it is not immediately obvious what the Ministers hoped to achieve by their insistence that the Consortium come to terms with the Chinese on a basis the banks considered unsatisfactory. Certainly the Ministers were concerned with the possibility of rival and less responsible syndicates appearing and demanding support; eventually, the argument might be expressed, a loan would be made to the Chinese by some syndicate on terms perhaps even more generous, that is, financially irresponsible, than the Chinese were now demanding. This combined with a desire to see development in China with the growth of trade and industrialization and the consequent benefit to the economy world-wide were factors which, in the momentum of the situation, pressed on the Foreign Ministers. No major foreign policy change may have been intended or admitted; the Ministers, however, could never again fall back to merely 'holding the ring'.

The Chinese too had to pay a price for their success. To the extent that bondholder recourse could now effectively be had only through their Governments, the Chinese faced the prospect of political confrontation as a consequence of mismanagement or other problems affecting repayment of the financial obligations.

The provincial problem

The provincial problem remained. Sheng Hsuan-huai had terminated the interview of April 5 by commenting that he 'half-hoped that some ground of disagreement would still be found, as otherwise he feared the business was going through and his troubles would then begin with the provinces'.[192]

Sheng's solution was a desperate one. He informed the bankers that an Imperial edict would nationalize the railways; after this he would finalize the Hukuang Loan agreement. As Sir John Jordan noted, 'The Government . . . has boldly faced the issue, and has faced it in a way which either compels acquiescence or invites rebellion. It is not difficult to predict the result . . .' Thus far Jordan was correct. The British Minister in Peking added, 'The provinces . . . will soon realize the necessity of yielding to firmness.'[193] He was mistaken.

The Hukuang Railways Loan had been publicly linked to railway nationalization – and to revolution. And although the loan agreement was signed, it was an inauspicious ending to years of negotiation or to the beginning of the cooperation necessary for efficient railway construction.

The provinces, faced not only with the unwanted foreign loan, but also with the forced nationalization of their companies, were not concerned with compromises. The discontent which had focused on the Hukuang Loan negotiations was more widespread, but the railway disturbances and ineffectual attempts to suppress them led to the incident in Hankow on the tenth day of the tenth month, known in history as the Double Tenth. This incident has been heralded as the beginning of the revolution which toppled the Ch'ing Dynasty and led to the establishment of the Chinese Republic.

Table 7.1 *The Hongkong and Shanghai Banking Corporation*
China: public loans and advances, 1905–1911
(discussed in Chapter 7)

Title and/or Purpose		Amount (millions)	Terms			
			(i)	(ii)	(iii)	(iv)
Advance to the Wuchang Viceroy 1905	Rights Recovery Canton–Hankow	£0.40[a]				
ICG 5–4½% Gold Loan of 1908	Rights Recovery Luhan Line	£5.00[b]	94[f]	98	30 yrs	BIC
Advance 7%	To meet the timing problem	Ts3.0				
ICG 5% Hukuang Railways Sinking Fund Gold Loan of 1911	Hukuang Railways	£6.00[c]	95[f]	100½	40 yrs	4 Power Consortium

(i) contract price to Chinese (ii) price issued to public
(iii) length of loan (iv) with whom or for whom issued

[f] Fixed [a] Temporary advance, part of Hong Kong Government loan of £1.1m.
[b] Of which £2.5 million issued in London.
[c] Four Power Groups Consortium Loan.
ICG Imperial Chinese Government.
BIC Banque de l'Indo-Chine.

8

SHANGHAI, REVOLUTION, AND THE REORGANIZATION LOAN, 1910–1914

We are, Sir, first and foremost a China Bank.
    Chairman, the First London Annual Dinner, 1908

The Hongkong Bank's interest in China was not confined to major development finance. The problems of modernization were reflected in the demands on both the private and provincial Government sectors which acquired crisis proportions both following the collapse of the boom in rubber and other shares on the Shanghai market in 1910 and then on the eve and aftermath of the 1911 revolution. The collapse of the Ch'ing Dynasty and the uncertainties of the next several years brought into question the future of the (Imperial) Chinese Maritime Customs and the collection and safekeeping of the revenues which secured the foreign loans. In the amelioration of these crises the Hongkong Bank was invited to assist.

Between 1912 and 1914, despite discussion of major schemes, only minor railway projects were actually financed *de novo*; previously completed loans were supplemented, but the main financial and political focus was on the Reorganization Loan of 1913 (see Tables 8.1 and 8.4).

With the outbreak of the Great War in August 1914, the Powers did not forget China; indeed, international rivalry in China and the financing of the China trade took on a new significance. But the European capital market was generally unreceptive to new overseas issues.

Certain of these developments adjust the focus from London and Peking, the two centres which dominated the history as told in Chapters 5–7, to include Hankow and Shanghai and, for a brief time, the Government based in Nanking. Shanghai had become the great International City it was to remain until the Pacific War, its 'feel' for provincial finance and everyday contact with Chinese merchants provided the Hongkong Bank with a base far superior to that of colonial Hong Kong; then too Shanghai's financial links with the world provided a base for currency arbitrage, its investment links with the region a base for share speculation.

Hong Kong was always the Bank's headquarters, maintaining a global control and key links into South China, but Shanghai retained and increased its relative importance in the Bank's China business, other than in the public loans managed by Charles Addis in London.

The revolution of 1911 was to leave its mark on Shanghai. Once again as in the post-Boxer years, an international commission of bankers had to be utilized, this time to protect the revenues pledged to redeem China's overseas borrowing. Nearby was the southern capital of Nanking, which for a brief period held the political spotlight and sought the resources which could alone sustain it. The bankers, who had worked for many years with many of China's post-Manchu leaders – Yuan Shih-k'ai, T'ang Shao-yi, and others in the North – had little knowledge of the 'revolutionaries'. Exceptionally, the Hongkong Bank was aware of the Hong Kong-educated revolutionary leader, Dr Sun Yat-sen, and of Cantonese frustrations, but the Powers followed the continuity which appeared to lie in Peking, a decision which the Bank was bound to accept, although keeping open its relations in the South and continuing the finance of the private sector from both Hong Kong and Shanghai.

Nor was the assessment, made by 'practical men of business', that China needed a strong central authority necessarily wrong; but the regime their finance supported proved incapable of controlling those provincial forces, themselves the result of many factors, railways included, which for many years to come would frustrate the creation of truly national authority.

As described in Chapter 7 the China Consortium, originally with three Power Groups, was joined by the United States and became a Four Power Groups Consortium in 1910; in the period covered by this chapter two further Powers joined, Russia and Japan. The expansion of the Consortium to include Six Power Groups, the financial requirements of China's new Government, and the growing indebtedness of China forced the British Government to once again provide exclusive support for a time to the British Group headed by the Hongkong Bank under the leadership of Charles Addis, from 1912 senior London Manager of the Bank.

Renewed British Government support was, however, obtained at a price. The British Group had to be expanded and by the end of 1912 the Hongkong Bank, while retaining the undisputed leadership, held only a one-third share in the syndicate. Finally, the pressures of miscellaneous lenders, mainly providing suppliers' credits, became too great and, much against Addis's advice, industrial loans were removed from the purview of the international Consortium.

These developments, misunderstood both in China and in Britain, continued the Hongkong Bank's close association with German financial interests to the very eve of the Great War, which caught Charles Addis in London

Table 8.1 *The Hongkong and Shanghai Banking Corporation*
China: loans and other advances, 1909–1913
(discussed in Chapter 8)

Title and/or purpose	Amount (millions) Total/HSBC	Terms			
		(i)	(ii)	(iii)	(iv)
1909					
Silver loan to the Hukuang Viceroy	Ts0.5	100	–	10	none
ditto A/c Chamber of Commerce	Ts0.5	100	–	–	none
1910					
Shanghai Tao-t'ai 4% loan to relieve banking and money market crisis in Shanghai	Ts3.5/0.8	100	na	5	+ 8 banks[e]
ICG 5% Tientsin–Pukow RR Supplementary Loan for £4.8m (1st tranche[a])	£3.0/1.11[b]	94.5[ff]	100½	30	DAB 3 Powers
Liang-Kiang Prov. 7% Silver Loan to relieve present state of the market	Ts3.0/1.0	100	na	6	DAB BI-C
1911					
Hupei Prov. 7% Silver Loan Repayment of other loans	Ts2.0/0.5	100	na	10	4 Power Groups

454

Loan	Amount	(i)	(ii)	(iii)	(iv)
Kwangtung Prov. 7% Silver Loan to relieve financial situation in money markets	$5.0/1.67[c]	100	na	5	DAB, BI-C
CMSNCo 6% Silver Loan (from Chapter 7)	Ts1.5	100	na	15	–
ICG 5% Hukuang Railways Sinking Fund Gold Loan (never issued, see Chapter 4)	£6.0/1.5	95[f]	101½	40	4 Power Groups
ICG 5% Currency Reform and Industrial Development Sinking Fund Gold Loan (never issued)	£10.0	95[f]	na	45	4 Power Groups
6% Advance against above	0.4/0.1	–	–	–	ditto
1912 Ts 12.1m (gold) Advances to Govt. against above	£1.8/.452	92½	–	1	4 Power Groups
1913 Chinese Government 5% Reorganization Gold Loan	£25.0/5.0[d]	84[fff]	90	47	5 Power Groups

(i) contract price to Chinese (ii) price issued to public
(iii) number of years (iv) Hongkong Bank plus banks listed

[f] Fixed [ff] points fixed at 5.5 [fff] 90 minimum, points fixed at 6.

[a] No further public loan made; balance of funds made available by banks.
[b] Hongkong Bank issued as agents for Chinese Central Railways.
[c] Payable and repayable in Hong Kong in banknotes.
[d] For the British Group; the actual London issue was £7,416,680; various advances were made against the payout of this loan.
[e] For list of banks, see footnote on page 459.
BI-C Banque de l'Indo-Chine.
ICG Imperial Chinese Government.
CMSNCo China Merchants' Steam Navigation Company.

unaware and almost disbelieving. August 4 marked the end of many things, among them the great international role which the Hongkong Bank had forged for itself in the East. Until that day, however, the Bank continued to serve the trade and finance of the East as it had from 1865 almost as if no adverse developments were present. The break in 1914 was as absolute for the Bank as it was for Europe itself, but for this reason the history of the Bank to August 4 need take little notice of the potential catastrophe, and the Great War, its prelude and its aftermath are thus subjects for subsequent chapters.

ON THE EVE OF REVOLUTION, 1910–1911

In the previous chapter the focus was on railway, that is, productive loans; here the focus is on administrative loans, and note should first be made of the Currency Loan of April 1911, against which an advance of £400,000 was authorized by the Four Power Groups the same month. Further advances would be made in 1912 and the loan was renegotiated as the Reorganization Loan in 1913.

While Charles Addis in London and E.G. Hillier in Peking pressed ahead with major development loans for China, the Hongkong Bank in China itself, especially in Hong Kong/Canton, Shanghai, and Hankow, faced both the periodic economic crises which typify a free economy and the mounting financial pressures under which local, and particularly provincial, Governments were operating. In Hankow where provincial opposition to the Hu-kuang Railways Loan was naturally centred, the Bank experienced one of several civil uprisings which were to disturb the trade of that great river port.

Financial crises – Hankow and Shanghai

The Hongkong Bank and, to a lesser extent, other exchange banks had become an integral part of China's domestic banking system and money markets through long-established relationships with the native banks through, *inter alia*, chop loans guaranteed by the exchange banks' compradores. China's foreign loans were paid through Shanghai and funds were held by the native banks there until due for deposit with the foreign servicing bank, usually the Hongkong Bank.[1] The 1909 crisis in Hankow and the 1910 crisis in Shanghai confirmed that the exchange banks had to support the system in difficulties or risk a chain of bankruptcies which would disrupt trade.

In Shanghai, the Hongkong Bank's actions proved that the Bank could deal directly with its Chinese constituents, but the methods employed highlighted the essential role the compradore was still playing in more normal times. The Hongkong Bank with others in the Exchange Banks Association attempted to use the occasion to effect reforms in the local banks (*ch'ien-chuang*) and did succeed in defining the proper use of local money market instruments, but there were limits to which foreign banks could 'reform' the Shanghai system; among these limits were the exchange banks' own lack of experience in major European money markets and their limited knowledge of central banking techniques.

Hankow, 1909

A Bank Inspector's report of 1912 noted that, in addition to the Hupei Provincial 7% Silver Loan of 1911 which will be considered below, there were outstanding on the books of the Bank's Hankow agency two Government 1909 loans: (i) to the Hukuang Viceroy for Ts5 lacs at 7% and repayable in ten years in Ts25,000 semi-annual instalments and (ii) Ts5 lacs at 5% on account of the Hankow Chamber of Commerce but guaranteed by the Viceroy. The timing suggests the same cause: the failure of native banks to which the Bank had in its normal course of business made 'chop' or clean loans.

The two Government loans had been sanctioned by the central authorities – the Wai-wu Pu and Prince Ch'ing respectively – and this sanction had been communicated to the British Minister; the former loan at least was signed in Hankow not only by the Viceroy and the Bank Manager, J.D. Taylor, but also by the British Consul. There were, however, no specific references to a full central Government guarantee, although for loans of this size this was not, presumably, thought necessary.

The 1909 native banking crisis in Hankow and the Bank's timely intervention serves to introduce the more serious but similar (although unconnected) crisis of 1910 in Shanghai.

Shanghai in 1910

Since the Boxer Uprising the total trade of Shanghai had increased over 30% to HkTs374 million, with imports since the pre-Boxer year of 1899 rising by the same percentage to Ts198 million by 1910. The Shanghai branch of the Hongkong Bank was under the able, if somewhat flamboyant, leadership of H.E.R. 'Harry' Hunter, and his Eastern staff numbering 30 – including A.S. Henchman and V.M. Grayburn – and there was a sub-agency in Hongkew with a staff of two. The focus was on the finance of the port's growing trade, but Hunter also handled vestigial activities of the Boxer Indemnity's International Commission of Bankers, the servicing of China's debts, with the related exchange transactions, and the overall supervision of Hankow and the northern Chinese branches.

Shanghai also had a stock market and from time to time new companies designed to open up tin mining in Malaya or a small factory in Shanghai were floated. During the rubber boom of early 1910, when prices reached 13s:8d per pound, nine new rubber companies were formed in London in February alone and the Hongkong Bank's H.E. Nixon (East in 1908) resigned to become a planter. The fever reached Shanghai for which market shares of new companies were reserved; in March, for example, of the 130,000 shares of the Kota Bahroe Rubber Estate Co., 20,000 at Ts9 were offered on the Shanghai market by the Hongkong Bank and were sixteen times over-subscribed in ten minutes.[2] This excitement spilt over into the rest of the market; there was considerable share speculation and, as previously noted, V.M. Grayburn resigned from the Hongkong Bank to join a firm of brokers. The boom burst before Grayburn's resignation became effective and he was permitted to withdraw it. Later he would be Chief Manager.

Key to the crisis was the failure of Yen I-pin's bank and associated banks as a consequence of complex financial dealings with the Shanghai Taotai, Ts'ai Nai-huang, involving speculation with central Government funds. These failures had repercussions throughout the 'native' money market, causing the failure of other banks and the refusal of those still solvent to honour their money orders or to issue further credit. The trade of Shanghai was brought to a standstill and the Chinese merchant community put pressure on the Taotai, to borrow funds from the foreign banks in order to restore confidence.

Two loans and other assistance

In June 1910 after consultations with Ts'ai Nai-huang, with the head of the Shanghai Chinese Chamber of Commerce, Chou Chin-chen, the Viceroy, Chang Jen-chün, and the Kiangsu Governor, Ch'eng Te-ch'uan, the Governor was persuaded to seek funds from the Ta-Ch'ing and Chiao-t'ung banks, but their response proved inadequate.[a]

On August 4, 1910, an unusual agreement was consequently signed between the Taotai and the Shanghai managers of nine foreign exchange banks. The agreement was unusual because (i) it called for a five-year loan of Ts3.5 million Shanghai sycee at 4%, a rate of interest at least 3% below market 'in view of this money being lent by the Banks in the interests of the trade of Shanghai' and (ii) the intervention of the Taotai, with the authority of the Nanking Viceroy and the sanction of an Imperial edict (communicated in the ordinary way by the Wai-wu Pu to the Legations), was perhaps the first direct involvement of this kind by a Shanghai Taotai relative to the business

---

[a] A Chinese newspaper report states that at this point the Hongkong Bank advanced Ts2 million for a year against property deeds, but, if so, it was likely to have been subsequently included in the Ts3.5 million loan from the nine banks. Alternatively the report could have confused this with the subsequent agreement to advance to individual Chinese merchants direct.[3]

activities of the community. It was a new departure, a recognition, albeit reluctant, of a new Government responsibility.[b]

The purposes of the loan were three: (i) to pay the native bank orders in the hands of the nine banks issued by the three most important bankrupt local banks – totalling approximately Ts1.4 million, (ii) to permit the prompt repayment of other unpaid native bank orders, and (iii) 'to render assistance to the Native Money Market in order to restore confidence generally'.

The first was promptly effected. The Taotai then turned to the third and deposited some Ts2 million in favoured banks, to the resentment, apparently, of the native banking community, which accordingly refused to respond to this injection of funds. The actual situation was difficult to determine; it is possible that the funds were available only at prohibitive rates of interest; it is equally possible that the prolonged and controversial bankruptcy proceedings, involving application to the Mixed Court, waiving of procedures relative to interrogation by the Taotai, etc., were legitimate reasons for delay.

W.G. Max Müller, the British chargé d'affaires in Peking, was able to report that by September 1910:

The assistance rendered by the foreign banks, headed by the Hongkong and Shanghai Banking Corporation . . . would appear to have had the desired effect . . . and there are grounds for hoping that the recent crisis may lead to the introduction of certain much needed reforms which will place the relations between foreigners and Chinese in this important trade centre on a sounder financial footing than has hitherto been the case.[4]

He was over-sanguine; there were at least two further rescue operations, one by the Hongkong Bank directly to Chinese merchants, the other a loan to the Nanking Viceroy.

Assistance to the local banks was only partly effective. The Hongkong Bank recognized that its Chinese constituents and other Chinese businesses needed funds on a loan basis, but the Bank's compradore was already over-extended and could not guarantee further loans. The only alternative was direct lending without the compradore's guarantee. In effecting this, the Bank took unusual steps which also revealed the real role the compradore played as an intermediary between the Bank and constituents whose business procedures and records would not permit them, in normal times, to make a satisfactory presentation on a Western basis.

The Hongkong Bank made Ts2 million available to Chinese businesses in

[b] The nine banks (and amounts) involved were the Hongkong and Shanghai Banking Corporation (Ts8 lacs); the Chartered Bank of India, Australia and China and the Deutsch-Asiatische Bank (Ts5 lacs each); the Russo-Chinese Bank (Ts4 lacs); the Yokohama Specie Bank, the Banque de l'Indo-Chine, and the International Banking Corporation (Ts3 lacs each); the Netherlands Trading Society (Ts2½ lacs); and the Banque Sino-Belge (Ts1½ lacs).

Shanghai through the Chinese Chamber of Commerce subject to the following agreed procedures: those who wished to borrow from the Bank within the Ts2 million scheme should (i) designate real property as security, (ii) provide full details thereof, with valuation etc., to the Chamber of Commerce, which would then provide an English language letter of introduction to the Bank outlining these details, (iii) go to the Hongkong Bank with an interpreter from the Chamber of Commerce where the documents would be considered and arrangements made for a valuation of the property by a foreign appraiser, and (iv) complete the documentation in English which would be attested by trustees designated by the Chamber of Commerce. For the use of translators, secretaries, paper, pens, typewriters, transportation etc., the Chamber charged a commission of Ts2.5 per mille.[5]

One stated reason for the December loan of Ts3 million to the Viceroy of the Liang-Kiang provinces, the Nanking Viceroy, was the continuing need to assist Shanghai. That loan, which was at the more usual rate of 7%, was made in equal amounts by the Hongkong Bank, the DAB, and the Banque de l'Indo-Chine for six years and was sanctioned by an Imperial edict, notified to the Legations by the Wai-wu Pu.[6] This combination of lenders is evidence that the loan was made within the framework of the Three Power Groups inter-bank agreement of 1909.

'Desultory provincial loans'

Turning now to a consideration of the advisability of the loans, the first, the two Ts500,000 in Hankow and Ts3.5 million to the Taotai, were necessitated by emergencies, pressed by the Chinese merchants, and resulted in the Hongkong Bank led rescue operation. Criticism focused on the need for a sound banking system, but the need was not confined to Hankow and Shanghai alone. The subsequent Hukuang provincial loan for Ts3 million, however, was already seen in the context of other provincial requests and worried both the Bank and the British Legation, the latter since a large number of small, miscellaneous administrative loans was difficult to assess and might result in numerous protests for repayment over the years.

As Sir John Jordan wrote to the Foreign Secretary:

This system of desultory provincial loans, the expenditure of which is probably very loosely controlled by the central Government, is, in my opinion, doubtful finance in the present condition of China, and I have suggested to the Hongkong and Shanghai Bank that future loans of this kind should be consolidated into one Imperial Loan. Mr Hillier seems to share these views.[7]

Referring back to the Taotai loan, Jordan added:

Kiangsu, for instance, does not see why it should have been saddled with the loan of Ts3.5 million made, it is alleged, to the Shanghai taotai in August last largely to cover up gambling debts of Chekiang (Ningpo) people in connection with rubber transactions, and the representatives of the province are making their views felt in Peking.[8]

Sir Edward Grey strongly endorsed these views.[9] The concept of what eventually became one of the basic intentions behind the Reorganization Loan of 1913 – although few had thought so far – was thus already in formulation.

'Provincial' vs 'Imperial' loans reconsidered

Until China's post-Boxer reform attempts, the central Government of the Empire routinely operated through the Viceroys and the provincial governors, who might, in such capacities as 'Northern Superintendent of Trade', for example, be acting as 'executive officers' for one of the Imperial 'boards', or for the provinces themselves. The key issue, however, was whether the loan was a sovereign risk loan, that is whether it could be truly stated that, whatever special security there might be listed, 'principal and interest [were] unconditionally guaranteed by the Imperial Government of China'.

In one sense the problem was relatively straightforward. The provincial authorities were forbidden by Imperial edict to borrow without Imperial authorization, such authorization carried with it the implication of sovereign responsibility and was duly accepted as such by the subscribing public after the loan had been notified through the Legation concerned. Provincial and local authorities did nevertheless borrow, but only directly from banks virtually in the normal course of business, and certainly the banks were in such cases without recourse to the established appeal procedures through the Legation to the Tsungli Yamen or, later, the Wai-wu Pu.

As larger public loans were required, direct access to Peking became a necessity, and thus the indemnity loans were negotiated by the Tsungli Yamen itself on behalf of the Imperial Chinese Government, but these loans too needed the Imperial edict. All authorized loans were thus sovereign risk loans. Not only did the provinces obtain permission to borrow, the borrowing was undertaken in the name of the Imperial Chinese Government; it could be argued that, although there were overdrafts and small advances, often for embryo industrial enterprises, there were no examples of unauthorized 'provincial' borrowing through a public issue.

Although this is perhaps overstating the situation, it is true that a new distinction arose when the provinces took on more independent administrative responsibilities commensurate with the growth of purely provincial developmental and reform projects. The ban on unapproved provincial borrowing remained, but when 'sanctioned' by an Imperial edict was this permissive only or did it carry the unconditional guarantee of the Imperial Government, did the loan qualify as a sovereign risk loan?

This is precisely the question asked in connection with the September 1910 claims of the London City and Midland Bank and Messrs Dunn, Fischer and Co. in relation to the Imperial Chinese Government 7% Peking–Hankow Railway Redemption Loan referred to briefly in the previous chapter.[10] E.G. Hillier, the Hongkong Bank's Peking Manager, now requested the Legation to make similar enquiries concerning the Liang-Kiang Provinces 7% Silver Loan of 1910.[11] Taylor's loans in Hankow and Hunter's loan to the Shanghai Taotai had been sanctioned but *not* guaranteed by the central Government, but as Hunter later explained in connection with the Shanghai loan, the matter was an emergency and the lending banks were aware of the risk. As for the Liang-Kiang Loan, this time they would make sure.[12]

In paragraph 8 of the Liang-Kiang Loan Agreement it is stated that the Viceroy is 'authorized to guarantee on behalf of the Imperial Chinese Government . . . that payment of interest and repayment of principal of this loan shall be duly made'. The Hongkong Bank, along with the DAB and Banque de l'Indo-Chine, had agreed in July 1910 not to lend without the central Government's unconditional guarantee; the question now arose as to whether paragraph 8 was such a guarantee and whether such an intimation could be read into the standard communication from the Wai-wu Pu to the Legation.[13]

Jordan himself refused to interpret the Chinese Government's intention, but he confessed to the Foreign Office that the paragraph and its subsequent endorsement by Prince Ch'ing could simply mean that the revenues of the province were pledged but that, if these should not be available, the revenues of the Empire were not necessarily available.

The endless vista of problems which this ambiguity evoked was but another reason why those responsible for financial relations with China thought in terms of a single, large administrative loan made unequivocally to the central Government.

The growing crisis, 1911

An incident in Hankow

Chinese opposition to the Hukuang Railways Loan was made manifestly clear when, on January 23, 1911, a mob attacked the Hongkong Bank in Hankow. Mrs J.D. Taylor, wife of the Bank's Hankow Agent, was reading to seven-year-old J.McG. Taylor and his brother in the Agent's flat above the office when a brick came flying through the window. But, recalled Taylor in a 1980 interview, she remained calm, only commenting, 'Oh, just schoolboys . . . these schoolboy pranks . . .', and she packed the two children off to bed, while the servants kept the mob at bay by hammering on the hands of those attempting to scale the high railing in front of the building. Mrs Taylor knew perfectly well what was happening, and the shouting and yelling were long remembered.[c]

The Bank was saved temporarily by the Volunteers, and eventually a German warship, the *Emden*, arrived. Captain von Müller came ashore and placed a guard of German Marines around the Bank; he then asked Mrs Taylor if she had any children. 'Two boys.' 'Could I see them please?' and so, concluded J.McG. Taylor, 'I have sat on the knee of Captain von Müller.' This was the same officer whose careful reading of the Shanghai and Hong Kong shipping news enabled him to intercept and sink several British merchant ships in the early days of the Great War.

Hankow was a centre both of development and of political agitation. The Hongkong Bank's compradore, Tang Kee Shang, was a director of the Government Cotton Mills at Wuchang, while revolutionary study societies were forming in Hupei.[14] One such group, the Kung-chin hui (Common Advancement Society) was loosely affiliated to the more widely based T'ung-meng hui; these two in cooperation began in September to plot revolt in Hankow; the plot was discovered on October 9. On the following day, October 10, 3,000 of a larger garrison revolted, and the Ch'ing fled – Wuchang, opposite the foreign settlements of Hankow on the Yangtze, fell. The foreign consuls declared their neutrality.

Finance in 1911

Following the signing of the Hukuang Railways Loan on May 20, 1911, the general political situation had deteriorated. On August 14 the Hongkong Bank with the DAB, the Banque de l'Indo-Chine, and the American Group, signed the Hupei Provincial 7% Silver Loan for Ts2 million. Later the same month, on August 30, the Bank together with the DAB and the Banque de l'Indo-Chine signed a loan with the Kwangtung provincial authorities for HK$5 million at 7% for five years. There may have been smaller advances made by the banks to provincial authorities, perhaps without the sanction and full repayment guarantee of an Imperial edict which characterized those referred to.

The Reorganization Loan assigned funds for the repayment of such provincial loans including those made (in addition to the loans specifically

---

[c] J.McG. Taylor's story of the 1911 riots is the earliest Bank-related memory orally recorded. He joined London Office in 1923, went East in 1925, and served in Sourabaya, Dairen, and Saigon; he was Accountant Jakarta, 1947–1949, and Manager 1950–1953; he was then appointed senior Sub-Manager in Singapore 1953–1955 from where he retired; he died in 1983.

His father, J.D. Taylor, joined London Office in 1883, went 'East' in 1884 (to the New York office) and then served in Hong Kong, Foochow, and Singapore; he was then Agent Colombo, Tientsin, and from 1907 in Hankow. His name features in many Foreign Office despatches, although he was joined by E.G. Hillier from Peking for the more critical negotiations. Taylor retired a few months after the incident described on grounds of health; he died 42 years later.

listed in this chapter) by the Hongkong Bank (Ts1.6 million), the Deutsch-Asiatische Bank, the Banque de l'Indo-Chine, the Russo-Asiatic Bank, and the Yokohama Specie Bank (Ts5.1 million) for a total outstanding in May 1913 of Ts8.2 million.[15]

The increasing inability of the provincial Governments to balance their budgets came at a time when Imperial direction was at last moving in terms of reform. The Currency Reform Loan (see Chapter 4) was never issued, but it acted as the administrative basis for the first *ad hoc* advances eventually consolidated in the Reorganization Loan of 1913. As such it was a factor motivating the Imperial Government in such reforms as the planned centralization of railways and the reorganization of the salt gabelle (independent of subsequent demands by foreign Powers). The Imperial Government under the Minister of Finance (President of the Hu Pu), Prince Tsai-tse, and associates of mixed background and reputation, for example, Sheng Hsuan-huai, were in fact 'reforming' the country from on top and without the sympathy or cooperation of either the gentry or the military leaders.

As in the 100 days of Reform, 1898, Imperial decrees ordering 'reform' could not be immediately implemented; the procedure was impractical and invited political reaction. The burden the several post-Boxer developments placed on the provinces and central authorities was reflected in these recurring demands for both major and piecemeal loans. The Government was unable to shift the incidence of taxation to the foreigners through an increase in the customs duties or raise sufficient funds domestically. This latter, rather than required indemnity and loan repayments, forced the Government to turn to further borrowing. But with the increasing reluctance of the exchange banks to be responsible for 'desultory, provincial loans' the course was set towards discussions for a major administrative loan.

The Hongkong Bank's involvement, despite its disapproval of provincial loans in principle, in the Kwangtung loan and its refusal to join the DAB in a loan to Shantung are illustrative of the considerations which were then thought important.

The Kwangtung Provincial Silver Loan of 1911
The emergency which precipitated a provincial loan to the Kwangtung Viceroy was a reported run on the Government-sponsored banks and the depreciation of their uncovered note issue. Indeed so urgent was the situation that H.E.R. Hunter, as the Hongkong Bank's Shanghai Manager, reported that the Ministry of Finance (Hu Pu) in Peking had transmitted through him Ts20 lacs for the Kwangtung Government and a further Ts5 lacs for the Canton office of the Chiao-t'ung Bank (Bank of Communications).

Hunter was meanwhile considering the Canton Viceroy's firm request for an advance of 70 lacs of taels while attempting, unsuccessfully, to persuade him to obtain the funds through a Bank loan to the central rather than the provincial Government. This attempt was in keeping with Bank and British Foreign Office policy; the Viceroy refused, 'his reason we can only guess at as being the sweating process the money would be subject to in Peking before it reached him'.[16] At the same time, Hunter as Shanghai Manager, in accord with Bank policy, coordinated with the representatives of the Four Power Groups.

To the concern of the Hong Kong Government, the Kwangtung loan was eventually made through the Four Power Groups and involved both French and German banks, whose participation in affairs close to the Colony was watched with suspicion by the colonial Government and the local branch of the China Association. As with the finance of the railways, local Chinese merchants and gentry, although protesting increasing foreign financial involvement, were as powerless as the Hong Kong Government to find a practical alternative. Schemes for a loan based in Hong Kong but subscribed by Canton and Hong Kong merchants were stillborn; the Hongkong Bank itself was bound by its agreements with the other Groups, and yet another international 'rescue' operation was required.

The terms of the Kwangtung loan agreement required payment and repayment in Hong Kong dollar banknotes, which brings to mind the discussion in Chapter 4 and the continuing premium on banknotes over legal tender coin.[17] The question of redeeming Canton banknotes was a recurring one; it became serious again in 1914 and a proposal was made by the Hong Kong Government to divert the £2 million assigned for reform of the Salt Administration for this purpose.[18]

Hunter referred to the reluctance of the Deutsch-Asiatische Bank to lend in silver and, indeed, for a time that bank had declined to participate unless the Kwangtung loan were repayable in gold. This is confirmation of the unusually favourable position of the Hongkong Bank in undertaking local silver operations and of the limits of local China-coast markets with reference to the absorption of Government silver loans; in consequence Hunter's prediction proved correct; the door for further provincial silver loans was, with the granting of the Kwangtung loan, virtually closed. And he noted, correctly as it turned out, 'the provinces may turn to gold'.

His comments specifically excepted the Japanese, but their aggressive lending policies are properly the subject of another history.

The Shantung Provincial Loan – a digression
In August 1911 the Governor of Shantung approached the Deutsch-Asia-

tische Bank for a gold loan of £200,000, and under the terms of the Four Power Groups Agreement, the other Groups were eligible for a participation, as indeed had happened in the Kwangtung, Hupei, and Liang-Kiang loans.[19] What in fact developed is a further illustration of the personal authority of the Hongkong Bank's London Manager, Charles Addis, in contesting with the Foreign Office the position taken by the British Minister in Peking. Although one may explain this by simply stating Addis's policy was the more sound, the important practical point is that he stated his views clearly and convincingly. In the process he made certain statements about Hongkong Bank policy which require comment.

The basic position of the British Government as stated, indeed by Sir John Jordan himself, was opposition to provincial loans.[20] Both the Hongkong Bank and the Foreign Office reacted automatically on the assumption, therefore, that the British Group should not participate in the Shantung loan. Addis communicated his views to the French and American Groups, who subsequently accepted them. His case was made easier by the frank explanation of Franz Urbig of the DAB that the loan was the consequence of factors outside his bank; he was subject to German political pressure.

Surprisingly Jordan argued in favour of participation; he felt apparently that as the Germans had participated in Yangtze Valley loans so now the British ought to confirm the 'open door' by participating in Shantung, thereby weakening the German exclusiveness in that province.[21]

Addis countered by noting the German Yangtze participation had been in a central Government loan and that Four Power involvement with the Germans in a Shantung provincial loan might seem to confirm rather than undermine the German position. The Foreign Office commented, significantly, that they could hardly ask the Hongkong Bank to lend its money where it did not wish to lend it.

Addis also remarked that as a rule the Hongkong Bank should confine its business to those parts of China from which orders could be expected by British firms, a rather incautious statement for a bank which had four German directors representing leading mercantile operations in China.[22] However British the Bank might be in London and with reference to its merchant banking operations, in Hong Kong and the East it catered to the trade requirements of all nationalities. Jordan did not, however, pick this up; rather he argued that the Chinese intended to use part of the funds for the development of Chefoo and Tsingtau, and particularly in the former (but also in the latter where the Bank was under pressure to establish an agency) British trade might prosper. And in any case, previous provincial loans, Jordan noted after consulting Hillier, had not resulted in orders for British goods.[23]

On September 5, 1911, Charles Addis countered in one of those letters which were the key to his negotiating success.[24] He made five basic points, which can be summarized as follows: (i) there were sound basic arguments against provincial loans, the very arguments originally advanced by Jordan, (ii) the Shantung loan was the first provincial *gold* loan and whereas it might not reach the European markets in view of German assurances, it was a dangerous precedent which could interfere with major loan proposals, (iii) that the previous provincial loans had failed to result in orders for British goods was irrelevant since their purpose was to prevent collapse of the money market and thus curtailment of trade in general, (iv) whatever the Chinese authorities said about funds for Chefoo and Tsingtau and Jordan's consequent belief that such moves 'ought' to benefit British trade, his comments reflected an act of faith in something unlikely to occur, and (v) the cooperation of the Four Powers would not suffer any more than from German abstention in the Luhan Line Redemption Loan.

Underlying this was Addis's belief that the overall impact of his having secured the abstention of the other Groups would be to discourage Germany, or indeed any Group, from lending again to provincial authorities on such terms.

Addis added, 'If in the opinion [of the Secretary of State] it is considered desirable for political reasons to accept the German offer, the Bank will do so at once.'[25]

After receipt of such a letter there was little possibility that the Foreign Office would urge the Bank further, even if Sir Edward Grey had disagreed with Addis. Addis quite obviously wished to retain the Bank's freedom of action but appear politically cooperative, his 'promise' was thus a sound conclusion to an incisive letter. It should not, however, be considered a statement of the Bank's position *vis-à-vis* the Foreign Office, nor did Addis so intend it. In a sense it was bravado.

Sir Francis A. Campbell and Sir Edward Grey agreed with Addis, and Jordan was so informed.[26] The British Group, like the French and American Groups, would not participate.

The China Merchants' Steam Navigation Co. Loan

In 1885 the Hongkong Bank, which had lent £300,000 to the China Merchants' Steam Navigation Co. (CMSNCo.), had been fully repaid, and there had been other dealings between the company and the Bank (see Chapter 5, see also Volume I, Chapter 14). In 1911 the Bank was again approached for financial assistance; apparently to cover an existing overdraft, and in September the Bank made a Ts1.5 million loan at 6% for fifteen years on the security of real property in Shanghai and elsewhere.[27]

The political implications of this loan were significant. The revolutionaries in Nanking were willing to sell out the company to Japanese interests to obtain funds. According to William D. Wray's account a deal for a Ts10 million loan against the mortgage of the fleet in favour of the NYK was practically accomplished at a February 1, 1911, shareholders' meeting, despite latent opposition. The deal had been aborted partly by the intervention of the anti-Japanese Yuan Shih-k'ai and partly by the Hongkong Bank's offer of funds. The Hongkong Bank had in turn been alerted by Butterfield and Swire, whose interest in the Chinese line was also of long standing.[28]

The resulting mortgage to the Hongkong Bank rendered the company less attractive and warded off further efforts by the Japanese, for example by the Okura Specie Bank Loan, to gain control through further lending, especially during a period of financial difficulties in mid-1914.

The mortgages had another benefit. During an attack on Hankow by Chinese forces, the consul authorized that the British flag be flown over the mortgaged property, thus minimizing the damage.[29] The revolutionaries were only temporarily frustrated; in 1912 the CMSNCo. was forced to make a political contribution of Ts0.5 million to the Nanking Government but was able for a time to surmount the consequent difficulties.[30]

A dollar transaction in Tientsin

The unsettled times undoubtedly caused many troop payment problems, and one, involving the Hongkong Bank in Tientsin, should be noted. The Imperial Government, even with funds available, was unable to lay down sufficient dollars in Tientsin to pay the Northern troops. There was in fact a shortage of silver dollars due to the natural tendency to hoard them in unsettled times. The Hongkong Bank's Acting Manager, H.G. Gardner, offered to procure British dollars, if these would meet requirements. As H.E. Muriel (East in 1909) recalls the events: 'The Chinese bankers discussed together in tea shops and over large belch-provoking meals and we were told Hong Kong [British] dollars would do very well. It has always been the Bank's policy to assist the Chinese Government as far as possible, and we did so now.'[31]

The transaction required the Shanghai branch of the Bank to buy silver bullion in San Francisco or London and ship it to Bombay where it would be minted into British dollars and shipped to Tientsin. At this point the dollar coins would be sold to the local bankers against payment in Tientsin taels with which the Hongkong Bank, Tientsin, would purchase an equivalent remittance in Shanghai taels, thus restoring the Shanghai branch's position.

Unfortunately, the Hongkong Bank left one link uncovered.

The series of transactions began with local bankers contracting, by several small individual agreements, to buy the dollar coins at a specified rate in

Tientsin taels. These contracts were made through the compradore, and Gardner should at the same time have covered himself by requiring these banks to sell him for forward delivery against the Tientsin tael amount an equivalent in TT on Shanghai at a rate agreed at the same time and satisfactory to the Bank, thus by closing the circuit ensuring a net profit.

By failing to take this last mentioned step, the Hongkong Bank was left open at two points: (i) the contracts themselves, to the extent they were signed by fictitious names, could be repudiated – the Bank would then find itself with silver dollars for which it had no use except to sell, perhaps to the same persons under a different name but at a less favourable price, (ii) since the rate for TT, Tientsin on Shanghai had not been fixed, the Bank had to accept whatever rate it could negotiate when the dollars had been sold, and this rate, negotiated at a time when the Bank's position and requirements were known, was bound to be unfavourable.

Muriel pointed this out to the acting Manager in Tientsin and was told, 'Never mind, it all goes into the pot.' But when the Manager, Duncan Mackintosh, returned from leave, he was more realistic. 'It doesn't go into the pot, Muriel, it comes out of the pot.'

THE CHINESE REPUBLIC, 1912–1914

The political background[32]

In 1907 two quite different 'reformers', the traditional scholar/official Chang Chih-tung and the younger, military oriented Yuan Shih-k'ai were taken from their provincial strongholds and made Grand Councillors in Peking. The Empress Dowager, the 'Old Buddha', died in November 1908; two days later the powerless Kuang-hsu Emperor died. He was succeeded, on the previous decision of the Empress Dowager, by the latter's three year old grand-nephew, P'u-i, the Hsuan-t'ung Emperor, with his father the second Prince Ch'un, Tsai-feng, as Regent. Prince Ch'ing remained Premier.

Sir Robert Hart returned to England in 1908, never to return; Yuan Shih-k'ai was dismissed from his posts in early 1909 and Chang Chih-tung died later in the year. The impact on railway politics had been noted with decreased power for Yuan's protégé, T'ang Shao-yi, and the regaining of authority by Sheng Hsuan-huai. In general the central Government was ill-equipped to meet the demands which its own minimal reform efforts had created. Representatives of sixteen provincial assemblies met in Peking in February 1910 and petitioned for a national parliament; this was rejected, but a cabinet was established in April 1911 – with eight Manchus, one Mongol bannerman, and only four Chinese.

Despite the obvious signs of unrest, the actual events at Wuchang on October 10, 1911, were not part of a premeditated plan and revolutionaries were caught unprepared. Sun Yat-sen, then in the United States, read of the uprising in the newspapers.

Between the uprising and January 1, 1912, when Sun Yat-sen became the first President of the Provisional Government of the Chinese Republic in Nanking, there had been significant developments. Rejecting the initial pleas of the Regent to resume office in Peking, Yuan Shih-ka'i waited for a grant of virtual full powers before returning to the capital. Troops under his command were successful in the Wuchang area but did not press further. Meanwhile, Yuan securing his power in the north negotiated with the revolutionaries in Nanking.

The leaders of the Nanking National Assembly recognized that they were not in a position to form an executive government in true parliamentary style; accordingly, with the full agreement of Sun Yat-sen, the Assembly on February 15, 1912, voted Yuan Shih-k'ai President of the Provisional Government, Sun stepped down, and Yuan took office on March 10. The Assembly had from the first made clear its anti-Manchu position, and P'u-i's mother, the Empress Hsiao-ting, who had become the virtual ruler of China, had authorized the abdication of the boy Emperor, thus ending over four thousand years of Imperial rule.

The Empress passed on the political succession to Yuan Shih-k'ai; he was appointed President by the last of three Imperial edicts, and he thus came to power with the legal sanction of continuity from Peking and with the freely given vote of the nation's only political assembly. Yuan took the oath of office in Peking; he did not come down to Nanking, and not unnaturally he did not adopt the approach of the elected official of a democratic republic; he sought and eventually obtained the authority of a dictator, although he lacked the control necessary to make that power effective throughout China.

In this Yuan Shih-k'ai rendered the Chinese nation a service, providing nominal continuity to which the foreign Powers could subscribe, thus preventing any immediately aggressive interference with the nation's sovereignty at least until the preoccupations of the Great War gave Japan a relatively free role. This service was, however, achieved at a cost which subsequent Chinese patriots have judged both unjustified and excessive.

As President, Yuan appointed a cabinet headed by the Cantonese T'ang Shao-yi, who thus became the first Premier of the Republic of China. The cabinet included members of the T'ung-meng hui, of whom the rising Sung Chiao-jen was one. During the period through October 1912, despite developing differences, including the resignation of T'ang and the T'ung-meng hui cabinet members in June, the façade of cooperation remained, and revolutionary leaders like Sun Yat-sen and Huang Hsing came north to Peking. Yuan, in fact, appointed Sun the Director of Railways and the latter was the author of a grand but totally impractical scheme for the development of a national railway system.

From mid-1912 there were political developments which could not be ignored. While Yuan Shih-k'ai was drawing power to himself through a compliant cabinet responsible to him as both chief of state and head of the Government (a presidential system), Sung Chiao-jen in Central China had succeeded in uniting various factions into the 'Kuo-min tang', or People's National Party (KMT), and was advocating a party Government responsible to the Parliament, a parliamentary system but with Yuan as head of state.

As the relationship between Yuan and the Nanking 'revolutionaries' deteriorated, the negotiations with foreign consortiums for administrative funds, which had been initiated independently by both Sun Yat-sen and Yuan Shih-k'ai, were continued by T'ang and Yuan and resulted, after a Belgian intervention, first, in the so-called Crisp Loan of August 30, 1912, and secondly, in the Reorganization Loan of April 26, 1913. The August loan has received little historical vituperation, partly because the Peking-Nanking relationship remained on an apparently acceptable basis and partly because the terms of the loan did not include foreign control provisions.

By April 1913, however, the situation had deteriorated. Yuan Shih-k'ai had achieved the assassination of Sung Chiao-jen on March 20, 1913, thereby creating a leadership vacuum in Nanking. Nevertheless the National Assembly desperately continued its efforts to control the President by insisting on the cabinet's responsibility to parliament. The proposed Reorganization Loan, required if a central Government authority were to continue in China, was seen by the Kuomintang leaders as an immediate means to force recognition of the relationship. Sun Yat-sen therefore informed the Hongkong Bank led Consortium that any such loan had to be approved by parliament.

Yuan argued that the loan had been approved in principle by the Assembly. The Peking Ministers of the then Consortium Powers – of the Five Power Groups (British, French, German, Russian, and Japanese) – instructed their nationals in the same sense, and the funds from the £25 million loan were made available to Yuan's Government in Peking on the same day that evidence of the complicity of his Administration in Sung's assassination was published in Shanghai.

The provisions of this new loan included the requirement that the salt revenues should not only be the security, as in the Crisp Loan, but that the Salt Administration should be co-administered by a foreigner. Thus the loan has been criticized on the grounds that (i) the loan infringed China's sovereign rights by control clauses, (ii) the loan was contracted by China by unconstitutional procedures, and (iii) that through the funds made available Yuan Shih-k'ai was enabled to remain in power on his own terms, and thus foreign funds made possible his successful betrayal of the revolution.

In 1913 there seemed to be and probably was no substitute for Yuan. If there were, it was not for foreign bankers to identify or support such a substitute. Despite his policies and by then apparent political goals, Yuan continued to receive important if reluctant support.

In July and August 1913 Yuan, having refused to make concessions to the Kuomintang, took the offensive, and Sun Yat-sen and Huang Hsing were soon defeated and in exile. In September Yuan formed a new cabinet in Peking bringing in moderate Kuomintang representatives and other Party leaders and on October 6 succeeded in having himself elected President of the Republic by Parliament according to the rules of that Parliament as established by the revolutionaries. The methods by which he achieved this constitutional goal included both bribery and intimidation, but the results were not open to dispute by normal diplomatic procedure and Yuan's international position was secured with the recognition by the Powers on October 7. Yuan was inaugurated on October 10, 1913, the second anniversary of the Wuchang Uprising.

President Yuan then ordered the Kuomintang disbanded and its members excluded from the Parliament which, now lacking a quorum, was dissolved – as were the provincial assemblies. The cabinet resigned in January 1914, and from May 1 Yuan ruled through a 'constitutional compact' which gave him dictatorial powers, subject to his ability to wield them. By the end of 1915 he had become President for life; he died on June 6, 1916.

China then entered a period of warlordism and unrest while the nucleus of a new Government formed fitfully in the South and the Powers continued recognition of whatever authority held Peking.

In this context the history of the Hongkong Bank in China, 1911–1914, must now be told.

The Hongkong Bank in the Chinese Republic

The Hongkong Bank changed the colours for its London sports teams from Imperial yellow with a black dragon to the red and white of the Republic. On other fronts the Bank found it less easy to meet both its obligations as a bank and to operate entirely without being associated with those forces which young nationalists saw as infringing on China's sovereign rights. The Bank's responsibilities to bondholders and to the Government of China on whose behalf it was often acting resulted in decisions which were unacceptable to those whose primary interest was political change.

Transactions undertaken in the initial confusion, advances made while Peking and Nanking retained an outwardly friendly relationship were denounced later when conditions had changed, and the Bank's actions were interpreted in a political context alien to the time at which the transactions took place. So important was the Bank's involvement in the Consortium agreements and the negotiation of the 1913 Reorganization Loan that this subject is reserved for full consideration in the final part of this chapter; other problems are considered here.

The Wuchang Uprising of October 1911 set off a chain of political events which triggered crises in the various local banking systems, the default on various loan repayments, and confusion in the matter of handling the revenues of the Chinese Maritime Customs, the greater portion of which was pledged as security for the repayment of the nation's foreign debt.

The Revolution, the Bank, and Tientsin

Although the total value of Tientsin's foreign trade in 1911 was only a tenth that of Shanghai, it had doubled since the immediate pre-Boxer days, the impetus of the railways being indicated by the post-1904 statistics. In fact, the port's trade, HkTs41 million in 1911, was approximately equivalent to that of all the other Yangtze ports combined. At this time the Hongkong Bank's Tientsin branch included seven Eastern staff headed by D.H. Mackintosh and including H.E. Muriel.

Muriel records incidents in a soldiers' uprising which destroyed much of the 'native' city.

Being young, foolish and vastly interested in other than my own business I joined with a company of like-minded idiots and went off to see the fun. . . . The mint was on fire, the chief shops were being looted of cash and goods . . . Looking down a side street we saw a soldier raging at a coolie, a looter, we walked along to see fair play – the soldier had forced the coolie to kneel on the ground and drew his sword – evidently to behead him, when from somewhere in the shadows who should appear but C.C. Barlow our Accountant. Barlow could not speak a word of Chinese but seized the man's uplifted arm saying, 'You can't do that you know, this man hasn't had a trial.'

The coolie was saved.

There was further intervention the following day. 'In came Mr Liu [the compradore's interpreter] tall and stout, usually very placid, now in a great fuss. He wanted me [Muriel] to go with him to the Compradore's house in the City and bring him and his family back to the Bank compound for safety and said transport was all laid on.' Accordingly the compradore, 'about six females, lots of children and a mass of baggage' progressed slowly in a truck with Muriel through the burning city to the borders of the foreign concession.

More directly related to banking was the fact that the Customs taotai had left Tientsin with all the funds, the machinery of collection had broken down, and there was nothing to pay the salaries and wages of Customs staff. The Deputy Commissioner of the Maritime Customs in Tientsin approached the Hongkong Bank, which accordingly advanced the necessary funds and undertook to hold the revenues.

As Muriel remembers the circumstances:

Mr Mackintosh called me in and said, 'Muriel, I want you to arrange with the Deputy Commissioner (waving his hand in the direction of a fat Frenchman with a long square-cut white beard) a system for collecting and accounting for the Customs Revenue of the port!!

To me, a junior of little more than two years' experience this seemed rather more than somewhat, but old Tosh airily waved aside any attempted expostulations and it was so.

Muriel adds that the compradore's department did most of the work – 'it was very good "face" for him' – and the young Hongkong Bank junior 'signed masses of Imperial yellow documents every day'.

A visit from the future Shanghai Manager, A.G. Stephen, would soon end Muriel's management of this operation – Stephen needed musical talent in Shanghai and Muriel could sing and sing well. He was, however, permitted as an exceptional favour to accept a gratuity of £40 from the Commissioner of Customs.

The first defaults and the Hongkong Bank's intervention

The various foreign loans of China were secured on a variety of revenues, including those of the Imperial Maritime Customs, but the actual handling of the Customs funds was undertaken by designated Chinese local banks and the repayment of the loans was not necessarily effected from the actual tax revenues designated as their security. With one or two early exceptions, in 1875 and 1883/84, which had been covered by advances by the Hongkong Bank, the Chinese had met their payments on schedule, and it was on this that their world credit standing was based.

The political and financial disturbances which immediately followed the Wuchang Uprising of 1911 resulted in China's defaulting on her debts, including both loans and the Boxer Indemnity payments. The Customs revenues were in fact collected, but they could not always be held or remitted in the traditional way, and banks, whether foreign or Chinese, were not empowered to make *ad hoc* decisions as to their disposal, but held them pending instructions from recognized authorities. The duties accounted for by Muriel and deposited in the Hongkong Bank in Tientsin could not be moved without orders from the Inspector-General of the Maritime Customs; that officer in turn could not issue new instructions except on orders from the Chinese executive authorities in Peking.

Although there were sufficient funds in the Shanghai branches of the loan-servicing banks, including the Hongkong Bank, to enable certain instalments to be made, in the absence of instructions no payment could be made and very soon the Indemnity payments were in default; defaults on several foreign loans followed. On December 10, 1911, a £224,000 payment on the 6% £3 million 1895 Gold Loan fell due; the Hongkong Bank advanced £24,000 to pay the interest coupons but repayment of the 2,000 £100 drawn bonds was delayed. Even the Hongkong Bank's Board of Directors took note of this state of affairs and instructed the Bank's Peking Agent, E.G. Hillier, to take (undesignated) action. Obviously emergency arrangements had to be made.

The Hongkong Bank's timely action had, however, an impact greater than the immediate payment of interest due. Referring to the published announcement that the Bank would buy the interest coupons at par (less income tax) even though the Chinese Government had not as yet put it in funds, Addis wrote to the Foreign Office:

> The announcement, which is as frank and straightforward as we could make it, has been well received, and the policy of thus taking the public into our confidence appears to have been justified by the result. The public argue that the Hongkong Bank, which they consider is in the best position to know, must have faith in the solvency of China or it would not purchase the coupons in default.[33]

Addis was correct; the quotations for Chinese loans dropped no more than ½ or ¾ of 1%. 'I doubt,' he added, 'if there is another country in the world of which the same could be said after the publication of a similar announcement.'[34] And the Foreign Office minuted, 'The H&S Bank may well be pleased with themselves.'[35]

So might China. The reaction in the market reflected confidence in Yuan Shih-k'ai, in the Chinese initiative in paying IMC revenues into the Hongkong Bank, and in the confirmation of these views by the leading British bank in China. The maintenance of China's credit would permit the continued financing of her requirements at prices which, while not highly favourable, were not as onerous as they might otherwise have been; in this China was partly indebted to the decisive London action taken by Charles Addis.

The Customs revenues – the official arrangements

On a longer run basis the Shanghai Commissioner of Customs proposed that the revenues collected be deposited in the Hongkong Bank and used to service foreign debts; the Shanghai Consuls recommended instead that the Commission of Bankers set up to handle Boxer Indemnity payments, of which the port's Hongkong Bank Manager was the British representative, should act. This proved unacceptable because the Customs revenues were pledged for certain loans and had to be deposited in advance of transfer to Europe in the loan-servicing banks. The Chinese Government proposed, through the Wai-wu Pu, that both Maritime and Native Customs revenues would be transmitted from the ports regularly and deposited in the first instance with the Hongkong and Shanghai Bank's Shanghai branch. To this the Powers, as represented by the Diplomatic Body in Peking, agreed.

These negotiations were still in progress, but the Inspector-General considered himself able to cable the London Office of the Customs:

> For Hongkong and Shanghai Bank for publication. No occasion for alarm. Net revenue collection for November and December deposited in Loan Service Accounts in receiving banks Shanghai Ts3 million . . . Arrangements for Bankers' Commission providing for weekly remittance of net collection to Loan Service Accounts now practically complete and payment will begin at early date.[36]

By the end of January 1912 the negotiations had been completed and the text of an agreement as proposed by the Wai-wu Pu was signed by the Dean of the Diplomatic Body on behalf of his colleagues.[37] The agreement called for the establishment of an international Commission of Bankers, consisting of the managers of the banks interested in the service of all outstanding loans secured by the Customs prior to 1900 and/or the Indemnity payments. The Commission was to have the right to determine, or rather 'certify to', the priority of loan repayments consistent with the legal priorities. The funds themselves, although received initially by the Hongkong Bank, were then redeposited in equal shares with the so-called 'custodian banks', the Hongkong Bank, the Deutsch-Asiatische Bank, and the Russo-Asiatic Bank, a decision, incidentally, which would mean that by the end of the Great War the Hongkong Bank was for a time the sole custodian bank.

Given the backlog of payments, and it was more than two years before the Indemnity payments were again on schedule, the above agreement with the new Republic of China did not in fact result in the custodian banks holding Customs revenues for any prolonged period, except as provided by the loan agreements. In any case, both the authorities in Peking and the Assembly in Nanking were, at the time of the agreement, seeking foreign financial support, which was naturally sought on reasonable terms. Therefore China's credit standing was given priority; in this context the Chinese Government's administrative decision to deposit funds directly with the Hongkong Bank was sound.[d]

---

[d] Later political observers would stress the impact of these arrangements on 'sovereignty', although it is difficult to understand how such an administrative arrangement proposed and approved by the competent authorities of the Chinese Republic could be considered an infringement of sovereignty. Eventually Chinese modern-style banks would become, with the Hongkong Bank, custodians of the Customs funds.

Financing the new Government

The Hongkong Bank and the Four Power Groups

In the night of November 13, 1911, three men met secretly with Charles Addis, London Manager of the Hongkong Bank, in his Primrose Hill house. Mrs Eba Addis recorded the event.

Edward Grenfell, 'General' Homer Lea, pale hunch-backed American visionary, and Sun Yat-sen, the future President of the proposed Chinese Republic dined with us – in great secrecy as Sun Yat-sen's life is at stake. A man of say 35, gentle, quiet, thoughtful and with the sweetest smile imaginable, he looked little like a rebel leader.[38]

The purpose of the meeting was to seek financial support for the proposed republic from the Hongkong Bank. Addis reacted on two levels: first he informed Dr Sun that he could not expect funds until a proper Government had been established, second he warned the Foreign Office of the grave danger of lending any funds to Yuan Shih-k'ai in the meantime.

In fact the Bank hesitated to advance funds until it was clear the Yuan Shih-k'ai party and the 'revolutionaries' in Nanking had reached an agreement. The British Government decision to permit its nationals to lend to the Provisional Government was forced by Japanese competition; the Bank remained uncommitted until a reconciliation had been effected between Yuan in Peking and Sun Yat-sen. As noted earlier, the Japanese had offered a loan to the Nanking leaders on the security of the China Merchants' Steam Navigation Co.; their motives were suspect and in view of the Hongkong Bank's prior financial interest, the situation was urgent. Nanking required 20 lacs of taels immediately; Yuan Shih-k'ai was negotiating for 70 lacs, but he agreed after consultation with Nanking that this should include the latter's required 20 lacs.[39]

On March 5, 1912, Addis recorded in his diary that he had been busy with 'projected financing of Yuan Shih-k'ai as president of the Chinese Provisional Republic', and the Bank's Board of Directors in Hong Kong noted approval of an advance to the 'provisional Government in Nanking . . . by arrangement with Yuan Shih-k'ai', which had in fact been agreed on February 29.

The Hongkong Bank was acting in concert with the German, French, and American Groups of the China Consortium. The first agreement with the Chinese authorities covered the advance of Ts70 lacs, of which only the Ts20 lacs required by Nanking was authorized for payment on March 5 – and of this, the Hongkong Bank's share was a proportionate Ts5 lacs. These and subsequent advances made on the urgent appeal of President Yuan to an eventual total of Ts12.1 million (see Table 8.2) were shared, retroactively where appropriate, with Russian and Japanese Groups. These Groups had

Table 8.2 *The Hongkong and Shanghai Banking*
Corporation
Terms of 7½% Treasury bill advances, 1912

Date	Shanghai taels (millions)	Exchange	Price	£ Face value £
28 ii	2.0	@ 2/8½ and 92½		= 292,793
9 iii	1.1	2/8	92½	158,559
17 v	3.0	2/9$\frac{11}{16}$	92½	455,236
12 vi	3.0	2/9¼	92½	449,324
18 vi	3.0	2/9½	92½	452,703
	Total: 12.1			1,808,615
	(of which Hongkong Bank = 2.01)			

Calculation: 292,793 × 0.925 × 7.385 = 2,000,000 £ per tael @ 2/8½ = £0.13541; reciprocal = 7.385
Source: Annexes A and B to Reorganization Loan. Agreement in MacMurray, II, 1017–18.

stated their intention of joining the Four Groups to constitute the Six Power Groups Consortium.

The later advances were subject to the 'regulations' accepted by Premier T'ang Shao-yi on May 17, including the auditing supervision of a Chinese-paid foreign staff. The final advance, on June 18, 1912, was confirmed at the meeting which established the enlarged Consortium.[40] The specific purposes are not always stated, but the June breakdown included Ts12 lacs to pay troops in Nanking and Shanghai; Ts4 lacs for Chefoo; Ts14 lacs for Peking and Kansu.

Although these advances would prove wholly inadequate to meet the continuing needs of the Provisional Government, they were, from the point of view of the participating banks, already significant. Their basis was, surprisingly, the Currency Loan Agreement of April 20, 1911 (see Chapter 4), although the participation of the Russian and Japanese Groups was anticipatory of the Reorganization Loan, which was the real security for the advances. The Currency Loan was never floated; it was, as already noted in Chapter 4, intended to be merged into the Reorganization Loan, but into the second tranche of a major Reorganization Loan of which only the first tranche of 1913 was issued. For the time being, then, the Currency Loan provided the formal as opposed to anticipatory cover, as it were, of the advances for the current administrative expenses of the new Government.

The advances themselves were negotiated initially with the Acting Finance Minister, that is with the cabinet Minister responsible. The advances were effected by the purchase of discounted Chinese Government Treasury bills payable in sterling issued in amounts sufficient to cover the tael advances at the agreed rate; the Treasury bills were thus gold obligations of the Chinese Government. As they were not repaid at the end of the first year, they continued to carry interest on the face amount at 7.5% until redemption.[41]

The Anglo-Belgian Syndicate

At the same time the Consortium Groups were making advances against an expected major Reorganization Loan, the Provisional Government in Peking were successfully negotiating for funds from foreign sources outside the Consortium.

First, there was the apparent success following negotiations in late 1911 for the Baron Cottu Loan totalling Fr150 million. The French Government, in support of the Consortium, refused to permit this loan to be quoted on the Bourse. It was successfully aborted. Second, the Banque Sino-Belge 5% Gold Loan of March 14, 1912, for £1 million, moved a stage further, and the Chinese actually received £250,000; third, there was the G. Birch Crisp and Co. 5% Gold Loan of August 30, 1912, for £10 million, of which only £5 million was paid over. The Anglo-Belgian loan will be considered immediately, the Crisp Loan later in this chapter.[42]

The Banque Sino-Belge Loan was negotiated in the names of 'Presidents Sun Wen [Sun Yat-sen] and Yuan Shih-k'ai' and effected by the purchase of Treasury bills discounted at 97, so that the yield to redemption was 8.2%. (The Chinese were paid $97 for a $100 Treasury bill redeemable after one year by repayment of the $100 face value plus 5% interest, or $8 in excess of the amount received.) The loan was made by an Anglo-Belgian syndicate, the British banks including the Eastern Bank (founded in 1909 by Sassoon interests, also represented in the Hongkong Bank), J. Henry Schröder and Co., and Brown, Shipley and Co. The large British involvement was to prove embarrassing for the Hongkong Bank, which was accused of cooperating with foreign groups while refusing to include other British banks in the 'British Group'.[43]

The acceptance of the £1 million loan from this syndicate was a breach of faith on the part of the Chinese Government engineered by the Premier, T'ang Shao-yi, and repudiated by President Yuan.[44] Willard Straight, the American representative in the Six Power Groups Consortium, has claimed that T'ang failed to inform the Council of Ministers in Peking of the March 9 undertaking; his subsequent failure to persuade the Belgians to carry out the disputed agreement led to his pleading a 'misunderstanding' which was rejected by the Ministers of the Powers involved. The Government consequently had no recourse but to admit officially that it had been guilty of a breach of faith.[45]

The Anglo-Belgian syndicate were left in equal discomfort, and the history of their efforts to secure Foreign Office support through protests from the Eastern Bank help to explain the actual nature of the so-called 'monopoly' support which the Hongkong Bank was supposedly receiving.

Virtually from the time of the Wuchang Uprising itself the Chinese political authorities, both in Nanking and Peking, were negotiating with the Hongkong Bank and, through them, with the Four Power Groups for a large administrative loan. The Foreign Office was not, however, committed to the support of the Hongkong Bank and informed Lord Balfour of Burleigh (a former Minister in recent Conservative Governments and then Chairman of the Eastern Bank) in early February that his bank would receive all the required assistance from the British Minister in Peking, but warned him that the transaction was for him to initiate with the Chinese and that the choice was theirs.

By late February the Four Groups' negotiations had reached the stage at which the representatives of the Powers in Peking were informed; the Foreign Office at this point did commit itself to the exclusive support of the British Group, that is, of the Hongkong Bank, of the Four Power Groups Consortium.

When this became known Lord Balfour and the Eastern Bank took two contrary positions: (i) in opposition to multi-national loans and (ii) insisting that the Foreign Office pressure the Hongkong Bank into sharing the Four Power Groups' loan on a 50/50 basis with his Anglo-Belgian syndicate. These two positions appeared indefensible when it was revealed that the Eastern Bank had made no communication with the Legation because their Peking negotiations were being conducted by the Russo-Asiatic Bank, thus involving French finance – and multi-national lending.

Aware that the Four Power Groups Consortium had made advances against the conclusion of a major loan, the Foreign Office had given its sole support to the Hongkong Bank, while 'encouraging' it to enlarge the British Group. The Foreign Office rebuffed the Eastern Bank's suggestion that the Foreign Secretary press the Hongkong Bank to accept them as a member of the enlarged British Group. British policy was (i) to approve nothing which would weaken the position of those now recognized to be negotiating the Reorganization Loan, (ii) to refuse interference in the composition of the British Group – other than to press the Hongkong Bank for its enlargement, and (iii) to deny any policy of monopoly or exclusive support – beyond the Reorganization Loan – for the British Group of the Consortium.

Refusing even to take official notice of the £1 million advance by the Anglo-Belgian Group, the Foreign Office replied to the Eastern Bank in very clear terms:

[The Foreign Secretary] feels bound to give due weight to the special position acquired by the Hongkong and Shanghai Bank by the fact that it was first in the field in regard to the present loan, and also that it was to a large extent instrumental in bringing about the present international combine which, it is hoped, will render effective the aim of His Majesty's Government to prevent any return to the former unprofitable policy of international competition in Chinese loans.

Under these circumstances, Sir Edward Grey feels that the Hongkong and Shanghai Bank can hardly be expected to give up the position of sole issuing bank in England for the present loan, and, though he would be glad to see you secure financial participation in the loan, he cannot urge the Hongkong and Shanghai Bank to share the issue with you or other banks.[46]

These loans and advances were all made during the period of outward cooperation between Peking and Nanking. They were designed as stopgaps, and the Four Power Groups augmented by the addition of Russian and Japanese Groups in June 1912 were planning a single, large loan, the Reorganization Loan, to replace the Currency Loan, to incorporate all the outstanding advances and arrears, and to provide funds for the intended administrative reforms of the Chinese Republic.

Domestic borrowing

The Chinese Government also attempted to raise funds domestically. In February and March 1913 regulations were promulgated relative to the issue of 6% National Bonds of the First Year of the Republic of China for $200 million at a maximum discount of 8%, which being typically grandiose in its purposes was relatively unsuccessful. In April 1914 a second Chinese Internal Loan for the more modest figure of $24 million was opened for subscription and, at the request of the Chinese Government:

Hongkong and Shanghai Bank have consented allow name appear in prospectus as prepared to receive subscriptions jointly with the Bank of China and the Bank of Communications for Chinese Government new 6 per cent Internal loan secured upon native customs and Shansi *li-kin*. . . . No agreement has been signed or has been ever contemplated, nor has any contract been entered into, and Hongkong and Shanghai Bank have no responsibility for any portion not subscribed by public.[47]

There had been rumours and the French Ambassador made enquiries. Was the Hongkong Bank about to break away from the Sextuple (Six Power) Groups Consortium and sign a major loan with the Chinese Government?[48] The above was designed to reassure; the Bank was merely acting as China's banker. There was nothing to share.

THE CONSORTIUM AND THE REORGANIZATION LOAN

The direct profit from negotiation and management of the issue of a loan is generally 'up-front' and arises from a commission which constitutes a part of the difference between the contract price and the price at which the loan is issued to the public. This differential, the so-called 'points', covered both the expenses to the issuing organizations and the commission or net profit, the latter often totalling 1.5% to 2% of the nominal value of the loan. The points also included the commission to the underwriters; if the issuing banks were willing to undertake this additional risk, then they might also receive this commission. In the case of the Reorganization Loan the return to the Hongkong Bank for both management and underwriting was approximately 0.5%. This small figure is explained by the fact that, despite its role as lead manager, the Bank represented one-third of the British Group in a Five Power Groups Agreement. This also explains why the Hongkong Bank, which, as Addis was anxious to point out, did all the work, was reluctant to share the profits with other British banks.

For the concession hunter, profits in the absolute amounts would undoubtedly constitute a sufficient inducement. The Chinese might later be persuaded to cancel the concession for a fee of similar proportions. For a bank closely connected with industrial firms, the profit on the loan *per se* was not the final desideratum.

The Hongkong Bank's involvement, while financial, was long-term. A loan was undoubtedly profitable in itself, but for the Bank it was a means to an end – the growth of the Chinese economy and the increased business this would bring. One loan was seen as part of a major responsibility, as one part of the financing of Chinese development.

From this several policies followed. The Bank was anxious to preserve the credit of China, not only for reasons of responsibility to present bondholders but also because the Bank knew that China would again be in the market. To preserve her credit the Bank saw the need to control what the market would consider ill-advised borrowing. The present International Bank for Reconstruction and Development (the World Bank) approaches the problem in this way, but neither the Hongkong Bank nor the Consortium had either the authority or the prestige of an accepted international organization.

Consequently, Charles Addis became convinced that, especially with financial loans, defined as non-project or administrative loans, control was necessary at the lending end. He came to London to find the Hongkong Bank/ DAB agreement in existence and the involvement of the French Group not far off; he came to believe that this 'Group' system, subject to support from their

Governments, was competent to rationalize lending to China on an a-political basis.

Addis's reluctance to broaden the base of the inter-bank agreements followed from the purpose of the combinations, to control lending. With the support of the respective Governments, if the key capital markets of London, Berlin, and Paris could be closed to those seeking unapproved funds for China, the Consortium would have achieved its purposes. This however was politically impractical, both domestically and internationally, and Addis witnessed the addition first of the somewhat reluctant American Group in 1910 (and their subsequent departure in 1913) and then the primarily political intervention of the Russian and Japanese Groups in 1912.

The Hongkong Bank and its associated companies, the British and Chinese Corporation and the Chinese Central Railways, operated in the context of China's post-Boxer commitments to undertake major overhead construction and political reform. Addis, in common with Bland and others, took the usual banking position that a loan intended for a specified purpose should involve detailed plans and controls sufficient to effect that purpose. Although accepted by firms in the private sector, such provisions were resented by leading Chinese, especially by those returned students, Young China, who had accepted exaggerated Western concepts of national sovereignty.

Irrational as their position might be in financial terms, it was popular politically and was an important factor in undermining well-intentioned efforts to ensure the sound use of funds. Controls would have both minimized the amounts borrowed overseas and secured the optimum terms from the market, but political factors dominated. Not surprisingly, Addis never achieved the controlling position he wished for the Consortium; there were always threats of competition, sometimes realized, from other groups in Europe; the Chinese themselves were usually negotiating with at least one other non-Consortium syndicate and, as in the case of the Hukuang Railways or the Reorganization Loan, one slip by the inter-bank Groups and months of negotiation could be wasted.

The one-time lender, the syndicate 'adventuring into China' on a one-time basis, would not be concerned with China's long-run position. Chinese political leaders were increasingly concerned with irrelevant and self-destructive political positions, complaining at the same time of the 'onerous terms' which such positions inevitably caused.

There was, however, another aspect to the overall problem. To preserve China's credit-worthiness was undoubtedly a policy of wisdom, although perhaps in view of Chinese political opposition somewhat quixotic. The bankers, however, were themselves investors in China's previous public issues and were directly involved; they were to an extent also responsible to other bondholders as trustees; on both counts they were properly concerned with a stable market for China loans.

This part of the Hongkong Bank's history recounts the efforts of Charles Addis to keep control of one important loan, the Reorganization Loan of 1913, as the membership in the Consortium varied, as the British Government vacillated on the support it would give the British Group, and as China itself considered and reconsidered the terms under which the funds would be made available against a background of growing (but unpredicted) political deterioration.

From Four Power to Six Power Groups Consortium

As early as November 1910 the Japanese had made enquiries relative to possible participation in the Four Power Groups Consortium; they had been discouraged by Charles Addis, with subsequent Foreign Office approval, on the grounds that they were unable to raise funds except on the London market.[49] Nevertheless, it was obvious that the Japanese remained interested and could upset the purposes of the Consortium by independent silver loans to China or, at least in theory, by guaranteeing Chinese loans on the London market issued through rival syndicates. Since Japanese credit was superior to that of China, such a guarantee would have the effect, other things being equal, of lowering the cost of the loan to China and possibly providing a margin for a commission to the Japanese.[50]

In the first months of the Republic, the Japanese pointedly made reference to their capabilities and again indicated their interest in the international Consortium.

Both Japan and Russia had objected to the intervention of the Consortium through the Currency Loan into Manchurian industrial development problems. Thus the Russians too were interested in joining the Consortium, but they quite clearly had an international group in mind, including J. Henry Schröder, who intended to issue part of any loan assigned to Russia on the London market.

This is sufficient to introduce both aspects of the 'composition' problem of the Consortium. The Four Power Groups – the British, French, German, and American Groups – could not prevent rival syndicates forming, especially those which were international in composition and thus touched several capital markets. American banks were not seriously interested in China, the French and German Groups were relatively comprehensive, but the Hongkong Bank stood alone. Nor did the British Government have the authority, as did the French, to close the London market to a particular issue. The British capital market was, therefore, exposed to infiltration by an international syndicate – the Russian Group, for example, with the Eastern Bank and Schröder's.

The admission of Japan and Russia

After lengthy negotiations, which appeared from time to time on the point of collapse, Japan and Russia signed an agreement on June 18, 1912, confirmed on June 20, with the existing Four Groups to form the Sextuple Groups Consortium having as its immediate purpose the negotiation with China of a reorganization loan or loans totalling some £60 million.

The danger of competition in the capital markets was overshadowed by the fear that national groups outside the Consortium might offer funds to China on terms (i) justifiable only in the context of political objectives, (ii) which could not be sustained on a long-run program basis, or (iii) which would widen the potential of conflict between Nanking and Peking in the early months of the Republic. Finance might deepen the rift rather than bring the two sides together. Despite their long-standing objections, by March 1912 the Four had accepted that, subject to acceptance of conditions, Japan and Russia would be brought into the inter-bank Group agreements.

Japan accordingly nominated the Yokohama Specie Bank as their sole representative, Russia, the Russo-Asiatic Bank, the capital of which was mainly French, as the lead bank of an international group of Belgian, French, and British banks (see Table 8.3).

In April 1912 the Germans made a proposal on behalf of Austrian membership, and indeed Austria was negotiating industrial loans to China. In early May the Italians made an offer, and the Belgians also expressed their interest, despite the confusion which the intrusion of the Banque Sino-Belge loan had created (see pp. 479–81). When the Netherlands also applied, one Russian observer commented, 'Et alors, cela deviendra la Tour de Babel!'[51]

Complex discussions between the Six Groups at a conference in London, May 14–16, 1912, reached no final conclusions. On the first day after eight hours of continuous sitting, a French delegate declared himself at 1:30 a.m. quite unfit to express an opinion on anything, and the meeting adjourned. On the second day it was obvious the meeting was hung on a few key points and that not even Addis's soothing after dinner speech was sufficient to move the issues.[52]

On June 8 a further conference was held, this time in Paris, and the Russians were given one week to agree to a clause relative to rights in Manchuria. Russia was told firmly that Schröder's would not be permitted to issue part of the Russian share in London, but a German compromise which would permit Russia partial access to the Belgian market was accepted.[53] Finally, as noted above, on June 18 the agreement bringing into existence the

Table 8.3 *The China Consortium: Sextuple Agreement of June 1912*
Members of the Six Groups

A. *British Group*
The Hongkong and Shanghai Banking Corporation
From December 14, 1912:
  The Hongkong and Shanghai Banking Corporation (33%)
  Baring Bros and Co. (25%)
  London County and Westminster Bank (14%)
  Parr's Bank (14%)
  J. Henry Schröder and Co. (14%)

B. *German Group*

Direction der Disconto-Gesellschaft	Nationalbank für Deutschland
S. Bleichröder	Deutsch-Asiatische Bank
Deutsche Bank	Jacob S. H. Stern
Berliner Handelsgesellschaft	Sal. Oppenheim Jr. & Cie
Bank für Handel & Industrie	Norddeutsche Bank in Hamburg
Mendelssohn & Co.	L. Behrens & Söhne
Dresdner Bank	Bayerische Hypotheken und
A. Schaffhausen'scher Bankverein	Wechselbank

C. *French Group*

Banque de l'Indo-Chine	Société Générale de Crédit Industriel &
Banque de Paris et de Pay-Bas	Commerciel
Comptoir National d'Escompte de Paris	Banque de l'Union Parisienne
Crédit Lyonnais	Banque Française pour le Commerce et
Société Générale pour favoriser le	l'Industrie
developpement du Commerce	Crédit Mobilier Français
et de l'Industrie en France	

D. *Russian Group*

Banque Russo-Asiatique	Société Belge d'Étude de Chemins de
A. Spitzer & Co.	fer en Chine
J. Henry Schröder & Co.[a]	Société Générale de Belgique
Eastern Bank Ltd.[b]	Banque d'Outremer[c]
Banque Sino-Belge	

E. *American Group (all of New York City)*[d]

Messrs J. P. Morgan & Co.	First National Bank of New York
Messrs Kuhn, Loeb & Co.	National City Bank

F. *Japanese Group*
The Yokohama Specie Bank

[a] British – later a member of the British Group.
[b] British – Sassoon interests.
[c] This bank is also Belgian.
[d] Represented in the United Kingdom by Messrs Morgan, Grenfell and Co., in France by Messrs Morgan, Harjes and Co., and in France and Germany by Messrs M. M. Warburg and Co. of Hamburg.

Six Power or Sextuple Groups Consortium was signed, although the meeting continued through until ratification on June 20, during which time minutes were drawn up to reflect certain compromises.

There had been two main issues. First, the question of the capital markets and the so-called 'internationalization' of any loan made under the agreement. The original Three Groups Inter-Bank Agreement had been among Powers capable of issuing their share of a China loan in their own markets; thus the internationalization, whereby bonds issued in one market might be bought and sold in another market was merely a matter of convenience. With the admission of the United States, this right had to be restricted; with the admission of Japan and Russia, it had to be severely limited.

The advantage to membership in the Six Power Groups Agreement was for the Japanese and Russians mainly political, but the Four Groups remained insistent that they were not competent to consider or take note of political issues or national policies, specifically those in regard to Manchuria and 'special rights'. The representatives of the Four Groups were aware that Russian objections to certain provisions of the Currency Loan agreement had, through French Foreign Ministry intervention, delayed payment of advances agreed under the terms of that loan. It was essential, therefore, that in admitting the two new members – any other applicants had been persuaded to withdraw or share a portion of any loan with their allies – the Four Power Groups should neither recognize special rights in Manchuria nor give the veto power to any Group.

These problems were met (i) by refusal to permit one Group to issue in the market of another, (ii) by including statements on rights in the minutes but not in any formal agreement, at the same time reiterating the fact that the Four Groups could take no note of them, and (iii) by granting the right of a Group to withdraw from participation in a particular loan, the right, that is, not to join a particular syndicate, in lieu of the previous insistence on unanimity. Non-participation in one project syndicate would not affect a Group's responsibilities relative to projects in which it had previously participated, the syndicate for which would naturally remain in existence as long as any responsibilities under the relevant agreement remained. (For a review of terms used, see the Introduction to Part II.)

The Sextuple Agreement, which remained like the other Group inter-bank agreements an agreement among banks not among governments, once concluded, the Groups were able to continue their consideration of the Reorganization Loan itself. This was facilitated by an important decision: the Groups appointed the London Office of the Hongkong Bank as their central office and authorized the employment of a secretary and the reimbursement of expenses in connection with the loan negotiations; at a subsequent meeting a specific contribution of £60 each on an annual basis to the Hongkong Bank for acting as a clearing house for the coupons and drawn bonds of the Chinese Reorganization Loan and £300 per annum each as a contribution towards the cost of the special work entailed in acting as central agency to the Consortium.[54] Charles Addis's role was formally confirmed and Murray Stewart, formerly on the Eastern staff of the Bank, became Addis's assistant in Consortium affairs.[e]

Early Reorganization Loan negotiations

Although the Sextuple Agreement was signed only on June 18, 1912, there had been a general expectation, at times almost frustrated, that such an agreement would be reached and, accordingly, there had been discussions relative to a major loan or loans to China for administrative purposes at least since March. Indeed, although the first 'advances' had been made by the banks party to the Four Power Groups Inter-Bank Agreement, they had later been shared even before the June agreement on a *pro rata* basis among the Six Groups.

The Groups were apparently in a strong position. In consideration of the advances agreed by March 9, that is, 'the assistance rendered by the Groups to China in the present emergency and of their services in supporting her credit on the foreign markets', President Yuan Shih-k'ai had, in a letter to the Hongkong Bank's Peking Agent, E.G. Hillier, dated March 9, 1912, assured the Groups of the 'firm option of undertaking the comprehensive loan for general reorganization purposes already proposed to them'. The first charge on such a loan would be the repayment of the advances previously made by the Groups against the sums eventually raised by the loan. However, Yuan's letter contained the proviso that 'terms be equally advantageous with those otherwise obtainable'.[55]

The acknowledged relationship between the projected loan and the advances was in fact one of the factors which determined the British and German Governments' sole support for the respective Groups until the conclusion of negotiations in connection with this major reorganization loan to China.

The Groups were not, as it might at first seem, in a wholly impregnable position. The very urgency of the Chinese requirements encouraged the

---

[e] Murray Stewart was the younger brother of Gershom Stewart, MP, another former Eastern staff member of the Bank. Murray went East for the Bank in 1890 serving in Shanghai, where he worked under Charles Addis, Tientsin and Hong Kong. During the Boxer Uprising he was sent to Tientsin carrying the mail. Later in 1900 Murray resigned from the Bank's service to join his brother as an exchange broker; he was also for a time the Hong Kong correspondent for *The Times* and active in the China Association. Returning to England he had become close to Addis and had earlier assisted him on an informal basis from time to time.

Chinese to undertake parallel negotiations with other syndicates, and, as already noted, an agreement with an Anglo-Belgian Group headed by the Banque Sino-Belge was signed on March 14, five days after the letter from Yuan to Hillier. Criticism of the Chinese Government's action, which was interpreted as a virtual breach of faith, fell most heavily on the Premier, T'ang Shih-yi, and implementation of the Belgian agreement was never fully effected. But it was a warning.

Although the focus of the early discussions was naturally on the terms of the inter-Group agreement, there had already developed a broad consensus on the Chinese need for some £60 million and for a first loan of some £25 million which would include provisions for the repayment – or payment – of (i) the advances on both the Currency Loan and the presently proposed loan, (ii) the Belgian loan, (iii) Boxer Indemnity arrears, and (iv) overdue loan interest and principal.

The provisions likely to become controversial were those involving control and accounting of expenditures and foreign supervision of the Salt Gabelle. There were two sources for reinforcing China's credit, the Customs and the Salt Gabelle; tariff rates had however been set in treaties agreed by China and, as unilateral action was politically inadvisable, any change required the agreement of the Treaty Powers; the salt tax depended on the implementation of reforms already underway. There was no indication, however, that the Powers would agree (and in fact they did not) to a tariff increase. This placed the entire burden of proving to the capital markets China's credit-worthiness on the potential increase in the salt revenues which, it was expected, would result from the planned reforms. For this reason and in the context of the proposed series of major reorganization loans, the impact of which would take considerable time to determine, the Groups considered that foreign co-supervision with the Chinese of the Salt Administration under overall Chinese political control was essential.

In this there were two dangers. First, such supervision seemed essential only to lenders concerned with China's long-term credit position over a series of loans. Thus an 'intruder', coming in with an offer of say £10 million and his profits up-front, would not be so demanding. This was another basis for Government 'sole support' of the Groups.

Virtually any offer made without controls of the kind envisaged by the Groups would appear to Chinese, of all parties, as coming within the exception provided for in President Yuan's letter of March 9; any terms offered which were without foreign controls would be preferred and could be interpreted as 'more advantageous' than those offered by the Groups.

The actual financial terms proposed by the Groups, 5% and 88 firm, were in fact competitive, as of mid-1912.

The Crisp Loan of August 30, 1912

Only a month after the confirmation of the Sextuple Agreement and the commencement of final negotiations for a Reorganization Loan planned originally for mid-July, the Chinese Minister of Finance, Hsiung Hsi-ling, signed a preliminary agreement on July 13 for a £10 million loan secured on the Salt Gabelle with the Jackson International Financial Syndicate represented in Peking by Edward F. Birchal. G.E. Morrison, who had recently quit *The Times* and was then going on leave to England prior to taking up his appointment as political adviser to Yuan Shih-k'ai, was asked by Yuan to investigate and comment on A.W. Jackson, an American financier; the results were negative, and it may have been largely due to Morrison's intervention that the loan was more respectably placed by the transfer of Jackson's rights to G. Birch Crisp and Co.[56] Morrison was later, when in Germany, to claim that the entire loan was his idea, but there is no evidence to substantiate this.[57]

In his account of the affair, Morrison compared Crisp, who had Russian financial connections, favourably to Sir Carl Meyer whom he characterized as a 'director' of the Hongkong Bank and a 'Hamburg Israelite'. Noting the support George Lloyd, MP, and Lloyds Bank were giving the Crisp Loan, Morrison attempted to make the point that the Crisp Syndicate was British while any loan made by the Six Groups would subject China to the requirements of Powers whose interests in China were inimicable to those of Britain.[f] 'And yet we still pin our faith to the Sextuple Group and consider that it is to our advantage . . . to block every British financial interest unless it be represented by the Hongkong and Shanghai Bank.'[59]

The Crisp Loan, the Chinese Government 5% Gold Loan of 1912, the proceeds of which were to be used *inter alia* for the repayment of existing loans, for the reorganization of the Government, and for productive works, was contracted for at 89 fixed. The agreement also provided for continuing privileges for the Syndicate; these, if granted, would have negated the purposes of the Sextuple Agreement. The final loan agreement was signed on

---

[f] Charles Birch Crisp (1867–1958) had become a member of the London Stock Exchange in 1897 and had been involved with South American railways. His international role came first in 1909; he and the London, City and Midland Bank placed £3.5 million Russian-guaranteed railway bonds on the London market. His Russian associations led eventually to his role in the Anglo-Russian Trust and his formation and chairmanship (1912–1927) of the British Bank for Foreign Trade. By the time he moved into China affairs, he had been joined by S.P. Cockerell, formerly of the Foreign Office, who made inaccurate statements relative to German shareholdings in the Hongkong Bank, while Morrison's support involved anti-Semitic attacks on Sir Carl Meyer, who was in any case only on the Bank's Consultative Committee. Crisp's Russian ventures ran into difficulties and he turned again to break the Consortium's monopoly on China affairs in 1918 and again in 1923. Despite his failures and his disservice to China, he chose a 'Chinese dragon' as part of his new armorial bearings in 1922.[58]

August 30, but only £5 million was ever issued to the public; the Syndicate found itself opposed both by the Hongkong Bank, thereby rendering transfers of silver funds to China expensive, and by the British Foreign Office. In the end Birch had to turn to the Hongkong Bank and make special arrangements for the transfer. It is not surprising, therefore, that, for a consideration of £150,000 to be paid by the Chinese Government, the Crisp Syndicate agreed on December 23, 1912, to cancel the agreement. At that point negotiations with the Six Power Groups reopened, continuing to the signing of the Reorganization Loan in April 1913.

The course of negotiations and the intervention of the Crisp Syndicate
The confusion and recriminations following Crisp's defiance of the Foreign Office seem almost a repetition of the 1909 German intervention in the Hukuang negotiations. The principles were the same and related events appear very similar.

An account has been given (see Chapter 7) of how, in 1909, Bland in Peking had felt it possible to negotiate from strength, aware of the Three Power Groups Protocol, assuming Germany's inability to handle the Hukuang loan on its own, and consequently weighing the strength of Chinese opposition to the control terms too lightly. He had rejected a Chinese offer, the Chinese had then declared themselves free to turn to other sources of finance. After two years of tedious negotiations, Addis in London and Hillier in Peking were at last ready to sign the Hukuang Railways Loan of 1911.

This time it was E.G. Hillier who acted precipitously. Once again the Peking representative felt secure; the Six Power Groups were the only sure source available to China for a loan of £60 million. Hillier was negotiating with the assurances of President Yuan Shih-k'ai, the sole support of the Foreign Office, and the cooperation of the Peking representatives of the other five banking Groups, who were in turn supported by their Foreign Ministries. If Hillier and his colleagues in Peking had one weak spot it was in the relative inflexibility of their instructions; referral to Addis in London was necessary.[60] As Bland before him, now Hillier in 1912 was to learn that a breakdown in communications could lead to disaster.

The Chinese Government in Peking probably recognized that only the Six Power Groups could provide £60 million, but others could provide £10 million. The Government needed funds immediately and was in any case unwilling to accept the control terms of the Six Power Groups. Taking action paralleling Chang Chih-tung's approach of 1909, therefore, the Government, searching for an alternative, negotiated with Edward W. Birchal, a British financial agent in Peking. As events developed, it was clear that the Chinese were uninformed as to the capabilities of Birchal's principals, the Jackson

Financial Syndicate, but that was not the point; the Chinese wanted an alternative – and they wanted the Six Power Groups to know they had an alternative.

Hillier like Bland before him failed to heed the signals. As the Six Power Groups continued their demand for controls, the Chinese moved closer to what had become the Crisp Syndicate; eventually they signed a final agreement for what came to be known as the 'Crisp Loan'. But it was not as yet effective.

The Chinese made one last counter-proposal to Hillier as representative of the Six Power Groups. Without reference either to Addis in London or Sir John Jordan in Peking, Hillier rejected it. The Crisp Agreement was immediately confirmed and activated. Charles Addis, who had presumably been on holiday during the key month of August, noted in his diary for September 23 and 24, 1912:

> [23rd] The blow has fallen. Hillier today rejected Chinese counter-proposal without reference to us. China has settled for a loan of £10 million with Birch Crisp, Lloyds, London, City and Midland and Chartered banks, so all the work of those weary months dashed at a stroke to the ground. Papers full of the Crisp Loan and defeat of the 6-Power Consortium.
> [24th] The Birch Crisp Loan is a pretty tangle. We have worked hard and hope against hope to the last. Alas! We are beaten. It comes out tomorrow.

The policy and terms of the Six Power Groups

The fact is that although Hillier might be faulted for failure to check with his principal in London, he had been given little reason to suppose that Addis would have reacted favourably to the Chinese counter-proposals. Addis and his colleagues in Europe had not had access to immediate up-to-date information on the progress of the Crisp negotiations; they probably assessed Crisp's capacity correctly, but they failed to accept that the Chinese would nevertheless push the matter to a crisis rather than accept the terms the Six Power Groups considered necessary for successful flotation of the loan.

The Six Power Groups were applying pressure at two levels: first, they were securing confirmation that their Governments would continue to give sole diplomatic support in Peking to their negotiations, at least until the first Reorganization Loan had been concluded; second, they were attempting to dry up the supply of small financial loans, disguised as 'industrial' or project loans, which were keeping the Chinese Government barely afloat on a month-to-month basis. Although the Groups were not wholly successful in this latter policy, it was clear that the Chinese need to find substantial funds in the immediate future led the Groups to feel safe in insisting on control terms.

Specifically, the Groups first refused to advance further funds except in the context of a comprehensive reorganization program; second, they required a five-year monopoly on future administrative loans for the full program of £60 million; and third, they required a role for foreigners, to be appointed by mutual consent, in the reorganization of the Salt Administration; the foreign appointees would have a supervisory authority, exercised in conjunction with Chinese officials, in the collection and disposal of salt revenues.

The object of these provisions was to ensure that the funds raised through a public issue, the purposes of which were advertised over the names of the issuing banks in the Prospectus, were seen by the public to have some credible security and that the purposes had some chance of implementation. Failure to act responsibly at this time would result in the bankruptcy of the Chinese Government and the possible consequent loss of several million pounds to European bondholders. Nor was the threat of a foreign rescue operation and the cost of sovereignty a wholly unrealistic possibility under such circumstances.

The Chinese rejected these terms.

Whatever reservations the Foreign Office might have over long-term support of the British Group or the failure of the Hongkong Bank to actively attempt to broaden the base of British representation, it had nothing favourable to say about either the Jackson or the Crisp Syndicates. Although aware of the stage the negotiations had reached with the Chinese, the Foreign Office as late as mid-September hoped that their opposition would be sufficient to cause the Chinese Government to renounce their as yet unactivated agreement with the Crisp Syndicate.[61] No doubt, this was a correct assumption – provided the Six Power Groups modified their terms sufficiently.

Despite French reluctance, the Six eventually agreed to renegotiate, and on September 19, 1912, talks with the Chinese were reopened. The impact of the Crisp threat was having the effect desired by the Chinese. The new offer from the Six Power Groups included the provision of an immediate advance of Ts1.5 million on condition that the Chinese (i) abandon the Crisp Loan and (ii) agree *in principle* to the idea of control. The Chinese were to propose 'any reasonable modification of terms which did not conflict with the maintenance of our reasonable requirements for the effective supervision of security and the control of expenditure'.[62] The fact that by this time the Chinese were committed to the Crisp Syndicate, which had advanced a portion of the loan on the 19th, did not deter the Chinese who nevertheless made counter-proposals to the Six on the 21st. These were rejected by Hillier.

The Crisp Loan and the consequences, September–December 1912

The expansion of the British Group

The confusion caused by the issue of the first tranche of the Crisp Loan was blamed on the Hongkong Bank's previous refusal to bring other British banks into the British Group. As Heinrich Cordes of the DAB in Peking wrote to his Berlin office, 'Addis should have been able to see this better than anyone else', to which the Reichskanzler added an explanatory note for the Archives – 'Addis ist ein eigensinniger Dickschädel.'[63]

The Hongkong Bank had failed to minimize opposition by including a sufficiently representative selection of banks in the British Group. As one French newspaper put it, 'The Hongkong Bank has shown itself very resolute not to share portions of the loan to be floated in England. Hence the tendency for English banks to offer loans outside the Consortium.'[64] And the Auswärtiges Amt was told from London, 'Two things make such adventurers possible in Chinese business. The faith of the British public in the Chinese Government and the animosity against the monopoly of the Hongkong Bank.'[65]

The DAB had expected the Hongkong Bank to invite in other banks; this was the assumption on which the 1895 Agreement was based. The formation of the British and Chinese Corporation in 1898 did not meet the requirement; at best it was an attempt at a British KfAG, which remained instead closely identified with the Bank and Jardine's. In 1910 Franz Urbig had been urging Charles Addis to form a comprehensive British Group, but, as the German Foreign Ministry commented in a marginal note, 'The Hongkong Bank is too stuck up [*hochnasig*] to bring in another bank.'[66]

Nevertheless even Addis was shaken by the events of September 1912 and the reaction of both the British banking community and Parliament. In October he wrote to his confidant, Dudley Mills:

The Press is against us, financial, Tory, radical, the last worst of all. . . . [Sir Edward] Grey is between the devil and the deep blue sea, or rather he was. His Party clamours against the monopoly and wish him to withdraw.

If he does, down goes the Six Power Consortium, and China is thrown to the Powers to scramble for. Accordingly he has taken his courage in both hands, and plumps, along with the other five powers, for the maintenance of the consortium.

Meanwhile [J.O.P.] Bland is off to lecture in America and incidentally to smash the consortium.[67]

The Government was asked questions not only about the monopoly of support given a 'British Group' however composed, but also of the 'monopoly' of the Hongkong Bank with its German associations *within* that Group, that is, the Hongkong Bank's 'monopoly' as being the sole member of the British

Group. The former 'monopoly', the sole support being given the British Group for financial loans to China until the completion of the Reorganization Loan – this the Foreign Office could and did defend; the Bank's British management, direction, and ownership it could also defend; but the 'monopoly' within the British Group had as a matter of practical politics to be ended.

Perhaps Addis was reminded of the Foreign Office warning, given in connection with the Eastern Bank affair the previous March:

The best method of obviating the difficulties in regard to your future business in China likely to arise from the competition of other British firms and the obvious impossibility of granting exclusive Government support to one British bank is the formation of a British Group somewhat on the lines of the French and German Groups.[68]

However valid the Hongkong Bank's arguments may have been, the Bank, and Charles Addis, yielded at last.

The Chartered Bank of India, Australia and China, which had associated itself with the Crisp Loan, was offered by the Hongkong Bank an equal participation in the British Group; the Chartered Bank rejected the offer on the grounds that it was not to be allowed a share in the loan servicing or the exchange, or, as their chairman Sir Montagu Turner put it in a letter to the Foreign Office, whose intervention they had requested, 'Mr Addis declines to recognize us as an Eastern Exchange Bank.'[69] Having just failed to manage the exchange operations of the Crisp Loan without Hongkong Bank assistance (see below), this was a difficult though understandable position to maintain. The Foreign Office confirmed that the composition of a group of private banks was one for the private banks to decide, but they kept Addis informed of all approaches.[70]

As noted in the Addis diary, 'the formation of the new British Group . . . taking up much time and strength'. Murray Stewart was helping, but with H.D.C. Jones, the new junior Manager, too often ill, Addis found himself on mail days doing much of the regular banking work of the London Office. Meanwhile Lord Revelstoke of Baring's had complained to Koch of Panmure Gordon that Addis was showing 'lack of confidence in his old friend' – Addis found encouragement from consultations with J.R.M. Smith.[71]

On December 14, 1912, the British Group was enlarged by agreement. In consequence, the British Group now comprised the Hongkong and Shanghai Banking Corporation (33%), Messrs Baring Bros and Co. (25%), London, County and Westminster Bank (14%), Messrs Parr's Bank (14%), and Messrs J. Henry Schröder and Co. (14%).[72] The inclusion of the last named caused their withdrawal from the Russian Group; the London and County Bank was the Hongkong Bank's clearer, and Parr's was the leading bank in the issue of Japanese loans with which the Hongkong Bank had long been associated. The Hongkong Bank had had sound relations with Baring Brothers.

The British Group would be enlarged again and by 1920 would include, in addition to the above, the Chartered Bank, N.M. Rothschild and Sons, and the British Trade Corporation. By then Parr's had merged into the London, County Westminster and Parr's Bank, Ltd.

Crisp's problems

When Crisp attempted in September to place a first series of £500,000 5% six months' bonds at 95, despite the opposition of the Foreign Office, he had only a moderate success. This was partially because Schröder's, then a member of the Russian Group in the Six Power Groups Consortium, had placed £1,250,000 worth of twelve months' bonds on the market at 94½ in order to ruin the Crisp issue.[73] On September 26 Crisp placed the issue of £5 million, half the Chinese loan, supported by the Chartered Bank, Lloyds Bank, and Crisp's Anglo-Russian Trust, but the Syndicate faced problems with exchange.

The Chartered Bank, despite the efforts of its Shanghai manager, was unable to obtain funds in China sufficient to carry out the exchange for the Crisp Loan at a reasonable rate, and the Chinese had to enter into direct negotiations with the Six Groups, who finally agreed to pay £130,000 in silver on October 31 against Chinese Government drafts on the gold raised by the Crisp issue. Negotiations were also entered upon for a further £500,000. These difficulties brought home to the Chinese how dependent they were on the facilities of the banks involved in the Sextuple Agreement; even if Crisp had been able to raise the full £10 million in Europe, a real possibility, and even if the Six Groups had not then recalled all their advances, Crisp would have been unable to lay down the funds in Shanghai, in silver at a reasonable rate, without their cooperation.[74]

Despite these advantages, the Six Groups considered their position far from satisfactory. Crisp himself continued to speak against the Hongkong Bank and he had friends in Parliament. The Hongkong Bank, fearing the pressure on the Foreign Office, suggested in October that the Consortium place the balance of the Crisp Loan themselves. At one low point, there was the feeling, reflecting undue pessimism, that the Foreign Office would have to transfer its support and that the Consortium would fall apart.[75]

Crisp withdraws

The action of the Consortium banks, principally the Hongkong Bank, in forcing up the exchange – resulting in China's receiving fewer silver taels for the gold funds borrowed – caused a strong reaction in the Chinese press. Eugene Chen, an 'Anglo-Chinese' as Jordan described him and a British-trained lawyer from the West Indies, wrote strong attacks in the English language *Peking Daily News*. As these were directed against Sir John Jordan personally, Jordan protested to President Yuan Shih-k'ai and Chen was, for the time being, silenced.[76]

At the same time there were reports from Hong Kong that a boycott against the Hongkong Bank was being urged, but Newton Stabb, the Chief Manager, claimed that there had been no boycott and that he did not know if the meetings of local and North China merchants had ever reached a decision. 'The Chinese are too good businessmen,' the German Consul wrote, 'to fail to see that the Hongkong Bank is the surest place for their money, and that, as the most important bank in Asia, it is able to offer facilities to its friends no other European bank can rival.'[77]

The real issue faced by all parties, by the Foreign Office, the Hongkong Bank and other banks in the Sextuple Agreement, the Crisp Syndicate, and the Chinese Government was how to resolve an impossible situation. The Chinese required funds urgently and they now realized only the banks participating in the Six Power Groups Consortium could supply them in full and at reasonable rates – and yet, the Crisp Agreement existed. The problem was not only the £10 million loan itself, but the preferential clauses which came automatically into operation when the funds had been fully provided. If Crisp were successful in transferring the total funds, the Chinese would be tied to his syndicate; without some special consideration, the Six Power Groups would be barred from assisting.

At an apparently stormy meeting in the Foreign Office Crisp had admitted he had been acting in defiance of British policy, but he had assumed correctly that he had public support and could float the first £5 million, even though the loan was refused recognition, that is, it was not registered by the Legation in Peking. The Foreign Office now took a stronger line; withdraw or face the full and open opposition of the British Government and the British Legation; with British encouragement, a full-scale conflict with the other five Governments would also be involved.[78]

The Foreign Secretary had stood firm. Britain would never support a loan 'without adequate safeguards for control of expenditures and proper security'.[79]

Crisp decided to withdraw.

Before any public announcement, however, Crisp called on Addis in November to urge the admission of his syndicate to the Consortium; after consultation Addis refused.[80] Crisp and, independently, the Consortium considered various half-measures, but eventually the problem was resolved in the simplest way: by an agreement signed on December 23, Crisp would be compensated £150,000 by the Chinese and would withdraw, defeated; the Hongkong Bank would enlarge the British Group; and the Chinese would be assured of immediate consideration of their requirements, but on terms satisfactory to the Six Groups.[81]

The Sextuple Groups emerged victorious, the intruder defeated, their Government support intact, and the Chinese Government more realistic about the terms necessary for the flotation of a loan on the European markets and the problems of transfer to China of the funds raised. Nevertheless, the Chinese did not permit the implementation of the Crisp withdrawal – not yet. There were further difficult negotiations with the Groups ahead.

The final negotiations and the signing of the Reorganization Loan

December 1912 through the American withdrawal, March 1913
The Hongkong Bank entered the final stages of the negotiations with the confidence that the Foreign Office would support the enlarged British Group for the whole run of the proposed £60 million Reorganization Loan series and for a sufficient time thereafter to effect the purposes of the loan. In order to obtain these assurances, however, the Bank had eventually to accept the need to separate financial from industrial loans, a distinction which, although difficult to make, was nevertheless being insisted on by the Governments of the other Groups.[82] At this point the Foreign Office was only requiring the removal of references to industrial projects from the mainly administrative Reorganization Loan; Addis's concern was a matter of practical banking; financial loans can be disguised as 'industrial' and suppliers' credits can be accumulated without control and eventually undermine a nation's credit-worthiness.

The Peking negotiations of early December 1912 had aroused the Chinese Government's expectations, but the European situation was deteriorating and the French and German Groups asked for a postponement of the mid-December Six Groups conference in Paris. This Addis opposed on precisely the grounds that China had been led to expect a speedy conclusion to the loan agreement. The meetings were held and considerable progress in fact made: (i) the elimination of industrial loans from the draft agreement, (ii) preference to be claimed for the Six Power Groups for financial loans only, (iii) as the first loan of £25 million was only part of the program, there would be a preference for two years in favour of the Consortium for further financial loans, and (iv) to protect the market, the Chinese Government would not proceed with any other Government-guaranteed loan, either financial or industrial, for a period of six months.[83] These terms were more favourable to the Chinese, but control requirements remained, and the Groups themselves were in dispute *inter alia* over the allocation of appointments by nationality to the various advisory and supervisory posts being created.

The meeting instructed the representatives of the banks in Peking to inform the Chinese that the rate of interest had been raised from 5% to 6%, later reduced to $5\frac{1}{2}$%, reflecting the increased rates on European Government and colonial securities. The price paid by the Groups to the Chinese for the loan would, however, be higher, partially offsetting the increase in interest.[84] Addis recorded in his diary, 'Unexpectedly good work done in bringing the six groups into line. All were gratified and surprised.' But he added, 'What the Chinese will do is another matter.'[85]

During the next two months the Groups shifted their positions, Newton Stabb in Hong Kong urged the independent action of the British Group, a proposal Addis strongly rejected; in fact, the task was continuous. Lord Revelstoke presented Charles Addis to King George V, and Addis noted that he had had a conversation with His Majesty about China and loan affairs. 'He seemed to be surprisingly interested.'[86] In March the Bank gave a dinner for Chinese Financial Commissioner, Tseng Yuen Chang, at which Addis spoke, Tseng responded, and a 'lively debate ensued' with Macrae, Jamieson, Koch, and McLeavy Brown.

At this point the American Group, which had never been financially enthusiastic, requested confirmation from the new Democratic Administration of Woodrow Wilson, and especially from his Populist Secretary of State, William Jennings Bryan, that the Government would continue to support American participation in the Sextuple Groups Consortium and the Reorganization Loan negotiations.

The response took the other Groups by surprise. President Wilson, while retaining American interest in the interference which the Currency Loan involved, took the extraordinary position that 'the conditions of the loan seem to us to touch very nearly the administrative independence of China itself, and this Administration does not feel that it ought, even by implication, to be a party to those conditions'.[87] Wilson professed to see that such involvement might lead eventually to direct interference, possibly military intervention. In fact, the controls required by the Six Power Groups were designed to ensure the security of the loan and thus prevent the very interference Wilson professed to oppose. The American Group retained its obligations under other Consortium agreements, and thus Wilson and his Administration, with Bryan gone, had a basis for a return to China Consortium affairs. By 1917 the American Government was negotiating the 'New Consortium' which would become effective after the Great War (see Volume III).

Although the Foreign Office considered the American statement under such terms a 'diplomatic outrage', the American Group decided to withdraw, but the loan negotiations were in no way impeded; they were continued by the five remaining Groups – the Quintuple Groups Consortium.

Final stages and the signing

The draft loan agreement, with an interest rate of 5%, had been agreed by the Chinese cabinet as early as September 1912, although it was not accepted by the Advisory Council until December 27, 1912. With the new interest rate of $5\frac{1}{2}$%, the Kuomintang members, who opposed any control terms and who were increasingly disillusioned with Yuan's administration, claimed that the loan had in fact been renegotiated and needed to be approved by the reconstituted National Assembly before being signed.

Yuan took another course. His Government needed the funds urgently; it was now clear that he had to deal with the remaining five Groups, and he accordingly approached them through the Japanese Group urging that the interest rate be reduced once again to the original 5%. The loan would then be substantially in the form agreed by the Council and there would be no impediment to signature.

The Five Groups agreed to the 5% rate on April 10. The President of the Chinese Republic then authorized the loan by a Presidential Order dated April 22, and the Five planned a final Paris meeting for April 26.[88] One topic would be the implications of the American withdrawal, especially the charge that the conditions were unacceptable.

Newton Stabb, the Hongkong Bank's Chief Manager, notified Addis urgently on April 25 that Sun Yat-sen had sent for the Bank's Shanghai Manager, A.G. Stephen, and informed him that, if the loan were signed without parliamentary approval, the southern provinces would revolt.[89] Stabb was naturally concerned whether, under the circumstances, the loan could be floated on the European markets. When the Five Groups met in Paris the following day, the Chairman read out a dramatic cable from Sun Yat-sen warning the representatives and confirming the threat that, if the loan were signed without the prior consent of the National Assembly, there would be Civil War.

Addis noted simply, 'Reading produced a profound impression.'[90]

Far from being unresponsive to Sun's dramatic cable, the Five Groups in Paris instructed their representatives in Peking not to make further advances to the Chinese Government, and the meeting adjourned to enable members to consult their Governments. Meanwhile, however, the agreement was being signed by the Chinese Government and the Five Groups' representatives in Peking. This would not, despite the drama surrounding the event, actually make the loan effective or the agreement binding, as those familiar with China loan proceedings well knew.

Nevertheless there was drama. The events were compared by Peking's *Daily Telegraph* to 'a Conan Doyle novel, with details reminiscent of Poe'.[91] As told from the capital, the story unfolded as follows.

The French and the Russians tried to obstruct the loan again at the last minute, but Sir John Jordan threatened that he would empower the Hongkong Bank to sign alone if necessary. The Chinese Finance Minister, Chou Hsueh-hsi, complaining that 'They want to eat my flesh', was in a state of terror and had to be brought back for the signing by a special train from Tientsin, where he was then in hiding.[92] At the last minute, the Chinese insisted that the Austrian Skoda (£3.2 million at 6% and 92) and the Belgian Pienlo (Fr250 million at 5% and 91) loans be included in the priority list for repayment from the Reorganization Loan amounts. Surprisingly, and despite the fact that these loans had been granted by 'interlopers', one of many industrial loan threats to the meaningfulness of the Consortium's supposed role, the Five agreed.[93]

At 3:00 p.m. on April 26 the agreement was initialled and the National Assembly informed.

At 10:00 p.m. the Finance Minister, the Foreign Minister, and President Yuan went to the office of the Hongkong Bank in Peking with a strong guard. A large group from the Senate also came to the Bank to issue further warnings, standing outside the Bank until about 3:00 the next morning. Finally, twenty minutes after the group from the Senate had left on the morning of April 27, the Reorganization Loan had been signed.[94] The Kuomintang members protested that the Assembly had not been consulted; they had voted not to ratify the agreement unless it were presented to them first.

The various foreign ministries advised the Groups that Yuan's action was valid, without which assurance from the Foreign Office the Hongkong Bank would not have proceeded further.[95] The Groups' Peking representatives advised that Sun's influence was waning and that his threats should not be taken seriously.[96] Accordingly the details were finalized and the agreement ratified by the Five Groups in London on May 13.

The Chinese National Assembly at first refused to ratify the agreement, but finally agreed after it had received declarations of its legality from the Five Groups.[97]

At this point a new problem arose. An Austrian loan for £3.5 million had been negotiated by Arnhold, Karberg & Co. – another interloper and one represented on the Board of the Hongkong Bank – and closed on April 10, *before* the Reorganization Loan. The Chinese claimed they could no longer back out of this loan but said that they hoped to be able to delay it in order to give the Consortium's loan priority on the markets. Arnhold, Karberg & Co. was contacted through its Hong Kong manager, who was on the Board of Directors of the Hongkong Bank; he in turn telegraphed his Tientsin office strongly recommending that the loan be delayed for six or more months.[98] The Five finally agreed to ratify the agreement on the condition that the Chinese did not try to issue the Austrian loan openly or privately within three months of the Reorganization Loan. Thus, on May 10, 1913, the Reorganization Loan was complete.[99]

Of the total loan £7,416,680 or 30% was issued in London; the Hongkong Bank's Hamburg Branch was, as usual in such cases, an issuing bank for a portion of the German share. The price to the public was 90; the banks had contracted on the basis of this as a minimum price and with a differential of six points. The Chinese Government accordingly received £84 for every £100 borrowed. The loan was not underwritten by an outside syndicate, but, as of May 21 when subscriptions were closed the loan was some four times over-subscribed in London, there was no loss to the Hongkong Bank on this account.

The Hongkong Bank's profit as reported to the Board of Directors was £103,000. This was presumably net of the direct expenses of issue but gross of such expenses as salaries, cables, cost of travel, and other items incurred during the negotiations. The London issue was £7.4 million and the Bank's share of the British Group was 33% plus a fee as lead managers. This suggests a commission of approximately 1.4% for (i) issuing and (ii) 'underwriting' the loan.

In absolute terms the Bank did not fare so well; the percentage on its share was adequate, but then its share was considerably smaller than when the Bank alone constituted the British Group.

There was, however, no costing of executive time. Were such items calculated and overheads included – Addis's and Hillier's salaries for example – and despite reimbursement of certain expenses by the other Groups, the net commission on the Reorganization Loan would have been considerably lower than the 1.4% quoted above.

The high cost of the loan to the Chinese reflected, at least in part, the high cost of money in Europe at the time. Reaction in Germany took note of this. The German press, for example, was not uniformly enthusiastic about the loan's success. The Balkan crisis persisted, and money was still short and expensive in Europe. At the same time, Germany was spending large amounts on armaments. Was this the time to export large amounts of capital to China, especially as the bonds were not internationalized so the money could not be retrieved easily by selling them on other markets later if needed?[100] Despite these objections, the German portion was five times over-subscribed.[101]

In any case, the Hongkong Bank had been successful. As Eba Addis loyally noted, 'Charlie receives congratulations for his courage and faith and able management in all these "delicate negotiations" from all kinds of people. How thankful we are it is over at last.'[102] More tangible was the reaction of the Hongkong Bank's Board of Directors who voted Charles Addis a bonus of £1,250 for his work on the loan; E.G. Hillier received an equal amount for his contribution in Peking; A.G. Stephen, the Shanghai Manager, received £500, H.D.C. Jones £600, and Murray Stewart £250 in London, R.C. Allen and S.F. Mayers respectively £750 and £250 in Peking – Mayers was the successor of Bland as representative of the British and Chinese Corporation, but presumably worked with Hillier on the Reorganization Loan. Those juniors in the cable departments – and coding and decoding the additional cables no doubt interfered with more healthy and pleasurable activities – were allocated a total of £300.

The Chinese Government 5% Reorganization Gold Loan[103]
Money was expensive in May 1913, and the nominal rate of interest unrealistically low; 6% would have better suited the market. But there was another reason why the Reorganization Loan had to be floated at 90. The purposes to which the proceeds were to be put were unproductive and unattractive as a long-run investment; the over-subscription suggested financial speculation. Even accepting the assumption, sincerely made by the Five Power Groups, that this was the first of a series, the loan was presented on its own merits and was judged on this basis.

A generous calculation suggests that 8% of the £25 million, say £2 million might be constructively employed. The balance, though essential to China, was unproductive from, to use a relevant term, the 'reorganization' point of view. How is this conclusion determined?

The net return to the Chinese was 84. As a consequence there was available to the Chinese Government only £21 million. From this must be subtracted the interest payable on the first coupon (for approximately 40 days equals say £130,000 + a service fee of ¼ of 1% or £325), which it was not worth sending out to China – and back.

There was also an agreement for advances at 7%; if it is assumed that the £2 million mentioned was in fact advanced for a year and that the interest was deducted from sums payable from the proceeds of the main loan, a further £140,000 would be accounted for. But this is a refinement; for present purposes the Chinese may be assumed to have started with £20,870,000.

Of this amount the following sums were required to meet existing financial obligations:

(i) Liabilities due by the Chinese Government, i.e.
    Arrears of Boxer Indemnity, Treasury bills,
    Belgian loan, various advances   £4,317,778: 9s:7d
(ii) Provincial loans, to be paid off   2,870,000: 0s:0d
(iii) Various liabilities maturing shortly   3,592,263:10s:3d

after which the Chinese Government had roughly £10,090,000. At this point there were funds available to pay off the troops, and sums under the heading 'disbandment of troops', details of which were to be handed confidentially to the banks, took up a further £3 million. Then there were the current and extraordinary expenses of administration, set out in great detail to a total of £5.5 million.

The loan agreement assigned £2 million to the 'Reorganization of the Salt Administration', but on the above calculations only £1.6 million remained for this purpose.

A wise investor might conclude that this was not a particularly sound operation. Even the most optimistic investor would require a relatively high rate of return and some assurance that the 8% of the Reorganization Loan actually earmarked for reorganization was in fact used wisely. This the bankers anticipated, and hence, in addition to the need to ensure the security, the insistence of foreign involvement in the administration of the Salt Gabelle. In this, and in this alone, China was fortunate. The Chinese had wanted a Dane named Oiesen, they accepted an Englishman named Dane.[104] Either would have served them well, but as it happened Richard Dane acted throughout in China's interests and rendered them signal service.[105]

The terms of the loan reflected not the rapacity of the banks, their return was reasonable, nor the greed of the subscribing public – if anything they were over-optimistic and purchased bonds at 90 which would soon depreciate to 88 and below. Rather the terms were unduly favourable to China in the circumstances and reflected the eternal optimism, except in periods of unlimited pessimism, aroused in foreigners on contemplation of the Middle Kingdom and its future.

The loan has been severely criticized. There is little justification for this. China had international obligations; the reorganization loans were designed to clear up the financial backlog, finance essential administrative tasks pending fiscal support from the provinces, and then, in subsequent loans, to finance real reorganization in preparation for economic development. To the Powers this seemed a reasonable program; the banks looked forward to a prosperous and efficient Chinese economy and were prepared to issue loans designed to achieve this end. The loans could be made only to the Government of China; this the Consortium banks did with the approval of that Government and of their own Governments.

Events did not develop as the bankers had expected. The bankers had taken serious note of the opposition to Yuan, but whatever their private opinions, the Hongkong Bank at least would not make political decisions. The loans were seen as economically viable propositions. In this estimate the Consortium banks were eventually proved wrong; the loss was borne by the bondholders, among whom were the Hongkong and other issuing banks. The loan, denominated in a gold unit of account, was made on the eve of the great appreciation of silver. The Chinese Government was never in a position to take advantage of this fact.

Money is fungible. The funds made available by the loan perhaps released other funds for other purposes. If that is what the critics are suggesting, they are citing but another example of the banker's fallacy. Project loans can only be controlled in the context of total budgetary control. That, in a sovereign state, is unacceptable; even the essential and minimal controls incorporated in the provisions of the Reorganization Loan were criticized. If the loan released undesirable forces, that is beyond the range of responsibility of the Five Power Groups who dealt, on the advice of their Governments, with the Government of the Republic of China.

Government support and the 'Reorganization Loan series'

Government and the Prospectus

As the Reorganization Loan Prospectus stated, the agreement for the loan was signed between the Government of the Republic of China of the one part and the Hongkong and Shanghai Banking Corporation . . . (and the other lead banks) of the other part. The Five Groups themselves were all banks in the private sector. And yet 'Government' pervades the document.[106]

The final loan agreement was 'officially communicated to the Ministers in Peking . . . by the Wai-chiao Pu' (the new name of the Chinese Foreign Ministry). This was a long-established pattern. But there were further Government interventions.

The loan not only designated the security but made provisions for identifiable repayment from the sources named. Thus certain provinces were obligated to pay over stated sums from the Salt Revenue and, the Prospectus continued, the British Legation had been officially notified that the 'obligations thus imposed have been officially recognized by the proper Provincial Authorities for the respective amounts assigned to each Province'.

The Legations were also involved in the terms under which the foreign directors and advisers were to be employed, the London-issued Prospectus stating that this had been arranged to the 'satisfaction of the Ministers of Great Britain [and the other powers] . . .'[107]

Finally and presumably in view of the highly publicized controversy over the Chinese signing of the loan, the London-issued Prospectus quoted a letter from the Foreign Office to the Hongkong Bank containing an unequivocal reassurance: '. . . The Chinese Government state that the contract in question constitutes a binding engagement on them and their successors. His Majesty's Government have taken note of this declaration and concur in the view expressed as to its binding character . . .' Similar letters, the Prospectus concluded, 'have been addressed to the Deutsch-Asiatische Bank [and to the other banks] . . . by the Governments of Germany [etc.] . . .'[108]

'Sole support' after the Reorganization Loan of 1913

'Sole support' indicates the level of involvement granted to only one contractor for any one loan; it can thus be seen as vital and valuable. With the Reorganization Loan of 1913 concluded, Charles Addis and the Hongkong Bank were naturally concerned, not without cause, about the future position of the British Government on this subject.

Support of the Hongkong Bank had required the well-publicized refusal to support British houses involved in the Anglo-Belgian Syndicate in March 1912 or the Crisp Syndicate in August 1913. The Government had countered charges of a Hongkong Bank 'monopoly' with the assurance that the 'sole support' was for the Reorganization Loan only and by insisting on a broader-based British Group.

In the Quintuple Agreement the Five Groups forming the Syndicate agreed that it was to continue in effect for a maximum of five years, or until the Groups decided that the reorganization series of loans had been issued or that no further such loans would be issued, whichever event came first. Addis was anxious to ensure that British Government support for the British Group covered the period of the agreement.

The reorganization loans were potentially all-embracing and the agreement covered all lending to China, including loans for industrial purposes, excluding only current banking business and loans which did not require a public issue. Under these terms the Peking Legation found itself unable to support British firms in smaller operations while observing that other Legations were not so reticent and that, in the case of project loans by Arnhold and Carlowitz, the German firms were actually represented on the Hongkong Bank's Board of Directors.

The British Government had not, even with the issuing of the 1913 Reorganization Loan, regained its 'freedom of action'.

The impossible political position of the British Government is reflected in the exchange between the Foreign Office and Charles Addis expressing views which reveal the pressures placed on the former by the Peking Legation and private firms seeking new concessions in China and on the latter by commitments to the British and Chinese Corporation and the Central Chinese Railways on the one hand and the other members of the several inter-bank agreements on the other.[109]

The basic concern was the possible bankruptcy of China and the intervention by the Powers they believed would inevitably have followed.

In late May Charles Addis confided to his old friend Dudley Mills that the Foreign Secretary had given notice that with the issue of the £25 million loan he intended to end his exclusive support for the British Group. 'Exit the Quintuple Group.'[110] Nevertheless before the final decision the Foreign Secretary, Sir Edward Grey, asked Addis for his opinion.

By mid-summer 1913 it was already obvious that the Reorganization Loan had not solved China's financial crisis and that indiscriminate borrowing was, if possible, to be prevented. This suggested continued support for the British Group in the Quintuple Agreement as argued by Addis. There were opportunities apparently opening up in China, a new scramble for concessions, new agreements between private firms and provincial authorities which, while threatening economic chaos, were not matters which could be restrained by the British Government acting alone. The sole support granted the British Group and the Hongkong Bank for the Reorganization Loan series as originally envisaged had become politically intolerable.

Addis was fighting a rearguard action, aware of the danger to China of any relaxing of the restraint imposed by the Powers' support of the Quintuple Agreement. He wrote two memorandums, the first of which was in part a full historical summary and the second argued the case for continued support.[111]

Addis's arguments in favour of continued and exclusive British support for the Quintuple Groups were based on the following points: (i) the Hongkong Bank had been instrumental in forming the international agreements which had brought some order to China loans, (ii) these moves had been not only countenanced by the British Government but in some cases, for example the broadening of the basis of the British Group, had been ordered by the Government as a condition of support, (iii) the Government had undertaken to support the Groups in their negotiations for the reorganization loans and the Groups had recently confirmed that this should be defined to include all loans to a total of some £60 million – a long-term commitment indeed – and (iv) Grey's proposed compromise, the separation of industrial from financial loans, was both undesirable and impractical.

Addis's response 'changed the mind of the Minister with regard to ending the Consortium'.

The letter was drafted formally renouncing exclusive support of the British Group and informal intimation of what was impending had been sent to Paris and Berlin. Happily along with the draft letter for signature the Secretary received my memo. Shortly after I received a telephonic message that Sir Edward Grey 'having read Mr A's memo had decided to make no change for the present in the Government's attitude *vis à vis* the Groups and would not sign the letter'.

It was a great, an unexpected deliverance or shall I say respite. We shall see after Jordan has had his say. It is a duel now, I fancy, between the British Minister and me.[112]

The debate was brought to a focus when Addis was informed that the British Legation had been supporting a proposal by Pauling and Co. and that this and other contracts might be lost if the conditions of support for the British Group were not relaxed.[113] On September 2, the Foreign Secretary, Sir Edward Grey, wrote Charles Addis a personal letter to accompany the official despatch. The Government asked to be relieved of its undertaking of exclusive support for industrial loans and Addis, while continuing to disagree, nevertheless accepted that the decision had been made and undertook to regain, at the next meeting of the Five Groups, the necessary freedom of action for the British Government.

I am deeply concerned [Addis wrote] to think that you should feel hampered by the pledges you gave me personally, at our interview a little over a month ago, in pursuing the policy you consider best fitted to serve the higher interests of Great Britain in China.

I am not prepared to accept without reservation the facts as stated in the official letter which accompanied your private note but I recognize that the time for arguments has passed and that a serious situation has arisen in China which calls for prompt action.

... as far as I am personally concerned, you may rely upon my doing everything in my power to give effect to your wish that I should assist in facilitating the recovery by HM Government at the earliest possible moment of their complete freedom of action with regard to industrial loans.[114]

In the meantime the Foreign Office made its position clear to the Governments of the other Groups, who were in complete agreement with the British position. On September 26, Addis was able to report that as a result of a meeting of the delegates of the relevant Groups (i) railway and industrial loans had been excluded from the scope of the Quintuple Groups and (ii) the Four Groups Agreement of 1910 and the Triple Groups Agreement of 1908 had been determined.[115] The obligations of these Groups qua syndicates relative to existing loan agreements remained.

Guaranteed support of the British Group was now restricted to 'financial and political' loans made in the context of the reorganization concept.

On October 21 the British Prime Minister H.H. Asquith wrote to Addis to ask whether he would accept a knighthood; he replied in the affirmative. The following day the Bank's new offices on Gracechurch Street opened. On October 23 *The Times* had something favourable to say at last of the Hongkong Bank's London Manager; he was a knight.[116]

Notes on the 'Reorganization Loan Series' to 1914

If the first Reorganization Loan were intended to do little more than clear up arrears, it was even in this a failure. Future proposed reorganization loans would still require provisions for past debts, indemnity payments, and Government current expenses. One early draft proposal for a second loan netting say £21¼ million to the Chinese recommended, for example, that £7.5 million be devoted to sundry liabilities of the central Government, £7.5 million to currency reform, and £6.25 million to redemption of provincial notes.[117] The central Government was, in fact, having difficulties in obtaining revenues from the provinces; Jordan was in favour of forcing the issue by limiting administrative loans, and the Five Power Groups had little choice but to delay action in the absence of suitable security.[118]

At this stage the potential for interference in China's internal affairs was limitless. A letter from the Deutsch-Asiatische Bank to Sir Charles Addis noted that no basic loan could be successful until China's floating debt were eliminated, and this in turn was pointless unless regulations were enacted to prevent current deficits being met by the printing of banknotes.[119] And after that . . .?

This reintroduced the subject of the Currency Loan. First, the Chinese had entered into obligations, at least partially in process of fulfilment of the required conditions, concerning currency reform; second, there had been a £400,000 advance outstanding, scheduled to be repaid under the terms of the Reorganization Loan but if held over would keep open the option to the provisions of the Currency Loan and its reform requirements; and third, the loan, having been signed in April 1911 carried with it a prior lien on the salt revenue, ahead that is of the Crisp Loan. The lien, if the Currency Loan were cancelled, would be available to opportunistic lenders and adventurers.[120]

The Currency Loan had included the United States but not Japan or Russia; the Four Power Groups Inter-Bank Agreement had been determined and the U.S. had effectually resigned participation in the Consortium; the State Department did not encourage its continued involvement in the Currency Loan – although President Wilson was later to claim otherwise. The remaining three Groups, the British, French, and Germans, consistent with the Consortium concept, agreed therefore to invite the participation of Japan and Russia; this was now accepted.

The role of the Five Power Groups as the 'China Consortium' and, as self-appointed and, to an extent, Government-encouraged custodians of China's credit, received setbacks in July and October 1913. Agreements were then signed relative to (i) a £10 million Chinese Government 5% Gold Loan for the Tatungfu–Chengtu Railway with the non-Consortium Société Belge de Chemins de fer en Chine and the Société Française de Construction et d'Exploitation de Chemins de fer en Chine and (ii) the Chinese Republic Government 5% Industrial Gold Loan of 1914 with the non-Consortium Banque Industrielle de Chine. The total amount for this latter loan was unspecified but the contract price was 84, and there is evidence that it was restricted to Fr100 million, or approximately £4 million, ostensibly for construction works including a harbour at Pukow and a bridge over the Yangtze at Hankow, but containing provisions for advances which suggested a 'financial loan' element.[121]

Addis took the position that while he would have preferred a British company to have won the contracts, he would rather the work were done by the French than not done at all. The prosperity of British business in China depended on the growth of China's economy, however that growth might be financed. Addis questioned, however, whether the Banque Industrielle could, given the tightness of the European markets, provide the funds. Later there were suggestions that the bank was obtaining funds from the Russo-Asiatic Bank; their intervention did have the impact of a financial loan and the Chinese refrained from dealing with the Five Power Groups while funds from this source were available.

There were also rumours of a new Crisp Loan, which Addis discounted, again on an estimate of the tight market and the lack of support such a loan would receive.

In the face of this competition real or threatened, there was little the Groups could do. China's salt revenues had increased, but not enough for successful flotation of a second £25 million loan. The Foreign Secretary accepted Jordan's recommendation that this was not the time to enhance the revenues by agreeing to an increase in tariffs. The Chinese Government proposed a smaller loan of perhaps £8 million to pay off short-term debts, a reflection of the financial position of the central authorities.[122]

As China was drifting into an unhappy financial and political state, Europe was moving towards war.

The associated companies, 1911–1914

The British and Chinese Corporation

With the ten for one share split in 1907 the British and Chinese Corporation's (B&CC's) £100 shares became £10 shares; by 1910 £5 had been paid up per share for a total capital of £125,000. In 1911 the Corporation was able to pay a dividend of 10%, or £12,500, but by the year ending June 1914 the peak profits of £23,000 had declined to £9,800. This decline reflects the fact that, although new loan agreements were signed (see below), the loans were not issued and there was consequently no commission; the fall in the price of China bonds would have made such an operation excessively expensive to the Chinese. Meanwhile, the advances made against the loans earned interest, but the funds were borrowed from the Hongkong Bank. With major construction work either completed or in abeyance, the commission on purchases of foreign materials was also diminished, although supervisory work continued and the cost of overheads, including the salary and other expenses of the Corporation's representative in China, S.F. Mayers, continued.

Despite the broadened base of the Corporation's ownership, it continued, for good reason, to be associated with Jardine Matheson and the Hongkong Bank, with whom agency agreements were renewed in 1912.

The major loans are discussed in Chapter 7; a list of additional loans and advances is found in Tables 8.4 and 8.5, the sterling amounts have been converted from silver equivalents where appropriate. The Hongkong Bank was opposed to *ad hoc* advances, but Addis did not object to silver advances for productive purposes as the Bank had idle funds in the East and they did not interfere with the Consortium's major loan program based on gold currencies in Europe.

The increased activity with railway loans reflects in part the success of Sir John Jordan in asserting Britain's Yangtze policy.[123] In this once again a British Minister's zeal and effectiveness exceeded the ability of the B&CC to find adequate funds in Europe and only considerable pressure from the Legation through E.G. Hillier on Newton Stabb and from the Foreign Office on the B&CC could force action at so unfavourable a time. Stabb, then the Bank's Chief Manager, made a major loan policy decision – the Hongkong Bank would undertake the necessary advances; he was interested in obtaining the exchange business. Nevertheless, the thin base of the B&CC's financial structure and support was revealed, and the Legation, free to deal with other British firms now that industrial loans had been removed from the British

Table 8.4 *The Hongkong and Shanghai Banking Corporation China: miscellaneous loans, 1912–1914**

Title and/or Purpose	Amount (thousands) Total/HSBC	Terms (i)	(ii)	(iii)	(iv)
1912/13					
5½% Shanghai Municipal	Ts500[a]	87 (?)		–	
6% Yuet–Han Railway Co.	Ts500	–		1 –	
Tientsin–Pukow Railway advance	£1,200/300	(repaid by 1920)		DAB CCR	
5% Pukow–Sinyang Railway Loan	£3,000[b]	5½ points	40	CCR	
against which 7% advance	£199	not repaid		CCR	
6% Shanghai–Nanking Railway Land Loan	£150	92		B&CC	
1914					
Shanghai–Fengching Mortgage Redemption Loan 6%	£375	91	20		
Chinese Government 5% Nanking–Hunan Railway Loan	£8,000[b]	4 points	45	B&CC	
against which 7% advance	$3,745			B&CC	
Pukow–Sinyang 7% advance	£8.464			B&CC	
Canton–Kowloon Railway 8%	£4.505			B&CC	
Two Government loans	£525[c]			B&CC	

[a] The Bank applied for the entire issue of these debentures.
[b] These loans were never issued, but see the advances related to them.
[c] Issued by private treaty and not on the market.
* See Table 8.1 for the loans discussed in this chapter and explanation of 'terms'.

Group's area of exclusive support, turned to the long-suffering Pauling and Co.[124]

The B&CC did negotiate the Chinese Government £8 million 5% Nanking–Hunan Railway Loan for 45 years to enable Government resumption of the Anhui Provincial Railway Company's works and for new construction.[125] As the B&CC itself put it, 'The profit of the Corporation was reduced to a possible one quarter of 1% and the Corporation as a commercial company was being sacrificed to political interests.'[126] The four points allowed the issuing corporation were undoubtedly the reason for the B&CC's complaint – the conditions were commercially unsound, but, although advances were made, the loan itself was never issued.

The Chinese Central Railways – performance
Although the Hukuang Railways Loan of June 1911 was made by the Four Power Groups, with the Hongkong Bank signing for the British Group, the transaction as far as the Bank was concerned was on account of the Chinese Central Railways (CCR). The company's 25% share of the loan was £1.5

Table 8.5 *The Hongkong and Shanghai Banking Corporation*
Advances against public loans and other advances

Date	Title	Amount (millions)	Amount £ (millions)
1905	Advance to Wuchang Viceroy		0.4
1908	7% Advance	Ts 3.0	
1912	7½% Treasury Bill Advance (Gold)	(Ts 12.1)	1.8/0.12[a]
1912/13	Tientsin–Pukow Railway Advance		1.21
1913	Pukow–Sinyang Railway		0.199
	(original loan: Pukow–Sinyang Railway Loan)		
1914	Nanking–Hunan Railway	$3.7	
	(original loan: Chinese Govt. 5% Nanking–Hunan Railway Loan never issued)		
1916	Pukow–Sinyang Railway (7% Advance)		0.846
1918	Canton–Kowloon Railway		0.450
1921	ICG 5% Currency Reform and Industrial Development Sinking Fund Gold Loan (6% Advance)		0.400
1929	Shanghai–Nanking Railway Rolling Stock Hire-Purchase Loan		0.156
1937	Chuchow Repair Shop Loan Advances		0.0205

[a] Total/Hongkong Bank participation.
ICG Imperial Chinese Government.

million and of this half was floated in London through the Hongkong Bank and half in Paris through the Banque de l'Indo-Chine (see Chapter 7).

In July 1911 the funds of the Tientsin–Pukow Railway, including the original loan of £5 million and the first series of the Supplementary Loan of £3 million, were nearly exhausted, and the Loan Syndicate, the DAB and the CCR, discussed the need for a further issue of £1.8 million. The Revolution intervened and the bonds could not be placed on the market. Instead the Syndicate advanced £1.2 million (of which the British Group was responsible for £300,000) against the right to take up loan bonds at a price of 88.[g] With the fall in the price of China bonds and the general high cost of funds this option proved impractical. The advance was due in any case to be repaid in March 1913, but that deadline passed and the company appealed to the British Minister, Sir John Jordan, in April 1914.[128] The records show that the advances were repaid at some time before 1920.

The CCR signed the 5% £3 million Pukow–Sinyang Railway Agreement for 40 years in November 1913; the loan was to be issued with a 5½ point differential and with the Hongkong Bank as agents. The agreement made

[g] Of the £300,000 advanced, the Hongkong Bank provided £126,000, the CCR £98,000, the B&CC £47,000, and Jardine Matheson £29,000.[127]

provision for advances, which are listed in Tables 8.4 and 8.5. The loan itself was never issued and the advances were not repaid.[129]

This summarizes the loan activities of the Chinese Central Railways.

As for the company's capital and dividends: by November 1907 50% of the £100,000 capital subscribed on account of the 100,000 ordinary shares was paid up and all of the £1,000 subscribed on account of the 1,000 deferred shares – giving a total paid-up capital of £51,000. The CCR became a private company in 1908. Its earnings were sufficient to permit the payment of dividends in 1908 (10s:0d per ordinary share), 1910 (2s:6d ordinary, £15 deferred), 1911 and 1912 (2s:6d ordinary, £12:10s:0d deferred), representing a total payout since the founding of the company in 1904 of £127,500.[130]

Although the average annual payout over the years through 1914 was some 23% of paid-up capital, this was an exaggerated statement of the financial capability of the company. The bunching of the dividends indicates the relationship of profit to the return from the provisions of the CCR's only effective loan agreements, those connected with the Tientsin–Pukow line and, through the Bank, with the Hukuang Railways. Furthermore, among the company's assets were advances to the Chinese Government subject to non-repayment and railway bonds subject to depreciation. The problems inherent in this situation will be considered in the following volumes.

The Pekin Syndicate in the CCR

The corporate history of the CCR in the four years before 1914 is complex and marks a deterioration in its relationship with the Pekin Syndicate which came under virtual French control. The CCR had been established in 1904 as a cooperative merger of British interests, specifically the B&CC and the Pekin Syndicate, on a 50:50 basis but with an identity close to the B&CC. The CCR at first used Jardine Matheson as their China agents, but in 1906 the company reached an agreement with the B&CC to share the latter's representative – J.O.P. Bland and then Mayers – while Jardine's remained the commercial agents and the Hongkong Bank was the company's banker. A further relationship had been established though Carl Meyer, the Pekin Syndicate chairman, and the Bank through Meyer's membership on the London Consultative Committee.

The expansion of the CCR to include French and Belgian Groups did not disturb the British status of the company (see Chapter 6), the relationship within the British Group which now also included the Yangtze Valley Company, nor the association of the CCR with the B&CC.

The Pekin Syndicate and the B&CC had an equal number of deferred shares entitling them to vote for the nine British directors; of the nine actually elected, four, including Carl Meyer, were on the board of the Pekin Syndicate, five on the board of the B&CC. The votes of the Yangtze Valley Company and the Belgian interests had been assigned in trust into the control of the two founding British companies.

The problem arose, as noted in Chapter 7, in 1910 when many British shareholders sold on a rising market and the consequent Continental majority successfully voted a requisition which led, as previously noted, to the resignation of Carl Meyer and his colleagues from the board of the Pekin Syndicate. They, however, refused to resign from the board of the CCR except under conditions which the Pekin Syndicate were unwilling or unable to fulfil – that the Syndicate's new board would nominate candidates acceptable to the then board of the CCR, the intention being to ensure the continued British balance. By electing directors friendly to the Pekin Syndicate's new French interests or directors with close connections to other syndicates, the whole purpose of the CCR as a 'Consortium-friendly', joint Anglo-French (and Belgian) venture, evenly divided but with a British casting vote, could have been undermined.[h] As the dispute continued, two of the CCR's directors from the B&CC board, J.G.H. Glass and William Keswick, died.

The problem remained unresolved through August 1914, despite the efforts of intermediaries. The CCR's directors had to be appointed jointly by the British Group, which, as noted above, comprised for voting purposes the B&CC and the Pekin Syndicate with equal votes. The B&CC proposed an agreement whereby the two deceased directors from the B&CC plus the four from the Pekin Syndicate should be replaced at the same time. Both sides were agreed that, as there were only three Pekin Syndicate directors who would meet the qualifications demanded by the B&CC, George Jamieson, the managing director of the CCR and a former Pekin Syndicate director and nominee, could be reelected.

The CCR did not remain powerless during this period, as the previous discussion on advances proves. Indeed, it was the very fear of a lack of a quorum, if the four Pekin Syndicate directors resigned in the normal way but without successors, which had led to their decision to retain their seats on the CCR board in these unorthodox circumstances. However, the long impasse and decline in the company's income brought the CCR further into the B&CC orbit, presumably with the agreement of the French and Belgian Groups. In 1913 the CCR became domiciled in Matheson and Co. and the secretaries and staffs of the two companies, the B&CC and the CCR, were

[h] In February 1911 the Pekin Syndicate submitted a list of its directors and asked the B&CC to choose among them, which task the latter refused as 'invidious'. The directors as listed were: Henry T. Anstruther, Sir Richard D. Awdrey, René de Cerenville, Comte du Chaylard, Chantrey Inchbald, Libert Oury, and Comte de Seguier.[131]

identical; they also, as noted above, shared the same representative in China.

The board room conflict reflected developments both on the Continent and in China. As the CCR moved closer to Matheson's so the Pekin Syndicate became further involved in French intrigue. New French/Belgian financial cooperation assisted the plans of Philippe Berthelot in his nationalistic approach to China finance. In 1913 his associate, Charles Victor, acquired a majority of the shares of the Pekin Syndicate; André Berthelot was then forced on the British shareholders as an 'administrateur-délégué' at the same time that plans for the creation of a new Chinese-French bank were being finalized. In this venture the Pekin Syndicate invested Fr5 million of a total Fr45 million, and thus the Banque Industrielle de Chine was established.[132]

This undermining of a key player in the British industrial group affected the whole structure of the several companies with which the Hongkong Bank was associated. Despite the concern of the French Government with these new developments, the founding of the Banque Industrielle signalled a danger to the China Consortium, its association with the Pekin Syndicate a danger to the CCR and to the B&CC. The agreements of 1905, including the CCR's region of operation within China, were being challenged. Illustrative of the consequences of the new developments were the attempts of the Pekin Syndicate to move outside areas agreed in 1905; specifically at stake was the line to Szechuan, the line which had brought the Groups into the CCR in the first place. The unanimous vote of the Pekin Syndicate's board in this matter led to the B&CC's withdrawing its previous approval of the candidacy of two Pekin Syndicate directors seeking election to the CCR board.[133]

In March 1914 the CCR, taking note of the fundamental implications of the new situation, proposed to the Pekin Syndicate the determination of the 1905 agreements as they affected the operations of the company. The CCR letter made specific reference to competition over the line to Szechuan and listed further reasons:

1st. The dissolution of the Consortium for industrial loans;
2nd. The active competition of companies of one nationality, British, French, and Belgian;
3rd. The marked disinclination which the Chinese authorities have recently displayed to do business with companies which partake of dual nationality.[134]

The Pekin Syndicate merely replied by noting that they would do nothing until they were properly represented on the CCR board.

The CCR's letter was in fact a message of defeat for the ideals of the China Consortium, but as for the CCR itself the impasse relative to the composition of its board of directors had worsened and would continue to do so.

The Hongkong Bank continued to be represented on the boards of both the B&CC and the CCR by Sir Charles Addis, who recognized the legitimacy of the call for Meyer and his associates to resign from the CCR board.[135] But Addis too was caught up in the problem of suitable replacements; to accept resignations before this question were resolved would mean either that the CCR's board would lack an operating quorum or it would be forced to accept French or Belgian directors in the British Group's quota.

By 1914 the Consortium, including the British Group with the Hongkong Bank, were without exclusive support except in the matter of a possible second reorganization loan (without industrial clauses), but such a loan was becoming less feasible with every new foreign obligation agreed by the Chinese Government.

Despite signs detected by Sir John Jordan that the Pekin Syndicate was returning to its British 'allegiance', this was a relatively small, though significant part of the newly developing scramble. The system the Hongkong Bank under Addis's leadership had built in association with Jardine Matheson, the DAB, KfAG, and the French Group headed by the Banque de l'Indo-Chine was in danger of total collapse. The Great War provided the necessary time for rethinking. One consequence would be the post-war New Consortium, which would, in its turn, be ineffective.

The Hongkong Bank, British policy, and Sir Charles Addis

The London Manager of the Hongkong Bank, Sir Charles Addis, had a vision: a modernized and efficient China achieved through controlled, a-political lending in the context of European financial cooperation. In the broadest context, this was British policy as well, and Addis would attempt to ensure that a fair share of the development did in fact come to British industry. As for the Hongkong Bank it would naturally benefit; Addis's task was to safeguard its interests from poachers who, caring little for China, sought to 'cash in' on negotiations the Bank had initiated.

Addis and the Bank were frustrated on all fronts. The task was too all-embracing to be tolerated by the borrowing country, China; its potential was too great to permit its accomplishment by a single bank even when linked to five other Groups representing major Powers. Addis had known China and the problems of loan negotiation from his junior years of responsibility in Peking and tedious days in Shanghai. By 1910 when the Four Groups signed the inter-bank agreement and China had accepted both reorganization and modernization, the China Addis knew and understood had reached its most receptive state. Had China continued on the familiar course Addis assumed, the international Consortium might have done much to implement the vision of orderly financing of China's requirements. But the strains of 1911 proved too great; other political forces of a complexity beyond Addis's studies were at work. The instrument of Addis's creation, the Consortium in the form of Five

Power Groups, made one great loan . . . and then sat waiting until the end in 1946.[i]

China was not as Addis or any foreigner perceived it, and as time passed Addis's insights were of less relevance, even as his knowledge and command of the City increased. The war in Europe and then the Warlord Period in China doomed Addis and the new post-war Consortium to pursue a policy of benign neglect, and possibly through this negative role to afford some protection to China's credit and China's resources.

Nothing could be done by the private sector alone; liaison with the British Government was essential. Communication between the Chinese Government and the banks, however initiated, became recognized only through the Legation. The Legation only assisted and registered agreements which were consistent with British foreign policy. Foreign policy could be influenced; the frequent contacts between Addis and the Foreign Office, between Hillier and Jordan were sessions of mutual influence.

Addis's influence depended first, on the role his Bank could play in the Chinese economy, and second, on his skill in presenting positive recommendations which were sufficiently in tune with British policy traditions to be considered seriously. There was one point, however, beyond which the British Government could not be induced to move – it would not create a monopoly, it would not entrust foreign economic policy in China to any single group. Ultimately the Bank had to compete in the market place.

The Government was nevertheless accused of granting the Hongkong Bank its exclusive support. The support the Bank actually received was far short of 'exclusive' and was due (i) to the undoubted command of resources with which the Bank could make initial contacts in China and compete in the market – thus the Bank, the B&CC, or the Chinese Central Railways was usually first to seek and therefore to receive official support and (ii) to the fact that the Reorganization Loan series bound the Government to a long-term support which despite repeated denials was seen, incorrectly, as 'exclusive' relative to all China loans.

Throughout this period, and subject to the framework of the Treaty system, China, in her relations with the private foreign firms, remained in control even

---

[i] The public at large, denied a role in high finance, could, however, still participate through party puzzles. For example, assume that the struggle for railway concessions by five syndicates was met by the Chinese Government's granting all five concessions. The five railways were required, however, to enter the city in a specific order by separate openings in the wall and proceed by the *shortest* route, but without crossing each other's lines, to their designated railway stations. The routes had to be determined before the concessions became operative, but, by the time a solution was found, the Chinese Government would have changed and the conditions would be altered. The specific terms *and the solution* to such a 'Chinese Railway Puzzle' can be found in H.E. Dudeney, *The Canterbury Puzzles and Other Curious Problems* (first published 1919, 4th ed. 1958), pp. 127, 224–25.

when she seemed least able to defend herself from their persistent demands. As Sir Edward Grey made clear to the Eastern Bank, the Chinese and not the Legation were the authority, and they set the terms. The struggle between Addis's vision and the hard realities of Chinese politics and emergency financial needs was an uneven one. China's loan negotiation tactics brought a steady improvement in terms which has been detailed, and this the foreigners accepted. Eventually the limit was reached, existing security was exhausted and control by lenders essential. Frustrated and determined to remain in control, the Chinese turned to *ad hoc* finance and to support from those who cared less about the country's long-term position.

The efforts of Addis, Urbig, and S. Simon in Europe, of Hillier, Cordes, and Casenave in Peking were brilliantly successful in themselves; they did not, they could not, fulfil the dreams of so many well-wishing foreigners – they could not reform China in their own image.

From these heights a return to the routine. Not only did the coupons have to be paid but the many detailed provisions of the loans had to be supervised; there were almost continuous disagreements, misunderstandings, reinterpretations, appeals to the Consul General or Minister, and all this designed to maintain clauses to which admittedly the Chinese had agreed but which required the Chinese to do something they did not in fact wish to do. In these negotiations local Bank managers were sometimes involved – certainly the Shanghai and Hankow branches were important points of contact, though even here Hillier came down from Peking from time to time to ensure continuity and control.

In an atmosphere of nationalism and of traditional anti-foreign attitudes reinforced by resentment at the terms of so-called 'unequal treaties', these frequent arguments and appeals to authority were the price the Bank paid for its dynamic overall policy, creating an attitude which would be resented. Yet in all this the Bank as agent and in a position of fiduciary trust had little choice.

In these petty disputes and controversies, in the Warlord Period when the Chinese state was divided and nationalism and anti-Treaty policies were all the several Governments and people had in common, the vision would be lost and the real promise of the 'Age of Imperialism' forgotten. Assistance would be seen as exploitation, attempts to control ill-advised borrowing as 'colonialism' – a manifestation of the 'informal Empire' concept. And yet, although the Bank's image suffered and to some its role became suspect, as one foreign observer had predicted, 'The Chinese are too good businessmen to fail to see that the Hongkong Bank . . . is able to offer facilities to its friends no other European bank can rival' – and, for a time, no Chinese bank could as yet offer.[136]

The Hongkong Bank and other foreign institutions however China-oriented would never be able to dispel entirely the image which dogmatic political theory had created for them. When, however, the Chinese banks were able to stand up to the Hongkong Bank, when bankers of the calibre of K.P. Chen and Tsuyee Pei became masters of deposit banking and foreign exchange, or when indeed China entered the Nanking Decade under the tutelage of the Kuomintang, the Hongkong Bank could again play a constructive, positive role in the economy of the Republic of China.

Part III

EPILOGUE: THE BANK, GERMANY, AND THE GREAT WAR

Daddy, what did *you* do in the Great War?
> Caption to an infamous British recruiting poster

A merchant from the Free and Hanseatic City of Hamburg, W. Nissen of Siemssen and Co., was a member of the founding Provisional Committee of the Hongkong Bank; he became Chairman of the Bank in 1867. During the Bank's crisis in 1875 the German merchant, Adolf von André of Melchers and Co. was Chairman, and of the six-member Board, a further two directors were German. An American was Deputy Chairman. That was the year the Board was searching for an 'English' director.

There is no question but that the extreme position in 1875, the year in which the Bank was without a British director from the United Kingdom, was untenable; the fact remains, however, that the Hongkong Bank was founded by a multi-national committee to serve the trading needs of a multi-national merchant community dealing together on the China coast. The 1875 position was untenable because (i) Hong Kong was a British colony and (ii) British trade predominated on the China coast. If the Hongkong Bank were to remain credible, its Board of Directors had to reflect these facts. Once they were recognized, the multi-national composition of the Board would once again make sense.

There were developments both on the China coast and world-wide, however, which over time and in a generation which had perhaps forgotten the origins of the Bank, brought the presence of Germans on the board of a bank self-proclaimed as 'British' into serious question.

The reasons for this are developed in Chapter 9, but in brief, by the 1900s the public concerns over the German role in the Hongkong Bank were (i) the Bank's financing of competitive German trade and (ii) the right of the Bank to be considered British in the context of Foreign Office support in China loan negotiations. Building on these concerns, the public during the Great War were encouraged by interested parties to wonder if the Hongkong Bank fully supported the purposes of that war, which they interpreted not so much in the context of idealistic declarations relative to safety for democracy in lands fit for heroes but rather in terms of the destruction of German trade on the China coast, with particular reference to the piece-goods business.

There was the carefully nurtured suspicion that the Bank, in view of its past German associations, was 'lenient' in its relations with enemy firms, especially the Deutsch-Asiatische Bank, and that the Bank harboured hopes for the reestablishment of post-war relations from which it would once again profit. The popular cry when deprived of rhetoric was above all self-seeking and came eventually to be adopted as official policy; the sacrifices at the Front were being endured to ensure the permanent exclusion of German trade from the China coast through continued prohibitions and sanctions in the post-war period.

The Bank as a corporation did not take so extreme a position, but rather through prompt execution of special Government commissions, through the deeds of its young employees at the Front, and by its adherence to its obligations, it proved its loyalty to Britain and the Allies. Suspicion and rumour are not, however, so easily countered.

Through its Chairman, David Landale, the Bank emphatically denied German influence and disassociated itself from its multi-national traditions. Those in the Bank who felt the capture of German trade a chimera based their views on general economic and political grounds, not on German influence in the Bank.

But these nice distinctions are not appreciated in time of war.

The Bank's management, facing what it considered totally false charges, was frustrated; its position was complex and its relations with the British Government endangered. Although Sir Charles Addis was successful in explaining matters to the Foreign Office, there would appear to have been no way to present an acceptable account of the Bank's activities to an increasingly emotional public.

The Great War had an impact on the Bank which can only be appreciated by first understanding what the Hongkong Bank had been, indeed, what Hong Kong had been – a great multi-national venture under British administration. Hong Kong's initial growth was not based on an exclusive policy; there was British sovereignty and British rule, but the harbour and its facilities, including its banks, were available to all. As for banking, it was this very openness of policy which prevented the successful development of the Deutsch-Asiatische Bank as the major source of German trade finance.

This indeed was the rationale for Hong Kong's cession in 1842.

In this context the Bank had forged relations with Germans and German firms of long standing; the Bank could not now, in August 1914, totally disentangle itself from these connections overnight. The Hamburg Branch existed, the Bank was trading in neutral countries, and international agreements involving the consortiums had to be honoured. The Bank was the agent of the neutral Government of the Republic of China; its role in the several international syndicates which issued the China loans was a continuing one. Thus accusations that the Bank persisted in its alleged German-leaning tendencies also continued; the Hongkong Bank remained on the defensive.

The task of Chapter 9 is to describe the historical relationship of the Hongkong Bank with German interests at three levels, the Board of Directors in Hong Kong and the finance of German trading companies, the Consortium relations in London and Peking (already covered in the previous four chapters), and the Hongkong Bank's branch in Hamburg. The history is one of sound commercial relationships established in the context of Hong Kong's free port traditions turning sour under the strain of political pressures which the Bank as a commercial corporation based in Hong Kong could not properly take into account.

With the coming of the Great War the Hongkong Bank's inescapable British character was revealed, forcing the obvious; its staff and its resources were devoted to the defeat of the Central Powers. Chapter 10 is an account of the Hongkong Bank during the period 1914–1918, its corporate performance, the policies of its Board and management, and the role of its staff both in banking and on active service – and the consequent coming of the ladies.

The positive contribution having been told, Chapter 11 will deal with the accusations, dealing with the enemy, of the quiet Peking walks of Cordes of the Deutsch-Asiatische and the blind Hillier, and of the problems created by the consortiums. This is told against an unpleasant background; those who resented the Bank and its success used the cover of patriotism to attack, sometimes openly, often subtly, whispering in the ear of Government. Not that the position of the Bank did not lend itself to legitimate concern; this too is discussed. But to specific accusations the Bank gave specific answers.

Throughout the War and totally beyond Hong Kong's control, the Hamburg Branch of the Hongkong Bank continued to operate. This story also is recounted in Chapter 11.

There were those in the Bank, it is true, who saw the War as a temporary madness, who knew that world economic interests following such a war would require the revival of all trade and who had the courage to say so. Unfortunately, given the previous accusations of German influence, this civilized position when stated by a Bank Manager was too often misinterpreted, and, as the War and loss of life continued, as the people of the Allied Powers became further embittered, the Bank was willingly directed into policies which, while understandably patriotic, were not wholly compatible with its history or wise even in the context of British trading interests in the East.

From this new position the Bank would have difficulty extricating itself in the inter-war period. Thus these three chapters are an epilogue to the Hongkong Bank in the formal traditions of its foundation.

As recounted in Volume III, the Bank would indeed reopen its doors to finance the commerce of all nations trading with the East, but symbolic of the impact of this Great War, the Bank would for over 60 years retain a wholly British directorate. The inter-war period was not a period of expansive thinking, for the Bank or for others; and yet, it could never remain British in any insular or narrow sense. At the same time it was British, it remained a China bank, alert to China's interests as its management understood them and, even as it withdrew tentatively from a major role in London, became ever more closely involved with the fate of the Chinese Republic.

Only after post World War II reconstruction and in the context of a new Hong Kong and a new China did the Bank move out once again from its region to take in the former Imperial Bank of Persia, the British Bank of the Middle East, and thus become an inter-regional banking group, having already consolidated its position in Asia by the purchase of the Mercantile Bank. Then after long negotiations the Hongkong Bank Group became multi-national in a different sense; it entered into a partnership with Marine Midland Banks, Inc. All this is recounted in Volume IV.

9

THE HONGKONG BANK AND GERMANY BEFORE 1914

The Hongkong Bank is largely German unfortunately. It is even thought by some that the majority of the shareholders are German.

G.E. Morrison, 1905

Perhaps the silliest of all the attacks is the attempt to make the Hongkong Bank out to be a German institution.

Charles Addis, 1912[1]

At the time of G.E. Morrison's 1905 accusation, the German shareholders of the Hongkong Bank numbered approximately 91, that is, 2.75% of the total.[a]

During the Great War when the Foreign Office was concerned with the charges of German influence in the Hongkong Bank, full details were compiled by Head Office: Germans held 5% of the shares outstanding, 1% of the deposit liabilities, 5% of secured and 1% of unsecured loans and advances, and 2.5% of bills and credits outstanding.[3]

The public, however, were subjected to a series of rumours and speculations in which 'confidential sources in the City' were said to have evidence of German control. That there could be such ill-informed discussion on this subject was at least in part the consequence of the Bank's policy of not revealing data on share holdings. Although this reticence was consistent with the Bank's rights under its own ordinance of incorporation (in contrast with the usual but inapplicable obligations stated in the Hong Kong Companies Ordinance), the Bank thereby subjected itself to unnecessary and invalid criticism. The image created by default was difficult to correct in times of stress, and from this developed pressures which caused the Bank significant problems in the Great War when, it might be argued, its whole effort should have been devoted to the cause, rationally defined.

---

[a] In determining whether a shareholder was or was not a German subject, some difficulty was encountered, especially in the case of shareholders with German-sounding names residing in Britain or on the China coast. Interestingly, the Bank had the same problem in 1915 and originally provided figures showing 7% of its shareholders had 'German-sounding names'; further analysis narrowed this down to 5% actually of German nationality. The figure provided for 1905 is of the correct magnitude.[2]

Appearances

The concern of the public relative to German influence in the Hongkong Bank was not totally irrational. In August 1914 the Bank had four German directors representing the leading German firms on the China coast: Arnhold, Karberg and Co. (from 1888), Carlowitz and Co. (from 1897), Melchers and Co. (from 1871), and Siemssen and Co. (from 1864). The modest German representation through Siemssen's, together with American, Norwegian, Parsee-Indian, and Jewish-Bombay members on an internationally composed Provisional Committee, consistent with the international composition of the China trade, had significantly increased.

Sassoon's also remained, but American interests were no longer directly represented. That the Bank thus appeared at best British *and* German seemed confirmed by the Board's invitation to Carlowitz as late as 1897; the more powerful of Britain's trading rivals had been consciously brought in to participate in the direction of a British exchange bank, one which as a merchant bank was claiming leadership in British China finance.

For nine years of its pre-1914 existence the Hongkong Bank had a German Chairman. As late as 1906 A. Haupt of Melchers and Co. was elected Chairman and in 1908 E. Goetz of Arnhold, Karberg and Co. was Deputy Chairman. Thus German chairmen would on occasion address the shareholders expressing favourable expectations for the growth of British trade. Appearances were confusing.

The appointment of directors lay in the hands of the shareholders at the semi-annual meetings. That four German directors could continue to be elected in a time of mounting trade rivalry seemed to confirm that Germans owned a percentage of the shares sufficient to decide the elections. In fact, a small combination of British interests actually attending the meetings could have easily blocked a fully coordinated German effort – had the latter been conceivable. Directors were, after all, first appointed by the Board as vacancies appeared and then proposed to the Annual Meeting; German directors who attempted to force a policy inimical to British interests could be rejected; but there was no reason why they should provoke opposition. The Hongkong Bank operated as a commercial institution; it served the legitimate financial requirements of its constituents, German or British; there was no conflict. And 'British interests' broadly defined extended beyond the immediate local concerns of British China-coast merchants.

The concern over the presence of German directors on the Board shows a misunderstanding of the role of the directors in the management of the Bank. In the imagination of the patriot the German director could be pictured discovering the secrets of British trading hongs and enabling Germans, provided with unlimited clandestine funds, to undermine British trade and capture British markets. It was the stuff political tracts are made of, but it is bad banking history.

The election of Bank chairmen was in the hands of the directors. It was accomplished in fact by a modified form of rotation by seniority; the post was non-executive. And it is at this point that even the Board showed an awareness of the Bank's public image; Stabb, in considering the succession, reflected the Board's views when he wrote in 1913, 'We cannot put up a German.'[4]

Those familiar with the structure of the Bank could have argued legitimately that the Board of Directors distanced themselves from purely banking decisions and that the composition of a board should reflect the diversity of a bank's principal constituents. This approach would however only shift the argument from 'ownership and direction of the Bank by Germans' to the 'finance of Germans'. On this latter subject the Bank remained true to the era of free trade; Charles Addis, in the letter quoted at the head of this chapter, had followed up his expression of indignation with the significant comment, 'As if it were not our pride that the Germans in China prefer to do business with the Hongkong Bank rather than with their own [Deutsch-Asiatische Bank]. It is the secret of our British colonizing success – equal opportunity for all nationalities.'[5]

Nor did Addis see this as inconsistent with the Hongkong Bank's British merchant banking operations, which, as none knew better than he, were directed *de facto* from London with the advice of a London Consultative Committee. Addis, however, did not represent the thinking of British jingoists.

The relationship of the Hongkong Bank with German trading interests also involved mutually satisfactory agency arrangements which do not appear to have been targets for criticism. Perhaps they were seen to be clearly in the interests of British trade; in any case, they should be noted: the Bank's first agency in Bangkok (from 1865 to 1883) was with the Hamburg firm of Pickenpack, Thies and Co.; Jucker, Sigg and Co., the Bank's second agent, was Swiss; in Vladivostok the Hamburg firm Kunst and Albers appears to have represented the Bank; in 1899 the Anglo-German firm with head office in Berlin of Arnhold, Karberg and Co. acted as the Bank's first agents in Tsingtau.[6]

THE GROWTH OF GERMAN TRADE AND INVESTMENT IN THE EAST[b]

Trade and banking

When the Bank was founded, Imperial Germany did not exist; Woldemar Nissen represented a firm from Hanseatic Hamburg; Julius Menke, the Bremer firm of Pustau and Co. They were trading firms and, with their Eastern partners based in Hong Kong, were natural constituents of the Hongkong Bank which specialized in trade finance. And these firms certainly did not confine themselves to German goods or even to trade with German ports; indeed, on the eve of the Great War more than half of Manchester exports to China were handled by German firms. This may help place the problem in perspective and explain why, despite their contribution to British industry, they and the bank that financed them would become subject to criticism – the vocal British elements were the rival trading and agency hongs. Manchester remained pointedly silent.

Table 9.1 confirms that British supremacy remained secure; if its percentage participation in the China trade declined, the major cause was not Germany alone. Chinese shipping grew in both numbers and tonnage; other nations became involved in the trade, especially Japan. The concern with Germany lies elsewhere.

With the defeat of France in the Franco-Prussian War in 1871 and the dismissal of German bank officers from the Comptoir d'Escompte, the Deutsche Bank made an abortive effort to establish Far Eastern branches.[7] After their withdrawal the Germans focused their efforts on the founding of their own specialist Far Eastern bank, the Deutsch-Asiatische (DAB). Although it was said to have been founded on principles similar to those of the Hongkong Bank, the similarities were superficial and its primary purpose was the furthering of German industrial investment in China; the finance of trade took second place.

Certainly the DAB kept its accounts in silver and had its head office in Shanghai, but its board sat in Berlin and its interests were often sacrificed to the requirements of the banks which participated in the owning consortium. The failure of the DAB to cater to the finance of German trade kept open the Hongkong Bank's opportunities; the failure of the DAB to establish a trading branch in a German port until 1905 gave the Hongkong Bank the opportunity to establish its own Hamburg office on a competitive basis. The German firms found the Hongkong Bank easier to deal with and its facilities of greater value;

---

[b] This section is particularly dependent on David J.S. King's report on the Hongkong Bank and Germany in the Hongkong Bank Group Archives.

Table 9.1 *China: British and German trade compared, 1880–1913*
(in millions of Haikwan taels or tons)

Year	Imports carried by various flags			Exports carried by various flags			Tonnage of vessels entered and cleared		
	British	German	Total	British	German	Total	British	German	Total
1880	68	2	82	51	3	80	10	1	16
1885	76	5	89	50	2	66	12	1	18
1890	78	10	129	47	2	89	16	1	25
1895	116	19	180	78	11	152	20	2	30
1900	129	22	222	76	19	170	23	4	41
1905	280	54	461	117	34	242	35	8	73
1910	241	39	477	136	47	394	34	7	89
1913[a]	270	47	586	144	50	419	39	6	93

[a] 1914 is a non-comparable year due to the outbreak of the War.
Imports and exports are for foreign trade only. Exports include re-exports.

Source: Liang-lin Hsiao, *China's Foreign Trade Statistics, 1864–1949* (Cambridge, MA: Harvard University Press, 1974), Tables 10a, 10b, and 10i respectively.

the Bank confirmed its interest by inviting the taipans of leading German hongs to seats on its Board of Directors.

Of the 25 German firms in Shanghai, only nine opened accounts with the DAB, and some of these still maintained their ties with the Hongkong Bank as well. In German Tsingtau it was the German firms who pressed for the establishment of an agency of the Hongkong Bank. This Charles Addis considered to be rather a matter for pride than for apology.[8]

Criticism of German trading methods

By the first decade of this century, something had gone sour. There were first of all those who for reasons not directly connected with the China trade, or indeed with trade in any area, considered war with Imperial Germany inevitable. Such was the foreign editor of *The Times*, Valentine Chirol, as also was that newspaper's Peking correspondent, G.E. Morrison. And in this context they turned on the Hongkong Bank.

In purely trading terms, however, the Germans in the East were faulted for unfair trading practices, for doing unspeakable things which were contrary to 'British methods'. The evidence advanced was conflicting, and a Hong Kong report by a young civil servant, G.R. Sayer, the father of the Hongkong Bank's executive Chairman (1972–1977), G.M. Sayer, presented data which suggested there had been no German state subsidies from secret service funds or elsewhere and no unfair competition.[9] His findings were consistent with British consular reports which had warned that the suspect German methods included a stricter attention to business, the learning of Chinese by German merchants located in key provincial towns, and direct contact with Chinese merchants and officials.

The papers presented to the General Committee of the China Association in London focused on two criticisms: (i) by granting Chinese importers long-term credit the Germans were encouraging unsound practices leading to waves of speculation and periodic trade depression following overtrading and (ii) the German firms were willing to assist the progress of negotiations by non-British methods, by bribery for example. Such uneconomic methods were, it was thought, impossible without Government subsidies and/or the finance of such banks as the Hongkong and Shanghai Banking Corporation which, as a bank which claimed to be British, ought to refrain from even marginal involvement in such practices.

Against this, however, was the undoubted fact that many British manufacturers were using German agents in preference to British. One of the principal qualifications H.D.C. Jones had for the junior joint-managership of the London Office, despite his personality incompatibility with his senior, Sir Charles Addis, was his ability to deal with Manchester constituents.[10] The established British hongs had their own legitimate complaints against manufacturers who expected too much of their agents, who withdrew agencies without sufficient cause, and who failed to perform as promised. They warned that British manufacturers were shortsighted and unaware of German long-run aims, but the fact remains that German merchants were agents for British exports by preference of British manufacturers and the Hongkong Bank was financing the trade. As the China Association chairman, George Jamieson, put it, 'The manufacturers are free agents and must be presumed to know their own business.'[11] Indeed even in 1918 British manufacturers were making it quite clear to the China Association that, on the conclusion of the War, they would if possible revert to German agents.[12]

A balanced summary concluded that German success was due to (i) lucrative agencies in such articles as dyes, watches, and cotton thread, (ii) granting of credit facilities to buyers due to exceptional facilities granted in London of which the Germans availed themselves, (iii) close cooperation with their Chinese staff, and (iv) great industry and close application to detail.[13]

The British Consul, Bertram Giles, reported from Changsha that:

... in many cases Germans seemed prepared to devote themselves more wholeheartedly to business than is the case with British merchants. For instance *all* the Germans in Changsha study Chinese, and some of them speak it remarkably well. They also engage in a large amount of free and unrestricted social intercourse with officials and with the directors of important commercial undertakings from whom they hope to obtain orders and in a variety of ways will give themselves infinite trouble by other than purely business methods to make business.[14]

Citing a specific case the Consul continued:

Carlowitz and Co. [represented on the Board of the Hongkong Bank] obtained the Hunan Provincial contract and took over the entire output of lead and zinc from the Shui-kuo-shan mines for a period of six years, but they had to advance Ts1.2 million to provincial authorities at no interest, and this they borrowed from the Hongkong and Shanghai Banking Corporation at normal interest.[15]

None of this proved convincing to the British merchants. The reference to the Hongkong Bank however seemed to confirm that the Bank was somehow implicated in a transaction adverse to British interests, defined as British China merchants' interests. Thus the concern over the Bank's 'pro-German' role persisted.

A.B. Lowson, the Hongkong Bank's Tientsin Agent in 1916, introduced a further category into the discussion. North China merchants, he reported, ascribed the growth of German trade over the previous ten years to the 'financial assistance which German houses have been able to secure through their home banks', and he made specific reference to two quite distinct situations.[16]

The first, finance for retail imports, could result as already noted in overtrading; the Germans, Lowson reported, when faced with non-payment by Chinese merchants, had persuaded the Chinese authorities to support them through the German-managed Guarantee Bank of Chihli.

But more important was the second category, the finance of large engineering contracts involving deferred payments. This, Lowson stated, was not the legitimate task of an exchange bank; funds were tied up for too long a period. The Home manufacturer should provide the finance; if he had difficulty doing so, there was an argument for either a state trade bank or for some combination of Home banks.[17]

The Germans, in other words, were not financing their exports within the traditional framework of exchange banking. Indeed, this could hardly be expected; the Deutsch-Asiatische Bank was founded by its own 'Home' banks to finance just such engineering exports through, for example, deferred payments. The Hongkong Bank, which was quite capable of competing with the DAB in ordinary trade finance, had defined itself – there were exceptions – out of an increasingly important market. Either British exchange banks had to reconsider their role or new institutions, a state trade bank, for example, were required.

There is thus no question but that the Germans were aggressive and that their diplomatic and consular officers played a positive role in promoting

German economic penetration. But with all this their percentage share in the China trade remained small; the concern with the Germans in China was part of a global concern.

This aggressiveness verging on intrigue was particularly apparent in Japan and Siam, but in the former the Hongkong Bank's role already matched the resources available consistent with Japanese regulations and in the latter German involvement was never a threat to the Hongkong Bank's secure position as the pioneering bank. German and British rivalry were apparent in railway construction, but all parties recognized that the Siamese Government had a policy of sharing its foreign dependence among the Powers. In the British Eastern colonies and protectorates German competition was feared but contained; China remained the principal area of concern.

In the midst of this anti-German controversy the China Association found themselves involved in a social exchange with their counterpart, the Deutsche Asiatische Gesellschaft, whose president had been a guest at the Association's annual dinner – now in 1913 it was A.M. Townsend's turn to visit Hamburg. In Jamieson's view this was all 'good for fellowship'.[18]

German finance and the Consortium

The founding of the Deutsch-Asiatische Bank

During the 1880s but after the closing of the Deutsche Bank's Eastern branches, the leadership of German financial interests in China was taken by the Disconto-Gesellschaft. The first efforts were made in London with Hermann Wallich approaching Jardine Matheson; overtures were also made through Rothschild's in London to the Hongkong Bank. These proved unsuccessful and the Germans, urged by their Minister in Peking, von Brandt, organized a loose consortium of the major German companies interested in East Asian industrial markets. In June 1885 A.H. Exner of the Deutsche Bank, C. Erich of the Disconto-Gesellschaft, and K. Bethge, a railway engineer, left for China. A month later A. von Hansemann met with the Hongkong Bank in London.

At the same time the Exner Commission was in Peking, another German group, the Warschauer Group, was negotiating the loan eventually issued in 1887 for five million marks. The two groups met but did not exchange information, yet it was only their eventual union through the mediation of the Frankfurt Rothschilds that made possible the formation of the Deutsch-Asiatische Bank in 1889. Meanwhile the Chihli Viceroy, Li Hung-chang, with his penchant for asking difficult questions, demanded to know of Exner whether he considered himself more intelligent than the Manager of the Hongkong Bank. Exner refused to be drawn.[19]

The delays in Germany reflected uncertainty over the purposes of the proposed Eastern bank and the likelihood of its profitability. The formal founding of the DAB in February 1889 was followed in 1890 by the opening of the bank's head office in Shanghai; the delay was due to the difficulties encountered in shipping out the bank's silver capital.

The consortium which founded the Deutsch-Asiatische Bank successfully combined all the German banks which had interests in *capital* investment in China. Slight alterations were required subsequently to admit new members and allow the Königliche Seehandlung to withdraw, and there was some dissatisfaction in the early 1900s when the Deutsche Bank resented the proportionately small share it had taken in the bank due to the hesitancy of Hermann Wallich to become too heavily involved in Chinese banking again.

However, in general, the DAB was successful in forming a comprehensive national monopoly in which all the interested capital forces of the country were fully represented. In 1890 a parallel consortium, the Konsortium für Asiatische Geschäfte (KfAG), was formed combining the major German banks interested in *industrial* projects in China, which included most of the same names as the DAB, while the DAB itself was also represented in the consortium with a 10% share (see Table 9.2). Due to their comprehensiveness, the two consortiums were able to lay claim to very strong Government support and were well-prepared to enter agreements with other countries, in which the financial interests of the countries as a whole could be delimited, without fear that German groups outside the consortiums would be able to circumvent these agreements.

The Hongkong Bank and the DAB

The first successful relationship between the two banks was arranged by Ewen Cameron in London following the failure of the Hongkong Bank and of Germany to obtain participation in the First Indemnity Loan of 1895. The continued existence of the agreement of 1895 as modified (see Chapters 5–8) became a subject of controversy; critics of the Bank complained that the fruits of British negotiation and diplomacy were thereby extended to German interests even in areas which the British considered within their own sphere of interest. The German activities in Shantung had unfavourable consequences to all concerned, but they also provided a popular anti-Imperialist basis for criticism of the banks' agreement.

Germany was unpopular, therefore the agreement was unpopular. But the Hongkong Bank was criticized further for its willingness to enter into international relationships and yet its outspoken reluctance to share with other British financial institutions by the formation of a representative British Group comparable to the German consortiums detailed in Table 9.2. The

Table 9.2 *German Far Eastern interests*

	Capital subscription (taels)
(I) German Banks involved in the founding of the DAB	
Disconto-Gesellschaft	805,000
Deutsche Bank	175,000
Königliche Seehandlung	555,000
S. Bleichröder & Co.	555,000
Berliner Handelsgesellschaft	470,000
Jacob S.H. Stern	470,000
Bank für Handel und Industrie	310,000
Robert Warschauer & Co.	310,000
Mendelsohn & Co.	310,000
A.M. Rothschild & Söhne (Frankfurt)	310,000
Norddeutsche Bank (Hamburg)	380,000
Sal. Oppenheim Jr & Cie.	175,000
Bayerische Hypotheken & Wechselbank	175,000

Dresdner Bank, A. Schaaffhausen'scher Bankverein, Nationalbank für Deutschland, and Born & Busse joined the consortiums later.

(II) German Banks in the Konsortium für Asiatische Geschäfte

Deutsch-Asiatische Bank	Bayerische Hypotheken und Wechselbank
Disconto-Gesellschaft	Königliche Seehandlung
Deutsche Bank	Dresdner Bank
S. Bleichröder & Co.	L. Behrens & Söhne
Darmstädter Bank	Nationalbank für Deutschland
Berliner Handelsgesellschaft	A. Schaafhausen'scher Bankverein
Jacob S.H. Stern	Born & Busse
Norddeutsche Bank	Bank für Handel und Industrie
Sal. Oppenheim Jr. & Cie.	

Source: D. J. S. King's research report 'On the relations of the Hongkong Bank with Germany, 1864–1948', p. 16, in Group Archives.

Bank's explanation that the British situation was better compared with the French, where only the Banque de l'Indo-Chine was directly represented, was neither understood nor accepted, and the Bank yielded to official and City pressure – but only in 1912.

The negotiations relative to indemnity loans, concessions, and railway loans received quite naturally a full coverage in the press, and the Bank's name was, therefore, continually before the public in conjunction with the Deutsch-Asiatische Bank and other German interests. Even when the negotiations were complete the Hongkong Bank had continuing business with the German consortiums. In 1913 on the occasion of Addis's knighthood, the *Banker* had written, 'As the head of the British Group [of the Consortium], Sir Charles Addis has borne a leading part in safeguarding British interests in the Far

East . . .'; that the contacts had been reported to be in defence of British interests seemed to some virtually irrelevant.[20]

But even accepting that the relationship of the Hongkong Bank with German interests might be overall beneficial to British interests, this would be true only if each of the several national groups were successful in restraining other national firms from operating in China contrary to the agreements they had signed. British interests complained that, while they had no voice in such agreements and received little support from the Legation and consulates in China, German firms such as Carlowitz and Co. were offering suppliers' credits, often in significantly large amounts, despite the restraints supposedly imposed by the German consortiums. And, to stress the relevance of such complaints, these German firms were represented on the Board of the Hongkong Bank.

These charges, explanations, and counter-charges have been stated in Chapters 5–8, and their merits are not further argued here. At this point the main concern is the perceived German connection of the Hongkong Bank. Simply put, that connection was based on business considerations of a commercial bank modified in the merchant banking field by the pressures of international political and economic relations. The Bank's primary concern was the interests of its shareholders and constituents; these were mainly British and consequently the Bank was overwhelmingly involved in the development of British trading and industrial interests. But it was also a Hong Kong bank, in which merchants of many nationalities had played a key founding and developmental role. These too were shareholders and con-stituents, and the Hongkong Bank met their requirements.

As for the DAB, the Hongkong Bank remained throughout a successful competitor. Indeed the Germans were as anxious as the Hongkong Bank to clear up any misunderstanding as to the non-German nature of the Bank! K.T. Stöpel supposed that the failure to open a German bank in Japan was due to the assumption that the Hongkong Bank, with its German directors, was at least partly a German institution.

This may have given the impression in interested circles that the Hongkong Bank is a half-German institution and thus pays attention to German interests. That is unfortunately not the case. What do you think of the situation in Japan in which only Englishmen and other nationalities fill responsible positions in the bank and not a single German? That in Hamburg, as an exception, Germans are hired is explicable on purely pragmatic grounds. The Germans on the Board of Directors of the Hongkong Bank should realize that there are capable German managers who could be used in Japan when the other managers leave![21]

In the Shanghai report for 1899, published in the *Handelsarchiv* in 1901, a similar view of, presumably, the Hongkong Bank, is found: 'It is worth noting, in order to correct a widespread error, that there is only one German bank in

China: the Deutsch-Asiatische Bank.'[22] However these two German references may be exceptional in their concern that the Hongkong Bank would be considered a 'German' bank. There are, on the contrary, numerous sources which refer to the presence of Germans on the Board of the Bank, and the Bank itself is referred to either as definitely English, or simply referred to in contrast to the German DAB.

The strong competitive drive of the Hongkong Bank was partially responsible for its commercial success over the DAB. The establishment of the Hamburg Branch was a major factor in this success, and to its history this chapter now turns.

THE HONGKONG AND SHANGHAI BANKING CORPORATION (HAMBURG BRANCH)

Julius Brüssel and the branch established[23]

The earliest source to mention the proposed establishment of a branch of the Hongkong Bank in Hamburg is found in the minutes of the Board of Directors of February 14, 1889: 'In view of a German bank commencing business in China, the desirability of opening a special agency in Hamburg was discussed.' The Chief Manager, G.E. Noble, stated that both Thomas Jackson and Ewen Cameron, the Bank's joint Managers in London, were in favour of the new agency and Noble suggested appointing as agent a German, Moritz Kalb, who had just retired from the British firm of Reiss and Co. in Shanghai.

The decision that the agent should be a national of the country and not a member of the Bank's regular staff is consistent with the precedent in which the Bank's Lyons agency was initially entrusted to a Frenchman. On February 28, 1889, on the urgent recommendations of the London Manager endorsed by two German members of the Board, it was decided to appoint Julius Brüssel instead.

Julius Brüssel was born on June 11, 1846, the son of the clothes merchant, Salomon Brüssel.[24] He went East for the Bank of Rotterdam and was posted to Singapore and then to Batavia where, as it happened, the bank was agent for the Hongkong Bank. With the withdrawal of the Bank of Rotterdam in 1873, Brüssel joined the German firm of Behn, Meyer and Co. and served as a junior partner in Batavia and Singapore. After marriage in 1879 Brüssel decided, in view of his wife's health, to leave the East; in 1881 he accepted the post of sub-manager of the International Bank of London, Ltd, which had been founded in 1880 with a subscribed capital of £400,000 as the successor to the International Bank of Hamburg and London. Thus although it did not specialize in Far Eastern business, this bank and, therefore, Brüssel had strong links with Hamburg and the Continent in general.

The DAB wanted Brüssel for Shanghai, but Brüssel himself preferred to remain in Europe and Jackson urged that he was 'by far the best man yet' and would be valuable even if the Bank had to pay an additional £500 a year to secure his services. He was accordingly offered a two-year contract from May 1, 1889, at £1,500 per annum or £500 more than would have been offered Kalb.[25]

Following the model that Harries was supposed to have used in San Francisco and Barnes in Manila, Brüssel first established his own firm in Hamburg, Firma J. Brüssel, to act as an independent agency for the Hongkong Bank. This firm was registered on September 20 and opened for business on September 24, 1889; a circular letter dated October 4 recommended that all Managers send Brüssel all drafts on Germany, not only those on Hamburg, in order to save two days' interest.[26]

On October 31, 1889, the Board of Directors decided that a full branch of the Bank should be established at Hamburg instead of Brüssel's independent agency and that Brüssel should become its Manager with a full power of attorney from the Bank. Hamburg Bürgermeister and State Senator Carl F. Petersen objected that the Hongkong Bank's motive was to forestall the DAB by becoming established first and by offering special concessions to customers. He complained that the Bank's Hamburg agency was already publishing daily its rates of exchange on Berlin. This protocol was duly forwarded to the appropriate department, but there was no basis for intervention. Thus on March 7, 1890, the Hongkong Bank became the first foreign bank to establish a branch in Hamburg; it was duly registered in Hamburg's *Handelsregister*. It was reregistered in 1904 with the full legal title of 'Hongkong and Shanghai Banking Corporation (Hamburg Branch)'.

In many ways Brüssel must have run the branch as a *German* branch of an 'international' (as opposed to 'British') bank, and he naturally had German interests, the interests of his constituents, at heart. In a letter to Ewen Cameron in 1893, for example, he complained about the difference between the buying and selling rates for German marks, which involved an extra 'squeeze' of $\frac{1}{4}$ of 1%: 'I do not see,' he wrote, 'why buyers of Mark remittances should be thus handicapped.' This is not to say that he ever put the interests of German firms before the interests of the Bank. His argument was that the extra payment was bad business, that sooner or later someone would offer a better rate, and that the Bank would lose business.

Brüssel established himself firmly in the Hamburg business community. In 1892 he became a Bürger of Hamburg, a special class of citizenship reserved for those of a certain status and income. In 1896, he requested a rise in his salary to bring it into line with offers he had received from a German bank, but the Hongkong Bank decided that it could not comply with his request as the volume of business in Hamburg did not justify it. However they reminded him that he would soon be receiving a bonus for his role in negotiating the 1896 Chinese Indemnity Loan.

Activities of Brüssel and the Hamburg Branch

After the Bank's 1895 Agreement to cooperate with the DAB in Chinese Government business, one of the tasks of the Hamburg Manager in the early years of the branch was to act as the Bank's representative in negotiations with the DAB and its associates. With the later illness of Brüssel and the dominance of Charles Addis, this role became less important, but the impact on the suspicious of a German representing the Hongkong Bank in negotiations with German financial consortiùms cannot have improved the Bank's British image.

In 1900 German merchants in Hamburg and Bremen with interests in East Asian trade joined together and founded an organization called the Ost-Asiatischer Verein (OAV). Brüssel was very active in this organization from the beginning. He signed its first membership list as Manager of the Hongkong Bank and, when he was elected its first treasurer, he naturally placed the organization's funds with the Bank.[27] In the first four years of the OAV's existence, meetings of its board of directors often took place in the offices of the Hongkong Bank. However as the treasurer was required to read out the account book at every meeting, it is easy to notice that Brüssel began to be absent more and more often as his health deteriorated. Although he was already very ill, he was re-elected treasurer in January 1904, but on September 6, 1905, Brüssel wrote to the board to announce his resignation due to ill health. He was replaced as treasurer by the representative of Carlowitz and Co., the former Hongkong Bank director (1898–1901) Paul Sachse, who moreover kept the organization's funds with the Hongkong Bank.

The DAB opened its branch in Hamburg in 1906; however its manager, Kochen, only became treasurer of the OAV in 1909, at which time he transferred some of the organization's funds to his own bank, the balance was transferred in 1910 and the OAV's board thanked the Hongkong Bank for its previous work.

Brüssel's health also rendered him on occasion unfit for work in the Bank; furthermore, A.J. Harold, who had come from London Office as Accountant in May 1889, had died in December 1902 and had not been replaced. This shortage in senior management prompted the emergency transfer of F.T. Koelle as the new Accountant in Hamburg. A member of the Eastern staff then stationed in Colombo, he had been educated in England; his mother was English but his German father had brought him up bilingual. Nevertheless he considered himself English; this was, in fact, his first visit to Germany. Koelle had been born in Turkey, and English citizenship could not be transmitted through the female line. Koelle, supposing himself stateless and having failed three times to acquire British nationality due to the technicalities connected with the residence requirement, asked if the Bank would object to his becoming a naturalized German subject.

Ewen Cameron replied, 'The fact of your becoming a German would make no difference to your career in the bank.'[28] In 1903 Koelle became a German subject. Koelle's citizenship was probably a factor in his being considered for the post of Manager in succession to Brüssel; it was certainly a factor in his forced retirement in 1920.

In November 1904 Charles Addis, then on leave from Shanghai, visited Hamburg at the request of Sir Ewen Cameron and made a trip to visit Brüssel at his sanatorium near Berlin. In his report to Cameron, he advised taking steps to prepare for the eventuality of Brüssel's death or at best only partial continuance in his office.[29] Addis took the position that Koelle would be able to carry on if Brüssel should be totally incapacitated, but that some better arrangements needed to be made relative to Powers of Attorney. Accordingly he suggested and Cameron and the Board agreed that Koelle be granted a full P/A by the Board of Directors in Hong Kong and that at the same time G.W. Butt in London Office be granted one to cover all emergencies. Butt had been Singapore Manager when Koelle was there on his first tour as a junior (see Volume I, Chapter 15). In addition the three senior German staff members were given a joint P/A, any two of them to be authorized to sign together.

Nevertheless, Addis did not suppose that Koelle, who was still relatively junior at 34 and remained a member of the Eastern staff, would automatically become Manager. He even approached an old Calcutta friend, Ferdinand Schiller, who, after some consideration turned down a tentative offer on the grounds that the Hamburg Manager should be a German subject. Schiller, who was a Swiss citizen possibly born in India, concluded with the thought that becoming a German subject was 'I think you will agree, a very serious move at my time of life.'[c]

An alternative to Koelle or an outsider was the promotion of a member of the German staff. Indeed, Addis reported that one member, Caspar, did have the necessary ability, but he was junior to two others, and Addis advised against promoting him over the heads of his seniors. But Addis did not

[c] There is a Ferdinand Schiller listed as 'German' and the promoter of the Port Canning Dock Scheme near Calcutta in the 1860s; the scheme was a failure and the land was taken over by Sassoon interests. Presumably Addis's friend was the son.[30]

recommend transferring another member of the Eastern staff. Thus the history of the Hamburg Branch does not parallel that of Lyons and Paris with de Bovis and his Eastern staff successors or, much later, New York with Kellogg and his successors. When Koelle succeeded Brüssel it was as a German; he was transferred from the Eastern staff. Events post-war were a consequence of feelings generated in time of war, and not until the 1980s would Hamburg again have a German Manager.

Brüssel resigned on grounds of ill-health in August 1905, and the Board voted him 20,000 marks in lieu of six months' salary plus a gratuity of 60,000 marks. But his health did not improve and he was drowned in the Alstersee on December 16, 1908.

The pre-war branch under Koelle

The second Manager of the Hamburg Branch was, then, F.T. Koelle, the Accountant in the last years of the Brüssel managership. His father, Dr S.W. Koelle of Würtemburg, was a German who, after training by the Basle Mission, had served 30 years in the Middle East with the Church of England. F.T. Koelle married an English woman and, despite his naturalization as a German, continued to be an active member of the Church of England serving on the Church committee in Hamburg. His early career, which was typical of that of a junior on the Eastern staff, has been described in Volume I.

The first detailed information that survives concerning the business done by the Hamburg Branch is contained in an Inspector's report of 1911. Unfortunately as the branch had been inspected only the year before, this report did not undertake a detailed analysis of the balance sheets. The Inspector found it difficult to estimate what proportion of German trade was coming through the Hongkong Bank as so much was financed via London, nor was it possible to determine whether the branch was keeping up in terms of the bills actually handled directly with Hamburg.

The German staff, all except one of whom had been hired and trained by Brüssel, though 'thoroughly loyal and hardworking', followed procedures initiated by Brüssel which the Bank Inspector found unusual and a consequence of Brüssel's 'mercantile training' – a suspicious factor to any banker – 'though sufficient for efficiency'. Brüssel's initial training had in fact been with a bank; his background was not entirely mercantile, but, exceptional among Bank Managers and Agents, he had not been trained in the Bank's London Office, and, therefore, when the Inspector noticed deviations from the norm, he automatically attributed them to Brüssel's years with a merchant firm. These deviations, he added, were being corrected by Koelle.

The staff at this time consisted of twelve Germans and the British

Accountant, R.E.N. Padfield. Padfield had joined London Office as a junior in 1896 and gone East to Hong Kong in 1901. He was presumably on his first leave when he was assigned to Hamburg; he never returned to the East; he was on leave when war broke out and was assigned to London where he remained, retiring as junior Manager in 1937. The information available suggests that he too was exceptionally young for the post and that the assignment may have been due to the emergency created by Brüssel's retirement, by Padfield's apparent unsuitability for the East, or both – the records provide no reason for his permanent transfer from the Eastern staff in 1905. He and Koelle did not work well together, an unfortunate circumstance in view of the fact that it was Padfield who was assigned the task of recommending the fate of the Hamburg Branch and, presumably, Koelle in the post-war atmosphere of 1919.[31]

In the early days the Hamburg Branch would appear to have had its own source of funds, even lending on occasion to London. Certainly the branch was less dependent on London before the War than in the inter-war period. Koelle however began the practice of keeping a large overdraft with the London Office from about 1908, thus avoiding the need to discount bills received on the German market. The rate of 4% current in Germany for discounting bills was considered a perfectly acceptable average return for these funds borrowed from the London Office.

The 1911 Inspector's report stated that, if the situation were watched carefully, there might be scope for the use of additional London funds in the local German market. This had been hampered previously by the Bank's internal bookkeeping system, especially by use of arbitrary crossrates which made the business appear less favourable in the Profit and Loss accounts of the branch. Under the existing system it was not possible to distinguish the profits from this activity from the interest regularly charged by London Office on the branch's overdraft.

The branch maintained, as was customary, a minimum credit balance of approximately RM100,000 with the Reichsbank, although no interest was allowed. This was to serve as a reserve fund and informal guarantee to the Reichsbank of the branch's financial position and was more than amply compensated for by the useful services and information provided by the Reichsbank. In addition, the branch maintained deposit accounts with the Deutsche Bank, which granted them interest at 2% below the bank rates regardless of the condition of the money market. The branch also lent money to first class brokerage firms against the deposit of approved acceptances and maintained small credits with various correspondent banks. Altogether the branch maintained between RM800,000 and 1,000,000 available at short call to meet demand liabilities.

In general the report was optimistic: German trade was growing rapidly, and the Inspector felt that if reasonable rates could be offered for D/P (Documents against Payment) bills, more of this business could be encouraged away from the London discount market as German firms were willing to pay slightly more for a direct draft; it saved them paper work, minimized commissions, and lessened the use of their name in London.

However there were problems. Since the branch had been established in 1889, several other banks with links to the East, including the DAB, had opened branches in Hamburg. At the time the report was being written, the Yokohama Specie Bank was planning to open a branch, threatening the Hongkong Bank's previous domination of Japanese business, which made up more than half of its total outward finance. Some of the Bank's methods were unnecessarily conservative: it might be argued that the Manager would be justified in, for example, accepting drafts without necessarily having full knowledge concerning the drawees, if the drawers were strong and the business appeared sound, at least until he received specific information to the contrary from an Eastern agent. The branch, the report stated, should serve as an information service for its better constituents; the Inspector had been surprised to discover that Koelle had not been receiving a full set of Semi-Official correspondence in which the officers of the Bank exchanged confidential information on trade conditions and the Bank's customers.

The Inspector concluded that the branch's future was promising and felt that Koelle was justified in proposing a move from their current, rather cramped quarters, into one of the new office buildings then being constructed.

THE HONGKONG BANK AND GERMANY – A SUMMARY, 1864–1914

German merchants maintained close links with the Hongkong and Shanghai Banking Corporation from its conception in 1864 until the outbreak of the First World War and beyond. This was due to a variety of factors which developed as conditions changed.

In the early years of the Bank's activity foreign trade had come to be dependent on the London discount market for financing. The Paris market began to assert itself with the formation of the Comptoir d'Escompte de Paris in 1860, however French trade was never very important in China. In 1870 the Germans, full of nationalistic fervour after their recent victories over the French and the ensuing national unification, established the Deutsche Bank in an attempt to provide German traders with facilities to finance their trade with Germany without passing their bills through the London market. The attempt, however, was doomed to failure, as the German discount market was not strong enough to offer competitive rates. German-Asian trade remained to a large extent dependent on the London market until the Great War, and, under changed circumstances after the War, became even more dependent on outside financing.

Until the 1880s the Hongkong Bank's activities were comparatively unhampered by politics and national rivalry. The Bank had been established to serve the interests of all the merchants in China, and there was no reason to discriminate among them. Although the executive staff of the Bank was almost entirely British, the Board of Directors remained international, reflecting the nationalities of the Bank's most important constituents. Industrial and financial business with the Chinese were still on a relatively small scale, and the Governments of the European Powers had not as yet begun to intervene to support the private business affairs of their nationals.

During the 1880s conditions began to change. The French tried unsuccessfully to insert a clause into the peace treaty concluding the Sino-French War in 1885 which would have required the Chinese to turn to the French for capital and materials if they should ever need foreign aid to build railways. At the same time, a consortium was being formed in Germany, with the approval and support of the German Government, which was also interested in railway and industrial projects in China.

These nationalistic stirrings constituted a threat to the Hongkong Bank's international character. Although the full implication of these developments was not and could not be fully appreciated in Hong Kong, the Bank, which was already dominant in Chinese Government business, nevertheless approached a German bank in an attempt to arrange for a subordinate participation in loan business at hand. This offer fell through, however, as the Germans in Germany saw the Hongkong Bank as a 'British' institution and, therefore, as a matter of German prestige in China could only agree to cooperate with them on the basis of full equality.

Until the mid-1880s the Chinese had resisted suggestions that they build railways and initiate other large-scale industrial projects. The only major contracts to this date had been for unproductive purposes, for example, the Government loans arranged by the Bank for various military campaigns. These had naturally been placed, when the Hong Kong and Shanghai capital markets proved insufficient, in London, not because the Hongkong Bank was 'British' and London was 'their' market, but because London was still the capital market of the world *par excellence*. It was not until 1887 that a German group placed a Chinese Government loan in Germany.

In 1885 German banks and companies interested in Chinese business formed an informal consortium and sent three representatives to China to investigate potential railway and other industrial business. German merchants were gradually encroaching upon the markets in China which the British tended to consider their special preserve.

In the 1890s these nationalistic tendencies intensified. In 1889, the Germans founded the Deutsch-Asiatische Bank (DAB), whose main concern was to negotiate large contracts for German industry and the German capital market, but which was meant also to finance German trade. After 1895 the French, Russians, Belgians, and Americans also became interested in securing contracts for their own nationals in China. That the Hongkong Bank, as a Hong Kong bank, would not participate on this basis was one of the main sources of the misunderstandings which persisted concerning its purposes and loyalty. The Bank approached British industry and with Jardine, Matheson and Co. organized the British and Chinese Corporation and, later, the Chinese Central Railways; the Bank assisted British interests in securing development contracts and obtaining the necessary finance, but the Hongkong Bank would not cancel its traditional China-coast associations, it would not throw over its constituents whatever their national allegiances.

Although 'government business' became increasingly politicized, ordinary trade continued in its accustomed channels. Many German merchants continued to deal with the Hongkong Bank despite the establishment of the German bank because they found the Hongkong Bank to be more attuned to their needs, especially after the Hongkong Bank founded its branch in the Hanseatic port city of Hamburg in 1889. As the Hongkong Bank was managed from Hong Kong, it could keep in touch with the local conditions and the needs of the merchants.

The DAB on the other hand was run from Berlin (even though its head office was in Shanghai), by men primarily interested in industry and Government finance rather than trade. Many of them had never been to China and had no idea of what was necessary in order to do business there. The Board of Directors of the DAB insisted on controlling all policy and even specific decisions from Berlin, and they could naturally only evaluate proposals by European standards. Furthermore they always had in mind the overriding consideration of the state of the money markets in Germany. Many practices normal in the China trade were unacceptable to the board of the DAB. They would not, for example, accept drafts at over three months' sight as these could not be discounted on German markets, and yet these were common in the China trade and essential to a merchant who wished to compete.

There were no merchant representatives, of German or any other nationality, on the Board of Directors of the DAB, but the major German firms in Hong Kong continued to be represented on the Board of the Hongkong Bank until the outbreak of World War I.

In 1895 China was defeated by the Japanese, and with the Indemnity Loans of 1895, 1896, and 1898 'government business' with the Chinese began on a large scale. For various reasons discussed in Chapters 4–8 the Hongkong Bank came to cooperate closely with German finance in this business; however this was not due, as suggested by some at the time, to the fact that German merchants were represented on the Bank's Board of Directors. As the new Government business became highly political, the Bank needed to keep in close touch with the British Foreign Office as well as the European capital markets. It is a credit to the flexibility of the management of the Hongkong Bank that it allowed the London Manager to control this profitable business, while control over the Bank as a whole remained in Hong Kong. This is the importance and relevance of seeing the Hongkong Bank in a sense as two banks: the one directed from Hong Kong and serving the interests of all merchants without discrimination and to which German merchants turned because the German bank was not willing to offer suitable conditions; the other 'Bank' in London, working through the British capital market and, though serving the requirements of China, focusing on those Eastern requirements which could be fulfilled in Britain primarily by British industry and capital. It was this latter 'Bank' which, because it was in the British national interest to have an ally in China against the Russo-French coalition, became closely linked with German finance.

Although these two relationships were in reality quite separate, they were confused by certain outside observers. The British, unable to recognize that their overwhelming economic predominance in China had been due partially to the temporary weakness of the rest of Europe and for this reason was bound to change, sought some other explanation for the remarkable growth of the German presence in China. Some at least, most notably the *Times* correspondent in China, G.E. Morrison, found an explanation in the close link between the Hongkong Bank and the German bank, which, he felt, could only be explained by the large German presence on the Board of Directors of the former.

The absurdity of this position was never fully exposed. It supposed that German merchants would force a bank in which they had strong financial and other interests to facilitate the operations of another bank, the DAB, which had not even been able to gain their support for normal banking business. Nor was there any prospect of German directors having the power to achieve such an end – that is not how the Hongkong Bank operated, it was not their purpose on the Board.

In the German press, these same German firms were accused of being the cause of the *weakness* of the Deutsch-Asiatische Bank.

In the two decades preceding the Great War the Powers struggled for political influence through a dominating position in Chinese finance and industrial development. Their competition to lend funds to China was restrained only by the fear that excessive borrowing would lead to bankruptcy and military intervention in China.

To diminish the danger of a one-sided intervention as well as to strengthen their own positions, the Powers formed various coalitions. These smaller alliances were superseded by a series of Groups, which at one point included all six major Powers competing in China. When the Great War broke out, Britain, Germany, France, Russia, and Japan were all members of a then active consortium. The cooperation which the Hongkong Bank and others fostered in China was nullified by jealousy and incompetence in Europe and vilified by those on the China coast who found any cooperation with Germany distasteful and had long concluded that war was inevitable.

It might be said that the Great War was not the Hongkong Bank's war. None of the various rivalries and tensions which led up to it were in the Bank's interests. The hostility between Britain and Germany was in part due to the intense trade rivalry and the competition in overseas investments. However the Hongkong Bank, and China, benefited just as much from the growth of German as it did from that of British commerce, and, in China, British and German finance worked together to the satisfaction of at least the Hongkong Bank. Furthermore, a significant percentage of the British export trade to China was handled by German merchant houses financed by the Hongkong Bank.

But the Great War was Britain's war and the Hongkong Bank was British. For reasons considered in this chapter there were those who saw the Bank, or who professed to see the Bank, as German-dominated. The actual and perceived activities of the Bank are considered in the next two chapters, but Sir Charles Addis's initial dream of a civilized approach to commercial affairs during the hostilities was a casualty of the length and bitterness of the fighting. The long years and the general hatred generated by the War had their effect; the casualties did not cease in 1918.

10

THE HONGKONG BANK IN THE GREAT WAR, 1914–1918, I: THE CORPORATION AND STAFF

> . . . as for Germany, she has reversed every idea I had conceived with respect to her. It is as if a friend, a strong, thoughtful, deliberate, sober-minded friend, had suddenly suffered some lesion of the brain, which, as sometimes happens, had turned every natural characteristic into its opposite. Deliberation into rashness, reflection into panic, health into hysteria.
>
> Sir Charles Addis, 1914[1]

There is a reluctant acceptance of war implied in the statement of the Hongkong Bank's London Manager, Sir Charles Addis. The hesitation, the sadness reflect the lingering influence of a great tradition based on the expectations of the merchants of the Free Port of Hong Kong and the economic philosophy of free trade, the soundness of which had for some years been debated. But Hong Kong was British and the Hongkong Bank was British. It was on this basis that Board, management, and staff approached the great problems before them.

Nevertheless, while all were eventually agreed on the short-term necessity of war, not all were agreed on its long-term implications. The Hongkong Bank had had German connections; did it not harbour hopes for German contacts in the future? Was now the time for the latent envy of the less successful to fuel public suspicion? While the Bank strove to meet its increased duties with a reduced staff, it was to bear the additional burden of defending itself from charges both specific and vaguely defined, charges which despite the Bank's successful defence came close to hampering its ability to fully serve the Allied cause.

And yet the record proves it did so. That is the subject of the present chapter.

The Board of Directors, once the German directors had resigned, remained virtually unchanged; the Bank's management remained in the capable hands of Newton Stabb in Hong Kong, A.G. Stephen in Shanghai, Sir Charles Addis in London, J.C. Peter in Singapore, and J.P. Wade Gard'ner in New York. But the staff with death, retirement, and calls from the

Front declined in numbers just as wartime tasks were placing an additional burden on those who financed vital British trade links with the East. How this was accomplished is an important chapter in the history of the Hongkong Bank – for this history remains the history of a bank, even in the dramatic times of war. Perhaps many readers, like the young Bankers themselves, would find the story of battlefields more exciting, nevertheless it is the Bank and banking which must remain the focus.

Throughout the War there had to be, after all, the routine of banking – decisions on new branches, the periodic discussions on the one-dollar note issue, dividend policy, the decrease in the market price of the securities which composed the Bank's sterling reserves, and all those problems which have hitherto comprised the subjects of this history. The Board, for example, continued its policy of writing down the Bank Premises Account, of paying a general bonus to all employees (except to members of the Hamburg staff) and special gratuities to key Managers, and of transferring funds from current gross earnings into contingency accounts. Yet even this routine took place in exceptional economic circumstances and from the first day of the War there were innovations both in London and in the East.

It is true that the balance sheet performance of the Hongkong Bank during the Great War was not spectacular and there were no new major policy decisions other than those arising from the need to counter the charges of pro-German dealings. The sterling value of shareholders' funds almost doubled in the period, but the small increase in their Hong Kong dollar value betrayed the cause – and the basic exchange banking problem of the War – the 85% increase in the price of silver, the consequent rise in the Eastern exchanges, and the significant fluctuations which required experienced Managers in control.

There is then a basis for approaching this period, despite drama on the battlefield, at least in part in a routine way. There are first the Board of Directors and the senior management, then the economic setting, and finally the chronology. At this point the events peculiar to the War – moratoriums, gun-running, and expansion to Vladivostok – have a place. And finally there must be a consideration of the impact of the War on the staff and staff policies of the Bank.

Despite the positive contributions the Bank made to the war effort, there was underlying it all an undercurrent of suspicion, of intercepted documents and charges and counter-charges; these are considered under the ominous title 'Trading with the enemy', and this chapter must therefore be followed by a study of the relations between the Hongkong Bank and Germany – both the charges, specific and general, and the reality. In Chapter 11 there is also a visit deep into enemy territory itself for a study of the dealings of the Hongkong and Shanghai Banking Corporation (Hamburg Branch).

THE CORPORATION

THE BOARD OF DIRECTORS AND THE SENIOR MANAGERS

Composition and role of the Board

Composition

The German directors were present at the meeting of the Board on August 4, 1914, but the following day the Board noted that F. Lieb and H.A. Siebs had resigned. C. Landgraf and J.E.A. Widmann were not then present but had asked whether a 'leave of absence' was perhaps all that was required. The Germans had long served the Hongkong Bank and the request was perhaps not as surprising as it seems in retrospect; after all, was there not a general expectation that the troops would be home by Christmas? But the Board resolved to advise Landgraf and Widmann that resignation was the best course, and the matter was concluded before the meeting of August 11. From that date the Hongkong Bank became for a period a wholly British bank in a wholly British colony.

The Bank was fortunate that Swire's had relented and that G.T. Edkins, the 'Head in the East' of Butterfield and Swire, had joined the Board and so broadened its base on the eve of the War. In early 1916 E.V.D. Parr was elected, thus incorporating once more talents from the P&O. Otherwise the only changes were substitutes in the representation of Jardine Matheson, Bradley and Co., and D. Sassoon's (see Table 10.1).

The Bank's first wartime Chairman was David Landale of Jardine, Matheson and Co., and he was re-elected, serving until early 1916. The elections of W.L. Pattenden of Gilman and Co., C.H. Dodwell, and P.H. Holyoak confirmed in general the traditional seniority principle; these directors were, in any case, taipans of leading hongs. It is difficult to suppose of a more effective system for a non-executive board in the circumstances of Hong Kong at that time.

Policies – the German question

The Bank's counsels relative to Germany were divided but the Board's room for manoeuvre was limited by prior accusations of German association, by the existence of the Hamburg Branch, the capture of correspondence between branches of the Bank and Hamburg, and by a somewhat non-friendly ('unfriendly' would perhaps be too strong) attitude in the City, where the

Table 10.1 *The Hongkong and Shanghai Banking Corporation Boards of Directors, 1914–1918*

August 1, 1914

D. Landale	Jardine, Matheson and Co.	*Chairman* 1914/16
W. L. Pattenden	Gilman and Co.	*Deputy Chairman* 1914/16
S. H. Dodwell	Dodwell and Co.	
C. Landgraf	Carlowitz and Co.	
H. A. Siebs	Siemssen and Co.	
F. Lieb	Arnhold, Karberg and Co.	
C. S. Gubbay	E. D. Sassoon and Co.	
J. A. Plummer	Bradley and Co.	
J. E. A. Widmann	Melchers and Co.	
E. Shellim	D. Sassoon, Sons and Co.	
P. H. Holyoak	Reiss and Co.	
G. T. M. Edkins	Butterfield and Swire	
12 members		

Resigned: J. E. A. Widmann (Melchers, August)
F. Lieb (Arnhold, Karberg and Co.)
H. A. Siebs (Siemssen and Co.)
C. Landgraf (Carlowitz and Co.)

February, 1915 and 1916

D. Landale	Jardine, Matheson and Co.	*Chairman* 1915/16
W. L. Pattenden	Gilman and Co.	*Deputy Chairman then Chairman* 1916/17
S. H. Dodwell	Dodwell and Co.	*Deputy Chairman* 1916/17
C. S. Gubbay	E. D. Sassoon and Co.	
J. A. Plummer	Bradley and Co.	
E. Shellim	D. Sassoon, Sons and Co.	
P. H. Holyoak	Reiss and Co.	
G. T. M. Edkins	Butterfield and Swire	
8 members		

There was no change in 1915/16; changes in 1916/17 are listed below.
Resigned: D. Landale   Elected: C. E. Anton
                                    E. V. D. Parr (P&O)

February, 1917

S. H. Dodwell	Dodwell and Co.	*Chairman* 1917/18
P. H. Holyoak	Reiss and Co.	*Deputy Chairman* 1917/18
C. S. Gubbay	E. D. Sassoon and Co.	
J. A. Plummer	Bradley and Co.	
E. Shellim	David Sassoon and Co.	
G. T. M. Edkins	Butterfield and Swire	
E. V. D. Parr	P. & O. Steam Navigation Co.	
C. E. Anton	Jardine, Matheson and Co.	
W. L. Pattenden	Gilman and Co.	
9 members		

Resigned: C. E. Anton   Elected: D. Landale
               J. A. Plummer   F. C. Butcher

February, 1918

P. H. Holyoak	Reiss and Co.	*Chairman* 1918/19
G. T. M. Edkins	Butterfield and Swire	*Deputy Chairman* 1918/19
C. S. Gubbay	E. D. Sassoon and Co.	
F. C. Butcher	Bradley and Co.	
E. Shellim	David Sassoon and Co.	

Table 10.1 – *cont.*

E. V. D. Parr	P. & O. Steam Navigation Co.
D. Landale	Jardine, Matheson and Co.
W. L. Pattenden	Gilman and Co.
S. H. Dodwell	Dodwell and Co.
9 members	

Resigned: E. Shellim	Elected: A. H. Compton
F. C. Butcher	J. A. Plummer

Bank's merchant banking successes and exclusiveness had been at times as unpopular as they were misunderstood.

There were three major aspects to the problem of German relations: (i) undue leniency in the winding up of German affairs and the liquidation of German firms, and consequent on this (ii) the suspicion that the Bank was acting in a way calculated to permit an early resumption of its business relations with German firms after the War, and (iii) trading with the enemy and the Bank's contacts with representatives of the Deutsch-Asiatische Bank in Peking.

The fact is that while the Chairman proclaimed publicly that the charges of leniency were false and that the Bank was not dealing with Germans except as required in neutral countries and by the terms of various loan agreements, no banking institution could satisfy the extreme sentiment which the War was generating. The Bank was operating in Hong Kong where the Governor, Sir Francis May, was also criticized for leniency, although Germans in Shanghai published a criticism of the severity of the Colony's liquidation policy. Meanwhile in London Sir Charles Addis was arguing that the capture of post-war German trade was a chimera; at the same time he urged, after critical sessions with 'Trading with the Enemy' bureaucrats, that the Bank must scrupulously follow the increasingly complex directives on the subject. But except for this reservation and the feeling that some moderation was in order, the Bank was guiltless of the charges made.

The Bank Chairmen's speeches were written in part by Addis and are concise summaries of significant economic events, of the Bank's problems, and of the Bank's position relative to the War. That they expressed patriotism is natural, but that they were often defensive is a consequence of the Bank's history. Discussing the events of 1915, David Landale, as Chairman, stressed the Bank's position in his annual address to shareholders:

I repudiate in the strongest manner the insinuations which have been circulated from time to time that the policy of the Bank or its officers has been in the direction of maintaining friendly relations with Germans with a view to resuming business with them after the war. On the contrary, our efforts to liquidate the German business standing in our books at the outbreak of the war have been so far successful that nothing more can be done till the various questions relating to cargo in captured or interned vessels have been settled and till the German Courts are again open to British claimants.

While on this subject I would like to refer to the assertion so frequently made by interested parties previous to the war that the Bank's policy was subject to German influences. These assertions are so absurd and wide of the mark that we have not hitherto considered it necessary to refer to them, but it now seems advisable to state that, apart from the local staff of the Hamburg Agency, no German was ever employed by the Bank in any capacity, and that the holdings of Bank shares by Germans have always been inconsiderable – at the outbreak of the war they amounted to under five percent of the share capital.[a]

We had, as was the case with almost every other British company in Hong Kong, directors of German nationality; these gentlemen resigned at the outbreak of war, and, unless future generations hold different views from the present one, no German is likely to be on the Directorate of this Bank again, nor, I hope, on that of any British Company.[2]

The Board supported, generously by the standards of the time, the various war charities while maintaining its involvement with local charitable concerns. But on the release of staff for active duty, the Board supported the position of management; British trade required banking facilities, banking required people. This problem will be considered below.

Banking policies

The rise in the value of silver and the consequent higher exchange rates resulted for the first time in shareholders on the Eastern share registers suffering from the depreciated value of sterling in terms of which dividends were quoted. Although over two-thirds of the shareholders were resident in Britain, half the shares were on the Eastern registers due to the long-standing restriction designed to retain control of the Bank in the East.

The fundamental policy of restricting the number of shares registered in London was not, apparently, discussed. Its effectiveness was selective; the Board and management had to consider its policies in the context of London opinion. But 'London' included the 'City' in general and not simply the shareholders. On the key question of the location of the Bank's head office and direction, the restrictions on the transfer of shares from the Eastern to the London registers prevented a 'drift' to London; the danger was probably most serious at the beginning of the century when merchant banking activities were of increasing importance and the Bank's ability to handle them not fully proved. The danger from shareholders receded as the advantages of a London base receded.

---

[a] Before 1903 F.T. Koelle was considered stateless; for a brief time after his naturalization he remained a member of the Eastern staff. H.H. Kopsch, who might be supposed German, was born in Britain of a German father and, according to reports, was very British. Sir Carl Meyer of the London Consultative Committee was a naturalized British subject.

Table 10.2 *The Hongkong and Shanghai Banking Corporation*
Certain wartime donations, 1914–1918[a]
and later war-related gifts

A. War related		
1914	Prince of Wales War Fund	£5,000
	National Relief Fund	£500
	St Johns Ambulance Brigade	£100
	Indian Soldiers Fund (India Day)	£100
	Central Committee for National Patriotic Organizations [CCNPO]	£10:10s
	Russian Red Cross Society	£26:10s
1915	Overseas Aircraft Fund	£2,000
	British Red Cross Society	£500
	Endsleigh Palace Hospital for officers	£250
	British Red Cross and St Johns Ambulance	$1,000
	Russian Red Cross Society	unspecified
1916[b]	CCNPO	£5:10s
	Russia Day	£105
	Seamen's Hospital, Greenwich	£105
	Lord Kitchener National Memorial Fund	£105
1917	St Dunstan's Hospital	£105
	King George's Fund for Sailors	£105
	YMCA Huts for Chinese Coolies in France	£600
1918	Red Cross	unspecified
	Their Majesties Silver Wedding Fund	£500
1919	Indian Soldiers Fund (India Day)	£105
	British Red Cross Society	£1,050
	Seamen's Hospital, Greenwich	£105
	Lord Kitchener ...	£105
	St Dunstan's Hospital	£105
	King's Funds for the Disabled	£250
	Marseilles British Merchant Seamen's Hospital	£105
	Ceylon War Memorial	Rs2,000
1920	Imperial War Relief Fund	£500
	Bombay War Memorial	Rs2000
	Hong Kong War Memorial	$50,000
	City of Verdun Lord Mayor's Appeal	£500
B. Others		
1914	West River Flood Relief	$10,000
1915	Kwangtung Flood Relief	$2,500
1918	University of London, Commerce Degree over period of five years	£1,000

[a] This table is incomplete as smaller donations may have been given for war purposes at the local level. Note the dates of the missing minute book.
[b] The minute book for 1916 through September 1918 is missing; the charities listed for these years are those in a list attached to the 1919 minute book – mainly for London Office.

The Board, however, were now concerned with the position of those residing in the East. Those on the Eastern registers living in London could opt for their dividends to be paid in sterling; the speculation was theirs to make. As the position of the Bank remained sound throughout the War and as the exchanges moved against sterling, the Board, given that dividends were as a matter of policy denominated in sterling, mitigated the problem faced by those in the East by recommending bonuses of increasing size. The bonuses benefited both gold and silver area residents but they were insufficient to prevent the fall in the silver value of the total annual payout. As Table 10.5A indicates, the sterling dividend payment rose from £4:11s in 1914 to £5:18s in 1918; nevertheless in the same period the dollar dividend fell from $50.08 to $35.51.

The War witnessed the fall in price of gilt-edged securities on the London market, and the Board agreed that these securities should accordingly be written down in the books to 'within' the market price. To maintain the level of the Bank's sterling reserves, to maintain the 'even keel', the Board had to purchase additional securities; the Bank was once again running to keep in the same place. The funds were taken from current earnings. The Bank, following the example of banks in England, eventually converted its reserves to the 5% War Loan which was issued at 97; during 1915 the Bank exceptionally retained the loan at this price on its books regardless of market fluctuations.

In August 1914 the Bank had two officers of the Eastern staff in Harbin and one in Dairen, working from offices provided by mercantile houses. By 1915 the Bank had opened its own agency in Harbin under the management of A.D. Brent, who had a working knowledge of Chinese and German. Otherwise the Bank remained in place until late 1918 when, under pressure from the British Government, the Board agreed to open an office in Vladivostok. The original justification was the need to meet the financial needs of those British forces supporting the mainly American intervention in Siberia, but in the long run the Board had been convinced of the possibilities of trade development and commercial viability.

With an increasing workload and a shortage of staff, a conservative policy was the only one practicable during the Great War.

London and the Consultative Committee

With the death of Sir Thomas Jackson in 1915 the purpose and composition of the London Consultative Committee was once again a question considered by both management and the Board of Directors.

The original purpose of the Committee was to provide the City with a substitute 'Board of Directors', not in any executive sense, but rather as a group of experienced and knowledgeable men of affairs who would be in the confidence of the Bank's directors in Hong Kong and, as it were, speak for them. The value of such a Committee to the Board (and, as the Board receded from active banking, to the management) was immediately apparent and the flow of information and advice went in both directions. But if the Committee were to represent the Bank in the City they had on occasion to defend it; before defending the Bank, however, they would insist on their opinions being heard and, in some cases, attended to.

As the Bank became better known, the Bank's London Managers could, to a greater extent, speak for themselves. Nevertheless the Committee was in London what the Board was becoming in Hong Kong, a guardian for the shareholders, the ultimate referee. The difference was that the Board spoke for the Bank by right, the Committee only by proxy. Yet as a means of contact between the London Office and the City it remained valuable.

The next stage was a resurgence of the London Committee's importance due to the Hongkong Bank's increased role in the London capital market as its China lending operations became of international significance. It is clear, as previous chapters have stated, that Sir Ewen Cameron and Sir Charles Addis referred to the Committee rather than Hong Kong many of the details relative to the issue of major loans, details which would normally be referred to a board of directors.

Not only the principal functions but also the composition of the London Committee and its relationship to the London Managers were changing, partly as a result of the developments listed but partly, and quite independently, by chance factors and decisions of the Board in Hong Kong. In 1889 the retirement of David McLean and his acceptance of the Board's offer of a seat put a former staff member on the London Committee; the return of William Keswick placed a former Bank Chairman on the Committee. And the Board confirmed the former decision by resolving that representation on the Committee by former staff was desirable.

With the appointment of Jackson as a permanent and salaried Chairman of the London Consultative Committee on his retirement from Hong Kong in 1902, a new dimension was introduced – the Committee now seemed to have a permanence and could therefore assume authority verging on the executive in London, if permitted to do so. Writers as well as financiers would see a 'chairman' on the one hand and 'managers' on the other; if they equated the former with the chairman of a joint-stock bank, there would be problems of status for the Hongkong Bank's London Manager or even for its distant Chief Manager and Board, problems minimized while the Managers were men of the calibre of Cameron, Addis, and, later, Stabb.

There was, however, an opposite problem. If the Committee were 'loaded' with old staff members, however capable they had been as bankers, the Committee would lose its independence and possibly its purpose. With a dominant Jackson and two Hongkong Bank retirees, there was a division in the membership which, while standard on an executive board of directors, was unsuitable for what was, after all, primarily an advisory body of City experts.

This led to the arguments relative to the seating of J.R.M. Smith and again, although with more reason, of A.M. Townsend. The latter's argument for membership was based on 'face'; even he had to accept that he had little in the way of independent advice based on City experience to offer. Thus despite the Board's previously expressed views that a retired member of the Bank staff – preferably, as in the case of Sir Ewen Cameron, the former senior London Manager – be appointed to the London Committee and despite the precedent of J.R.M. Smith's appointment on retirement, Addis successfully blocked the immediate appointment of A.M. Townsend, the Chief Manager's father-in-law, when Townsend retired in 1912. 'One hates wounding the feelings of an old servant of the Bank,' Addis wrote in his diary, 'but from the Bank's point of view he would be of no use to management.'[3] Smith and Jackson were already members and Townsend would add little or nothing. In this Addis was supported by Carl Meyer, and Jackson certainly did not disapprove.

When Sir Thomas Jackson died in 1915 an opportunity was created for reconsideration of the Committee's composition. The middle of a Great War is not the best time for dispassionate deliberation; nevertheless the alternatives were considered.

Charles Addis proposed to the Chief Manager, Newton Stabb, that the Committee be reorganized with himself as permanent Chairman. His exact recommendations have to be inferred from Stabb's reply, but it would appear as if Addis still expected to remain a member of the staff, unlike Jackson, and to retain the senior London managership. Underlying this was his desire to be free from the routine – and also of H.D.C. Jones, whose appointment as junior London Manager he had resisted from the first.[4]

Stabb rejected Addis's proposals as impractical under the existing circumstances, shortage of available senior staff, and on grounds of policy. Stabb wanted the Committee to remain independent not only for the sake of the Committee but also because he wished all executive authority to remain clearly in the Bank and subject to the Chief Manager; he sensed that with Addis as a virtually full-time Chairman while still a member of the staff, the Committee, given Addis's strong position and the importance of London, would tend to become executive, perhaps threatening the authority of the Board in Hong Kong. At best the Committee would be advising Addis as its Chairman rather than the Board of Directors through the London management or, more realistically, Stabb through Addis.

Table 10.3 *The Hongkong and Shanghai Banking Corporation*
London Consultative Committee, membership, 1914–1918[a]

1914	
Sir Thomas Jackson, Bart, Chairman	
Director, Westminster Bank, and formerly Chief Manager, HSBC −1915	
Sir Carl Meyer, Bart	*company chairman*[b] −1916
William G. Rathbone	*director, P&O SN Co.* −1919
J. R. M. Smith	*formerly Chief Manager, HSBC* −1918
Henry Keswick	*director, Matheson and Co.* −1919
Changes in the Committee:	
1915	
Sir Thomas Jackson, died	
1916	
A. M. Townsend, appointed	*retired London Manager* −1932
Sir Carl Meyer, resigned	
1918	
J. R. M. Smith, died	
The Committee at the end of 1918:	
William G. Rathbone, Henry Keswick, and A. M. Townsend	

[a]   See Table 1.2, p. 28, for 1903–1914 membership.
[b]   Carl Meyer was no longer on the Board of the Pekin Syndicate.

Stabb went further. In February 1916, with the approval of the Board, he appointed A.M. Townsend to replace Jackson although as an ordinary member not as a designated Chairman, and he did this without consulting either Addis or the London Committee. He had, he wrote, misplaced the previous correspondence and could not conceive of any valid reason why Townsend's membership would not be acceptable.[5] The London Committee 'acquiesced', and Addis professed himself glad that the 'painful business' had been settled.[6] Townsend was aware of the Committee's feelings, but accepted; he at last had been fairly dealt with.[7]

And for good measure Stabb made a strong defence of Jones and urged Addis 'as a personal favour' to ensure that the two joint Managers 'pull together'. As one concession Stabb, recognizing the increasing burden of Addis's position, suggested an enhanced role for Murray Stewart, who was at that time paid entirely by funds from the Consortium.[8]

Stabb would have preferred Smith's taking over the chairmanship of the Committee, presumably with an agreement similar to Jackson's, although this is not explicitly stated. But Smith, as expected, refused; he had never fully recovered his health after his return from Hong Kong.

The Chief Manager had asserted his authority and the London Consultative Committee had been left independent in an effort to assure its continued advisory function and pre-empt the possibility of a misunderstanding of its role. There is, it must be recorded, no evidence that the Committee had ever harboured ambitious intentions or overstepped the role assigned it at any particular time. Rather the problems were latent and existed only in the context of City life and theoretical possibilities.

In July 1915 Sir Carl Meyer, suffering from insomnia and a general breakdown in health, had retired to a rest home, his spirit broken by the wave of anti-German feeling which included British subjects of German origin.[9] (His son was then serving with British forces at the Front.) In September 1916 the Chief Manager, Newton Stabb, wrote to Meyer 'suggesting' that he retire in view of the sentiment against 'Germans, even naturalized Germans'. Meyer showed the letter to Addis, who recorded the fact without comment in his diary.[10] In November Meyer resigned from the Committee, 'a painful business', saying good-bye to all members except Addis. 'Perhaps he thinks I did it!' Addis wrote.[11]

In consequence of Stabb's decision, Meyer's resignation, and other wholly unforeseen circumstances the London Consultative Committee virtually disappeared. Henry Keswick had accepted a commission and was rarely able to attend meetings. With Meyer gone, the decline in W.G. Rathbone's health, the absence on active service of Keswick, and the death of Smith in 1918, the Committee had reached a critical state; in fact the Attendance Book shows that there were rarely more than two members present, one of whom would be Townsend, and often he signed the book alone.

On the recommendation of Addis and with the agreement of the Board, the Committee was reinvigorated in 1919 with Addis as *ex-officio* Chairman. On the eve of his retirement as Chief Manager in 1920, Stabb himself would make recommendations reversing his wartime decisions; Addis would eventually become the paid full-time Chairman – but only upon his own retirement. In 1933 under very different conditions, the senior London Manager again became *ex-officio* Chairman of the Committee.

During the last years of the War, however, the London Committee of the Hongkong Bank was for all practical purposes inoperative.

THE CHRONOLOGY, 1914–1918

The setting

Overwhelming all other factors were the rise of silver and the extreme fluctuations in exchange which accompanied this phenomenon. The principal cause would appear to have been the continued and indeed increasing demand for silver for coinage in countries which, like India, were on a gold exchange standard. The British Government was finding consumer resistance to the one-pound Bank of England note. The increasing reliance

Table 10.4 *The price of silver and the Hong Kong exchange, 1914–1918*

Year	Price per fine ounce of silver	$=x$ s/d^a	% change in 6	12 months
1872 June	60.0	4/6	–	
1877 October	54.6	3/11$\frac{1}{8}$^{b}	–	
1901 December	25.8	1/10$\frac{1}{4}$	–	
1914 June	26.3	1/10$\frac{5}{8}$	–	
1914 December	23.3	1/9$\frac{1}{8}$	–6.6	–8.9
1915 June	22.9	1/9$\frac{5}{16}$	0.9	–
1915 December	27.1	1/11	7.9	8.9
1916 June	30.0	2/1$\frac{1}{8}$	9.2	–
1916 December	37.0	2/4$\frac{3}{4}$	14.4	25.0
1917 June	39.9	2/6$\frac{1}{4}$	5.2	–
1917 December	43.5	3/0	19.0	25.2
1918 June	49.3	3/3$\frac{3}{4}$	9.0	–
1918 December	48.8	3/4$\frac{1}{4}$	2.5	11.8
1919 December	76.0	4/10$\frac{1}{2}$	–	45.3

Silver: 1914 (June) –1918 (Dec.)	85.6
1872 (June) –1919 (Dec.)	26.7
Exchange: 1914 (June) –1918 (Dec.)	77.9
1872 (June) –1919 (Dec.)	8.3

^{a} Rate quoted in HSBC annual reports.
^{b} Temporary high.

on fiduciary issues, especially in the United States, did not relieve the demand for coins, and as silver prices began to rise, certain countries, including India and the United States, imposed controls on the export of the metal. China became an important source of monetary silver, but with her export trade encouraged by new demands from the United States and her imports curtailed by shortages of shipping, silver could only be obtained with higher exchange rates, which accordingly fluctuated on an upward trend to meet an increasing but erratic demand.

As silver rose 85.6% between June 1914 and December 1918, the Hong Kong exchange rate rose by 77.9% from 1s:9⅛d to 3s:4¼d. A year later the Bank's accounts would be based on an exchange of 4s:10½d, an even higher rate than the pre-1874 rate of 4s:6d (see Table 10.4).

The problem is to determine how the Bank reacted to this development. Unfortunately it is at this point that the fact of the missing 1916–1918 Board Minute Book becomes of importance; without it the question is extremely difficult to resolve. This much is apparent from the published accounts – the

Bank maintained the dollar value of the sterling reserves as written down to within their market value and converted at the arbitrary book rate of 2s:0d, a rate which had been set as a conservative figure in the days of depreciating silver.

There is also a feeling that neither Stabb nor the Board expected that the higher prices of silver would prevail; certainly this became generally accepted in 1919/20 when silver reached a modern high of 89½d in February 1920. Not that anyone necessarily anticipated the 12d silver price of exactly eleven years later; it was simply that the extreme highs could not be sustained and, therefore, the Bank, ever-conscious of its sterling image and of the consequent importance of the sound positioning of reserves (broadly interpreted, that is, not only funds officially designated as 'reserves') as between gold and silver areas, decided to lean towards a stronger sterling position.

The increase in the sterling value of shareholders' funds, after allowing for the 'real' increase, the growth in terms of the dollar unit-of-account, was considerably less than the percentage increase in the exchange rate. From this alone one would conclude that the Bank in this period did not make a determined speculation in anticipation of a later decline in the price of silver.

In considering the Bank's overall reserve policy and interpreting the figures in the tables, it should be noted that the dollar value of the sterling Reserve Fund (narrowly defined) was kept at $15 million, although allocations from net earnings were transferred at year-end 1916, 1917, and 1918 to augment the silver reserves. This does not mean that the Bank was anticipating a further increase in the price of silver. As stated above, funds had been transferred to the sterling reserves from *gross* as opposed to *net* earnings and the sterling reserves had thus been affected, first, by writing down their sterling value and then buying securities to offset this decrease. The adjustment was not complete because the reserves were valued at 2s:0d. The reserve policy retained a modified 'even keel' tradition. But as suggested by the terms 'broadly defined' and 'narrowly defined' the story is not yet complete; the Bank held sterling securities other than those in the Reserve Fund and thus the overall position is still undetermined.

In consequence, the annual accounts become difficult to put into a trend. Such key indicators as total assets, cash/assets ratios, and total deposits are sensitive to the relative value of sterling and dollars, which was changing at a rate which the Bank could not immediately counter and which resulted, therefore, in arbitrary totals at any particular moment, including December 31.

The second major factor affecting the performance of the Hongkong Bank was the financial arrangements resulting from the War itself. Thus the decision whether to rediscount or hold bills was affected by London interest rates, and these were controlled by the Bank of England in the context of overall control of British financial resources. The Hongkong Bank in London was part of the London market and as such conformed, in the tradition of the City, to the prevailing financial policy.

The Bank's annual reports tend to be bullish relative to China's potential, although the death of Yuan Shih-k'ai, the attempt to restore the Manchus in 1917, and the rise of the *tu-chuns* or 'warlords' were seen as adverse factors. Indeed, the detailed discussion of Chinese affairs, which Nationalists would come later to find objectionable – especially when frankly critical – was a new dimension to the report and illustrates the Addis touch throughout.

Particular reference is made to the increased revenue from the Salt Gabelle; to this extent the focus is on China's credit-worthiness. The rise in the exchange was favourable to China as a debtor nation and a surplus developed in the Customs and Salt accounts; outstanding short-term debts were paid off. The entry of China into the Great War on the side of the Allies and the consequent adjustment of Boxer Indemnity payments, including suspension of payment for five years, permitted China to withdraw now surplus funds from the loan-service accounts, after disputes with the representatives of the Powers in Peking in which the Hongkong Bank argued for China's right to withdraw. These released funds were used in part to improve the position of the modern banking sector, including a rescue of the Bank of China and the beginning of a limited currency reform.

The Bank was unable, however, to take advantage of China's improved credit-worthiness. The old Consortium was in disarray, the capital markets unavailable for China loans, and the Japanese, with their export surplus, were anxious to exploit their unique position by imposing their financial authority on China. There was, however, much discussion. These developments, along with the fear of increased bureaucratic control in Europe post-war, were also topics covered as integral parts of the Bank's annual reports; they were part of the setting in which the Bank operated during the Great War.

From the annual accounts (Tables 10.5, 10.6, and 10.7)

'London', Sir Charles Addis wrote in his diary on August 5, 1914, 'is in a turmoil. There was a queue of people last Friday [July 31] at the Bank of England demanding gold for notes . . .'[12]

At the outbreak of war the Chief Manager, Newton Stabb, was in Britain on leave; Stephen was acting in Hong Kong, and J.D. Smart was acting for Stephen in Shanghai. Behind Stephen was A.H. Barlow, the Hong Kong Sub-Manager; he had ten years yet to wait for his own appointment as Chief Manager.

The day before war was declared, Stephen, as noted earlier, had cabled Stabb that in his opinion the danger spot was London, adding, 'I think in view of gravity of situation you should resume charge here and I proceed Shanghai unless in your opinion your presence more necessary in London in general

Table 10.5 *The Hongkong and Shanghai Banking Corporation*
Key indicators, 1914–1918

(in millions of dollars except as indicated)

Year	Assets $	= £	Reserves[a] (i) + (ii)		Net earnings	To reserves	To dividends[e]		Rate $1=xs/d
						(semi-annual)			
1914 June	419.8	39.6	15.0	18.0	3.5	0.35	@£2:3[b]	2.7	1/0⅝
						(annual)			
1914 December	435.2	38.3	15.0	18.0	7.3	0.00	@£4:11[c]	6.0	1/9⅛
1915 December	436.2	41.8	15.0	18.0	6.9	0.00	@£4:11	5.9	1/11
1916 December	402.8	48.2	15.0	18.5	7.1	0.50	@£4:16	5.8	2/4¾
1917 December	418.9	62.7	15.0	19.5	6.7	1.00	@£5:6	4.5	3/0
1918 December	432.0	72.4	15.0	21.0	6.6	1.50	@£5:18[d]	4.3	3/4¼

Shareholders' funds (1914 June) = $50,340,000 (@1/10⅝=£4,746,000)   Change 8.3%
Shareholders' funds (1918 December) = $54,530,000 (@3/4¼ =£9,145,000)   (92.7%)
(i) silver reserves   (ii) gold reserves·

[a] The figure for the Reserve Fund *includes* the amount transferred at the end of the period as approved by the shareholders at the subsequent meeting.
[b] Initial semi-annual rate of £2:3s but *not* tax paid, and the three shillings was designed as compensation. Add bonus where applicable.
[c] Quoted on an annual basis, i.e. an interim and a year-end regular dividend equal to £4:6s plus bonus at year-end. Note that the Hong Kong dollar value of the interim dividend is calculated at a rate appropriate to the date as shown in Table 10.5A.
[d] The final dividend was increased to £2:5s. The interim dividend was unchanged at £2:3s for a total of £4:8s regular plus a bonus. For 1918 the bonus was £1:10s.
[e] For the details of dividends see Table 10.5A.

interests HSBC.'[13] The Head Office of the Hongkong Bank was in Hong Kong; the Bank's Chief Manager returned to take charge.

During the first months of the War the Bank devoted considerable effort to clearing up the details of financial transactions connected with trade affected by the hostilities, and in the Chairman's annual statement for *1914* the need for contingencies and a strong reserve position in view of continued uncertainty was naturally stressed. Consequently the sterling securities were, as previously noted, written down to within market price and their value in sterling maintained by the purchase of additional securities from current earnings; at the same time $1.25 million was placed in unappropriated contingencies accounts. But the semi-annual dividend was maintained at £2:3s plus a year-end bonus of 5s:0d for a total payout in 1914 of £4:11s per share. As exchange rose the sterling-quoted dividend meant a lower dollar payout for shareholders in the East; the bonus was to counter, in part, their disquiet.

For the impact of changing exchange rates on the cost of the dividend, see Table 10.5A.

Table 10.5A *The Hongkong and Shanghai Banking Corporation Dividends, 1914–1918*

Year	Interim £ @	= $	Final £ @	= $	Bonus[a] £	= $	Total £	= $	Total payout £ (millions)	= $	Total payout %	Total dividend as % of book value £	$ (per cent)
1914	2:03 $1/10\tfrac{5}{8}$	22.81	2:03 $1/9\tfrac{1}{8}$	24.43	0:05	2.84	4:11	50.08	0.55	6.01	82	12.2	11.8
1915	2:03 $1/9\tfrac{5}{16}$	24.21	2:03 $1/11$	22.44	0:05	2.61	4:11	49.26	0.55	5.91	86	11.1	11.5
1916	2:03 $2/1\tfrac{1}{8}$	20.54	2:03 $2/4\tfrac{3}{4}$	17.95	0:10	4.17	4:16	42.66	0.58	5.12	82	9.3	9.9
1917	2:03 $2/6\tfrac{1}{4}$	17.06	2:03 $3/0$	14.33	1:00	6.67	5:06	38.06	0.64	4.57	67	8.0	8.6
1918	2:03 $3/3\tfrac{1}{4}$	13.15	2:05 $3/4\tfrac{1}{4}$	13.42	1:10	8.94	5:18	35.51	0.71	4.26	65	7.7	7.8

Bold face = $ equivalent.

[a] Bonus is at same rate of exchange as final dividend.

After these allocations from Profit and Loss Account had been made there were no funds remaining for transfer to the published reserves, although an unallocated balance in this account of $2.6 million was carried forward.

The news of the outbreak of hostilities caused a run on the banks in Hong Kong and Shanghai, but depositors, after an initial period when they withdrew silver (and then redeposited it for want of a safekeeping place) demanded the right to take their funds in banknotes. In the context of the Bank's obligation to deposit silver dollar for dollar against an increase in the 'excess' note issue, the Bank requested and was granted permission to consider its Shanghai silver reserves, which would be placed under the custody of the Consul-General, as part of the 'backing' of the excess issue. This development is reflected in the larger total note issue of $27.2 million at the end of 1914 (see Table 10.6).

In Japan the shipping problem cut back on exports and the balance of trade turned sharply against her. The Hongkong Bank found itself unable to cover its Japanese branches' oversold position in sterling, its resources strained by other war-related financial requirements. The solution was to ship Chinese and/or Japanese gold to North America, despite war risks and unfavourable crossrates; there it could be sold, at a cost, against sterling. In consequence the Bank's bullion 'in hand and in transit' rose from $3.4 million at the end of June 1914 to $5.4 million at the end of the year and $7.6 million at the end of 1915, but this included gold shipments from Shanghai. There was some concern at this point that the Germans were using commercial channels for the shipment of gold purchased in China from Boxer Indemnity and other official payments; the Hongkong Bank, in common with other banks, was shown to be exporting more gold than it had apparently purchased on the market, and the business was commented on adversely by the British authorities in view of the possibility the enemy was being aided.[14]

Meanwhile in Hong Kong the Bank was carrying, or 'dry-nursing' as one Government despatch put it, many of the trading hongs which were in temporary difficulties. Their problems were to a large extent caused by the initial delays following the banking moratorium declared in Britain at the outbreak of the War, by lost documents, and diverted cargoes. These matters took time to sort out.[15]

The Bank's policy of carrying constituents is reflected in the accounts. The consequent difficulty in interpreting the figures is illustrated by noting the considerable increase in bills receivable, which would suggest an increase in trade financed. But the end-1914 figure is compiled on the basis of figures from the branches which closed their books on different dates and at exchange rates open to discussion. The payments moratorium was still in effect when London closed its books – the figure is, therefore, non-comparable.

Another complexity arises from the fact that the differentiation between

(in millions)

Table 10.6 *The Hongkong and Shanghai Banking Corporation*
Cash, selected balance sheet items, and ratios, 1914–1918

Year	Assets $	Index 1914=100	Cash and bullion $[a]	C/A ratio	Net E $	E as % of A	Excess notes $[b]	Deposits total $	Loans etc. $	Loan/D ratio	Bills rec. $	Bills pay. $
1914 December	435.2	100	97.4	0.22	7.3	1.68	12.2	329.3	141.5	43	150.9	17.4
1915 December	436.2	100	99.9	0.23	6.9	1.58	10.6	329.7	133.5	40	150.7	20.9
1916 December	402.8	93	69.1	0.17	7.1	1.76	14.3	303.1	145.5	48	143.7	11.9
1917 December	418.9	96	91.7	0.22	6.7	1.60	9.9	314.0	131.6	42	146.1	17.4
1918 December	432.0	99	80.0	0.19	6.6	1.53	10.3	341.2	151.8	44	154.8	5.7
1919 December	425.8	98	82.1	0.19	7.4	1.74	15.5	337.2	154.7	46	154.6	4.4

[a] Includes $15.5 million against the note issue   E = earnings   D = deposits
[b] Add $15m for total note issue   A = assets   Bills rec. = BR = bills receivable
                                                     Loans etc. = Bills discounted, loans, and credits

Bills pay = BP = bills payable, incl. 'drafts on London Bankers and short sight drawings on our London Office against bills receivable and bullion shipments'.

Table 10.7 *The Hongkong and Shanghai Banking Corporation
Earnings and share prices, 1914–1918*

Year	(i) Net earnings (million)	(ii) Dividend/ share £:s	(iii) Book value $	(iv) £	(v) Share price London	(vi) M/B ratio £	(vii) Rate $1=xs/d
1914 December	7.3	4:11	424	37.3	80	2.14	1/9⅛
1915 December	6.9	4:11	427	40.9	84	2.05	1/11
1916 December	7.1	4:16	433	51.4	78	1.52	2/4¾
1917 December	6.7	5:6	441	65.0	84	1.29	3/0
1918 December	6.6	5:18	454	74.1	103	1.39	3/4¼

(i)   Net annual earnings in millions of Hong Kong dollars.
(ii) Annual dividends declared in pounds sterling.
(iii) Book value = shareholders' funds, i.e. paid-up capital + reserves (including amounts paid in from net earnings) + retained profits, divided by the number of shares outstanding.
(iv) Column (iii) converted into pounds sterling at rate in annual report.
(v)   London prices for shares on the London register.
(vi) Equivalent to (v) divided by (iv).
(vii) The rate used in the annual Hongkong Bank accounts.

'gold' and 'silver' liabilities had lost its full significance since accounts in traditional silver standard countries, Siam and the Straits Settlements for example, had for some time been related closely to sterling and yet continued to be listed in the 'silver' category. Rather than redefine the status of each agency, the Board decided to eliminate the distinction from the published abstract of accounts.

The *1914* accounts carried the signature of A.C. Hynes as acting Chief Accountant. He was the first to hold this post who would rise to the chief managership, a position he achieved in 1927 after the relatively brief tenures of Stephen and Barlow.

The end-*1915* accounts state that the Bank's entire Sterling Reserve Fund investments of £1.5 million were in 4½% War Loan bonds at par and exchange of 2s:0d, which rate was still above the 1s:11d rate used in the accounts. Although no funds were transferred from net earnings to augment the reserves, $1.2 million had been transferred from gross profits to offset the fall in price of the Bank's and London Office's sterling investments and Indian Government rupee paper, while another $1.5 million had been transferred to the Contingencies Account. The balance carried forward exceeded $3 million. The dividend, as denominated in sterling, remained unchanged.

It was in the annual address covering these activities that the Chairman refuted the allegation that the Bank was or had been under German influence; the relevant section has been quoted above. The Chairman also detailed the contacts the Bank had been required to make with the Deutsch-Asiatische Bank in Peking in connection with the various international loan agreements.

The Hongkong Bank prospered financially during *1916*, and, despite the several allocations necessary to maintain various reserve accounts at book level, was able to double the bonus from 5s to 10s for reasons already noted and to augment the silver reserves.

The Board continued the practice of quoting sterling reserves at 2s:0d despite the exchange of 2s:4¾d on the balance sheet, but in the absence of the Board's Minutes the reason for this must be assumed to rest on the fact that exchange was already falling, temporarily as it turned out, when the accounts were brought to the Board, and that there was in any case an argument (although not a particularly sound one) in favour of a stable rate for this particular account. It is true that the Bank had more than an offset in its unallocated Contingencies Account, but this particular item is overvalued in dollars. The published accounts indicate this fact quite clearly.

Transfers from gross profits were again necessary to offset the write-down of sterling securities to within market value. Building projects in Calcutta and Hankow argued for the transfer of $750,000 from net profits to write down the Premises Account, and this the shareholders approved at the annual meeting in February 1917.

The year *1916* was marked by the increased export of silver from China to meet the problem of financing India's exports and coinage requirements. This is reflected in the particularly low cash and bullion position of the Bank as shown in Table 10.6.

The issuing by the Indian Government of 'Special Councils' had virtually ceased; this practice had enabled banks requiring funds in India to pay for exports to purchase Special Councils, defined as bills issued by the India Council which were purchased by banks in sterling against a deposit to their credit in rupees. (The impact of this change of procedure will be seen in the case study of the Colombo branch below.) With this simple facility eliminated, the alternative was the shipment of silver bullion to India. The silver could at first be obtained from China, but as China's exports were in increasing demand and with China's currency needs growing, the expectations were for an increased price of silver and with it higher exchange rates on China.

China joined the War in 1917 on the side of the Allies.

Net earnings for *1917* showed a small decline in part due to the squeeze in London between the rate of discount for three months' bills and the rate for call money, the former being closely related to the rate for Treasury bills and therefore artificially low to minimize the cost of Government borrowing. Another impact of the War was the increased level of bills payable, a consequence of slow mails and lengthened time on the water rather than increased trade. Nevertheless the Bank was able to write $1 million off Premises Account, transfer $1 million to silver reserves, maintain the value of the Sterling Reserve Fund, which, although written down to 95, was still on the books at an exchange of 2s:0d, compared to the 3s:0d rate being used for the balance of the accounts.

In addition the Board approved an increase in the bonus dividend at the end of the year to £1. This was due in part to pressure from Eastern shareholders who saw the dollar value of their dividends declining; the decision was apparently not unanimously approved. At the annual meeting of shareholders A.H. Harris, the shareholder seconding the Chairman's motion, noted that some might have preferred that the funds be transferred to reserves and commented, 'If our friend the Chief Manager happens to be among that number I hope that he can feel some compensation for his disappointment by the very general approval of the shareholders with this action.'[16]

Apparently the Chief Manager, Stabb, had been overruled.

The controversial one-dollar note issue, which had been increased with Treasury approval to a limit of $350,000 in 1912, was further increased to $400,000, subject to unconditional withdrawal. The higher limit was finally granted in July 1917, not on its own merit, but rather as a counter to the competitive threat of the one-dollar issue of the Banco Nacional Ultramarino in Macau. The 1% banknote tax was waived for the duration of the War. By the end of the War the one-dollar note issue limit had been raised to $1.2 million.[17]

During *1918* the British Government was able to borrow at 1¼% less than previously by lowering the interest paid by the Bank of England on bank deposits and restricting banks to 3% maximum on their customers' deposits. There was, however, a special dispensation for Eastern banks; current deposits might be renewed at existing rates of interest. The result was a further profit squeeze, and the Bank's net earnings totalled $6.6 million. In considering this figure, however, it should be noted that unpublished profits before allocation were in the order of $7.2 million, from which $1.25 million had been already transferred to Contingencies Account and $150,000 allocated to cover the depreciation of investments before publishing the net earnings.

From published net earnings $1.5 million was transferred to Silver Reserves and a further $750,000 to Premises Account; this latter was in excess of expenditures and marked preparations for the already planned new Shanghai building. The regular year-end dividend was raised to £1:5s and the bonus to £1:10s, for a total payout per share of £5:18s. Although this was 12s:0d in excess of the payout in 1917, the dollar equivalent, given the rise in the exchange to 3s:4¼d, was smaller. That the Board felt able to grant the unusually generous bonus was possibly due to the end of the War and to the consequent elimination of wartime risks. The Bank ended the War with a strong inner reserve position of at least $10.8 million, an enhanced published Reserve Fund, and $3.3 million carried forward on Profit and Loss Account.

Special events

The continuity of events in the years 1914–1918 is provided by the War itself and by the modified routine of business which underlies the special events described above. But in times of war there are special and often unexpected demands, perhaps disruptions, in which the resources of the Bank are especially tested. The following are selected incidents in the history of the Bank at war.

Gun-running – out of China

Britain was not fully prepared for the Great War. But, by jingo, the Bank gave the men and it gave the money, too. It didn't have the guns but was asked to get them.

Two proposals to obtain small arms were put to Charles Addis as London Manager of the Hongkong Bank: the first involved conversion of an empty building in Hong Kong into an arms factory and transport of the products via the Trans-Siberian railway, the second was a scheme for smuggling rifles out of neutral China. On the first Addis merely commented that the scheme suggested the Government were preparing for a long war. On the second he cabled Stabb in early 1915 requesting him to ascertain whether he could obtain a 'large quantity of Mauser or other modern rifles and not less than 500 rounds per rifle'.[18] Addis added the caution that Stabb should not contact the central Government of China but work through the 'Viceroys', the provincial authorities, and through Landale and C.H. Ross of Jardine's.

This was a dangerous scheme in view of China's neutrality and the likelihood of agents leaking information; Stabb cabled to ask whether it was worth the risk. He was informed that the War Office knew the risk before it made the request; consequently Stabb initiated enquiries, the purport of which reached the Legation in Peking through Hillier; Jordan, the British Minister, contacted the Foreign Office in London. The War Office had, however, neglected to mention the plan to the Foreign Office, and Addis was summoned; for a brief period he was in a difficult position.

Meanwhile Stabb had located 26,000 old-style Muratas and was quoted a price FOB Tokyo, but the War Office held out for modern rifles. In February 1915 he finally cabled Addis that the Bank could obtain 16,000 Mauser rifles, 1888 vintage (apparently modern), 7.9mm, with delivery off Saddle Island

(Ma-an lieh-tao), outside Hangchow Bay (see insert, Map 2).[19] The business was concluded satisfactorily later in the year with arrangements finalized for the delivery of £2 million worth of rifles and machine guns – 'grand stroke of business for both Governments, also for HSBC'.[20]

So much for gun-running *out* of China. For the less popular gun-running *into* China see Volume III.

Relations with the Treasury

During 1915 Charles Addis was involved with the terms of renewed Treasury Chest business -- in competing with other banks for official remittance business the Hongkong Bank in Shanghai was always successful, to the point that the Chartered and Yokohama Specie Banks, the main competitors, refused to bid, thus undermining the Treasury system. An agreement covering Hong Kong Treasury business was concluded in June, and in June and July standard agreements were signed for Treasury Chest business in the Straits Settlements and China respectively. The provision requiring the Treasury Chest officer to respect commercial custom in Hong Kong, in particular the premium on banknotes, was included.[21] This settled the matter until new negotiations were completed at the end of 1919.

The Hongkong Bank and the Chartered Bank were appointed to receive funds under certain provisions of the 'Trading with the Enemy (Amendment) Regulations, 1915'.[22]

On March 22, 1915, Addis received the Treasury's warrant dated March 19 permitting the Bank to open branches and/or agencies in Harbin (1915), Vladivostok (1918), Haiphong (1922), Kedah (Sungei Patani, 1922), Tokyo (1924), Nanking (1947), Changsha, Changchun, Delhi (1982), and Karachi (1982). The list was merely permissive; the actual year of opening (if any) of the new agencies is shown in parenthesis.

The list suggests Addis's assumption of an extensive China network, but the Bank specifically rejected the suggestion of a Changsha branch, despite railway finance, and it opened in Nanking only after World War II. In early 1918 G.G.S. Forsyth was sent to Chefoo and Chungking, cities on earlier Treasury lists, and his reports provide excellent surveys of the local economies and their banking potential; the return trip down the Yangtze was eventful in that his steamer was subjected to small-arms fire and the Captain killed, but his recommendation against a branch in Chungking was based firmly on business considerations.

Following Forsyth's suggestions, the Board of Directors did authorize a sub-agency in Chefoo in 1922. The 1918 opening of the Vladivostok branch is a separate story.

The Bank did not attempt geographical expansion in India until it took over the business of the Mercantile Bank in the late 1970s.

During the War there was considerable discussion relative to the Hongkong Bank's note issue: (i) the size of the one-dollar issue, originally limited to $3½ lacs and (ii) the security, specifically the possibility of releasing urgently required silver against the deposit of additional approved securities. The one-dollar note issue was enlarged on two occasions but the discussions on the latter suggestion, referred to by Stabb as 'criminal folly', were inconclusive.[23]

There is evidence in the Colonial Office files that the Hongkong Bank continued to advise and assist on such varied matters as subsidiary coinage and Hong Kong Government finance relative to the War.[24]

Bullion movements – gold
Throughout the War the Hongkong Bank was involved in exceptional bullion movements arising from the dislocation of trade, the consequent disruptive imbalances of accounts requiring settlement in bullion, and the continued demand for silver for coinage, especially in India.

In late 1914 the focus was on covering Japan's purchases of sterling by shipping gold to North America, described above.

Japanese exports to Siberia were paid for by the Russians in roubles sold in Europe, converted into sterling, and available to the Japanese for the purchase of gold for shipment to Japan. The Hongkong Bank was involved in this business, but, by agreement with the Treasury, limited its shipments to prevent compounding the factors which were threatening to force the Bank of England to suspend specie payments.[25]

Also in December 1915 the Hongkong Bank was permitted to assist the Java Bank in Batavia to obtain gold from the United States.

By mid-1916 the gold flow back to the East appeared to be increasing and the Bank of England requested British banks not to become involved; gold shipments were for England only and Chinese purchases were to be discouraged. A.G. Stephen complied but complained that other banks remained in the trade whereas the Hongkong Bank was not permitted by London Office to complete a contract already concluded; it had to be passed to the International Banking Corporation.[26]

In July of 1917 in fact Stephen was acknowledging a request from Addis for shipment of gold bullion from China. The Chinese had been buying gold and, as the market tightened, Stephen expected they would have to sell, but he could not guarantee the quantity.[27] During the War Britain nevertheless was able to increase her gold reserves from £40 to £107 million.

At the request of the Foreign Office the Bank took responsibility for the transshipment to Australia of 1,000 boxes of Russian raw gold on instructions received in May 1918.[28]

But the Bank's main business was in silver.

Bullion movements – silver from the Philippines

The initial wartime demands for silver bullion came not from China but from the exceptional requirements for financing military operations in the Middle East and East Africa, coupled with the underlying demand for silver for coinage in England and coinage and hoarding in India. In its search to meet these demands, the Hongkong Bank learned of surplus silver coins in the Philippines.

The first operation would appear to have resulted from a visit to Manila in late 1915 by A.G. Stephen, who had been the Bank's Manila Manager from 1906 to 1909. He was informed that the Bureau of the Treasury was intending to dispose of silver coins with a face value of Pesos 20 million. The coins were shipped to Shanghai where the face value of the coins being greater than their intrinsic value, they were defaced by two specially purchased machines as part of the agreement, the operation being supervised by Philippine officials. The silver was then shipped to Bombay.[29]

In a follow-up operation in May 1916, Newton Stabb in Hong Kong underbid offers for a further $Gold3 million in coins. This time the coins were shipped to Hong Kong at which point the Hongkong Bank was paid by the India Council to the credit of the Hong Kong office's account with the Bank in London for just over 4 million ounces at 35d an ounce. Addis explained to Stabb that he would then debit Hong Kong and credit the Philippine Government account with Chase National Bank in New York at the rate of $Gold4.76 to the pound sterling. 'We have secured exchange on New York for £500,000 of the £608,288:8s:9d,' he wrote, 'which balance is at risk of Council.'[30]

Bullion movements – silver to London

The British Government requested Addis to find silver; the Hongkong Bank delivered. In the three months before June 20, 1916, the Bank's Shanghai office sold £3.5 million of silver bullion to London and A.G. Stephen wrote to Addis that the Government must consider him a 'silver King' and a 'factor to be reckoned with to produce so much in a short time'.[31]

The circumstances were exceptional. The demand for silver raised its price on the Shanghai market, Hong Kong was unable to remit to Shanghai thus driving up the price of the Shanghai tael. Consequently, it became profitable to finance North China's exports to South China by shipping silver – bullion, old coins, cut dollars etc. – to Shanghai rather than remitting through the

21 The Hamburg Managers.
(*top*) Julius Brüssel (1889–1905).
(*below*) F. T. Koelle (1905–1920).

ABSTRACT OF ASSETS AND LIABILITIES, HONGKONG & SHANGHAI BANKING CORPORATION,
31st December, 1918.

LIABILITIES.

PAID-UP CAPITAL,	$15,000,000.00
STERLING RESERVE FUND, £1,500,000 @ ex. 2/-,	15,000,000.00
SILVER RESERVE FUND,	19,500,000.00
MARINE INSURANCE ACCOUNT,	250,000.00

NOTES IN CIRCULATION:—
(Authorised Issue against Securities and Coin deposited with the Crown Agents for the Colonies and their Trustees,) $15,000,000.00
Additional Issue authorised by Hongkong Ordinances against Coin lodged with the Hongkong Government, ... 10,305,644.00
— 25,305,644.00

CURRENT ACCOUNTS,	235,089,857.94
FIXED DEPOSITS,	106,080,904.07

BILLS PAYABLE:—
(Including Call Loans and Short Sight Drawings on London Office), ...$ 5,125,479.89
Drafts on London Bankers, ... 574,836.09
— 5,700,315.98

ACCEPTANCES ON ACCOUNT OF CONSTITUENTS,	1,824,504.00
PROFIT AND LOSS ACCOUNT,	8,212,841.30

Liability on Bills of Exchange re-discounted, £4,673,748. 6s. 10d. of which £4,663,848. 6s. 2d. have since run off.

$431,964,067.29

ASSETS.

CASH (including $15,500,000 Coin lodged with the Hongkong Government against authorised and/or excess note circulation), ...$77,443,150.35

BULLION IN HAND AND IN TRANSIT, ... 2,543,588.61

BRITISH GOVERNMENT, INDIAN, COLONIAL AND OTHER SECURITIES, ... 21,918,123.86

STERLING RESERVE FUND INVESTMENTS, viz.:—
£1,578,947 7s. 5d. 5% War Loan 1929/47 @ 95 = £1,500,000 @ ex. 2/-, ... 15,000,000.00

BILLS DISCOUNTED, LOANS AND CREDITS,	151,796,213.59
BILLS RECEIVABLE,	154,814,717.28

LIABILITIES OF CONSTITUENTS for acceptances, per contra, ... 1,824,504.00

BANK PREMISES, ... 6,623,767.60

$431,964,067.29

GENERAL PROFIT AND LOSS ACCOUNT, HONGKONG & SHANGHAI BANKING CORPORATION,
31st December, 1918.

Dr.   **Cr.**

To INTERIM DIVIDEND:—
Paid on 12th August 1918
£2-3/- per Share on 120,000
Shares = £258,000 @ 3/3½ = ...$1,577,579.62

REMUNERATION TO DIRECTORS, ... 30,000.00

FINAL DIVIDEND:—
£2. 5/- per Share on 120,000 Shares = £270,000 at 3/4½ = ...$1,609,937.89
Bonus of £1 10s. per Share on 120,000 Shares = £180,000 at 3/4½ = ...1,073,291.93
— 2,683,229.82

TRANSFER TO SILVER RESERVE FUND,	1,500,000.00
TRANSFER TO BANK PREMISES ACCOUNT,	750,000.00
BALANCE forward to next year,	3,379,611.48
	8,212,841.30

$ 9,820,420.92

By Balance of Undivided Profits, 31st December, 1917, ...$ 3,223,238.18

Amount of Net Profits for the Year ending 31st December, 1918, after making provision for bad and doubtful debts and contingencies, deducting all Expenses and Interest paid and due, ... 6,597,182.74
— $ 9,820,420.92

$ 9,820,420.92

STERLING RESERVE FUND.

To Balance, ... £1,500,000 @ ex. 2/-, ... $15,000,000.00
(invested in 5% War Loan 1929/1947).

By Balance 31st December, 1917, £1,500,000 @ ex. 2/-, $15,000,000.00

$15,000,000.00   **$15,000,000.00**

SILVER RESERVE FUND.

To Balance, ... $21,000,000.00

By Balance 31st December, 1917, ...$19,500,000.00
Transfer from Profit & Loss Account.................. 1,500,000.00

$21,000,000.00   **$21,000,000.00**

N. J. STABB, *Chief Manager.*

H. C. SANDFORD, *Acting Chief Accountant.*

P. H. HOLYOAK,
DAVID LANDALE, } *Directors.*
J. A. PLUMMER,

We have compared the above Statement with the Books, Vouchers and Securities at the Head Office, and with the Returns from the various Branches and Agencies, (with the exception of the Hamburg Office from which no Statement of Accounts has been received since 1914) and have found the same to be correct.
With the exception of certain distant offices, where the year is closed on 31st October or 30th November, all Branch and Agency accounts are made up to 31st December.

HONGKONG, *11th February, 1919.*

F. MAITLAND,
E. A. M. WILLIAMS, A.S.A.A. } *Auditors.*

22 Abstract of assets and liabilities and other accounts, December 31, 1918. The figures clearly reflect the unusually high exchange rate. The securities held indicate the consequence of wartime investment policies.

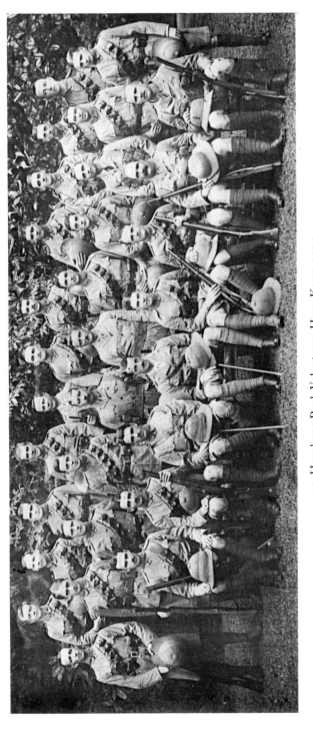

23 Hongkong Bank Volunteers, Hong Kong, 1915.
Left to right: (*back row*) F. A. Gace, R. E. Sedgewick, G. E. Towns, H. E. Muriel, A. C. Hynes, R. T. Barton, H. R. Northey, E. Wilken, W. C. Cowan, M. A. Murray, G. B. Dunnett; (*middle row*) H. Bates, A. Morse, P. S. Leigh–Bennett, D. Jackson, N. J. Stabb, A. H. Barlow, J. A. Ridgway, H. G. Jennison, R. P. Thursfield, A. C. Leith, D. M. Ross; (*front row*) P. S. Cassidy, J. H. Ramsay, W. M. Sutherland, L. N. Murphy, H. G. Hegarty, W. H. Stewart, F. H. Thomas, H. C. Sandford.

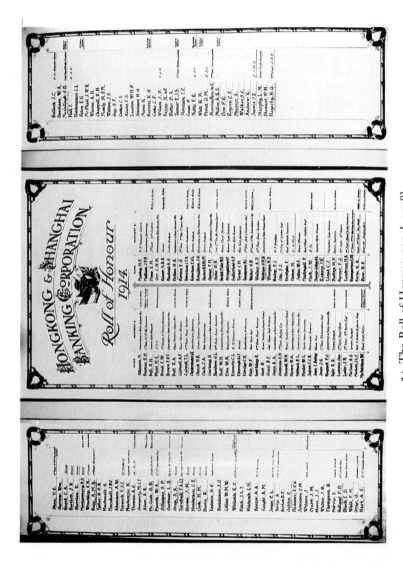

24 The Roll of Honour, 1914[-1918].
The list includes both Eastern and Home staffs, the first to volunteer being listed alphabetically in the centre.

banks. Stephen bought, but, as he confessed to Addis, the sudden demand from London saved him from an embarrassing situation. Indeed, in addition to the London sales Stephen sold India Ts194 lacs.

Shanghai was by this time left with sufficient silver for its own requirements, but little more. Stephen predicted that he would soon be buying, a fact which would have alerted the Bank to the likely continued increase in the price of silver.[32]

German-inspired runs on the Hongkong Bank – Shanghai and Bangkok

One consequence of these silver transactions was a German attempt to embarrass the Bank by causing a run on its Shanghai office. The pro-German Shanghai *Tao-yin* wired the Peking authorities that the Hongkong Bank had closed in Hong Kong and Shanghai and that Newton Stabb had left his office and disappeared. The great volume of the silver shipments was generally known in Shanghai and the ostensible explanation for the Bank's alleged failure was that the Germans had sunk many of the ships carrying the Bank's silver.

The Foreign Affairs Commissioner in Shanghai, Yan Tseng, sent a counter-wire and the *Tao-yin* eventually resigned. Little damage had been done; few apparently believed the elaborately designed story. Stephen distributed silver dollars to the native banks with instructions to cash at par any Hongkong Bank banknotes presented; at the time the Bank's Shanghai office had virtually 100% cover in dollar coin against the Shanghai note issue. Stephen was left wondering what the Germans had hoped to achieve.[33]

This form of harassment continued and the *Peking Gazette* published further rumours in November 1916, although these may have been inspired by the Bank's attitude towards the note-redemption policies of the Bank of China.

A more serious German effort to embarrass the Bank developed in Bangkok on November 27, 1916, when depositors, responding to a rumour, began to withdraw funds from the Bank. The British Minister protested to the Siamese Foreign Ministry, the latter responded by cancelling instructions for a routine withdrawal of Ticals 200,000 in order to provide the public with a convincing statement of the Government's confidence in the Bank.[34]

The Germans had also been operating in Siam through the Siam Commercial Bank and related local banks. The DAB and other German interests had since the origins of this bank, which had expectations of eventually becoming the state bank, retained a political interest in the potential influence it might wield, and the manager was until 1917 a German. After confidential conversations with the King and his officials, the British Minister, H. Dering, was able to secure the promise that a British manager would be accepted, and the Hongkong Bank expressed a willingness for its Bangkok Accountant G.H. Ardron to take over the management, despite the fact that no replacement could be sent out under the manpower stringencies of the War. Ardron was co-opted but given the right, at the end of the War, to return to the Hongkong Bank; he chose, however, to remain in the service of Siam until his retirement in 1927.[35]

The proposed British silver loan in China – and other happenings

For the remainder of the War A.G. Stephen attempted to keep sufficient silver in Shanghai to meet the needs of China's trade. In 1918 he would seem to have lost contact with the silver markets, and he had other problems.

In early 1917 the British Minister called a meeting attended, Stephen reported, by 100 compradores and 100 prominent Chinese to urge support of the War Savings Association; a regular contribution would be invested in (depreciating) British Government securities. There was little interest.

The next proposal was for a British Government $10 million silver loan to be subscribed in China, although, as Stephen rightly asked, by whom? An analysis of the silver position and past experience suggested that such a British loan would fail in the market. Neither British banks nor British businesses in China had funds for the purpose and success thus depended on Chinese support. A Hong Kong Government silver loan had received little support from Chinese in South China and Hong Kong; Shanghai Municipal debentures were at 89, and Stephen doubted that in 1917 the Municipality would be able to borrow as much as Ts16 lacs at 7% without the 'assistance', that is, the virtual underwriting, of the Bank. All these proposals would, if carried through, strain the already overextended silver supply.[36]

In explaining this to E.G. Hillier, Stephen stated that it was Stabb in Hong Kong who did much effective work in convincing the British Government to cancel the silver loan proposal.

Chinese official concern over the silver situation led to Government suggestions that there be an embargo on silver exports. The exchange banks, including the Hongkong Bank, argued in opposition to this and agreed that they would do all possible, in their own best interests, if for no other reason, to maintain sufficient silver for currency and trade purposes. The inflow of gold into China as a factor in the equation was also touched on.

In April 1918 the United States Congress passed the Pittman Act which permitted the Government to melt down silver coins against the withdrawal of an equivalent value of silver certificates. This silver was then available for export, but the timing and regulations were not clearly understood in the East, and the Hongkong Bank's New York and San Francisco Agents would appear to have been unable to keep Stephen informed. Major shipments appeared destined for India, but Stephen pleaded with Addis to press for British Treasury support in urging the American Government to sell silver to the Bank in Shanghai. Meanwhile other banks had apparently obtained access to the market, and Stephen, who would appear to have lost contact with the market, had to withdraw his pleas of crisis. Addis had made various elaborate proposals, including substituting securities for a high percentage of the coin lodged against the note issue.[37] Although his devices were not approved, China's need as at first conveyed by Stephen was acknowledged by the British authorities; Addis, who had thus convinced the Treasury, expressed annoyance when the actual position was revealed.

The wartime build up of sterling balances was a potential for the disruption of immediate post-war trade; the immediate rise in the price of commodities, especially the dramatic increase in the price of silver, was the consequence of removing controls against the unrequited wartime demand and the consequent overbought position in sterling common to most exchange banks.

Roubles and the opening of the Vladivostok agency

In 1915 the Hongkong Bank had positioned itself in Harbin in an attempt to gain access to the finance of trade between Northern Manchuria, Siberia, and the markets to the south. With A.D. Brent as Agent and the Russian-speaking J.P. McGillivray as the number two, the Bank was well-represented. Stephen, under whom the agency operated, considered this presence sufficient for commercial purposes, expecting that the political and consequent economic activities in Siberia would decrease after the War. The establishment of the White Russian Government in Omsk and the potential of Allied involvement in Siberia changed the situation dramatically.

The British Government advised the Hongkong Bank through Sir Charles Addis in London that it intended to finance an expeditionary force in Siberia through the purchase of rouble notes, which purchase was to be undertaken on Government account to a total of £10 to £15 million through the Hongkong Bank; the Foreign Office urged the Bank, at the same time Stephen was urging Addis to clarify the Government's position, to open an office in Vladivostok. The British purpose was to 'discourage by every means possible' the use of yen in Manchuria and to minimize the effectiveness of Japanese intervention.[38] With this the Americans, who also sent an expeditionary force to Siberia, were in complete agreement.

The Hongkong Bank under Stephen's management in Shanghai obtained the roubles.

The main difficulty as Stephen saw it was the fact that the establishment of such a branch of a foreign bank was forbidden by Russian law. He asked Addis to obtain official British assurances that the Bank would be protected. As a former Philippine Manager Stephen was familiar with the Jurado case, 'I don't want Manila all over again,' he wrote. Vologodsky, speaking for the Omsk Government, declared that any contract with the Bank would be held invalid.[39] Stephen had nevertheless sent D.C. Edmondston (East in 1912) and Mr Gregory, a Greek from the Hongkew agency, to Harbin in readiness; Stephen reported to Addis that between the two of them they spoke all the languages of Europe. By October 15, 1918, the Vladivostok agency was established and operating; on October 24 that opening was authorized formally by the British High Commissioner.

Stephen did wonder about events after the British withdrew. By that time, as it happened, Omsk was not the problem.[40]

THE HONGKONG BANK, CHINA, AND THE CONSORTIUM

August 1914 found the Hongkong Bank not only with four Germans on its Board of Directors but with multiple and complex international agreements concerning its relations with the Deutsch-Asiatische Bank. Relations with the DAB as commercial bank could be handled under 'Trading with the Enemy' and are so considered below, but relations between the Inter-Bank Groups on the one hand and the Chinese Republic on the other had to be maintained and this involved continued contact with the DAB. These contacts related to past agreements; the problem arose therefore as to what financial arrangements might be made with China without German participation and yet without disturbing, to the detriment of the Allied Powers, the existing arrangements.

For the Hongkong Bank there were further problems, paralleling those described in Chapters 7–8. These included the responsibilities inherent in the various loan agreements relative to the handling of Chinese Government funds deposited in the Bank, the extent to which new loan agreements might be negotiated with China and approved by the British Treasury, the formation of new international groupings which would include the United States but exclude Germany, and the expansion of the British Group to include the Chartered Bank.

The details are extensive, but the correspondence and negotiations under wartime conditions resulted in very little concrete achievement. Although they involved the close attention of the Hongkong Bank's top management – Sir Charles Addis in London, Newton Stabb in Hong Kong, and E.G. Hillier in Peking – their failure to have long-term impact on the Bank suggests an abbreviated treatment in the history.

The $24 million 7% internal Chinese loan of 1915
In March 1915 Liang Shih-yi, Comptroller-General, Bureau of National

Loans of the Chinese Government, wrote to E.G. Hillier in Peking requesting that the Hongkong Bank agree to a 2% commission to receive subscriptions for a proposed $24 million 7% internal loan. The Bank was to share the task with the Bank of China and the Bank of Communications and its area of coverage included China, Hong Kong, the Philippines, Japan, and the Straits Settlements. The Bank agreed.[41]

This brought protests, based however on inaccurate information, from the Banque de l'Indo-Chine who supposed that the Bank were underwriting or otherwise participating in the loan. This would have violated the Inter-Group agreements which called for the opportunity of equal participation. After considerable correspondence the matter was cleared up and the protest withdrawn. The British Minister, who had not been consulted, expressed his agreement with the Bank's action; the loan might strengthen China's credit at a time when she was in any case unable to obtain outside financial assistance and would thereby lessen her dependence on foreign Powers.[42]

The proposed 'Second Reorganization Loan'

The £25 million Reorganization Loan of 1913 was intended as the first tranche of a total £60 million, and negotiations for a second loan were underway when the War broke out. The loan was never made, but the urgent financial requirements of the Peking Government put pressure on the Powers to make advances against either the proposed second loan or the partially negotiated Currency Loan. During the course of the War various proposals were made, but in the event it was the Japanese who made the advances alone. The Hongkong Bank, as the leader of the British Group, urged acquiescence, the Yokohama Specie Bank having made it quite clear that, in the absence of agreement among the Group banks, the Japanese Government would probably meet Chinese requests for funds directly.[43]

To prevent total domination of Chinese external finance by the Japanese, Sir Charles Addis continued negotiations. Inter-Group meetings were held, with Murray Stewart as Secretary, and a Belgian Group was admitted to the Consortium in December 1917. The British Group had been reconstituted by an agreement dated December 7, 1916, and indications from the American Ambassador in London were that a new American Group would join in order to make possible a new major loan to China of between Ts10 and 20 million, probably at 6% and 84.[44]

The Foreign Office wrote to the Treasury in support of the loan, even suggesting that if the American Group were not prepared in time for participation, the British Group would subscribe their share on a temporary basis. The American participation was considered essential for the success of the loan. The British Treasury, however, while accepting the danger of leaving the field to the Japanese alone, forbade the participation of the British Group on overall financial grounds.[45] The Treasury's decision made the conditional approval of President Woodrow Wilson for the formation and participation of a new American Group of no immediate practical consequence; nevertheless, correspondence was initiated in Europe and the United States by mid-1918, and the foundations for the post-war 'New Consortium', without German involvement, were laid. The details will be considered in Volume III.[46] Britain could do little to assist China during the War, but American interests were already negotiating with the Peking Government when the War ended.

The British Group as reconstituted included the Hongkong Bank (33%), Baring Bros and Co. (23%), London County and Westminster Bank (11%), Parr's Bank (11%), J. Henry Schröder and Co. (11%), and the Chartered Bank of India, Australia and China (11%). The Hongkong Bank was the head of the Group and responsible for management, for which it was to receive a negotiating commission of $\frac{1}{2}$ of 1%. The Chartered Bank was, however, to receive recognition as an Eastern exchange bank with custody of 25% of the loan funds, compared to the Hongkong Bank's 75%, and a proportionate amount of the service fees.[47]

Addis's private reaction to the inclusion of the Chartered Bank was petulant – like a professor who continues to judge a university on the basis of an old-boy sports rivalry. In fairness Addis's private expressions of annoyance may have resulted from the arrogant position being taken by the Foreign Office, where all success of the British and Chinese Corporation, the Hongkong Bank, Sir Charles Addis, and the Inter-Bank Groups between 1895 and 1916 was ascribed in the minutes to the alleged consistent and strong support which the Foreign Office and the British Minister in Peking had without fail provided.[48] Although it is unlikely that Addis saw such minutes, he would have sensed the atmosphere, and such a travesty must have been excessively annoying to the principal actor.

Quite understandably the Hongkong Bank was reluctant to share the profits of its own endeavours indiscriminately with all comers and its annoyance with the minor role played by the Chartered Bank during the Crisp negotiations was understandable at the time. But the Hongkong Bank argued the need for exclusive Group dealings with the Chinese Government, and the British Government would never tolerate long-run support for a Group which was not broadly based or which gave (or appeared to give) a monopoly to the Hongkong Bank alone. Thus the Bank's own insistence on long-run Government support forced its acceptance of broader participation in the British Group, and this alone both justified and necessitated the Chartered Bank's involvement.

Miscellaneous financial assistance to China

Although the major loan negotiations were inconclusive and major advances were restricted to those made by the Japanese, with lesser assistance directly from the United States, the Hongkong Bank did participate in smaller transactions.

In 1915, for example, the Bank agreed to advance to the Postal Department up to $120,000 by overdrafts at 7% on the daily balance; this was grandly entitled the 'Post Office Premises Hankow Loan', made against security of property titles.

In December 1915 the British and Chinese Corporation, of which the Bank was one of the two joint-managers in China and acted as the Corporation's bankers, advanced ShTs2.1 million at 7% to the Chinese Government. This took advantage of silver bullion then on hand in the Shanghai branch of the Bank, and the proceeds were used to pay off sums due on various international loans which would otherwise have been in default.[49]

The following March the Hongkong Bank and the Russo-Asiatic Bank authorized overdrafts to a total of ShTs450,000 at 7% for conservancy works on the Liao River at the Port of Newchwang in Manchuria.

As a consequence of serious floods in and near Tientsin in 1917, the Chinese Minister of Finance, Liang Ch'i-ch'ao, sought funds for river conservancy and related flood works totalling $6 million. This sum was reduced to the more realistic figure of ShTs700,000, and seven banks, including the Hongkong Bank, advanced $138,289 (@ 69=Hongping taels 95,419.4 which @ 104.8=ShTs100,000) each.

China was in a position to secure such an advance against surplus Salt Gabelle revenues expected to be paid into the lending banks from April to August 1918, during which months the advances would be repaid by internal transfers within the banks themselves with interest at 7% per annum.

There is a real possibility that the above fails to include all the actual small and short-term advances, *ad hoc* in nature, which the Bank made available to the Chinese Government from time to time. For example, E.G. Hillier confirmed in October 1916 that the Hongkong Bank would make available to the Chinese Minister in London an immediate sum of £5,000 plus £800 per month for six months thereafter at 6% per annum. Repayments were to be made from the release of surplus salt revenue funds.[50] And there were others, all tending to confirm the informed opinion that the Chinese Government in Peking was living 'from hand to mouth'.

Loan for plague prevention

On January 18, 1918, the Hongkong Bank together with the Banque de l'Indo-Chine, the Yokohama Specie Bank, and the Russo-Asiatic Bank agreed to a credit of $1 million to be advanced in three instalments of ShTs240,000 each for the purposes of plague prevention. These sums would be held at the subscribing banks pending the joint order of Chinese and Foreign Treasurers, with the receipts signed by the Ministry of Finance. Interest was at 7% per annum from the receipt date of each instalment, and repayment was to begin in June 1918 at the rate of ShTs100,000 per month which the banks were authorized to deduct from the monthly pay-in of funds from the Salt Gabelle. The loan was unconditionally guaranteed by the Chinese Government for full repayment by the end of January 1919.[51]

By the standards of the period from 1895 to 1913 this was not a large loan, but it is the only one recorded in MacMurray's *Treaties* during the War period of 1914–1918 in which the Hongkong Bank is involved. It was signed by Hillier in Peking, together with St Pierre of the Banque de l'Indo-Chine and de Hoyer of the Russo-Asiatic Bank, two men who had over the past few years done much in an attempt to damage Hillier's reputation. But that story and an explanation of Hillier's relations with Heinrich Cordes of the Deutsch-Asiatische Bank are told in Chapter 11.

THE COLOMBO BRANCH DURING THE GREAT WAR – A CASE STUDY[b]

The burden of rearranging international finance to keep the Eastern trade, especially trade in essential items, flowing during a period of war was the responsibility of the Eastern exchange banks, including the Hongkong Bank. The Bank's Chairman would each year praise the role of the Managers – they had to cope with the unusual problems that arose, and it was in the branches that the details had to be worked out. The Hongkong Bank was not the leading bank in Colombo – particularly in the business of import-financing. The Bank's failure to establish an agency in Madras would prove a negative factor, and the pressure of the Eastern branches and Head Office to use on their own account the financial facilities available increased the burden of the Colombo Manager. This case study of Ceylon is a continuation of the branch history in Chapter 2 and has been chosen to illustrate the confusion caused by one break in a complex link and the methods by which a Hongkong Bank Manager – in this case W.R. McCallum (East in 1889) – surmounted, as best he could, the problems he confronted.

With four German directors and a branch in Hamburg, the Hongkong Bank had considerable German business even in Ceylon; the War involved

---

[b] This section is indebted to H.L.D. Selvaratnam's research report undertaken as part of the Hongkong Bank History Project through the MARGA Institute, Colombo, Sri Lanka; the report is available in Group Archives. Also consulted were the Bank's Colombo S/O correspondence and Inspectors' reports.

Colombo as it did most other branches. First, there was the problem of enemy ships being held in Colombo harbour as 'prizes of war'. Since German merchants handled a high percentage of British exports to the East and as these were financed by the Bank, it was British trade and the Hongkong Bank's fund management which were inconvenienced. The Bank, together with the other exchange banks, complained in London to the Trading with the Enemy Committee: the cargoes must be released urgently and not held until there had been Prize Court decisions. 'Financing cargoes from India [and Ceylon] we buy in the East Bills of Exchange with relative Bills of Lading attached covering produce . . . to India [and Ceylon] we advance in London against relative Bills of Exchange with Bills of Lading attached.'[52]

Second, in line with jingoist accusations that the Bank was in communication with Hamburg, Colombo confessed in 1915, following the revelations in documents captured by the French (see Chapter 4), that it too had been 'guilty'. That the communications concerned business of interest to the British and that, unlike the Kobe branch's correspondence referred to below, it had been passed through the Chief Censor, who in turn had passed it through the Bank's Amsterdam agents Hope and Co., meant little to the single-minded. Colombo was informed that the practice must cease; the Kobe indiscretion and the accusations which followed had forced the Bank, on the advice of Sir Charles Addis, the London Manager, to curtail even legally authorized contacts.

Ironically one item of enemy property held by Colombo branch was a current account credit to F.T. Koelle, the branch's sometime Accountant and presently the Hongkong Bank's Hamburg Manager.

The Bank's main problems developed from its inability to increase its role in the competitive financing of Ceylon's imports and the consequent problems of being overbought in sterling. There were two dangers here, the first one immediate. As the overbought position was consequent to an inability to sell sterling against rupee funds, the Colombo branch found it difficult to provide its major Ceylon constituents with the local funds required for estate maintenance or to meet production costs.

The second danger was longer term. With an overbought position in sterling a rise in the exchange, that is, a costlier rupee in terms of sterling, would mean a book loss for the Colombo branch. In 1915 at a point when Colombo office was financing exports by transfers from Calcutta, Head Office lent Colombo Rs5 lacs from its Calcutta account and later in the year sold Rs5 lacs from Bombay against credit in sterling in London, but this could not continue, and Colombo, unable to obtain cover, found its overbought position in sterling continuing to grow. To some extent the danger from exchange exposure was covered by an agreement of the Indian Government to sell rupees post-war at a currently fixed rate to the extent of the overbought position, provided the exchange banks cooperated in using their resources to finance only priority items. These problems and their partial solutions become clearer if their development over time, especially in 1917 and 1918, is considered.

Banking competition in Colombo was severe and London Office worked hard to obtain accounts. 'With further reference to your Mr Padfield's call upon me ...' wrote the chairman of the Dairy Company, Ltd. There were cold calls (and unwelcome calls); in London the Hongkong Bank did not wait for potential customers to drop by. In 1915 London succeeded in having the Westminster Bank, the Hongkong Bank's clearer, transfer their Colombo account from the National Bank of India and there was increased, but difficult, business with Dunlop. Early in 1916 Colombo Manager W.R. McCallum wrote, 'I will have a detailed list of all the best importing firms here made out as you suggest and will get our head shroff [=compradore, then C Namasivayan] to get into touch with some native firms and endeavour to get them to have their business financed through us.'[53]

By the beginning of 1917 it was apparent that improved marketing policies would not alone solve the branch's funding problems. Wartime conditions limited the volume of imports from Europe and the Indian Government was cutting back on the total sales of Council bills as well as limiting further the portion of these allocated to Ceylon. Even more potentially serious to the economy were the imposition of exchange controls and the restriction of food imports from India itself. Meanwhile Ceylon estates naturally continued to produce for export. If they could not finance exports by selling sterling bills for rupees to the Colombo banks, they could sell their drafts to the banks in Colombo, take credit in sterling in London, and then instruct their London agents to buy TT on Colombo, the consequence of which was that the banks were still required to provide rupees. Obviously McCallum had to instruct London to restrict its drawings on Colombo.

One attempted solution was for the Bank to buy estate finance bills in sufficient quantities to provide an estate with funds for essential rupee expenditures but to refuse to negotiate for the total value of the exports. This resulted in drafts for the balance being sold in what might be termed a 'grey' market at an unfavourable rate of exchange, contrary to Government intentions.

Eventually two policies evolved. First, the Ceylon Government resolved to reduce the rupee coin balance required for the note issue from 50% to 25% and to increase the currency supply (and thus the overall money supply) by buying TT from the banks against credits in local funds and depositing the sterling as a special reserve for the note issue with the Bank of England.

The second solution was in a sense only partial and depended on mercantile cooperation during a time of war. Both banks and estates and their parent companies had to be willing to permit the build up of sterling deposits in London; they had, in other words, to restrict uneconomically their demand for rupees. As a consequence the volume and price of exchange operations would no longer be determined solely by market factors, and so to avoid arbitrary allocation a list of priority exports was drawn up, the finance of which was facilitated by the sale of Councils by India and by the purchase of TTs on London by the Ceylon Government. Meanwhile exchange facilities between India and Ceylon were improved by special arrangements with the Bank of Madras. And, eventually, reinforcing all this was, as previously noted, the Indian Government's agreement to reduce the exchange banks' overbought sterling position at equal rates post-war to an extent defined by agreement.

With the War continuing in Europe the British Government was eventually moved to limit unrestricted export finance to the benefit of the most urgent requirement, tea, a beverage surprisingly popular with those involved in the War effort. Accordingly the Ministry of Food undertook to purchase 32% of the output of each Ceylon tea estate payable in India in rupees at 50 cents per pound. Shippers were to draw four months' sterling drafts on the Ministry of Food; the banks were to meet these in rupees to the extent of 35 cents per pound, involving a commitment by the four Colombo exchange banks of £300,000 a month equivalent. London Office instructed McCallum that this business was to get absolute priority over every other export of national importance from Ceylon. To achieve these ends Special Councils were sold in London, but their allocation was to be a continuing source of argument. At first the Hongkong Bank's Colombo branch was allocated Rs10 lacs, or one-quarter of those sold, but at one point the Hongkong Bank was entirely omitted from the list. The branch had not fully utilized its previous allocation and then Head Office had apparently assigned the proceeds of a portion of the Councils to Eastern branches to the annoyance of the Indian Government.

Certain of the above policies suggest, correctly, an inflationary impact, and between 1913 and 1923 wages doubled while the cost of a 160 pound bag of rice rose from Rs10 to Rs14.5. However, inflation did not lead to the same degree of labour unrest which characterized the period following the Second World War.

While patching up the triangular finance system was key to the continued operation of the branch, there were other events of note during the war years. The Colombo branch, for example, worked out a system of financing the export of Java sugar for a Ceylon refinery. At the same time there were mixed and conflicting events which affected the Bank. The Government distributed more evenly accounts which had been kept solely in the Bank of Madras, providing the Hongkong Bank's Colombo branch with surplus funds it could not at that point use but which promised well for the post-war years. At the same time patriots in England were forcing the colonies to help pay for the War through loans to which the banks were invited to subscribe and which threatened withdrawal of deposits – 'cheap funds' as the Manager rightly termed them. And throughout this period the branch attempted to improve its local position relative to its competitors.

As for the expatriate staff, they could expect little consideration during the War and, indeed, their work increased dramatically due primarily to the increased number of sterling drafts issued, reflecting the changing method of financing exports. As part of their contribution to the War effort, there were in addition daily military drills![c]

HONGKONG BANKERS DURING THE GREAT WAR

There is no bank whose policy and whose whole staff is more thoroughly anti-German than ours.

Newton Stabb, 1915

The staff position – a summary

During the Great War the Eastern staff of the Hongkong Bank declined in numbers from 214 to 183. This was the natural consequence of the initial surge to volunteer and the continuing drain of men to the armed forces despite the pleas of management and the pronouncements of the Government. In the East there were losses through retirement and illness, but the records show that fewer than twenty juniors left London during the total four years of war, compared with say fifteen each year in the immediately previous period. Even then, some eight of the twenty sailed in 1918 and one at least, V.A. Mason, arrived after the Armistice had been signed.

In consequence of this shortage of staff, leaves were cancelled or postponed and men stayed East for longer periods. During 1917, for example, only six of the Eastern staff were on regular leave compared with 27 in July 1914. The normal 'tour' of duty was still five years, but of those who were at their desks when war broke out five served a tour of ten years or more, 77 served between seven and nine years, and another four served for six years.

This is hardly surprising. Replacements could only come from those physically unfit for or discharged from the services, and few of these were

---

[c] Participation in the War effort reached all sections of the community. More specifically, London Office was instructed to debit the account of the Chief Shroff, Namasivayam, with £500, being the cost of an ambulance he was donating to the cause.

likely candidates for life in the East, although there were notable exceptions, for example, Sir Arthur Morse (retired as Chairman and Chief Manager, 1953) and V.A. Mason (retired as Manager Japan, 1951).

Even this overstates the potential availability of men for the East. The Bank's London Office juniors had traditionally served an apprenticeship in some other company, usually a bank, but the London banks had agreed not to compete for each others' former employees discharged from the service. Mason, for example, had to resign from his bank, find temporary employment in a non-banking firm, and then apply to the Hongkong Bank before he could be accepted. Perhaps not all potential candidates were so determined.

The impact of the War on the tenure of the Bank's Eastern branches, agencies, and sub-agencies is difficult to determine because, as discussed in Volume I, Chapter 15, the Bank had often left offices in charge of senior men for long periods, and, there being no compulsory retirement age, length of service in the East would not provide relevant evidence. The opportunities for transfer were few and there were positive advantages in having an agent well-established in a local merchant community which itself tended towards lengthy tenures. Certainly wartime conditions would add a further factor in favour of extended assignments, as, indeed, Table 10.8 confirms – the list there represents approximately two-thirds of the Eastern offices. The American and European agencies were always exceptional.

The London Office also had manpower problems. There were volunteers from the Home staff itself. And no matter how over-supplied the office had been with juniors waiting for their 'orders' for the East, their absence was serious; they did provide essential services, undoubtedly learning more in the process than they were later ready to admit.

There was, however, a reservoir of potential talent, the ladies, who had replenished the London staff virtually before the end of 1914. In the brief interim there were Eastern staff members on leave, in fact some fourteen of them including the Chief Manager, and they could be drawn on before they either joined up or returned East. Later there were men who might be temporarily recruited, and the Board of Directors made reference to three such in the 1919 minutes, awarding them each a gold watch, but unfortunately neglecting to state where they had been working. From the value of the gift one can assume that they did responsible work perhaps for a nominal salary. Retirees of the Bank do not appear to have been recalled; this may be because the London Office department heads in 1914 were all quite senior and would have been able to remain at their jobs.

Table 10.8 *The Hongkong and Shanghai Banking Corporation Managers: extended assignments which include the Great War*

		Years
Shanghai	A. G. Stephen, 1912–19	8
Peking	E. G. Hillier, 1891–1923	32
Foochow	C. H. Balfour, 1905–20	16
Hankow	H. G. Gardner, 1912–20	9
Amoy	I. Turner, 1916–21	6
Canton	D. Forbes, 1914–23	10
Yokohama	R. T. Wright, 1911–23	13
Kobe	G. H. Stitt, 1913–19	7
Saigon	J. Kennedy, 1915–20	6
Manila	A. M. Reith, 1911–19	9
Singapore	Sir John C. Peter, 1911–22	12
Johore	G. W. Wood, 1913–19	7
Malacca	J. H. Courtney, 1914–21	8
Batavia	J. C. Nicholson, 1909–21	13
Sourabaya	W. Drysdale, 1896–1917	22
Bangkok	E. W. Townend, 1914–19	6
Calcutta	W. K. Dods, 1905–21	17
Bombay	C. H. Wilson, 1907–20	14
Rangoon	R. C. D. Guinness, 1911–21	11
Hong Kong	Sir Newton J. Stabb, Sub-Manager, 1909–10 Chief Manager, 1911–20	12
	A. H. Barlow, Sub-Manager, 1911–23, Chief Manager, 1924–27	17
London	Sir Charles S. Addis, 1905–21	16
	H. D. C. Jones, 1912–32	31
Hamburg	F. T. Koelle, 1906–20	15
Lyons	F. de Bovis, 1893–1922	30
New York	J. P. Wade Gard'ner, 1902–19	18
San Francisco	T. S. Baker, 1912–21	10

War service – statistics

During the Great War, of a total 169 members of the Home (London) and Eastern staffs of the Hongkong Bank who joined the British forces, 40 were either killed or listed as missing in action. The statistics for local staffs overseas have not, regrettably, been located.

Of those who died, two came from the Home staff, the rest from the Eastern staff, including perhaps as many as 31 who had not in fact been East.

Some 29 men who had served in the East joined the forces, most of them while on leave at Home, the remainder resigned while still in the East and returned to England to volunteer; of these six were killed in action; H.E.

Blunt, who had used his Chinese with the Labour Corps in France, died of pneumonia at the War's end.

On the basis of information in the Bank's official war service list (Table 10.9), there would appear to be many young men destined for the East who were in London Office too short a time to get their names on the office employment registers. Men like G.E. Bruce Tytler and T.J.J. Fenwick – and 24 others in the same category – appear only after the War when they are already in the East; their experiences are related below.

In other cases a man might join the Bank, stay a few weeks, volunteer, and then not return to the Bank's service or remain too short a time to appear on the office records. That there should be wartime dropouts is hardly surprising. Most London Office juniors knew little of banking as a career and even in times of peace the dropout rate was high; during the War men would suffer and mature, learn of other professions, or become too ill to go East. Among those who survived the War are the names of 48 men who do not appear to have been employed by the Hongkong Bank after the War.

Neither the record of what these men did on active duty nor the circumstances under which they performed acts of heroism or met their deaths have been compiled. 'There are few ways in which a man can be more innocently employed,' wrote Dr Johnson, 'than in getting money.' The Great War was not made by bankers. These young Hongkong Bankers paid heavily for the failure in political leadership.

As for the continuity of the Hongkong Bank, the statistics suggest that it was timing and 'bunching' which would cause the problems. There were certainly enough juniors for the Bank in the 1920s, and most of them had joined the Bank in the usual way; the War for those who survived had been an interlude, delaying their 'orders' to the East. The Board of Directors noted the names of the dead at their several meetings and made reference to the loss of potentially able officers, but the Bank continued.

What has been said of those who died need not be here repeated. They were remembered. On May 24, 1923, the Governor and his escort, a guard of honour furnished by the Navy and Army, having left the Hong Kong cenotaph, proceeded directly to the Bank at 1, Queen's Road, Central. There full military honours were performed before the Bank's own memorial which had been placed facing the Praya, corresponding with the position of the statue of Sir Thomas Jackson, Bart.

Not all casualties were War-related. Members of the Eastern staff died in the course of duty, as in 1915 did Addis's former Calcutta assistant, E.M. Bishop, by then a junior in the Shanghai branch. Perhaps the most dramatic and tragic were the deaths caused by the collapse and consequent burning of the mat-shed stands at the Hong Kong race course in February 1918. Newton Stabb's account of this disaster, written in a semi-official letter to Sir Charles Addis as senior Manager in London, provides an insight into the Bank's relations with its Chinese staff – of the respect for them and of the separateness of the communities:

I regret to say we lost several shroffs, coolies and office boys. Our No. 2 shroff and his wife lost their lives – he had been with us for many years and was an experienced and valuable servant of this Bank and very much liked by all who knew him. [Those who have served in Hong Kong will] remember him under the name of Tan.[54]

The death of J.R.M. Smith

After his return from the East in 1910, Smith would appear never to have fully regained his health. He remained close to the Bank, and Addis referred frequently to informal consultations with Smith, whom he both admired and trusted. After some discussion Smith had been made a member of the London Consultative Committee and was frequently in London office.

He died in August 1918. On receiving the news, Newton Stabb wrote to Addis, 'It is with feelings of deepest regret that I received your wire. He was a man of exceptional ability whose sound and wise advice was always valuable and a staunch and sympathetic friend. . . . His kindly and generous nature endeared him to all who knew him and his loss will be very much felt by us all.'[55]

Smith was a banker's banker. The story told in Chapter 1 of his unobtrusive inclusion in the team photograph at New Beckenham perhaps typifies his public image. It would have been difficult to top Jackson in the public eye; the Bank was fortunate in selecting a successor to the great TJ who would not attempt to do so. That was not the way he operated; the Board could front for him, the Chairman speak for him. And under his management the Bank had flourished.

Volunteers and the Bank's policy

The first rush

Of the total Bank staff at least 169 joined the British forces – others would join the French, the American, and, in fairness to a loyal staff, the forces of Imperial Germany; in the end even the Hamburg Manager was called up.

On August 6, 1914, members of the London staff who had qualified as 'efficient' in the Territorial Forces and had been called up for military service were informed that they would be granted leave, retained on the staff, and receive half-pay while on military duty. The original exodus included 45 out of 75 Eastern staff juniors, and many more were to follow. The leakage from the

East, however, was minimal. Appeals to patriotism included arguments for staying at one's profession, but the task of convincing the younger men was increasingly difficult and thankless. Enlistment for those in the East required not only resignation but payment of passage Home, if passage could be found on ships whose shore managers might be friends of the Bank. Nor was the man's conscience eased with the coming of conscription; the decision still rested with the individual. Conscription did not apply to those living overseas.

The reason for what seemed to the young as discrimination against eligible overseas bankers is not hard to find. With German trade seriously hindered from the beginning of the War, many British merchants saw this as an opportune time to take over and develop that trade to their own advantage. They were hampered by the shortage of shipping and were in a continuous struggle to retain their British staff, although as the Shanghai Consul General tried to point out to the over-zealous, '. . . were all to throw over those duties in order to go and fight, the sinews of war would soon fail.'[56]

The Board of Trade were from the first in an unequal battle with the ladies with white feathers. Those who heeded the former were hounded by the latter. The Government accepted the need to retain men in essential positions, which included work in overseas exchange banks; the ladies, however, had taken it upon themselves both on the streets and in the music halls to make the life of any young man seen in civilian attire uncomfortable – unless, as in the case of Bruce Tytler (see below), he appeared too young.

Nor could Managers fail to sympathize with a man's desire to volunteer. There was an official position, but once the deed was done, once the junior had joined, he was virtually congratulated – at least in the beginning and until the position in the East became more serious.

Bruce Tytler (retired from the East as Manager Bombay in 1951) was eighteen when he faced 'Jumpy' Jones and had the usual questions fired at him. 'Rugger or soccer?' 'Soccer.' 'We play Rugger here but I expect you'll soon pick it up.'[57] Tytler was accepted, but war broke out and he attempted to enlist immediately in his Scottish Territorial unit. The adjutant was an old friend of Tytler's father; the father intervened and, on the argument that the War would be over by Christmas, convinced the young man that enlistment was unnecessary; he should join the Hongkong Bank.

On return to London I found that all the Territorials had been called up and their places taken by cheroot-smoking Eastern staff on leave called in to fill the gap. They did not actually put their feet on the desk, perhaps because there were no natives to do the work, but they made frequent excursions across the street for coffees and 'quick ones'. Notices posted in the wash-rooms signed by the President of the Board of Trade exhorted us to remain with the Bank so as to help carry on Empire and overseas trade without which the War could not be won. Despite this, men drifted off in ones and twos. I looked so young that I was never the recipient of a white feather from patriotic young ladies, but I was unhappy as I averted my gaze from Kitchener's eyes and pointing finger which accused from every hoarding.[58]

But the War continued past Christmas, Tytler's father withdrew his advice against military service, and, signs in the washroom notwithstanding, Tytler left the office to enlist. Afterwards he reported to the head of his department. 'Oh, that's all right, I knew where you would be. Only wish I were young enough myself: but you'd better make your peace with the Sub-Manager.' There, after the Bank's official position had been restated, the Sub-Manager said he too wished he were young enough to enlist.[59]

The pattern is repeated in the case of T.J.J. Fenwick (retired in 1951 as the Bank's Chief Inspector). He too was discouraged by parents from joining up; the War would be over by Christmas, and instead he joined the Bank as a London Office junior, breaking his apprenticeship with the North of Scotland and Town and County Bank.

Then I got fed up with being hounded, feathers and things in London, after a very few months, and we'd been told that if we wanted to join the Army, we would have to resign. So one weekend I went off and joined the Army as a Tommy, and on the Monday I wrote out my resignation and went in to see Sir Charles [Addis] . . .[60]

The policy reaction and its consequences

After the initial permission to members of the Volunteers and the consequent exodus, the Bank's Board of Directors had to preserve the remainder at just the time when, with the outlook for a long war becoming clearer, the young men were reconsidering their initial decisions, as in the cases of Tytler and Fenwick. The official Board policy was stated in unequivocal terms: '. . . while fully sympathizing with the desire of men to enlist, the exigencies of the service made it impossible to grant permission to any of the Eastern Staff to volunteer for active service and all applications would have to be declined.'[61]

Those who insisted on volunteering had no choice but to resign from the Bank; the Bank, after the War, had no real choice but to take them back, and consider itself fortunate to be able to do so.

By mid-1916 the Bank's official policy had reached the cognizance of the editor of the London *Morning Post*; a British bank was threatening to discharge patriotic staff who wished to fight the Germans. Sir Charles Addis was asked to confirm whether this was so.[62] The Bank's alleged German sympathies had by this time been given some coverage and here, it seemed, was some specific confirmation.

The Bank, due to A.G. Stephen's foresight, was prepared. The problem faced by staff of military age was not confined to the present, to gifts of white feathers, but also to the fears of the future, of young children around the fire on a winter's evening asking expectantly, 'Daddy, what did *you* do in the Great War?'

For just this question – which, as it happened, would rarely be asked – A.G. Stephen had obtained an official answer.

Stephen, who was regarded even by critics of the Bank's 'Germanity' as a 'real Britisher', had put the situation to Consul-General Fraser in Shanghai stating frankly that only the conviction of the value of their services kept the members of the Bank's Eastern staff at their desks, but, he added, 'This conviction has in some cases been shaken by outside influences and we have lost men . . . whose services we could very ill afford to spare.'[63] What the Bank needed was an official statement from His Britannic Majesty's Consul-General as to the importance of their service.

Fraser accepted that the Bank's staff was depleted and that the services were essential. He concluded:

I have heard that some men, thus denying themselves [the right to volunteer] are uneasy lest after the War they be despised for want of ardour. To any man who needs it, I am willing to give an official certificate that he did not go to the war solely because of his duty to his employers and because I was of the opinion that his bounden service lay at his post in Shanghai.[64]

'People's memories,' Stephen wrote to Addis, 'are even shorter in these days than in normal times.' Government policy was quite clear, but to forestall 'some stupid attack on the Bank', Stephen sent a copy of the correspondence to Addis with the suggestion that he 'refresh' the memory of the *Morning Post*.[65]

The problem was, however, a continuing one, especially as the War dragged on and casualties mounted.

The Hongkong Bank's Chairman, W.L. Pattenden, informed the Annual Meeting in March 1917 that the Board recognized 'the responsibility placed on us by refusing the many applications from Eastern Staff for leave to proceed home to fight' and he reiterated the importance of 'serving their country in a different field'.

Nevertheless the whole problem re-emerged in 1918 when the country's military manpower problem was recognized by the raising of the age limit for enlistment to 51 years. Although the situation appeared to be under control in China, the Bank was particularly concerned that staff in Japan might volunteer.[66]

In some colonies a Government committee was organized to rule officially on whether the work being done was in fact essential. A deputation of the Hongkong Bank staff attended the Hong Kong General Chamber of Commerce to inform them that they had handed in their resignations and appealed to the Governor to release them for active service. The Government was asked to revive the Military Service Commission to classify British subjects who could be spared from essential service and to send them to India for training.

Other nations, other armies

The Bank's manpower situation was aggravated by such developments as the 'requisition' in 1917 of A.G. Kellogg, an American citizen, for a War assignment, and by the success of a recruiting drive in New York which forced Addis to consider sending additional British staff to handle that agency's important business. One of those so recruited was Vincent Youmans; he was involved with music in the Army and on demobilization became a composer of, among other hits, the musical 'No, No, Nanette'. Bank juniors assigned to post-war New York remember him for his gift of tickets to Broadway shows.

On the other side of the world G.H. Ardron (East in 1899), the Accountant in Bangkok, was leaving at the request of the Foreign Office and with the agreement of the Bank to take over the managership of the Siam Commercial Bank, which had been under German influence. The New York problem prevented Addis from sending a replacement to Bangkok.

C.L. Edwards had joined London Office as a junior in 1912. As a volunteer in a naval unit he found himself interned in Holland. He was permitted to work with Hope and Co., the Hongkong Bank's correspondents in Amsterdam, throughout the War.

In Germany there were three problems: (i) the fate of the London Office junior who had been caught there in August 1914, (ii) the call-up of the Bank staff, and (iii) the call-up of the Hamburg Manager, F.T. Koelle.

Although the German authorities knew that German bankers, with a few exceptions, were still exempt from internment in England, they did not exempt British bankers from the November 1914 order that all enemy males between the ages of 17 and 55 be interned.

St G.H. Phillips joined the London Office as a junior for the Eastern staff in 1911 and after London training had been sent to Hamburg for further experience before going East; he had chosen voluntarily to remain at his post at the branch rather than try to escape back to England while that was still possible at the beginning of the War. On November 6, 1914, he was ordered to report to the police and was then taken to an internment camp at Ruhleben, where, with one short break from April to July 1915, he remained till the end of the War. In 1917, F.T. Koelle wished to apply for Phillips's temporary release so that he could help prepare the branch's half-yearly balance, as by this time most of the branch's German staff had been called up for military service.[67] The British staff of some of the other banks in Hamburg had been granted such permission under similar circumstances; however Koelle was not permitted by the trustees assigned by the German authorities to oversee the operations of the branch to forward his application.

Koelle visited Phillips during his internment and kept him as well supplied as possible, and there is a touching letter of appreciation in the files, but unfortunately, on Phillips's release and return to England at the end of the War, he was found unfit for Eastern service and so left the Bank with a gratuity in 1919.

Koelle, as a German citizen, was subject to German military service. By April 30, 1915, he had been examined medically and declared fit for infantry field service. He then made several successful applications for deferment, but on February 15, 1916, the trustees no longer found it in their consciences to support his application for deferment. W. Carstens and F. Spandau, two senior members of the German staff of the branch who held a joint power of attorney, would however remain in Hamburg as the former at age $47\frac{1}{2}$ was too old and the latter was medically unqualified for active service.

In December 1916, Koelle was finally called up for training, but it had been arranged that this should be done near Hamburg, so that he could occasionally check back at the branch. His first duty was also in Hamburg at the Hauptbahnhof. In December 1917 he was transferred to the island of Sylt, but even there he was able to keep in contact with branch business by mail and when he returned to Hamburg on furlough. After the 'revolution' of November 8, 1918, Koelle was, on November 20, one of the 'patriarchs', the first to be disbanded from the army, and he immediately returned for duty at the branch.[68]

Bank salaries and related problems

As far as official recognition to its staff for services rendered, all the Bank could offer was the assurances provided by the Government and the offer of a letter from the Consul-General – or some equivalent.

The Board, however, made provision for a staff bonus of up to 20% in addition to specific allowances for inflation. Managers received their regular bonus on the basis of performance. Compensation was paid for postponed leave by providing a gratuity of one fifth of one year's full pay for every year's service from the time leave was due, effective Spring 1915.

Salaries themselves were adjusted in 1918 due to the increased cost of living which approximately doubled in England during the War. Adjustments for juniors included special increases after twelve and fourteen years' service. The more senior had their basic salaries increased between 5 and 6%. For London staff messengers and ladies this was a 50% rise; for others it varied but was not less than a one-third increase.

The relevant circulars express the belief that the need for the rise may not be permanent; it was to meet a 'special and it is hoped a temporary state of affairs'. The difference between those in the East and in London reflects (i) the rise in the exchanges, (ii) the smaller increase in the cost of living, and (iii) the larger proportion of income in kind, for example, housing.

From July 1917 the luncheon provided by the London Office Lunch Club was free of charge, subject to the same strict economy being practised in the future as in the past, but from August 1918 staff were asked not to use the lift on the way down; there was to be economy in the use of electricity.

The Board intended that members of the German staff in Hamburg would be excluded from the bonus. In this matter, Koelle does indeed appear to have gone against the orders of the Board of Directors. In 1914 and 1915 he granted the bonus without instructions but could excuse this on the grounds that he would have received the instructions had it been possible. But in 1916 he was in possession of the speech by David Landale, the Chairman of the Hongkong Bank, quoted in the *Economist*, in which he stated that 'needless to say, the Hamburg Office is not included in the bonus, but British members of that staff [Phillips] will receive their share in due course'.[69] Koelle considered this statement to have been intended to protect the directors from the charge of making a gratuitous payment to enemy employees and felt justified in granting the German staff a 'scarcity allowance' in lieu of the bonus, something which in any case the other banks had been granting as an offset to the rising cost of living in Hamburg.

Similarly the question of what salaries should be paid by enemy banks to local staff members drafted into the army was resolved with reference to the arrangements made by the German banks in England in 1916. In England a system had been established whereby fixed percentages of the regular salaries were paid depending on whether the employee was married and the number of his children. This information was brought to Germany by the returned manager of the London branch of the Disconto-Gesellschaft and the Hongkong Bank in Hamburg had no choice but to accept the system. In addition Koelle again decided to raise salaries in the face of the rising cost of living. He appears however to have been very conservative in this, seeking only to alleviate real hardships, as he was very conscious of the fact that the branch was making no profits and had very limited realizable assets.

The threat that the Hamburg Branch might be liquidated became more real after ordinances were passed in July and August 1916 expressly excepting bills, if collected by a liquidator, from the protection of previous ordinances regarding payments to enemy banks.[70] Therefore at the request of the German staff and with the approval of the trustees, Koelle paid the staff their

Officers Provident Fund (retirement fund), which would not have constituted a priority claim in the event of a liquidation.

A War tribute to the staff

In March 1919 the Board were able to put matters in perspective by a three-tiered tribute.

First, there was the Board's 'admiration for the heroism of those . . . who served with His Majesty's Forces . . .'

Second, there was 'deep regret at the loss of those who laid down their lives . . . and sincere and heartfelt sympathy with the bereaved'.

And there was also a third category for whom the Board expressed 'their high appreciation and recognition of the self-abregation and loyal devotion to duty of most members of the staff who could not be spared and who remained at their posts in the Bank, bearing uncomplainingly the extra strain thrown on them by the exigencies of the service in the War.'

There was some correspondence with the Government as to the handling of those who volunteered without permission. The Foreign Office unfortunately used language which Addis interpreted as suggesting the decision to permit staff to resign had been based on a balance between the needs of the country and the requirements of the Bank; Addis insisted that Newton Stabb's problem had been in weighing the merits of two responsibilities to the nation, one military and the other economic.

The conflicting interests, therefore, were not, as you seem to imply, those of the Bank and those of the military Authorities. Mr Stabb was given the difficult task of judging between the economic and military needs in Hong Kong of the British Empire, complicated by the unanimous assertion of his staff of their right to render personal service in the field.[71]

In the end, that is, by October 1919, returning veterans were reinstated at their previous seniority without penalty.

London Office ladies staff

During the War London Office changed forever. There had indeed been one or two ladies employed by the Hongkong Bank before the War – even in Shanghai the Manager had employed a lady secretary, a Miss L. McInnes, since 1908; she retired in 1921 with a pension of £75 per annum. In 1918 Addis had, with considerable difficulty, booked a passage for a Miss Broomhall who was to be employed in the Shanghai office, on terms unspecified but left to the discretion of A.G. Stephen, the Manager.

The mass exodus of juniors, relieved on a very temporary basis by Eastern staff on leave, forced Sir Charles Addis to make a more wide-ranging decision. By the end of the year the records show some 49 lady typists and coupon clerks; there were seventeen Eastern staff juniors remaining, and most of these would go East in 1915, the rest would resign, although some rejoined with a 1919 seniority.

In 1917 Sir Charles Addis addressed himself to the question of a fair remuneration for the 'female staff'. He began with what would appear to be an unexceptional statement: 'The general principle we have kept before us is equality of remuneration for male and female labour of equal efficiency.'[72] The problem arises with the term 'equal efficiency', because, after careful examination, Addis concluded that the ladies were only two-thirds as efficient as the men. While admitting that in the then state of knowledge generalization was particularly dangerous, he felt justified in taking 'due account of the inability of the female sex to stand a prolonged strain, their more frequent absence from work, [and] their liability to nervous breakdown in face of sudden emergency'.

Sir Charles did not cite his evidence.

In consequence the approximate average weekly wage for the first year was 34s:9d for males and 28s:9d for females, the latter being lower with reference to money wages, higher with reference to efficiency as calculated by Addis. The ladies' wages were more generous than in other Eastern banks, but Addis nevertheless proposed a 25% bonus and began consideration of the free 'lunch table' noted above.

With the recruitment of new London Office juniors for the Eastern staff in 1919, the number of ladies declined immediately and sharply, but some stayed on, were promoted, and are remembered by retirees as efficient and able teachers. W.A. Stewart (East in 1933), for example, recalls the names of five ladies remaining on the 1929 staff who had been recruited during the Great War.[73]

The call on the ladies was not a solution practical in the East where a pool of such assistance was non-existent. Nevertheless the threat was sufficient in Hong Kong in 1917 to cause the Portuguese staff to threaten a strike if this solution were attempted.

Hongkong Bankers in the East

In Hong Kong, the Chief Manager, Newton Stabb had a Head Office staff of Sub-Manager and Chief Accountant but with only 17 'banker's assistants' or 'juniors' in August 1918 compared with 26 immediately pre-War. The Sub-Manager was **A.H. Barlow** (East in 1891), but in 1920 he would be passed over as the Bank's next Chief Manager in favour of Stephen. **H.C. Sandford** (East in 1899), who would resign as Manager Manila in 1924, was the Chief Accountant, a position which was not yet the necessary preliminary to the Chief Managership. Last on the Hong Kong list was **Arthur Morse**.

Shanghai's 'juniors' were down to 19 from 25, one of whom was **F.W. Barff** (recruited as an 'Eastern junior', seniority 1880), the second most senior man on the Eastern staff after **J.P. Wade Gard'ner** (East in 1873). François de Bovis, who went East in 1872, was senior to them both, but he was no longer on the Eastern staff as then defined. The branch's Sub-Manager at the end of the War was **A.C. Hynes**; at the beginning of the War he had been the Bank's Chief Accountant in Hong Kong; in 1927 he would succeed Barlow as Chief Manager. **V.M. Grayburn** and **A.S. Henchman**, who would dominate the Bank in the 1930s, were juniors in Singapore (under **J.C. Peter**) and Manila (under **A.M. Reith**) respectively. Also in Manila for part of the War was **A.G. Kellogg**, who as an American was until 1917 the citizen of a neutral country and thus better able to deal with Germans at the counter. His declaration to his loyal British colleagues of 'neutrality' during Ireland's 1916 Easter Rising was not so much appreciated.

The Shanghai branch was dominated by **A.G. Stephen**, who was also chairman of the China Association's local branch, advised on currency, was responsible for the North China operations of the Bank and the opening of the Bank's first offices in the Northeast, and generally a very impressive figure. Stephen was, as earlier noted, considerably senior to the Chief Manager, Newton Stabb, and he had already served as Manager Manila and Inspector of Branches. While in Bombay in 1895 he had, with special Board permission as he had not yet reached the position of Accountant, married a Spanish lady, reputed to be an excellent violinist. The couple were in fact both musical. Stephen was in addition both a student of Shakespeare (and quotations from the Bard's works appear in his letters) and an art connoisseur, all this giving an unusual tone to their social activities in Shanghai.

The veteran **E.G. Hillier** presided in Peking although he was turning more and more responsibility over to his Accountant **R.C. Allen** (East in 1902). His first wife was dying in England and Hillier was one of the few granted leave to return Home; in 1919 he would be married again, to Eleanor Richard, who had been his secretary; she was the daughter of the well-known missionary, Timothy Richard. Allen's tenure as Acting Agent was successful in difficult times, and Sir John Jordan wrote specifically in praise of his role in dealing with complex loan problems, including his handling of the delicate relations with the Deutsch-Asiatische Bank's representative in Peking.[74]

In the United States, **J.P. Wade Gard'ner**, who had been Acting Chief Manager of the Bank for a few months in 1890, had then served in the key post of Shanghai but had been passed over for the London managership in 1905 and 1911, remained in New York. Another senior man, **T.S. Baker**, who had managed Singapore during the currency crisis, was in San Francisco.

And **J.C. Nicholson**, who had returned to the East for his health after an initial retirement and position in London Office, was Agent in Batavia. His work for the local Church of England – the creation of the Java Chaplaincy Fund for the finance of a chaplain through the diocese of Singapore – following as it did on F.T. Koelle's earlier efforts, was particularly memorable, as was his interest in horse racing and his refusal to attend the races on the Lord's Day. That he had been more senior in the Bank was well-known, and he was particularly respected by the Dutch bankers for his command of exchange problems. Those who knew him in Batavia have recorded their memories of him, proving their high regard for this long-serving agent of the Bank. He came, he told them, from Norfolk. At his initial interview with the Bank he gave his father as 'gentleman farmer'; 'Nonsense, my boy,' the (nameless) Manager had said, 'no such thing – is your father a gentleman or a farmer?'[75]

In Hankow, A.G. Stephen's Board-approved building program got under-way in late 1917 with what the *Central China Post* referred to as an 'interesting little ceremony'.[76] The post-war requirements of the Bank had not been forgotten; indeed, in this case they had been exaggerated. With the site cleared for a grand new building, with the stone unloaded and all ready for the foundations, **Mrs Geary Gardner**, wife of the Bank's Hankow Manager, was asked to turn the first sod before a gathering of notables, which included Fraser, HBM's Consul-General, and the staff and friends of the Bank. The ground was pounded so hard that an English spade in the hands of a lady refused to make an impression on it, but when Mrs Gardner, not to be defeated, smote it with a native matlock the sod was well and truly turned, as the Consul-General declared. He called for three cheers for Mrs Gardner, which were heartily given, and Mr Fraser wished all prosperity to the Bank and its new building when completed – which would be in two years' time at an estimated cost of six lacs of taels; it would be under-utilized and consequently known locally (and inevitably) as 'Geary's Folly'.

The building will be heard of again in this history.

Return to the East

The pattern of movements

In August 1918 there were seven of the Eastern staff on regular leave, granted at least in part for compassionate reasons; a further two were on sick leave. The following year there were 40 (including J.C. Nicholson) on Home leave;

'Return to the East' should perhaps have been entitled 'Return Home'. There were, however, 50 men of 1919 seniority who reached the East, although there must have been some ill-matching movements and counter-movements with consequently short-staffed offices during periods of that first year of peace.

But the story runs ahead of itself.

In 1916 there was only one addition to the Eastern staff, **A.R.M. Blackhall**. He had in fact joined London Office in 1902 and gone 'East' in 1905. His first assignments were in New York and San Francisco; in 1911 he moved on to Hong Kong, resigning on his first leave. He rejoined the Bank in San Francisco in 1916 and remained there until 1921 when he was transferred to Shanghai, his only Asian posting in this second period of employment. From 1927 he was Accountant San Francisco and from 1938 Agent. He retired in 1947 and there is the obvious inference that he was or had become an American citizen.

To the East on probation

In May 1918 with his staff appealing to the Governor for permission to enlist, Stabb wrote to Addis approving the idea of employing men on contract for 'the duration and one year, £400 plus quarters and return passage plus £50 for outfit' – and sending them East in effect on probation, as the need for additional staff would continue, Stabb noted, after the War.[77] The records do not differentiate, but this is the explanation of how men without London Office experience were in fact sent out in 1918.

The last to go was **V.A. Mason**, who retired in 1951 as Manager Japan (in Tokyo). He had approached the Bank early in the War before enlisting but had been told he was too young; after he was released from the army in 1916 he rejoined the Union of London and Smiths Bank, his previous employer. The Hongkong Bank was bound by an agreement with the other banks as noted above, but by mid-summer 1918 he was in a position to apply once again to the Bank.

He was told quite simply, 'There's a boat leaving for Hong Kong on the 20th of October; if you'd like to catch that you can go, the salary will be £400 a year.' Mason scrambled to put his things together with the benefit of a £50 clothing allowance and, after a very cursory medical examination, reported to Sir Charles Addis that he was leaving for Hong Kong. 'When I went in and he wished me goodbye and good luck, he said, "The last man who went out East two or three weeks ago hasn't been heard from. So whether he's gone down, I don't know." '[78] The trip took ten weeks. Mason sailed on the 3000 ton 'Kamakura' and reached Cape Town in time to celebrate the Armistice on November 11 – there was a festive atmosphere despite the heavy loss of life in the influenza epidemic in Cape Province. Then on to the China coast.

I arrived in Hong Kong at night time, and when I woke up at daylight we were in Hong Kong harbour, and I was looking over to the hills and waiting to see what happened. . . . After all the formalities were done with, George, the Bank's sailor, alerted the 'Wayfoong' and it came alongside to collect me. It was a beautiful shining object, painted white, and about 80 feet long . . . I wondered whether the Lord Mayor of London ever travelled in a more beautiful state than I was travelling. . . .

I was brought off the launch at Statue Pier and taken up to the old Office, which was a beautiful building, and introduced to Newton Stabb and Barlow and to Sandford the Accountant, who waved me onwards to one of the junior types who was told to take me up to the Peak mess. The accountant handed me a pass for the Peak tram, and so off we shot up to the top-side Mess.[79]

The Hongkong Bank's inter-war history had begun.

11

THE HONGKONG BANK IN THE GREAT WAR, 1914–1918, II: THE HONGKONG BANK'S RELATIONS WITH GERMANY

> I find the imputation hard to bear that a Bank, which has done twice as much as its neighbours in the way of recruiting, has been lax to prosecute the War in other directions or reluctant to assist H M Government to unloose the bonds of the financial and commercial arrangements, many of which date from the Anglo-German Agreement of 1895.
>
> Sir Charles Addis to War Trade Department, 1915

The War record of the Hongkong Bank and of Hongkong Bankers as recounted in the previous chapter would seem to need no apology. And yet throughout the War the Hongkong Bank had to counter an underlying current of suspicion, of unfounded charges, of vague innuendos circulated by influential men in public affairs and allowed to remain unchallenged by those in the City who knew better. The Bank's close ties with Government made the suspicions all the more serious and a matter for official concern; indeed, this was the purpose of the rumours – to disengage the Government from their long but erratic support of the Bank and the British and Chinese Corporation.

Now that the nation was at war with Imperial Germany, those that had long anticipated such a war, those who had done much to make it inevitable, turned on the Hongkong Bank for associations which had been made in the common interests of Britain and Germany with the full sanction of the Foreign Office. The Foreign Office knew this, but being continually subjected to both British and Allied representations, they too were partly on the defensive. Sir Charles Addis, London Manager of the Hongkong Bank, was frequently called in to give, once again, the answers the Foreign Office had long before accepted.

Addis's statement of the war sacrifices made by young Bankers and sons of Bankers is illustrative of the seriousness of the situation and the concern felt by the Bank. This was surprising enough, but Addis felt constrained to develop the theme; not only the young Bankers but the sons of the Managers and the sons of members of the Consultative Committee are mentioned. Addis's presentation is a dramatic if indirect statement of the impact which suspicion and rumour had achieved and of the sense of frustration felt by the Hongkong Bank.

I hope you will not consider it irrelevant if I add to what I have already written on the subject that 98 of our London Staff have enlisted for the War and that the percentage of those who were eligible for military service when War broke out and who have enlisted since amounts to 72¾%. This compares with the 30% to 40% of enlistments contributed, I understand, by the London Joint Stock Banks.

My colleagues in the Management have each a son in the Army; I have two, one in the Army and another in the Navy. The Chairman of our London Committee [Sir Thomas Jackson] has four sons in the Army. Of the other members of the Committee Mr Henry Keswick, M.P., has himself obtained a commission in the Army, Sir Carl Meyer's only son is with the Yeomanry in Egypt and a son of Mr W.G. Rathbone is fighting in the Cameroons.

I am not seeking credit for this. It is our duty, or rather our privilege, to bear our part in the great conflict, but I confess . . .[1]

Failure to round off figures appropriately is unusual. The '¾' in the above may be assumed, therefore, to express cold fury.

Addis concluded his letter with the statement quoted at the head of this chapter. Had he waited, he could have mentioned that Townsend's second son – the first had died after the siege of the Peking Legations – had been killed in action, Jackson lost one of his four sons, and that other senior Managers, including Sir Charles Addis, A.G. Stephen, and E.G. Hillier, were similarly deprived.

Although it was Addis himself who was taking the most constructive approach to British-German relations, and who thus might well have been the main target of abuse, the charges never touched him. He was a valued adviser of Government; in addition to the specific banking advice he gave the Foreign Office and the Board of Trade, he was in 1917 appointed a member of the Committee on Currency and Foreign Exchanges, and after the War, the Cunliffe Committee; in 1918 he was elected a director of the Bank of England.

IN DEFENCE OF A RATIONAL POLICY

Countering a 'chimera' – the Bank and long-run trade policy

A reluctant convert to war

Charles Addis was slow to bow to prevailing hysteria. In June 1914 Franz Urbig of the Deutsch-Asiatische Bank had sent him a friendly message, 'Please accept many good wishes for the new world citizen.'[a] In February 1920

---

[a] The reference is to the new-born (Sir) John Addis, sometime HBM's Ambassador to the People's Republic of China and member of the Bank's London Consultative Committee.[2]

the Committee for United Prayer and Peace praised Addis for suggesting publicly that by following the Christian law of mercifulness 'towards the Germans, the English surely would not be thought to show a sign of weakness . . .' – this struck the Committee as being both noble and wise.[3]

Although on August 9, 1914, Addis wrote to his confidant, Dudley Mills, that Sir Edward Grey, the British Foreign Minister, had 'at last . . . made a tardy and reluctant convert of me – Yes, we had to fight, but what a hateful necessity. I suppose Germany, our best customer, will be beaten. And what then?'[4]

He qualified himself by stating, 'After all Germany stands for a great deal of what is best in civilization. If she is wiped out, the damage moral and intellectual as well as economic will be enormous.'[5] And shortly after this a German friend of Addis was seized on board a ship docking in England; Addis took him to dine at the Reform Club – 'as an enemy alien ought not to have done so'.[6]

A Free Trader's position and charges of German influence

Addis was convinced that the dream of seizing German trade was just that and any attempt to achieve this by restrictions against the post-war Germans was in effect to protect the incompetent and inefficient.

The capture of German trade is a chimera. More than half the Manchester trade with China is distributed by German firms. There is not available at present either the British capital or the British personnel required to take their place. If the German firms are wiped out the result will be the diminution of British trade . . .[7]

Addis predicted correctly that the attempt to check German trade would result in chaotic conditions; German firms would deal through a British partner and by other means.[8] 'The only way for the British to capture German trade is to beat them on their grounds in efficiency. The British should seek to gain naturally.'[9] His was the classic position of a Free Trader, a man who believed in the efficacy of trade as a guarantee of peace and free market development – and in the importance of the banking institutions which financed that trade.

But this was a new war, a Great War. Events were occurring which forced Addis to temporarily modify his position to meet renewed attacks on the Hongkong Bank. Captured documents reinforced complaints by British critics and foreign representatives relative to the Bank's post-war intentions and, after an interview in the Foreign Office in December 1915, Addis cabled Stabb that he should take immediate steps to dispel any impression the Bank was pro-German, that he should stress 'the essentially British nature of the institution and its earnest intention of cooperating in the policy of HM

Government which has for its object the suppression of German trading in the Far East and its transfer into British hands.'[10]

To be fair to Addis, he maintained throughout the difficult interview that 'he doubted himself whether any boycott of Germans at the end of the war would be effective . . .'[11] But facing evidence that the Bank's Kobe branch had been in unauthorized contact with Hamburg, that the French were threatening to boycott the Bank after the War, and unable to state exactly the German influence in the Bank, Addis was in a weak position.

When a few days later Addis supplied the Foreign Office with the information on the very limited German shareholding and other interests, both the Foreign Office and the War Trade Department expressed surprise; the facts did much to assist the Bank in regaining the confidence of the Government for the time being.[b]

Newton Stabb responded by urging Addis to inform the Foreign Office that the Bank was subjected to criticism based on 'general impressions', always difficult to handle. 'There is no bank whose policy and whose whole staff is more thoroughly anti-German than ours.'[13]

Indeed, A.G. Stephen, the Manager in Shanghai and chairman of the China Association's local branch, wrote in a similar tone: 'Our experience of the bad faith of the majority of German firms will make it impossible for us to resume relations with them in any circumstances . . .' and he would hold to that long into his own chief managership.[14] In 1919 he was urging in the most severe terms a harsh liquidation of the Deutsch-Asiatische Bank and supporting measures to require German citizens to be returned to Europe, writing, as it were, in direct opposition to the position Addis was taking in London.[15]

This recalled a further criticism of the Hongkong Bank – it had been dilatory and permissive in its liquidation of German firms in Hong Kong. In fact the process was handled according to established regulations; it was through adherence to these that the Bank was criticized by those who felt the entire Government policy, especially in Hong Kong, was too 'weak'.

Charges and suspicions – the price of the Hongkong Bank's success

How is one to defend oneself from a 'tendency to hope'?
Sir Charles Addis to Newton Stabb, November 1916

Addis's position, however, was well-known in the City; the Hongkong Bank's continued relations with German firms were first distorted and then over-

---

[b] The figures given in Chapter 9, p. 527, are repeated: at the outbreak of the War, Germans held 5% of the shares outstanding, and 1% of the deposit liabilities of the Bank, 5% of secured and 1% of unsecured loans and advances and 2.5% of bills and credits outstanding were on German account.[12]

publicized despite the Government's understanding of the Bank's true position; the enemies of Addis and the Bank combined and were sufficiently effective to cause the Bank serious concern for its future – such that, years later when Addis was invited to become the British director of the reconstructed Reichsbank in 1924, A.H. Barlow had been hesitant to authorize acceptance; he remembered the years of the hate campaign against the Bank and was still reluctant to have the Bank's name in any way connected with Germany.

The Bank under the London managership of Sir Charles Addis had been too successful; over the years since 1905 the cold logic of the Addis memorandums had brushed aside specious arguments from competitors seeking official patronage or a share in the hard-earned gains of the Hongkong Bank. There was little sympathy from rivals in the City when the Bank was attacked by old enemies: J.O.P. Bland took the opportunity to strike back at Addis and the Bank with a libellous letter to the Foreign Secretary in which he repeated old arguments supported by false inferences and half-truths; the Peking agent of the Russo-Asiatic Bank, L. de Hoyer, struck at his rival, E.G. Hillier; even Hillier's friend, R. St Pierre, the manager of the Banque de l'Indo-Chine, gave credence to charges of collaboration.[c]

A friendship in Peking – Hillier and the Bank under attack
An opportunity to attack the Bank's activities in Peking came with the continued friendship between Hillier, the Bank's Agent, and Heinrich Cordes, the representative in China of the Deutsch-Asiatische Bank. Cordes had narrowly missed assassination by the Boxers when Baron von Kettler was shot; in 1914 Cordes was the German representative on the Peking Commission Administrative du Quartier Diplomatique, which retained its international composition in the early years of the War. At a time when the Hongkong Bank was being urged, despite its international loan obligations (to be considered below), to find a way to avoid all contacts with the DAB, Cordes regularly called on Hillier and assisted him, in consideration of his blindness, on his daily exercise, as he had for many years past.

A despatch to the French Foreign Ministry from Alexandre Conty, the fiery French Minister, who deplored Cordes's presence, quoted G.E. Morrison as complaining that one could not enter the Hongkong Bank without running into Cordes.[18]

---

[c] The impact of all this on the Foreign Office was minimized by their knowledge of the writers: 'We should be careful', one relevant minute reads, 'how we deal with Mr Bland who will do anything to injure the H & S Bank and particularly Sir C. Addis'.[16] On de Hoyer, the French representative M. Picot agreed with Langley (Foreign Office) that no charge with that origin would carry any weight whatever.[17]

French archives suggest something of a barrage of anti-Hongkong Bank correspondence, based to some extent on Hillier's alleged German contacts. But specific references are inevitably limited to either the Consortium question or the personal friendship of Hillier and Cordes. Underlying this and fully expressed in several letters was the jealousy of the French officials and bankers towards the Hongkong Bank and its pre-war financial dominance in the East. Writing about R.C. Allen, who took over the Peking agency of the Bank during Hillier's leave, Conty, the French Minister, stated that he was an adept follower of the dogma that the Hongkong Bank was a superior institution, essential and fundamental, around which all financiers, business-men, and merchants who are admitted to see the light of day in the Far East must gravitate.[19]

The impact of all this led eventually to Sir John Jordan, also a long standing friend of Hillier's, requiring Hillier to inform Cordes that he could no longer enter the Hongkong Bank except by invitation and then only for Inter-Group meetings. In explanation Jordan cabled the Foreign Office that Cordes was the German agent behind the financing of scurrilous Press attacks on British interests and leading personalities in China. Jordan was having trouble restraining the Press, especially the *Times* correspondent and the Reuters agent, from bringing these personal meetings to public attention.[20]

Addis, after a consultation at the Foreign Office, confirmed to Hillier that the meetings were 'not convenient' and 'liable to be misunderstood' but suggested that the remedy was extreme. Hillier need only inform Cordes privately of the matter.[21] The suggestion in Addis's letter became distorted in reports – Addis had instructed Hillier to disregard the Minister's orders and to continue meetings with Cordes.[22]

That such an apparently trivial, even personal, incident requires recording in the history of the Hongkong Bank is a reflection of the times.

Continuing harassment, continued suspicion

The innuendos were a continuing nuisance. When Hillier left Peking for Britain on leave, the British-oriented *North-China Herald* reprinted a speculation in the notorious *Peking Daily News* that Hillier had been recalled to 'head office' to be questioned on his 'continued association with the D.A. Bank'. A.G. Stephen, the Bank's Shanghai Manager, labelled this 'an entirely false and misleading expression'. In a stinging rebuke Stephen further stated that (i) the Bank's head office was in Hong Kong, London being a 'subordinate office' and (ii) Hillier's wife was dying; it was this that took him back to England.[23]

But, more important to the Bank, Hillier's activities in Peking, although wholly innocent, provided the excuse for criticism from both the French and

Russian Governments.[24] Even where the Bank had acted promptly and correctly, a subtle interpretation could be made. For example, the German directors of the Hongkong Bank, it is true, resigned on the advice of their English colleagues. But, the critics asserted, the Board did not replace them – they were waiting to reinstate them at the end of the War. When the Board did invite a new member, from the P&O Co., the critics merely noted that the Board was planning to invite three instead of four Germans post-war.[25] That all this made no sense in the context of the Bank's 'charter' and Deed of Settlement was irrelevant; it was one more harmful rumour.

These representations from Allied Governments, already fuelled by evidence revealed in the captured documents of Hongkong Bank/German trade contacts – contacts for the most part authorized by the relevant British regulations, but contacts nevertheless – were more serious in the eyes of the Foreign Office than the obviously biased and personal attacks which they had already discredited.

The role of the Bank's London Manager
Of all this Sir Charles Addis took the brunt. The Chairman and directors were all in distant Hong Kong; the Chief Manager, Newton Stabb, was busy keeping the Bank on an 'even keel' during the dramatic and erratic movements of silver, adjusting the operations of the Bank to war conditions, meeting Imperial requirements for bullion shipments, solving system-wide staff problems, attempting to solve difficulties created by the premium on Hong Kong dollar banknotes, keeping abreast of currency problems in China and particularly in the Canton region – and generally being a banker. Thus as far as the British authorities were concerned, when complaints were made or explanations required, Charles Addis was 'the Bank', and it was Addis who was ordered to the Board of Trade, to the Treasury, the Bank of England, the Foreign Office, or the Colonial Office and required to explain and rectify.

To take one example: documents captured by the French revealed that the Kobe branch of the Bank had been corresponding directly with the Hamburg Branch. Addis was called in and an explanation demanded. The minutes of the meeting reveal that Addis spoke with authority; he would obtain an explanation from Kobe, he would issue instructions, etc. And he followed through. As it happened the correspondence dealt with subjects which, if the letter had been sent through London, would have been approved by the authorities and forwarded to Germany in an acceptable way. Nevertheless, Addis acknowledged the error of judgement and reported that he had taken steps to prevent reoccurrences.[26]

The underlying problem – relations with Government

There are important implications in this state of affairs. The British Group at this time still had the exclusive support of the British Government and the Hongkong Bank was head of the British Group in the Five Power Groups Consortium responsible for loan negotiations with China. The Bank was seen as close to the Government; the full history of the relationship and its limitations were not a matter of consideration; the fact of Government support was sufficient, justifying the representations of Allied Governments relative to the Bank's activities.

If the Bank were to retain its international position in the China consortiums, it had either to move its head office to London or to have an officer in London who could act for the Bank without reference to Hong Kong. This was nothing new, but previously it had been possible to separate merchant banking activities relative to major public loans issued in London from the other activities of the Bank based in Hong Kong and the East. Now Addis was acting for the Bank in all matters.

If Addis failed, the future of the Bank as a bank with an international role was apparently in jeopardy. If Addis succeeded in causing branch Managers, with whom he corresponded directly, to respond to the demands of the British Government, he was in danger of usurping, or perhaps 'pre-empting' the role of the Chief Manager, acting, indeed, as if he were an executive chairman of the Bank. Hence in later years, when Addis as the Chairman of the London Consultative Committee was referred to as 'the Chairman of the Hongkong Bank', there was resentment in Hong Kong. Perhaps Stabb had the 'image' problem in mind when he refused to consider recommending to the Board of Directors Addis's 1916 proposal to be made a full-time, paid Chairman of the London Consultative Committee; the Committee could too easily be mistaken for a board of directors with Addis as the Chairman of the Bank. With the majority of the Bank's shareholders resident in the United Kingdom, with the public criticism of the Bank's activities expressed in London and focusing on Government relations as implemented by London Office, there was once again the danger of a forced move to London.

Yet the success of Addis in meeting official (as opposed to Press) concern may have saved the Bank for Hong Kong. His ability to speak and 'deliver' for the Bank without reference to and without operating through a distant head office convinced the British authorities, at that time, that the Hongkong Bank, although its head office might be in Hong Kong, was a British bank and responded as such to Government representations as effectively as if its head office had been in the City. Any move thus became irrelevant.

This is not to say that the contentious issues affecting the Bank's image were ever fully resolved. The attacks on the Bank continued throughout the War. But although junior Government officials wrote tentative minutes speculating on Addis's dismissal, the charges when they reached experienced levels in the Foreign Office were placed in perspective. There were problems, but the Bank also had difficulties, and the purpose of the attacks was understood.

Addis was able to counter or correct specific issues, but he was never able to overcome the general impression that the Hongkong Bank was somehow too favourably inclined to the Germans. Frustrated, he requested an independent enquiry, but the Foreign Office hesitated; what would be the purpose of such an enquiry? They knew it would confirm what they already accepted; the facts would support Addis and the Bank.

But the Foreign Office also knew Addis. His approach to post-war relations made his protestations of support for a thorough anti-German policy vulnerable to continued suspicion. More revealing than an investigation of the Hongkong Bank, one frustrated official minuted, would be 'an inquiry into the state of Sir C. Addis's mind'.[27]

There are, at this point and before a final summary, two aspects of the Bank's relations with Germany which require specific exposition: the first is 'Trading with the Enemy'; the second is the history of the Hamburg Branch, which remained in operation throughout the War under the isolated management of F.T. Koelle.

TRADING WITH THE ENEMY

The original belief was that the War would end by Christmas, 1914. Although trading with the enemy was prohibited from the first, the actual regulations became progressively more severe as the War continued and sentiments relative to the Germans hardened. On August 28, 1914, for example, and following a clarification of terms in London, Charles Addis was able to cable the Bank's Shanghai office, 'His Majesty's Government now give permission to trade with Germans Austrians resident British Colonies Neutral countries. Re foregoing we take bills on German Austrian firms for collection only.'[28]

At the request of Shanghai, this was confirmed directly by the Foreign Office with the Consul-General.[29] The matter was of immediate concern because many firms, both British and German, were in financial straits as a result of uncertainty and consequently non-payment of sums due, and, as Shanghai Consul-General Fraser put it, 'If anything can be done to help the [Hongkong] bank, which is "dry-nursing" very many China firms through this crisis, I hope you will let me know and I'll pass it on.'[30]

The difficulty of complying with the Trading with the Enemy Regulations lay first in their complexity and consequent intra-government disputes as to their meaning and second, in the continuous outpouring of changes which made one day's attempt to serve a long-standing constituent appear tomorrow's unpatriotic action. As Addis cabled Stabb in Hong Kong,

The Board of Trade, the Treasury and the Foreign Office are all interested from different points of view and, as they do not appear to be agreed among themselves, it is impossible to lay down with any degree of exactitude the precautions branches should take . . . Proclamations on this subject [Trading with the Enemy] continue to follow each other in a bewildering succession . . .[31]

Citizens of Germany and Austria were not originally considered 'enemies' solely by reason of their nationality even if civilly domiciled in their native land; the test was 'commercial domicile'. If this latter was shown to be, for example, neutral China (including the various international settlements of which China was the sovereign of the soil), then trade with such German firms in dealings with other neutral countries or Allied territory was, under most circumstances, permitted.

Despite the over-simplication of this exposition, it is sufficient to show that the Hongkong Bank with its pre-war contacts would have broad scope to deal with enemy nationals and that it would not willingly abandon its constituents. The contacts in fact took several forms: (i) winding up of pre-war business, (ii) involvement in trade finance permitted by the regulations as issued from time to time, and (iii) relations with the DAB which were consequent on international loan agreements. All involved problems of interpretation, but the first category was virtually concluded by mid-1915 and the second was minimized and finally forbidden by redefinitions and successively more restricted regulations. The third, however, remained virtually to the end of the War.

Pre-war business

Liquidation of the Hong Kong branch of the DAB

The Hongkong Bank's contacts under the category 'pre-war business' nevertheless affected the public image of the Bank, seeming to confirm the German influence which was alleged to control the management.

For example, the Bank was accused of delaying the liquidation of the Hong Kong branch of the Deutsch-Asiatische Bank.[32] In fact, the Hongkong Bank, specifically H.C. Sandford and G.G.S. Forsyth, were merely supervising the process which the DAB was to carry out itself; the funds realized were not to be transferred to Germany. The Government instructions stated, '. . . the interests of the enemy aliens whose affairs you are winding up must be considered in every possible way. The object of deporting and interning

German and Austrian subjects is not to obtain their trade.'[33] This clear statement was consistent with tradition and with Addis's position; it was not popular. It was totally opposed to the position of the China Association and those British merchants who saw the War as an opportunity to deny Germans access to world trade. As the War continued and hatred mounted, the narrowly nationalistic views prevailed; the supposed pro-German position of the Bank continued under attack.

The bulk of the work relative to the DAB's liquidation was in fact completed expeditiously. The Hong Kong Government, however, held up the sale of the DAB's Hong Kong office building. The situation had become standard; the Bank was accused of pro-German action, Addis supplied full explanations to the Foreign Office, these were accepted and the incident closed – but the accusation lingered in the public mind, forming part of that 'general atmosphere' of criticism which the Bank could not counter.[34]

Manchester vs the China Association

In August 1914 the Hongkong, Chartered, and Mercantile Banks requested the Hong Kong Government to permit German firms to continue business in order to dispose of stocks in the finance of which the exchange banks were involved.[35] Again no funds would be remitted to Germany, but again the Hongkong Bank's name was linked with German business in the East; that the two other British exchange banks were equally involved was irrelevant to those who had established for their own purposes the Hongkong Bank as their target. G.E. Morrison, for example, in writing to C. Clementi Smith, then active in the China Association, London, singled out the Hongkong Bank for comment: 'Enemy trading still continues in China. It is inevitable seeing that the Hongkong and Shanghai Bank is so inextricably bound up with German trade in China, German trade is being kept alive in the interests of this Bank but now so much outcry is being raised that the policy is under reconsideration.'[36] He then continued on a theme arising from his support of the Crisp Loan – 'It is always one of the unexplained enigmas why the Chartered Bank should be boycotted by the British Legation in China and a monopoly of support given to the Hongkong and Shanghai Bank who are responsible more than any other agency for the growth of German trade in China.'[37]

While all of Morrison's statements in the above two quotations are factually incorrect, he fails to mention that all exchange banks in China faced the same problem of uncompleted trade finance ultimately beneficial to British interests. The Hongkong Bank being larger was more involved, which is perhaps why Morrison himself banked with the Hongkong and Shanghai Banking Corporation.

The pressure to fulfil contracts with German firms came in fact not from the banks but from Manchester; the Hongkong Bank at first refused to finance shipments to Germans; later, presumably after the representations to the Hong Kong Government referred to above, Manchester was permitted to complete German orders from the East under documentary credits issued by the Hongkong Bank; this the Bank did for reliable British firms of high repute. When the Proclamation of June 25, 1915, prohibited all trade with Germans in China, the Hongkong Bank ceased this practice and faced general complaints from Manchester firms.

This, at least, was the position of H.D.C. Jones, junior Manager of the Bank's London Office. And he shared none of Addis's long-term hopes for the post-war world. Indeed Jones wrote to Stabb, 'I am heartily in accord that nothing too much or too drastic can be done to root out and ruin German trade all over the world . . .', but, he said, 'we know Bland's motives . . .'[38]

Special cases

In the case of one Hong Kong liquidation, that of Leopold Casella and Co., correspondence on the subject of deposits with the Reichsbank did get through from F.T. Koelle, the Bank's Hamburg Manager.[39] The discussion of what the German firm had done in Hamburg, indeed what action the Hamburg Branch had initiated on its own or on the instructions of its trustees, became a matter of concern to the Hongkong Bank in China; they might be setting funds aside in both Shanghai or Hong Kong and Hamburg with the possibility of confusion post-war. Despite requests for special consideration, the British authorities, concerned with the problems of precedents, refused to modify procedures.[40]

Koelle, as will be shown below, was equally frustrated.

In the wind-up of pre-war business there were unusual situations, as, for example, a cargo of armaments shipped by Carlowitz and Co., financed by the Hongkong Bank, and consigned to the Government of China. Caught in the neutral port of Genoa at the outbreak of war, the cargo was detained and the Bank sought to have it released in view of its destination; Carlowitz cooperating sought to have the relevant bill of exchange withdrawn. The British authorities failed to appreciate the complexity of the problem, pointing out that China should instruct its Minister in Rome to claim ownership. The shipment had been made, however, by provincial authorities without the sanction of the central Government and under a system of kickbacks and bribes which they preferred not to detail. Consequently, the cargo sat in Genoa until unloaded for reasons of safety; the Bank's position remained unresolved.[41]

Interpretation

The second category involved the interpretation of complex regulations.

One local Bank Agent, H.G. Gardner in Hankow, sought advice from the British Consul; the latter unwisely gave it. Gardner notified Shanghai that he had been advised not to undertake the transaction; Shanghai office overruled him; and in the end the files suggest that the original information had not been complete – the transaction, though marginal, was legal. Sir John Jordan, however, warned his consul that, while personally agreeing with the advice given on the basis of the original information, it was no duty of a consul to interpret the regulations – they were too complex.[42] A bank manager, faced with a decision usually made on the spot, was in a difficult position.

Despite this, the specific instances of doubtful Hongkong Bank transactions as recorded in the relevant Foreign Office files are fewer than five, and the amounts involved are small.[43] Had it been any bank but the Hongkong Bank, the matter would have aroused no interest beyond that of the legal position itself. The Foreign Office took the position that a Bank so closely connected with the Government should be totally free from suspicion, but this, as Addis continually reminded his contacts, was impossible.[44] As the regulations came to forbid all contacts with the nationals of the Central Powers and with China's entry into the War in the Allied cause, the nice problems which had previously confronted the Bank's local agents were automatically resolved.

A clear example of this is provided in the case of a borderline transaction involving the Bank in Siam; the Bank was placed temporarily on a 'blacklist', but no further action was taken because the Board of Trade considered that new regulations which were then about to be promulgated would totally rule out contacts with Germans in the East and thus eliminate the problem. As the Board of Trade observed, 'So long as trading by firms in this city with branches of German firms in countries outside Europe is permitted, the Board feel some difficulty in taking exception to the financing of such transactions by British banks.'[45]

The Hongkong Bank's main problem in this category would seem to have arisen from the continued preference of Manchester firms to deal with German merchant agents in China, despite the efforts of the British-merchant dominated China Association to have such agencies transferred to British firms. Exports from Britain were on a bills for collection basis, the financing thus being undertaken by the manufacturer and the role of the Hongkong Bank in handling these bills confined to collecting for the British manufacturer, transactions wholly within the regulations. This failure to secure British export trade by competitive means led the Shanghai branch of the China Association and other British firms to urge successfully for a more stringent definition of 'enemy' and eliminate all dealings with German and Austrian firms, directly or through neutral 'fronts'. In the meantime if the Hongkong Bank could not be faulted on legal grounds, it could be criticized for playing a role in a trade the British China merchants considered German, but which the Bank and apparently the Board of Trade might quite as legitimately have considered British.[46]

Relations with the DAB

The question of the Deutsch-Asiatische Bank, however, was not so simply resolved.

The two banks were initially involved in such matters as commercial dealings originating pre-war and consequences of Consortium dealings. Although the DAB had its head office in Shanghai and might, therefore, be considered as commercially domiciled in China, there is no evidence that this interpretation was relied on by the Hongkong Bank in justification for any relationship. Obviously in Hong Kong, where the DAB was under process of liquidation, the problem was of a different nature; this discussion is, therefore, focused on China.

First problems

The difficulties began in London when Addis reported that a British firm, Waterlow and Sons, Ltd, having won the bid for the engraving of the bonds for the entire £25 million Reorganization Loan of 1913 against keen German competition, had now completed the work and the bonds, including those of the Berlin issue, had to be delivered. Could the German issue be sent to Berlin? The final decision was that they could be sent only through a neutral country – the decision was made thirteen months later after protracted discussion in which the Bank was once again seen as wishing to deal with Germany.[47] The Hongkong Bank was acting as agent for the Chinese Government, but this was the first of a series of increasingly contentious problems relative to the Deutsch-Asiatische Bank which plagued the Hongkong Bank throughout the War.

The Hongkong Bank as agent of the Chinese Government

The focus is shifted to China. By international agreement the Hongkong Bank and other banks in Shanghai were the depositories of Chinese Government funds required to service loans and execute indemnity payments, but in certain cases the Hongkong Bank was the initial depository, the funds being then transferred from a Shanghai branch current account, operated by the

Inspector-General of the Chinese Maritime Customs, to the other issuing or custodian banks, including the Deutsch-Asiatische Bank.

Sir John Jordan, the British Minister in Peking, noted the obligation under which the Hongkong Bank found itself and alerted the Foreign Office. Addis saw immediately that these transactions might be in contravention of Trading with the Enemy regulations, and the Foreign Office after acknowledging the Bank's problem authorized Sir John Jordan to issue the Bank a licence.[48] Addis however deprecated the idea, fearing it would lead to public misunderstanding and might even cause Hongkong Bank officers to act with less caution.[49] The authorities then concluded that the Bank, acting in a neutral country as the agent of that country, was not contravening the regulations and therefore did not require a licence.[50] This was ruled to hold even under the stricter regulations subsequently issued.[51]

This did not, however, end the Bank's problems. When cables from URBIGSBANK through CHINABANK to WAYFONG, transmitted from Amsterdam by Hope and Co., were intercepted they were regarded with suspicion and Addis was requested to explain. The first was the code for the Disconto-Gesellschaft of which Urbig was a director, the second was for the DAB of which Urbig was chairman, the third for the Hongkong Bank, and Hope and Co. were the Bank's correspondents in Amsterdam; the cable itself dealt with clearing house problems of the kind already approved.[52]

The problem of British-held bonds of German issue

There was, however, a further complication. The bonds of specified China loans, the Hukuang Railways Loan, for example, were issued in London, Paris, and Berlin. They could be and in fact were purchased in these centres by investors of any nationality – that is, British subjects might buy bonds of the German issue; Germans might buy bonds issued in London. The Hongkong Bank and the DAB were agents of the Chinese Government. As such each bank received funds for the payment of interest due on bonds issued in London or Berlin respectively; but as direct contact between the nationals of the two countries was not permitted, the Chinese Government permitted the Hongkong Bank to pay all British holders of bonds whether issued in London or Berlin, the DAB all German holders. However, there were more British with Berlin-issued bonds than Germans with London-issued bonds; therefore, as Addis put it, the Hongkong Bank stood ready to receive funds from the DAB to cover the difference. In fact, the DAB paid into the Hongkong Bank sufficient in gold to permit the latter to pay the interest due to British bondholders of the German issue.

As pressure began to mount on the Government to take action with regard to the Bank's alleged pro-German proclivities, the Foreign Office for political reasons was anxious to be seen as 'strict' in enforcing the regulations. Since, however, the receipt of funds from the DAB was to the advantage of the British bondholder, the Bank could not be asked to cease its relations with the DAB until an alternative solution to the interest payments could be found. The obvious solution was for China to make the allocation among the issuing banks calculated on a basis of nationality of ownership rather than place of issue. This, given the complexity of the situation, China declined to do.

The pressure to eliminate this source of contact came primarily from the French – and from the Russians, in particular the Peking manager of the Russo-Asiatic Bank.[53] The willingness of the DAB to pay gold into the Hongkong Bank for British bondholders might seem a gracious act in time of war, but it was interpreted as a way to keep in contact with the Hongkong Bank and so prepare for immediate cooperation once the War was over. This interpretation was consistent with the known tendencies of Sir Charles Addis. Such post-war cooperation in its most significant aspect would come in the renewed activities of the Five Power Groups, and since the Hongkong Bank's role depended on continued exclusive Foreign Office support, the Foreign Office had the means to influence the Bank's immediate policy.

In the meantime the Foreign office delayed; they were aware that China was on the verge of declaring war on Germany. The problem would then cease to exist.[54]

Indeed, the Hongkong Bank and Addis in particular were accused by the French in the *Journal de Pekin* of informing the American Group that their proposal to advance funds to the Chinese on behalf of the Consortium could only be made after Addis had consulted the Germans, implying that Addis on behalf of the Bank would make such a consultation. Hillier replied to the editor of the *Peking Daily News*, which had reprinted the French allegations with reservations. This letter was based on Addis's response to an urgent request from Hillier for information: Addis informed him that the Americans had made a loan proposal in the context of the Six-Power Groups, but that any such proposal by the Americans met with two difficulties found to be insuperable: (i) the British and French could not deal with the Germans in the Consortium and (ii) the Americans as neutrals could not ignore them. The American proposal was in consequence dropped.[55]

Nevertheless, the Hongkong Bank was still bound by international agreements which included German interests. Letters dealing with the Hukuang Railways Loan, for example, were sent to the Chinese authorities bearing the names and signatures of all parties, including H. Cordes for the DAB.

The consequence of these events and pressure from the Foreign Office was the formulation of a policy of support for the so-called New Consortium, which would include the United States and exclude Germany, with an opening for participation by Chinese banks, as the Yokohama Specie Bank had participated in international loans to Japan. This and related matters have been discussed above. Here it is sufficient to recall that the Foreign Office warned the Bank that such a Consortium would have to include a British Group with even wider membership, including the Chartered Bank and the Midland Bank, than that involved in the Reorganization Loan of 1913.[56]

In fairness it is unreasonable to suppose that regulations and attitudes which prevailed, barely, at the commencement of hostilities could last through four years of slaughter. The Hongkong Bank while obeying the regulations had become so enmeshed in international trade and investment agreements that it could not shake itself free nor could it suddenly abandon the principles on which it had operated, with the support of its shareholders as represented by its directors, since its founding in 1865. In the end the increasing strictness of the regulations guided the Bank into practices more acceptable to the emotional environment in which it operated; thus the Bank did not have to forgo voluntarily, as was at some point expected, commercial opportunities permitted by the particular interpretations of 'domicile' and 'enemy' which, while consistent with the traditions of nations at war and legally explicable, were unacceptable to those vocal elements of the public convinced of the pro-German tradition of the Bank.

The initial Foreign Office concern over these accusations against a bank with which it had associated itself was virtually eliminated by the revelations submitted by Sir Charles Addis and detailed at the beginning of this chapter. German equity investment in the Bank was negligible; outstandings were equally minimal. The whole basis of suspicion was erroneous. The Foreign Office was convinced, but there were members of the public who were anxious that criticism of the Bank should continue; there were Allied Governments who felt aggrieved, and as Addis and Stabb argued, there was no way to defend the Bank from general opinion when all specific instances were proven false.

Meanwhile the Bank continued to operate in Hamburg.

THE HAMBURG BRANCH DURING THE GREAT WAR[57]

Prelude to war
Although the build up of tension among the Powers had been observed closely in Hamburg, England's actual declaration of war on Germany on August 4, 1914, came as a surprise and a shock. The correspondence of many Hamburg merchant firms was inextricably tied up with the English, whether because they were dependent on the London discount market for the financing of their

trade or because they were involved in shipping English goods or in trade with England. Only on July 31 did the order come through to the Hamburg Branch of the Bank that the Eastern banks had decided that all insurance policies must now cover 'war risk'. Until then procedures had been perfectly normal. Similarly it was only during that last week that the Deutsch-Asiatische Bank (DAB) had decided to stop drawing bills on London and that the London banks had withdrawn their credits to the German bank.[58]

There would be no time to withdraw the British staff and no recognition of any need to do so. The British staff of the Hamburg Branch at that time was limited to two officers, R.E.N. Padfield, the Accountant, who was on leave in England, and St G.H. Phillips, the London Office junior. On July 31 Koelle received instructions from London Office to continue discounting and remitting freely, and London Office even offered to send Padfield back if he was required. Koelle replied that he did not yet need him, as he felt that 'with our business entirely stopped, as appeared likely, it would be a pity to recall him when London Office might be glad of his services'.[59]

The first hint of the changing conditions came on July 31 when the branch was instructed by the German authorities to cable only in German and without using codes. Koelle wired London Office to request that the other Hongkong Bank branches be instructed to send their wires to Hamburg if possible in German and certainly without code. On August 1 mail was returned with instructions that it was to be sent with the covers open, however even when these instructions were followed most mail was never received overseas.

On August 4, Koelle sent a wire, which was later returned undelivered by the military authorities despite having been previously passed by the German censors, in which he advised London Office of the DAB's urgent request for £50,000 to be sent to Calcutta, for which the DAB had conditionally deposited one million Marks at the Reichsbank to the joint credit of the Hamburg Branch and the Chartered Bank.

The DAB made a proposal to the Hongkong Bank that they agree to attempt the safeguard of each other's interests; the DAB would undertake without responsibility to help the Bank in Hamburg and Tsingtau, while the Hongkong Bank would do the same for the DAB in Calcutta, Singapore, and Hong Kong. Koelle's advice on this matter was that, in his lawyers' opinion, it was out of the question that the Hamburg Branch would be closed by the Germans as the calling in of the Bank's assets would cause grave hardship to several important German firms. These firms were otherwise protected by the Foreign Bills Moratorium of August 10, 1914, the Prohibition of Payments against England of September 30, 1914, and subsequent legislation. He therefore had refused to pledge the Bank in any way. This cable too was never delivered, but the DAB made a similar offer to the Bank in Hong Kong, where it received a similar rejection.

The first impact

Correspondence with London during the War was naturally difficult. From the beginning, it was hampered by regulations and from mid-August 1914 mail began to be returned to the Hamburg Branch. But when the branch was put under the control of German trustees, they were allowed to communicate regularly with London, although, as the letters had to be sent open, and the contents were censored so as not to prejudice German interests by giving information which might lead to claims against German firms or concerning the location of German ships, little could be said. There is however no record that these letters were ever delivered in London, and they are not to be found in the files of semi-official (S/O) letters in the London Office archives.

German banks claimed in February 1916 that they were unable to obtain any information from their branches in England, and this led to still further restrictions. The branch also received only sporadic correspondence from London Office; Koelle complained that the Chartered Bank was permitted to communicate more regularly. Most correspondence was sent via Hope and Co. in Amsterdam, but in November 1917 the Hamburg Branch heard that this link might soon be closed.

At the end of 1914 Koelle had been able to convince the German authorities that it was in German interests that Bills of Lading for goods against which Hongkong Bank drafts had been drawn should be sent to London when the relevant ships were in hostile ports in order to provide the Bank the opportunity to claim for these goods in the Prize Courts.·

The Hamburg Branch as a British bank

To help the plight of refugees who could in any way prove their respectability in trying to leave the country, the five British banks with branches in Hamburg – the Hongkong Bank, the Anglo South American Bank, the British Bank of West Africa, the Chartered Bank, and the Standard Bank of South Africa – each deposited 500 Marks into a guarantee fund at the Hamburg Branch of the Hongkong Bank to allow the branch to advance money, thereby relieving the heavily overworked American consulate. These funds were reclaimed after the War.[60]

At the same time the Anglican Church building was placed at the disposal of the Red Cross, and again the five British banks acted together in donating money to fit up the Church with hospital beds. Later, as it turned out, the Church was not used, but this act did much to enhance the goodwill towards the banks in the local press.

Koelle also served British interests during the War by making enquiries regarding British officers, by assisting wherever possible in safeguarding the personal property of interned British citizens, and by visiting them in the camps. He also tried to arrange the exchange of the interned manager of the

Standard Bank of South Africa for the manager of Disconto-Gesellschaft in London, who was released without the exchange in 1917.[61]

Koelle's policy from the beginning (in the absence of instructions of any sort from London) was to continue the Bank's pre-war policy of unbiased loyalty to the firms it served regardless of nationality. His first concern was to maintain sufficient liquidity to be able to meet any liabilities, thereby hoping to avoid giving the German authorities any excuse to close down or liquidate the branch or even to submit it to the control of trustees. In this last aim he was not successful, as the German authorities appointed a controller for the branch on September 5, 1914, although there had been no complaint concerning its activities.

Koelle also kept in close touch with the managers of the other British banks in Hamburg for as long as they were free to function and discussed his ideas for financing the branch with them. On August 5, for example, after such a discussion Koelle transferred 100,000 Marks of the Bank's funds into a Reichsbank account in his own name to serve as an emergency fund for the payment of salaries, charges, etc., should the Bank no longer be able to handle its own funds. However, he withdrew the money again on September 7 without waiting to be ordered to do so by the trustee.

From Koelle's own account of his activities during the War, there is no reason to doubt his continued loyalty to the principles the Bank had stood for since its founding. During that whole period he had to act for the most part without any form of communication with his superiors and was thus unaware of the anti-Bank feeling among certain interested British nor was he able to appreciate the growing anti-German attitude in the Bank itself.

In keeping with this policy, Koelle loyally kept up payments on the Bank's demand liabilities as they became due. To the British this was the equivalent of 'Trading with the Enemy' although the regulations could hardly reach into enemy territory and control the actions of an enemy national. No new business was undertaken during the War, but to Koelle the meeting of current obligations was merely a question of maintaining the Bank's good name with its traditional customers despite the transient impediment of the War. Moreover Koelle had little choice but to comply, as the branch was subjected to first one and then two trustees. By thus winding up his business in a fair and honest way, Koelle was able to maintain the branch largely under his own control. If he had attempted to refuse payments to enemy nationals, the trustees would most certainly have done so in his name, and there would then have been a greater possibility of the branch being liquidated.

Payment of dividends

When reports were received concerning the dividends paid by the Bank to shareholders in Allied and neutral territory, the trustees insisted that German shareholders also be accommodated. Koelle assumed that the dividends owed to German shareholders would be held in special accounts by the Bank until after the War, and therefore arranged to 'advance' the equivalent amount in Germany, charging the same amount of interest as would be allowed to accrue on the special accounts in the Bank.

However he later learned that the Hongkong Bank was required to pay these dividends into an account with the Public Trustee which received no interest. This in effect meant that the Bank paid these dividends twice, in Germany and again to the Public Trustee. Koelle attempted to protect the Bank against possible losses, but the German authorities prevented the insertion of the necessary qualifying clauses.[62]

Koelle was careful in such cases to obtain written evidence that he was only complying with express orders from the German controllers, as this would put the Bank in a position to make a claim for compensation after the War. In this particular case Koelle did not feel that the Bank was losing interest on the Hamburg funds 'advanced' against the dividends, as it was impossible for a foreign bank to place funds at interest during most of the War.

In 1916 Koelle received a communication from London asking for information concerning these dividend payments, but the German controllers would not allow him to send more than the total amounts paid out. The controllers felt that to give the names of German shareholders in the Bank and other such details would give the British information which might put German shareholders at a disadvantage if it should come to a confiscation of German property. Thus Koelle could not send sufficient information to London to make it possible for the Bank to reclaim the dividend funds which had been paid over to the Public Trustee.

Koelle and the German trustees

Koelle's relationship with the German trustees appointed to oversee the branch during the War remained cordial throughout, so much so that at one point the trustees agreed voluntarily to reduce the salaries the branch was forced to pay them. The trustees had the right to examine anything in the branch but, Koelle reported, never abused this to gain access to confidential S/Os or materials not directly connected with the carrying out of their supervisory functions.[d] At various times Koelle protested that the Hamburg

---

[d] In 1917, Garrels, one of the trustees, who had been chairman of the Deputation for Trade and Shipping, resigned his position to become a Hamburg State senator. He was replaced by his business partner Börner, of the firm Garrels & Börner – a long-standing constituent of the Hongkong Bank.[63]

German trustees of the Hamburg Branch during the Great War:

E. Guttmann	Sept 4, 1914–July 23, 1919
J.H. Garrels	Sept 23, 1914–Jan 22, 1917
H. Börner	Jan 23, 1917–Dec 10, 1918

Branch was burdened with two controllers whereas other enemy banks, the Chartered Bank for example, never had more than one. But the German authorities claimed that this was necessary as the volume of the Hongkong Bank's business with Germany justified the extra supervision.

The treatment of the British banks in Germany depended to some extent on reports received concerning the treatment of the German banks in England. Suspecting that the obverse would also be true in England, Koelle at various times sent messages to England to stress that they received good treatment from the German authorities, that private property was being respected, and that the British in Germany might be subject to reprisals if this were not also the case in England.

Banking problems

Koelle managed to keep the branch liquid until 1917, but it was a difficult task. Various regulations limited his ability to present or discount bills, although some companies voluntarily chose to pay their bills punctually even though they were under no legal compulsion. However, Koelle had discounted as many bills as possible before the restrictions were imposed and had been able to work out an arrangement in 1914 whereby the Reichsbank granted the branch credits against the remaining bills which had been drawn to the order of Hamburg Branch directly; however, they would not accept those which had been endorsed over to the branch by other offices of the Bank or by enemy firms.

In addition the branch had fortuitously received a large deposit in current account on August 1, 1914, of 1,823,000 Marks from the Siamese Government, but this proved more of an embarrassment than a boon as Koelle could never be sure when it might be withdrawn.[64]

The Reichsbank had, as we have seen, never allowed the branch interest on current account, but in 1914 the other German banks also agreed among themselves not to allow interest on deposits from English banks. This decision was modified later, however, and some British banks, though apparently not the Hongkong Bank, were allowed 1% on the credit balances they had shown at the outbreak of War. In May 1916, after consulting with the other banks, the Deutsche Bank agreed to pay the branch $3\frac{1}{2}$% per annum (the amount offered to the liquidators of foreign firms) on funds taken in *after* the branch had been put under control. Koelle was then able to place funds again at interest not only with the Deutsche Bank but also with the Dresdner and Norddeutsche Banks.

Koelle also tried to supplement the branch's income by subletting a portion of the premises to a Government department (potatoes); however, their landlord objected on the grounds that the large crowds which would have gathered at such an office would damage the reputation of the house and make his other tenants give notice.[65]

The threat that the branch might be liquidated became more real after ordinances were passed in July and August 1916 expressly excepting bills, if collected by a liquidator, from the protection of previous ordinances regarding payments to enemy banks.[66] Koelle, with the approval of the trustees and at the request of the staff, paid out their Officers Provident Fund to avoid any loss on liquidation.

Koelle consulted his lawyers as to the advisability of applying to be appointed liquidator himself, but they advised him not to agitate in this direction until the situation developed. Various firms made representations in Berlin to protest against any liquidation of the British banks in Hamburg. Koelle pointed out that, aside from the office furniture, the Bank had few realizable assets in Germany. A liquidation would have amounted to in effect a transfer of funds from German drawees to German drawers causing great hardship to the former, who were for the most part not in receipt of the goods in question.[67]

A further threat to the branch's financial position came from the possibility that German firms might attempt to 'arrest' funds belonging to the Hamburg Branch proportionate to the amounts which the British Custodian of Enemy Property had confiscated from them from their assets with the Hongkong Bank elsewhere. In fact only a few firms attempted this. However from the amounts involved, it is clear that the branch could not have accommodated many further suits. The first and most important case of this sort was brought by Leopold Cassella & Co. (Frankfurt). On April 22, 1915, they were successful in obtaining a court order to arrest 900,000 Marks of the branch's funds at the Reichsbank for amounts held in a suspense account for their correspondent firm Sander, Wieler and Co. in the Hongkong Bank in Hong Kong. Koelle decided not to protest this decision but made sure that the Bank would retain the right to file a protest after the War. He feared that publicity might encourage other German firms.[68]

In January 1916, a Munich customer of the Standard Bank of South Africa had a similar arrest put on that bank for his securities in safe custody in London. Koelle protested that the Standard Bank had been allowed to communicate this embargo to London, whereas the Hongkong Bank had not 'in spite of the Hongkong Bank's German connections, shareholders and directors'.[69] The trustees said they would look into the matter, but the branch was never allowed to inform London.

During the War, the branch was subject to various taxes. It is noteworthy that, in the case of the *Wehrsteuer*, or Imperial Defence Tax, of 1913, Koelle was able to persuade the German authorities to reduce the tax assessment on the branch from 18,255 to 9,600 Marks. In September 1917, an extraordinary tax was levied on the assets of enemy banks and firms. The branch was assessed for 141,110 Marks which was paid under protest in October. The branch also engaged in several lawsuits during the War in order either to establish the basis for a claim by the Bank after the War or to set a precedent.

Koelle's every action suggests that he, like Addis, was considering the post-war period and the resumption of normal business. To the extent possible he protected the Bank and reserved its rights. The relatively moderate policy pursued by the German authorities gives, in one sense, a credence to Allied views that Germany expected its trading relations to be reestablished; German firms would still need financial assistance, and the Hongkong Bank would be one source of funds. In this they were to prove correct, but under circumstances that neither side envisaged.

The tragedy is personal. Koelle remained loyal to the Bank. The Bank, however, would find it impolitic to remain loyal to Koelle.

SUMMARY: THE HONGKONG BANK AT WAR

The Hongkong Bank with a functioning branch in Hamburg, continuing contacts with the Deutsch-Asiatische Bank, and traditional relations with German trading firms was never able to completely clear itself of general and often vague assertions of 'German influence' – in the public mind. The Bank's London Manager, who like Koelle himself, was a Christian and the son of a preacher, had a vision – economic development facilitated by the international cooperation of leading banking groups, a concert of Europe to assist in the growth and to foster the prosperity of China and the East. The Great War was a reluctant necessity to purge Germany of a temporary aberration before a return to a pre-war world and the pre-war vision. That he held these views was widely known; for some the Addis view confirmed the image of the Hongkong Bank which its enemies were fostering.

And yet the enmity and campaign of vilification had little practical effect. The Hongkong Bank erred in only a small number of cases, the Foreign Office became convinced of its integrity and British orientation, the financial capabilities of its staff and the facilities it made available were essential to Britain and its Allies in the East, and the Bank's performance as reflected in its dividend payments and the growth of its reserves was evidence that it remained the premier exchange bank in the East.

The Bank, however, survived the 'hate' campaign at a price. It committed itself publicly to becoming 'British' in the narrow sense of 'anti-' German – eventually even marriage to a foreigner would be seriously questioned.

Already virtually totally British as far as executive staff were concerned, the Bank proclaimed this policy as the price of acceptance. For a time it played down its international base, but then Hong Kong itself chose to forget its international purpose in providing equal opportunities to all traders; although it continued, perforce, to do so. Hong Kong sank into the background and the inter-war focus was on Shanghai, the great international city on the edge of the vast Yangtze Valley of China, but the Bank was both Hong Kong and Shanghai, and to the extent permitted by the economic realities of their world, prospered. The Bank was, after all, primarily a China bank.

Such attitudes could not and would not last in their fullness. The memory of the 'hate' campaign would, however, remain and affect the history of the Bank as recounted in Volume III.

Whatever doubts the jingoists had of the Bank's corporate background, whatever aspersions were cast at its British image, there was no question of the loyalty of its British staff and management and of the role they played in the Great War.

It was unanimously decided to place on record the thankfulness and profound satisfaction felt by the directors on the receipt of the news that an Armistice had been signed on November 11, 1918, terminating the fighting in the titanic struggle, also their appreciation and admiration for the heroism and staunchness displayed by all ranks of the British and Allied Armies and Navies to whose united efforts, aided by the whole-hearted cooperation of the Governments and civilian populations of the Allied countries, the Victorious termination of this long and bloody struggle is due.

Board of Directors, 12 November 1918.

NOTES

Material from the Hongkong Bank Group Archives is not fully cited; the archives were in the process of cataloguing during the writing of this history. Sufficient information has been provided to permit the Archives staff to locate the material. The 'F.H. King letters' are those selected by F.H. 'Towkay' King from the then London Office Archives for the use of J.R. Jones in preparing for the centenary history.

Abbreviations used in the notes

AA	Germany, Federal Republic, Ministry of Foreign Affairs, Archives, Bonn (Auswärtiges Amt)
BT	Board of Trade records in the PRO
cf	compare
CO	Colonial Office records in the PRO
DG	Disconto-Gesellschaft
DNB	*Dictionary of National Biography*
f	folio
ff	folios; following pages
FO	Foreign Office records in the PRO
Group Archives	Archives of the Hongkong Bank Group, Head Office, Hong Kong
HSBC	Hongkong and Shanghai Banking Corporation
ibid	the same
IG	Inspector General (of the Imperial Maritime Customs)
IMC	Imperial [*then* Chinese] Maritime Customs
IOR	India Office Records, London
LOSO	London Office Standing Orders, Hongkong Bank
MA	Massachusetts
MI	Michigan
NA	National Association
n.d.	no date
p	page
pp	pages
P&O	Peninsular and Oriental Steam Navigation Company
P.I.	Philippine Islands
PP.MS.14	[Sir Charles] Addis Papers, Library, School of Oriental and African Studies, University of London

PRO	Public Record Office, London
PROHK	Public Records Office, Hong Kong
SNA	Singapore National Archives
s/o	'semi-official' intra-Bank correspondence
SOAS	School of Oriental and African Studies, University of London
SS	Straits Settlements
SSLCP	*Straits Settlements Legislative Council Proceedings*
T	Treasury records in the PRO
trans	translator
Ts	Taels
USNA	National Archives of the United States
Vol	Volume

Part I. There are no notes to the Introduction to Part I.

I THE CORPORATION, 1902–1914

1 H.E. Nixon to J.R. Jones, in 'Personalities and Narratives', Hongkong Bank Group Archives, Hong Kong.

2 Newton J. Stabb to Charles S. Addis, 27 August 1910, PP.MS.14/364, [Sir Charles] Addis Papers, Library, School of Oriental and African Studies, University of London.

3 See letters dealing with Jackson's acceptance of the Chairmanship of the Imperial Bank of Persia in Jackson box, Group Archives.

4 Addis diary, 27 July 1903, PP.MS.14/21.

5 Ibid, 17 October 1906, PP.MS.14/24.

6 Ibid, 6 December 1906, PP.MS.14/24.

7 Under 'Stabb' in J.R. Jones, 'Personalities and Narratives', Group Archives.

8 Addis diary, 30 June 1902, PP.MS.14/20.

9 Stabb to J. Swire, 17 October 1913, in the Archive of John Swire and Sons, Ltd, the Library, SOAS. Edkins became a member of the Board.

10 For reaction to the Bank's refusal to permit its Shanghai Manager to stand for election, see China Association, Minutes, 11 March 1913, and the subsequent explanatory letter from Hongkong Bank Chairman Stanley H. Dodwell dated 29 September, in Archive of the China Association, the Library, SOAS. For the Hong Kong Governor's despatch on this subject, see Sir Francis May to Secretary of State, 7 March 1913, CO 129/400, ff. 42–43. I am indebted to Dr Norman Miners for the latter reference. See also Chapter 3 on this subject.

11 Stabb to Addis, 22 January 1913, in Group Archives from London.

12 See, for example, Morrison's Reuters cable and the exchange between E.G. Hillier and G.E. Morrison, 26 and 27 July 1909 (letters 313, 315–16, 318), in *The Correspondence of G.E. Morrison, 1895–1920*, edited by Hui-min Lo (Cambridge, 1978), I, 505–10, and *passim*.

13 D. McLean to James Greig, 16 July 1875, in McLean Private Letters (London), I, 3, McLean Papers, MS 380401, SOAS.

14 Addis, 'Journal', PP.MS.14/674, photocopy.

15 G.E. Morrison, letter no. 556, 15 November 1912, in his *Correspondence*, II, 54–55.

16 A.M. Townsend to Treasury, 3 August 1904, T.1/10138A.

17 Addis to Treasury, 21 August 1906, T.1/10518B; the file contains other relevant material.

18 Minutes of a meeting (the 8th) held at the Wai-wu Pu, 25 October 1906, on

the Kowloon–Canton Railway, in CO 129/336, f. 435, and 'Agreement for the issue and regulation of a loan for the construction of the Canton–Kowloon Railway', 7 March 1907, in John V.A. MacMurray, comp. and ed. *Treaties and Agreements with and concerning China, 1894–1919* (New York, 1921), I, 623.

19 Addis to J.R.M. Smith, 7 November 1904, PP.MS.14/352.
20 HSBC Inspector's Report, in Group Archives.
21 China Association, Minute Book for 3 February 1903, in China Association Archive, SOAS.
22 Ibid.
23 Rosemary Quested, *The Russo-Chinese Bank* (Birmingham, 1977), p. 3.
24 Harold van B. Cleveland and Thomas F. Huertas, *Citibank, 1812–1970* (Cambridge, MA, 1985), pp. 80–81; Frank M. Tamagna, *Banking and Finance in China* (New York, 1942), pp. 20–28, 35–42.
25 Takashi Masuda, *Japan, its Commercial Developments and Prospects* (London, n.d.), p. 77.
26 Quoted in *Yushin Nippon* (Kobe, 1 June 1926).
27 J.A. Chinoy to Sir Thomas Jackson, 6 December 1906, in 'Personalities', Group Archives. The draft and notes for the ceremony of the statue are found in the Nathan Papers, Rhodes House Library, Oxford, 350a–b, f. 38.
28 J.R.M. Smith to T. Smith, Colonial Secretary, 18 January 1907, CO 129/339, ff. 573–75.
29 CO 129/339, f. 259, 18 February 1907; see also ff. 260–63.
30 Treasury to Colonial Office, 28 February 1907, CO 129/342, ff. 415–17.
31 J.R.M. Smith to F.H. May, Colonial Secretary, 7 March 1907, CO 129/339, ff. 576–77.
32 *Hongkong Hansard* (1907), pp. 11 and 16.
33 See Addis to Colonial Office, CO 129/342, f. 420, and discussion in CO 129/340, ff. 42–52 and 649–51, and CO 129/342, ff. 407–23. The proclamations are found in CO 129/340, ff. 652–55.
34 Telegram book, KG 1/1, Group Archives.
35 Ibid.
36 This section is taken from Carl T. Smith, 'Compradores of The Hongkong Bank', in King, ed. *Eastern Banking* (London, 1983), pp. 109–10.
37 Data from India Office (Purchase of Silver), *Return of any Correspondence with the Bank of England and Messrs Samuel Montagu and Company, relating to purchases of Silver in 1912* (London; HMSO, 1912); see India Office Records (IOR), L/F/7/21, p. 2, 'Events of 1912'.
38 Ibid. The story is taken from the correspondence and commentary reprinted in the above cited work, including correspondence to and from the Hongkong Bank.
39 See Marcello de Cecco, *Money and Empire: the International Gold Standard, 1890–1914* (Oxford, 1974).
40 Mocatta and Goldsmid archives, MS18,653, Guildhall Library, City of London and Addis diary; see also IOR L/F/7/222 on the Specie Bank's speculations in silver and L/F/7/231 on the bankruptcy.
41 For the 1910 Canton affair, see correspondence in CO 129/367, ff. 129, 150–57; CO 129/368, ff. 159–62; CO 129/368, ff. 447–53 and 464 referring specifically to a representation of the Hongkong Bank dated 10 August 1910; and CO 129/385, f. 52.
42 Letter addressed to F.H. May, 12 December 1912, in CO 129/394, ff. 73–74.
43 Jordan to Sir Edward Grey, 5 December 1912, CO 129/405, ff. 109–10.
44 12 December 1912, CO 129/405, ff. 215–16.

45 See the discussion in Stanley F. Wright, *Hart and the Chinese Customs* (Belfast, 1950), pp. 842–46.
46 Morrison to O.M. Green, 21 December 1912, letter No. 563, in Morrison, II, 70.
47 Personnel records in Group Archives.
48 From a verbatim transcript made for the Hongkong Bank, now in Group Archives.
49 Taken from CO 129/124 and abbreviated without notation.
50 T.A. Lee, 'The Financial Statements of The Hongkong and Shanghai Banking Corporation', in King, ed. *Eastern Banking*, p. 78.
51 From the verbatim transcript, cited.
52 Noted in the Board of Directors Minutes.
53 Claude Severn, Officer Administering the Government of Hong Kong, to Secretary of State Harcourt, 26 June 1912, CO 129/390, ff. 411–16, with enclosed report of the Finance Committee of the Legislative Council, dated 22 May 1884 and signed by T. Jackson and others, ff. 417–20.
54 Ibid.
55 Treasury to Colonial Office, 5 June 1911, CO 129/386, ff. 131–32.
56 CO 129/397, ff. 91–94, esp. letter from Treasury to Colonial Office, dated 2 September 1912, f. 91.
57 See correspondence in CO 129/391, ff. 248–62. The authorization for the purchase of the Gracechurch Street property was signed by F.H. May as the Officer Administering the Government, 29 September 1910 (f. 252); the Bank's submission of its property list was on 26 July 1912.
58 Memo dated 15 May 1914, CO 129/411, f. 254.
59 The Governor's letter is dated 4 June 1914 and includes a draft of the circular to shareholders giving the detailed amendment proposals for the Extraordinary Meeting, CO 129/411, ff. 251–57.
60 See Executive Council minutes for 10 September 1914 in CO 131/49, f. 323, and Legislative Council minutes of 18 September 1914, *Hongkong Hansard*, p. 97; for the commentary of the Hong Kong Government following passage of the Bill, see CO 129/413, ff. 324–27. The Government had the proposed amendments advertised in the *Hongkong Daily Press* and the *Chung Ngoi San Po*.
61 Addis diary, 4 July 1914, PP.MS.14/32.
62 Ibid, 14 December 1910, PP.MS.14/28.

2 BRANCHES AND AGENCIES – AN ILLUSTRATIVE SURVEY

1 I am indebted to Professor Patrick Tuck, University of Liverpool, for introducing me to this aspect of the Bank's activities and for contacting Fr J. Verinaud, Archivist of the Missions étrangères de Paris, Aix-en-Provence, on my behalf. The references have been provided through the courtesy of Fr Verinaud and are quoted with permission.
2 Based on information in the letters of Mgr Colombert to Père Lemonnier, Procureur Générale in Hong Kong (1877–1891), 1 October 1882 and 6 February 1883, nos 100 and 109 respectively in Volume 759 (Cochinchine Occidentale), Archives of the Missions étrangères de Paris.
3 Ibid, 9 November 1885 (No. 191).
4 Quotation kindly supplied by Professor T. Hamashita.
5 For the background history of this company and its failure see H.S. Williams, 'Demon-tiles', *Mainichi Daily News* (25 June 1960), reprinted in his *Foreigners in Mikadoland* (Tokyo, 1963), pp. 202–06.
6 Information in a letter from Professor Hamashita.

7 References in this section come from a research paper in Group Archives, David J.S. King, 'The Hongkong Bank and Germany, Part I, The History – excluding the China Loans', Chapter IV, 'Japan – a brief survey'. See Maximilian Müller-Jabusch, *Fünfzig Jahre Deutsch-Asiatische Bank, 1890–1939* (Berlin, 1940), p. 207.

8 Auswärtiges Amt, Bonn [AA], Japan no. 3. Finances. Vol. 5, A.S. 373, AA minute after a conversation with Roland-Lücke of the DB on 18 and 21 March 1905.

9 Ibid, A 4816, AA minute after a conversation with Roland-Lücke, 22 March 1905.

10 Diary entry by Mrs Addis, 31 March 1905, PP.MS.14/23, [Sir] Charles Addis Papers, Library, School of Oriental and African Studies, University of London.

11 See note 9.

12 Müller-Jabusch, 1940, p. 208; AA, Japan no. 3. *Finances*. Vol. 5, A 4893105, minutes of their discussion.

13 AA, Japan no. 3. Finances. Vol. 6, A 11080, 26 June 1905.

14 Ibid, A 11128, AA Note, 27 June 1905.

15 Müller-Jabusch, 1940, p. 209.

16 AA, Japan no. 3. *Finances*. Vol. 6, A 12222, AA minute of a conversation with Erich of the DAB, 12 July 1905; ibid, A 20368, AA Note, 16 November 1905.

17 For the Anglo-Japanese Bank see BT 31/11517/88771, for the British and Japanese Finance Corporation see BT 31/11248/85937.

18 David McLean to Jackson, 16 March 1877, Private Letters (London), I, 219, in McLean Papers, MS 380401, the Library, School of Oriental and African Studies, University of London.

19 Sir Compton Mackenzie, *Realms of Silver, One Hundred Years of Banking in the East* (London, 1954), p. 134. This is a commissioned history of the Chartered Bank of India, Australia and China.

20 See Renato Constantino, *A History of the Philippines: from the Spanish Colonization to the Second World War* (New York, 1975), pp. 192–201; S.V. Epistola, 'The Hong Kong Junta', *Philippine Social Sciences and Humanities Review* 24: 3–12, 23–33 (March 1961). I am indebted to Professor Grant Goodman, University of Kansas, for these and the following references.

21 Suit No. 31 of (21 April) 1898, cited in J.R.M. Taylor, comp. *The Philippine Insurrection Against the United States. A Compilation of Documents with Notes and Introduction* (Washington, 1906), I, 467.

22 See references in note 19 above.

23 F.C.B. Black, oral history, recalling in 1980 the story as told him in 1932 while assigned as a junior to the Manila branch. In this account the insurgent leader is given as 'Rizal'; if 'José Rizal' it becomes quite a story of historical interest.

24 A.G. Kellogg to Arthur Morse, 11 August 1945, in Group Archives with F.H. King letters, K1.18. An article from the *Shanghai Evening Post* recalling the event was enclosed.

25 Townsend to Secretary of War Russell A. Alger, USNA, RG350, File 1988, in National Archives of the United States, Washington, DC.

26 Charles Dawes to Secretary of War, 29 July 1901, USNA, RG350, File 2879.

27 Report of the Treasurer, file date 27 May 1901, USNA, Bureau of Insular Affairs, RG350, File 2879.

28 War Department, Division of Insular Affairs, Memoranda of statistics and comments by P.I. Officials on condition and methods of banks doing business at Manila, P.I., Memorandum for Colonel Edwards [Chief of Division] endorsed for forwarding to the Comptroller of the Currency, 18 July 1901, USNA, Bureau of Insular Affairs, RG350, File 2879.

29 Walter H. Young, *A Merry Banker in the Far East* (London, 1916), pp. 58–59.
30 General Otis to War Department, August 1899; see note 28.
31 R.P. Thursfield, *Topical Verses* (Shanghai, 1914).
32 Bankers Association of the Philippines, *History of Banking in the Philippines* (Manila, 1957), p. 7.
33 From Reports of the Bank Examiner, Bureau of the Treasury; USNA, Record Group 350. Also from Annual Reports of the Bank Commissioner of the Philippines to Secretary of Finance, various fiscal years.
34 Vicente Valdepeñas and Gemilino Bautista, *The Emergence of the Philippine Economy* (Manila, 1977), pp. 115–16. The references are taken from Roy C. Ybañez, 'The Hongkong Bank in the Philippines, 1899–1941', in King, ed. *Eastern Banking* (London, 1983), pp. 452–53.
35 [Smith, Bell and Co.], *Under Four Flags, the Story of Smith, Bell & Company in the Philippines* (privately published in England, n.d. but early 1970s), Chapter 7, 'The Sugar Crisis', pp. 30–35.
36 David McLean to Thomas Jackson, 3, 10, 24 February 1888, in Private Letters (London), VI, 92, 93, and 95 respectively.
37 *Encyclopaedia Britannica*, V, 180.
38 See H.A. de S. Gunasekera, *From Dependent Currency to Central Banking in Ceylon* (1960).
39 *Bangkok Times* (24 October 1888). Certain of these references are from Thiravet Pramuanratkarn, 'The Hongkong Bank in Thailand: a Case of a Pioneering Bank', in King, ed. *Eastern Banking*, pp. 421–34.
40 Letter from the former Ambassador and Thai-language student, then in Mombassa, to J.R. Jones, who was collecting material for the Hongkong Bank centenary history.
41 *Bangkok Times* (7 February 1894).
42 Trade figures are from James C. Ingram, *Economic Change in Thailand since 1850* (Stanford, 1955), and Paul Sithi-Amnuai, *Finance and Banking in Thailand, a study of the commercial system, 1888–1963* (Bangkok, 1964).
43 Information on the loans is taken from (i) the prospectuses, (ii) memorandums prepared for J.R. Jones, and (iii) a reply from Mme Suparb of the Bank of Thailand using Ministry of Finance files, all in Group Archives.
44 Addis diary, 25 March 1905, PP.MS.14/23.
45 Addis diary, 18 February 1905, PP.MS.14/23.
46 Addis diary, 14 March 1905, PP.MS.14/23.
47 W.R.D. Beckett to Secretary of State Sir Edward Grey, dated 7 November 1906, in T.1/11845.
48 The references to German sources are found in D.J.S. King's report on the Hongkong Bank and Germany, cited, Chapter V 'Siam: Intrigues and Rivalries', specifically, AA, Siam No. 1. General Situation, Vol. 30, items dated 4, 11, 12, 16, 23 January 1907.
49 Ibid.
50 Letourneur (Lyons) to Maillard (London branch of Crédit Lyonnais), 10 January 1884, quoted in J. Bouvier, *Le Crédit Lyonnais de 1865 à 1882*, p. 282n4. See also, ibid, p. 281n9.
51 R. Brun de la Valette, *Lyon et ses rues* (Lyon, 1969), p. 116.
52 Ministry of Finance, Paris, Archives: F 30.370. Hongkong Bank (Lyons) Ministry of Finance, 30 April 1907, 1 February, and 30 July 1908.
53 There are many references in de Bovis's letters. See also Louis Gueneau, *Lyon et le commerce de la soie* (Lyons, 1932), pp. 167–70.
54 See W.W. Syrett, *Finance of Overseas Trade*, 3rd ed. (London, 1957), pp. 56–67.

55 De Bovis to J.C. Peter (Sub-Manager, Hong Kong), 16 November 1906, Group Archives.
56 Banque de France, Paris, Archives: Rapport d'Inspection de la Succursale de Lyon, 1910.
57 Hongkong Bank Inspector's report on Lyons agency, 18 March 1918, p. 12.
58 De Bovis to H.D.C. Jones (London), 9 June 1913.
59 De Bovis to A.H. Barlow (Hong Kong), 12 December 1913.
60 De Bovis to J.H. MacLaren (Sub-Manager, Yokohama), 28 November 1913.
61 De Bovis to MacLaren, 5 December 1913.
62 Banque de France, Paris, Archives: Rapport d'Inspection de la Succursale de Lyon. See reports for 1890, 1892, and 1899.
63 Ibid. Reports for 1890 through 1900 respectively.
64 De Bovis to Peter, 13 September 1907 in Group Archives.
65 Banque de France, Paris, Archives: Rapport d'Inspection de la Succursale de Lyon, 1908.
66 For the history, see the references of C. Fivel-Démoret as follows: John F. Laffey, 'Municipal Imperialism in Nineteenth Century France', *Historical reflections – réflexions historiques* 1, 1: 81–113 (1974); 'Municipal Imperialism in France: The Lyon Chamber of Commerce 1900–1914', *Proceedings of the American Philosophical Society* 119, 1: 8–23 (1975); 'Municipal Imperialism: The Lyon Chamber of Commerce 1914–1925', *Journal of European Economic History* 4, 1: 95–120 (1975); 'Municipal Imperialism in Decline: The Lyon Chamber of Commerce 1925–1938', *French Historical Studies* 9, 2: 329–53 (1975); 'The Lyon Chamber of Commerce and Indochina during the Third Republic', *Canadian Journal of History* 10, 3: 325–48 (1975).
67 Laffey, pp. 331–33. See also Michel Bruguière, 'Le chemin de fer du Yunnan: Paul Doumer et la politique d'intervention française en Chine, 1899–1902', *Revue d'Histoire Diplomatique* (1963), pp. 23–61, 129–62, and 252–78, especially pp. 262–78.
68 De Bovis to Peter, 15 and 29 June, 20 July; then 15 and 18 May, 29 June 1906, 20 July, and 14 December 1906 and to R.R. Hynd (Hong Kong), 28 December 1906 in Group Archives. A semi-official publication praised the concern as a path-breaking agent for French trade in Indochina, see Maurice Zimmerman, 'Lyon colonial', in *Lyon et la région lyonnaise en 1906* (Lyon, 1906), p. 275.
69 De Bovis to Peter, 14 December 1906.
70 De Bovis to R.R. Hynd (Sub-Accountant, Hong Kong), 28 December 1906.
71 De Bovis to Peter, 7 February 1907.
72 This list is based upon one compiled by J.R. Jones in Group Archives under 'Branches'; it has been checked against a list in a translation of a study by the Bank of Chosen, *Past and Present of the Hongkong and Shanghai Banking Corporation* (1915), and with David J.S. King's research report cited in note 7 above.

3 HONGKONG BANKERS, 1900–1914

1 The quotation is from the Hongkong Bank Board minutes for 24 October 1905.
2 F.H. May to the Secretary of State, 7 March 1913, CO 129/400, ff. 42–43. See Chapter 1, note 10.
3 Circulars, Vol. X, 17 June 1913, H.D.C. Jones to China Association; Minute Book, 1911–22, 16 May 1911; 11 March, 8 April 1913, in Archive of the China Association, the Library, School of Oriental and African Studies, University of London.

4 Addis diary, 17 December 1908, PP.MS.14/26, [Sir Charles] Addis Papers, SOAS.
5 Addis to Mills, 26 December 1908, PP.MS.14/169.
6 Addis diary, 16, 18, and 24 December 1908, PP.MS.14/26.
7 Ibid, 23 October 1913, PP.MS.14/31.
8 Ibid, Eba's [Lady Addis's] entry, 25 October 1913, PP.MS.14/31.
9 Sir Carl Meyer to Astley's, Plumstead, 23 October 1913, in his letters Vol. IV, quoted through the courtesy of Sir Anthony Meyer, MP.
10 References from H.E. Muriel are either from his autobiography or from his contribution to the collection entitled 'Personalities and Narratives', compiled by J.R. Jones in connection with the centenary history and arranged alphabetically without continuous pagination. Both are in the Hongkong Bank Group Archives. This quotation is from the autobiography.
11 'Personalities'; this information is under 'Wood'.
12 H.E. Muriel, in his autobiography, Group Archives.
13 Addis to his father, 27 February 1886, PP.MS.14/64/19. See discussion in Volume I, Chapter 9.
14 Muriel, autobiography.
15 Ibid.
16 J.C. Peter in 'Personalities'.
17 Florence C. Hawkins to Charles Addis, 29 September 1892, PP.MS.14/115.
18 Stabb to Addis, 27 August 1910, PP.MS.14/364.
19 Ibid, 19 February 1912, PP.MS.14/368.
20 Eba Addis, diary, 29 December 1900, PP.MS.14/18.
21 Mrs T. Jackson, Chislehurst, Kent, to Charles Addis, 3 November 1887, PP.MS.14/107.
22 Addis to Mills, 26 July 1896, PP.MS.14/157. See biography of Veitch in Volume I, Chapter 15.
23 George Addis to Charles Addis, 7 November 1889, PP.MS.14/79.
24 Addis to Mills, 26 July 1896, PP.MS.14/157.
25 George Addis to Charles Addis, 27 July 1886, PP.MS.14/76; Ewen Cameron to Charles Addis, 19 June 1901, PP.MS.14/118 – Cameron had known George in Calcutta; J.H. Simpson of the Bank of Liverpool to Charles Addis, 22 August 1901, PP.MS.14/162; see also PP.MS.14/162, 11 August 1901.
26 PP.MS.14/118.
27 For the International Banking Corporation offer, see Eba Addis's diary entry, 4 December 1902, PP.MS.14/20.
28 PP.MS.14/163, 13 August 1902.
29 PP.MS.14/354, 3 March 1905.
30 PP.MS.14/354, 6 March 1905.
31 P.G. Wodehouse, 'My Banking Career', *The Hongkong Bank Group Magazine* No. 6 (summer 1975), p. 14.
32 Diary, 19 January 1909, PP.MS.14/27.
33 Information for this section, unless otherwise stated, is taken from the 'Personalities' file compiled by J.R. Jones, Group Archives.
34 PP.MS.14/117.
35 Diary, 22 June 1908, PP.MS.14/26.
36 Chirol to G.E. Morrison, 12 April 1906, in Hui-min Lo, ed. *The Correspondence of G.E. Morrison* (Cambridge, 1976), I, 363.
37 The quote refers specifically to the earlier illness, see Addis to Mills, 19 June 1905, PP.MS.14/166.
38 Diary, 10 December 1908, PP.MS.14/26.

39 Ibid, 13 June 1911, PP.MS.14/29.
40 Ibid, 9 December 1911, PP.MS.14/29.
41 Ibid, 11 January 1912, PP.MS.14/30; the actual letter is PP.MS.14/368, same date.
42 Addis to Mills, 19 June 1905, PP.MS.14/166.
43 Diary, 11 January 1908, PP.MS.14/26.
44 Ibid, 11 March and 17 June 1915, PP.MS.14/33.
45 Addis to Stabb, 24 December 1915, PP.MS.14/377.
46 Sir Newton Stabb to Lady Stabb, 25 December 1915, in the F.H. King collection of letters, Group Archives.
47 On Amoy, see Arnold Wright, ed. *Twentieth Century Impressions of Hongkong, Shanghai and other Treaty Ports of China* (London, 1908), p. 821; Addis diary, 16 October 1937, PP.MS.14/55.
48 A.S. Henchman to J.R. Jones, in Personalities file, Group Archives and Geoffrey Jones, *Banking and Empire in Iran*, Vol. I of his *The History of the British Bank of the Middle East* (Cambridge 1986), p. 166.
49 See under 'Hillier' in Personalities file.
50 For Hewat's dislike of Peking, see Hewat to Addis, 5 July 1890, PP.MS.14/112.
51 Biographical sketch by Hillier's second wife, Eleanor Richard Hillier, in Personalities file.
52 *The Times* (15 April 1924).
53 Eleanor Hillier on E.G. Hillier, see note 51 above.
54 Sir Robert Hart at the Bank's Second Annual Dinner, January 1909, in London Office II materials dealing with the dinners, Group Archives.
55 A.M. Townsend, 'Early Days of the Hongkong and Shanghai Bank' (1937), p. 16, in Group Archives.
56 Biographical notes by Townsend in Personalities file, Group Archives.
57 Addis diary, 13 April 1909, PP.MS.14/27.
58 Ibid, PP.MS.14/24.
59 Ibid, 20 September 1907, PP.MS.14/25.
60 Ibid, 30 July 1913, PP.MS.14/31.
61 Ibid, 8 February 1910, PP.MS.14/28.
62 Materials on First Annual Dinner, in London Office II files, Group Archives.
63 Materials on Third Annual Dinner, in ibid; also *Supplement to the London and China Express* (24 December 1909), pp. 1–2.
64 'Hongkong and Shanghai Banking [*sic*], The New Office', *The Bankers', Insurance Managers' and Agents' Magazine* 96, 837: 734–42 (December 1913).
65 Addis to Stabb, 8 September 1915, in F.H. King letters, Group Archives.
66 A.S. Adamson to J.R. Jones, 8 November 1953, in Personalities file, Group Archives.
67 London Office Standing Orders (LOSO), 6 Vols, 1880–1958, Vol. II (1896–1907) and Vol. III (1907–1922), in Group Archives LOH2 169 to 174.
68 Ibid.
69 Ibid.
70 Personalities file, Group Archives.
71 Ibid, under F.E. Nicoll.
72 P.G. Wodehouse to J.R. Jones, 15 October 1954, in Personalities file.
73 Miss Robina Addis, OBE, the youngest daughter of Sir Charles and Lady Addis, told me this story during a visit to the family home in Frant, Sussex, in 1980.
74 13 January 1941, PP.MS.14/59.
75 LOSO, Vol. III, 15 August 1913.
76 P.G. Wodehouse, *Psmith in the City*, p. 17.

77 Ibid, p. 24.
78 Ibid, p. 26.
79 Ibid, p. 32.
80 Ibid, p. 34.
81 Ibid, p. 157.
82 P.G. Wodehouse, 'My Banking Career', *The Hongkong Bank Group Magazine*, No. 6 (Summer 1975), pp. 13–16. See also, Wodehouse to J.R. Jones, 15 October 1954. For other Wodehouse comments on the Bank see, e.g. 'Wooster Looks at London', *Time and Tide* and 'Something Clever', *Punch* (6 October 1954).
83 Wodehouse, 'My Banking Career', pp. 13–16.
84 LOSO, 1907.
85 H. Hewat to H.E.R. Hunter, 4 July 1900, p. 3, under 'Hunter' in Personalities file, Group Archives.
86 See, for example, Addis, 'Leaves from a Diary', 30 October 1901, PP.MS.14/67/148.
87 Murray Stewart to Addis, 18 May 1900, and 21 August 1901, PP.MS.14/231 and 232.
88 George Addis to Charles Addis, 15 September 1887, PP.MS.14/77.
89 Ibid, 26 March 1891, PP.MS.14/81.
90 Addis diary, 20 October 1899, PP.MS.14/17.
91 Supplement to the *London and China Express* (24 December 1909), p. 1.
92 Ibid.
93 Ibid.
94 Ibid.
95 Addis diary, 20 November 1911, PP.MS.14/29.
96 'Personalities' under '[F.E.] Nicoll', Group Archives.
97 Oral history interview by Christopher Cook, 18 February 1981, in Group Archives.
98 Oral history interview by Christopher Cook, 18 August 1980, in Group Archives.
99 Addis to Cameron, 18 November 1904, PP.MS.14/352.
100 LOSO, announcing the new school, 1900.
101 George Addis to Charles Addis, 7 November 1889, PP.MS.14/79.
102 In 'Memorandum of C.S. Addis . . .', Appendix III, Report of the Committee on Oriental Studies in London, 1908; see also, testimony of Charles Addis, 21 May 1908, ibid, pp. 184–89, PP.MS.14/643.
103 Charles Addis to Colin C. Scott of Swire's, 18 November 1904, Box 1183, Archive of John Swire and Sons, the Library, SOAS.
104 A.M. Reith, Hankow, to Charles Addis, 17 May 1906, PP.MS.14/360.
105 Addis to Cameron, 18 November 1904, PP.MS.14/352.
106 LOSO, 11 October 1909. This order refers only to Part I, but for the few that passed Part II, a similar award was in fact made.
107 Personalities file, F.E. Nicoll, in Group Archives.
108 For a biographical sketch of Bernard H. Leach, including his months as a London Office junior with the Hongkong Bank, see Sue Bond, 'Portrait of a Potter', *Hongkong Bank Group Magazine*, No. 8 (Summer 1976), pp. 25–28.
109 My interview with Sir Arthur Morse in his garden flat overlooking Green Park, London, in 1966.

4 CURRENCY AND BANKING REFORMS

1 Debate on the Currency Note Amendment Bill, 13 November 1908, Singapore National Archives (SNA), *SSLCP* (*Straits Settlements Legislative Council Papers*), p. B139.
2 Addis to Mills, 7 March 1914, PP.MS.14/175, [Sir Charles] Addis Papers, Library, School of Oriental and African Studies, University of London.
3 For a discussion of this subject see Takeshi Hamashita, 'A History of the Japanese Silver Yen and The Hongkong and Shanghai Banking Corporation, 1871–1913', in King, ed. *Eastern Banking* (London, 1983), pp. 322–38. The Agreement for the minting of the British Dollar was signed by G.E. Noble for the Hongkong Bank in London, 14 December 1894, in IOR/V/6/333.
4 FO 371/861, ff. 1–3, 12–14, 20–24.
5 For effectiveness of provincial regulations see FO 371/856, ff. 226–29, esp. report of W.G. Max Müller to Grey, ff. 227–28.
6 Ibid.
7 China Association, Minute Book, 30 July 1912, in Archive of the China Association, SOAS.
8 China Association, Circular, Minutes of the Customs and Inland Taxation Sub-committee, Shanghai Branch, 9 December 1915, pp. 11–14.
9 Information on the silver content of sycee, exchange rates, etc. taken from Edward Kann, *The Currencies of China* (Shanghai, 1927).
10 China Association, Circulars, 17 April 1909, Vol. III, p. 307, and Vol. VI, 20 July 1910.
11 E.D. Sanders (Shanghai) to D.H. Mackintosh (Tientsin), 9 August 1909, in S/O files, Hongkong Bank Group Archives.
12 Memorandum: 'Currency Reform in China', July 1906, in FO 371/21, ff. 92–101.
13 Addis diary, 10 March 1903, PP.MS.14/21. Addis had recently turned down an offer from the International Banking Corporation, see entries for 4 and 5 December 1902, PP.MS.14/20.
14 'Memorandum by Mr Hillier on the proposed New Currency Regulations', FO 371/21, ff. 31–32; the edicts are on ff. 29–31.
15 FO 371/1068, ff. 211–15, 253–63, including minutes of the Brussels Conference of the Inter-Bank Groups, 18 March 1911, at which preliminary arrangements for the Currency Loan were made.
16 The agreement is available in FO 371/1068, ff. 313–29. For the French concern, see ibid, ff. 403–04, 413–18 in May 1911. Their objections were eventually withdrawn and the advances proceeded with, see Addis to Foreign Office, 30 May 1911, f. 495.
17 'Report of the Chinese Currency Committee and Minutes of the Meeting', July 31–August 4, 1911, in FO 371/1069, ff. 163–91. On the difficult position of Dr Ch'en, see pp. 41–42 of the report.
18 Ibid, pp. 21–22 of the minutes, or ff. 175–76 of the FO file.
19 Charles Addis to Foreign Office, 5 September 1911, FO 371/1069, f. 233.
20 Dr Ch'en claimed that the Chinese Government was appointing Vissering independently of the Loan Agreement (see 'Report of the Chinese currency Committee . . .', p. 31), however the Inter-Bank Group subsequently negotiated with Dr Vissering and 'nominated' him; see the minutes of a meeting in Berlin, 23 September 1911, FO 371/1069, f. 260. For an outline of the Currency Reform provisions and Vissering's role, see E. Kann, *The Currencies of China* (Shanghai, 1927), pp. 384–95; for Vissering's own study, see his *On Chinese Currency*, 2 vols (Amsterdam, 1912 and 1914).

21 FO 371/1313, f. 285.
22 A.M. Townsend refers to this in his autobiography, 'Early Days of the Hongkong and Shanghai Bank', p. 15. See also Hamashita, p. 325.
23 Dated 31 March 1877 and as translated in CO 129/177, ff 557–59.
24 The expert opinion on the Japanese yen is found in CO 129/186, ff. 128–52, September 1879; see also T.W. Kinder, Master of the Osaka Mint, a report included in *Minutes of Evidence Taken before the Select Committee on Depreciation of Silver* (London, 1877), p. 138, and cited in Hamashita, p. 324.
25 The 1877 proposals are set out in a letter from the Hong Kong bank managers, including Thomas Jackson, dated 16 February, in CO 129/177, ff. 145–48, see also ff. 156–160. A copy of the 1877 petition was sent to the Colonial Office with the 1893 correspondence on the subject, see CO 129/259, f. 361. The offer of the Hongkong Bank to operate the Hong Kong mint is in CO 129/129, ff. 445–48, see discussion in Volume I, Chapter 5.
26 See letter of J.J. Keswick, writing as a director of the Hongkong Bank, to the Governor of Hong Kong, 7 July 1893, CO 129/259, ff. 355–56, and Keswick as chairman of the Chamber of Commerce on 13 July 1893, f. 357, and related correspondence on ff. 346–61.
27 IOR V/6/332, Financial No. 151, 16 August 1894, pp. 15–18; for a memorandum see Enclosure 2 of 4 July 1894 on p. 17. The negotiations continued through November 1894, as recorded in Financial No. 213, 15 November 1894, pp. 73–82; the Order in Council is found in Financial No. 38, 7 March 1895, Enclosure No. 1, p. 36.
28 See IOR V/6/333, Financial No. 6, 10 January 1895; for the draft agreement see Enclosure No. 12, pp. 17–18.
29 An India Office letter of 1 September 1905, quoted in a memo, 'Coinage of the British dollar for use in China at the Indian mints', FO 371/33, ff. 373–80.
30 Colonial Office, 'Coinage of a British Dollar for Circulation in Hong Kong and the Straits Settlements', Eastern No. 62, CO 882/5, November 1894; for Cameron's testimony see p. 27. The Agreement for the minting of the British dollar was signed by G.E. Noble for the Hongkong Bank in London, 14 December 1894, in IOR V/6/333 (see also 332). For other relevant IOR material see V/6/333, Financial No. 63, 25 April 1895, pp. 63–66, and IOR V/6/334, Financial No. 201, 21 November 1895, pp. 62–64. See also the correspondence in CO 129/265, ff. 567–76 together with draft orders in council; CO 129/267, ff. 210–20, 683–87; see also CO 129/270, ff. 20–21 and 42–49. These files include letters from G.E. Noble. For the comment on Singapore see SNA, SSLCP, No. 71 Appendix, pp. C194–95, 2 October 1900.
31 The Jackson letters are dated 22 April and 21 June 1895, CO 129/267, ff. 217–18 and 687.
32 India Office to Foreign Office, 5 October 1906, FO 371/33, ff. 386–87.
33 See Harry Hunter, acting Chief Manager, to Governor Sir Matthew Nathan, 12 July 1906, in FO 371/33, f. 384, with enclosures covering developments.
34 Harries to 'Comision' [*sic*], 12 January 1906, in FO 371/33, ff. 358–60.
35 Smith to Nathan, 5 March 1906, FO 371/33, ff. 361–62.
36 Ibid, f. 380.
37 For the Mercantile Bank and related topics, see Treasury file T.1/11495. For the Chartered Bank, see Compton Mackenzie, *Realms of Silver* (London, 1954), p. 220.
38 Sessions of the Hong Kong Legislative Council on 19 July and 24 September 1909, for which see CO 131/43, ff. 123–34 and 147 respectively.

39 The relevant Treasury file is T.1/11495 which covers most of the statements made in this section.
40 J.R.M. Smith's letter, dated 29 January 1910, was written while he was on leave and is addressed to Charles Addis, the Bank's London Manager, and is found in T.1/11495.
41 File T.1/11495 includes the memo of 28 April 1910 by R.G. Hawtrey of the Treasury.
42 In Smith's letter cited, see note 35 above.
43 See Charles Addis to Treasury, 16 February 1915, in London Office S/O file, Group Archives. The overall situation is best described in a private memorandum of the Chief Manager, Newton Stabb, 9 June 1915, in CO 129/422, ff. 555–57.
44 Major-General F.H. Kelly to Sir F.H. May, 9 January, and May to Secretary of State, 27 January 1915, in CO 129/420, ff. 176–85.
45 Addis to Treasury, 16 February 1915, see note 43.
46 Governor May; letter of 27 January 1915, cited in note 44.
47 British Parliamentary Papers, *Report of Treasury Committee on the Mode of Issuing the Dollar in the East*, 2 vols (London, 1913); the report is also found in IOR L/F/7/499.
48 Ibid; testimony of C.S. Addis, second day, 30 April 1913, II, 16–21.
49 Ibid, question 477, p. 18.
50 Postmaster General to the Officer Commanding 26th Punjabis, Hong Kong, CO 129/420, f. 182.
51 Addis's testimony, question 476, *Committee on the Mode of Issuing the Dollar in the East*, IOR L/F/7/499, II, 18.
52 N.J. Stabb, 9 June 1915, CO 129/422, ff. 555–57.
53 Ibid, f. 557.
54 Ibid.
55 For a description of the copper sector of the Chinese monetary system, see Frank H.H. King, *Money and Monetary Policy in China, 1845–1895* (Cambridge, MA, 1965), Chapter 2, pp. 51–68.
56 See Frank H.H. King, 'Appendix: an Outline of the Problems of The Hongkong and Shanghai Banking Corporation's Note Issue', in King, ed. *Eastern Banking*, pp. 150–54, esp. p. 154.
57 Governor Nathan to the British Chargé d'Affaires, Peking, 26 June 1906, FO 371/33, ff. 326–27.
58 Memorandum, J.C. Peter to Chief Manager, 14 July 1906, in FO 371/33, ff. 328–29.
59 Ibid, f. 329.
60 Quoted in US War Dept, Division of Insular Affairs, 'Memorandum for the Secretary of War on Currency and Exchange in the Philippines' (1900), p. 15.
61 Ibid, pp. 49–50.
62 Ibid, pp. 46–47.
63 Ibid, p. 33, 13 September 1899.
64 China Association, Minute Book, 3 February 1903.
65 Charles A. Conant, *Coinage and Banking in the Philippine Islands* (Washington, DC, 1901), in USNA, Bureau of Insular Affairs, RG350, File 3197. H.D.C. Jones was on leave at the time of the interview.
66 Ibid, 24 September 1901, pp. 85–95.
67 Conant to Edwards, 7 October 1901, RG350, File 3197.
68 Townsend to Forbes, 21 February 1902, in ibid.
69 Conant report cited in note 65, 29 April 1901.

70 The earlier history depends on W. Evan Nelson, 'The Hongkong and Shanghai Banking Corporation Factor in the Progress Toward a Straits Settlements Government Note Issue, 1881–1889', in King, ed. *Eastern Banking*, pp. 155–79.

71 Governor C.B.H. Mitchell to Secretary of State, 22 July 1896, *SSLCP* (1896), Appendix 60, 'Government Notes Issue', SS 336, pp. C 363–C 365.

72 G.W. Butt, Manager, Hongkong Bank, Singapore, to Acting Colonial Secretary, Straits Settlements, 4 August 1898, in Straits Settlements No. 34, Papers laid before . . ., 7 November 1898, 'Gold Currency for the Straits Settlements', *SSLCP*, p. C 423; for the Chartered Bank response see pp. 422–23.

73 Ibid. On the debt of gratitude, see 'Address of . . . Sir Alexander Swettenham . . . 2 October 1900', in *SSLCP*, p. C 195.

74 See Frank H.H. King, *Money in British East Asia* (London, 1957), pp. 11–14, *Report of the Straits Settlements Currency Committee*, Cd 1556 (London, 1903), and J.O. Anthonisz, *Currency Reform in the Straits Settlements* (London, ca 1916).

75 Hongkong Bank, London Manager, to Colonial Office, 13 October 1903, located in SS 350, file 139 for October–December 1903, SNA.

76 Baker's contributions in Committee can be seen in, e.g. *SSLCP*, 1908, B 147–51, but see his dissent to the Report of the Select Committee on 'The Currency Note Bill' on p. C 154.

77 The key debate, from which the quotation at the head of this chapter was taken, was on the Currency Note Ordinance Amendment Bill, 13 November 1908, in *SSLCP*, pp. B 138–46.

78 Government of Ceylon, Report of the Ceylon Currency Commission, 1902.

79 Diary, 5 September 1902, PP.MS.14/20; for information on Bredon and Taylor see references in, e.g. Stanley F. Wright, *Hart and the Chinese Customs* (Belfast, 1950).

80 For a discussion of these issues as they concern the development of Indian banking, see Frank H.H. King, *Survey our Empire! Robert Montgomery Martin (1801?–1868): a bio-bibliography* (Hong Kong, 1979), pp. 150–77.

81 IOR L/F/5/71, 3 February 1900.

82 Addis to Mills, 7 March 1914, PP.MS.14/175.

83 Junpei Shinobu, *The Korean Peninsula* (in Japanese; 1901), p. 51; the author was Japanese consul in Korea. There are passing references to the Hongkong Bank's agencies in the Japanese consular reports, e.g. Foreign Office, August 1900, No. 2511, Annual Series, Diplomatic and Consular Reports, 'Trade of Corea for the year 1899', also 1902. References supplied by Professor T. Hamashita. See also the Hakadote Chamber of Commerce *Report on a tour of inspection of trade to China, Korea and Russia* (in Japanese; 1904), p. 259.

84 Addis to Wade Gard'ner, 17 November 1896, PP.MS.14/67/121. The description of McLeavy Brown is from Addis's letter to Mills, 21 October 1896, PP.MS.14/67/122.

85 Addis to Wade Gard'ner, 17 November 1896, see note 84. See also diary entries for 29 September, 3, 23, 29 October and 2 November 1896, PP.MS.14/14.

86 18 October 1903, PP.MS.14/51/70.

87 See note 85 and diary entry for 29 October 1896, PP.MS.14/14.

88 Addis to Murray Stewart, 9 January 1897, PP.MS.14/227.

89 Charles A. Conant, *Coinage and Banking in the Philippine Islands* (Washington, DC, 1901), pp. 51–52, in USNA, Bureau of Insular Affairs, RG350, File 3197.

90 Ibid, p. 91.

91 For Oram's reply, see ibid, p. 90; for the Treasury letter referred to see SNA, Treasury to Colonial Office, 19 April 1884.

92 Ibid, p. 91.

93 These developments are described in the documents filed under PRO Treasury file, T.1/11845. The Addis reference is from his diary, 17 and 18 April 1907, PP.MS.14/25.

PART II THE HONGKONG BANK AND CHINA, 1895–1914

The general comments in the introduction to Part II have profited from the points made in the following articles and thesis: E.W. Edwards, 'The Origins of British Financial Co-operation with France in China, 1903–6', *English Historical Review* 86:285–317 (1971), and his 'British Policy in China 1913–1914; Rivalry with France in the Yangtze Valley', *Journal of Oriental Studies* 40:20–36 (1977) – see also his more recent *British Diplomacy and Finance in China, 1895–1914* (Oxford, 1987), although he has failed to consult newly available material in the Honkong Bank and other archives; K.C. Chan, 'British Policy in the Reorganization Loan to China, 1912–13', *Modern Asian Studies* 5:355–72 (1971); David McLean, 'Finance and "Informal Empire" before the First World War', *Economic History Review* 29:291–305 (1976), and his 'British Banking and Government in China: the Foreign Office and the Hongkong and Shanghai Bank, 1895–1914', PhD thesis, Cambridge University (1973).

1 See references cited by Edwards, p. 300n3.
2 Abstract of a Report by Alfred Bonzon, formerly Manager, Crédit Lyonnais, 23 November 1913, transmitted by the Ministry of Finance to the Ministry of Foreign Affairs, No. 432 in F30.371, China 2, Situation économique et financière, 1900–1913, French Foreign Ministry Archives, Paris.
3 Bapst to Stephen Pichon, Minister of Foreign Affairs, Peking, 20 March 1908, F30.371, China 1, Situation économique et financière, 1886–1914, in French Foreign Ministry Archives, Paris.
4 A similar question was asked in a Foreign Office minute dated 11 April 1904, FO 17/1637, quoted in Edwards, p. 300.
5 Ministry of Foreign Affairs to Minister of Finance, 11 December 1909, 'au sujet des chemins de fer chinois', Asie No. 1422, in F30.371, China 2, Situation économique et financière, 1900–1913.

5 DEFEAT, INDEMNITY, AND RAILWAYS, 1895–1900

1 Cable books of the Tientsin office dating back to 1893 have survived and are in Hongkong Bank Group Archives. The quotation at the head of the chapter is dated 7 November 1894, the quote noted is 31 December 1894. Later cable books contain mainly routine matters as negotiations shifted to Peking, then in direct communication with Shanghai and London.
2 General sources consulted for this and the following sections are: Chen Chung-sieu, 'British Loans to China from 1860 to 1913, with special reference to the period 1894–1913' (PhD thesis, University of London, 1940); David J.S. King, 'On the Relations of the Hongkong Bank with Germany, 1864–1948', Part II, 'The China Loans', deposited in Group Archives; J.R. Jones, ed. 'Chinese Loans', in Group Archives; J.R. Jones, comp. bound collections of agreements and some related correspondence, in Group Archives; John V.A. MacMurray, comp. and ed. *Treaties and Agreements with and concerning China, 1894–1919* (New York, 1921) 2 vols; Stanley F. Wright, *Hart and the Chinese Customs* (Belfast, 1950); and Maximilian Müller-Jabusch, *Fünfzig Jahre Deutsch-Asiatische Bank, 1890–1939* (Berlin, 1940).
3 In addition to the sources in note 2 above, this section depends on the continuity provided by [Dr] David McLean, 'The Foreign Office and the First Chinese

Indemnity Loan, 1895', *The Historical Journal* (1973), pp. 303–21; see particularly references in FO 17/1253.

4 See McLean, cited, and also Hart to Campbell, 21 April 1895, letter No. 969, in John K. Fairbank *et al*, eds. *The I.G. in Peking* (Cambridge, MA, 1975), II, 1014–15 and *passim*.

5 Memorandum by Sanderson, 13 May 1895, FO 17/1253, cited in McLean.

6 Ibid, 15 May 1895.

7 Ewen Cameron to Lord Kimberley, 19 May 1895, in ibid.

8 Cameron to Sanderson, 20 May 1895, in ibid.

9 Memorandum by Sanderson, 20 May 1895, in ibid.

10 Cameron to Kimberley, 21 May 1895, in ibid.

11 Cameron to Sanderson, 22 May 1895, in ibid.

12 Auswärtiges Amt [AA], China no. 3, *Finances*. Münster in Paris to AA, A 5633, 23 May 1895; Archives of the German Ministry of Foreign Affairs, Bonn.

13 Paul Graf von Hatzfeldt, *Botschafter Paul Graf von Hatzfeldt: Nachgelassene Papiere, 1838–1901*, ed. Gerhard Ebel, 2 vols (Boppard am Rhein, 1976), p. 1044.

14 Note 12, Rothschild to von Hansemann, 19 June 1895.

15 Wright, p. 659.

16 Note 12, von Hatzfeldt to AA, 22 June 1895.

17 AA, China no. 3. *Finances*. Vol. 8, The report on the meeting by Otto Franke, the German interpreter in Peking, 22 June 1895.

18 AA, China no. 3. *Finances*. Vol. 6, N.M. Rothschild to von Hansemann, 26 June 1895.

19 Ibid, Vol. 7. Letter from the Hongkong Bank (London) to the DAB (Berlin), 2 July 1895.

20 Ibid, Rehders to the DAB (Berlin).

21 Ibid, Vol. 8. Private Letter from Lord Salisbury to Hatzfeldt, 5 July 1895.

22 Charles Addis to Dudley Mills, 11 October and 10 November 1898, PP.MS.14/159 and PP.MS.14/67/128, Addis Papers, the Library, School of Oriental and African Studies, University of London.

23 A copy of the Agreement is in the Hongkong Bank Group Archives.

24 *Cf* FO 371/181, ff. 268 and *passim*.

25 AA, China no. 4. *Railways*. Vol. 1, March (of Carlowitz and Co.) to von Schenk, 10 August 1895; Mackintosh to Cameron, 30 March 1896, in Group Archives, Shanghai II, 37.

26 AA, China no. 3. *Finances*. Vol. 10, A 11866 and A 11867, the DAB to von Brandt, 9 and 15 October 1895.

27 For the loan agreement, see MacMurray, I, 55–59. Drafts and comments are in FO 233/120, ff. 360–64, a memo dated 25 December 1895 on f. 389 [? faded] dealing with the reasons for the poor terms offered in the context of the price of existing loans with better security, and FO 233/121, ff. 7–61.

28 AA, China no. 3. *Finances*. Vol. 12, A 5138, von Schenck to the AA, 31 March 1896.

29 Otto Franke, *Erinnerungen aus zwei Welten* (Berlin, 1954), pp. 77ff.

30 AA, China no. 3. *Finances*. Vol. 9, A 11405, von Schenck to AA, 24 October 1895.

31 Ibid, Vol. 10, A 11618, von Schenck to AA, 29 October 1895.

32 Ibid, Brüssel to the Disconto-Gesellschaft, 11 November 1895.

33 Ibid, A 12544, von Schenck to the AA, 12 November 1895.

34 Ibid, A 350, von Schenck to the AA, forwarding a memo by E.G. Hillier outlining the joint offer, 25 November 1895.

35 Ibid, Vol. 11, Hillier to Cameron, 17 December 1895.

36 Cable, Hamburg Office, Hongkong Bank, to Peking, 21 January 1896.

37 Cable from London Office, Hongkong Bank, 13 January 1896. The complete exchange of telegrams with the Hamburg Office relevant to this loan has been transferred from the Hamburg Branch Archives to Group Archives in Hong Kong.

38 AA, China, no. 3. *Finances.* Vol. 12, Hillier to von Schenck, 19 February 1896.

39 Ibid, Vol. 11, Hongkong Bank, London Office, to Brüssel, 5 March 1896.

40 Ibid, Vol. 10, A 1776, Münster (in Paris) to the AA, 17 February 1896.

41 Ibid, Vol. 11, von Schenck to AA.

42 Ibid, Vol. 12, Hart to von Schenck, 6 March 1896.

43 Sir Robert Hart to Campbell, 22 March 1896, Letter No. 1013, in Fairbank *et al*, eds. II, 1056–57.

44 See FO 233/121, ff. 28–54 (preliminary); ff. 55–61 (for definitive agreement).

45 Hart to Campbell, 16 August 1896, letter 1032, in Fairbank *et al*, eds. II, 1079, quoting a cable previously sent.

46 Maximilian Müller-Jabusch, *Franz Urbig zum 23-ten Januar 1939* (Deutsche Bank, 1939), pp. 47–48, translated by D.J.S. King.

47 Ibid.

48 This account is in Group Archives in J.R. Jones, 'Personalities and Narratives'.

49 MacMurray, I, 107–12; see also FO 233/129, ff. 165–74.

50 Quoted in Wright, p. 664.

51 AA, China no. 3. *Finances.* Vol. 14, A 6289, von Heyking to Reischskanzler, 24 March 1897.

52 Ibid.

53 Quoted in Wright, pp. 664–65.

54 See Hart to Campbell, letter 1094, 30 January 1898, in Fairbank *et al*, II, 1149–50; see also China no. 3. *Finances.* Vol. 17, A S 1273, von Heyking to the AA, 4 March 1898.

55 See Hui-min Lo, ed. *The Correspondence of G.E. Morrison* (Cambridge, 1976), I, 74.

56 Letters dated 7 January and 11 February 1898, in FO 17/1356, quoted in David McLean, 'International Banking and its Political Implications: The Hongkong and Shanghai Banking Corporation and The Imperial Bank of Persia, 1889–1914', in King, ed. *Eastern Banking* (London, 1983), p. 3.

57 Quoted in J.R. Jones's article on the Indemnity loans in 'Chinese Loans', p. 10.

58 MacMurray, I, 105.

59 MacMurray, I, 104.

60 Hart to Campbell, 13 February 1898, letter 1096, in Fairbank *et al*, eds. I, 1151–52.

61 Jones, p. 13.

62 AA, China no. 3. *Finances*, Vol. 17, A S 562, Betzold (Paris) to von Hansemann, 25 February 1898.

63 E.G. Hillier to G.E. Morrison, 9 March 1898, in Hui-min Lo, ed. pp. 72–73.

64 26 March 1898, quoted in Chen, p. 83.

65 Hart to Campbell, 6 March 1898, letter 1098, in Fairbank *et al*, eds. II, 1153–54.

66 *Banker's Magazine* (1898), p. 863, quoted in Chen, p. 83.

67 This account follows the correspondence in Japan, Ministry of Foreign Affairs, *Compiled Documents on Japanese Foreign Affairs* (Tokyo, 1954), Vol. 29, Section 17, External Loans and Miscellaneous Items, pp. 562–64, 567–68, 570–83, 590–93, 614–15, 618–23, and 646–49.

68 See Wright, pp. 666–67.

69 Kia-ngau Chang, *China's Struggle for Railroad Development* (New York, 1943), pp. 26 and 46. In addition to the works listed in note 2 above, the following were

utilized for continuity: Ralph W. Huenemann, *The Dragon and the Iron Horse, the Economics of Railroads in China, 1876–1937* (Cambridge, MA, 1984), E-tu Zen Sun, *Chinese Railways and British Interests, 1898–1911* (New York, 1954), and En-han Lee, *China's Quest for Railway Autonomy, 1904–1911* (Singapore, 1977). The Agreements are in MacMurray, cited, and in Group Archives. Other standard collections exist.

70 This estimate was made by Vera Schmidt, *Die deutsche Eisenbahnpolitik in Shantung, 1898–1914. Ein Beitrag zur Geschichte des deutschen Imperialismus in China* (Wiesbaden, 1976), p. 10.

71 United States, House of Representatives, Hearings before a Subcommittee of the Committee on Government Operations, 96th Congress, second session, 15 May and 25 June 1980, p. 89.

72 Materials for a corporate history are found in the appropriate files at Companies Registry House, London, and in the archives of the company secretaries, Matheson and Co. For B&CC see file 57,491.

73 G. Kurgan-van Hentenryk, *Léopold II et les groupes financiers belges en Chine: la politique royale et ses prolongements (1895–1914)* (Bruxelles, 1972), pp. 227 and 440–41. J.R. Jones, 'The Chinese Loans', in Group Archives, contains a summary of the B&CC's annual reports.

74 Information on the B&KC is found in BT 31/9319/69261. A memo providing a summary history of the B&KC together with annual reports was provided to Charles Addis when he succeeded Cameron on the B&CC Board in 1905; these are in Group Archives.

75 See references in ibid, and in Tim Wright, *Coal Mining in China's Economy and Society, 1895–1937* (Cambridge, 1984), pp. 128, 130, 142, 148, and 152. The Board of Trade file could not be located, but certain material is in the CCR file, *q.v.*, Chapter 6; for a hint of the relationship between Luzzatti and Meyer, see the personal letter of Meyer addressed to Burgenstock, 15 August 1899, in Letter Book of Carl Meyer, 1894–1899, in possession of Sir Anthony Meyer, MP; for the reference to J.P. Morgan interests, see letter of 28 August 1899 in ibid.

76 The basic files are BT31/31836/68872 for the Yangtze Valley Company, BT31/8611/62743 for the Upper Yangtze Valley Syndicate, and BT31/8558/62317 for the Yangtze Valley Syndicate. See also, for information on the Hongkong Tramways, *Hongkong Government Gazette* (1883), pp. 491–527, and the Russell and Co. bankruptcy file, Statement of R.G. Shewan, 4 August 1903, HKRS 62, Public Records Office of Hong Kong (PROHK).

77 MacMurray, I, 173–83; for the list of previous advances, see p. 181.

78 The Russian comment is in B.A. Romanov, *Russia and Manchuria*, trans. Susan Wilbur Jones (Ann Arbor, MI, 1952), p. 126; for the note on Hu, see A. Feuerwerker, *China's Early Industrialization: Sheng Hsuan-huai (1844–1916) and Mandarin Enterprise* (Cambridge, MA, 1958), p. 270n50.

79 This intervention in Tientsin is partially documented by the Tientsin cable books, see 16 December 1898 and following. The almost total involvement in such matters is seen also in the Addis papers and diaries.

80 H.B. Morse to Detring, 20 May 1886, ff. 22–25, in Morse Papers, MS Chinese 3.1, Houghton Library, Harvard University; see also (all in ibid) letter of resignation, 1 December 1886, ff. 114–16; Morse to Detring, 2 December 1886, ff. 120–21, 3 August 1887, ff. 204–05, and 10 August 1887, ff. 210–12.

81 A.D. Bruce to E.G. Hillier, 5 January 1900; translation of a memorial by Chang Yen-mao, 25 January 1899; and other correspondence in file, 'Government Loans, Railway Loans, Correspondence 1898–1900', SHG 255.1, in Group Archives.

82 MacMurray, I, 205.

83 Addis diary, 3 September 1903, PP.MS.14/21.

84 Müller-Jabusch (1940), pp. 103ff; see also Müller-Jabusch (1939), pp. 54ff.

85 Cameron to Foreign Office, 4 April 1898, in China No. 1, Affairs of China 1899, p. 4, No. 5.

86 Müller-Jabusch (1940), p. 117.

87 AA, China no. 4, no. 1. Secret. *Railways*. Vol. 2, Rothschild forwarded Cameron's letter on 23 June 1898.

88 The text of the Agreement (or 'Arrangement') is in MacMurray, I, 266–67.

89 Ibid, p. 266.

90 AA, China no. 4. *Railways*. Vol. 8, A S 2561, von Hansemann to von Bülow, 21 December 1899.

91 A summary of the negotiations as they are documented in British Foreign Office records was the subject of a memorandum by Sir Ernest Satow, dated 17 November 1905, in FO 371/21, ff. 264–85; the British official side, which includes correspondence from the Hongkong Bank, is told here based primarily on this source.

92 The characters for 'Yung Wing' are romanized (in Wade-Giles) as 'Jung Hung'. His autobiography covers the railway problem very briefly; see Yung Wing, *My Life in China and America* (New York, 1909), pp. 236–38.

93 AA, China no. 4, no. 1. Secret. *Railways*. Vol. 5, A S 2721, 2900, von Heyking to the AA, 20 August, 3 September 1898; Vol. 2, A S 1602, von Hansemann memo on his conversation with Rothstein, 28 May 1898.

94 Ibid, A S 146, von Heyking to the AA, 19 January 1899, see also AA, China no. 4, no. 1. Secret. *Railways*. Vol. 6, A S 542, von Heyking to the AA, 24 January 1899.

95 AA, China no. 4, no. 1. Secret. *Railways*. Vol. 7, A S 889, von Heyking to the AA, 30 April 1899.

6 BOXERS, INDEMNITY, AND RAILWAYS, 1900–1908

1 Diary of Charles Addis, PP.MS.14/16, [Sir Charles] Addis Papers, the Library, School of Oriental and African Studies, University of London. Charles Addis's wife Eba on occasion kept his diary, as in the instance cited.

2 General references to the Boxer Uprising are: Peter Fleming, *The Siege at Peking* (London, 1959); Victor Purcell, *The Boxer Uprising, a background study* (Cambridge, 1963); Stanley F. Wright, *Hart and the Chinese Customs* (Belfast, 1950), pp. 730–42; the A.D. Brent papers in Hongkong Bank Group Archives; J.R. Jones collection of 'Personalities and Narratives' also in Group Archives, esp. under H.E.R. Hunter, copies of letters of the Hongkong Bank's Tientsin Agent, H. Hewat.

3 Quoted in Fleming, p. 132.

4 E.G. Hillier to Sir Claude MacDonald, copy to G.E. Morrison, 6 October 1898, in Hui-min Lo, ed. *The Correspondence of G.E. Morrison* (Cambridge, 1976), I, 95–96.

5 British Parliamentary Papers, 'Reports from HM Minister in China Respecting Events at Peking', Cd 364, December 1900, p. 58.

6 Brent's account was published as 'The Siege of Peking by one who went through it, Diary of a besieged resident', in the *Daily News* (London, 16 October 1900), p. 4.

7 E.G. Hillier, Peking, to Messrs Chubb and Co., 17 October 1900, provided by the courtesy of the latter and reproduced in Noel Currer-Briggs, *Contemporary*

Observations on Security from the Chubb Collectanea, 1818–1968 (London, n.d., privately published).

8 Addis diary, 8 September 1902, PP.MS.14/20.
9 H. Hewat to H.E.R. Hunter, 1 July 1900, in J.R. Jones, Group Archives.
10 [A.D. Brent], letter to editor signed 'Overworked Bank Clerk', *Peking and Tientsin Times* (23 February 1901).
11 Cable dated 18 July 1900, FO 17/1768, f. 73; see also Wright, pp. 733–34 and 786n73.
12 The main Treasury file for this loan is T.1/9590B, and the specific reference is to a letter from Francis Bertie in the Foreign Office to the Treasury dated 10 August 1900.
13 Bertie to Spring Rice, 31 August 1900, T.1/9590B.
14 Affairs of China, No. 1, Shanghai, 5 September, Enclosure 1, 'Memorandum by Mr Hillier respecting the Loan for £75,000 made by the Hongkong and Shanghai Bank, under British Government guarantee, to Chang Chih-tung, Viceroy of Wuchang, for the Payment of Provincial troops', in T.1/9590B.
15 30 August 1900, in T.1/9590B.
16 For the Cameron quote above see Cameron to Campbell, dated 10 June 1901, enclosed in Bertie to Lascelles, Paper of Sir F. Lascelles, FO 800/6, f. 497. For the final Protocol, see John V.A. MacMurray, *Treaties and Agreements with and concerning China, 1894–1919* (New York, 1921), I, 278–84, and annexes thereto on pp. 285–308.
17 Ibid, p. 281. For discussion, see Wright, pp. 744–46, 766–67.
18 Foreign Office to Treasury, 1 May 1902, and E.G. Hillier to Marquess of Lansdowne, 30 April 1902 in T.1/9590B.
19 Foreign Office to Chairman, Chartered Bank of India, Australia and China, 7 December 1901, in FO 17/1736, f. 292.
20 Commission of Bankers, Minutes of recommendations, and Hillier to Sir Ernest Satow, 23 January 1902, in T.1/9915A – the main file for the present discussions by the Commission.
21 Quoted in Hillier to the Secretary of State for Foreign Affairs, 10 March 1902, printed in 'Affairs of China', 15 April, No. 1, in T.1/9915A.
22 Hillier to Marquess of Lansdowne, 7 April 1902, in T.1/9915A.
23 See, for example, the advertisement in *The Times* (31 July 1902).
24 Hillier to Sir Ewen Cameron, 18 July 1902, in T.1/9915A.
25 Hillier's expense account for January–August 1902, dated 23 August, is in T.1/9915B.
26 A letter of 10 January 1906, for example, is signed 'H. Hunter', British Delegate; see FO 371/18, f. 392. The vast routine of the payment of the indemnity and its transfer to England, etc., is found in the FO 371 files. On the appointment of Oram, see the letter of recommendation on his behalf, written from the Peking Legation for the Treasury, 23 June 1906, FO 371/18, f. 497.
27 See 'Exchange of Notes regarding Final Settlement of the Question of the Boxer Indemnity', 2 July 1905, in MacMurray, I, 319–20.
28 Minutes of the Board of Directors, Hongkong Bank, 7 and 14 February 1905.
29 Sir Robert Hart to Campbell, 22 January 1905, letter No. 1360, in Fairbank *et al*, eds. *The I.G. in Peking* (Cambridge, MA, 1975), II, 1449.
30 See, for example, *The Times*, Morrison's article of 4 February 1905.
31 References from the Auswärtiges Amt [AA] are as follows: China no. 3, *Finances*, Vol. 21, A 10179, Mumm von Schwarzenstein to the AA, 7 December 1904; AA minutes of Schoeller's meeting, 11 January 1905; A 1847, Erich of the DAB to the AA, 2 February 1905; Hongkong Bank, Hamburg Branch, to the DAB

(Berlin), 1 February 1905, and Cordes (DAB Peking) to DAB (Berlin), 1 February 1905. The material is found in D.J.S. King's research report, 'The Hongkong Bank and Germany. Vol. II The China Loans', Chapter VI, 'The HSBC–DAB Loan of 1905', pp. 77–78, in Group Archives.

32 Hillier to Mumm von Schwarzenstein, 25 March 1905, in AA, China no. 3, *Finances*, Vol. 21.
33 G.E. Morrison to V. Chirol, Peking, 25 March 1905, in Lo, ed. pp. 294–96.
34 Ibid, 5 May 1905, pp. 300–01, and 8 June 1905, p. 317.
35 *London and China Express* (10 February 1905).
36 Bernstorff (London) to the AA, 28 May 1905, in AA, China no. 3, *Finances*, Vol. 21, A 9347.
37 Addis diary, 5 February 1905, PP.MS.14/23.
38 See correspondence in FO 233/128, ff. 199–210.
39 General sources consulted for this and the following sections are: Chen Chung-sieu, 'British Loans to China from 1860 to 1913, with special reference to the period 1894–1913' (PhD thesis, University of London, 1940); David J.S. King, 'On the relations of the Hongkong Bank with Germany, 1864–1948', Part II, 'The China Loans', deposited in Hongkong Bank Group Archives; J.R. Jones, ed. 'Chinese Loans', in Group Archives; J.R. Jones, comp. bound collections of agreements and some related correspondence, in Group Archives; Maximilian Müller-Jabusch, *Fünfzig Jahre Deutsch-Asiatische Bank, 1890–1939* (Berlin, 1940); E-tu Zen Sun, *Chinese Railways and British Interests, 1898–1911* (New York, 1954), and En-Han Lee, *China's Quest for Railway Autonomy, 1904–1911* (Singapore, 1977). The agreements are in MacMurray, cited, and in Group Archives.
40 FO 371/418, ff. 241–42.
41 Information from the CCR file, BT 31/36256.
42 In a letter dated 26 February 1904 from PRO, Satow papers, 30/33/7/4, and cited in E.W. Edwards, 'The Origins of British Financial Co-operation with France in China, 1903–6', *English Historical Review* 84: 285–317 (1971), esp. p. 297.
43 MacMurray, I, 55.
44 This account follows Edwards' study of British–French cooperation, cited.
45 Chinese Central Railways to Foreign Office, 8 November 1905, annex 2 in FO 405/157, cited in G. Kurgan–van Hentenryk, *Léopold II et les groupes financiers belges en Chine; la politique royale et ses prolongements (1895–1914)* (Bruxelles, 1972), p. 722n3.
46 For the details of Belgian investment in China, see Kurgan-van Hentenryk, esp. pp. 725 and 764. The companies are listed in the index.
47 The agreement is in CO 129/344, ff. 630–42. The Pekin Syndicate's meetings were reported in *The Times*, see especially 1 February 1907, p. 10b; the continuing controversy is reflected in the B&CC Archives, Matheson and Co., London.
48 FO 371/27, ff. 444–59, February–April.
49 Addis diary, 5 September 1903, PP.MS.14/21.
50 J.O.P. Bland to Charles Addis, 8 August 1906, in Box 23, J.O.P. Bland Collection, Fisher Rare Book Library, University of Toronto, Toronto, Ontario, Canada.
51 Governor of Hong Kong, cable, 28 June 1905, in FO 17/1762, f. 223; Sir Ernest Satow to Foreign Office, cable, 7 June 1905, f. 161, and related documents.
52 A.M. Townsend, Hongkong Bank senior London Manager, to Foreign Office, 12 July 1905, FO 17/1762, ff. 232–33, and Foreign Office memo, f. 234.
53 In FO 17/1762, f. 238.

54 See Satow memorandum, p. 26, in FO 371/21, f. 276.
55 For the action of Fraser, see telegram of 15 July 1905, Governor of Hong Kong to Secretary of State, in CO 129/329, f. 60.
56 Townsend to F.A. Campbell, Foreign Office, 25 October 1906, FO 371/40, ff. 246–47. Note, there is reference to a similar situation in Canton in 1904.
57 Campbell to Manager, Hongkong Bank, London, FO 371/40, ff. 250–51 and related papers, ff. 224–52.
58 British Consul-General, Hankow, to Sir John Jordan, British Minister, Peking, 18 August 1909, FO 371/641, ff. 303–06, and the agreement, ff. 307–14, signed by J.D. Taylor, Hongkong Bank Agent, Hankow.
59 Carnegie in Peking to Sir Edward Grey, 27 July 1906, FO 371/27, f. 465 and related correspondence, ff. 460–92.
60 Addis diary, 4 September 1905, PP.MS.14/23.
61 The draft agreement is in FO 371/181, ff. 277–78; the final agreement is in Group Archives.
62 AA, China no. 3, *Finances*, Vol. 22, see the printed Minutes of the Meeting (in English), 4 October 1905.
63 Addis diary, 7 October 1905, PP.MS.14/23.
64 Hart's general position on domestic loans and the role of the Hongkong Bank can be found in Wright, pp. 363–67.
65 This summary is taken from Chen Chung-sieu's dissertation, 'British Loans to China from 1860 to 1913', p. 202.
66 Addis to Bland, 5 July 1906, in Bland Collection.
67 15 November 1905, PP.MS.14/166. Addis used the earlier railway names; for 'Pukow', he wrote 'Chinkiang', for 'Shanghai–Hangchow', 'Soochow–Ningpo'.
68 The edict was issued on 9 May. For the unfolding of the story as seen by Hart, see his letters nos 1406–23 in Fairbank *et al*, eds. II, 1507–23. See also Wright, pp. 818–30. See Legation despatch of 14 May 1906 in FO 371/181, ff. 122–31. The 181 file contains the complete Foreign Office record of the case.
69 Addis for the Hongkong and Shanghai Banking Corporation to the Secretary of State for Foreign Affairs, 10 May 1906, FO 371/181, f. 13.
70 Hillier's cable was dated 12 May and conveyed to the Foreign Office in a letter from Addis dated 14 May, FO 371/181, f. 21; see also ff. 23–24; also cable of 14 May, conveyed by A.M. Townsend, f. 39A.
71 Hillier to Addis, 1, 2, and 10 August 1906, FO 371/181, ff. 194–200, 236–37; *The Times* (4 and 6 June and 1 August 1906) with comments in FO 371/181, ff. 101–04 and 186–88; the China Association memorandum, signed by R.S. Gundry, together with copies of cables from Hong Kong etc. is in FO 371/181, ff. 293–300, with comments in *The Times* (8 September 1906) and in the Foreign Office files, FO 371/181, ff. 321–24; for questions in Parliament, see, e.g. FO 371/181, ff. 43–48 (15 and 16 May 1906), ff. 111–12 (12 June 1906), ff. 140–43 (3 July 1906).
72 Carnegie to Sir Edward Grey, 17 May 1906, FO 371/181, ff. 133–38.
73 29 July 1906, in FO 371/181, f. 349.
74 Ibid.
75 The minutes of the meeting with Addis are in FO 371/181, ff. 256–62; Addis's memorandum, f. 263.
76 20 August 1906, FO 371/181, ff. 264–66, and Hart's reaction, ff. 304–05.
77 Quoted in Wright, p. 828.
78 Hillier (Tientsin) to G.E. Morrison, 8 October 1900, in Hui-min Lo, ed. pp. 145–47.
79 See MacMurray, I, 331–32.

80 Quoted in E-tu Zen Sun, p. 50.

81 See MacMurray, I, 387–402.

82 Foreign Office minute reporting private information from Sir Ewen Cameron, in FO 371/418, f. 253. This information was also cabled to Tientsin.

83 Information in cables to Tientsin dated 29 June and 20 July 1903, Tientsin cable books, Group Archives.

84 Bland to Addis, 15 November 1906, and Addis to Bland, 27 December 1906, in Bland Collection.

85 Ibid.

86 Addis to Bland, 11 January 1907, Bland Collection.

87 Ibid, 28 January 1907.

88 See MacMurray, I, 408–09.

89 Cable, Tientsin to Shanghai; Shanghai to Tientsin, 2 June 1904, in Tientsin cable books, Group Archives.

90 See MacMurray, I, 131.

91 Ibid, pp. 615–25.

92 Memorandum of points for discussion between His Excellency the Officer Administering the Government of Hong Kong and the Chief Manager of the Hongkong and Shanghai Banking Corporation in connection with the proposed Canton–Kowloon Railway, CO 129/322, ff. 73–74, with letter from F.H. May to Alfred Lyttelton, 15 January 1904, CO 129/322, ff. 67–72, and minutes on f. 66; see also FO 17/1761, ff. 116–19.

93 CO 129/322, f. 792.

94 C. Chatterton Wilcox, Chairman, China Association, Hong Kong branch, to F.H. May as Colonial Secretary, 12 October 1904, CO 129/324, ff. 160–62.

95 China Association, Minute Book, 1901–06, entry for 15 November 1905, Archive of the China Association, the Library, SOAS.

96 Letter from the Viceroy of the Liang-Kwang provinces to the Consul-General, Canton, in CO 129/337, ff. 171–72.

97 Sir Matthew Nathan, Governor of Hong Kong, to the Secretary of State, 18 October 1905, CO 129/329, ff. 530–31.

98 In CO 129/329, ff. 483–84.

99 21 June 1905, in CO 129/331, ff. 40–41.

100 Letters of 30 December 1905 and 30 January 1906 in CO 129/333, ff. 39 and 345; see also correspondence of the Governor with the Earl of Elgin and related matters, FO 371/24, ff. 128–39, January–April 1906.

101 T'ang Shao-yi to Viceroy of Canton, translated in a despatch of Sir John Jordan to Sir Edward Grey, 13 March 1907, enclosure No. 2, FO 371/210, ff. 561–62. Enclosure No. 1 is the loan agreement, for which see ff. 565–71.

102 J.O.P. Bland to C.S. Addis, 16 January 1907, and Addis to Bland, 18 January 1907, Bland Collection.

103 See note 101 above.

104 Art. I, see MacMurray, I, 388.

105 See note 101 above.

106 Minutes of the 7th meeting, 22 October 1906, CO 129/338, ff. 415–16 and 9th meeting, 31 October 1906, f. 423.

107 For the text of the agreement, see MacMurray, I, 702–09.

108 Ibid, p. 319.

109 Minutes of the 7th meeting, 22 October 1906, CO 129/338, ff. 413–14.

110 Addis to F.A. Campbell, 25 October 1906, FO 371/24, f. 514; there is a copy in the Bland Collection.

111 Ibid.

112 F.A. Campbell to Addis, 25 October 1906, FO 371/24, f. 515, or copy in Bland Collection.
113 Addis diary, 26 April 1907, PP.MS.14/25.
114 Other and wilder charges against the Bank are discussed and dismissed in Ralph William Huenemann, *The Dragon and the Iron Horse, the Economics of Railroads in China, 1876–1937* (Cambridge, MA, 1984), pp. 110–22.
115 This is a continuation of the account in Chapter 5. British official sources, including Hongkong Bank correspondence with officials, to 1906 depend on the Satow memorandum dated 25 November 1905 in FO 371/21 cited, which should be consulted if the full history of the negotiations is of interest.
116 For the agreements see MacMurray, I, 684–97; for the details of Addis's decisions, see Addis to Bland, 18 March 1908, Bland Collection.
117 Addis to Bland, 1 April 1908, Bland Collection.
118 For the terms of the Chinese allocation, see Art. 13, MacMurray, I, 688; for the cables, see Tientsin cable book, Shanghai (from London) to Tientsin, 25 March, Tientsin to London, and London to Tientsin, 2 April 1908, in Group Archives.
119 E-tu Zen Sun, p. 137.
120 Loan agreements and prospectuses are in FO 371/845, ff. 490–95 and 505–19, see also MacMurray for the advances, I, 814–27.
121 F.A. Campbell to Lascelles, 28 March 1903, FO 800/6, ff. 521–22.
122 Bland to Addis, 3 July 1906, Bland Collection.
123 Statement of the German Minister, Count Rex, with Bland's letter to Addis dated, Peking, 16 April 1907, Bland Collection.
124 Addis to Hillier, 13 December 1907, copy with covering letter Addis to Bland of same date, Bland Collection.
125 AA, China no. 4, no. 1. Secret. *Railways*. Vol. 18, A 14052, Knappe's report to the AA, 25 August 1908.
126 The views expressed here are a reflection of the exchange of views in the Bland/Addis correspondence throughout 1908, until, in his letter of 17 December 1908, Bland reminds Addis that he has received instructions from the board of the B&CC (and presumably the CCR) not to communicate official matters except through the board.
127 On replacement of Cordes, see Secretary, Chinese Central Railways, to Foreign Office, 8 August 1907, FO 371/225, f. 273; on Bland – he was told of the appointment in an interview with Addis but typically made no comment at the time; he wrote to Addis later on the eve of his departure for Berlin, see Bland to Addis, 10 August 1907, Bland Collection.
128 For the British comment on Cordes, see Sir John Jordan to Sir Edward Grey, 20 August 1907, in FO 371/225, f. 320; for the German comments on Hillier, see AA, China no. 4, no. 1. Secret. *Railways*. Vol. 17, A 13239, Erich of the DAB to the AA, 14 August 1907.
129 Addis to Bland, 13 August 1907, Bland Collection.
130 Sir John Jordan to Sir Edward Grey, cable, 13 September 1907, FO 371/225, ff. 305–11, also Jordan to Grey, 18 September 1907, f. 377.
131 Foreign Office minute, 22 February 1907, FO 371/225, f. 344.
132 Addis to Bland, 3 October 1907, Bland Collection.
133 AA, China no. 4, no. 1. Secret. *Railways*. Vol. 18, A 11522, Cordes to Knappe, 31 August 1908. See also Foreign Office Confidential Print 405/181, No. 31, enclosure, 'Notes of Cordes', cited in En-han Lee, pp. 179–80; and summary of Jordan to Grey, 2 September 1907, FO 371/225, f. 345.
134 AA, China no. 4, no. 1. Secret. *Railways*. Erich of DAB to AA, 16 October 1906.

135 Addis diary, 1 December 1906, PP.MS.14/24.
136 See, e.g. Metternich to Foreign Office, 24 March 1907, FO 371/225, f. 75.
137 *The Times* (14 January 1908), reprinted in Hui-min Lo, ed. p. 438n2.
138 Kia-ngau Chang, pp. 98–104.
139 The 99 figure is from the Prospectus; there is a 98¾ figure in the minutes of the Board of Directors; the 5½ points is from the agreement as published in MacMurray, see I, 707; the alternative figures are quoted, e.g. in Lee, p. 25, and compiled from a collection of authoritative materials which are cited in Lee's study, and from J.R. Jones's collected material on the China Loans, although this latter source is not authoritative.
140 This account follows E-tu Zen Sun, *Chinese Railways and British Interests, 1898–1911* (New York, 1954), pp. 61–72. See also her 'The Shanghai–Hangchow–Ningpo Railway Loan of 1908', *Far Eastern Quarterly* 10, 3 (1951).
141 Addis to Bland, 25 May 1906, Bland Collection.
142 Ibid, 6 December 1907.

7 RAILWAYS – RIGHTS RECOVERY, FINANCE, AND THE CONSORTIUM, 1905–1911

1 Opinion of the B&CC's Counsel, 14 November 1908, in FO 371/430, ff. 405–06.
2 For the 1907 understanding, see FO 371/418, f. 244; for the recriminations, see Émile d'Erlanger to Sir Francis Campbell, Foreign Office, FO 371/622, ff. 125–27; see also William Keswick as Chairman, B&CC, to d'Erlanger, 19 February 1909, in ibid, f. 312.
3 See especially the following letters of G.E. Morrison: (i) to V. Chirol, 25 March 1905, (ii) to L.G. Fraser, 22 May 1905, and (iii) to J.O.P. Bland, 25 May 1905, Hui-min Lo, ed. *The Correspondence of G.E. Morrison*, I, 295–96, 306, and 307 respectively.
4 Charles Addis, memorandum, 4 June 1920, FO 371/1319, ff. 79–84, and related correspondence to and from Sir Francis Bertie in ibid, ff. 64–78.
5 For the Belgian involvement see G. Kurgan-van Hentenryk, *Léopold II et les groups financiers belges en Chine* (Bruxelles, 1972); for reference see index under 'American China Development Company', by which title it is generally referred to in the literature.
6 Comment by Viceroy Chang Chih-tung, quoted in E-tu Zen Sun, *Chinese Railways and British Interests, 1898–1911* (New York, 1954), p. 80. The present chapter depends for continuity on her study.
7 See, for example, Governor of Hong Kong to Secretary of State, 8 September 1905, copy in FO 17/1762, ff. 406–08.
8 For a copy of cables to and from the British Minister, Sir Ernest Satow, in Peking see FO 17/1762, f. 181; see also Governor of Hong Kong cable of 28 June 1905, in ibid, f. 223.
9 Satow to Governor of Hong Kong in ibid, f. 224, 28 June 1905.
10 FO 17/1762.
11 John V.A. MacMurray, comp. and ed. *Treaties and Agreements with and concerning China, 1894–1919* (New York, 1921), I, 530–31.
12 See developments in FO 17/1/1762, ff. 406–08, 427–33, and 445–47.
13 'Agreement for a loan for the redemption of the Canton–Hankow Railway concession, September 9, 1905', Art. 7, MacMurray, I, 529.
14 Correspondence under cover of 22 September 1905, FO 17/1762, ff. 353–54.

15 The origins of the loan and the actual lender were subjects of considerable correspondence, for which see, for example, Satow to Sir Matthew Nathan (Governor of Hong Kong), 18 August 1905, FO 17/1762, ff. 431–32; Marquess of Lansdowne (Foreign Secretary) to Sir Francis Bertie, British Ambassador in Paris, 18 October 1905, FO 17/1762, f. 451 and also f. 454; Hongkong Bank to S. Simon, Banque de l'Indo-Chine, Paris, FO 17/1762, ff. 386–87.

16 For a draft prospectus dated 14 February 1906, see CO 129/336, f. 500; there is considerable discussion on the inadequacy of the enabling ordinance and other features of the loan, for which see, e.g. Colonial Office to Governor, 26 January 1906, in CO 129/336, ff. 467–500.

17 MacMurray, I, 747–55; for the Prospectus, see FO 371/422, ff. 337–78.

18 Sir John Jordan to Sir Edward Grey, Secretary of State for Foreign Affairs, 27 October 1908, CO 239/360, f. 25.

19 MacMurray, I, 756–59, for the agreement; for the discussion of its status, see FO 371/871, ff. 367–97, 406–07, October–December 1910.

20 The loan agreement of 10 November 1908 is included as No. 1 in despatch of Jordan of 1 January 1909, FO 371/622, ff. 30–31; see also, FO 371/422, f. 332.

21 1 January 1909, FO 371/622, f. 30.

22 S. Simon to Charles Addis, 5 May 1908, enclosed with Addis to Bland, 6 May 1908, in the J.O.P. Bland Collection, Thomas Fisher Rare Book Library, University of Toronto, Toronto, Ontario, Canada.

23 Auswärtiges Amt [AA], China, no. 3. *Finances*. Vol. 23, A 18707, Baron von Rex, German Minister in Peking, to the AA, 24 October 1908.

24 Kurgan-van Hentenryk, pp. 737–48.

25 Addis to Bland, Bland Collection.

26 Chinese Central Railways [CCR] to Bland, 10 June 1908, in CO 129/352, ff. 594–95, incl. 2.

27 Addis to Sir Francis Campbell, Foreign Office, 21 July 1908, FO 371/422, f. 170.

28 CO 129/352, ff. 593–97, despatch dated 7 July 1908 with enclosures, including Bland to CCR and CCR to Bland.

29 Jordan to Sir Edward Grey, 7 July 1908, CO 129/352, ff. 593–94.

30 Addis to Cailloux, 19 June 1908, CO 129/352, ff. 7–8; see also, Grey to Bertie, 8 April 1908, FO 371/422, f. 48.

31 See E.G. Hillier's warning cable, Hillier to Hongkong Bank, London, 1 July 1908 in CO 129/352, f. 595.

32 2 July 1908, CO 129/352, ff. 595–96. The Germans decided not to participate, Hongkong Bank London to Hillier, 10 July 1908, in ibid, f. 600.

33 In a cable to Peking, 10 July 1908, FO 371/422, f. 159.

34 Grey to Jordan, 9 September 1908, CO 129/352, f. 602.

35 See e.g. Grey to Jordan, 9 September 1908, CO 129/352, f. 602; Jordan to Grey, CO 129/353, ff. 288–89, 16 September 1908.

36 Exchange between Addis and O. Homberg of the Banque de l'Indo-Chine, in FO 371/422, ff. 295–96; for the leak see Addis to Homberg, 17 September 1908, CO 129/353, f. 145.

37 Cables between Addis and Hillier in CO 129/353, ff. 148–50.

38 Kurgan-van Hentenryk, cited, and En-han Lee, *China's Quest for Railway Autonomy, 1904–1911* (Singapore, 1977), p. 223.

39 Addis diary, 20 October 1908, PP.MS.14/26, in Addis Papers, the Library, School of Oriental and African Studies, University of London.

40 For the agreement, see MacMurray, I, 707; for the Keswick letter see FO 371/430, f. 382.

41 FO 371/430, ff. 401 and 405–06; refer also to note 1 and related discussion above.

42 Addis to Fanqui (French syndicate), 20 February 1908, FO 371/422, f. 13.

43 Hillier to A.M. Townsend, 12 July 1907, CO 129/345, ff. 271–73, the comment is from p. 2, line 2; memo of the negotiations, 4 July 1908, FO 371/431, ff. 79–92.

44 FO 371/622, f. 22.

45 Ibid, f. 26.

46 Ibid, f. 57.

47 This information was sent to the Colonial Office on 27 January 1909, see FO 371/622, f. 77.

48 Ibid, f. 58.

49 Addis's memorandum on the negotiations of 25–27 and 28 January in Paris and Berlin respectively in ibid, ff. 163–64 or CO 129/360, ff. 316–24, esp. f. 320.

50 CO 129/360, f. 321.

51 Grey to Sir Francis Bertie, Paris, 1 February 1909, FO 800/163, ff. 64–65; Grey to Cambon, 15 February 1909, FO 371/622, ff. 218–19.

52 4 February 1909, FO 371/622, ff. 179–80.

53 Addis to Sir Francis Campbell, 1 February 1909, and accompanying memorandum, FO 371/622, ff. 184–85.

54 Addis to Dudley Mills, 6 March 1909, PP.MS.14/170.

55 DAB to Addis, 5 March 1909, FO 371/622, f. 419.

56 9 March 1909, FO 371/622, f. 471; for a complete list of cables and for the communication from Addis, 19 March 1909, see FO 371/623, ff. 148–49.

57 Addis to Mills, 6 March 1909, PP.MS.14/170.

58 Addis diary, 5 March 1909, PP.MS.14/27.

59 On the pressure from the Ministry, see Foreign Office to Addis, 5 February 1909, FO 371/622, ff. 202–03; for the resentment, see Jordan to Grey, 2 February 1909, FO 371/622, f. 198.

60 Quoted in Sun, p. 103.

61 Jordan to Grey, 10 March 1909, FO 371/622, f. 467.

62 FO 371/622, ff. 407–08.

63 Ibid, f. 425.

64 Addis to Murray Stewart, 20 June 1909, PP.MS.14/228.

65 This is based on a survey of the German reaction, see David J.S. King's research report, 'On the Relations of the Hongkong Bank with Germany, 1864–1948 – the China Loans', p. 90n46, in the Hongkong Bank Group Archives.

66 FO 371/622, f. 471.

67 Addis to Mills, 14 March 1909, PP.MS.14/170.

68 Minutes, in FO 371/622, ff. 526–28.

69 FO 371/623, ff. 3–5.

70 See Notes, dated 24 March, on letter from the DAB of 20 March 1909 in FO 371/623, ff. 75–76.

71 FO 371/623, ff. 55–56 or 65–66.

72 Addis to Alston, 22 March 1909, ibid, ff. 57–58.

73 These agreements are found in draft form in FO 371/623, ff. 178–91.

74 FO 371/263, ff. 108–14, 119–21, 141–42, 147–49, 156–58.

75 A shorthand transcript of the proceedings was sent by Addis to the FO, see FO 371/623, ff. 317–58, but see also Addis's personal account in his letter to Mills, 9 April 1909, PP.MS.14/170.

76 Ibid, f. 351.

77 FO 371/623, f. 349.

78 FO 371/623, f. 242.
79 Minute of 5 April 1909, FO 371/263, ff. 272–79, including the account in *The Times* for 5 April, which Addis said was accurate.
80 Addis diary, 8 April 1909, PP.MS.14/27.
81 The official accounts are in FO 371/236, ff. 233–36. The minutes of the meeting are in ibid, ff. 240–42.
82 See exchange of cables with Addis and Hillier; the control was the essential point; the channel of control of lesser significance, FO 371/623, f. 410, for views of counsel see ibid, ff. 412–13.
83 Grey to Jordan, 7 May 1909, FO 371/624, f. 24, and Addis Papers.
84 Hongkong Bank to Addis; Addis to Hongkong Bank, 8 April 1909, FO 371/623, f. 296.
85 9 May 1909, FO 371/624, f. 36.
86 AA, China no. 3. *Finances*. Vol. 24, 22 March 1909.
87 Addis to Sir Francis Campbell, 5 April 1909, FO 371/623, f. 209.
88 Addis to Mills, 2 May 1909, PP.MS.14/170; see also Jordan to Grey, 30 April 1909, FO 371/623, f. 472.
89 S. Simon to Addis, 3 May 1909, FO 371/624, f. 2.
90 For a summary see Jordan to Grey, 22 April 1909, FO 371/624, ff. 44–46.
91 Grey to Jordan, 12 May 1909, FO 371/624, f. 143.
92 FO 371/624, f. 144.
93 Addis to Murray Stewart, 20 June 1909, PP.MS.14/228.
94 J. de Salis to Sir Edward Grey, Berlin, 15 May 1909, FO 371/624, f. 125. The memorandum of agreement is in FO 371/624, ff. 156–58, the minutes are ff. 221–26. See also Addis's letter to Langley of the Foreign Office, 17 August 1909, FO 371/625, f. 260.
95 Von Bülow to the Kaiser, 15 May 1909, Lepsius, vol. 32, p. 5, Nr 11604, quoted in D.J.S. King, p. 93.
96 Commentary with Hukuang Railways loan, 'Correspondence between Mr Hillier and Deputies Kao [Ling-yu] and Tseng [Kuang-jung]', both of whom were officials of Hupei, the former Commissioner of Education, the latter Taotai of Shih Ho, in FO 371/625, ff. 28–30.
97 Sir John Jordan to Sir Edward Grey, 6 June 1909, FO 371/624, f. 280; see FO 371/625, ff. 2–3 for exchange between Hillier and the Chinese delegates on this subject.
98 FO 371/624, f. 297.
99 Jordan to Grey, 8 June 1909, FO 371/625, f. 2.
100 Grey to Count Benckendorff, 27 July 1909, FO 371/625, f. 147.
101 Addis diary, entries by his wife, Eba Addis, 3, 10 December 1907, PP.MS.14/25.
102 Grey to Benckendorff, 27 July 1909, FO 371/625, f. 147.
103 For the March 1909 negotiations of Pauling and Co., see FO 371/634, ff. 343–54.
104 The initial full criticism of Hillier is found in Bland to Addis, 23 December 1907; for the development of the problems, see Bland to Addis, 17, 23, and 31 May 1908 and, for the later criticism of Hillier, 26 June 1908, in Correspondence with C.S. Addis, Volume 23, item 23B, in J.O.P. Bland Collection, Thomas Fisher Rare Book Library, University of Toronto.
105 Addis diary, 27 August and 17 September 1908, PP.MS.14/27.
106 Bland to Addis, 5 September from London and 2 November 1908 from Peking; a response from Addis to this latter letter, 24 November 1908; and a response from Bland, 17 December 1908 in J.O.P. Bland Collection, cited.
107 The cable was sent on 17 May 1909, see Eba Addis's diary entry for that date,

PP.MS.14/28; for the post-dismissal reaction, see Charles Addis's diary entries for 31 March and 7 November 1910 in ibid and references in Chapter 8, note 67 and Chapter 11, note 16, and Bland, *Recent Events and Present Policies in China* (London, 1912).

108 See the file entitled 'My case against the British and Chinese Corporation', Bland Collection, Volume 24, Correspondence 'in' and 'out', Box II (item D). For the motion to wind up the B&CC, see Addis diary, 24 November 1910, PP.MS.14/29. A fuller report of the meeting, including Bland's own presentation of the case against the Hongkong Bank, is in *The Times* (25 November 1910), p. 22 d–e.

109 Addis to Bland, 15 November 1909, in Bland Collection, cited.

110 For a reference to J.R.M. Smith, see Bland to Addis, 9 July 1908, in ibid.

111 The agreement between the B&CC and the Hongkong Bank can be found in 'My case . . .', Bland Collection, also in Group Archives and in the B&CC archives with Matheson and Co.

112 Bland to Addis, 6 June 1906 and Addis to Bland, 20 February 1907, Bland Collection, cited.

113 British and Chinese Corporation to J.O.P. Bland, 17 October 1905, in 'My case . . .'.

114 Landale to Bland, Shanghai, 18 September 1907, and other letters in the file 'British and Chinese Corporation (correspondence with Jardine, Matheson)', Bland Collection, Vol. 24.

115 Lord ffrench to Pauling and Co., London, 14 August 1908, British and Chinese Corporation (Relations with Messrs Pauling and Co.), item 23-D, Vol. 24, Bland Collection.

116 The draft and related information is contained in a memorandum by F. Rutherford Harris to Pauling's dated 10 September 1908 and marked 'Personal and strictly confidential'; the actual letter, signed by George Pauling, was dated 14 September. For the proposed role of Erlanger, see Harris to Bland, 11 September 1908, in ibid.

117 Harris to Bland, 13 November 1908, in ibid.

118 Bland to Harris, 24 November 1908, in ibid.

119 Addis diary, 26 January and 18 February 1909, PP.MS.14/28.

120 Secretary, Board of Directors, Pauling and Co. to Secretary, Board of Directors, B&CC, 28 January 1909, in ibid.

121 Addis diary, 19 February 1909, PP.MS.14/28 and Keswick to d'Erlanger, 19 February, in Bland Collection.

122 Addis diary, 18, 25, 26, and 27 February 1909, PP.MS.14/28.

123 Thomas Gilbert, Secretary CCR, to Bland, 10 June 1908, in Correspondence with the Chinese Central Railways, Volume 24, Bland Collection.

124 Dated 12 June 1908, in ibid.

125 Jamieson (on CCR stationery) to Bland, 23 December 1908, in ibid.

126 Jordan to Grey, 8 June 1909, FO 371/625, f. 2.

127 Memorandum dated July 1908 and marked 'Mr Addis' in the file 'My case . . .', see note 108. The copy in the Bland Collection was sent to Bland officially by the board secretary by a covering letter dated 28 August 1908; a copy of Macrae's opposing memorandum was also enclosed.

128 Addis diary, 31 July 1908, PP.MS.14/27.

129 The contract continuation is found in B&CC to Bland, 16 October 1908, in 'My case . . .'; Bland's accusation of Addis's dissent is in Bland to Addis, 2 November, the rebuttal in Addis to Bland, 24 November 1908, in Correspondence to and from C.S. Addis in the Bland Collection, cited.

130 Hillier to Bland, 13 November 1908, in 'My case . . .'.

131 Keswick to Bland, 26 March 1909, in ibid.
132 Bland to Keswick, 17 April 1909, in ibid.
133 Bland to Harris, 31 March 1909, in the file 'Relations with Messrs Pauling and Co.', in the Bland Collection, cited.
134 Chang Chih-tung to E.H. Fraser, Consul-General, Hankow, 13 February and reply of Fraser, 16 February 1909, copies of the cables in 'My case . . .'.
135 Bland to 'E.G. Hillier, Esq., CMG, Agent, The Hongkong and Shanghai Banking Corporation, Peking', 26 May 1909, in ibid.
136 The cable was copied in a letter, Bland to the Board of the B&CC, 29 May 1909, in ibid.
137 Bland to 'Agent [Hillier], Hongkong & Shanghai Banking Corporation, Peking', 2 June 1909, in ibid.
138 Hillier to Bland, 7 June 1909, in ibid.
139 Addis diary, Eba's entry for 27 May, Charles Addis's entries for 1, 2 and 5 June 1909, PP.MS.14/28.
140 Ibid, Eba's entry, 10 June, Charles Addis's entry for 2 July 1909.
141 Memorandum dated 10 June 1909, in 'My case . . .'.
142 Addis diary, 19 July 1909, PP.MS.14/28.
143 Keswick to Bland, 20 July 1909, in 'My case . . .'.
144 Bland to William Graham (his legal adviser), 20 July 1909, in ibid.
145 'Terms of Arrangement between The British and Chinese Corporation Limited and J.O.P. Bland', 1 September 1909, in ibid.
146 Bland to the B&CC Board of Directors, 16 December 1909, in ibid.
147 Instructive in this context is Hillier's description of the Chinese reaction to Taft's message, see Hillier to Addis, 23 July 1909, FO 371/625, ff. 197–98.
148 Addis to Foreign Office, 24 July 1909, FO 371/625, f. 169.
149 Quoted by Hillier in his letter to Addis, describing Bland's activities before his departure from China in company with V. Chirol of *The Times*; the letter is dated 23 June 1909, and a copy is in FO 371/625, ff. 129–30.
150 M. Boissonnas, chargé d'affaires de la République française en Chine, and Stephen Pichon, ministre des affaires étrangères, 30 June 1909, Asie 779, FO 30.372, Archives of the Ministry of Foreign Affairs, Paris.
151 Quoted in Lo, I, 505n1, and FO 371/625, f. 234; the full Morrison version is in ibid, f. 233.
152 N.d., but 'PS' dated 30 July 1909, see ibid, f. 228.
153 H. Cordes to G.E. Morrison, 26 July 1909, Hillier to Morrison, 26, 27 July, in Lo, I, 505–06.
154 Morrison to Hillier, 27 July 1909, in ibid, I, 507–08.
155 FO 371/625, f. 235.
156 See Morrison to Hillier, 27 July 1909, in Lo, I, 507–08, and Hillier's comments thereon to Addis, in FO 371/625, f. 229.
157 Baron von Rex to AA, 21 June 1909, AA, China no. 4, *Railways*, Vol. 20, A 10577, in D.J.S. King, p. 94.
158 On the *Times* takeover, see C.F. Moberly Bell to Morrison, 23 September 1908, in Lo, I, 463–73, and for Koch's role, see p. 270; for Koch as a member of Panmure Gordon, see p. 515.
159 Chirol to Morrison, 10 August 1909, Addis to Langley, 17 August 1909, FO 371/625, ff. 260–63. Bland's incorrect version as leaked to the French in Peking is found in the letter to the French Ministry of Foreign Affairs, cited in note 150 above.
160 Chirol to Morrison, 19 August 1909, Lo, I, 514–15; FO 371/625, ff. 374–79;

Chirol to Grey, 6 September 1909, ibid, ff. 375–76; memo in ibid, ff. 377–79.

161 Chirol to Morrison, 27 August 1909, Lo, I, 519.

162 Von Rex to the AA, 28 July 1909, AA, China no. 3, *Finances*, Vol. 21, A 12494, cited in D.J.S. King, p. 96.

163 Von Rex to the AA, 4 September 1909, in ibid, A 15459.

164 MacMurray, I, 866–79, and Minutes of the Board of Directors.

165 'Hukuang Railways, Official Translation of Despatch from the Minister of Communications [Chu Chi-chien]', 'To the Representatives of the Deutsch–Asiatische Bank, the Hongkong & Shanghai Banking Corporation, the Banque de l'Indo-Chine and the American Group', Peking, 1 March 1913, and reply of 3 March 1913, in B&CC archives, Matheson and Co., London.

166 See Addis to S. Simon, 25 September 1909, FO 371/625, ff. 468–71.

167 Memo by Addis in reply to French, 14 October 1909, FO 371/626, ff. 71–72; see also G. Jamieson, Managing Director, CCR, to Simon, 22 December 1909, in FO 371/626, f. 232.

168 24 January 1910, FO 371/842, f. 172.

169 FO 371/851, f. 293.

170 FO 371/851, ff. 27–55; Jordan to Grey, 22 December 1909, f. 49; minute referred to, f. 48.

171 Jordan to Prince Ch'ing, 12 February 1910, in ibid.

172 See e.g. Addis to Foreign Office, 30 March 1910, FO 371/851, f. 257, and Max-Müller to Grey, 4 May 1910, ibid, f. 380; see also, ibid, ff. 447–55.

173 *Cf* Sun, pp. 113–19; her assessment that the foreign bankers 'completely disregarded' the seriousness of provincial objections is mistaken.

174 For correspondence on the Shanghai–Ningpo problems see FO 371/858, ff. 42–78, 105–107, 144–63.

175 FO 371/851, f. 305. For the agreement, see MacMurray, I, 266–67 and Chapter 4 above.

176 FO 371/851, ff. 305–08, 318–25.

177 Addis to Foreign Office, 23 April 1910, FO 371/851, f. 319.

178 FO 371/851, ff. 360, 371–73; for the agreement, minutes, and related comments, see ibid, ff. 392–444.

179 Addis to Sir Francis Campbell, 27 May 1910, CO 129/372, f. 241.

180 Addis to Langley in Foreign Office, 12 August 1910, FO 371/851, f. 533. The response of the Wai-wu Pu is dated 1 August and is in ibid, f. 539.

181 FO 371/851, f. 560.

182 Addis to Sir Francis Campbell enclosed telegram from Peking and E.G. Hillier etc., 10 March 1911, CO 129/383, f. 117.

183 CO 129/382, ff. 266–67.

184 Addis memo with his covering letter to FO of 19 April 1911, CO 129/383, f. 290.

185 Minutes of an interview at Prince Ch'ing's residence, 5 April 1911, in CO 129/383, ff. 336–37.

186 Jordan to Grey, 9 April 1911, CO 129/383, f. 336. See also Albert Feuerwerker's biography of Sheng, *China's Early Industrialization, Sheng Hsuan-huai (1844–1916) and Mandarin Enterprise* (Cambridge, MA, 1958).

187 On gambling with exchanges, see Hongkong Bank, Peking, to Addis, 21 April 1911, CO 129/383, f. 291. See also, the comment by Stanley Wright in *China's Customs Revenue since the Revolution of 1911* (Shanghai, 1935), p. 109.

188 See Jordan to Grey, commenting on discussions with Hillier, 21 April 1911, in CO 129/383, f. 518.

189 Notes of a meeting held at Yu-ch'uan Pu, 7 April 1911, CO 129/383, ff. 337–38.

190 CO 129/383, f. 518; CO 129/382, ff. 284–85; see also note 188.
191 22 April 1911, CO 129/383, f. 332; see also, Addis to Foreign Office, 24 April 1911, ibid.
192 Quoted by Jordan in Jordan to Grey, 9 April 1911, CO 129/383, f. 336.
193 Jordan to Grey, 10 May 1911, FO 129/384, f. 119.

8 SHANGHAI, REVOLUTION, AND THE REORGANIZATION LOAN, 1910–1914

1 Since the Shanghai banking system has been so completely described by Andrea Lee McElderry in her *Shanghai Old-Style Banks (Ch'ien-chuang), 1800–1935; a Traditional Institution in a Changing Society* (Ann Arbor, 1976), Michigan Papers in Chinese Studies, No. 25, the following narrative is confined to matters directly involving the Hongkong and Shanghai Bank.
2 Belgian Consul-General, Shanghai, to Minister of Foreign Affairs, 30 March 1910, Dossier no. 2822 (V–VIII)–2823 (I–VIII), National Archives, Brussels.
3 See McElderry, esp. pp. 98–99, 105–12. The reference to the Chinese newspaper is in *Tung-fang tza-chih* 7, 10 (October 1910), pp. 130–31. A comprehensive study of these events has been made by Marie-Claire Bergère, *Une Crise financière à Shanghai à la fin de l'ancien régime* (Paris, 1964) and placed in context by McElderry, see note 1 above.
4 Despatch to Foreign Secretary of 6 September 1910, FO 371/873, ff. 99–107, esp. f. 100.
5 *Tung-fang tza-chih* 7, 11 (1910).
6 Sir John Jordan to Sir Edward Grey, 22 December 1910, FO 371/1068, ff. 23–26, 41–42. The actual loan agreement was between the Financial Commissioner of Nanking, Fan Tseng-hsiang, and H.E.R. Hunter for the Hongkong Bank and the other bank representatives in Shanghai.
7 22 December 1910, FO 371/1068, f. 24.
8 Ibid.
9 Ibid, ff. 41–42.
10 John V.A. MacMurray, comp. and ed. *Treaties and Agreements with and concerning China, 1894–1919* (New York, 1924), I, 755–57.
11 Referred to in Sir John Jordan to Sir Edward Grey, 22 December 1910, FO 371/1068, f. 24.
12 H.E.R. Hunter to acting Peking Agent A.D. Brent, 28 June 1911, FO 371/1092, f. 277.
13 See agreement dated 11 December 1910, with ibid, ff. 24–25.
14 Arnold Wright, ed. *Twentieth Century Impressions of Hongkong, Shanghai and the other Treaty Ports of China* (London, 1908), 'Hankow'.
15 Reorganization Loan of 1913, Annex B, see MacMurray, I, 1018.
16 Hunter to acting Agent A.D. Brent in Peking, 28 June 1911, FO 371/1092, f. 277.
17 The agreement is in MacMurray, I, 906–09, also, with other relevant information, in Jordan to Grey, 30 September 1911, FO 371/1092, f. 295.
18 See Chapter 3 for further comments.
19 A.M. Townsend to Foreign Office, 26 August 1911, FO 371/1069, f. 193; see also cables to and from Hong Kong, and between Addis and F. Urbig, ibid, ff. 196–200.
20 22 December 1910, FO 371/1068, f. 24.
21 See minutes and correspondence in FO 371/1069, ff. 201–19.
22 Quoted in Grey to Jordan, 31 August 1911, ibid, f. 204.

23 Jordan to Grey, 1 September 1911, ibid, f. 211.
24 Addis to Sir F. Campbell, 5 September 1911, FO 371/1069, f. 220.
25 Ibid.
26 Grey to Jordan, 5 September 1911, FO 371/1069, f. 221.
27 For the overdraft comments, see Morrison to D.D. Braham, 16 February 1912, in Hui-min Lo, ed. *The Correspondence of G.E. Morrison* (Cambridge, 1976), I, 737. The Board of Directors minute gives the interest rate as 6½%, but all other sources state 6%. See A. Feuerwerker, *China's Early Industrialization: Sheng Hsuan-huai (1844–1916) and Mandarin Enterprise* (Cambridge, MA, 1958), p. 135.
28 William D. Wray, *Mitsubishi and the N.Y.K., 1870–1914* (Cambridge, MA, 1984), pp. 396–97. Wray cites HSBC to Foreign Office, 30 January 1912, FO 371/1312, f. 87 and 1 February 1912, f. 82.
29 *Yin-hang chou-pao* (Banking weekly, Shanghai) 12, 15:9–10 (24 April 1928).
30 Sir Claude MacDonald to Sir Edward Grey, 26 January 1912, FO 371/1311, f. 439 (also cited by Wray, see note 28), and Feuerwerker, cited.
31 H.E. Muriel in autobiographical letter to J.R. Jones in 'Personalities', Hongkong Bank Group Archives. There is also his full length and more recent autobiography in the Archives.
32 For a definitive biography for Yuan Shih-k'ai, see Ernest P. Young, *The Presidency of Yuan Shih-k'ai* (Ann Arbor, 1977); the outline in this chapter is also indebted to John K. Fairbank, Edwin O. Reischauer, and Albert M. Craig, *East Asia, the Modern Transformation* (Boston, 1965).
33 Addis to Lindley at the Foreign Office, 23 December 1911, FO 371/1098, f. 348; for the announcement, see ibid, f. 351.
34 Ibid.
35 Ibid, f. 347.
36 Stanley F. Wright, *China's Customs Revenue since the Revolution of 1911* (Shanghai, 1935), China, Maritime Customs, II. Special Series: No. 41, 3rd ed. p. 111n1. This section is based on information from Wright's study, esp. pp. 3–10 and 111–47.
37 MacMurray, II, 946.
38 Addis diary, 13 November 1911, PP.MS.14/29, [Sir Charles] Addis Papers, the Library, School of Oriental and African Studies, University of London.
39 Hongkong Bank, Peking, to Four Groups, cable, 24 February 1912, FO 371/1313, f. 394. Jordan's concern over Japanese competition and his conclusion that British lending to the Provisional Government should be permitted is in his cable to Sir Edward Grey, 23 February 1912, ibid, f. 319.
40 The confirmation is found on p. 3 of the minutes, for which see FO 371/1319, f. 451; the regulations are in a letter from T'ang to Finance Minister Hsiung Hsi-ling, 17 May 1912, Enclosure 5, in Addis to Foreign Office, 24 June 1912, ibid, ff. 490–91.
41 See Yuan Shih-k'ai to E.G. Hillier, 'Letter of Agreement for Advance upon Currency Loan, March 9, 1912', in MacMurray, I, 852. There were similar letters dated 15 April and 18 June.
42 The Cottu Loan is referred to with important references in G. Kurgan-van Hentenryk, *Léopold II et les groupes financiers belges en Chine: la politique royale et ses prolongements (1895–1914)* (Bruxelles, 1972), p. 772. For the Anglo-Belgian loan, see ibid, 773–87.
43 Compton Mackenzie, *Realms of Silver, One Hundred Years of Banking in the East* (London, 1954), p. 207.
44 For a discussion on the responsibility for this breach of faith as between Yuan and

T'ang, see Kit-ching Chan Lau, *Anglo-Chinese Diplomacy in the Careers of Sir John Jordan and Yuan Shih-k'ai, 1906–1920* (Hong Kong, 1978), pp. 56–57.

45 Willard D. Straight, *China's Loan Negotiations*, pp. 12–13; see also, Chan, p. 57.
46 British Parliamentary Papers, China, No. 2 (1912), 'Correspondence respecting Chinese Loan Negotiations', Cd. 6446, pp. 11–12; see also ibid, pp. 4–5, 13, and *passim*.
47 Cable from Hongkong Bank, Shanghai, to Addis, London, quoted in Addis to Banque de l'Indo-Chine, in FO 405/219, f. 14.
48 This is presumably the Third Year Domestic Loan, originally for $16 million but raised to $24 million. However, the dates would not appear to be consistent with those in MacMurray, for which see II, 1150–52.
49 C.S. Addis to Foreign Office, 22 November 1910, with enclosures, FO 371/874, f. 35; see also, minutes of 17 November 1910, FO 371/873, f. 546; for the withdrawal, see Addis to Foreign Office, 2 December 1910, FO 371/874, f. 93.
50 Germany, Auswärtiges Amt, [AA], China no. 3, *Finances*. Vol. 30, in the printed minutes of the meeting.
51 Ibid, Vol. 31, A 8814, Poutalès in St Petersburg to the AA, 18 May 1912.
52 Addis diary, 14–16 May 1912, PP.MS.14/30.
53 AA, China no. 3, *Finances*, Vol. 32, A 1198, AA note of 26 June 1912.
54 Minutes of 20 June 1912 meeting of the Sextuple Groups, FO 371/1319, f. 488; minutes of the 7 July 1913 meeting of the Quintuple Groups, FO 371/1594, f. 366, p. 2.
55 Reprinted in MacMurray, I, 852.
56 For a Foreign Office minute on the Jackson Syndicate, see FO 371/1322, ff. 102–03, 13 September 1912, and Morrison's letter to O.M. Green, editor of the *North-China Daily News* (Shanghai) and correspondent of *The Times*, 21 December 1912, in Lo, II, 64–72.
57 AA, China no. 3, *Finances*, Vol. 34, A 16675, Montgelas (who had known Morrison in Japan), AA note after a conversation with Morrison at the AA, 27 September 1912.
58 R.P.T. Davenport-Hines, biography of Crisp, in David Jeremy, ed. *Dictionary of Business Biography*, I, 822–26. London, 1984.
59 Morrison to O.M. Green, cited in note 56 above. See also, Morrison to Jordan, possibly never sent, undated but between 12 and 16 March 1914, in Lo, II, 297–303.
60 AA, China no. 3, *Finances*, Vol. 35, A 19523, Urbig memo, 6 November 1912.
61 Foreign Office to Jordan, 13 September 1912, FO 371/1322, f. 124.
62 Draft telegram to Peking, 13 September 1912, FO 371/1322, f. 127, and AA, China no. 3, *Finances*, Vol. 34, A 16589, Montgelas, AA minute after a conversation with Urbig, 27 September 1912.
63 AA, China no. 3, *Finances*, Vol. 35, A 19587, Haxhausen in Peking to AA, 24 October 1912.
64 Ibid, Vol. 34, A 15939, in *Le journal des débats* (16 September 1912).
65 Ibid, A 16301, Kühlmann in London to AA, 19 September 1912.
66 Ibid, A 16661, Urbig to Montgelas of the AA, 28 September 1912; and 26 October 1910, FO 371/873, ff. 452–54.
67 Addis to Mills, 23 October 1912, PP.MS.14/173.
68 *British Parliamentary Papers*, China, No. 2 (1912), 'Correspondence respecting Chinese Loan Negotiations', Cd. 6446, pp. 11–12.
69 Addis to Foreign Office, 12 December 1912, and Sir Montagu Turner to Foreign Office, 10 December 1912, FO 371/1325, f. 180.
70 See e.g. FO 371/1325, a folio following f. 97.

71 Addis diary, 31 October and 23 November 1912, PP.MS.14/30.
72 FO 371/1325, f. 226; for related documents, see also ff. 223–31, under minute dated 16 December 1912.
73 AA, China no. 3, *Finances*, Vol. 34, A 16301, Kühlmann to the AA, 19 September 1912.
74 Ibid, Vol. 36, A 20586, Curt in Shanghai to AA, 5 November 1912; reference might also be made to the Morrison letters cited in note 56.
75 Ibid, Vol. 35, the DAB in London to the DAB in Berlin, 17 October 1912.
76 Jordan to Grey, 8 October 1912, FO 371/1323, ff. 243–47.
77 AA, British Possessions in the Far East. Hong Kong. Vol. 3, A 20759, German Consul in Hong Kong to the AA, 25 October 1912.
78 China, No. 2 (1912), 'Correspondence respecting Chinese Loan Negotiations', Cd. 6446, p. 15.
79 Ibid, p. 13.
80 Addis diary, 27 November 1912, PP.MS.14/30.
81 MacMurray, II, 967n; FO 371/1324, f. 311; FO 371/1325, f. 64 and *passim*.
82 Grey to Jordan, FO 371/1325, f. 117, 13 December 1912, and Langley to Hongkong Bank, 21 December 1912, ibid, f. 232.
83 Addis to Foreign Office, 16 December 1912, FO 371/1325, f. 200.
84 Ibid.
85 Addis diary, 14 December 1912, PP.MS.14/30.
86 Addis diary, 26 February 1913, PP.MS.14/31.
87 Statement, 18 March 1913, reprinted in MacMurray, II, 1025. For America's continued involvement in currency reform, see a statement of the American Legation, Peking, 15 April 1917, reprinted in MacMurray, I, 852.
88 Young, p. 128.
89 FO 405/211, p. 385.
90 Addis diary, 26 April 1913, PP.MS.14/31.
91 Haxthausen to the AA, Nr 11969, 29 April 1913, in AA, Lepsius, Vol. 32, pp. 395–97.
92 Young, p. 287n68.
93 See MacMurray, II, 1004–06 and 977 respectively.
94 AA, China no. 3, *Finances*, Vol. 38, from articles in the *Frankfurter Zeitung* and the *Kölnische Zeitung*, 29 and 30 April 1913, respectively. These newspapers used the Peking *Daily Telegraph* as sources.
95 Charles Addis in FO 405/211, pp. 262–63.
96 Ibid, p. 389.
97 AA, China no. 3, *Finances*, Vol. 39, A 9550, Urbig to Montgelas of the AA, 8 May 1913.
98 Ibid, AA marginal note commenting on a note from the Chinese Finance Ministry to the DAB, 4 May 1913.
99 Ibid, A 9696, Hongkong Bank, London, to DAB, 10 May 1913.
100 Ibid, A 10464, in the *Bayerischer Kurier und Müncher Fremdenblatt* (22 May 1913).
101 Ibid, from *The Times* (22 May 1913).
102 Addis diary, 21 May 1913, PP.MS.14/31.
103 For the agreement and annexes, etc., see MacMurray, II, 1007–38.
104 Jordan to Grey, 11 December 1911, FO 371/1325, f. 119.
105 See the definitive study, S.A.M. Adshead, *The Modernization of the Chinese Salt Administration, 1900–1920* (Cambridge, MA, 1970). The dates are a reminder that reform did not begin with Sir Richard Dane, although his contribution was of great importance.
106 A copy of the Prospectus is in FO 371/1594, ff. 183–85.

107 Ibid.
108 W. Langley to the Hongkong Bank, 8 May 1913, reproduced in the Prospectus, for which see FO 371/1594, f. 183.
109 These exchanges, including key memoranda, are in the Addis Papers, PP.MS.14/342.
110 Addis to Dudley Mills, 29 May 1913, PP.MS.14/174.
111 Memorandums of 24 June and 30 July 1913, PP.MS.14/372.
112 Addis to Dudley Mills, 3 July 1913, PP.MS.14/174.
113 Ibid, 5 August 1913.
114 FO 371/1594, ff. 515–18; the official despatch, dated 3 September, is in ibid, ff. 519–20.
115 H.D.C. Jones to Foreign Office, forwarding information from Addis in Paris, 26 September 1913, FO 371/1595, f. 83.
116 Addis diary, 23 and 25 October 1913, PP.MS.14/31.
117 Draft scheme contained in letter from Sir Charles Addis to FO, 13 December 1913, in FO 371/1595, f. 336.
118 Addis diary, 8 November 1913, PP.MS.14/31.
119 November 1913, FO 371/1595, f. 166.
120 This discussion is found in correspondence throughout, particularly file FO 371/1602, but the specific reference to the £400,000 advance is in ibid, Addis to Chou Hsuch-hsi, Minister of Finance, 16 April 1913, in ibid, ff. 265–66; see also f. 264, dated 1 May 1913.
121 S. Simon to Addis, 10 November 1913, and Addis to Foreign Office, 11 November 1913, in FO 371/1623; for the loan agreements, see MacMurray, II, 1042–53 and 1055–66.
122 Cable from Hongkong Bank, Peking, 9 June 1914, FO 371/1938, f. 104.
123 For Jordan's strong feelings on the failure of the B&CC to respond to his policy, see Sir John Jordan to Sir W. Langley in the latter's private papers, FO 800/31, ff. 146–50.
124 See correspondence between Sir Edward Grey and Sir John Jordan in the first half of 1914, e.g. 5 February, 18, 20, and 30 March, 30 April, 13 May, 30 June in FO 405/216; on the B&CC's financial position and the Hongkong Bank see Addis to Stabb, 21 March 1914, enclosure No. 3 in No. 186, FO 405/216, and related correspondence.
125 MacMurray, II, 1113–23.
126 J.R. Jones, 'Chinese Loans', section on the British and Chinese Corporation, p. 5, in Group Archives.
127 From the CCR board minutes of 16 December 1915, as quoted in a 'history' of the company, i.e. a summary memorandum of major events, in CCR Archives, Matheson and Co., London.
128 Mayers to Jordan, Peking, 18 April 1914, with Memorandum of same date, in ibid.
129 MacMurray, II, 1068–77.
130 For the capital structure see Chinese Central Railways file, BT31/36256/79679, in PRO; for dividends, see company file in Matheson and Co., London.
131 Thomas Gilbert, Secretary, Pekin Syndicate, to Secretary, B&CC, 23 February 1911, and reply of A.N. Frewer, Secretary, B&CC, 8 June 1911, in B&CC/CCR archives, Matheson and Co., London.
132 G. Kurgan-van Hentenryk, pp. 808–09.
133 Correspondence between the two company secretaries between 3 July and 25 May 1914, in B&CC/CCR archives, Matheson and Co., London.

134 G. Jamieson, Managing Director, CCR, to the Pekin Syndicate, Ltd, 30 March 1914, and reply of Thos Gilbert, Secretary, Pekin Syndicate of 21 April 1914 in B&CC/CCR archives, Matheson and Co., London. One further fruitless exchange dated 8 and 25 May has been located.

135 Addis diary, 11 February 1915, PP.MS.14/33.

136 See note 77.

9 THE HONGKONG BANK AND GERMANY BEFORE 1914

1 G.E. Morrison to V. Chirol, 25 March 1905, in Hui-min Lo, ed. *The Correspondence of G.E. Morrison* (Cambridge, 1976), I, 296; Charles Addis to Mills, 23 October 1912, PP.MS.14/173, in Addis Papers, the Library, School of Oriental and African Studies, University of London.

2 From a List of Shareholders, dated 31 December 1905, found in the Toyo Bunko, Tokyo. For a general discussion of this list, see Chapter 1.

3 Addis to G.W. Russell, Trade Clearing House, 22 December 1915, in F.H. King letters, Hongkong Bank Group Archives, or the memorandum submitted by Sir Charles Addis, dated 8 December 1915, in FO 371/2342, f. 201. See also note 2 above.

4 Newton Stabb to Addis, 22 January 1913, London Office files in Group Archives.

5 Addis to Dudley Mills, 23 October 1912, PP.MS.14/173.

6 The actual arrangement with Kunst & Albers in Vladivostok is not fully documented.

7 Manfred Pohl, *The Deutsche Bank's East Asian Business, 1870–1875...*, Studies on Economic and Monetary Problems and on Banking History 15 (1977).

8 M. Müller-Jabusch, *Fünfzig Jahre Deutsch-Asiatische Bank, 1890–1939* (Berlin, 1940), p. 50.

9 China Association, Circular 208, 9 October 1915, Archive of the China Association, in the Library, SOAS.

10 Stabb to Addis, 17 February 1916, PP.MS.14/379.

11 China Association, Minutes, 12 December 1911, Archive of the China Association.

12 Ibid, in Circulars, Vol. 16, Memorandum of May 1918.

13 Ibid, Vol. 13, 1915.

14 Ibid, Vol. 9, 16 August 1912.

15 Ibid.

16 Lowson to Addis, 25 May 1916, 5HG II, No. 39, Group Archives.

17 Ibid.

18 China Association, Minutes, 11 March 1913.

19 Quoted in Müller-Jabusch, *Fünfzig Jahre,* . . . p. 18.

20 See 'Hongkong and Shanghai Banking, the New Office' *The Bankers' Insurance Managers' and Agents' Magazine* 96, 837: 734–42 (December 1913).

21 Karl T. Stöpel, *Ueber Japanisches Bankwesen und Deutschlands Anteil am Welthandle und der Industrie Japans* (Halle, 1898), p. 27, as cited in D.J.S. King's research report on the Hongkong Bank and Germany in Group Archives, p. 22.

22 D.J.S. King, p. 22.

23 This section is taken from D.J.S. King's 'The Hamburg Branch: the German Period, 1889–1920', in King, ed. *Eastern Banking*, esp. pp. 522–26 and 528–29.

24 Quoted in D.J.S. King, p. 522, from Hamburg Staatsarchiv.

25 Hongkong Bank Board of Directors Minutes, Group Archives.

26 Information from Hongkong Bank Group Archives.

27 See the Protocol books of the OAV at their offices in Hamburg.
28 Correspondence regarding F.T. Koelle, file in Group Archives.
29 Addis to Sir Ewen Cameron, 4 November 1904, PP.MS.14/352.
30 Schiller to Addis, 18 August 1905, PP.MS.14/358.
31 Addis diary, 28 March 1907, PP.MS.14/25.

10 THE HONGKONG BANK IN THE GREAT WAR, 1914–1918, I: THE CORPORATION AND STAFF

1 Sir Charles Addis to Dudley Mills, 9 August 1914, PP.MS.14/175, [Sir Charles] Addis Papers, the Library, School of Oriental and African Studies, University of London.
2 Chairman's speech at the Annual Shareholders Meeting, 19 February 1916, reported in the *North-China Herald* (4 March 1916), p. 593.
3 Addis diary, 26 June 1912, PP.MS.14/30.
4 Inferred from Newton Stabb to Addis, 17 February 1916, PP.MS.14/379.
5 Stabb's decisions as recorded in ibid.
6 Addis diary, 10 February 1916, PP.MS.14/34.
7 Ibid, 14 February 1916.
8 Stabb to Addis, see note 4.
9 Addis diary, 22 July 1915, PP.MS.14/33; Addis to Stabb, cable books, 1916, Hongkong Bank Group Archives.
10 Addis diary, 21 September 1916, PP.MS.14/34.
11 Ibid, 2 November 1916.
12 Ibid, 5 August 1914, PP.MS.14/32.
13 A.G. Stephen to Stabb, 3 August 1914, cables book, 1914, Group Archives.
14 See correspondence Addis to A.G. Stephen, LO II, Box 2, items 27 and 28, Group Archives.
15 Consul-General Fraser to Langley, Foreign Office, 1 December 1914, FO 371/2298, ff. 35–37.
16 Report of the Annual Meeting, February 1918, p. 11, Group Archives.
17 Stabb to Colonial Secretary, 3 April 1917, and subsequent correspondence, CO 129/442.
18 Cable books, 1914–18, in Group Archives.
19 Ibid, 8 February 1915.
20 Addis diary, 15 September 1915, PP.MS.14/33.
21 Correspondence between HM Office of Works and the Treasury, August 1914 and January 1915 in T.1/11765; see also F.H. King letters for 1915 in Group Archives.
22 Sir John Jordan to Sir Edward Grey, FO 371/2303, f. 18.
23 Stabb to Colonial Secretary, Hong Kong, 3 April, and Governor to Secretary of State, 21 May 1917, CO 129/442, ff. 340 and 338 respectively, Treasury paper of 27 July 1917 and related correspondence in CO 129/446, ff. 8–11, and 12 June and 2 July 1918 in CO 129/449, ff. 4–9; for material on the release of silver from holdings against the Bank's note issue and its use for India and China, see correspondence between the India Office, the Treasury, the Colonial Office, and the Bank, in CO 129/446, file 255/6/7/8, 20 September 1917, and minutes etc. on ff. 265–69, CO 129/448, f. 605, and *passim*.
24 See, e.g. CO 120/433, f. 392.
25 Addis to Stabb, 10 December 1915, F.H. King letters, Group Archives.

26 Stephen to Addis, copy in London to Peking file, LO II, Box 2, Shanghai Semi-official correspondence (s/os).

27 Addis to Stephen, 26 July 1917, London Office II, Box 2.

28 4 May 1918, cables book, Group Archives.

29 'Branches' file, compiled by J.R. Jones, Group Archives.

30 Addis to Stabb, 19 May 1916, F.H. King letters.

31 See note 25.

32 Stephen to Stabb, 20 June 1916, in LO II, Box 2, Shanghai s/o file London, Group Archives.

33 Ibid.

34 Quoted in Thiravet Pramuanratkarn, 'The Hongkong Bank in Thailand: A Case of a Pioneering Bank', in King, ed. *Eastern Banking*, pp. 18–19; see also related correspondence in file 6060 in FO 371/3026.

35 Correspondence in file 151641, FO 371/3026, T.1/11845, Frank H.H. King, 'The Foreign Exchange Banks in Siam, 1888–1918, and the National Bank Question', in papers presented at the 'International Conference on Thai Studies', (Bangkok, 1984), Vol. I, pp. 14–17 (each paper is separately paginated); Ardron's emotional retirement letter is quoted on p. 17 from the files of the Siam Commercial Bank.

36 Stephen to Hillier, 3 March 1917, in F.H. King letters.

37 For Stabb's reaction to the Addis proposal, see Stabb to Addis, 30 August and 19 September 1918, CO 129/450, ff. 66–71; see also Addis to Stabb, 28 August 1918, CO 129/452, f. 285.

38 Addis to Stephen in several letters dated October 1918, in F.H. King letters, Group Archives.

39 The Vologodsky declaration is reported by Sir Charles Addis to the Foreign Office, 12 December 1918, in FO 371/3366, ff. 345–46. For developments see ibid, ff. 348–49, 370–71.

40 Stephen to Addis, 15 October 1918, F.H. King letters.

41 Liang Shih-yi to E.G. Hillier, 31 March 1915, in FO 405/219, f. 21.

42 Stabb to Addis, 14 April, and Hongkong Bank to Banque de l'Indo-Chine, 15 April and Jordan to Grey, 19 and 21 April 1915, FO 405/219, ff. 14 and 21.

43 Tatsumi (Yokohama Specie Bank) to Addis, 22 October 1917, FO 405/223, f. 48.

44 Addis to FO, 7 December 1916, FO 405/221, f. 51, Foreign Office to Hongkong Bank, 3 December, Foreign Office to Treasury, 8 December, Minutes of Meeting of Inter-Bank Group, 11 December 1917, and related correspondence in FO 405/223, ff. 38, 48, 55–56, p. 108.

45 Treasury to Foreign Office, FO 405/223, p. 108.

46 A convenient collection of relevant correspondence is found in *The Consortium, an official text of the Four-Power Agreement for a Loan to China and Relevant Documents* (Washington, DC, 1921), Carnegie Endowment for International Peace, Division of International Law, Pamphlet Series, No. 40, esp. pp. 1–18.

47 Addis to Foreign Office, 7 December 1916, FO 405/221, f. 51.

48 For one such imaginative effort by B. Alston and others, see FO 371/2651, ff. 10–17.

49 Liang Tun-yen, Minister of Communications, to S.F. Mayers, British and Chinese Corporation, 4 December 1916, FO 405/221, f. 10.

50 Hillier to Ch'en Chin-t'ao, Minister of Finance, 2 October 1916, FO 371/2657, f. 239.

51 John V.A. MacMurray, *Treaties and Agreements with and concerning China, 1894–1919* (New York, 1921), II, 1405–06.
52 Exchange Banks Association to J. Simon, Attorney General, Chairman, Trading with the Enemy Committee, 2 October 1914, in Ceylon report cited, Group Archives.
53 From s/o cited in Ceylon Report, Group Archives.
54 Stabb to Addis, 1 March 1918, F.H. King letters, Group Archives.
55 Stabb to Addis, 16 August 1918, in ibid.
56 E.H. Fraser to A.G. Stephen, 11 January 1916, in ibid, Group Archives.
57 Bruce Tytler, *Here, There & (Nearly) Everywhere* (London: Weidenfeld and Nicolson, 1979), p. 22. The work was published posthumously and does not mention the Hongkong Bank by name.
58 Ibid, p. 25.
59 Ibid.
60 T.J.J. Fenwick, oral history interview by Frank H.H. King in Cape Town, Republic of South Africa, 4 June 1981, p. 2; deposited in Group Archives.
61 Board of Directors, special meeting, 5 August 1914.
62 Addis to Stabb recounting the affair, in cable books, June 1916.
63 Stephen to Fraser, 11 January 1916, F.H. King letters, Group Archives.
64 Fraser to Stephen, 11 January 1916, in ibid.
65 Stephen to Addis, 19 October 1916, in ibid.
66 Stabb to Addis, cable dated 2 May 1918, and Addis to Sir Walter Langley, Foreign Office, 2 May 1918, FO 371/3463.
67 F.T. Koelle's 'War Report', p. 35, in Group Archives, quoted in David J.S. King, 'The Hamburg Branch: the German Period', in King, ed. *Eastern Banking*, p. 534.
68 Ibid, p. 537.
69 Koelle's 'War Report', p. 31, cited in ibid, p. 533.
70 Ibid, p. 536.
71 Addis to Foreign Office, 24 September 1919, FO 371/3702, f. 59; see also related documents in ibid, ff. 47–64.
72 Sir Charles Addis, memorandum on 'London Office Female Staff', Group Archives.
73 W.A. Stewart, oral history interview by Christopher Cook, 18 December 1981, p. 5; deposited in Group Archives.
74 Quoted in a letter from E.G. Hillier to N.J. Stabb, Group Archives.
75 'Personalities' file, compiled by J.R. Jones, in Group Archives.
76 Quoted in the *Peking Chronicle* (6 November 1917), in the William S. Ridge Papers, Archives of the Hoover Institution, Stanford, California.
77 The details are set out in Addis to Stabb, cable dated 16 May 1918, cable books, Group Archives.
78 V.A. Mason, oral history interview by Christopher Cook in Toronto, Canada, 29 March 1980, edited in association with Mason by Gary Watson, p. 3; in Group Archives.
79 Ibid, pp. 9–10.

11 THE HONGKONG BANK IN THE GREAT WAR, 1914–1918, II: THE HONGKONG BANK'S RELATIONS WITH GERMANY

1 Sir Charles Addis to Geoffrey W. Russell, War Trade Department, 13 December 1915, in F.H. King letters, Hongkong Bank Group Archives.

2 F. Urbig to Addis, 11 June 1914, PP.MS.14/124, in [Sir Charles] Addis Papers, the Library, School of Oriental and African Studies, University of London (SOAS).
3 Comite v/d Oproep tot Gebedscemeenschap to Addis, 2 February 1920, PP.MS.14/125.
4 Addis to Mills, 9 August 1914, PP.MS.14/175.
5 Ibid.
6 Addis diary, 2 September 1914, PP.MS.14/32.
7 Addis to E.G. Hillier, enclosed in a letter to D. Mills, 9 January 1915, PP.MS.14/176.
8 See e.g. the complaints of British merchants in FO 371/2300, ff. 189–223, April 1915.
9 Sent to Foreign Office, enclosed with letter of Mills of 9 January 1915, PP.MS.14/176.
10 Cables in FO 371/2342, ff. 180–96, first paper in the file dated 6 December 1915; minute of the meeting dated 8 December.
11 Ibid, f. 189.
12 The information is in a memo dated 8 December 1915 and on f. 201 of FO 371/2342; the letter is f. 198, 10 December 1915, War Trade Department to Sir Walter Langley, FO, supplemented by letter of 24 December 1915, f. 204, Addis to Geoffrey W. Russell, War Trade Department.
13 See note 10.
14 Stephen to Stabb, letter in Group Archives.
15 Stephen to Sir John Jordan, 22 January 1919, in Stephen file, Group Archives.
16 Minute is on f. 84; J.O.P. Bland to Gregory, Board of Trade, 21 October 1916, in FO 371/2652, ff. 85–86.
17 FO 371/2651, 6 March 1916, f. 1.
18 French Foreign Ministry archives were searched by Claude Fivel-Démoret in connection with the Hongkong Bank History Project, and translations were made by David J.S. King. The key report is: Ministère de la Guerre, Commission Militaire de Contrôle Postal, 'Rapport sur la Deutsch-Asiatische Bank son activité en Extrême Orient au cours des exercise 1915–1916', based on documents captured from the Norwegian ship 'Leif Gunderson'. This is supplemented by correspondence in Ministère des Affaires Étrangères, Archives Diplomatiques, especially despatches from the French Legation in Peking to the French Foreign Ministry. The Morrison quote is taken from a despatch dated 5 January 1916. See also the amusing description of the situation by the Italian Président de la Commission, Daniele Varé, in his *Laughing Diplomat* (London, 1938), pp. 116–17.
19 A. Conty, French Minister in Peking, to French Foreign Ministry, 5 May 1916.
20 Jordan to Foreign Office, 22 December 1915, FO 371/2342, f. 217. The articles were written, according to G.E. Morrison, by A.J. Eggeling, then Peking manager of the DAB, see Hui-min Lo, ed. *The Correspondence of G.E. Morrison* (Cambridge, 1976), II, 564.
21 Hillier to Addis, and Addis to Hillier, 20 December 1915, FO 371/2342, ff. 213–14.
22 See references in notes 18 and 19 above.
23 Stephen to Editor (Clark) of *North-China Herald*, 7 January 1917, Shanghai Manager's Private Letter Books, 1914–1916, Group Archives.
24 See minutes in file dated 20 January 1916, FO 371/2650, ff. 570–73.

25 Copy of a letter from de Hoyer, Manager of the Russo-Asiatic Bank in Peking to Petrograd Head Office, 5 January 1916, found in the French Archives, see note 18 above.

26 Addis to Russell, Board of Trade, 8 December 1915, FO 371/2342, ff. 199–200.

27 B. Alston, 6 March 1916, FO 371/2651, f. 3.

28 FO 371/1949, f. 9.

29 Ibid, f. 11.

30 Fraser to Langley, 1 December 1914, FO 371/2298, ff. 35–37.

31 15 January 1915, F.H. King letters, Group Archives.

32 Governor May to Colonial Office, 14 August 1914, CO 129/412, f. 396. For a full survey of the initial developments, see Government of Hong Kong, 'Correspondence with the Secretary of State for the Colonies and other Correspondence on the subject of Trading with the Enemy and the Liquidation of the Deutsch-Asiatische Bank during August and September 1914', printed in Hong Kong and marked 'very confidential'; found in CO 129/421, ff. 316–42.

33 30 October 1914, CO 129/414, f. 126. The full regulations are incorporated in Ordinance No. 28 of 1914, An Ordinance to Provide for the Winding up of the Affairs of Certain Enemy Aliens. A report on this is found in CO 129/415, ff. 65–67.

34 For a long Addis letter on this and other incidents, see Addis to Foreign Office, 24 November 1916, FO 371/2652, ff. 149–57.

35 15 August 1914, CO 129/412, f. 399.

36 Morrison, see Lo, ed. *Correspondence*, II, 407.

37 Ibid, pp. 407–08.

38 H.D.C. Jones to Stabb, 19 January 1916, Group Archives history file.

39 Manager Hamburg to Manager London, s/o letter, 10 May 1915, in CO 129/424, f. 119.

40 See correspondence of the Governor of Hong Kong, 11 August 1915, in T.1/11968, file 23622, and between the Bank and Sir Everard Fraser, British Consul-General in Shanghai, 14 February 1917, Hillier and the Legation in Peking, and related documents in T.1/12084, file 12469.

41 FO 371/2321, ff. 231–37, file dated 22 January 1915; for the internal Chinese arrangements, see comments in Fraser to Langley, 1 December 1914, FO 371/2298, f. 35.

42 Harry H. Fox, Consul-General, Hankow, to Sir John Jordan, 26 February 1915, FO 371/2300, ff. 175–77, and related documents, ff. 178–81, and legal opinion etc., ff. 312–19.

43 This statement is made after a search of the FO 371 files and other relevant records in the PRO, London.

44 See the minutes relating to a case of Bank finance in Siam in file 62153, dated 18 May 1915, FO 371/2463.

45 This is the case cited above, file 62153, Board of Trade to Foreign Office, 10 June 1915, FO 371/2463.

46 See, e.g. China Association, Shanghai Branch, to China Association, London, 19 February 1915, in FO 371/2300, ff. 200–03.

47 Addis to Foreign Office, 1 December 1914, and related files in T.1/11721.

48 Cable, Jordan to Foreign Office, 27 February 1915, and Addis to Alston, 10 March 1915, and related documents, FO 371/2300, ff. 81–85, 112–17, 164–69.

49 Minute of an interview with Addis, 30 March 1915, FO 371/2300, f. 164.

50 Foreign Office to Sir John Jordan, 8 April 1915, FO 371/2300, ff. 241–44.

51 Hillier to Jordan, 13 July 1915, and reply in FO 371/2302, ff. 362–68, file dated 10 August 1915; see also, file dated 19 August 1915, FO 371/2303, ff. 79–81.

52 FO 371/2651, f. 94, Addis to Sir Walter Langley, 14 April 1916, the cable is on f. 95.

53 The Peking Manager's letter is translated in FO 371/2907, ff. 410–14, dated 14/27 November 1916.

54 Foreign Office minute, 9 February 1917, FO 371/2907, f. 407.

55 Hillier to Editor of the *Peking Daily News*, 9 November 1916, FO 371/2652, ff. 158–60, included in a lengthy exposition of the Hongkong Bank's position, dated 24 November, ff. 149–57.

56 Minutes dated 24 March 1916, file No. 12458, FO 371/2651, ff. 28–31.

57 This section is taken from D.J.S. King, 'The Hongkong Bank in Hamburg . . .' cited, pp. 529–37. This is heavily indebted to the 'War Report' of F.T. Koelle, which he sent to London immediately after the War. It would appear to be wholly reliable and is now in Group Archives.

58 Müller-Jabusch (1940) p. 240.

59 Koelle's War Report, p. 2.

60 Saville of the Board of Trade to the London Office, 2 December 1919, in the Archives of the HSBC, London Office, now in Group Archives, Hong Kong.

61 Koelle's War Report, pp. 4 and 27.

62 Ibid, pp. 27–28.

63 Ibid, p. 36.

64 Ibid, p. 7.

65 Ibid, p. 37.

66 Ibid, p. 48; the two Ordinances were No. 5365 of 31 July 1916 and No. 5406 of 24 August 1916.

67 In a notebook with the heading 'Manager's Notes' in the Hamburg Branch.

68 Koelle's War Report, pp. 16 and 34.

69 Ibid, p. 29.

GLOSSARY OF TERMS

For current standard banking terms, see F.E. Perry, *A Dictionary of Banking*, 2nd ed. London, 1983; for terms special to the earlier period, see the works of W.F. Spalding cited in the Bibliography and earlier editions of standard exchange manuals, e.g. *Tate's Modern Cambist*. For Chinese terms and events, see, among others, Samuel Couling, ed. *The Encyclopaedia Sinica* (rpt Hong Kong, 1983), the works of Edward Kann, and the biographical collection of Arthur W. Hummel, ed. *Eminent Chinese of the Ch'ing Period* (Washington, DC, 1943).

ACCOUNTANT   the Hongkong Bank officer responsible, *inter alia*, for administration of the office; originally and in smaller agencies, the second-ranking officer; the actual accounting was done by the officer in charge of 'books'.

AMAH   Chinese female domestic servant.

BANTO   office manager (Japan).

CASH   a Chinese copper coin, worth in theory 1,000th of a tael.

CHETTIAR   'chetty' – a South Indian caste of 'native' banker found also in Ceylon and the Straits Settlements.

CHOP   a mark or brand name.

CHUMMERY   a bachelors' mess, usually in India, but the term was sometimes used by foreign firms in China.

COMPRADORE   the Chinese manager who also guaranteed transactions with Chinese customers; the word had other meanings in common usage, see Volume I, Chapter 14.

CONCESSION   in an appropriate context, the term refers to some area near a Chinese city which is under foreign administration, either separate or joint, as in Hankow and Tientsin. See also, French Concession, International Settlement.

CONSTITUENT   the term used by the Hongkong Bank for 'Customer', suggesting the close relationship desired and the responsibility implied in becoming a Customer's 'banker'.

DIGS   rented room or flat.

EXTRATERRITORIALITY, EXTERRITORIALITY, EXTRALITY   used in this history in two particular senses: (i) the concept that the 'traveller' carries his own law with him or the fiction that he remains outside the territory of the state in which he resides and therefore is not amenable to its laws but remains subject to the laws of his own Sovereign, an arrangement formalized by treaty with, e.g. the governments of China, Japan, and Siam, (ii) the policy relative to the authority of a British colonial legislature outside the territory of the particular colony.

FRENCH CONCESSION   the part of Shanghai administered by French authorities;

673

the French Concession and the International Settlement, *q.v.*, constituted foreign-administered Shanghai.

GATEKEEPER   a bank regulator without authority to require a particular policy 'a', but who is able to force acceptance of 'a' when a bank requests permission for some approval 'b' over which the regulator does have authority.

GODOWN   warehouse.

GUARANTEE SHROFF   in Ceylon, the compradore, *q.v.*

HOLD OR KEEP THE RING, TO   the policy designed to ensure that the rules of the contest (or commercial competition) are maintained but not to intervene otherwise.

HONG   company.

HUKUANG PROVINCES   Hunan and Hupei provinces.

HU PU   Board of Revenue/Ministry of Finance.

INTERNATIONAL SETTLEMENT   stated without qualification, the term refers to that portion of Shanghai delineated (for the British Settlement) by the Land Regulations of 1845, amended in 1854 to establish the Shanghai Municipal Council, and subject since 1863 to joint British/American jurisdiction (thus including the American Settlement) as subsequently modified. See also, French Concession.

JOSS   pidgin-English from 'dios': local gods; by extension, their protection and consequent good luck.

LAC [LAKH]   one hundred thousand, written: 1,00,000.

LI   Ts0.001, i.e. a one-thousandth part of a tael.

LIANG   the Chinese for 'tael', *q.v.*

LIANG KIANG   Kiangsi and Kiangsu provinces.

LIANG KWANG   Kwangtung and Kwangsi provinces.

LIKIN   a tax on goods in inland transit.

LORCHA   small boat with Western design hull and Chinese masts and sails.

MAFOO   groom.

MIXED COURT (OF SHANGHAI)   'tribunal for the decision of cases in which foreigners were either directly or indirectly involved'.

OPEN PORTS   ports at which foreign trade and residence is permitted, see Treaty Ports.

PEAK DISTRICT   residential district on Hong Kong Island along the western end of the dividing ridge.

PEON   office attendant (Hongkong Bank usage).

PIDGIN   business.

SHROFF   an employee responsible for handling the cash; sometimes 'the shroff', i.e. the second ranking Chinese after the compradore, *q.v.* *Cf* the Hongkong Bank use of 'Accountant'. See also, guarantee shroff.

SYCEE   Chinese monetary silver, usually coined into the shape resembling a Chinese shoe, hence, 'shoe of sycee'.

TAEL   a 'liang' or Chinese unit of weight; a Chinese silver unit of account. The tael weight and the silver content of the tael unit of account varied from place to place and market to market; the term had therefore to be qualified except where context made this unnecessary. *Cf* ounce Troy and ounce avoirdupois; pound sterling and lira. See also, various taels under Shanghai, Haikwan, Kuping.

TAEL, HAIKWAN   an imaginary unit of account in which foreign Customs Revenues were denominated (HkTs100=ShTs111.4).

TAEL, KUPING [K'U-P'ING]   Treasury tael (Kuping Ts=ShTs107.4).

TAEL, SHANGHAI   an imaginary unit of account in which Shanghai-based commercial transactions were denominated (ShTs72=$100).

TAIPAN   chief executive.

TAOTAI [TAO-T'AI]   district officer/magistrate.

TAO-YIN   intendant of a circuit.

TIFFIN   the noon meal; sometimes also a light snack.

TRANCHE   section or portion (of a loan); a 'drawing down' of an instalment or tranche of the sum agreed.

TREATY PORTS   before the first Sino-British War China had successfully limited Western sea-borne trade to the port of Canton; under the terms of subsequent treaties the Chinese agreed to open further ports – and in some cases opened them without foreign inducement (the so-called 'self-opened' ports). These were designated 'Treaty Ports' or 'open ports'. Until 1895 foreigners were free to settle only in designated areas of the open ports, in some cases under a local foreign administration, the foreign concessions.

TSUNGLI YAMEN   the Imperial office in Peking serving as the equivalent to a foreign ministry; succeeded by the Wai-wu Pu, *q.v.*

UP-FRONT PROFIT   profit from a transaction, which, despite the extended period of the transaction itself, is taken at the commencement.

WAI-CHIAO PU   Ministry (Board) of Foreign Affairs, successor to the Wai-wu Pu.

WAI-WU PU   Ministry (Board) of Foreign Affairs, successor to the Tsungli Yamen.

YU-CH'UAN PU   Board of Posts and Communications.

CHINESE GLOSSARY

(Chinese names and terms are arranged alphabetically by syllables or characters according to the version found in the text. Wade-Giles romanization has been added where useful. The pinyin romanization and the actual characters are also provided. The compilation was completed with the assistance of Kitty Yu Wai Hing 余蕙卿, Cathy Wong Lin Yau 黃蓮有 , and Anita Lau Po Ling 劉寶凌.)

AS IN TEXT WADE-GILES	PINYIN	CHARACTERS
Aigun	Aihun	愛渾
Amoy		
Hsiamen	Xiamen	廈門
Anhui (Anhwei)	Anhui	安徽
Canton	Guangzhou	廣州
Chang Chih-tung	Zhang Zhidong	張之洞
Changchun	Changchun	長春
Chang Jen-chün	Zhang renjun	張人駿
Chang Yen-mao	Zhang Yinmou	張燕謀
Changsha	Changsha	長沙
Chao Erh-shun	Zhao Ersun	趙爾巽
Chao Kang (Bank)	Zhaokang	兆康
Chefoo	Zhifu	芝罘
Chekiang	Xijiang	浙江
Chen, Eugene		
Ch'en Yu-jen	Chen Youren	陳友仁
Chen, K.P.		
Ch'en Kuang-p'u	Chen Guongpu	陳光甫
Ch'en Chin-t'ao	Chen Jintao	陳錦濤
Ch'en-chou	Chenzhou	陳州
Ch'en K'uei-lung	Chen Guilong	陳夔龍
Chengtu	Chengdu	成都
Cheng Yuan Bank	Zhengyuan chienzhuang	正元錢莊
Ch'eng Te-ch'uan	Cheng Dequan	程德全
Chiao-t'ung Bank	Jiaotong Yinhang	交通銀行
Chientang	Chientang	錢塘
Chien Yü Bank	Qianyu chienzhuang	謙餘錢莊

AS IN TEXT WADE-GILES	PINYIN	CHARACTERS
ch'ien	qian	錢
ch'ien-chuang	qianzhuang	錢莊
Chihli	Zhidi	直隸
Chinchow	Jinzhou	金州
Chinkiang	Zhenjiang	鎮江
Chinghua	Qinghua	清化
Chingmen	Jingmen	荊門
Ching–Yu (Yamchow–Chungking Railway)		
Ch'in(-chou)–Yü(-chou)	Qin(zhou)–Yü(zhou)	欽(州)—渝(州)
Ch'ing	Qing	清
Ch'ing, Prince	Qing Qinwang	慶親王
Chou Chin-chen		
Chou Chin-piao	Zhou Jinbiao	周晉鑣
Chou Hsueh-hsi	Zhou Xuexi	周學熙
Chuchow	Zhuzhou	株州
Chuangchow	Zhuangzhou	莊州
Chün-chi Ch'u	Junji chu	軍機處
Chungking	Congqing	重慶
formerly *Yü-chou*	Yuzhou	渝州
Chung-kuo t'ung-shang yin-hang	Zhongguo tongshang yinhang	中國通商銀行
'Chung Ngoi S Po'		
Chung-wai hsin-pao	Zhong Wai Shen Bao	中外新報
Dairen (Dalny)		
Ta-lien	Dalian	大連
Fan Tseng-hsiang	Fan Zengxiang	樊增祥
Fengching	Fengjing	楓涇
Fengtien (Mukden)	Fengtian	奉天
Foochow	Fuzhou	福州
Haikwan	Haiguan	海關
Han	Han	漢
Hankow	Hankou	漢口
Hanyang	Hanyang	漢陽
Hangchow	Hangzhou	杭州
Harbin	Ha'erbin	哈爾濱
Ho Fuk		
Ho Fu	He Fu	何福
Ho Leung		
Ho Liang	He Liang	何亮
Honan	Henan	河南
Ho Sai Iu		
Ho Shih-yao	He Shiyao	何世耀
Ho Sai Ki		
Ho Shih-chi	He Shiji	何世基
Ho Sai Kwong		
Ho Shih-kuang	He Shiguang	何世光
Ho Sai Wa		
Ho Shih-hua	He Shihua	何世華
Ho Sai Wing (Ho Wing)		
Ho Shih-yung (Ho Yung)	He Shirong (He Rong)	何世榮(何榮)

AS IN TEXT WADE-GILES	PINYIN	CHARACTERS
Ho Tung	He Dong	何東
hong	hang	行
Hongkew		
Hung-k'ou	Hongkou	虹口
Hongping taels		
Hang-p'ing hua-pao-yin	Hangping huabaoyin	行平化寶銀
Hsiao-ting, Empress		
Hsiao-ting-ching huang-hou	Xiaodingjing huanghou	孝定皇后
Hsiao yin	xiao yin	小銀
Hsinmintun	Xinmintun	新民屯
Hsiung Hsi-ling	Xiong Xiling	熊希齡
Hukuang Railways	Huguang Tielu	湖廣鐵路
Hupei	Hubei	湖北
Hu Pu	Hubu	戶部
Hu Yü-fen (Yün-mei)	Hu Yufen (Yunmei)	胡橘棻(芸楣)
Huang Hsing	Huang Xing	黃興
Ichang		
I-ch'ang	Yichang	宜昌
I-ho ch'üan	Yihequan	義和拳
I-K'uang (Prince Ch'ing)	Yi Kuang	奕劻
Jung-lu	Rong Lu	榮祿
Kaifeng	Kaifeng	開封
formerly *Pien-liang*	Bianliang	汴梁
see also *Pienlo*		
Kaiping	Kaiping	開平
Kansu	Gansu	甘肅
Kang-i	Gang Yi	剛毅
K'ang Yu-wei	Kang Youwei	康有爲
Kiangnan	Jiangnan	江南
Kiangsi	Jiangxi	江西
Kiangsu	Jiangsu	江蘇
Kiaochow	Jiaozhou	膠州
Kinchow, see *Chinchow*		
Kirin	Jilin	吉林
Kiukiang	Jiujiang	九江
Kowloon		
Chiu-lung	Jiulong	九龍
Kuling	Jiuling	九嶺
kuping		
k'u-p'ing	Kuping	庫平
Kuang-hsu	Guangxu	光緒
Kuang-shui	Guangshui	廣水
Kuei-chou-fu	Guizhoufu	桂州府
Kung-chin hui	Gongjinhui	共進會
Kung, Prince		
Kung Ch'in-wang	Gong Qinwang	恭親王
kung-ku	gongu	公估
Kuomintang	Guomindang	國民黨
Kwangsi	Guangxi	廣西
Kwangtung	Guangdong	廣東

AS IN TEXT WADE-GILES	PINYIN	CHARACTERS
Kweilin	Guilin	桂林
Lau Kung Mow		
Lao Kung-mou	Lao Gongmao	老公茂
Lau Pun Chiu		
Liu Pan-ch'iao	Liu Banqiao	劉伴樵
Lau Wai Chun		
Liu Wei-ch'uan	Liu Weichuan	劉渭川
li	li	厘
Li Ching-fang	Li Jingfang	李經方
Li Hung-chang	Li Hongzhang	李鴻章
likin	lijin	厘金
liang (taels)	liang	両
Liang Ch'i-ch'ao	Liang Qichao	梁啟超
Liang Kiang	Liang Jiang	兩江
Liang Kwang	Liang Guang	兩廣
Liang Shih-i	Liang Shiyi	梁士詒
Liang Tun-yen	Liang Dunyan	梁敦彥
Liao River	Liaohe	遼河
Liaotung	Liaodong	遼東
Liu K'un-i	Liu Kunyi	劉坤一
Liu Yü-lin	Liu Yulin	劉玉麟
Lo Sow Sung		
Lo Shou-sung	Lou Shuosong	羅壽嵩
Lowu	Luohu	羅湖
Loyang	Luoyang	洛陽
see also *Pienlo*		
Luhan (Railway)		
Lu(-kou-ch'iao–Han(-k'ou)	Lu(gouqiao)–Han(-kou)	盧(溝橋)—漢(口)
Lunghai (Railway)	Long–Hai	隴海
Ma-an lieh-tao	Ma'an liedao	馬鞍列島
ma-chen kuan	mazhen guan	媽振館
mafoo	mafu	馬夫
Manchu	Manzhou	滿州
Manchuria		
Tung-san-shêng	Dongsansheng	東三省
Meihsien	Meixian	梅縣
Mok Kon Sang		
Mo Kan-sheng	Mo Gansheng	莫幹生
Mukden		
Mu-ting	Muding	穆鼎
see also *Fengtien, Shenyang*		
Nanchang	Nanchang	南昌
Nanking	Nanjing	南京
Nanpiao	Nanpiao	南票
Newchwang	Niuzhuang	牛莊
Ningpo	Ningbo	寧波
Pei Ho	Beihe	北河
Peitaiho	Beidaihe	北戴河
Pei T'ang	Beitang	北塘
Pei Tsu-yi (Tsuyee Pei)	Bei Zuyi	貝祖詒

AS IN TEXT WADE-GILES	PINYIN	CHARACTERS
Peking	Beijing	北京
Pienlo (Railway)		
Pien(-liang)–Lo(-yang)	Bian(liang)–Luo(yang)	汴（梁）—洛（陽）
see also *Kaifeng*		
Pingtu	Pingdu	平度
Pokwan	Baiguan	百官
Pukow	Pukou	浦口
P'u-i (Hsuan-t'ung)	Puyi (Xuantong)	溥儀（宣統）
Shameen	Shamian	沙面
Shasi	Shashi	沙市
Shanhaikwan	Shanhaiguan	山海關
Shansi	Shanxi	山西
Shantung	Shandong	山東
Shanghai–Nanking (Railway)		
Hu–Ning	Hu–Ning	滬寧
Shenyang (Mukden)	Shenyang	瀋陽
Sheng Hsuan-huai	Sheng Xuanhuai	盛宣懷
literary *Tzu-yi*	Ciyi	杏蓀
Shih Chao Tseng (Alfred Sze)		
Shih Chao-chi	Shi Shaoji	施肇基
Shingyi		
Hsing-i	Xingyi	興義
Shui-k'ou-shan	Shuikoushan	水口山
Shui-wu Ch'u	Shuiwuchu	稅務處
Shumchun	Shenzhen	深圳
Sinyang	Xinyang	信陽
Soochow	Suzhou	蘇州
Soochow Creek		
Wu-sung-kiang	Wusong Jiang	吳淞江
Sun Yat-sen	Sun Yixian	孫逸仙
Sung Chiao-jen	Song Jiaoren	宋教仁
sycee		
hsi-ssû	xisi	細絲
Sze, Alfred, see *Shih Chao Tseng*		
Szechuan	Sichuan	四川
Ta Ch'ing (or Ta Ts'ing)	Da Qing	大清
Taku	Dagu	大沽
Talienwan	Dalianwan	大連灣
Tatung	Datong	大同
ta yin	da yin	大銀
taipan		
ta-pan	daban	大班
Taipei	Taibei	台北
Tamsui	Danshui	淡水
Tang Kee Shang		
Têng Chi-ch'ang	Deng Jichang	鄧紀常
Tangku		
T'ang-ku	Tanggu	塘沽
Tangshan (T'ang-shan)	Tangshan	唐山
T'ang Shao-yi	Tang Shaoyi	唐紹儀

AS IN TEXT WADE-GILES	PINYIN	CHARACTERS
Taokow	Daokou	道口
taotai		
tao-t'ai	daotai	道臺
tao-yin	daoyin	道尹
T'ieh liang	Tie Liang	鐵良
Tientsin	Tianjin	天津
Tientsin–Pukow (or –Chinkiang)		
Chin-P'u (–Chen)	Jin–Pu (–Zhen)	津浦(鎮)
Tong, T(sung) P(oi)		
T'ang Tsung-pao	Tang Zongbao	唐宗保
Tsai-feng (Prince Ch'un)	Zai Feng	戴澧
Tsai Nai-huang	Cai Naihuang	蔡乃煌
Tsai-tse	Zai Ze	戴澤
Ts'en Ch'un-hsüan	Cen Chunxuan	岑春煊
Tseng Yuen Chang		
probably *Tseng Tsung-chien*	Zeng Zongjian	曾宗鑑
Tsim Sha Tsui	Jianshazui	尖沙咀
Tsinan	Jinan	濟南
Tsingtau	Qingdao	青島
Tsungli Yamen	Zongli Yamen	總理衙門
tuchun	dujun	督軍
Tüan, Prince		
Tuan Chin-wang	Duan Qinwang	端親王
Tungchow	Tongzhou	通州
T'ung-meng hui	Tongmenghui	同盟會
Tz'u-hsi	Ci Xi	慈禧
Wai-chiao Pu	Waijiaobu	外交部
Wai-wu Pu	Waiwubu	外務部
Wang Wen-shao	Wang Wenshao	王文韶
Wayfoong		
Hui-feng	Huifeng	匯豐
Weihaiwei	Weihaiwei	威海衛
Whampoa	Huangpu	黃埔
Whangpoo River at Shanghai		
Huang-p'u	Huangpu	黃浦
Woosung	Wusong	吳淞
Wuchang	Wuchang	武昌
Wu Mao-ting	Wu Maoding	吳懋鼎
Yamchow		
Ch'in-chou	Qinzhou	欽州
See also *Ching–Yu (Railway)*		
Yan Tseng		
Yang Shêng	Yang Sheng	楊晟
Yang Chin-tsin		
Yang Ch'ang-pao	Yang Changbao	楊昌濬
yang-li	yangli	洋例
Yen Cheng	Yencheng	鄆城
Yi-chang-hsien	Yichangxian	宜昌縣
Yo-chou	Yuezhou	岳州
Yu-ch'uan Pu	Youchuanbu	郵傳部

AS IN TEXT WADE-GILES	PINYIN	CHARACTERS
Yü-hsien	Yu Xian	毓賢
Yuan-feng-jun Bank	Yuanfengrun Yinhao	源豐潤銀號
Yuan Shih-k'ai	Yuan Shikai	袁世凱
Yüeh (or Yuet)–Han	Yue–Han	粵漢
Yunnan	Yunnan	雲南
Yung Wing (Jung Hung)	Rong Hong	容閎
Zakow	Zhakou	閘口

JAPANESE GLOSSARY

AS IN TEXT	CHARACTERS
Asano Sōichirō	浅野総一郎
habutai	羽二重
Hamashita Takeshi	浜下武志
Hiogo (Hyōgo)	兵庫
Iwasaki Yanosuke	岩崎弥之助
Iwasaki Yatarō	岩崎弥太郎
Katō Takaaki	加藤高明
Kondo Rempei	近藤廉平
Masuda Takashi	益田孝
Mitsubishi Bank	三菱銀行
Mitsubishi Zaibatsu	三菱財閥
Mitsui Bussan	三井物産
Nagasaki	長崎
Nichi-Ei Ginkō	日英銀行
Nichi-Ei Kinyū Gaisha	日英金融会社
Nippon Kōgyō Ginkō	日本興業銀行
Nippon Yūsen Kaisha (N.Y.K.)	日本郵船
Ōkura Kihachirō	大倉喜八郎
Shibusawa Eiichi	渋沢栄一
Shimoda Kikutarō	下田菊太郎
Takahashi Korekiyo	高橋是清
Tōa Dōbun Shoin	東亜同文書院
Yokohama Specie Bank	横浜正金銀行

BIBLIOGRAPHY

The 'bibliography' is primarily a list of works consulted, prefaced by an explanation and a description of archival material obtained for the history. The list covers only those materials relevant to Volume II of the history of the Hongkong Bank. A separate bibliography is provided for each volume.

CHINESE SOURCE MATERIAL

In Volume I, I explained that, despite a search of various collections and biographies, we had found little relevant Chinese material which focused sufficiently on the history of the Hongkong Bank.

The various loans described in Part II of this Volume must have been accompanied by internal communications within the Chinese Government. They would add to our knowledge of the total loan history, but not necessarily to the history of the Bank. Files in Group Archives and in the PRO contain translations of relevant Chinese documents. The A.N. Young papers in the Hoover Institution contain summaries which appear accurate. There are other compilations cited in the list of works consulted. The history of the loans, as told in this history, is an extension of European economic history; it describes the problems faced by the Bank and its associates. The sources have been selected with this priority in mind.

ARCHIVAL COLLECTIONS – GENERAL

The most important source for the history of the Hongkong Bank is the Bank's own records in the Hongkong Bank Group Archives. These, however, had not been assembled when the project began, and as yet full use has not been made of them. Briefly, they include for the period covered by Volume II: the Minute Books of the Board of Directors with gaps noted, the semi-annual (later annual) reports of the directors and abstracts of accounts, limited inter-branch correspondence, Shanghai and London share registers, miscellaneous charges books, ledgers from several branches, personnel reports, early photographs, and occasional letters. There are files on the various loans and an increasing number of Inspector's Reports.

There are the compilations of J.R. Jones made in the process of collecting material for the Bank's centenary history (see list of works consulted). Included in this category are the 'F.H. King letters', the result of a search of the more important letters then in London Office. F.H. 'Towkay' King (no relation) was a retired member of the Bank's Eastern staff. There are other bound reports and boxes of personal memorials, manuscripts etc. which are part social history, part banking.

The Bank's archives were enriched by the shipment of material from Shanghai, but that comprehended only that material actually taken from the Bund to the godown in 1955 and for the most part deals with post-1920 events. Other branch materials depend for their coverage on the chances of preservation, often confined to a 'sample' ledger or, as in Bangkok, to the first.

The oral histories are more important in later volumes, but quotations are taken here from the transcripts of T.J.J. Fenwick, V.A. Mason, and W.A. Stewart. The latter two were interviewed by Christopher Cook.

In this period, therefore, the Bank's material must be supplemented by documents preserved elsewhere.

Research associates have studied the materials in the national archives of Sri Lanka, the Philippines (and I have searched the Insular records of the National Archives in the United States), and Singapore (the Straits Settlements). In Thailand access was granted to the Royal files in the National Archives and the Siam Commercial Bank made material available relative to early relations with the Hongkong Bank. In France access was obtained to the archives of the Foreign Ministry and the Finance Ministry; the reports of the Banque de France relative to the Bank's Lyons branch were also seen. The German material requires separate comment below.

Fr J. Verin provided material through Professor P. Tuck from the Missions Étrangères de Paris.

Interest in the various British syndicates resulted in research in the files in Companies House, London, the Board of Trade files, and the Archives of the British and Chinese Corporation and the Chinese Central Railways held by Matheson and Co. The Addis/Bland, Bland/Pauling and Co., and other relevant correspondence was found in the J.O.P. Bland Collection in the Thomas Fisher Rare Book Library, University of Toronto. The Bank's earlier involvement with the China Merchants' Steam Navigation Company is noted in the H.B. Morse Papers, Houghton Library, Harvard University.

The Hoover Institution archives proved essential for Volume III, but a reference from the William S. Ridge Papers is included in Volume II. There is also an early use of materials from the Thomas Lamont Collection, Baker Library, Harvard Business School, relative to American participation in the China Consortium.

There is a link between South African and China finance; the key, as far as the Hongkong Bank is concerned, would be Sir Carl Meyer, but his letter books, as kindly provided by his grandson, Sir Anthony Meyer, MP, were almost entirely personal. One or two insights were, however, obtained.

A search of the Nathan Papers in Rhodes House, Oxford, was made, with one minor reference obtained.

Considerable use is made, as in Volume I, of the material in the manuscript collections of the Library, the School of Oriental and African Studies, University of London.

The earliest materials are the David McLean Papers; McLean was the Bank's first Shanghai Manager, and he was subsequently London Manager until 1889. The most important collection for Volume II is that of Sir Charles Addis; his papers (PP.MS.14) are vital as a source for the Bank's history, broadly defined, from 1884 to 1944; the collection comprises a remarkable record of diaries, correspondence, and clippings, concerning which see Margaret Harcourt Williams, *Catalogue of the Papers of Sir Charles Addis* (London, 1986). Also consulted were the archive of John Swire and Sons Ltd (see Elizabeth Hook, *A Guide to the Papers of John Swire and Sons Ltd*, London, 1977), and the China Association Archive, including minute books and correspondence.

For the Hongkong Bank's relations with the Hong Kong and British Governments, particularly important in this period, the Public Record Office, London, is the main source. Only one or two isolated documents have survived in Hong Kong and are in the Public Records Office here. The main files consulted were those of the Colonial Office (CO 129), the Foreign Office (FO 17), and the Treasury (T.1), but there is material as recorded in the end-notes in many other files, including the private papers of important diplomats, e.g. Satow and Jordan, and the company records under the Board of Trade. There is relevant material in the India Office Library and Records especially in relation to specific bullion operations. In India the Hongkong Bank did not, otherwise, play a leading role; the Bank's agents co-signed letters from the Exchange Banks Association on matters of public policy.

City materials are found in the Guildhall Library, and use is made of the archives of Baring Brothers, the London Stock Exchange, and Mocatta and Goldsmid.

As noted at the beginning of the 'end-notes', certain material was uncatalogued when consulted. Efforts have been made to insert the proper reference numbers later, especially in the case of the Addis Papers. However, this has not proved practical relative to the Hongkong Bank Archives. Material cited is hopefully sufficiently well identified to be located by the Archives staff.

ARCHIVAL COLLECTIONS – GERMANY

The Hongkong Bank's close relationships with German economic and political development are described in Chapter 9. Material on Germany intrudes, however, throughout the history. This is the result of the research efforts of David J.S. King, and his documentation, as found in his research reports, cited, is thorough. This has not always been fully reproduced and, therefore, the following summary of archives visited and persons consulted, based on his own account, will be useful.

An appreciation of the early days of German banking involvement in the East and with the Hongkong Bank in particular depends on (i) the archives of Siemssen and Co. and (ii) the papers of Hermann Wallich, now in the possession of Dr Henry Wallich. From this base David King moved to other material in Germany.

David King reported:

The archives of the Bank's German clients have almost all been destroyed by the bombing in the war, or simply to make room for new more relevant documents, with the exception of certain fragmentary remains in the archives of Siemssen and Co. in Hamburg. Therefore pre-war public relations publications by these firms are useful in getting some idea of their activities, although naturally such publications seldom include much business detail.

The archives of the Deutsch-Asiatische Bank were in Berlin and were in the Russian zone of occupation at the end of the war. It is unknown how much survives, although it is assumed that most of the documents were destroyed in the bombing. Fortunately there is a well-written history of the DAB by Maximilian Müller-Jabusch which was published in 1940. Although this work tends to play down periods when the DAB was not successful and does not include any footnotes or other indications of sources, the author is generally accurate; he clearly had complete access to the archives of the DAB and of the Deutsche Bank–Disconto-Gesellschaft merger, which have also been lost. These two banks were the most likely ones in the consortium to retain useful information concerning the DAB. Evidently, the archives of the Disconto-Gesellschaft were for the most part discarded when the two banks merged in 1929, and unfortunately little material concerning China or the DAB survives in the DB archives.

The most useful archival source still available in Germany is the archives of the

Political Division of the Foreign Office (Auswärtiges Amt AA). These are fairly complete for the period up until the First World War, but then become very fragmentary. The 'Commercial–Political' Division of the AA is to be found in Potsdam, in the German Democratic Republic, but I was unable to get permission to use those materials.

In addition there are the contemporary newspaper reports, the annual reports of the banks, publications by men close to the events, and more general contemporary works on banking and Asian trade. However many of these suffer from the lack of access to accurate sources, some of the books and articles referred to in older bibliographies are now very hard to find, and some of them are apparently now only available, if anywhere, in the Staatsbibliothek in Leipzig.

From the Hamburg Branch itself unfortunately only fragments remain, for example, the complete exchange of telegrams concerning the Indemnity Loans in 1895 and 1896, but, although the other materials survived the war, they were destroyed in the late 1960s to facilitate a move. Fortunately, London Office has saved its copies of semi-official correspondence with the Hamburg Branch (as well as with other branches, much of which also discusses German business) for the period following 1913, and this allows a very detailed view of the business the Branch was doing in the inter-war period. Also in London are preserved Inspectors' Reports for the branch from 1911, 1919, and 1924 (they are now with Group Archives in Hong Kong).

GERMAN ARCHIVES:

Bonn:	Political Archives of the Foreign Office (Auswärtiges Amt)
Bremen:	Archives of the Chamber of Commerce (Bremer Handelskammer)
	Bremen State archives (Staatsarchiv)
	Archives of C. Melchers and Co. (Destroyed in the war)
Frankfurt:	Archives of the Deutsche Bank. (Very little on the DAB, and most of the Disconto-Gesellschaft papers were destroyed at the time of the merger.)
	Archives of the Deutsche Bundesbank
Hamburg	Archives of Arnold Otto Meyer
	Archives of Carlowitz and Co. (Destroyed in the war)
	Archives of the Chamber of Commerce (in the Commerzbibliothek)
	Archives of the HSBC (Hamburg Branch)
	Archives of the Ost-Asiatischer Verein
	Archives of Siemssen and Co.
	Hamburg State archives (Hamburger Staatsarchiv)
Koblenz:	German National Archives (Bundesarchiv)

LIBRARIES:

Bonn:	Bonn University Library
Bremen:	Bremen University Library
Cologne:	Cologne University Library
Frankfurt:	Deutsche Bibliothek
	Frankfurt University Library
	Library of the Frankfurt Chamber of Commerce
	(Handels- und Industrie-kammer)
Hamburg:	Commerz-Bibliothek (in the Chamber of Commerce)
	Hamburg University Library
	Hamburg Welt-Wirtschaftsarchiv Library

LIST OF WORKS CONSULTED

* indicates a sometime member of the Hongkong Bank staff

*Addis, *Sir* Charles S. 'The Daily Exchange Quotations'. *North-China Herald* (11 February 1903), pp. 285–89.
'The Finance of China'. *Edinburgh Review* 230 (October 1919).
Adshead, S.A.M. *The Modernization of the Chinese Salt Administration.* Cambridge, MA, 1970.
Ahrens, Karl. *Die deutschen Auslandsbanken.* Würzburg-Aumühle, 1939.
Allen, G.C. and Audrey G. Donnithorne. *Western Enterprise in Far Eastern Economic Development. China and Japan.* London, 1954.
Western Enterprise in Indonesia and Malaya. London, 1957.
Andree, H.V. *Progress of Banking in Ceylon.* Colombo, 1864.
Anthonisz, J.O. *Currency Reform in the Straits Settlements.* London, ca 1916.
Armstrong, F.E. *The Book of the Stock Exchange.* London, 1934.
Ayres, G.L. 'Fluctuations in New Capital Issues in the London Capital Market, 1899 to 1913'. MSc Thesis, University of London, 1934.
Baasch, Ernst. *Quellen zur Geschichte von Hamburgs Handel und Schiffahrt, im 17., 18., 19. Jahrhundert.* Hamburg, 1910. .
Bangkok Times. 1888–1894.
[Bank of Chosen.] *Past and Present of The Hongkong and Shanghai Banking Corporation.* Bank of Chosen, 1915.
[Bankers Association of the Philippines.] *History of Banking in the Philippines.* Manila, 1957.
Bankers Magazine [title varies]. London, 1895–1918.
Baster, A.S.J. *Imperial Banks.* London, 1929.
[Behn Meyer and Co.] *Zur Geschichte der Firmen Behn Meyer & Co. und Arnold Otto Meyer.* 2 vols. Hamburg, 1957.
Benfey, F. *Die neuere Entwicklung des deutschen Auslandsbankwesens, 1914–1925.* Berlin, 1925.
Bergère, Marie Claire. *Une Crise financière à Shanghai à la fin de l'ancien régime.* Paris, 1964.
Bericht der China Studiumkommission des Reichsverbandes der deutschen Industrie. Berlin, 1930.
Berliner Börsen-courier.
Beutler, Heinz. *Hundert Jahre Carlowitz & Co., Hamburg und China.* Diss. Hamburg, 1948.
Bland, J.O.P. *Recent Events and Present Policies in China.* London, 1912.
Bond, Sue. 'Portrait of a Potter'. *Hongkong Bank Group Magazine*, No. 8 (Summer 1976), pp. 25–28.
Born, Karl Erich. *International Banking in the 19th and 20th Centuries.* Leamington Spa, England, 1983. German ed. *Geld und Banken.* . . . Stuttgart, 1977.
Borsa, Giorgio. *Italia e Cina nel secolo xix.* Milan, 1961.
Bouvier, Jean. *Le Crédit Lyonnais de 1865 à 1882: les années de formation d'une banque de dépôts.* 1961. Vol. II.
Brandt, Max von. *Drei Jahre Ostasiatischer Politik, 1894–97.* Stuttgart, 1897.
China und seine Handelsbeziehungen zum Auslande. Berlin, 1899.
Industrielle und Eisenbahn Unternehmungen in China. Berlin, 1899.
33 Jahre in Ost Asien. Erinnerungen eines deutschen Diplomaten. 3 vols. Leipzig, 1901.
*[Brent, A.D.] 'The Siege of Peking by one who went through it; diary of a besieged resident'. *Daily News* (London, 16 October 1900), p. 4.

'To the Editor', [signed] 'Over Worked Bank Clerk'. *Peking and Tientsin Times* (23 February 1901).

Bruguière, Michel. 'Le Chemin de fer du Yunnan: Paul Doumer et la politique d'intervention française en Chine, 1899–1902'. *Revue d'Histoire Diplomatique* (1963).

Buckley, Charles B. *An Anecdotal History of Old Times in Singapore, 1819–1867*. Singapore, 1902. Rpt Kuala Lumpur, 1965.

Bullionist (London).

C. Melchers & Co. Bremen, Melchers & Co. China: Firmenschrift. Bremen, 1909.

'Carlowitz & Co'. *Historisch-biographische Blätter der Stadt Hamburg.* Berlin, 1905/06.

Carlowitz & Co. China, Hong Kong, Hamburg. Hamburg–Zwickau, 1925.

Carlowitz & Co. Hamburg, Hong Kong, New York, China und Japan. Hamburg, 1906.

[Carlowitz & Co.] *Kurzer Auszug aus der Geschichte der Firma Carlowitz & Co.* Shanghai, 1937.

Carlson, Ellsworth C. *The Kaiping Mines (1877–1912)*. Cambridge, MA, 1957.

Cassis, Youssef. *Les Banquiers de la City à l'époque Edouardienne*. Geneva, 1984.

Cecco, Marcello de. *Money and Empire: the International Gold Standard, 1890–1914*. Oxford, 1974.

Celestial Empire. Shanghai.

Ceylon, Government of. 'Report of the Swettenham Currency Commission', 1893. Report of the Ceylon Currency Commission, 1902.

Ceylon Observer [article on Koelle], 10 January 1903.

Chan, Kit-ching Lau. 'British Policy and the Reorganization Loan to China, 1912–13'. *Modern Asian Studies*, 5 (1971).

    Anglo-Chinese Diplomacy in the Careers of Sir John Jordan and Yuan Shih-k'ai, 1906–1920. Hong Kong, 1978.

Chandler, Alfred D., Jr. *The Visible Hand; the Managerial Revolution in American Business.* Cambridge, MA, 1977.

Chang, John K. *Industrial Development in Pre-Communist China.* Edinburgh, 1969.

Chang, Kia-ngau. *China's Struggle for Railroad Development.* New York, 1943.

Chapman, S.D. 'British-based Investment Groups before 1914'. *Economic History Review* 38:230–51 (1985).

Chen, Chi. *Die Beziehungen zwischen Deutschland und China bis 1933.* Hamburg, 1973.

Chen, Chia Tsün. *Das chinesische Bankwesen unter Berücksichtigung der neuen chinesischen Banken.* Berlin, 1938.

Chen, Chung-sieu. 'British Loans to China from 1860 to 1913, with special reference to the period 1894–1913'. Diss. University of London, 1940.

Ch'en, Gideon. 'The Early History of China's External Debt'. *Yenching Journal of Social Studies* 2:637–60 (1939).

China. Maritime Customs. *Documents Illustrative of the Origin, Development, and Activities of the Chinese Customs Service.* 7 vols. Shanghai, 1940.

China Association. Minute Books. 1889–1902. Archive of the China Association, the Library, School of Oriental and African Studies, London.

Die China Export- Import- und Bank-Compagnie. Hamburg, 1959.

China Mail (Hong Kong).

Chronicle and Directory for China, Japan, the Straits Settlements, Indo-China, Philippines, etc. Shanghai, 1891–1914.

Chung-kuo jen-min yin-hang Shang-hai-shih fen-hang 中國人民銀行上海市分行 (The Chinese People's Bank, Shanghai), comp. *Shang-hai ch'ien-chuang Shih-liao* 上海錢莊史料 (Historical materials on the native banks in Shanghai). Shanghai, 1960.

Cleveland, Harold van B. and Thomas F. Huertas. *Citibank, 1812–1970.* Harvard Studies in Business History, No. 37. Cambridge, MA, 1970.

Coates, Austin. *Whampoa, Ships on the Shore.* Hong Kong, 1980.

Cole, W.A. 'The Relations between Banks and the Stock Exchange'. *Journal of the Institute of Bankers* (1899).

Collis, Maurice. *Wayfoong. The Hongkong and Shanghai Banking Corporation.* London, 1965. Reprinted with additional material by the Hongkong Bank, 1978.

Conant, Charles A. *Coinage and Banking in the Philippine Islands.* Washington, DC, 1901.

The Consortium, an official text of the Four-Power Agreement for a loan to China and Relevant Documents. Carnegie Endowment for International Peace, Division of International Law. Pamphlet Series, No. 40. Washington, DC, 1921.

Constantino, Renato. *A History of the Philippines: from the Spanish Colonization to the Second World War.* New York, 1975.

Cook, Christopher. 'The Hongkong and Shanghai Banking Corporation on Lombard Street'. In *Eastern Banking: Essays in the History of The Hongkong and Shanghai Banking Corporation.* Ed. Frank H.H. King. London, 1983. Pp. 193–203.

Coons, A.G. *The Foreign Public Debt of China.* Philadelphia, 1930.

Couling, Samuel. Ed. *Encyclopaedia Sinica.* Shanghai, 1917. Reprinted, Hong Kong, 1983.

Currer-Briggs, Noel. *Contemporary Observations on Security from the Chubb Collectanea, 1818–1968.* London, n.d. Privately published.

Däbritz, W. *David Hansemann und Adolf von Hansemann.* Deutsche Bank, 1954.

Daily Advertiser. Hong Kong.

Daily Press. Hong Kong.

Davenport-Hines, R.P.T. 'Birch Crisp'. In David Jeremy, ed. *Dictionary of Business Biography*, I, 822–26. London, 1984.

Dayer, Roberta A. 'The Young Charles S. Addis: Poet or Banker?' In *Eastern Banking: Essays in the History of The Hongkong and Shanghai Banking Corporation.* Ed. Frank H.H. King. London, 1983. Pp. 14–31.

Dénis, Etienne. *Bordeaux et le Cochinchine sous la restauration et le second empire.* Bordeaux, 1965.

Deutsch-Asiatische Bank. *Jahresberichte.* 1905–1952.

Deutsche Bank. *Geschäftsberichte der Direction der Deutschen Bank.* 1872–1875, 1889–1894, 1908.

Dewall, Wolf von. 'Die Vorgeschichte der Canton–Hankow Eisenbahn'. In *Archiv für Eisenbahnwesen* 31 (1908). Pp. 1313–69.

Dictionary of National Biography.

Disconto-Gesellschaft. *Die Discontogesellschaft 1851 bis 1901: Denkschrift zum fünfzig-jährigen Jubiläum.* Berlin, 1901.

Dorpmüller, Julius. 'Vom Eisenbahnbau in China'. In *Archiv für Eisenbahnwesen* 51:1097–1140 (1928).

Drumm, Ulrich and Alfons W. Henseler, eds. *Historische Wertpapiere*; Bd. II, *Chinesische Anleihen und Aktien.* Frankfurt/M, 1976.

Dudeney, H.E. *The Canterbury Puzzles and Other Curious Problems.* London, 1919. 4th ed. 1958.

Easton, Harry Tucker. *The History of a Banking House (Smith, Payne and Smiths).* London, 1903.

Eckardstein, Hermann Freiherr von. *Lebenserinnerungen und politische Denkwürdigkeiten.* 3 vols. Leipzig, 1919–21.

Economist. London.

Edwards, E.W. 'The Origins of British Financial Co-operation with France in China, 1903–6'. *English Historical Review* 86:285–317 (1971).

'British Policy in China, 1913–1914: Rivalry with France in the Yangtze Valley'. *Journal of Oriental Studies* 40:20–36 (1977).

Endacott, George B. *A History of Hong Kong.* London, 1958.

Epistola, S.V. 'The Hong Kong Junta'. *Philippine Social Sciences and Humanities Review* 24:3–12, 23–33 (March 1961).

Fairbank, John K., Edwin O. Reischauer, Albert M. Craig. *East Asia, the Modern Transformation.* Boston, 1965.

See also Hart, Sir Robert

Feavearyear, Sir Albert. *The Pound Sterling: a History of English Money.* 2nd ed. Revised by E. Victor Morgan. Oxford, 1963.

Feldwick, W., ed. *Present Day Impressions of the Far East.* London, 1917.

Feuerwerker, Albert. *China's Early Industrialization: Sheng Hsuan-huai (1844–1916) and Mandarin Enterprise.* Cambridge, MA, 1958.

The Chinese Economy, ca. 1870–1911. Michigan Papers in Chinese Studies, No. 5. Ann Arbor, Michigan, 1969.

The Foreign Establishment in China in the Early Twentieth Century. Michigan Papers in Chinese Studies. Ann Arbor, Michigan, 1976.

Fieldhouse, D.K. *Economics and Empire, 1830–1914.* London, 1973.

Fivel-Démoret, Claude. 'The Hongkong Bank in Lyon, 1891–1954: Busy, but too Discreet?' In *Eastern Banking: Essays in the History of The Hongkong and Shanghai Banking Corporation.* Ed. Frank H.H. King. London, 1983. Pp. 467–516.

Fleming, Peter. *The Siege at Peking.* London, 1959.

Franke, Otto. *Erinnerungen aus zwei Welten.* Berlin, 1954.

Die Frankfurter Zeitung, 1912–21.

Frey, Werner. *Sir Valentine Chirol: Die Britische Position und Politik in Asien, 1895–1925.* Diss. Zürich, 1976.

[Gillett Bros Discount House.] *The Bill on London.* London, 1952.

Glade, Dieter. *Bremen und der Ferne Osten.* Bremen, 1966.

Graham, John. *The Lowe Bingham Story, 1902–1977.* Hong Kong: privately published, 1978.

Griser, Norman. 'The British Investor and his Sources of Information'. MSc Thesis, University of London, 1940.

Gueneau, Louis. *Lyon et le commerce de la soie.* Lyons, 1932.

Gunasekera, H.A. de S. *From Dependent Currency to Central Banking in Ceylon.* Colombo, 1960.

Gundry, R.S. *China Past and Present.* London, 1895.

Hall, A.R. *The Export of Capital from Britain, 1870–1914.* 1968.

Hallgarten, George W. *Imperialismus vor 1914.* Munich, 1963.

Hamashita, Takeshi. 'A History of the Japanese Silver Yen and The Hongkong and Shanghai Banking Corporation, 1871–1913'. *Eastern Banking: Essays in the History of The Hongkong and Shanghai Banking Corporation.* Ed. Frank H.H. King. London, 1983. Pp. 321–49.

'The Role of Intermediaries in Local and National Chinese Finance, 1898–1916'. Paper read at the Eighth International Economic History Congress. Budapest, 1982.

Hamburgische Börsenhalle.

Handelsnachrichten. Stuttgart, Marburg.

Hänisch, Adolf van. *Jebsen & Co. Hong Kong: Chinas Handel im Wechsel der Zeiten, 1895–1945.* Apenrade, 1970.

Hao, Yen-P'ing. *The Comprador in Nineteenth Century China: Bridge between East and West.* Cambridge, MA, 1970.

Hart, Sir Robert. *The I.G. in Peking: Letters of Robert Hart, Chinese Maritime Customs, 1868–1907.* Eds. John K. Fairbank *et al.* 2 vols. Cambridge, MA, 1975.

Hatzfeldt, Paul Graf von. *Botschafter Paul Graf von Hatsfeldt: Nachgelassene Papiere, 1838–1901.* Ed. Gerhard Ebel. 2 vols. Boppard am Rhein, 1976.

Helferrich, Karl. *Georg von Siemens. Ein Lebensbild aus Deutschlands Großer Zeit.* 3 vols. Berlin, 1973.

Henseler, A.W. 'Die deutsche Beteiligung an chinesischen Anleihen'. In *Bankhistorisches Archiv*, No. 11, 1976.

Herrick, Tracy G. *Bank Analyst's Handbook.* New York, 1978.

Hieke, Ernst. *Die Reederei M. Jebsen A.G.* Apenrade, 1953.

Hodsoll, Frank. 'Hongkong and Shanghai Banking Corporation'. In *Britain in the Philippines.* An address to the members of the American Association of the Philippines, U.S. Embassy, Manila, December 1, 1954. Pp. 18–21.

Hoffman, R.J.S. *Great Britain and the German Trade Rivalry, 1875–1914.* Philadelphia, 1933.

Hong Kong, Government of. *Hongkong Government Gazette.*

Legislative Council Sessional Papers.

'Correspondence respecting the Issue of One Dollar Notes, presented to the Legislative Council by Command of HE the Governor'. 1884.

Legislative Council Proceedings, 1899.

Correspondence with the Secretary of State for the Colonies and other Correspondence on the Subject of Trading with the Enemy and the Liquidation of the Deutsch-Asiatische Bank during August and September, 1914. In CO 129/421, ff. 316–42.

'Hongkong and Shanghai Banking [*sic*], the New Office'. *The Banker's, Insurance Managers' and Agents' Magazine* 96, 837: 734–42 (December 1913).

Hongkong and Shanghai Banking Corporation. Semi-annual and annual reports. 1865–1985.

Hongkong Daily Press.

Hong Kong Hansard.

Hou, Chi-ming. *Foreign Investment and Economic Development in China, 1840–1937.* Cambridge, MA, 1965.

——— and Tzong-shian Yu, eds. *Modern Chinese Economic History.* Taipei, Taiwan, 1979.

Hsiao, Liang-lin. *China's Foreign Trade Statistics, 1864–1949.* Cambridge, MA, 1974.

Hsü, Leonard Shih-lien, and others. *Silver and Prices in China: report of the committee for the study of silver values and commodity prices, Ministry of Industries.* Shanghai, 1935.

Hsu, Moughton Chih. *Railway Problems in China.* New York, 1915.

Hsü I-sheng 徐義生. *Chung-kuo chin-tai wai-chai shih t'ung-chi tzu-liao, 1853–1927* 中國近代外債史統計資料 (Statistical materials on the history of China's foreign loans, 1853–1927). Peking, 1962.

Huang, Feng-hua. *Public Debts in China.* Studies in History, Economics and Public Law, Vol. LXXXV, No. 2. New York, 1919.

Huenemann, Ralph W. *The Dragon and the Iron Horse, the Economics of Railroads in China, 1876–1937.* Cambridge, MA, 1984.

Hummel, Arthur W., ed. *Eminent Chinese of the Ch'ing Period (1644–1912).* 2 vols. Washington, D.C., 1943.

Hyde, Francis E. *Far Eastern Trade, 1860–1914.* London, 1973.

Ingram, James C. *Economic Change in Thailand since 1850.* Stanford, 1955.

Investors Monthly Manual published with the *Economist.*

Jackson, Stanley. *The Sassoons.* New York, 1965.

Japan. Ministry of Foreign Affairs. *Compiled Documents on Japanese Foreign Affairs.* Tokyo, 1954.

Jones, Geoffrey. *Banking and Empire in Iran.* Vol. I of his *The History of the British Bank of the Middle East.* Hongkong Bank Group History Series, No. 3. Cambridge, 1986.

*Jones, J.R. History Collections in the Hongkong Bank Group Archives:
  'Personalities and Narratives'.
  'The Bank, 1876–1942'.
  'Branches'.
  'Chinese Loans'.

Journal of the Institute of Bankers.

Journal of the Money Market and Commercial Digest.

Kann, Edward. *The Currencies of China.* Shanghai, 1927.
  'Early History of China's External Debt'. *Yenching Journal of Social Studies* 2:637–60.
  'The Foreign Loans of China'. *Finance and Commerce.* Vol. XIX, No. 85.
  The History of China's Internal Loan Issues. Shanghai, 1934.

Kent, P.H. *Railway Enterprise in China.* London, 1907.

Keswick, Maggie, ed. *The Thistle and the Jade: a Celebration of 150 Years of Jardine, Matheson and Co.* London, 1982.

King, Catherine E. 'The First Trip East – P&O via Suez'. In *Eastern Banking: Essays in the History of The Hongkong and Shanghai Banking Corporation.* Ed. Frank H.H. King. London, 1983. Pp. 204–29.

King, David J.S. 'China's First Public Loan: The Hongkong Bank and the Chinese Imperial Government "Foochow" Loan of 1874'. In *Eastern Banking: Essays in the History of The Hongkong and Shanghai Banking Corporation.* Ed. Frank H.H. King. London, 1983. Pp. 230–64.
  'The Hamburg Branch: The German Period, 1889–1920'. In *Eastern Banking: Essays in the History of The Hongkong and Shanghai Banking Corporation.* Ed. Frank H.H. King. London, 1983. Pp. 517–44.
  'China's Early Loans, 1874–95, and the Role of The Hongkong and Shanghai Banking Corporation'. Research report in Hongkong Bank Group Archives, Hong Kong.
  'On the Relations of the Hongkong Bank with Germany'. 2 vols. Research report, 1981, in Hongkong Bank Group Archives, Hong Kong.

King, Frank H.H. *Money in British East Asia.* London, 1957.
  Money and Monetary Policy in China, 1845–1895. Cambridge, MA, 1965.
  Survey our Empire! Robert Montgomery Martin (1801?–1868), a bio-bibliography. Hong Kong, 1979.
  and Prescott Clarke. *A Research Guide to China-coast Newspapers, 1822–1911.* Cambridge, MA, 1965.
  ed. *Eastern Banking: Essays in the History of The Hongkong and Shanghai Banking Corporation.* Hongkong Bank Group History Series, No. 1. London, 1983.
  'Appendix: an Outline of the Problems of The Hongkong and Shanghai Banking Corporation's Note Issue'. In *Eastern Banking: Essays in the History of The Hongkong and Shanghai Banking Corporation.* Ed. Frank H.H. King. London, 1983. Pp. 150–54.
  'The Foreign Exchange Banks in Siam, 1888–1918, and the National Bank Question'. In International Conference on Thai Studies, *Papers.* Bangkok, 1984. Volume I, pp. 14–17 (separate pagination).
  'Extra-Regional Banks and Investment in China, with comments relative to other

Far Eastern Territories, 1870–1914'. In Rondo Cameron, ed. Proceedings of a Conference on International Banking and Industrial Finance, Bellagio, 1985 (in the press).

King, W.T.C. *A History of the London Discount Market*. London, 1936.

Korff, Baron. *Weltreise II: Japan, China, 1893–1894*. Berlin, 1896.

Kreig, Hans. *Bernhard Buschmann: Die Geschichte eines Ostasienhauses*. Hamburg, 1952.

Kuhlmann, Wilhelm. *China's Foreign Debt*. Hannover, 1983.

[Kunst & Albers] 'Auszüge aus der von Dr. Alfred Albers 1939 verfaßten Firmengeschichte, betreffend die Jahre 1864–1898'. In *Ostasiatische Rundschau*, 21. Jahrgang, Nr. 4, 5/6 und 7, 1940, S. 84ff.

'Die Hamburgische Firma Kunst & Albers in Wladivostok, 1864–1914'. In *Vierteljahrsschrift für Sozial-und Wirtschaftsgeschichte*, 34 (1941). Pp. 268–99.

Kurgan-van Hentenryk, G. *Léopold II et les groupes financiers belges en Chine: la politique royale et ses prolongements (1895–1914)*. Bruxelles, 1972.

Landes, David. *Bankers and Pashas, International Finance and Economic Imperialism in Egypt*. London, 1958.

Lau, Kit-ching Chan, *see* Chan

Lavington, F. *The English Capital Market*. London, 1921.

Lee, En-han. *China's Quest for Railway Autonomy, 1904–1911*. Singapore, 1977.

Lee, Kuochi. *Die chinesische Politik zum Einspruch von Shimonoseki und gegen die Erwerbung der Kiautschou Bucht*. Münster, 1966.

Lee, T.A. 'The Financial Statements of The Hongkong and Shanghai Banking Corporation, 1865–1980'. In *Eastern Banking: Essays in the History of The Hongkong and Shanghai Banking Corporation*. Ed. Frank H.H. King. London, 1983. Pp. 77–92.

Lim, Chee Peng, *et al.* 'The History and Development of The Hongkong and Shanghai Banking Corporation in Peninsular Malaysia'. In *Eastern Banking: Essays in the History of The Hongkong and Shanghai Banking Corporation*. Ed. Frank H.H. King. London, 1983. Pp. 350–91.

Little, A.J. *Through the Yang-tze Gorges or Trade and Travel in Western China*. London, 1898.

Liu, S.Y. 'China's Debts and Their Readjustment'. *Chinese Economic Journal* 5:735–49 (1929).

Lo, Hui-min, *see* Morrison

London and China Express (London).

Loney, Nicholas. *A Britisher in the Philippines or the Letters of Nicholas Loney*. Introduction by Margaret Hoskyn and Biographical Note by Consul José Ma. Espino. Manila, 1964.

Lu, Ku Sui. *Die Form bankmäßiger Transaktionen im inneren chinesichen Verkehr*. Hamburg, 1926.

Lyon, Chambre de Commerce. *La Mission Lyonnaise d'exploration commerciale en Chine, 1895–97*. Lyon, 1898.

Macau, Government of. *Boletim da Provincia de Macau e Timor*.

MacDermot, B.H.D. *Panmure Gordon & Co. 1876–1976. A Century of Stockbroking*. London (privately published by the company), 1976.

McElderry, Andrea Lee. *Shanghai Old-Style Banks (Ch'ien-chuang), 1800–1935: a Traditional Institution in a Changing Society*. Ann Arbor, Michigan, 1976.

Mackenzie, Compton. *Realms of Silver: One Hundred Years of Banking in the East*. London, 1954.

McLean, David. 'Commerce, Finance, and British Diplomatic Support in China, 1885–1886'. *Economic History Review* 26:464–76 (1973).

'The Foreign Office and the First Chinese Indemnity Loan, 1895'. *The Historical Journal* 16:303–21 (1973).

'British Banking and Government in China: the Foreign Office and the Hongkong and Shanghai Bank'. PhD Thesis, Cambridge University, 1976.

'Finance and "Informal Empire" before the First World War'. *Economic History Review* 29:291–305 (1976).

'International Banking and its Political Implications: The Hongkong and Shanghai Banking Corporation and The Imperial Bank of Persia, 1889–1914'. In *Eastern Banking: Essays in the History of The Hongkong and Shanghai Banking Corporation.* Ed. Frank H.H. King. London, 1983. Pp. 1–13.

MacMurray, John V.A., comp. and ed. *Treaties and Agreements with and concerning China, 1894–1919.* 2 vols. New York, 1921.

Mai Chung-hua 麥仲華, ed. *Huang-ch'ao ching-shih-wen hsin-pien* 皇朝經世文新編 Vol. I. Taiwan rpt: 1965.

Makepeace, W.M., G.F. Brooke and R.St.J. Braddell. *One Hundred Years of Singapore.* London, 1921.

Marriner, Sheila and Francis E. Hyde. *The Senior, John Samuel Swire, 1825–98.* Liverpool, 1967.

Masuda, Takashi. *Japan, its Commercial Development and Prospects.* London, n.d.

Molsen, Käthie. *C. Illies & Co. 1859–1959: Ein Beitrag zur Geschichte des deutsch–japanischen Handels.* Hamburg, 1959.

Morgan, E. Victor. *The Stock Exchange. Its History and Functions.* London, 1962.

Möring, Maria. *Siemssen & Co. 1846–1971.* Hamburg, n.d.

Morrison, G.E. *The Correspondence of G.E. Morrison.* 2 vols. Ed. Hui-min Lo. Cambridge, 1976.

Morse, H.B. *The International Relations of the Chinese Empire.* London, 1918.

Müller-Jabusch, Maximilian. *Franz Urbig zum 23 Januar 1939.* Deutsche Bank, 1939.

Fünfzig Jahre Deutsch-Asiatische Bank, 1890–1939. Berlin, 1940.

Münch, Hermann. *Adolph von Hansemann.* München, 1932.

*Muriel, H.E. Autobiography. TS in Hongkong Bank Group Archives.

Myers, Ramon H. *The Chinese Economy, Past and Present.* Belmont, CA, 1980.

Nelson, W. Evan. 'The Hongkong and Shanghai Banking Corporation Factor in the Progress toward a Straits Settlements Government Note Issue, 1881–1889'. In *Eastern Banking: Essays in the History of The Hongkong and Shanghai Banking Corporation.* Ed. Frank H.H. King. London, 1983. Pp. 155–79.

'The Imperial Administration of Currency and British Banking in the Straits Settlements, 1867–1908'. Diss. Duke University, 1984.

North-China Herald (Shanghai). 1895–1918.

Ostasiatischer Lloyd.

Ostasiatischer Verein Hamburg–Bremen zum 60-jährigen Bestehen. Hamburg, 1960.

Ostasien.

Paish, F.W. 'The London New Issue Market'. *Economica* 18:1–17 (1951).

Pan, Am. *Die Beteilung der Banken am chinesischen Außenhandel.* Diss. Jena: Universitäts-Buchdrückerei Neuenhahn, 1932.

Pekinger Deutscher Zeitung (2 copies for 1901 in the British Library).

[Pekin Syndicate.] *A Few Facts concerning the Pekin Syndicate: showing the Origin of the Syndicate, its rights, prospects, and progress.* London, 1904.

Pelcovits, Nathan A. *Old China Hands and the Foreign Office.* New York, 1948.

Perry, F.E. *A Dictionary of Banking.* 2nd ed. London, 1983.

Pohl, Manfred. *The Deutsche Bank's East Asian Business, 1870–1875: Proposals and preparations for establishing branches in Shanghai, Hong Kong and Yokohama.* Studies on Economic and Monetary Problems and on Banking History, 15. Frankfurt/M, 1977.

Powell, Ifor B. 'The British in the Philippines in the American Era, 1898–1946, (ii): the Banks'. *Bulletin of the American Historical Collection* 9,3:39–52 (July–September 1981). Manila.

Pramuanratkarn, Thiravet. 'The Hongkong Bank in Thailand: A Case of a Pioneering Bank'. In *Eastern Banking: Essays in the History of The Hongkong and Shanghai Banking Corporation.* Ed. Frank H.H. King. London, 1983. Pp. 421–34.

Protest der deutschen Firmen Hongkongs gegen die Maßnahmen der englischen Regierung. Shanghai, 1915.

Purcell, Victor. *The Boxer Uprising, a background study.* Cambridge, 1963.

[Pustau, Carl Wilhelm von.] 'Aus dem Lebenslauf von Carl Wilhelm von Pustau . . . Zusamengestellt aus Erinnerungen der Kinder, Urkunden und Zeitschriften in 1939'. (unpubl. located in Commerz-bibliothek, Hamburg.)

Quested, Rosemary. *The Russo-Chinese Bank.* Birmingham, 1977.

Radandt, Hans. 'Hundert Jahre Deutsche Bank: Eine typische Konzerngeschichte'. In *Jahrbuch für Wirtschaftsgeschichte.* Berlin (East), 1972. Pp. 37–62.

Raggi, G. Salvago. 'La Memorie di Salvago Raggi, ambasciatore italiano in Cina'. In Glauco Licato, *Notabili della Terza Italia.* Rome, 1968.

Reed, Richard. *National Westminster Bank, a short history.* London, 1983.

Reiß, Auguste. 'Das Bankwesen in China'. In *China, Wirtschaft und Wirtschaftsgrundlagen.* Ed. Josef Hellauer. Berlin/Leipzig, 1921.

Richthofen, Ferdinand von. *Tagebücher aus China.* Berlin, 1907.

Romanov, B.A. *Russia and Manchuria.* Trans. Susan Wilbur Jones (of *Rossiya v Manchzuria).* Ann Arbor, MI, 1952.

Roth, Cecil. *The Sassoon Dynasty.* London, 1941.

Ryder, F.R. and D.B. Jenkins. *Thomson's Dictionary of Banking.* 12th ed. London, 1974.

Sayer, Geoffrey R. *Hong Kong, 1862–1919: years of discretion.* Hong Kong, 1975.

Schmidt, Ernst Wilhelm. *Männer der Deutschen Bank und der Discontogesellschaft.* Deutsche Bank, 1957.

Schmidt, Vera. *Die deutsche Eisenbahnpolitik in Shantung, 1899–1914. Ein Beitrag zur Geschichte des deutschen Imperialismus in China.* Wiesbaden, 1976.

Schmollers Jahrbuch.

Schrecker, John E. *Imperialism and Chinese Nationalism, Germany in Shantung.* Cambridge, MA, 1971.

Sear, Judith. 'Variety in the Note Issues of The Hongkong and Shanghai Banking Corporation, 1865–1891'. In *Eastern Banking: Essays in the History of The Hongkong and Shanghai Banking Corporation.* Ed. Frank H.H. King. London, 1983. Pp. 139–49.

Seidenzahl, Fritz. 'Als in Europa noch chinesische Anleihen aufgelegt wurden'. In *Beiträge zu Wirtschafts- und Währungs-fragen und zur Bankgeschichte.* Deutsche Bank, 1966.

Hundert Jahre Deutsche Bank, 1870–1970. Frankfurt: Deutsche Bank: Im Selbstverlag, 1970.

Selvaratnam, H.L.D. 'The Guarantee Shroffs, the Chettiars, and The Hongkong Bank in Ceylon'. In *Eastern Banking: Essays in the History of The Hongkong and Shanghai Banking Corporation.* Ed. Frank H.H. King. London, 1983. Pp. 409–20.

'Servicos de Finanças: *Inventario* do Codice de "Minutas do Oficios Expedidos em 1890" '. In *Arquivos de Macau.* Vol. I, 1983.

Shanghaier Nachrichten.

Sheng Hsuan-huai 盛宣懷, *Hsin-hai ke-ming ch'ien-hou* 辛亥革命前後 *Sheng Hsuan-*

huai tang-an tzu-liao hsüan-chi 盛宣懷檔案資料選輯, eds. Chen Xulu (Ch'en Hsü-lu 陳旭麓, Gu Tinglong (Ku T'ing-lung)顧廷龍, Wang Xi (Wang Hsi) 汪熙. Shanghai, 1980.

*Chia-wa Chung-Jih chan-cheng*甲午中日戰爭, 2 Vols. Eds. Chen Xulu 陳旭麓 *et al.* Shanghai, 1980.

Shenoy, B.R. *Ceylon Currency and Banking.* London, 1941.

Shinobu Junpei 崔聖淵. 開港과洋舘歷程 (The Korean Peninsula, 1901).

Sithi-Amnuai, Paul. *Finance and Banking in Thailand, a study of the commercial system. 1888–1963.* Bangkok, 1964.

[Smith, Bell & Company.] *Under Four Flags, the Story of Smith, Bell & Company in the Philippines.* Privately published in England, nd, but early 1970s.

Smith, Carl T. 'Compradores of The Hongkong Bank'. In *Eastern Banking: Essays in the History of The Hongkong and Shanghai Banking Corporation.* Ed. Frank H.H. King. London, 1983. Pp. 93–111.

*Spalding, W.F. *Eastern Exchange, Currency and Finance.* 3rd ed. London, 1920.
Dictionary of the World's Currencies and Foreign Exchanges. London, 1928.

Statist. London.

Stingl, Werner. *Der Ferne Osten in der deutschen Politik vor dem ersten Weltkrieg (1902– 1914).* 2 vols. Frankfurt/M, 1978.

Stöcker, Helmuth. 'Dokumente zur deutschen Politik in der Frage der Industrialisierung Chinas (1889–1894)'. In *Zeitschrift für Geschichtswissenschaft,* 5 (1957). Pp. 603–06.
Deutschland und China im 19. Jahrhundert. Berlin (East), 1958.

Stöpel, Karl T. *Ueber Japanisches Bankwesen und Deutschlands Anteil am Welthandel und der Industrie Japans.* Halle, 1898.

Straits Settlements, Government of. *Report of the Straits Settlements Currency Committee.* Cd 1556. London, 1903.

Strasser, Karl. *Die deutschen Banken im Ausland.* München, 1924.

Sun, E-tu Zen. *Chinese Railways and British Interests, 1898–1911.* New York, 1954.
'The Shanghai–Hangchow–Ningpo Railway Loan of 1908'. *Far Eastern Quarterly* 10, 3 (1951).

Syrett, W.W. *Finance of Overseas Trade.* 3rd ed. London, 1957.

Tamagna, Frank M. *Banking and Finance in China.* New York, 1942.

Taylor, J.R.M., comp. *The Philippine Insurrection Against the United States. A Compilation of Documents with Notes and Introduction.* Washington, 1906.

Teng, Ssu-yü and John K. Fairbank. *China's Response to the West: a Documentary Survey, 1839–1923.* Cambridge, MA, 1954.

*Thursfield, R.P. *Topical Verses.* Shanghai, 1914.

The Times.

Times of Ceylon.

Times of India.

*Townsend, A.M. 'Early Days of the Hongkong and Shanghai Bank'. Privately reproduced. Copy in the Hongkong Bank Group Archives, Hong Kong.

Townsend, M.E. *The Rise and Fall of Germany's Colonial Empire, 1884–1918.* New York, 1930.

Treue, Wilhelm. 'Die Geschichte des Bremer Handelshauses C. Melchers & Co. von seiner Gründung bis zum Ende des ersten Weltkrieges'. In *Beiträge zur Bremischen Firmengeschichte.* München, 1966. Pp. 33–46.
'Rez. V. Schmidt. Die deutsche Eisenbahnpolitik in Shantung'. In *Vierteljahrsschrift für Sozial- und Wirtschaftsgeschichte.* 1978. Pp. 110–14.

Tsingtauer Neueste Nachrichten, 1904–11.

Tung-fang tza-chih 東方雜誌 (Oriental magazine). Vol. 7, No. 11 (1910).
*Tytler, Bruce. *Here, There & (Nearly) Everywhere.* London, 1979.
Uebersicht über die Bestände des deutschen Zentralarchivs Potsdam. Berlin, 1957.
United Kingdom. British Parliamentary Papers.
   Reports of HM Minister in China Respecting Events in Peking, 1900.
   Report of the Straits Settlements Currency Committee. Cd 1556. London, 1903.
   Report of the Committee on Oriental Studies in London, 1908.
   'Coinage of a British Dollar for Circulation in Hong Kong and the Straits Settlements'. Eastern No. 62. CO 882/5.
   Report of the Chinese Currency Committee. 1911.
   Return of any Correspondence with the Bank of England and Messrs Samuel Montagu and Company, relating to purchases of Silver in 1912. London: HMSO, 1912.
   Report of Treasury Committee on the Mode of Issuing the Dollar in the East. 2 vols. London, 1913.
   China, No. 2. 1916. *Correspondence respecting Chinese Loan Negotiations.* Cd 6446.
United States. 'Memorandum for the Secretary of War on Currency and Exchange in the Philippines'. U.S. War Department, Division of Insular Affairs, 1900.
Valdepeñas, Vicente and Gemilino Bautista. *The Emergence of the Philippine Economy.* Manila, 1977.
Valette, R. Brun de la. *Lyon et ses rues.* Lyon, 1969.
Varé, Daniele. *Laughing Diplomat.* London, 1938.
Vissering, G. *On Chinese Currency.* 2 vols. Amsterdam, 1912 and 1914.
Wagel, Srinivas R. *Finance in China.* Shanghai, 1914.
Wallich, Hermann. 'Aus meinem Leben'. In *Zwei Generationen im deutschen Bankwesen.* Schriftenreihe des Instituts für Bankhistorische Forschung e.v., Vol. II. Frankfurt/M, 1978.
Wang, Chin-chun, T.T. Linn, and E.W. Chang, comps. *Railway Loan Agreements of China.* Railway Department, Ministry of Communications, Peking, 1922.
Weerasooria, W.S. *The Nattukottai Chettiar: Merchant Bankers in Ceylon.* Colombo, n.d.
Wesley-Smith, Peter. 'The Hongkong Bank and the Extraterritorial Problem, 1865–1890'. In *Eastern Banking: Essays in the History of The Hongkong and Shanghai Banking Corporation.* Ed. Frank H.H. King. London, 1983. Pp. 66–76.
Whale, P. Barrett. *Joint Stock Banking in Germany.* London, 1968.
Williams, H.S. 'Demon-tiles'. *Mainichi Daily News* (25 June 1960).
Williams, Margaret Harcourt. *Catalogue of the Papers of Sir Charles Addis.* Hongkong Bank Group History Series, No. 2. London, 1986.
Wing, Yung (Jung Hung). *My Life in China and America.* New York, 1909.
Witte, Graf. *Erinnerungen.* Trans. Herbert Hoemer. Berlin, 1923.
*Wodehouse, P.G. 'Over Seventy, an autobiography with digressions'. In *Wodehouse on Wodehouse.* London, 1981. Pp. 467–645.
   Psmith in the City. London, 1910. Penguin ed. 1970.
   'My Banking Career'. *The Hongkong Bank Group Magazine.* No. 6 (summer, 1975), pp. 13–16.
Wong, Kwai Lam. 'Anglo-Chinese Trade and Finance, 1854–1914'. PhD Thesis. University of Leicester, 1976.
Wray, William D. *Mitsubishi and the N.Y.K., 1870–1914.* Cambridge, MA, 1984.
Wright, Arnold, ed. *Twentieth Century Impressions of Hongkong, Shanghai, and other Treaty Ports of China: Their History, People, Commerce, Industries, and Resources.* London, 1908.
   and H.A. Cartwright. *Twentieth Century Impressions of British Malaya.* 1908.

Wright, Stanley F. *China's Customs Revenue since the Revolution of 1911*. 3rd edition, revised by John H. Cubbon. Shanghai: Inspectorate General of Customs, 1935. *Hart and the Chinese Customs*. Belfast, 1950.

Wright, Tim. *Coal Mining in China's Economy and Society, 1895–1937*. Cambridge, 1984.

Ybañez, Roy C. 'The Hongkong Bank in the Philippines, 1899–1941'. In *Eastern Banking: Essays in the History of The Hongkong and Shanghai Banking Corporation*. Ed. Frank H.H. King. London, 1983. Pp. 435–66.

Young, Ernest P. *The Presidency of Yuan Shih-k'ai*. Ann Arbor, MI, 1977.

Young, Walter. *A Merry Banker in the Far East*. London, 1916.

Zimmerman, Maurice. 'Lyon colonial'. *Lyon et la région lyonnaise en 1906*. Lyon, 1906.

Zühlke, Herbert. 'Die Rolle des Fernen Ostens in den politischen Beziehungen der Mächte, 1895–1905'. Reprinted in *Historische Studien* 186 (1965).

INDEX

[Alphabetization is by *letter*. Names of Chinese cited in Chinese format (without comma) are accordingly alphabetized on the basis of their entire name. Names of Hongkong Bank staff are marked by an asterisk. Hongkong Bank branches are listed under the appropriate cities.]

health, 14, 15, 16, 17, 33, 153, 154, 155–
56, 157, 160–61, 165–66, 167–70, 188,
192, 283, 317, 356, (retirement for
reasons of) 156, 160–61, 463n, 542
Hong Kong office, life in, 151, 182, 184
ladies, 587, 597–98
leaves, 586
marriage, 153, 156, 186
promotion and career, 33, 116, 190,
463n, 488n, 538–39, 540–41, 542, 586,
588, 598–600, (mid-career problems)
152, 153–55, 184, 488n
recruitment, 8, 18, 164, 173–75, 183,
194, 538–39, 541, 586, 587, 588, 591,
598–600, 601–02, (examination) 173–
74, (policy) 171, 541, (porridge trap)
173
size, 7, 147, 150, 152, (during Great
War) 550, 586, 588
sports, 99, 174–75, 472, (at New
Beckenham) 12, 172, 174–75, 184, 193
'three-tier system', 7, 91n, 127, 128, 176
training, 174, 183, 185–88, 192–93, 542,
(up-grading and professionalism) 8,
182, 185–89, 357, 417
staff, remuneration: bonus and gratuities,
60, 62, 72, 80, 82, 99, 282, 290, 317,
318, 503, 540; during Great War, 587,
595–97, (ladies) 598; Officers Good
Service Fund, 70, 73; Provident Fund,
625; retirement and/or death benefits,
70, 80, 156, 160, 542, 625; salaries, 99,
159, 165, 282, 539–40, 598,
(compradore) 75
Hongkong and Whampoa Dock Co., 74
Hongkong Bank, Board of Directors, 158;
chairmen, 21, 523, 528, 551–53,
(speech) 88–89, 553–54; composition,
20–27, 328, 501–02, 528–29, 549, 551–
53; on Legislative Council, 21; policies,
64–67, 89, 251, 550, 619, (banking) 52,
80, 303, 554–56, (charity) 70, 187, 554,
555, (Chief Manager and other
appointments) 8, 13–15, 15–16, 37,
161–62, 356, (control, inspection,
frauds) 74, 92–93, 94, 105, 125–26,
356, (during Great War) 553–54, 587,
589, 592, 595–96, 597, 627, (during
Great War, relative to Germany) 551–
54, (on location of Head Office) 7, 19,
28–29, 554, (public role for staff) 21n,
148–50, 228; role of, 18–19, 27, 30, 70,
81, 94, 95, 97, 274, 296, 328, 338, 356,
417, 475, 477, 528–29, 557, 560, 590.
See also Germans
Hongkong Bank, Chief Manager, 3, 8–9,
211–12, 344; refusal to be, 17;

remuneration, 8, 37; role of, 8; selection
and succession, 12–18. *See also* Kresser;
Greig; Jackson; Noble; de Bovis; Smith;
Stabb; Stephen; Barlow, Hynes;
Grayburn; Morse; Turner
Hongkong Bank/Deutsch–Asiatische Bank
Agreement of 1895 and revisions, xxv,
243, 247, 249, 254, 272–75, 282, 284,
299, 306–09, 327–29, 337, 339–40,
348, 374, 380, 381, 386, 391, 400, 401–
02, 407, 415, 444, 494, 535, 540;
Declaration of 1898, 307–08, 311, 343–
45, 407, 444. *See also* Deutsch-
Asiatische Bank
Hongkong Bank, London Advisory
(Consultative) Committee: advice or
pressure from, xxv, 30, 66, 98, 149, 159,
260; as 'Board of Directors', 557, 610;
composition, 28–30, 33, 157, 158, 168,
261, 298, 303, 331, 490n, 514, 557–60,
610; role of, 8, 19, 27–31, 171, 296,
416, 556–57, 558, 559–60, 610
Hong Kong General Chamber of
Commerce, 593–94
Hong Kong Government, 7, 21, 56, 261,
358–59, 376; and Germans (Great
War), 531–32, 606, 612–13, 614;
Kowloon–Canton Railway (British
Sector), 355–56, 358–59, 380–81;
legislation, (No. 5 of 1866) 66, 67, 81,
84, 87, (No. 6 of 1907) 68–69, (No. 11
of 1905) 359, (No. 65 of 1911) 208n,
(No. 24 of 1914) 88; Hongkong
Tramways Ordinance of 1883, 303
Hongkong Telegraph, 107
Hongkong Tramways, 303, 334
Hooley-Jamieson Syndicate, 285
Hope and Co., 583, 594, 617, 621
Ho Sai Iu, 75
*Ho Sai Ki, 75
*Ho Sai Kwong, 75
*Ho Sai Wa, 75
*Ho Sai Wing (Ho Wing), 75
Ho Tung, *Sir* Robert, 75
*Howard, J.W.L., 188
de Hoyer, L., 582, 607
hsiao-yin, 'small silver', 215
Hsinmintun, 244
Hsiung Hsi-ling, 490
Huang Hsing, 472
Hubbard, T.H., 41
Hukuang Viceroy, term explained, 344n,
388n
Hunan, 445
*Hunter, H.E.R., 16–17, 38, 62, 71, 121,
148, 161, 163–64, 326, 420, 424, 465
Hunter, W.B., 237

HONGKONG BANK GROUP HISTORY SERIES

General Editor: FRANK H.H. KING

1 *Eastern Banking: Essays in the History of The Hongkong and Shanghai Banking Corporation* Edited by FRANK H.H. KING.

2 *Catalogue of the Papers of Sir Charles Addis* by MARGARET HARCOURT WILLIAMS, with an introduction by Roberta A. Dayer.

3 *The History of The British Bank of the Middle East* by GEOFFREY JONES.
   Volume I. *Banking and Empire in Iran.*
   Volume II. *Banking and Oil.*

4 *The History of The Hongkong and Shanghai Banking Corporation* by FRANK H.H. KING. 4 vols.